To the
VICTOR
the SPOILS

The author Sean Longden studied History at the
University of London. He has had a varied career
mixing work in historical photographic archives
and international press agencies. The inspiration
for this book came from his desire to link historical
events to real lives and he has spent over three years
writing and researching the book, much of which is
based on original research, interviews with war veterans and unpublished source material. He is married with two children and lives in Surrey.

To the
VICTOR
the SPOILS

D-DAY TO VE DAY,
THE REALITY BEHIND
THE HEROISM

Sean Longden

ARRIS BOOKS
An imprint of Arris Publishing Ltd
GLOUCESTERSHIRE

First published in Great Britain in 2004
by
ARRIS BOOKS
An imprint of Arris Publishing Ltd
12 Adlestrop, Moreton in Marsh
Gloucestershire GL56 0YN
www.arrisbooks.com
Published in paperback 2005
Text copyright © Sean Longden 2004

ISBN 1-84437-058-5

Printed and bound in Great Britain by Biddles Ltd, King's Lynn

Telephone:01608 659328
Visit our website at www.arrisbooks.com or email us at info@arrisbooks.com

Contents

Acknowledgements

I would like to thank all those people without whose help this book could not have been written. Particular thanks must be given to Mrs Dolores Baron and her son Nick for allowing me to quote from the unpublished memoirs of Alexander Baron and giving me access to his wartime letters. Other individuals went 'beyond the call of duty' including Mr and Mrs Lutter who gave me my first contacts in the British Legion at Rushden. Dr Ken Tout answered questionnaires, gave permission to quote his published works and found me many contacts from the 1st Northants Yeomanry. Eric Davies arranged contacts in the Norwich area and gave much more help and advice. Roy Merrett kindly sent out questionnaires to his comrades in the 43rd Reconnaissance Regiment Old Comrades Association and regularly sent me copies of their newsletter 'Spearhead'. Ken Moore who kindly invited me to a 5th Kings Regiment reunion and introduced me to his former comrades. John Majendie and Stan Procter helped with contacts in the 4th Somerset Light Infantry. Eric 'Bill' Sykes who kept up regular contact from his home in America. Sydney Jary who answered my questions and agreed to let me quote from his book *18 Platoon*.

Many others agreed to be interviewed including Len Bennett, Joe Ekins, Ken Hardy, Michael Hunt, Arthur Jarvis, John Mercer, John Reynolds, Ken Squires, Jack Teare, Les Toogood, and John Longfield and his 5th Kings comrades. Thanks are also due to Major Douglas Goddard and Jack Oakley who sent copies of their wartime diaries and Jack Woods who sent a copy of his unpublished memoirs *A Trooper's Tale*.

Other veterans took time to fill in questionnaires and send letters, including Wilf Allen, Lord Boardman, Patrick Delaforce, Harry Free, John Groves, Ian Hammerton, Arthur Heyworth, George Marsden, R.G. Mead, William Partridge, Arthur Rowley, Alec Simons, Jim Sims, R.W. Siriett, Cyril Spencer, Fred Sylvester, Colonel John Waddy, Charles Whiting and G. Worthington.

Thanks must also be given to Rick Colls for allowing me access to his father Doug's memoirs *The Past Is Always Present* and to Veronica Taylor who very kindly sent me letters about the post-war experiences of her late husband Clifford.

I must also thank and praise the staff of the Public Record Office for helping me find all the necessary files. Also I must thank the staff and Trustees of the Imperial War Museum for access to a number of collections within the Department of Documents. Particular thanks go to Amanda Mason for assistance with clearing copyright for the use of quotations. My thanks go to the following veterans for allowing me to quote from their private papers held at the museum: Bill Bampton, Michael Bendix, Andrew Charles, Tom Gore, James Hendrik Witte. Thanks are also due to the following: Dr Gwenda Barer for allowing access to the papers of her late husband Captain R. Barer, to Cynthia Beadle for permission to quote from the memoirs of her late uncle W.A. Blackman, to Eileen Charters for permission to quote from the letters of her late husband C.J. Charters, to Valerie Hills for permission to quote the memoirs of her late father Major A.J. Forrest, to Margot Taylor for permission to quote from the papers of her late father Lieutenant Colonel W.S. Brownlie, to Peter White for permission to quote the diary of his late father John White. In the case of the papers of Jim Sims and Reverend Cullingford the museum made every effort to trace the copyright holders but were unable to do so.

Further thanks go to the following organisations: to Robert Hale Ltd for permission to quote from *The Commandos – D-Day and After* by Donald Gilchrist, to Harper Collins for permission to quote from *A Full Life* by Lt General Sir Brian Horrocks, to Lord Carrington and James Gill at PFD for permission to quote from *Reflect on Things Past* by Lord Carrington, to David Higham Associates for permission to quote from *The Unfinished Man* by James Byrom, to the editor of *The Spectator* for permission to quote from a 1944 letter to the magazine, to Pen and Sword Books Ltd for permission to quote from *Summon Up The Blood* by J.A. Womack and Celia Wolfe.

Finally, my thanks go to Katrina and Graeme whose enthusiasm for the project helped spur me on from day one, and to my long-suffering wife Claire whose support allowed me time to research and complete the book.

Timeline

1944

5 June	Allied Expeditionary Force departs for France by sea and air.
6 June	Airborne landings east of River Orne. Capture of Pegasus Bridge and destruction of Merville Battery. British land at 'Sword' and 'Gold' Beaches, Canadians land at 'Juno'.
7 June	Bayeux liberated by British 50th Division.
8 June	General Montgomery arrives in France.
26 June	'Operation Epsom' launched in an attempt to capture Caen.
1 July	'Epsom' halted, Caen remains in enemy hands.
8 July	'Operation Charnwood' launched in a further attempt to capture Caen.
9 July	British and Canadian 3rd Divisions capture northern part of Caen. The south and east remain in German hands. 43rd Division begin assault on Hill 112.
18 July	'Operation Goodwood' launched in attempt to encircle Caen from east and breakout towards Falaise.
20 July	'Goodwood' halted, Caen captured by Canadian 3rd Division. British armour fail to capture Bourgebus ridge and advance towards Falaise halted.
22 July	43rd Division clear remaining Germans from Hill 112.
25 July	Canadians launch 'Operation Spring' in support of US army's 'Operation Cobra'.
7 August	Canadian II Corps launch 'Operation Totalize' night time advance towards Falaise.
11 August	'Totalize' halted with failure to advance on Falaise
14 August	Canadians launch 'Operation Tractable', attempting to reach Falaise.
20 August	Polish and Canadian troops close 'Falaise Pocket' trapping 50,000 German troops.
25 August	43rd Division cross River Seine at Vernon.
29 August	XXX Corps launch 'The Swan', the rapid advance from the Vernon bridgehead towards Belgium.
3 September	Brussels liberated by Guards Armoured Division.
4 September	Antwerp liberated by 11th Armoured Division.
9 September	Ostend liberated.
10 September	Guards Armoured Division capture bridge over Meuse-Escaut canal at Neerpelt in Belgium. 49th and 51st Divisions attack Le Havre. First supply ships arrive at Dieppe.
12 September	Le Havre liberated by British and Canadian forces. 12,000 prisoners taken.

13 September	Boulogne and Calais captured. 15th Division secure bridgehead over Meuse-Escaut canal near Gheel.
17 September	'Operation Market Garden' launched in an attempt to cross the Rhine at Arnhem in Holland. Airborne forces fail to capture bridge at Arnhem. XXX Corps advance towards Arnhem from Meuse-Escaut canal. Canadian 3rd Division launch assault on Boulogne.
18 September	Eindhoven liberated by Guards Armoured Divison and US paratroopers.
20 September	Guards Armoured Division cross Nijmegen bridge but are unable to advance towards Arnhem.
21 September	Airborne troops at Arnhem bridge finally surrender.
22 September	German garrison at Boulogne surrenders. Canadians take over 9,000 prisoners.
25-26 September	1st Airborne Division withdrawn from Oosterbeek and evacuated across the Neder Rijn.
30 September	Calais surrenders to the Canadians who take 10,000 prisoners.
1 October	1st Canadian Army launches operation to clear Scheldt estuary.
12 October	Start of operations to clear Germans from west bank of River Meuse. Overloon captured by 3rd Division.
19 October	Venray captured by 3rd Division.
1 November	Commandos and 52nd Division land at island of Walcheren in the mouth of the Scheldt estuary.
4 November	Royal Navy minesweepers begin to clear Scheldt estuary.
8 November	Walcheren finally clear of enemy troops.
28 November	First supply convoys arrive at Antwerp.
16 December	Germans launch offensive against Americans in the Ardennes.
19 December	XXX Corps move south to prevent Germans crossing River Meuse.

1945

4 January	XXX Corps and 6th Airborne Division advance into the Ardennes.
15-28 January	XII Corps clear 'Roermond Triangle' in preparation for assault on the Rhineland.
8 February	1st Canadian Army, including British XXX Corps, launch 'Operation Veritable', attacking into the Reichswald forest to advance up to the banks of the Rhine.
23 February	US forces launch attacks in Rhineland in support of 'Operation Veritable'.

10 March	German troops retreat across Rhine at Wesel.
23 March	'Operation Plunder', the crossing of the Rhine by 51st Division at Rees and 1st Commando Brigade at Wesel, begins under cover of darkness.
24 March	Rhine crossings continue. 6th Airborne Division lands around Hamminkeln in 'Operation Varsity' and links up with ground forces.
April	2nd British Army begins advance towards River Elbe. 1st Canadian Army advances into Holland and northern Germany.
13 April	11th Armoured Division liberate Bergen-Belsen concentration camp.
14 April	49th Division captures Arnhem.
26 April	Bremen captured.
29 April	15th Division cross River Elbe.
2 May	6th Airborne Division reach Wismar on the Baltic coast. 11th Armoured Division enter Lubeck.
3 May	7th Armoured Division take surrender of Hamburg. German delegation arrives at Field Marshal Montgomery's HQ at Luneburg to discuss surrender.
4 May	Ceasefire signed. 21st Army Group told to halt offensive operations.
5 May	Surrender comes into effect at 8 a.m.
6 May	General Jodl signs formal surrender at Reims.
7 May	49th Division liberate Amsterdam and Utrecht.
8 May	Formal surrender comes into effect from midnight. The war in Europe is over.
25 August	21st Army Group dissolved, becoming The British Army Of The Rhine.

Introduction

The Second World War was not won by an army – nor was it won by generals, spies, politicians, scientists or codebreakers. It was not even won by professional soldiers. All played their part, all suffered, all excelled themselves, and all helped to change and shape the world we now live in. But on the whole they did not fight the battles, nor shed the blood that brought victory.

The Second World War was won by men. Ordinary men, often little more than boys, with unspectacular pasts and unspectacular futures.

This is not an ordinary story of war. This is not a list of victories and defeats, or of tactics and strategy, but the story of the lives of the men who fought the battles in north-west Europe between D-Day and VE Day. It is the story of the men of Field Marshal Montgomery's 21st Army Group, of what they thought and how they behaved. These were men who aspired simply to survive to the end of another day, hopefully to get some sleep and hot food at nightfall – men who went for weeks without a bath or a change of clothes.

They lived a life few could have imagined when they first landed in Europe. The battles drained the soldiers of both their physical and mental strength. For eleven months they experienced the full range of human emotions. At one moment they could be ruthlessly vindictive towards their enemies, at the next they were caring and forgiving. For most killing was an unpleasant necessity, required to ensure survival. However, others relished the violence and unleashed a wave of crime that shocked their leaders.

Naïve young men, who had hardly taken a drink before they joined the army, found themselves at war's end managing and drinking dry German breweries and distilleries. Thousands stood eagerly in queues outside brothels whilst others deserted to run them. They were saints and sinners, heroes and villains. They fought hard, got drunk, looted, took drugs to keep themselves awake, left an unprecedented trail of destruction across Europe, and finally defeated the enemy. And they fought knowing one thing – the only way to get home was to get the job done.

Yet despite the heroics performed by the men of 21st Army Group, somewhere in the following years much of their story has been forgotten. Their exploits never caught the attention of the public. For all their sufferings and sacrifices history seems to have been unkind to the European campaign. E xcepting a few notable events such as D-Day and the battle at Arnhem – other military feats were not destined to capture the heart of the nation.

Masterful strokes of naval skill, such as the trapping of the *Graf Spee* or the sinking of the *Bismarck* had been ideal candidates for public adulation. They seemed to fit into the typically British notion of the underdog – small forces taking on a mighty enemy and triumphing against the odds. The Battle of Britain, the Blitz and the return of the BEF from the beaches of Dunkirk were much the same – in the nation's darkest hour David had somehow defeated Goliath. These were the legends that grew in the post-war world, recorded forever in books and films that celebrated the victories. Even POWs entered the public consciousness for their adventurous spirit and their efforts to escape against all the odds.

The early war years had been a catalogue of unmitigated disasters for the army with defeats in France, Greece, North Africa and Burma. Only in 1942, after the defeat at El Alamein of Rommel's seemingly invincible Afrika Korps did the public find new heroes – the men of the Eighth Army. The tide had been turned, a chink of light had appeared and from that moment onwards victory seemed inevitable. No longer were they the underdogs. Now, side by side with the Americans and their economic might, they were part of a successful winning team.

With the success of the D-Day landings of June 1944 the public seemed to think the battle was over and after the initial outpourings of joy interest seemed to wane. Only with the airborne landings at Arnhem was interest revived. Once more the British soldiers were the underdogs as the undergunned, undersupplied 'Davids' of the 1st Airborne Division did battle with the 'Goliath' of the SS. Only this time Goliath was victorious. Then, with the coming of winter and the failure to 'bring the boys home by Christmas', the public again seemed to lose interest.

It was not to say that the British public did not care, most families had men serving in Europe, but they had no obvious symbols to latch onto. June 1944 to May 1945 saw not a series of climactic battles but an almost never-ending slog. These were not stirring battles to capture fortresses, culminating in victorious flag waving ceremonies, but messy battles to capture anonymous villages, nameless hills and seemingly insignificant bridges, forests or fields.

For all the bloodshed and heartache there were few remarkable images to capture the public imagination. There was no defining moment caught for posterity by photographers with which to identify with their fighting men. Then, in face of the relentless wartime and post-war publicity given to American involvement in the campaign it seemed somehow inevitable that the British and Canadian role would fade into the background.

How could they compete? Everything seemed to favour their US allies. Without a doubt D-Day's most dramatic story came at Omaha Beach where gallant GIs struggled against appalling odds to gain a foothold in France. Nothing endured that day by any other army could compare to the scale of the slaughter of those first hours.

Then was it not the Americans who first broke out of the Normandy bridgehead to strike deep into occupied France? The speed of General Patton's drive to capture Brittany and then sweep to encircle the German army was the stuff of headlines. This was the drama the public wanted.

When the British launched their own breakout from Normandy it failed to have the same impact. General Horrocks' 30 Corps raced from the Seine to the Scheldt in little over a week, outstripping in speed and distance the heroics of General Patton, yet the British efforts lacked the resonance of the earlier advance. Patton went on to become an American icon, revered by the public and immortalised by Hollywood. Brian Horrocks went on to become 'Black Rod', a prestigious yet purely ceremonial figure at British State occasions.

This was iconography versus modesty, it seemed the campaign was designed for a nation that celebrates understatement. The list was endless. GIs liberated Europe's most fashionable capital – Paris. The British and Canadians took its least fashionable – Brussels. In the two most notable battles of the campaign, the Americans fought heroically in the Battle of The Bulge and emerged victorious, whilst the British were defeated at Arnhem. Whilst the Americans used speed and guile to snatch the last bridge over the Rhine at Remagen, 21st Army Group laboured to build up vast supplies for what, to outside observers, appeared an unnecessarily massive operation to breach the Reich's last natural border. Even in victory the story was the same. The Americans finished the war in the breathtaking scenery of the Bavarian Alps whilst for 21st Army Group the climax was reached on the uninspiring plains and heaths of northern Germany.

It is easy to see why much of the campaign was quickly forgotten. Post-war Britain was a land exhausted by war. All but bankrupt, its Empire dissolving, both industry and the workforce worn out, tormented by years of rationing, Britain was a country in need of change. It was time to look forward and not to the past. Whilst American industrial power reigned supreme and Germany rose from the ashes of defeat, Britain struggled to climb from the ruins of its own victory.

Exhausted by war, there was little will to remember or celebrate and as memories faded the truth faded with them. The veterans shared their memories with each other but few shared such information with their own families. Thousands of sons grew up knowing little of their fathers' experiences. Confronted with Hollywood heroics, and faced with the reticence of their own fathers to admit to having played anything other than a minor role in the drama, a whole generation seemed to emerge uncertain of their nation's role in the defeat of the Nazis. In time one of Britain's greatest military victories became relegated to a footnote in history.

Yet the reality was that it had been an incredible journey – one that cost the lives of 39,599 British and Canadian soldiers and saw the wounding of countless others. It was an experience few would ever forget and that few of the civilians would ever really understand. This was a generation of men whose experiences of the extremes of life and death were to surpass that of any previous generation, or that of any who followed them. In those long months the men of 21st Army Group suffered great hardship and deprivation, enjoyed comradeship and lost friends. They were both killers and saviours, destructors and builders, men who laughed and cried, ate, slept, gambled, made love, got drunk and quite often died.

Here is their story. Read it and you'll never look at your grandfather in the same way again.

I

The Landscape of Battle

'The smell of death was totally in the air – like going into a morgue. But you got used to that smell. It got into your clothes and it was there continuously, so you didn't notice it in the end.' (1)

By 1944 the army had evolved into something almost unrecognisable from that which had existed in 1939. The 21st Army Group that included the British Western European Force, and later the British Liberation Army, was far removed from the British Expeditionary Force that had gone to France in 1939. Consisting of General Dempsey's 2nd Army and General Crerar's 1st Canadian Army, 21st Army Group was under the command of General Bernard Montgomery, the fabled victor of Alamein. Under his command the mixed force of British and Canadians – supplemented with smaller detachments of men from throughout occupied Europe – was to win a victory equal to any in Britain's long military history.

Although consisting almost entirely of conscripts and 'hostilities only' volunteers the army displayed a professionalism little seen in previous years. In the years before the outbreak of war the regular army, though made up of volunteers rather than conscripts, was like a club for some of its members – an organisation joined out of tradition, because for generations the family had sent one son into a particular regiment. Territorial battalions were a mirror of the societies in which they were raised, in rural areas the landowners, magistrates and merchants served as officers whilst gamekeepers and farm hands provided the other ranks.

With the influx of conscripts the army underwent a rebirth. No longer would new officers arrive at their regiments to be given instructions that they should not marry until the age of twenty-five and should go foxhunting twice a week. Instead, the army had evolved into a modern and potent fighting force. The defeats in France, Greece and North Africa had been a violent education. But the mistakes had been learned from, and the army had kept learning all the way across North Africa, through Italy, and by June 1944 stood poised to strike at the German war machine. The army that had gone to France in 1939 full of high hopes to 'Hang out the washing on the Siegfried Line' was set to return with more realistic aspirations.

On the evening of 5 June 1944, as 21st Army Group began its journey towards France, few could have imagined what lay ahead. The airborne forces in their gliders and transport planes, the infantrymen, engineers and tank crews in their landing craft – all could look around at the faces of their colleagues and wonder how many might still be alive the next day. Yet for all their fears few betrayed their inner feelings – about to take part in the greatest military endeavour in history the soldiers did their best to pass it off with an air of studied indifference. Some read books or newspapers, others slept, played cards, chatted idly with their mates. As the hours ticked by so the mood changed, the mask of nonchalance began to slip – silence deepened as their thoughts raced around the fate that awaited them. Those who still talked made less sense and now few were still sleeping although some feigned slumber in an attempt to calm themselves. As some would later comment, they were like actors waiting for their cue to take the stage; uncertain as to whether it would be their greatest performance or an unmitigated disaster.

This was not an easy campaign, it was not a case of land in France and just push the enemy back towards Berlin. There were to be eleven months of fighting during which the soldiers suffered the sunburn of summer, the rains of autumn, the frostbite of winter, and finally – and appropriately – the awakenings of spring.

Right from the start the British and Canadians set a standard for the pattern of advance. From before the first man set foot on the landing beaches, right up until the final defeat of the enemy they unleashed an unprecedented weight of firepower upon the enemy with rocket firing fighter bombers, heavy and medium artillery, mortars, tanks, heavy machine guns, heavy bombers and even battleships. In the parlance of the fighting men this was 'The Full Monty' – named after their general whose preferred method of assault was to batter the enemy into virtual submission before unleashing the infantry and tanks. It was unglamorous, but Monty and his generals knew war wasn't about glamour, instead it was about making sure your men survived to see the final victory.

In their battles the Allies had one great advantage over the enemy – morale. There was one simple detail that kept the soldiers fighting: they could see victory ahead and knew that victory would allow them to go home. Victory was their passport home to their families. For the Germans there was no such luxury. Defeat would mean the destruction of their homeland, the death of thousands of soldiers and civilians and the dislocation of their entire way of life.

But still they fought. Obeying the orders of their Führer, the Germans defended almost every inch of land, even when military logic dictated withdrawing and reforming to fight in natural defensive positions. However logic wasn't the order of the day. After the initial shock of the D-Day landings the Wehrmacht composed itself, improvised defences and hung on tenaciously, even when surrounded. This was not an army prepared to give up without a fight and this was to remain the pattern. Even when short of ammunition or when they were hungry and morale had dipped and when they should have given up, the Germans did the unthinkable and counter-attacked. With a vigour and tenacity displayed by few armies, the Germans were the masters of the counter-attack, waiting for the Allied forces to capture a position then bringing down artillery fire and throwing forward their reserves. For the men of the British and Canadian armies these tactics made their lives uncomfortable, fractured their morale and made survival a luxury.

Throughout the campaign the story was to be the same. There were few glorious battlefield victories, the stuff of which the dreams of armchair generals are made. In truth, much of the time it was a vicious slog as both sides attempted to wear out the opposition. When journalists announced to the world that 'a quiet day has passed at the front' scores of men were dying to capture anonymous and soon to be forgotten villages and fields.

In the early battles every mile advanced was bought at a cost in men and tanks. This was not a clean, orderly battlefield but a state of confusion. Snipers and pockets of cut-off German infantry appeared behind the Allied lines, hiding out in woods and abandoned houses, sneaking out to hit targets of opportunity. At times there was little certainty over who was really in control in many areas. The only certainty was that no one wanted to be a target for the desperate, tenacious and, eventually, surrounded Nazis.

From the start everyone frantically had to learn the realities of war, some senior officers had to relearn what they already knew and those who had fought in the desert had to learn this was a very different war. They discovered the shortcomings of their tactics, had to learn how tanks and infantry should work together and how the airforce could best assist the land war. But it was in the front lines where the lessons were the most vital and certain ones stood out above all others – war was not what the soldiers expected nor would their war bear much resemblance to that recorded by much of history. Where they expected order they found chaos. Where history records advances they remember a hard-fought slogging match. Where history records victory they remember pain and death.

At first many of the inexperienced soldiers had little idea of how to behave. They were slow to dig in, sometimes slept above ground and even stood up to watch nearby actions. These were bad habits that had to be lost quickly if they were to live. As well as being terrifying, the first encounter with enemy fire was often an uncertain experience. It took time to learn when incoming fire was likely to land nearby and when it was necessary to take cover. Only the fortunate ones had the time to learn. One of those 'lucky' men was Wilf Allen who experienced incoming fire on the day he joined the 1st Royal Dragoons from a holding unit:

> We were about three miles back from the front line, the German long range guns would send over about half a dozen shells two or three times a day, I was not aware of this and was walking to my billet with some of my kit when some of these shells started to go over my head landing about a hundred yards away, I carried on walking thinking this is a bit 'hot'. Arriving at my billet nobody was to be seen, after the barrage had finished my driver appeared from a cellar and wanted to know what I was doing outside, they were all taking cover as usual … was certainly afraid of the shells but at that time I was more afraid of being seen as scared than anything else. I soon learned to take cover. (2)

Learning to take cover was just one lesson. There would be many more surprises for them. Despite the mechanised nature of modern warfare, the technical innovations designed to increase firepower and protect the infantryman, the battlefield was a surprisingly lonely place. Whilst death stalked their every move, the soldiers seldom saw the people firing at them and visibility was restricted to little more than a few yards around. For all the noise of the battlefields of Europe the soldiers who inhabited them discovered they were curiously empty places. The rule was never to show yourself, unless absolutely necessary, for a visible man was a dead man. For infantrymen battle could be lonely. Swirls of smoke obscured both friend and foe, and flashes of tracer gave the only indication of the enemy's location and their own inevitable destination. The only sight of the enemy would be a distant blur of movement or a muzzle flash. Many infantrymen found themselves lost in their own world. It was only in the final moments, when the enemy positions were reached, that anyone would be visible. As one infantryman explained: 'You looked around and thought "What the hell am I doing here?" You couldn't see the big picture, you had tunnel vision. You just saw your bit. Before you went into an attack you knew who was on your right and who was on your left. Outsiders were faceless.' (3)

Whenever an advance halted, even for minutes, soldiers dug in and crouched in their slit trench awaiting orders. When the line was static men crouched for days in the slit trenches they shared with a mate, hardly seeing anyone from their own sections let alone the enemy. Their world became the view of the bare earth walls of their trench, maybe a row of bushes, some trees or the corner of a field. Their only contact with the outside world might be a slit trench a few yards away, the sight of friendly helmets indicating the location of their mates. In close countryside the world of the footsloggers was severely restricted. The crash of unseen artillery and the roar of anonymous tank engines were the stimuli experienced by the infantryman.

It was little different for the tank crews, only the commander in his elevated position having any real idea of their surroundings. Under fire the driver and co-driver viewed the world through letter-box sized slits and the gunner through his gunsights. The radio operator/loader had an even more restricted view, seeing nothing but the steel walls that surrounded him. Like the infantryman the tank crews became enclosed in their own small world.

In the chaos and confusion of battle it was little wonder many tragic mistakes were made on the battlefield. In the fog of war, accidents now known as 'friendly fire', but then called 'blue on blue', were commonplace. Throughout the campaign the story was the same – harassed officers misread maps, confused soldiers fired on anything that moved and airmen misidentified targets. The soldiers made plenty of mistakes, as one remembered: 'A chap said to me "There's a Jerry up that tree" so I upped my rifle, took a shot and saw him fall. About an hour later I discovered I'd shot one of our own snipers. Nothing was made of it, these things happen, it wasn't done on purpose. I very much regretted it but you can't dwell on it. I was lucky I didn't know who it was.' (4)

Of all the mistakes it was the failings of the Allied airforces that were to have the most profound affect. Within days of the landings in France officers were reporting their positions attacked by Allied aircraft and in some particularly tragic cases wave after wave of heavy bombers pounded friendly positions. In one incident nearly four hundred Canadians were killed or wounded by Allied bombers supposedly supporting their attack. Every unit had stories about attack by their own planes. Some officers ordered their men to open fire on any planes that attacked them – indeed some were even shot down by irate infantrymen – while others insisted they should receive no aerial support for fear of the damage it might do.

If that were not bad enough the troops also encountered serious problems with civilians. Although for much of the campaign the troops received a welcome few could have dreamed of – smothered in kisses, garlanded with flowers, given food, drink and love – it was not always the case. The reaction differed from place to place – in the words of one soldier: 'The French were generally indifferent, the Belgians welcoming, the Dutch ecstatic and the Germans suspicious.' (5) In France few of the villagers whose homes were destroyed during the Allied advance gave anything like the welcome expected. Understandably they were often sullen and openly hostile; having seen friends and family killed and their homes and farms ruined by war, what did they have to celebrate? A handful even took their hostility to extreme lengths, attacking the advancing armies. Some drivers even sang 'La Marseillaise' as they passed through villages in the hope of protecting themselves from attack.

Civilian snipers were reported, often thought to be women whose German boyfriends had been killed. Just days after D-Day Arthur Jarvis was sent on a sniper hunt: 'Some of the French people were shooting at us on the beach. They gave me six men and we found one of the houses where they were firing at us from. We got a chap with a Bren gun firing at the windows and I went with the others round the back. We crept up the stairs and threw a grenade in. We found two lads who looked about fifteen and we killed them.' He later asked a French woman about the civilian reaction and she told him: 'The Germans have been here four years and we've not lost anything. You've been here three or four days and we've got nothing left.' (6)

Such problems just added to the uncertainty of the men on the battlefield, enhancing their confusion. However, they were little more than an irritation compared to two things that cut through the fog of war, penetrating and permeating the senses – smell and sound. The smell of the battlefield is something few soldiers can ever forget and that many find difficult to describe to outsiders who have never experienced such an intense assault on the senses. There was the unique aroma of cordite that lingered over the battlefield after every explosion and every round fired. Its sickly sweet fumes seemed to hang at ground level, combining with the smell of dead bodies and phosphorus. Some men found the cocktail of odours was so revolting they felt constantly sick. In addition to these were the smells of dead, and often rotting farm animals, the odour of dried sweat on unwashed uniforms and bodies, and the stench of unburied human faeces. The impact was explained by one infantryman: 'The smell of death was totally in the air – like going into a morgue. But you got used to that smell. It got into your clothes and it was there continuously, so you didn't notice it in the end. Then you'd go out of the line for a couple of days – forget it – then when you returned it would hit you again. Terrible.' (7)

Overpowering though it was for infantrymen, the senses of the tank crews were pushed to the very limit. Enclosed in their 'tin horses' there was no escape from their own body odour, the cordite as they fired their guns, the diesel or petrol of their engines and even the urine they passed into empty shell cases to be emptied out through the hatches when a suitable moment came.

The sounds of war laid almost permanent siege on the eardrums. At its height noise could be so intense that it seemed to merge into a blanket of sound that enveloped the soldiers. The lack of definition between sounds, in which friendly or enemy fire became indistinguishable, offered an unlikely protection from fear for some men. Deprived of the sense of hearing they could no longer hear approaching danger and thus they no longer worried about it. With time the noise merged into the background with soldiers able to distinguish the noises that really mattered, and eventually some soldiers found the roar of artillery almost like a lullaby – a background noise that accompanied their drifting off to sleep. An infantry NCO tried to explain the effect of noise:

> The mortars would be throwing shells over, the 25 pounders would be firing, the Brens would be firing. It was all noise. And coming back the other way would be shells. So you had the whistle of shells all day. Tanks rolling, tanks firing right alongside you. When I was in the Bren carrier the gun was going 'dack, dack, dack, dack' right by my ear. So the noise was absolutely amazing. When you were under a barrage you were cocooned within it. You could go for days and not hear what you were saying – just the chatter of the guns. Terrible, when an attack was going in. (8)

Some found the intensity of noise affected more than just the ears, seeming to assault the skin. With every explosion they felt the vibration and heat of the blast rippling across their faces. Even the ground beneath their feet shook. The artillerymen who fired the massed barrages that were to become a feature of 21st Army Group's offensives were left deafened for hours afterwards. Even shorter fire orders would leave a ringing in their ears. Others found themselves suffering from intense headaches caused by the noise that enveloped them. For men under heavy artillery fire conversation became impossible. The soldiers listened intently for the noise of incoming shell or mortar fire. They soon learned the tell-tale signs that meant a round was heading for them and 'hit the deck' accordingly – if shells made a short, sharp, swishing noise they should take cover, if the noise was more leisurely the rounds would land some distance away. In time those lucky enough to survive would consider themselves to have developed a sixth sense about incoming artillery. Some men noticed how they walked with a stoop and one ear cocked to the air as if ready to hit the ground at the first sign of incoming fire.

These sounds that heralded danger had to be listened out for amongst the rumble of friendly artillery and the crash of distant explosions. There was also the noise of the close support aircraft that could appear overhead to batter enemy positions, and in the first weeks after D-Day, the terrifying rumble of naval gunfire and the deafening accompaniment of large calibre projectiles. Most frightening of all was the screams of the wounded, the less serious cases calling for medics and stretcher bearers, the more serious crying incoherently for their mothers. These were the awful sounds that could go on long after the fighting was over as dying men lay in no man's land pleading for assistance. With the dangers of proceeding into no man's land too great, men had to sit tight and listen to hours of crying as their friends lay dying. It was unnerving for their friends but no compensation to know the sounds were irritating to their enemies. And at the end of it all a surreal peace descended over the battlefield – birds could be heard singing, dogs barking, cows mooing and insects buzzing – for a brief period it seemed as if the world had regained its sanity.

Despite all the mechanised madness of war the soldiers' lives became closely tied in with nature. Often living in holes in the ground they became attuned to a very basic life. Their days were controlled by the hours of daylight, their night time activities controlled by cloud and moon. The weather influenced them to a degree they had never previously experienced. In the sun of summer they sweated, their clothes rubbed, their skin burned and everything smelt worse. In the wet of spring and autumn the damp penetrated their clothing, water seeped into their boots and their skin turned soft and puffy. Then in winter the cold penetrated their bones making them ache. Gloved fingers could hardly move for cold and ears, noses and toes all risked frostbite. The wind dried their skin, leaving their cheeks stinging and lips chapped. If a change of season was a respite it was merely a prelude to more misery to follow.

The summer sun brought more than just the discomfort of sunburn to the men who fought in Normandy – they were also plagued by insects. The rivers and streams were the breeding ground for swarms of mosquitoes that assaulted the troops. In the heat of summer the soldiers had to keep their shirts buttoned up to the collar to keep out the insects and wore camouflage netting as scarves to try to keep them out. Yet somehow the persistent insects always managed to find a way inside, creeping up sleeves or trouser legs to reinforce the discomfort. Those soldiers occupying positions in view of the enemy dared not even move to swat insects for fear of alerting the enemy of their position. Instead they suffered in silence, reluctantly counting the growing number of bites covering their exposed skin. To deter the mosquitoes the army issued the men with cream that was designed to repel them. Instead most users found the insects attracted to it and joked that the best use of the cream was just to open the pot and leave it nearby to lure the mosquitoes away.

Other insects swarmed around their positions including virulent wasps and horseflies. Soon many soldiers were covered in infected bites, their skin red raw and itching. To find twenty mosquito bites on the back of one hand was not unusual and it looked as if they had measles. It became impossible for some soldiers to shave and bites around the eyes left others unable to see properly.

Worse than the irritation of the bites was the fact the insects fed on the thousands of corpses – animal and human – that littered the Normandy countryside, spreading disease and infection amongst the already weakened soldiers. In the unsanitary conditions of the battlefield many soldiers found the bites becoming seriously infected. There was little else the medics could do but clean up infected bites, give them antibiotics and return them to their unit. In the bitter fighting that followed D-Day there were few enough reinforcements coming in to fill the gaps left by the wounded and killed for a unit to be able to spare a man as a result of boils. Insects were also blamed for the spread of dysentery that was to have such a debilitating effect on so many soldiers that summer. Some units recorded as much as 75 per cent of their men suffering from dysentery.

The winter of 1944-45 was among the coldest in living memory and left the men of 21st Army Group floundering in the frozen and flooded Dutch country-side. It was an experience few ever wished to repeat. Men woke in the mornings to find their clothing or blankets frozen to the ground. As one officer complained to the War Office: 'No one in this theatre of ops will ever again say hard things about the English climate.' (9)

The worst of winter saw thousands of British troops struggling through snow and ice, seldom with sufficient winter clothing in the frozen Ardennes, helping to roll back the advances made by the Germans during the Battle of the Bulge. The severity of the winter brought a drop in morale among members of all the armies fighting in Europe, and the British and Canadians were no exception. The extremes of weather brought physical discomfort – coughs, colds, respiratory illnesses, frostbite, trench foot and exposure.

It also brought with it the psychological impact of knowing that they wouldn't be home for Christmas. Hot food was often scarce and men became caught up in a cycle of discomfort where the lack of food meant they couldn't keep warm, unable to keep warm they couldn't sleep and the lack of sleep made them feel colder still.

These conditions lowered morale and in time discipline began to suffer. Ken Hardy, a subaltern in the 49th Division, recalled the latter months of 1944:

That winter morale dropped, it was very difficult to get blokes to go forward, very difficult to get blokes to do anything, by that time of course it was after Arnhem, and people really expected the war to be over soon and they didn't want to miss out on it. Christmas is a bad time, I was on 'the island' for quite a lot of the time during that winter, it was very, very depressing. 'The island' wasn't too bad to get blokes to do things because it was terribly static. But the Ardennes, when we really thought the Germans might get to the channel ports and we weren't going to get out, that was a really low ebb. It was really difficult to get blokes to do anything. Morale was very, very low. I don't think it's made enough of in the history books. Afterwards when we were going to go through the Reichswald morale really lifted up because you were doing something. But when it just wallows around ... I think there was drift, from top to bottom. Officers were not unaffected either, and men soon catch up if their officers are drifting, and don't really know where the hell they're going. I can remember an occasion when a fellow officer of mine said 'If you go back now I'll shoot you' and he meant it. Discipline became rock hard, 'if you do that I'll shoot you'. It was an awful time. It occurs to me that the idea that morale was high from beginning to end is rubbish. During that winter it was very low, when we were messing around doing nothing. (10)

Even following the low of the winter cold there was more to come. While many civilians were already beginning to think of life post-war, planning their victory celebrations and the inevitable return to normality, thousands of British and Canadian troops, under the command of the Canadian General Crerar, were advancing into the Reichswald forest. With the snow thawing they fought from village to village, clearing woods and farms, always in the cold and rain, their every move plagued by a sea of mud which engulfed roads and bogged down tanks, some even to the height of their turret. Damage to the flood defences of the Rhine left vast areas flooded and patrols had to be undertaken by boat and troops moved by amphibious carriers – it was an experience few would ever forget.

The interaction with the environment endured by the men of 21st Army Group was a discomfort, an irritation and sometimes drove men to the brink of mental and physical exhaustion. Yet for some this communing with nature had a more horrific impact. There were moments when the natural way of the world affected even the most hardened soldier, as one veteran of North Africa, Sicily, Italy and north-west Europe remembered: 'I can't stand rats because I've seen what they can do to a body. Within minutes of a man getting killed the bloody rats were there. They can reduce a body in minutes, they come in hordes. They're in a pack, they wait and all of a sudden they go and the body is stripped within minutes. Then they're gone.' (11)

Just as the natural world plagued their existence so too did the technical world. The men of 21st Army Group fought with weapons that were seldom up to their task. Their Lee Enfield No 4 rifles were reliable and accurate but outdated – relying on a bolt action rather than the semi automatic fire favoured by the Americans. The automatic weapons used by the British and Canadians were also less than popular. The most common sub-machinegun – the Sten – was one of the most unreliable weapons ever issued, jamming when it was most needed and firing by accident at other times. Some men drew up lists of the Sten's best points and concluded that the magazine catch was good for opening beer bottles, the return spring house cap could be used for measuring a rum ration and the barrel could be removed to use as a straw for drinking from wine vats.

If that was bad, their revolvers were even worse and few frontline officers bothered to carry them. They were inaccurate, heavy, difficult to fire and lacked penetrative power. One officer even fired six shots at a charging goat and failed to hit with a single round. The overwhelmingly low opinion of these weapons led to the War Office concluding that the .38 Enfield was 'useless', and in tests 50 per cent of rounds failed to penetrate a petrol tin at a range of twenty-five yards. (12)

Not only weapons were a problem. Binoculars were so underpowered most officers preferred to use ones captured from the Germans. Signals equipment also proved less than popular. In official reports one wireless was described as: 'A bad set for battle. Netting device too fragile for rough work of infantry in action. Very limited performance but has proved useful on occasions … It is most inadequate for Mobile Fire Control work in our mortar platoon. Not a success in tanks as a means of communication to infantry.' The No18 set was described as 'quite useless' and other sets were: 'Difficult to obtain and very inferior in quality.' Not only were the radios considered poor but there were few enough trained operators, with many of the reinforcements having little or no knowledge of the No19 set – a set which curiously required operators to carry a sixpence with which to tighten the locking screws and keep it on frequency. Little wonder the overall assessment of signals equipment given by one battalion commander was: 'most unsatisfactory'. (13)

Of course not everything was bad. Their mortars were generally accepted as efficient and reliable, as were grenades – with the '36' grenade described as 'top notch' in official reports. The Bren light machinegun was among the best in the world, beloved by all who used it. As the War Office reported: 'This weapon performed excellently. No adverse comments whatsoever. Considered the finest weapon they had to use.' (14) The British had also acquired an unequalled reputation for artillery fire. The performance of the Royal Artillery and their Canadian counterparts was the very basis of the success of the army's operations, and in the 25 pounder field gun they had one of the best weapons of the whole war. It was the envy of other armies, both Allied and enemy. It was the ideal weapon – accurate, reliable and mobile – one which both gunner and infantryman could have complete confidence in. And the infantry really did have faith in the artillery– riflemen cheered and applauded as the gun limbers drove past them in the knowledge that these were the people who blasted a path for the advance. In the words of one veteran, the gunners were: 'the most professionally competent people in the British Army'. (15)

The British Army had also developed some of the most modern specialist equipment in the world. They had 'Flail' tanks that could beat a path through minefields, fearsome flamethrowing 'Crocodile' tanks that struck terror into the hearts of the enemy defenders and amphibious tanks that rose from the surf on D-Day to confound the enemy gunners. Added to this was the best military bridging equipment available to any army, tanks that could lay carpets across soft ground, fill anti-tank ditches or deliver explosive charges to flatten concrete defences.

Yet for all of these advancements they were hampered by one great technological failing. The tanks of 21st Army Group were years behind those of the enemy, something that soon caused dismay among the troops and cost the lives of hundreds of young tank crews. Even before the invasion of France the matter was raised in parliament but, not wanting to spread panic, the politicians did their best to cover up the realities of the situation. In parliament Churchill evaded the issue and stated that when British tank crews next went to war: 'They will be found to be equipped in a manner at least equal to the forces of any other country in the world.' (16)

Yet as Churchill and many observers knew, he was, in the language of parliamentarians, being 'economical with the truth', and once the fighting in Normandy got underway the truth soon became apparent. The main tanks in use by the men of 21st Army Group were the American-made Sherman and the British-made Cromwell. With its 75mm gun, the Sherman was unable to penetrate the frontal armour of the German Tigers and Panthers, and was often ineffective against their side armour. Its own high profile made it an easy target for enemy tanks or anti-tank guns and its thin armour offered little protection against the guns deployed by the Germans. The only positive claims made for the Sherman was its high speed and the fact that it could be easily repaired or replaced.

Like the Sherman, the British-made Cromwell was also fast, its high speed supposedly allowing it to break out quickly across open countryside, causing havoc among the enemy. Of course the reality of war in Europe offered little opportunity for such displays. Instead the crews of the Cromwell tanks often found themselves inching through narrow streets or carefully manoeuvring along country lanes, ever on the lookout for enemy troops.

The stories about the failure of armour soon began to circulate, and some senior officers expected there to be open dissent in tank units as a result of the inequality. As Wilfred Allen, a veteran of 1st Royal Dragoons, recalled: 'The mere whisper of Tiger tanks and things went very quiet.' (17) One tank commander tried to console his gunner who had complained about the failure of their 75mm gun to penetrate German tank armour, telling him that at least inside a tank they were better protected than the infantry. The gunner wasn't convinced and replied: 'What would the infantry do if they were sent into action with rifles which wouldn't penetrate the enemy's uniforms?' (18)

Montgomery attempted to suppress criticism of the tanks, fearing the rumours would damage morale. He even banned the writing of reports by senior officers on the subject for fear of their contents being leaked. Despite this General Dempsey called for reports on the failure of the tank guns and concluded that at thirty yards a 75mm gunner couldn't penetrate German armour, and the Tiger was declared to be 'practically immune' to the Shermans and Cromwells. The reports concluded the Tigers and Panthers were 'infinitely superior' to the tanks of 21st Army Group and it was admitted that: 'At the present time our armour is fighting under a considerable handicap.' (19)

For the men inside the tanks the only short-term alternative was to find ways to give themselves additional protection. Mechanics spent hours welding spare tracks onto the front of tanks in the hope that they might help to deflect the shells of the enemy guns, and fitted racks that could be filled with sandbags to absorb the punch of the enemy's hand-held anti-tank weapons. They also backed their tanks into defensive positions so that the engine would protect them from the penetrative power of the enemy guns – they did not mind if their vehicle was disabled, they just wanted to survive.

The saving grace for British tank crews was the appearance of the upgunned Sherman Firefly. At least Firefly crews could go into battle with a measure of optimism since it carried a British 17 pounder gun which was actually capable of penetrating enemy armour. The accepted method of using the Firefly was one per troop of four tanks with the three 75mm Shermans attempting to protect the Firefly until it could get a clear and effective shot at the enemy. It would only be in the latter months of the campaign, with the introduction of the Comet that the British finally had a tank capable of competing on equal terms with the enemy.

This was one of the lessons learnt by the troops – everything takes time. War was a learning process for everyone – generals and privates alike. And everything they were learning about would influence their life. The terror and uncertainty of battle, the ups and downs of relationships with civilians, the failings of weapons and accidents on the battlefield all helped mould the attitudes and behaviour of the soldiers. They found this landscape of battle was not a comfortable place, but they would do their utmost to live through the experience as best they could.

2

The Ordinary Men

'I'm very glad to be off at last … The sooner we get across and finish it, the sooner we shall all return to our homes, and I'll be with you all again.' (1)

Any attempt to summarise the attitudes of the soldiers who fought in the European campaign is bound to upset someone. Some might find assessments of the situation fail to reflect their own views – to them most interpretations will be wrong. And what of those whose friends and relatives died? Any writer runs the risk of destroying cherished memories of how the soldiers behaved and what they thought of war. With such a diverse range of men serving in the army who could hope to reflect the attitudes of them all – influenced, as they were, by pre-war experiences and post-war aspirations? By highlighting the views of a man who fought not for 'King and Country' but only for his own survival may offend those for whom patriotism is an end in itself. It is a thankless task to attempt to summarise the attitudes of an army where nobility rubbed shoulders with communists, where grandfathers fought alongside teenagers, and where former secondary schoolboys commanded men from the top public schools.

By June 1944 the whole of society was at war. Soldiers were fighting in Italy and Burma. The Royal Navy patrolled the seas and the merchant fleet carried the supplies that would be moulded into weapons of war. Women were working in factories to turn these raw materials into weapons, whilst bomber crews flattened the cities of the Reich. Farmers and the girls of the Land Army were reaping and sowing to feed the country. A population of millions was working towards the common goal – victory.

Yet for all the millions playing their part in the war effort, few would pay a higher price than the soldiers who fought the victorious battles. Among the men at the apex of the advance all of society was represented – they came *From the City, From the Plough* (2) and were destined to return there, if they were lucky. Some were brave, some were cowards – but most were unsure which they were.

All types of men were in khaki. There were timid, unassuming men who became callous, hard-hearted killers – whilst unit bullies were reduced to crying and shaking with fear. Similarly, there were long-serving senior NCOs who were unable to endure the rigours of battle whilst 'long-haired, silk-scarved types' became valiant commando officers.

When assessing the behaviour and attitudes of the troops of the 21st Army Group it becomes necessary to cast away the long-held public perceptions of soldiers during the Second World War. There exists an image of cheekily cheerful privates, overwhelmingly working class, with strong regional accents, stoically following orders and accepting their destiny with a fateful sense of duty. This image, fostered by films, television programmes and countless comic books, only paints part of the picture. The army had become a melting pot as class and social barriers were eroded by war. University graduates rubbed shoulders with illiterates, public schoolboys with grammar schoolboys. The old pre-war elite served alongside men who had known long years of unemployment in the 1930s. Young men, many of whom were still schoolboys when war broke out, mixed with worldly-wise men, including First World War veterans. Amidst the massed wave of men were devoted husbands, serial womanisers, homosexuals, rapists, the sexually voracious and the virtually monastic.

Artilleryman John Mercer recalled: 'In the army you met an enormous variety of people, like a university in a way. I was a bank clerk. George had started as a lighterman, Dennis was a tailor's cutter from Leeds. Most of the soldiers weren't professionals, they had come from all walks of life. One of the gunners with me was a housemaster at Eton. He wouldn't take a commission, he was just an ordinary gunner.' (3)

In the days before mass travel, this social and geographical mix surprised many men, as one explained:

> Quite frankly, I couldn't understand some of them. We had some Welshmen in our lot and they used to get up a corner and jabber away in Welsh. We also had a lad from somewhere to the north of Inverness and he had such a thick accent you just couldn't understand him. When you think of lads who had never been anywhere … I suppose the farthest away from my hometown of Norwich that I'd been was Great Yarmouth, and that was on an evening trip! (4)

It was not just men representing British society who served in the campaign. Montgomery's 21st Army Group consisted of two armies – the British 2nd Army under Lieutenant General Dempsey and the Canadian 1st Army under Lieutenant General Crerar. The Canadians of Crerar's 1st Army had a mixed reputation, known to be ferocious in battle and a nightmare for any authority figures who tried to keep them under control. Even one of their own number described many as: 'mavericks and misfits from a depression-ravaged land'. (5)

The Canadians were not just serving with their own army. Some had volunteered to be platoon leaders in British infantry regiments under the Canloan scheme. These were to prove themselves among the best of the junior officers of the 21st Army Group whose battle honours and casualty rate reflected their outstanding contribution.

Even the so called 'British army' was also populated by thousands of foreigners. There was a Polish armoured division, Belgian and Dutch infantry brigades and a Czech armoured brigade and French, Danish, Spanish and Norwegian commando units. More than ten thousand foreigners had joined as individuals and were scattered among the troops, included among them were Irishmen, Yugoslavs, Romanians, Hungarians, Italians, Russians and Americans. Most surprisingly, more than 4,000 German and Austrian Jewish exiles had also joined the British army.

This mix of men was to influence attitudes and behaviour. Some tried to make sense of what they saw around them and construct an overview of the men they served with. In a 1944 essay entitled 'What the Soldier Thinks' one anonymous officer wrote to the *Spectator* magazine of his observations. He found them less than optimistic about the future, expecting another European war within twenty years. They thought others were sentimental towards the enemy as they themselves had been prior to combat: 'knowing that his hatred will only endure until he hears the first German baby ask him for chocolate'. They seemed genuinely cynical about the past, present and future. The fighting men were afraid for their future after demobilisation, thinking that with high wages having been paid to those in war work they themselves would be left behind. With regard to the war industries at home they felt that big business was profiteering and that there was a strong case for nationalisation. Ever distrustful of politicians, they were sceptical of the Beveridge Report that promised them health care and pensions in the post-war world, since they thought there must be a catch in it. As for the subject of religion it: 'scarcely touches the fringes of his life'. In summing up the soldiers the writer felt: 'He is tough, hard, honest, intelligent, cynical, kind, soft hearted, sentimental and completely disillusioned. He is fighting not for any ideal .... But because he knows that Germany must be utterly defeated before he can get home to his family, his football, his beer and his fireside.' (6)

There was little of the traditional motivation perceived by so many people. Few were fighting for King, Country and Empire. For most there were more basic considerations. This personal rather than patriotic motivation was summed up by one veteran:

We agree that we went to war because it was an unavoidable duty which we never expected to last so long, and about which we could not have imagined the reality. When we first joined up it was with excitement, not knowing what to expect. We did not consider ourselves pacifists when we discovered too late that it was not what we expected – we did the job but felt that no one in authority knew what they were doing. We are all in agreement about the degree of comradeship that arose among those who were in service, a bond that still exists today. I have never been a Royalist and I never thought of fighting for King and Country. I joined up because my friends were going, also my brother and sister. If I had any ideals, it was for my family and to preserve our way of life in my home town, that I was fighting for. If all my comrades fought for their home town then this could be interpreted as being patriotic. (7)

He and his friends explained their experiences:

It was an adventure you see, that was the biggest thing in your mind. I was 16 or 17 years old, hardly been out of the village. My brother had gone into the army, then my sister went and I was the only one left. All my friends from school were thinking about going. So that was the main reason I volunteered, so as not to be at home on my own. But it was also an adventure. We could see ourselves with two guns – like cowboys. We were brought up on cowboy films.(8) (His friend continued): I was at school when war started and I think we got these romantic ideas at school. I volunteered simply because I knew I had to go in any case, so I thought I'd go into something of my choosing. Certainly any thought of romance and adventure went by the board. (9)

Others had no intention of volunteering. On 3 September 1939 Arthur Jarvis was in church to hear the banns read out in advance of his wedding. Any thought of war was far from his mind when the vicar interrupted the service to listen to Chamberlain's radio broadcast announcing the opening of hostilities:

> I was twenty-years-old when the war started. I got married on 9 September. I wasn't going for anything, I was forced to go. I had no choice. When you got to twenty you were registered to do six months service under the military act. I got a letter to say they didn't need me, then within a week I got another letter to say I was registered and I was to go for my medical! So I was only married for three weeks before I was called up. (10)

Viewed en masse, the stereotypical image of the infantrymen does persist, with their comradely behaviour and jovial voices, the massed khaki ranks helped to cement the image. The flippant behaviour of soldiers helped reinforce the stereotype of a carefree, phlegmatic approach to war. It was not uncommon for infantrymen, whether experienced soldiers or unblooded recent recruits, to recognise that they were cannon fodder and take risks that would have been unthinkable in the peacetime army. Many felt the red infantry flash worn on their sleeves made them feel like gladiators who were about to enter the arena. They knew they could face no greater punishment than to be allowed to continue on their journey to the front.

Whether baaing like sheep as they queued to board troopships or shouting insults at passing MPs there was often a childishness to their behaviour. Troops aboard landing craft heading for Normandy hung over the sides gesturing rudely or shouting insults at the boats they passed. Even once the fighting was underway some continued to display an irreverent outlook. When soldiers of the Royal Scots Fusiliers occupied a small hill to the north of Arnhem, they were seen running to the top, dancing around and singing 'I'm the King of the Castle'.

In this anonymous mass of khaki were soldiers desperate to exert their independence. Everywhere they went walls were marked with graffiti – their own names, the names of their wives and girlfriends, or complaints about army life. They carved lovehearts into trees, scrawled obscene doggerel on walls, and scribbled cartoons of glamour girls. Crews of tanks and armoured vehicles took to painting names and slogans on their craft. Some were patriotic exhortations to victorious endeavour – such as 'Our Revenge' – although more usually the slogans showed a longing for home or were just plain rude. Acronyms were also popular, such as 'FUJIAR' that stood for 'Fuck You Jack I'm Alright'. (11) These were all reminders of their existence, embellishments that displayed their links to a civilian life to which they longed to return.

The attitudes of the new recruits to the armed forces was such that few were prepared to see themselves first and foremost as soldiers. Instead many viewed themselves simply as civilians in uniform and many recognised that they weren't suited to the enforced regimentation of army life. They were prepared to do their duty but intended to do it on their own terms, not the army's. Joe Ekins of the 1st Northants Yeomanry was one such 'civilian soldier'. Anxious to avoid the infantry he volunteered for tanks at the age of seventeen, but soon realised he was not suited to army life:

> I was sent to Bovington which was the premier tank training centre. I went down there and I realised that I wasn't going to be a soldier in the way they wanted me to be a soldier. I didn't fit in with doing the things they wanted. The first day, we got to Wool station which is about 4 or 5 miles away from the camp and they decided we were going to run all the way. I've got two suitcases! I took far more kit than I needed. So that wasn't all that hot for a start off. But the actual training I loved. I liked the driving, I liked the wireless operating, I liked the gunnery. But the bullshit, I just couldn't stand it. I'd never liked to waste my time. I considered that at least 50, possibly 60 per cent of it was an absolute waste. Didn't do me any good, didn't make me a better soldier. Later when we were based in a park, anyone could have got in, and there were two of us walking around all night to guard it. Absolutely stupid it was, waste of time and effort. Between the guns we had tarpaulin tank sheets, that made a lovely bed. I got caught asleep on guard. So that's the attitude I went to war with. Generally speaking, I had no time for the army. All the bullshit were an absolute waste of time. I knew what I were doing regards my job. First thing we did when we got over there was throw away the machine gun ammunition and fill the boxes with fags. (11)

Ekins and his later crewmates retained this attitude from Normandy through to the Rhine crossing: 'just making the best of it and skiving out of as much work as you could. We were always in trouble and we were always scheming to get out of work.' (12) Despite the conscious decision to reject military discipline his attitude had little effect on his abilities as a tank gunner. During Operation Totalize his tank engaged a formation of Tiger tanks. When the battle was finished the Germans had lost three of their precious tanks, and in one of them their foremost tank ace of the war, SS Captain Michael Wittmann. Trooper Ekins, who devoted so much of his army career to skiving, had proved his worth in battle.

The failure of many soldiers to accept some of the more excessive demands of authority made it increasingly difficult for the army to get its men to adhere to some of the most basic disciplinary rules. Many believed they were exempt from saluting when on exercises, on leave, or in the field and officers calculated that two-thirds of soldiers failed to salute their superiors. The soldiers of democracy were prepared to salute the man where respect was due but had little intention of saluting the uniform unless it could not be avoided.

Most soldiers had little desire to take part in any military activity when off duty and some were lucky to find there was little restriction on their behaviour. Stan Procter was a signaller at 214 Brigade HQ whose duties included spending time attached to infantry units:

> The funny thing is being attached to an infantry battalion and not having our own officers anywhere near us, I was a sort of free agent. As long as I did my job for the battalion, they didn't exercise any discipline over me. We were just attached to them

and our officers were elsewhere. Incredibly when we were on the way up to Arnhem we went off and had a breakfast in a farm. Anything could have happened and we weren't there. It's extraordinary we'd disappear for half a day or something like that. This is whilst the war's on. Quite amazing. (13)

Few soldiers were willing to allow the military authorities to interfere with personal relationships and thus the manner in which men could be posted away from their comrades caused friction between soldiers and the authorities – they felt the army was their employer rather than their master. Private soldiers even raised petitions amongst their colleagues to prevent the transfer of popular officers. Once they had a commander they could trust in battle they had little desire to lose him to an unknown replacement. Likewise, wounded men who were deemed fit to return to the front wanted to rejoin their own units. What they feared was life in holding units or transit camps from where they might be posted to another unit, where as an unknown replacement they might die before anyone learned their name. Instead the option favoured by some was to go AWOL and hitch back to their units. There they could catch up on gossip, celebrate life with their surviving mates and mourn the loss of those who had passed. In Northern Ireland a group of recuperating officers, from various regiments, were sent to join the South Lancashire Regiment. Even airborne officers were told to hand in their coveted red berets. To a man they refused. The CO realised that an error had been made. In face of a mutiny he backed down and the officers were returned to their own units.

Despite the retention of a civilian outlook many of the new soldiers impressed their professional superiors. Thousands were carried along on the tide of war, not necessarily wanting to kill or to risk their own lives, but enjoying the physical tests endured in training. They wanted to be able to run as fast or carry as much as their mates, or complete assault courses in record time and be the best shot in the company. Plenty of men who had never imagined themselves as soldiers threw themselves wholeheartedly into training. One group adopted the catchphrase that: 'an NCO was no good unless a third of his men referred to him as "that bastard"'. The man who coined the phrase, Alexander Baron, went on to explain:

> This proposition is not as unpleasant as it looks. I coined it to catch the attention of my listeners. It should be reversed. In a good unit the NCO ought to be able to convince most of his men that they will be safer and more effective if they become a good team. In any human group it is realistic to assume that some will remain anti-social but in war most of these will be carried on by the will and tempo of the majority, and by the need to survive. NCOs had to learn that they would now be doing their men a bad turn if during a training period they took them behind the sheds to pass the time with a quiet smoke. The corporal who kept his men trotting in a circle and dropping flat every time he shouted 'Down!' was not a sadist but was teaching them how to save their lives. (14)

Such attitudes were to impress many professional officers. Colonel John Waddy, a pre-war regular, explained why he felt they made good soldiers:

By '44 most of our soldiers had been in the Army for 4 to 5 years and were soldiers and not civilians in uniform! There was a different spirit during the war and they regarded themselves as professionals. Many 'civvies' did a lot better in fighting than some regulars. Despite the outward appearance of being a peace loving nation the British have done a lot of fighting over the past 300 to 400 years. How do you think we gained and maintained an Empire? Soldiering is in the blood. (15)

Tensions existed between soldiers of all ranks – whether regulars, territorials or conscripts. For all the glamour of the elite regiments few of the new breed of 'civilian soldiers' were truly impressed by them. Men of the Royal Tank Regiments complained that it always seemed to be their task to break through the enemy defences whilst the Guards were detailed to break out and exploit lightly defended interior positions. With humour they called out to Guardsmen to take care not to scratch their paintwork or get their vehicles dirty. They watched in awe at the way some Guards officers sauntered about the battlefield, but although admiring their resolve there was little respect for the 'bullshit' that accompanied it. It was not just the elite of the army that were sometimes viewed with hostility. John Majendie, a regular officer serving in the Somerset Light Infantry, noticed the differences:

There was a certain antipathy from Territorials towards us regulars. I spent time in a couple of TA battalions before we went to France and I know one where they rather liked to think that they were the good part time soldiers and they didn't really appreciate someone who happened to be a regular. It was not unpleasant but one realized. Occasionally senior NCOs looked down a bit on the chaps, conscripts, who'd come in rather unwillingly. But when the war got going I think everyone became equal. (16)

Differences were apparent in many units. Some members of armoured cavalry units looked down on the 'professional' tankmen of the Royal Tank Regiment, whom they considered to be unworthy successors to their mantle as the leaders of lightning charges. The professionals in turn looked at the cavalrymen as privileged amateurs and referred to them as 'donkey wallopers' (17), more suited to the polo field than the modern battlefield. Despite their differences both groups agreed on one thing. Newly trained tank crews, who could end up in either cavalry regiments or a Royal Tank Regiment, viewed posting to another group with trepidation. As a tank commander noted in his memoirs, only 'heroes and headcases' (18) joined a reconnaissance regiment, since patrolling ahead or on the flanks of the advance was too dangerous for most to consider.

For all the tensions that existed between various units, there grew increasingly close links between many officers and their men. To many observers the key to the whole operation of the vast machinery of warfare was the subalterns and NCOs. This was the teamwork the army relied on for success. If the leaders performed badly the men wouldn't respond. If the men didn't respond the infantry were doomed, and if they were doomed so was the entire campaign. For all the rhetoric of the senior commanders, good or bad, it was the subalterns whose job it was to carry out their orders. It would hardly be an exaggeration to say they were the glue that held the army together.

There was little doubt such glue was vital to the army. Officers had to build close relationships since the men made it clear they had little trust for many of the generals – some openly joked about how both British and German generals had probably gone to the same schools. It was a little unfair, more suited to the Great War when the Kaiser and King George were cousins, but it showed a questioning of authority. The best of the officers were devoted to their men, caring for them like sons or younger brothers, shepherding them through the trials and tribulations of army life. The two-way relationship between officers and their men bred a devotion that continued even after being transferred away. When one officer of the 23rd Hussars heard of the losses in his former Yeomanry squadron he simply told his CO he was returning to his old unit to take command. No consultation, no waiting for orders, just a straightforward return to help those he cared for.

The best officers were able to rally their men to carry out unthinkable tasks. Discipline was irrelevant, they could order a man to advance but that was mere words – the real measure of a platoon commander was respect. Sydney Jary who led his platoon from Normandy until the end of the war, tried to explain the relationship:

> The major factor was undoubtedly the confidence and trust that existed between me and my NCOs. 18 Platoon could not have achieved what it did without our wonderful NCOs. Other officers did not copy my methods. You cannot do this. Leadership is a very personal and individual art and the ethos of a group of people cannot be replicated. ... I did not try to stamp my individuality on my platoon. Had I done so they would probably have resisted. It all just happened and came naturally. The outcome certainly gave us our own distinctive identity – rather like conductors and a symphony orchestra. (19)

However, with all the changes that had taken place between the outbreak of war and the summer of 1944 many pre-war officers were surprised by the familiarity between junior officers and their men. The diminishing gap between officers and other ranks led to some most unmilitary displays of informality. Captain John Majendie, a pre-war graduate of Sandhurst, noticed the changes:

> I was rather shocked once. In each battalion we had half a dozen or so 'Canloans', officers on loan from Canada. One was called Deziel and I remember hearing a private in the slit trenches calling him 'Dizzy'. I didn't think that was quite correct. But I don't think anybody would be very popular if they tried to start bollocking people for relaxing. Discipline at Sandhurst was very tight indeed, and you just didn't think of it any other way. I was a little surprised when things were let slip a bit. (20)

This new army was not riven by the old class divide that characterised the army of the Great War. It was by no means an egalitarian organisation but the mood and ethos of earlier years had changed beyond all recognition. Many of the platoon commanders were little different from the men they commanded. This new breed of infantry officer was no longer separated from his men by class, education and breeding. Illustrative of this was Ken Hardy. Hardy was one of a rare breed of infantry officers – a platoon commander who was at the front from June 1944 to March 1945 and survived. Raised in the London suburb of Thornton Heath, he had little thought of becoming an officer. Surely, he thought, officers were men who went to public schools? He was soon proved wrong:

> I went to secondary school in Croydon. Came out of school and went into a bank. I can't tell you how keen I was to get into the army. The war made me, it came along at exactly the right time. I enjoyed it. I had the ability to be a good infantryman. Forget all about being an officer – just the ability to be a good infantryman. Suddenly I realised, here was something I could do. After six weeks training the Sergeant in charge of my squad came up, said I was officer material and asked would I do it? I said 'No thanks' – I was quite happy doing what I was doing. He said they'd come back to me later. Again they came back and said would I consider becoming an officer. By this time I was in the Kings Royal Rifle Corps, which was a snobby lot. They made it quite clear if I got a commission I wasn't going to be commissioned into them. I said no, I was quite happy being a driver. The trouble was I went home on leave and my mother heard I'd been approached and she never let me hear the last of it. In the end, just to get her off my back, I said yes. So I joined OCTU. It was a strange experience because I was the youngest person in my squad by miles. They all thought I had absolutely no chance at all. In fact I was the only one to come through. I really wanted to do it. I went to Aldershot at the end of '43, by Feb '44 I was commissioned and by June, which ain't long, I was out there leading a platoon. (21)

Once in France the big question was whether the twenty-one-year old Hardy would be able to handle his men in action. Would they be able to respect him? He soon found the answer: 'There were no problems whatsoever. In fact I think my background helped. I think we could identify with each other. You weren't all that distant from them.' (22)

For all the examples set by such officers there was only so much they could do to ensure the soldiers followed them. They could coax their men, offer praise, and lead heroically from the front, but the success of the army was reliant upon personal motivation. They needed to find inspiration from somewhere to send them forward into battle.

It came down to the question of how much the soldiers wanted to win the war. Many of the new soldiers were men whose own fathers had fought in the Great War and came home with a less than generous view of the army. Len Bennett recalled his final moments before leaving to report for basic training: 'My father was a very uncommunicative man – he never spoke about his experiences in the Great War. The only time I saw him get upset was when I went away. He said to me "Keep your head down, boy".' (23) Many had taught their sons about the horrors of war and encouraged them never to go into uniform. Others were disgruntled about the failure of inter-war gove rnments to live up to the promises of 1918. Was Britain a land fit for heroes? Plenty thought not, and when war came it was uncertain how men would react.

Certainly by 1944 most of the men of 21st Army Group were ready to get into battle. They were sick of the training and the hanging around. Most just wanted the war over as soon as possible. They didn't want to be in the thick of the fighting, risking their lives, but they remained realistic. They wanted to get the war over and get out of uniform, and there was only one way of doing that – defeating the enemy.

For all their desire to get the war finished there were still important questions to be asked of the men of the British and Canadian armies – how would attitudes change once the fighting had started?

The answers started to become evident in the final days before D-Day. Few but the most hopeful expected the Germans to give in without a long protracted fight and there seemed little point in rushing in when what might be the last few days of life were left to be savoured. Despite the obvious desire of some senior officers to have their units at the forefront of the battle plenty of their subordinates were less aggressively minded.

One man, who landed on Gold Beach on D-Day, recalled a speech by a major telling his men what an honour it was to be part of the invasion force: 'I think most of us felt that we could have stood the disgrace of being left out of it.' (24)

The men who expressed these emotions were not without motivation but they had a subdued sense of duty. They were willing to get the job done, but with a minimum of fuss. Many shared these feelings – as the ramp of his landing craft dropped into the surf off Normandy an officer of the Hertfordshire Regiment noted how rather than calling out 'Charge', 'Berlin or bust', or any suitably martial war c ry he uttered the somewhat less memorable words 'I think we'll go in now'. (25)

Despite this reserve, plenty of men initially showed a genuine enthusiasm for war. Soldiers whose landing craft were hit on the approach to the Normandy beaches and were left floundering in the channel felt despair that they were missing out on an historic moment. These were mixed emotions – some men wanted to be in the thick of the action, some wanted to be alongside their mates, others just wanted to be in a situation where they were not helpless and could at least have some influence over their own destiny. In the early days of the campaign many of the inexperienced soldiers were desperate to see action, they thought they were part of something special and didn't want to miss out on the honour of battle. When officers of the 6th Airborne Division had to make the difficult decision to leave out some men to prevent the overburdening of gliders there was an extreme reaction. Some of the toughest men in the British army were left in tears, pleading to be allowed to go into battle alongside their comrades.

Initially, the desire to get the war finished carried many men forward into battle with a sense of purpose. Those men left out of battle were often keen to get the chance to prove themselves, to the extent of wondering how they might get the chance to be involved. During the fighting in Normandy, Northants Yeoman Ken Tout found himself as a spare tank commander. He explained how he felt as he waited for the chance to go into action: 'Tank crews lived and trained together for a considerable time before entering battle so there was general desire to be in the "first team"; partly as in a football squad and partly because one did not wish the bad experiences on such close comrades.' (26) The desire left him hoping that someone would be wounded, even though it would probably be a friend. He found himself wishing that if he had to step into a dead man's shoes it should be one of the least popular NCOs who made way for him. The problem with expressing such outwardly morbid views was that the reality of the situation could soon make itself apparent: 'If one had wished the worst on a comrade, usually on a rather severe sergeant or badly spoken of corporal, and then that man was wounded or killed, there was a great deal of anguish in the hearts and minds of those who had wished them ill. The wish was superficial. No one really meant it.' (27)

Despite the initial enthusiasm it did not take long for most to change their opinions. At first the men at the front had no time to consider their situation – fear, motivation, morality and mortality – were all subsumed beneath an all-consuming burden of work. Three days after D-Day Alexander Baron finally found time to stop and write home to his family: 'We didn't have time for any high-falutin' sentiments. We were far too busy at first and far too exhausted afterwards. It is only today, resting in a pleasant meadow smoking a cigarette, and with a good hot meal inside me that I've had time to reflect at all on everything that's been happening.' (28)

Many soldiers grew uncertain about their feelings since many conflicting emotions were at play. The paradox was neatly summed up by Willie Whitelaw. In 1944 Whitelaw was a junior officer in the Scots Guards. In his memoirs he recalled: 'I have always thought that it is one of the strange aspects of war that away from the action one longs for battle, as soon as the horrors of battle are experienced one secretly craves to leave the action again as soon as possible.' (29)

Against a background of heavy fighting, hesitant advances, stubborn enemy resistance – the chaos and confusion of war – it was no surprise that the men at the front of the advance began to change their attitudes. It was easy for them to grow pessimistic and cynical as the advance was paid for in blood. They became increasingly cautious in the knowledge that every hedgerow and every farmhouse might be concealing the enemy. The infantrymen had learned that showing themselves on the battlefield was to court danger. Instead they stayed hidden, only venturing out of cover when it was absolutely necessary.

As morale was slowly eroded the troops at the front began to complain to each other about their situation. It was a situation that was not fully appreciated by outsiders. General Horrocks later wrote of the infantrymen: 'I have always regarded the forward area of the battlefield as the most exclusive club in the world, inhabited by the cream of the nation's manhood – the men who actually do the fighting.' (30) Despite the well-deserved flattery most would have given anything to be somewhere else – it was an 'exclusive club' whose membership they would happily forego. Dirty, dishevelled, frightened men sat quietly in shell holes and slit trenches listening to the incoming enemy fire and bemoaned their fate. The same questions came to mind time and time again – why hadn't they volunteered for the artillery, why weren't they storemen or drivers or clerks? Always the same question and always the same answer – someone had to do it.

The men in the front lines found it easy to mistrust their leaders. Too often they had heard an assignment would be easy only for it to turn out to be a 'sticky' job – where the advance was bought in blood. In this atmosphere of distrust they thought an issue of beer must mean they were being 'buttered up' for an unpleasant task and were mistrustful of all rumours that sounded appealing. When word went round that Bremen was home to 130,000 bottles of champagne the assaulting troops immediately thought it was just a ruse to encourage them to take the town quickly.

It soon became the wish of most soldiers not to be involved in any major battles – they could happily leave the hard fighting to someone else. When tank crews saw a Highland regiment coming into their area they realised they were facing a tough assignment, as one later wrote: 'They attract rotten jobs. Bloody battles .... we're going into something special if the Highland Jocks are in on it.' (31)

With the increasingly pessimistic men at the front learning the realities of war it was often only the fear of letting down their mates that prevented them from running away. The sense of comradeship that bound the men together was a mix of personal emotions and circumstances that could never be entirely defined. In his memoirs Lord Carrington outlined his own feelings about how best to survive a war: 'The two most important things in war are to participate under the command of people who know their job; and to spend it with friends. The first gives a decent chance of preparedness, even survival, even success, even honour. The second ensures that amidst the most disagreeable circumstances there will still be laughter and affection.' (32) For others camaraderie meant respect for their leaders, trust between friends, bonding by common experience, or even a shared mistrust of outsiders. More often than not this spirit was not based around larger formations – corps, divisions, brigades – nor even around their regiments. Instead their loyalty was more personal. Staff at 21st Army Group's 'A' branch noted such behaviour in a report from Normandy regarding the behaviour of Royal Engineers wounded on D-Day. They were: 'extremely keen to get back to their own units in battle as soon as possible, and were willing to make light of their wounds or sickness to do so .... The desire to return to their units was based on a sub unit standard ie. they wanted to get back to their own squadron, not so much their own Regt or formation.' (33) It was in these small groups that men learned respect for each other and showed an affection that was incomprehensible to outsiders.

For a unit to function it was vital to develop this sense of cohesion. Ken Squires of the 1st Northants Yeomanry explained the spirit that held them together:

> Everything had to be done right. If you took a parade you did it properly, well as properly as Yeoman can. We were as good as the Guards. But it was done in such a gentle way. Nothing was ever 'You've got to do it!' It was all done in this nice 'countryfied' atmosphere. Most of the officers were country gentlemen. It was a wonderful regiment to belong to. Because of that I think we had a good reputation in the various battles we fought.

His wartime colleague Michael Hunt agreed:

> I think there was something special in the unit. They say a unit is only as good as its officers and NCOs, but I think with us it went right down to the roots. Discipline was slack, but you did what you were told. In barracks if you had creased trousers, or your boots were dirty, you were told. But it wasn't officious. There was a sort of gentleness. Which is why everyone did everything for everyone else. When people ask what was it that kept us going? It was the comradeship, you wouldn't let your mates down. That type of spirit lasts forever. Sixty years on those of us who are left are still good mates. (34)

The desire to be among friends was essential to morale. Signaller Stan Procter experienced the camaraderie of infantry life. Whilst serving at battalion HQ he was anxious not to be sent forward to handle infantry communications, at one point even offering to give up his stripes. Yet once at the front the situation changed:

> There were times when I thought 'Why the hell can't they take me back to Brigade headquarters for a little while, for a rest?' But when the chance came for me to go I thought 'I don't want to leave these chaps'. I got on so well with the chaps from the infantry, from the Worcesters. When you are together with people, who are all in the same boat as yourself, you know you are all going to look after each other. (35)

Some men even turned down cushy jobs since it meant leaving friends behind – Pioneer Corporal Alexander Baron turned down promotion to sergeant and the post of guard commander at the NAAFI in Brussels in order not be split from his friends. The reward for his loyalty was daunting, and he soon found himself transferred to an infantry holding camp ready to be sent forward as a reinforcement.

At times this sense of camaraderie worked to the detriment of outsiders who were attached to units, who found themselves being given the most dangerous jobs, even to the extent of being sent into visible positions to draw fire. Some infantrymen openly suggested that newly-arrived reinforcements should be given the worst assignments to allow the veterans some peace. It may have seemed callous but if someone was going to die they figured it best to be a reinforcement – quite simply the death of a stranger was easier to cope with.

With so many men in uniform there was always going to be a diverse range in attitudes towards war. Though the central issue of war was killing it was the one area few soldiers had any real desire to be involved in and one isue which many veterans remain unwilling to discuss. The stumbling block was that few men held a particular animosity towards the enemy. Yes, they hated Hitler and his cronies, and wanted to see Europe free from Nazi tyranny, but they had little hatred towards individual Germans. New recruits, who proclaimed their aim to kill as many Germans as possible were laughed at by their more experienced comrades, who told them their job was not to kill but to stay alive.

This attitude was evident in the aftermath of battle. Once the fighting stopped, and they saw the enemy up close, they realised how little difference there was between them. It was common for the British and Canadian troops to take pity on their opposite numbers in the Wehrmacht. They were young, frightened, hungry, almost certainly critical of their leaders, and all would have preferred to be at home getting on with their lives. Both sides prayed to the same god for protection when they were scared, both sides cried for their mothers when they were dying. Tank man Ken Tout was one of those soldiers who shared this emotion. Looking from his tank he saw a young German soldier paralysed with fear – he knew he could fire and kill the boy but it seemed pointless since he felt no malice towards him. His words reflected how so many of his comrades felt: 'It is only Stan and Harvey and I passing by. Just ordinary, inoffensive youths like himself.' (36)

Understanding these similarities made killing difficult. In the words of a veteran of the Royal Ulster Rifles: 'Shooting people? Well this is the big question now. I may have shot a lot of people. And it's a thing I would like to have avoided, to be shooting anybody .... I shot .... I got quite a few of them. ... I had to do it you know.' (37) Many soldiers openly admitted guilt over the deaths of enemy soldiers and some avoided killing wherever possible. Sergeant William Partridge of the 4th Battalion Somerset Light Infantry went to war with just that attitude. Despite fighting in some of Normandy's bloodiest battles and earning a battlefield commission, he had little intention of personally harming the enemy: 'I never killed anyone. By reporting the positions of sightings, sounds, and other indicators to the Intelligence Officer I was able to bring about artillery or aircraft fire on enemy positions. In this way I was responsible – to a certain extent – for the deaths of enemy soldiers. Since this action saved the lives of my comrades I had no regrets.' (38)

Another veteran explained his feelings:

> I was a yokel, yet they taught me to kill in six weeks. Unbelievable. I would never have killed anybody in a million years. There's no two ways about it, you get acclimatised to killing, it's just another piece of work. First of all I killed with a Bren gun – so that was from far away – you never saw them close up, you just saw them dropping. As time went on you got nearer and nearer, you had to close your mind to it. I was squeamish when I first did hand to hand fighting – when I did my first bayonet attack. And especially when I had to go out on patrol at night and stick them in the back. But I was good at closing my mind. You weren't killing anybody you were getting rid of somebody so that you can go where you want to go. You must remember it's kill or be killed, always. If you think they won't do it to you, you're dead. So whether he's going to shoot you or not, you've to be first in. (39)

Yet though soldiers became used to the act of killing only a handful ever grew to enjoy it. Among those who saw killing as an unpleasant part of the job was platoon commander Ken Hardy, who explained:

> I never liked it. I never enjoyed the idea of shooting to kill. In the heat of the moment there were times when it was easy to do it. But it had to be in an impersonal way. I never enjoyed the idea of killing a German. The men did what they had to do, but I don't think the men enjoyed killing. Pushed to the point, they could all do it. Sometimes it was either you or him, but there was no joy in it. (40)

With such attitudes so prevalent it was little surprise to find men who when asked if they had hit anything replied 'I hope not'. Others learned how to say 'I'm sorry' in German in order to apologise to men they had wounded. Recognising this lack of martial spirit and aggression men joked that the war would over quicker if everyone who killed a German was sent home – it would give them the incentive to be more aggressive and get the job done more quickly.

Though most soldiers grew used to killing the enemy in the heat of battle, cold-blooded killings remained something few soldiers could accept. The rarest of breeds was the soldier who deliberately went out of his way to find ways to attack the enemy. These were the men who carried out personal vendettas against the Germans. Some volunteered for as many patrols as possible, others merely snuck off into the dark of night armed with knives, searching for an opportunity to make a kill. Many were remembered as quiet men, saying little but letting their actions speak for them. Often they were men who had lost homes and families to the bombing of British towns and cities, and who, after years of waiting wanted to take revenge.

Of the few soldiers who could remain blasé about killing in cold blood many belonged to a particular group – the snipers. Snipers had to be ruthless about killing. It was their job to line up their sights on a man's head and pull the trigger. It had to be approached in a calm manner and there was little room for emotion. Some would shoot enemies who were obviously drunk, legitimising their behaviour with the knowledge that the next day the men would be sober. A few even went as far as to keep 'Game Books' in which they logged their daily 'bag'. Snipers operating in the large houses of Oosterbeek outside Arnhem used pencils to scratch their daily scores onto the furniture or walls of the homes they occupied, leaving returning civilians with a bloody reminder of the battles fought within their homes.

In his memoirs of Operation Market Garden paratrooper James Sims noted the behaviour of his fellow soldiers who were blasé about the act of killing. As he watched a wounded German pulling himself along the ground: 'A rifle barked next to me and I watched in disbelief as the wounded German fell back, shot through the head. To me it was little short of murder.' (41) As Sims later explained: 'Snipers were altogether different and seemed to enjoy killing their enemies, and were disliked as much by their own side as their enemies.' (42)

For all the distaste for the work of the snipers, they themselves knew they had an important job to do. They were killing the enemy to make the battlefield safe for their comrades – something they could not afford to feel emotional about. They needed to be brutal, they needed to be calculating, they needed to be without mercy – in short they needed to be killers. One of their number explained their work. Sergeant Les Toogood had joined the army in the late 1930s, been evacuated via Dunkirk, trained hard for four years and then returned to France on D-Day. Although many of the infantrymen might have considered his work callous and arbitrary, Toogood explained the sniper's vital role: 'I knew the first things we would come across were either OPs for the Mortars or the machine guns. We would have snipers out, we would know where they were. And we would have a crack at them first, before the attack. If we found it was heavily covered by machine guns the attack wouldn't go in that day, we would have a go at them at dusk.' Although it was clear their work was vital it was essential snipers be fully motivated to be able to line up their sights on another man's head – even if he was smoking, laughing, or relaxing – and pull the trigger. Toogood explained:

> I've had blokes that can't shoot. They are good shots, they can shoot at a target, but not at a man's head. You could see them freeze. We'd take them to the first aid post and the chaps who couldn't kill would realise what the Germans were doing to our boys. Then they'd get a bit niggley. When I lost a man the replacement came but he'd never do any firing, he'd just carry the grenades and stuff, until he got used to the facts. At 100 or 200 yards, that was what we'd call a fair shoot, and the new blokes would see afterwards that it was only a target. How did I come to be good at it? I was at Dunkirk. I was brought up on a farm, I was used to killing. I saw no difference between a man and an animal, I just saw them as a target.(43)

With the campaign progressing and even the most reluctant soldiers growing used to killing other men, most remained sentimental about animals. Officers who gave their men orders to put wounded animals out of their misery found no one willing to carry out the order, instead insisting they could not hurt an animal. Men who could step unconcernedly over the bodies of dead men could be brought to tears by the plight of animals. Unable to show real affection to their mates the soldiers instead showered affection on the creatures they found on the battlefield, as one infantryman recalled: 'On one of our carriers they had a stray dog they had found. It went everywhere with them, it rode on the top of the carrier. Eventually, it got hit by a shellburst. They showed more emotion that day than they ever showed for a mate getting killed.' (44)

Whilst the troops were getting emotional over the suffering of animals many were suffering conflicting feelings about their own safety. Though they desperately wanted to get through the war unscathed most realised this was unlikely. They realised the odds were stacked against them remaining unhurt and instead began to look at the alternatives. The choice was bleak – their only escape was on a stretcher or in a coffin. When Rex Wingfield, a veteran of the 7th Armoured Division, sat down to write his memoirs he could have chosen no more apt a title than *The Only Way Out*. This one short simple phrase tells us more about the attitude and feelings of the soldiers than could be found in reading official histories or the memoirs of generals and politicians. These four short words speak for both the resilience and resignation of those who had to do the fighting – men who had accepted their lot and had little choice but to become fatalistic.

Once the men at the front realised they would probably fall victim to enemy action at some point, they soon began thinking what type of injury they would like. The overwhelming desire was to get what was called 'a blighty wound'. This was a wound sufficient to ensure evacuation yet not bad enough to leave them seriously disabled. Memoirs of the period are littered with references to clean, safe wounds, with men calling to each other: 'Cheer up, we might get a blighty.' (45)

With these attitudes prevailing, the walking wounded were among the most cheerful men on the battlefield. Advancing troops would be greeted by the sight of bandaged men moving towards aid posts. Happily collecting their personal effects they rejoiced in the knowledge that their wounds were serious enough to send them home but had not incapacitated them. Even men who lost limbs made light of their wounds, celebrating the fact they were out of the war for good. Some wounded men picked up their kit and nonchalantly strolled back to the aid post disregarding the fact that they were in the full view of the enemy. Others pulled books from their packs and sat reading until medics arrived. It was an act of defiance, as if to say 'I've done my bit and now I'm going home'. Those walking wounded who appeared forlorn received encouragement rather than sympathy from men envious that the wounded were heading home. As the waiting soldiers watched the evacuation of their mates they realised how confusing their jealousy was – thinking it strange when a man was considered lucky if he lost a foot.

Many found their wounds were not the hoped for guarantee of safety. As Michael Hunt remembered, wounds did not always mean a ticket back home: 'When I first joined the squadron we were "stonked" in a field. I caught a bit of shrapnel in my arm. So I went down to the Aid Post. I thought that was it I'm out, I'm home. The bloke cut off my shirt, put a bit of sticking plaster on it and said "Bugger off".' (46) The introduction of penicillin also meant hospital stays were not as protracted as the men hoped. The War Office recognised the false hopes of the wounded men and addressed the problem:

> This means a man with a straightforward flesh wound is out of hospital in approximately a fortnight from the date of wounding and after a week or two at Convalescent Depot is ready to return to duty in a month to six weeks. … The reaction was at first not entirely enthusiastic – as a wound is still looked on as a 'ticket for UK' but the introduction of short leave for this type of case will doubtless do much to counteract any adverse psychological effect produced by improved surgical methods. (47)

Even soldiers facing amputations were often able to cope with surprising fortitude. The thought of losing an arm may have been a terrible prospect but compared to death it seemed minor. This notion of amputation became a vital part of many soldiers' defence against their own fears. Everyone had their own way of dealing with their crazy situation. Whilst some men genuinely hoped to die rather than be crippled or mutilated, others began to weigh up the pros and cons of losing a limb, pondering how they would happily cope with disability. Like the notion of a 'blighty wound' the idea of amputation grew to fascinate some men. They asked themselves which limbs would they surrender in return for survival? Would they prefer to lose a leg or an arm? If so which arm? And so it went on – personal bargains made in the hope of staying alive.

The depth of their concern were explained by one veteran NCO:

> You didn't think of death. But you didn't want it to be messy. You didn't want a belly wound because you knew that was the end of you. But you didn't mind losing an arm or a leg. We always used to talk about it – arms, legs – ok – but eyes? That would be worse than anything. You thought if you lose your arm or your leg, you're back home.

But we were all afraid of being blinded. You didn't mind being killed, but you didn't want to be blinded. (48)

Even those not yearning to be evacuated realised their wounds were a blessing. Many found they were mentally and physically exhausted and their wounds had probably saved their lives. After convalescence Sergeant William Partridge, who had been wounded during the crossing of the Seine at Vernon, was posted to a training battalion:

> I was glad to be in England and contributing towards winning the war as much as I would were I still fighting. I wasn't posted to a training battalion as a member of staff but earned that position by my ability to instruct on weapon training and field craft. The need to have properly trained replacements was far greater than any contribution that I could make on the battlefield. I was glad to be out of the war. There would be very few left in 'D' Company who knew me and those who did would have moved on 100 years since I left them. (49)

For others the prospect they would not fight again weighed heavy on their minds. As a regular officer John Majendie felt it was his duty to be at the front, not languishing in hospital: ' Initially I felt terribly depressed. I hadn't completed what I had been trained to do. To start with I was anxious to get back. But later I think I was more worried that I didn't particularly want to go back. I couldn't have gone back and shouldn't have wanted to go back any more than I did.' (50)

Hand in hand with the hope of evacuation came a wave of fatalism that penetrated into the psyche of many. Whatever their attitudes, there were few who did not cross the channel in a mood of quiet contemplation and homesickness. Those last moments, as the English coast slipped into the distance, were a chance to look back on life and everything that was being left behind. The soldiers made peace with themselves as they prepared their minds for war.

Ken Hardy contemplated his future as he set sail:

> When I went out to France I didn't expect to come back. It was my twenty-first birthday, my parents had sent me a little present – which I received on the boat – and I thought, goodbye I won't be coming back. No way did I ever expect to survive. And, although it sounds terribly heroic, I really wasn't afraid to die. Honestly. In Normandy I never expected to come out alive. It's much easier to lead by example if you have that attitude. I went to a secondary school in Croydon and I came out without a great deal of prospects. My prospects in 1939 were pretty grim, so I didn't leave a hell of a lot behind. The true belief that I wouldn't come back made it much easier. It sustained me for a long time. Of course, as days go by Russian roulette comes into it and it gets worse and worse. I can remember by the time I got to Holland I was waking up every morning and thinking 'It must be my last day! It can't go on any longer!' By that time I was the only subaltern left in the Division from Normandy. All the others were gone. I thought 'It can't go on any longer! Today must be the day! It can't go on much longer!' That's when it gets really hard. (51)

This sense of pessimism spread. Soldiers looked at the reality of their situation – friends and foes alike being slaughtered in their hundreds – and their future seemed bleak. When they walked past corpses they saw the same battered black boots sticking out from beneath blankets. It was easy to make the connection – it could so easily be them. As one infantryman explained: 'I thought I'm not going to last the day, this is bloody dangerous. You accepted it. You didn't think about it. You were going to go into the advance and so many people were going to die. So you didn't expect to get through. I wake up now and if I'm not in the obituary in the newspaper then I know I'm alright!' (52)

Not everyone was so certain of their fate. Some felt certain they would survive – the immortal dreams of youth casting away any fears of death. At eighteen or nineteen they were certain they would not be killed, instead they felt immortal. They convinced themselves it would always be someone else. This was what gave them the hope and the ability to fight on, even when the odds were stacked against survival. Their certainty suppressed their fears, gave them strength and kept the war machine rolling forward.

Many fatalists made the conscious decision to enjoy whatever time they had left. It made sense to drink whatever they could find, or have sex whenever possible, since they might never get another opportunity. At times it could appear excessive, sometimes even hedonistic, but they had to seize the moment. When one soldier found himself in a shattered building in the outskirts of Arnhem he started a fire on the floor and began to cook a rabbit. His comrades thought it mad – surely he would set fire to the house? They tried to reason with him but he stood his ground, telling them they might all be dead after the next attack and he wanted to die with his belly full.

Many tank crews followed a similar strategy. Tank gunner Joe Ekins was a dedicated fatalist, existing in what he called a 'never, never state':

> I quickly became a fatalist. If you didn't then you just went barmy, like a lot of them did. Luckily my crews felt the same. I don't see any other way of keeping sane. If you thought 'I'm gonna get shot this morning', and thought 'If I get shot, I get shot. If I don't, I don't.' It becomes a fact of l i fe. We didn't give a damn. We would cook in the tank, rather than go outside and risk getting hit by a shell. It was dange rous, using a meths stove in there with all the petrol fumes around you. (53)

Such was the realistic approach to the conduct of war that some men divided jobs between themselves on the flip of a coin. Games of chance could mean the difference between clearing a minefield and watching a friend do it. Luck became the deciding factor between life and death, because they accepted the job would have to get done. They knew that life in the front line was a lottery – however careful they were, however alert or well prepared, they couldn't determine whether a sniper fired or a shell landed nearby. All they could do was hope and pray, then leave the outcome to fate.

The resignation with which such soldiers accepted their fate whilst faithfully continuing to do their duty might have seemed almost spiritual. The notion of leaving the outcome of the battles in the hands of outside influences might have looked as if they were happily preparing to 'meet their maker' – Onward Christian

Soldiers? Nothing could have been further from the truth. In face of the mental strain of war it would have been unsurprising if soldiers had turned away from the physical world and placed their hopes in the realms of spirituality. That said, religion was surprisingly unimportant for many of the soldiers. Like most people of their generation the soldiers came from nominally religious backgrounds and many had regularly attended church. It was a matter of course that they filled in forms stating their religious denominations, but for many it remained an irrelevance. The majority of British soldiers were Church of England – by May 1944 there were almost two million serving in the army as opposed to almost 300,000 Roman Catholics, 240,000 Church of Scotland and 160,000 Methodists. Virtually every recognised religion was represented – Jews, Unitarians, Salvationists, Orthodox, Mormons, Plymouth Brethren, Moslems and Hindus. There were even over 14,00 Christian Scientists and 500 Quakers, a supposedly pacifist organisation. All of the smaller gospel religions were also represented, as were churches whose names were as obscure as their beliefs – Cremationists, Rationalists, Pithenians, Mosaics and the bizarrely named Peculiar People. Ten men had even classified themselves as Druids.

Whatever it said on their service records it was only at the times of greatest stress that most turned to prayer. On the landing ships heading towards Normandy men surprised themselves by attending religious ceremonies, often regardless of the denomination. The attitude seemed to be that in the face of death there was no harm in taking the sacrament just in case – as most padres noted every man in a slit trench is a Christian. They were right – men who hadn't prayed for years started again, it was a case of 'any port in a storm'. One explained his feelings: 'I believed but I was not what you would call religious, but when you are near death and you see your mates get killed you have to have something to believe in, I laugh and say I am a religious atheist, so I edge my bets just in case.' (54)

For many, religious convictions entered a state of flux – at one minute waning as their minds absorbed the reality of war, the next surging at the prospect of imminent death. Believer or atheist, forsaker or convert – there was no average for the men of 21st Army Group. If the 'normal' religious belief of the soldier could be identified it might fit the words of one NCO:

> We had church parades and I went to them, but I was not a religious person. During battles I prayed, that's the hypocritical part of it. I suppose I prayed it would be the other bloke and not you. You didn't want him to die, but rather he die than you. When we needed it we prayed, but it was not fervent prayers. That sounds very bad, but you had to have something to hold onto. Like a rock. I know there's something up there, but what, I don't know? A lot of people said it was a lot of nonsense, because of what was going on around them – why would God let this happen? A tremendous amount of people thought like that. Whenever there was a church parade, if we were out of the line, a majority would say 'No fear. I'm going to have a sleep.' But I think 99 per cent said a prayer – they won't admit it – whether they were religious or not. It was just something to hold onto. (55)

The heat of battle was when most prayers were offered. With death so close some openly fingered rosaries, offering a prayer for their salvation. Others sat in the midst of battle reading their bibles. In this atmosphere of uncertainty even the non-religious men realised it might not help but it could do no harm. John Majendie, who commanded a rifle company on Hill 112, explained his own feelings towards religion:

> My father and grandfather were parsons. So I'd always been brought up as a church-goer, but I suppose I was average C of E. So one jolly well said one's prayers at times – when you're in a slit trench and a lot of 'muck' comes down, one does send up a prayer. I wish I had been like the people who were very religious, it did them an enormous amount of good. They felt your fate was decided for you and so be it. (56)

One of those religious men was Sergeant William Partridge, whose actions on the battlefield were influenced by his beliefs:

> Personally religious faith was, if anything, strengthened. Faith in divine protection and inspiration played an important part, as did the fear of God. My actions were influenced not to incur the 'wrath of God' in case he withdrew his protection! Restricted to living in slit trenches, under sporadic mortar fire, my platoon nevertheless requested the Padre to visit and hold a prayer service. (57)

Some men, having survived the ferocity of battle, began to feel their prayers had been answered. They listened to the sermons of their padres and it made sense – had they not survived against all the odds, maybe someone was watching over them? Inevitably some began to take a closer interest in religion. John Mercer was among those whose attitudes changed:

> We were quite philosophical. We talked about religion, about God, about the stars, about the future, about the past. I was brought up irreligious but I was actually confirmed into the Church of England whilst in the army. To some extent experience had changed my attitude. The padre came round and spoke to us, we were in a foxhole at the time, and asked us if we wanted to be confirmed. I thought 'Why not?' The confirmation took place in Eindhoven. All these soldiers – dirty boots, stained uniforms, – were confirmed by the Bishop of Dover. Unbelievable. Some had been involved with religion before, but I hadn't. I went on to become a lay reader in the church for thirty years. (58)

Others had the opposite reaction and the notion that God might exist was an anathema. Their opinions were based upon their personal experience of war. They watched the death and destruction and figured that a God who could allow such suffering was not worthy of their prayers, having abandoned those most in the need of his protection. Paratrooper Eric 'Bill' Sykes was among them: 'After experiencing the tragedies of war I became more and more detached from religion, and all of the religious learnings and teachings, to a point of complete disbelief in a supreme being and the biblical theories and endorsements as portrayed and promoted by the clergy, and remain so to this very day.' (59)

Ken Tout was one of those men with strong religious views whose experiences, though not undermining his belief in God, shaped his view of religion:

> I was a registered theological student before I joined up. The horrors of war encouraged me to continue training for some vocational cause, and subsequently I worked with the Salvation Army for 20 years, mainly overseas. However, battle sights, including civilian and animal dead, changed my outlook generally from purely theological/evangelical into a more 'Social Gospel' attitude, which led to further service with Oxfam, Help The Aged International and the United Nations Unit on Ageing. (60)

With traditional religious beliefs under challenge, the soldiers needed something else to look to – if they could not ask God for help, who would be there to protect them? Superstitions became increasingly important to many as rituals were maintained and lucky charms carried. Four leaf clovers, lucky heather, St Christopher medals – all had their place inside the wallets of the fighting men. Most kept their lucky charms hidden, secretly carrying into battle small items to remind them of home and, hopefully, bring them luck. Such was the importance of lucky charms that some men were unable to cope with their loss. Men of the 1st Royal Dragoons watched as one of their number became increasingly attached to an animal: 'During the winter of 1944-45 my car commander's lucky mascot, a white rabbit which he kept in our scout car, vanished on Christmas Day, he never went out on patrol with me again. I had a new car commander for the rest of the war.' (61)

Along with superstitions came the belief in divine intervention and guardian angels. Regardless of specific religion some soldiers experienced lucky excapes that seemed too strange to attribute to fortune, as one explained:

> One time we were shifting our position, the carriers were laid out overlooking a hedgerow. I knew the Germans were there and they were going to come at us at minute because we could hear the tanks. All of a sudden I turned to the driver and said 'Take us back and go left.' So he put her into reverse and moved back. By the time we'd stopped there was a bloody great big shell hole where we'd been. Now, why did I say to reverse? Three times that happened to me. Why? So, grasping at straws, I thought I'd got a guardian angel – someone who's looking after me. You clutched at things – silly things. Anything daft. That was all the religion I had. (62)

The idea of a 'guardian angel' could bring more than just comfort. It could mean a soldier started to believe he was destined to survive. Sydney Jary explained the only way he could have survived for so long as a platoon commander: 'I have been assured that my survival was a statistical impossibility. Seriously, I consider that I had – and still have – a guardian angel.' (63)

Even the fatalists found that a lucky escape meant they had cheated death. Harry Free began to realise that he might actually survive the war:

> The only time my attitude changed and I really believed I was destined to survive was after an incident that happened about a month before the end of the war. We were on a recce and pulled up in a lane. A group of us disembarked and we did a foot patrol to see if the Germans were in a nearby farmhouse. Half way across the field the

> Germans opened fire on us. We fell to the ground as bullets whizzed overhead. I tried
> to return fire with my Bren but it jammed! Typical. We retreated crawling backwards
> to the lane where the rest of the patrol was waiting. Walking backwards up the lane,
> I reached my car and the gunner informed me that he'd tried to open fire on me as I
> approached thinking I was a German – and the gun had jammed. A close shave and
> one that made me re-think my ideas about my destiny! (64)

With such quirks of fate defining a man's destiny it became easy for the soldiers to experience major changes in their attitudes and behaviour. The sights of the battlefields – dead men, dead animals, burning vehicles, wrecked buildings – became the norm, and they grew accustomed to some parts of the experience. The soldiers adapted to the routine. They learned when the enemy was likely to shell them, when they would be on duty, what time they would go to sleep, and when they would stand-to in the morning. It could seem like the routine of any job, except that people were trying to kill them.

No longer was it a shock for them to see a man fall from a bullet wound. All the old civilian values had been swept away. Life had been proved cheap, death was everywhere, and if they could accept their own fate, why should they worry about killing?

Although large numbers of the soldiers were unenthusiastic about killing, attitudes did change. Few grew happy to shoot their enemies, but most became less concerned by their actions. It became clear this was not the army of innocents who had stepped ashore on D-Day. Their increasing callousness caused a sense of shame for some of the soldiers. They didn't perceive themselves as people who could disregard pain, suffering and death – but that's exactly what they did.

They developed a casual attitude to death that would have shocked them in the past. Targets once considered worthless would be hit – bringing down artillery fire on the enemy as they sang Christmas carols or firing at men as they went to the toilet. For many of the soldiers compassion was something to be used sparingly. The moral dilemma of what made a suitable target was a serious issue, for example was there sufficient justification for shooting at a retreating enemy? Gradually it became easier to overcome worries about shooting the Germans in the back – they learnt the enemy had usually prepared secondary defence lines which it was safer not to allow them to reach. It may not have been chivalrous but it was certainly logical. When a reconnaissance tank of the 1st RTR pursued three Germans fleeing across a field, the commander recorded: 'We were now all reduced to the level of primaeval animals running their quarry down, so thin is our veneer of civilisation. I was baying over the intercom, the gunner was drooling, and the driver was beating his steed for the utmost effort.' (65)

Such behaviour was the reality of war. They settled into killing as a routine – as much a part of their day as eating and sleeping. The chivalry of days gone by had been by-passed – some officers refused to accept ceasefires to allow the enemy to collect their wounded. Others used ceasefires and the cover of the white flag to scout around enemy positions and pick up information. By the time the army reached the German border soldiers were seen sniping at targets regardless of whether they were armed, in uniform, or simply civilians living near the front.

Hand in hand with the acceptance of killing there came an encroaching disrespect for the corpses of enemy soldiers, who could no longer routinely expect a proper burial. Right from the early days in Normandy corpses had been searched for cigarettes and money before being buried, but as the war continued the attitudes of some individuals changed. In winter, rather than dig a hole in frozen ground, soldiers were seen using machetes to cut off limbs and make enemy corpses fit any available hole. It was gruesome but quick, allowing the soldiers to get on with their lives. In the Ardennes, one man was spotted lighting a fire underneath the frozen body of a German who he had strung up from a tree in an attempt to defrost the body and steal his boots. Some desecrated corpses in the search for loot. These 'ghouls' – as they were referred to by their revolted comrades – hacked at corpses, cutting off their fingers to get gold rings or pull out gold teeth.

Along with this behaviour came a ghoulish humour that shocked many inexperienced observers – in the Ardennes British soldiers were seen stopping to shake hands with frozen enemy corpses. Even the deaths of close friends were passed off with throwaway quips: 'Oh well, that's more food for the rest of us!' (66) Although the desecration of corpses would never become common, these extremes of behaviour increased as the war dragged on. If the British and Canadians could laugh about their dead comrades why would they worry about the fate of their enemies?

Despite the callous disregard for death and suffering it did not mean the soldiers were hardened by their experiences. Despite their best efforts, there were certain sights that brought their emotions welling up to the surface. The personal possessions of the dead – family photographs, teddy bears, lucky charms and letters from home – littering the ground in the aftermath of battle, were often enough to reduce strong men to tears. The sufferings of civilians, in particular children, appalled them. Deep down many cursed how war had turned them into cold-hearted killers, themselves responsible for much death and destruction. For most, their callous attitudes were not a genuine surrendering of emotion, instead it was a suppression of their feelings. They cast aside thoughts of the past and the future and lived for the moment, concentrating on getting the war won so that they would be free to enjoy the future.

With death shadowing their every move, who could blame the soldiers if they found humour in the least humorous of situations? The ability to laugh at their circumstances became essential in suppressing their true feelings and maintaining morale. Some of the jokes were corny, and many were dark, black humour revelling in the sense of misfortune. They laughed at people who stood on mines, saying 'Give the Germans an inch and they take a foot'.

The soldiers could not help joke about their fate. When the force they were part of was christened the 'British Western European Force' – BWEF – they said it stood for 'Burma When Europe's Finished'. When the army changed the title to 'British Liberation Army' – BLA – they claimed it stood for 'Burma Looms Ahead'.

Nowhere was this sense of humour seen more than by the antics of the infantrymen who struggled to stay sane. These urges would lead to some very unmilitary displays, as one veteran NCO recalled:

> You've got your mates with you, you do an attack, and I suppose at least 25 per cent of you haven't made it through. Your mate's dead and you go pick his kit up and you make jokes about it. But it wasn't against him it was just black humour. If you didn't make jokes about it you'd break down – that would be the end of you. If you were going forward and a mine goes off and a bloke's head gets sliced off – but he's still walking – you take bets on how far he's going to walk! I wouldn't expect anybody to understand it. It was a way of expressing yourself. (67)

In eleven months of war their attitudes were in a constant state of flux. Whether abandoning God or embracing faith, whether laughing at death or crying at misfortune, whether becoming a callous killer or being unwilling to kill, one thing was certain. The ordinary men would never be ordinary again.

3

Dutch Courage & the Calvados Campaign

'We came upon a cider still and got pissed on raw cider. We filled our water cans with cider rather than water that day. We were all as sick as dogs.' (1)

Most men across the world are united by one thing – their appreciation of alcohol. Throughout history – from the drunken excesses of Roman orgies to today's lager louts – alcohol has played an influential role and this was no exception for the soldiers of 21st Army Group. The Victorian temperance movement had failed to take a grip on the hearts and minds of most of the population and social drinking remained the focus of most communities – whether in the village inn, city lounge bar, or working men's clubs.

Although war had brought changes to the British public houses, their atmosphere remained the same. Canadians arriving from across the Atlantic were shocked by what they discovered in Britain. They were used to dark windowless taverns where respectable people did not go and women dared not enter. They looked on in awe at British women who entered pubs unaccompanied and confidently ordered their own drinks. Glasses were in short supply but men simply took along empty jam jars and asked for them to be filled with beer. Beer itself was also in short supply, so customers had to go on pub crawls – nipping from pub to pub – to find enough beer. Spirits were all but unknown, unless the customers had connections. The problem was not merely a shortage of alcohol caused by rationing but also a shortage of time. In the months before the invasion soldiers began to realise there might be precious little time left to enjoy themselves. Many drank as much as they could because their future was so uncertain. There was an almost forced desire to fill the ever diminishing days of peace and freedom – living life to the full and emptying pubs of drink.

Officially the British and Canadians were only allowed a certain amount of alcohol once they arrived on the Continent. The tradition of giving soldiers a tot of rum before going into action in cold weather remained and the arrival of the rum barrel was a source of delight to the men waiting expectantly with their tin mugs. The quarter pint ration was just enough to steady their nerves but not enough to make them drunk. The rum warmed them and loosened inhibitions just sufficiently to make them prepared to face the imminent danger. The ration was not reliable, it was not a daily event, but it existed – and who could begrudge such a small consolation to men about to face death?

Despite the popularity of the rum ration, many soldiers were suspicious of it.

Brought up on their fathers' stories of Great War infantrymen given rum then sent into battle 'half cut', they had little desire to risk battle with anything other than a clear head. It was an admirable and wise sentiment, although it did not prevent thousands of men enjoying army issue rum and any other drinks they could lay their hands on.

Before setting off for France there was a rush to visit pubs as the troops made the most of these final opportunities. When Royal Marine Commandos were ordered to prepare for movement to France they were granted 'shore leave'. The next morning the officers and men all seemed to exhibit signs of hangovers, much to the disgust of some senior officers. Even after this 'last night ashore', as it was known to the Marines, they were lucky enough to be excused for one final drink. Those wanting a final beer before departure were marched from their camp to a nearby hotel, kept from any contact with civilians, assembled in the hotel garden and issued two pints per man.

As some of the soldiers were enjoying a final beer, others were already beginning their journey to France. On the night of 5 June 1944 the first men of the D-Day invasion force began their journey towards France, cramped inside Dakotas and Horsa gliders. They sat silently, waiting for the green light that was their signal to drop into the darkness below. With little idea of what the future might bring, they were restrained and showed little emotion. Many of their leaders had banned them from drinking alcohol for twenty-four hours before their departure knowing that a drunken soldier might cross the line between cautious and reckless behaviour. Colonel Terence Otway, whose men had the vital task of neutralising the Merville Battery which could fire on Sword Beach, was one such leader. Yet as they crossed the channel he passed around a bottle of whisky to the men in his plane. The aim was to allow them just enough to calm their nerves and occupy their minds as they approached the landing zones. Such was the sense of expectation, none of the men over-indulged and the bottle was returned to Otway before it was empty. When his turn came to jump he handed the half empty bottle to the RAF despatcher. Such restraint was admirable but it would take more than just willpower to keep up such high standards in the months to follow.

As the planes and gliders flew steadily forward they passed over the lines of vehicles waiting to board ships and later the landing craft as they steadily made their way across the channel. Those heading for France on American ships found the craft surprisingly comfortable but there was one thing missing – alcohol. Men able to withstand seasickness found the food exceptional but unlike the Royal Navy, the US Navy was teetotal and there was no chance of a few sips of 'Dutch Courage'. Some Canadians found a solution by consuming the methylated spirit contained within the cookers in their ration packs. In contrast to the Americans the Royal Navy were generous to their 'visitors', issuing double rum rations and anything else they had to share. Sailors treated some men to breakfasts of whisky and Mars bars. A group of officers serving in the Border Regiment even shared a bottle of champagne. With the bottle empty they put a sheet of paper, signed by all of them, inside requesting the finder to send the bottle on to the Regimental

Museum, then flung it overboard.

While the invasion force slipped silently across the Channel some paratroopers, spearheading the invasion, were already sampling local hospitality. The British drop was scattered across a wide area, and many airborne men were left wandering around the countryside. Two lost medics teamed up with a pair of fighting soldiers. Forced to take refuge in a French farmhouse they were treated to celebratory drinks of cognac and calvados by their hosts. Eventually the medics were guided through the marshes and attempted to make their way back to their unit. The two supposed fighting men were left behind, in the hayloft, sleeping off the effects of their hosts' hospitality.

The airborne troops holding Pegasus Bridge became involved in the campaign's most famous drinking session. After liberating the first house in France, the Gondrée Café in Benouville, the proprietor promptly dug up his stock of champagne which he had buried in 1940 to prevent it falling into German hands. He wanted to share it with his liberators. The café had been designated as the aid post for the troops but not only the wounded found excuses to make their way there to join the celebrations. Major John Howard, commanding the company at the bridge, soon put a stop to the drinking knowing his men could expect a German counter-attack at any time. He returned the men to their positions, but not before he too had drunk a glass.

As the first waves of troops hit the Normandy beaches few had anything but survival on their minds. Sea sickness had been enough to prevent the soldiers from even thinking about eating or drinking. Most just wanted to be clear of the surf, across the beach and achieving their objectives. However in the chaos of those first few hours there were many opportunities for soldiers to be distracted from the realities of war by the chance of taking a drink. There was little thought of over-indulgence, soldiers simply took quick nips from bottles then moved on. On Gold Beach the Beachmaster handed out tots of rum to the soldiers he asked to walk his dog. Canadian tank commander Sergeant Leo Gariepy's crew had their first drinks before leaving the beach. They found themselves unable to advance because the way forward was blocked by an anti-tank ditch. Whilst waiting for engineers to bridge the gap Gariepy ordered his crew to heat up some soup and passed around a bottle of rum. With battle hardly started – and not even their first objective reached – the crew were enjoying the drink until they realised they were parked right next to a German gun emplacement. The party broke up and they returned to war, destroying the German gun. By 9 a.m., with the invasion beaches hardly cleared, a café in Bernières sur Mer was open for business selling wine to the passing soldiers. Within hours of landing men of the East Yorks Regiment had captured their first objective and with it liberated a number of crates of German beer. It fell to their CSM to keep the men under control to prevent what he feared would turn into a drunken orgy.

For Allied soldiers, many of whom had never been away from home before, the vast supplies and types of drinks available came as a surprise. Coming from Britain where there were constant beer shortages and almost no spirits on sale, the delights of France were a great temptation. As soon as men arrived in Normandy they found vast quantities of alcohol in captured German positions. Troops entering the captured 'Hillman' bunker found numerous bottles of champagne. For the soldiers it was a day of firsts – their first time in action and their first taste of exotic foreign drinks. One young soldier, taking his first taste of champagne was confused by the light bubbly taste and asked for more cider.

Once safely established in France, the authorities realised care would have to be taken to prevent drunkenness and appeals were made to show respect for their hosts and avoid excesses. The Assistant Provost Marshal of 1st Corps issued an order stressing that: 'Drunkenness is not a common French vice and "drunks" are looked on with contempt.' (2)

There were plenty of bars in close proximity to the battlefield and throughout the Normandy campaign troops made the most of opportunities to visit them. Brief interludes in the fighting allowed the more fortunate to take a well-earned break. In small groups they made their way to cafés and sat in virtual silence, still clutching their weapons. Few drank heavily, most just relaxing with a few glasses of cider and enjoying the change of scene.

It was not necessary to visit cafés to get a drink. The whole of Normandy seemed covered in orchards, with hundreds of small farms producing cider from their own apples. Summer saw the trees heavy with fruit and the soldiers picked apples from the branches to eat as they marched. As tanks moved beneath the low hanging branches the fruit tumbled through the open hatches providing them with something to snack on. But it was the product of this fruit that most interested them. Cider was one of the region's biggest exports and with the battle raging the farmers were isolated from their usual markets. At first civilians were eager to give it to their liberators but later they sold it by the gallon to thirsty soldiers. Farmers admitted with pride they only charged British soldiers fifteen francs but had charged Germans twenty. When the soldiers found abandoned farms they searched out the cider barrels and filled their water bottles and whatever spare vessels they could find. Men of the 43rd Reconnaissance Regiment had to be ordered to desist from carrying cider in the water jerrycans on their vehicles, and Northants Yeomanry tank crews came across a stock of cider that was not yet ready for consumption. As one of their gunners recalled: 'We came upon a cider still and all got pissed on raw cider. We filled our water cans with cider rather than water that day. We were all as sick as dogs.' (3)

Despite their enthusiasm most soldiers took care, as one recalled: 'It's true I drank the cider when we came across it. But we weren't trying to get drunk. I suppose we started soon after we landed in France, while we were waiting around for something to happen. No, I never saw anybody drunk. I doubt if we would have passed the breathalyser test, but we weren't drunk. I think everyone had enough sense to be careful – they'd be dead for a start.' (4) Fortunately most French cider tended to be weaker than English variants and was less likely to cause drunkenness than calvados or captured German spirits, although some was so rough it corroded the jerrycans the soldiers stored it in. Rough or smooth, the fermented apple juice made an ideal refreshing drink for soldiers tired of consuming warm chlorinated water.

Apart from cider there was another drink long remembered by those who tasted it – calvados. An exceptionally potent brandy made from apples, calvados is strong enough in its finished form, but in its raw state – as consumed by many that summer – it was little short of deadly. Almost every farm seemed to have its own still and most of the towns a distillery. However farmers tended to hide the finished product underground, leaving only the immature drink in vats above ground, so soldiers pinched the non-aged clear liquid rather than its amber-coloured aged variant. At around seventy per cent proof it had to be treated carefully. Some likened the spirit to liquid dynamite, liquid flame or even metal polish. It was so strong it also became popular for use in cigarette lighters, where it burned with a clear blue flame.

A commando serving in Normandy vividly recalled his introduction to the drink: 'It was a powerful sensation. There was a sudden shock of fiery fluid burning its way deep into the system to reach my feet and twitch my toes, then surging up and scorching my belly, a furnace of flames reaching my face from a witch's cauldron, creating a hot sun.' (5) Alcohol and armies are a lethal combination and it was a formidable task for any officer to keep his men from sampling this 'fire water'. Such was the effect of the spirit that drunks were sometimes thought to be battle exhaustion casualties, wandering the empty streets of villages, haphazardly firing their weapons, shouting to a non-existent enemy. As one diarist recorded: 'a lot of the boys were zig-zag on it'. (6)

Despite an initial reluctance many soon developed a taste for it. Ken Squires, serving in a tank crew of the Northants Yeomanry, remembered how they received the spirit: 'If you'd liberated a little village they'd all be there with their flasks. You'd put your mug out and they'd fill it up, then you'd drink it down – and it was calvados! Couldn't drive a tank straight after that!' (7)

Consumption of the spirit was a risky business. One gunner was reported to have died after the raw spirit attacked the enamel lining of his water bottle and the resulting mixture of calvados, enamel and lead entered his bloodstream, poisoning him. Rumours abounded that a Canadian unit was hit by a German counter-attack with dire results as its men were drunk on calvados. Stretcher bearer Jack Oakley was among a group of men who put themselves in danger after an afternoon drinking calvados:

> I don't remember very much about this incident but we soon began to feel a little worse than merry, in fact downright ill. Wandering about we soon got lost until an infantryman popped up and stopped us, wanting to know who we were and where we had come from. I think the general vague answer was 'Over there' pointing in the direction from which we had come. He told us we were dead lucky for there were no British troops in front of him. He pointed out our way back and having arrived we all collapsed in some sort of stupor. During the night I was sick all over my rifle and awoke next morning with the grandfather of all hangovers and I saw the metal parts of my rifle had gone green. It took a long time to clean it. We did, however, boast that last night we had made 100 yards for the Allies. (8)

In some units distribution of 'liberated' supplies became part of the day-to-day routine. One driver was sent to fill up the water truck for a regiment of tanks and returned much later than expected and noticeably drunk. When the water was tested it turned out to be calvados in its rawest form, only recently distilled, not having been aged and remained at over a hundred per cent proof. Somewhat unexpectedly the officers were pleased with the driver who explained he had 'liberated' four hundred gallons from a distillery. Rather than waste the drink a deal was struck with a neighbouring unit who accepted a daily ration in exchange for providing the tank crews with water.

With both cider and calvados in plentiful supply and stocks of German beer and spirits found in captured positions there was plenty of temptation for the British and Canadians. Luckily most soldiers at the front were careful about consuming alcohol. Even if they could get drink, which was not easy when they were sheltering in slit trenches under almost constant fire, they did not want to risk drinking to excess. Few officers ever recall seeing their men 'worse for wear' during this period. Men like Jack Oakley were the exception and most at the front preferred to keep a clear head. They knew the dangers of losing concentration, falling asleep, or indulging in foolhardy acts of bravery.

Instead they kept their drinking for when they were out of the front lines. During a rest period following the slaughter of Hill 112 men of the 43rd Division concocted a cocktail known as 'Stuporjuice' – a mix of calvados with either wine or cider. Its effects were sufficient to allow the soldiers plenty of sleep before they were next sent into battle.

Weakened by the rigours of warfare some men found their ability to handle alcohol diminished. With the potency of calvados it was unsurprising some men collapsed or suffered alcohol poisoning. One man who had been seen drinking calvados as if it were wine was found unconscious. For three whole days he drifted in and out of a coma-like state, occasionally rising from his bed to scream and shout at his friends. To avoid the attentions of their officers he was kept hidden and forcibly restrained whenever he attempted to leave. Despite the temptations, and occasional lapses there were relatively few incidents of alcohol-fuelled indiscipline. Some drunks threatened MPs with guns when they attempted to accost them, but such incidents rarely ended in violence. When soldiers were so drunk they dared to brandish weapons they had usually consumed so much they were easily disarmed and arrested.

Not all incidents ended peacefully and in some cases good natured celebrations erupted into violence. One Guardsman, convicted of the murder of a Royal Engineer outside a Normandy café, was sentenced to death. The sentence was later commuted to fifteen years penal servitude, most likely as a result of the revelations heard by the court about the amount of alcohol consumed by all those involved in the case. The Guardsman had gone to the café after an afternoon spent drinking calvados with civilians. By his own calculations he then drank at least two bottles of champagne. His drinking partners estimated the five-man group had consumed eight bottles of champagne, three bottles of calvados, and about forty glasses of cognac and witnesses revealed one man was sprawled on the floor, senselessly drunk. Little wonder those involved had little recollection of the events leading up to the murder. Even the first witness to arrive on the scene, who was passing in a jeep, admitted to being drunk.

Disregard for the people they were liberating could also cause problems. Troops had not been told about local customs and some cared little about them. They treated what they found as their own, often regardless of whether the rightful owner was there to prevent them. Such attitudes caused conflict with local farmers. Soldiers often smashed open narrow necked bottles of calvados containing a pear which were bottles saved for years to be given to their first son upon his marriage. One Frenchman recruited tank crews to dig up his stock of wine which had been hidden underground to keep it from the Germans. At the end of their labours the farmer attempted to pay the soldiers with a solitary bottle of wine. They were outraged – all that work for a mouthful of wine? Ken Tout recorded the scene: 'A mass of baying, shouting troopers pushes past the old man and begins the process of extracting bottles..... Hands pass the bottles to other hands. Legs scamper in the darkening night. Troopers at ground level gently elevate bottles .... And troopers on turrets just as carefully store bottles away in racks intended for more militant purposes.' (9) The farmer complained to their CO who of course made all the right noises, threatening a full investigation, whilst hiding a bottle beneath his stool.

As the battle for Normandy came to a close there was to be a brief respite. With the closing of the Falaise Gap some units were able to relax and take stock. With many units surrendering their transport to be loaned to 30 Corps for the advance towards Belgium they found themselves static. For a few precious days they had a chance to indulge without the fear of being left drunk and incapable. Although there was little extreme drunkenness, men certainly could drink with a clear conscience. The Poles were even lucky enough to reacquaint themselves with their favourite tipple, vodka, courtesy of stocks abandoned by the Wehrmacht. Gallons of cider were consumed, as were innumerable glasses of calvados. Wine was so plentiful villagers would bring it out to their liberators in buckets. It was an all too brief interlude before returning to the business of war.

Whilst their comrades were resting, General Horrocks' 30 Corps hit the road. The 'Swan' – the rapid advance to Brussels and Antwerp – was a period of great relief for the men who had fought so long and hard in Normandy. No longer were they fighting static battles, constantly fearing enemy counter-attacks. No longer were thousands of artillery shells fired, and tons of high explosive dropped, only for attacks to stall as soon as the Germans climbed from their bunkers and manned their guns. This was a rapid advance, seldom meeting more than half-hearted resistance. Not only were advancing troops greeted by enemy soldiers with their arms raised above their heads, but also by joyous civilians. These were not the sullen Norman farmers whose homes were being wrecked and lives disrupted by war. Instead, these people had suffered little during liberation – and were ready to celebrate. Troops found themselves facing almost constant temptation from civilians wanting to party. Despite the temptations most managed to remain well disciplined – apart from those whose vehicles miraculously 'broke down' outside cafés. Even when some men drank to excess their officers happily packed them off to barns and haylofts to sleep it off. This was a time to turn a blind eye to excess in the hope when hard fighting restarted troops would be able to return to the standards of discipline they had shown in Normandy.

Every woman, young or old, wanted to kiss their liberators, children wanted chocolate and cap badges as souvenirs, fruit was thrown to soldiers and flowers festooned their vehicles. Resistance fighters would fire their weapons into the air in celebration and everyone wanted to share carefully hoarded stocks of alcohol. These were the scenes that greeted the men of the 4/7th Royal Dragoon Guards on their entry into Lille. The advance was held up whilst the men joined in the celebrations until word came that the enemy was nearby. As the square cleared and the men remounted their tanks it was noticed such was the effect of the celebrations that very few climbed back into their vehicles with the same ease as they had dismounted. This was not the deliberate, sustained drinking of alcoholics but a joyous mood of celebration, a sense of relief and abandon that a major town had fallen without a fight. The alcohol took its toll on men since they were often exhausted, having driven for days inside stuffy tanks, seldom pausing except to refuel and catch a few hours sleep.

One armoured car commander had a solution to the temptations on offer – he accepted calvados from civilians and promptly emptied them through a hole in the vehicle floor. The hole was designed to drain rainwater from the vehicle but also helped keep the soldier 'dry'.

For the first time it seemed that the war might really be over by Christmas. There was little serious fighting to be done and the rapid advance brought in vast quantities of loot from abandoned enemy stores. The soldiers' favourite loot was alcohol. The first tank crews into the French town of Seclin discovered a store crammed with champagne, wine and brandy. The loot was quickly transferred to their tanks, hidden inside the crew's bedrolls that hung from the back of turrets. When word got around of the haul of drink an order was given for the quartermaster to reclaim the loot and for it to be assimilated into official supplies. However, all the quartermaster could find were bottles of white wine, which were generally unpopular with the troops. The rest remained hidden, ready to be consumed at the first opportunity.

When the 'Swan' came to an end the Guards Armoured Division had liberated Brussels. At Louvain they overran the principal German military champagne store, and at Holsbeek a dump was located housing around fifteen thousand bottles of spirits. Tankmen were soon helping themselves to crates of champagne, emptying their supply trucks of ammunition to transport more 'liberated' champagne. All ranks joined in from guardsmen to colonels. Soon MPs were placed on guard to prevent outsiders from getting in to join the looting frenzy. The champagne was sufficient to last for months and in some units was recorded as: 'flowing like water'. (10) One distinguished liberator, the Earl of Kimberley, later admitted the liberation of Brussels had been the beginning of his eventual slide into alcoholism. From then until the end of the war he maintained a constant supply of champagne within his tank, regularly drinking it from a tin mug. He later claimed he spent much of the war 'tight' and was unable to stop once it was over.

For the rest of 1944 periods of rest enjoyed by the Guardsmen were marked by the drinking of vast amounts of champagne. Visits by friends or comrades around the various tank squadrons were always an occasion to break open a bottle and it was consumed at a rate most could only ever have dreamed of. For a short period a party atmosphere reigned. Such were the stocks of champagne that surplus bottles were fed to captured geese they were fattening up for Christmas.

When 11th Armoured Division captured the port of Antwerp, they had advanced four hundred miles in just eight days. For a few days they stayed in the city and relaxed. General Horrocks, the commander of 30 Corps, was so pleased with the advance he sent up a dozen cases of champagne and one lieutenant colonel recorded having champagne with his lunch for three days, then leaving Antwerp in possession of eight hundred bottles of claret, eight dozen bottles of Cointreau, and eight dozen bottles of brandy. This was no surprise, since the division had acquired up the contents of a local Customs store – earning eight hundred bottles of wine and eight thousand cigars per regiment. Even artillery observers joined in whilst manning their positions. One recalled observing from an Antwerp office whilst listening to pre-war blues records and drinking coffee and brandy brought to him by a member of the office staff. Others ordered drinks by telephone, to be sent up from the parties below.

Whilst 30 Corps enjoyed the fruits of victory, other units dealt with those Germans who had been bypassed. British and Canadian forces advancing along the coast were fighting hard to secure the channel ports from which the German garrisons had not retreated. The culmination of the successful assaults on the ports was an orgy of plunder. When Le Havre fell sufficient stocks of champagne were found to fill the cooks' trucks of the 2nd Battalion of the Gloucestershire Regiment. There was also enough beer for two bottles to be issued to each man in the battalion. In total, around one million bottles were thought by some to have been found in Le Havre, much of which was sent for consumption in the military hospitals. British soldiers were seen wandering the streets of the liberated town swigging cherry brandy and Benedictine from the bottle. As they downed their drinks empty bottles were smashed against the wall. Scottish soldiers were drinking champagne from tin mugs before engaging in energetic sprees of looting and a drunken Canadian was seen riding a horse through minefields. Such was the availability of loot that news of the haul spread quickly through the army and the town was soon besieged by hordes of desperate looters. The liberators were forced to put guards on the approaches to the town and some joked how it had become harder to get into the town after the liberation than before.

Some soldiers made detours to find the drinks they craved. Outside Le Havre soldiers went to buy Benedictine from the monks at Fécamp. Northants Yeoman Ken Squires found himself drinking the liqueur:

We were outside Le Havre, after the town had surrendered, and about six of us went on a quick night out to Fécamp. We'd heard the place to go was an 'estaminet', 'cause that's where the 'crumpet' was. So off we go. We found an estaminet but the place was deserted. So we sit down and we wait, eventually someone comes out. We asked for some beer, no beer. We asked for wine, no. They only had one thing – so we all had a bottle of Benedictine each! How we ever got back on the lorry to get back to where we should have been, god above only knows. All thoughts of 'crumpet' went out the window. (11)

Ken Hardy also recalled his first encounter with the drink: 'I discovered Benedictine and it was a revelation to me ... I was so ignorant of the right things to do, I had no experience of booze really, none at all, and I didn't really know how to behave towards it. We were in the top floor of a barn and I said to the blokes "Here, share that amongst you". When I came back most of them didn't like it and those that did were drinking it out of pint glasses!' (12)

With the slow-down of the advance and the end of summer, the issue of rum became an increasingly regular occurrence. Thousands of gallons of the spirit were consumed – in one month the 53rd Infantry Division consumed 1,228 gallons of ration rum. On cold mornings, before they went into action, men crowded around their NCOs to get the quarter pint of rum that was supposed to calm their nerves. Some took the ration but preferred not to drink it – figuring the effects of alcohol might cause them to become too reckless once the fighting had started. Often they swapped the precious liquid for cigarettes with comrades who wanted to suppress their fears with alcohol. Others chose to pour the rum into their water bottles, saving it for after the battle and using it to aid relaxation.

In cold, damp conditions soldiers needed something to warm and cheer them before any concerted activity. With morale starting to 'drift' officers were well aware of rum's recuperative power. Ken Hardy was in command of an infantry platoon facing the worst of the Dutch winter: 'We had lots of black rum. When we were on "the island", outside Arnhem, the issue of rum for night patrols became very much the thing. Partly because people hated going out in the dark. They were very frightened. So they doubled our rum ration. It was lovely stuff, the best rum I've ever had. Black as pitch and twice as strong.' (13)

Of course, not everyone was so keen, as Northants Yeoman Michael Hunt recalled: 'I wasn't a drinker in those days. I can remember my first rum. We'd been out all night. It was pouring with rain and we were all soaking wet. And Major Bevan said "Pass the rum round". We all had our tot of rum but I couldn't drink it. I did my best but it was vile – very earthy. Yet when we were in Germany, Harry Graham came back from leave and brought a bottle of Captain Morgan rum. He dished it out to everyone in the troop. That was much better.' (14) Despite such reservations few were going to waste such a valuable product, Hunt's mate Ken Squires was always happy to see the rum jar: 'I used to swig it out of the jar. The Quartermaster Sgt used to come up and say "Here, have a swig". Yeah, you're 18 or 19 years of age, you don't know what kind of trouble you're going to be in. But there was no drunkenness, no way.' (15)

Recognising the soothing effects of alcohol, officers increasingly took to saving rum to be served once the fighting had finished. Patrols often returned from behind enemy lines to find tots of rum waiting for them, which they drank as intelligence officers listened to the information they had gathered. Often it was served in tea, the combination of heat and alcohol helping to soothe the troubled men. The rum stopped hands shaking, teeth chattering and bodies shaking – in minutes they would be back to normal.

For all the benefits of rum it was not really what the men craved. What they really wanted was something more familiar – beer. The issue of beer rations were much heralded occasions. Soldiers talked among themselves about when beer rations would arrive. Anxious for such simple reminders of home they longed to hear the familiar clinking of glass that heralded its arrival. Corporal Worthington of the 1st Royal Dragoons recalled: 'It came about once a month, some men, or boys if you like, used to exchange cigs for beer and sometimes they would dance with each other.' (16)

Most of the time there was little access to home-produced alcohol and they had to do with whatever local brews they could find. In Holland they came across 'Arrack' distilled from date palms, Bols, and the unfamiliar Dutch gin, Genever. In Germany they sampled 'Danziger Goldwasser' that, when held up to the light, shimmered with reflections from hundreds of tiny pieces of gold leaf floating in the spirit.

Finding such spirits unpalatable they were mixed to make cocktails. Ken Squires was rapidly becoming acquainted with many of Europe's favourite drinks:

> Once I got promoted to Sergeant I became a part of the Mess – mind you I was always in a mess! You always got a good liquor ration every month – couple of bottles of Scotch or a couple of bottles of gin. This all went straight to the Mess, so you could have a drink for nothing. And a round used to be six Marks, whatever you were going to drink would be the same price. At that time we were getting forty Marks to the Pound, so six of you would go in and order a round of drinks. But you never got to the sixth person, particularly if you were drinking champagne. 'Cause you'd drink a whole bottle on each round, so it never got to the sixth person. So you made sure you were on the end, then it didn't cost you anything! One particular drink I remember was Noilly Pratt – we laughed 'Who's got an oily prat?' – it turned out to be bloody vermouth! We couldn't drink it, it wasn't to our taste at all. So we used that to make cocktails. (17)

Soldiers who only had access to an occasional bottle of beer and the rum ration had to make efforts to obtain anything stronger. At times the inexperienced drinkers were unaware of the possible results of overindulgence in strong spirits. Many had been too young to drink when the war started, and shortages meant they were unused to spirits and some treated them without caution. They poured wine and spirits into their pint mugs and swigged them like beer, expecting they would be able to consume as much as they would at home. Some experimented with the bottles kept by officers. Fred Sylvester was among them: 'My car commander managed to acquire a bottle of whisky which he left with me whilst he went off with his sergeant cronies. Fearful that it might evaporate before he returned I felt compelled to drink it. I don't remember much after that!' (18)

The results were dreadful, many of the youngsters collapsed in drunken stupors and experienced headaches the like of which they had never known. It was only the care and attention of fellow soldiers that kept them away from the prying eyes of officers and senior NCOs.

In many instances such drunkenness was less the result of wilful ill discipline and more the result of unfamiliarity. One soldier recalled his first encounter with a bottle he and his friends had obtained: 'this resulted in my driver losing his false teeth out of the window and me being very ill, I've not drunk cognac since'. (19)

Those units stationed in towns and villages soon 'took over' their own cafés and bars in which outsiders were made to feel unwelcome. In many areas there was an unwritten rule that only men of one nation's army should use certain bars. Canadians avoided British bars and vice versa. In particular the rule applied in areas where the men of 21st Army Group served alongside US formations. Attempts by GIs to use British bars were like a red rag to a bull. The nightmare that their wives, girlfriends, daughters and even mothers, might be seduced by the lure of rich Americans was bad enough. However, the thought GIs might now muscle in on their bars, buying all the drink and 'pulling' the local girls was enough to ensure a hostile reception. In one incident British troops did their best to ignore the provocation until their officers had departed. As soon as the door closed behind the officers the mood changed, and confrontation became inevitable. It was only at parade the next morning that the result of the fracas became known. Men were seen sporting black eyes, broken noses, bloodied faces, bruised knuckles and toothless gums. All claimed their injuries were the result of sporting accidents or night time trips and falls. Everyone knew the real reason for the injuries was the fight to evict unwanted Americans from the bar. Even the company commander winked when he loudly proclaimed he would not tolerate his men fighting among themselves. The implications for morale – keeping the bar safe for his men to use peacefully – outweighed the worries of a few bruises and broken teeth.

The story was repeated in towns where the troops were sent on leave. As one officer on leave noted in his memoirs: 'Tradition demanded that in such a situation a pair of young subalterns should get a little drunk.' (20) MPs soon noticed how many young soldiers did more than get a 'little drunk' and seemed unable to restrain themselves when they had a night out. One 'Redcap' wrote up the arrest of a soldier he had found 'making merry' on his first night of freedom in Belgium: 'Pte Farmer – drunk – trying to perform traffic policeman's duties – wearing collar and tie against regulations – claiming his mother gave him permission to do so.' (21)

Not all behaviour did credit to the good name of the British and Canadian armies, in fact the antics of some soured relations between the liberators and the liberated. A Tilburg coal merchant reported an unpleasant encounter with two

The Ordinary Men
By 1944 the army included men from all walks of life. This group of
Gordon Highlanders reflects that mix. *Normandy, June 1944.*

The Ordinary Men
A typical British 'Tommy', Private John Ward of the 1st
Herefords. *Holland, March 1945.*

The Landscape of Battle
The men soon learned the chaotic nature of war. Here infantrymen are seen
at a tense moment during streetfighting in Geilinkirchen, Germany.

The Ordinary Men
This British corporal, though wounded by a mine, is still smiling.
He has a 'Blighty Wound' and knows he is going home.

The Ordinary Men

'Any silly thing goes…You'd come out of a house with the saucepan on your head…or they'd pick up a woman's handbag and wear knickers and a brassière over their uniform. They'd come out of the house to where everybody was and just strut around. That was a lovely spellbreaker, especially if you've had a rough time. It keeps you sane'.

The Landscape of Battle

In the course of the campaign the men endured all the extremes of weather.
This army fireman is protecting himself from the summer sun.
Normandy, August 1944 .

Dutch Courage and the Calvados Campaign
The rum ration proved popular during cold
weather. Here Rifleman Burrel of the 1st
Battalion The Rifle Brigade delivers the
ration for Christmas.

Dutch Courage and the Calvados Campaign
During the Normandy campaign cider
became the favourite tipple of the troops.
Here Bombardier Thomas and Gunner
Pollard sample from a vat found in a
farmhouse. *August 1944.*

Dutch courage and the Calvados Campaign
Troops resting during the advance into Holland, their sleep
aided by the contents of the bottles around them.

drunken British officers who had beaten on his door and demanded admittance. When he opened the door he was held at gunpoint and ordered to find them a woman. Fearing for his life he led them down a side street where he was able to struggle free. As he escaped into the shadows the officers opened fire at him, fortunately missing. As the Dutchman admitted they were probably too drunk to shoot straight. On Christmas Eve, as the Battle of the Bulge raged to their east the Royal Ulster Rifles were awaiting a possible German breakthrough. At midnight shots were heard and troops prepared for an attack. However closer inspection found a weather vane being used for target practice by drunken officers. It was also easy for soldiers to resent the behaviour of some officers, especially when their antics impinged on valuable rest periods. They objected to being told to behave themselves yet seeing officers misbehave.

Whilst discreet drunkenness was tolerated by many officers, open drunkenness was deemed unacceptable. It was one thing for a soldier to drink himself into a stupor quietly whilst in a safe area but quite another to be seen wandering openly in a state of intoxication. In such cases officers and NCOs felt obliged to act and many offenders faced court martial. Those men who succumbed to temptation and allowed themselves to get drunk whilst on duty faced little more than token punishment – ten days field punishment and loss of forty days pay was a typical award. Officers however faced stiffer penalties. As a result of drunkenness they could be reduced to the ranks. The problems came when the men facing charges were experienced men who were vital to the unit. Some officers argued against charging them, knowing if the indiscretion was not overlooked the efficiency of their unit might be compromised. Others argue if drunkenness was not clamped down on they might face a wave of over-indulgence and the spread of alcohol fuelled indiscipline.

Drunkenness in the forward areas never reached unmanageable levels. Many officers carried hip flasks but few overdid it. Instead they were ideal for an invigorating 'nip' in times of trouble, when a warming mouthful of spirits was just enough to steady the nerves. Some officer carried bottles of brandy euphemistically known as 'medicinal comforts'. Similarly, some men carried waterbottles full of whatever spirits they could find. Some even took to wearing a second waterbottle to ensure they could also carry enough water.

Most were well aware of the risks involved and steered clear of them. The effects of alcohol were always a danger to the fighting soldier – loss of fear, a slowing of reactions, impaired ability to judge distance, and a tendency towards irrational and dangerous behaviour. All of these could bring a soldier's fighting career to a rapid end. The fine line between Dutch courage and foolhardiness meant the stakes were too high for front line soldiers. If drunkenness was seldom apparent at the front there can be no better reason than that given by a Canadian engineer who was offered a drink of whisky whilst sheltering on Juno Beach. He simply admitted he was concerned the drink would make him brave. Some drunks took chances with their lives, marching around in full view of the enemy, exhorting their comrades to the vigorous pursuit of war.

Those who took their chances and got drunk were often those who were growing increasingly desperate. With their nerves in tatters and the prospect of death seldom far from their minds they consciously over-indulged. Anything that blotted out reality was positive. They had little fear of repercussions. Punishments were not fierce and to many offending men a brief period of detention would mean a period away from the dangers of the front. It was a chance for their nerves to settle and to recover what little courage they had left. Though few in number, some succumbed to the lure of alcohol and drinking to steady their nerves became habitual. For some it was to be the start of a lifetime of submerging their awful memories of war.

Stan Proctor was one of those men who usually only ever drank sparingly, seldom saw anybody else drinking and had only one experience of a soldier being drunk on duty – himself. Procter celebrated his birthday and Christmas 1944 together, marking the occasion with a cocktail prepared in a pint mug by his sergeant: 'With short-sighted and idiotic bravado I sank it almost in one gulp. I remembered nothing after that until I was dragged back to my billet, was sick all over my bedroom floor and woke up in the morning with a head that did not allow me to get up till lunchtime. .... I was due for duty in the afternoon. 2nd Lt. Johnson, our 2nd in command, saw what a state I was in and did my duty for me. I went back to bed. Sgt Dodds' cocktail had consisted of whisky, cognac, gin, beer and sherry. I was told that I had imitated Churchill with five cigars in my hand and read Morse at an impossible speed.' (22)

For some, dangers came from attempting to find alcohol rather than actually drinking it. The desire to locate sources of alcohol led officers and other ranks to concoct elaborate schemes and even put other men at risk. A 43rd Division chaplain was asked to go under cover of a white flag to bury some fallen comrades. Whilst digging the graves the major who had requested him to carry out the burial appeared. He made his way into a nearby house, making the Germans suspicious. The ceasefire was broken and the Germans opened fire. Upon return to the British lines it was found the officer had been in the house looking for wine. The chaplain wrote: 'I am still convinced that the wine ..... was the real reason for that request for burial in broad daylight and in full view of the enemy. I was furious, and went straight to the C.O. and told him that I did not mind sticking my neck out when necessary, but that I strongly objected to being used as a stalking horse in a wine foraging lark.' (23)

Others used alcohol as a distraction, hoping the mental rather than physical effects of a strong drink might help keep the men calm. Some officers and senior NCOs toured positions under fire offering drink to the men sheltering from the enemy. The intention was to break their concentration, making them focus on something other than the danger they faced. With a drink inside them they could relax and think back to nights in pubs back home and of happier occasions when alcohol was linked to celebration. Anything rather than think of death.

During most of the campaign men in the front lines were fortunate enough not to be faced with temptation. They fought through fields and shattered villages and, apart from the cider filled farmhouses of Normandy, seldom found anything worth consuming in the forward areas. Much of Europe was racked by shortages, the Germans having confiscated much of the drink already. If they were not fortunate enough to liberate the German stocks there was precious little left in civilian hands.

This state of affairs was to be reversed for one short period of the campaign – Operation Market Garden. The men of the 1st Airborne Division reversed the usual roles. They were not the attacking force, trying to storm the town under the cover of artillery fire and air support. Instead they were the defenders, valiantly holding out against superior odds and facing the might of the German army. It was not the usual landscape of shattered homes and farms, but a peaceful town where they waited for war to come to them. And come it did.

Paratroops advancing into Arnhem were met by joyous crowds, cheering, singing, throwing flowers, offering them fruit and drinks of gin. One inebriated Dutchman rode towards the troops with a stone bottle only to be met by a British officer who threatened to shoot both him and any soldier who accepted a drink. Others were prepared for victory and one senior officer landed in Holland carrying bottles of gin, sherry and whisky, with which he envisaged entertaining the local resistance leaders.

As the battle progressed the situation changed, with the Germans cutting off the water supply to the houses the paratroopers were occupying. At first the soldiers resorted to drinking the water from the radiators and central heating systems. Once this was exhausted a new source had to be located – the bottles of wine and gin found in cellars. At the Hartenstein Hotel, functioning as Divisional HQ, the water shortage was offset by the contents of the wine cellar. Wracked by hunger and thirst their tolerance of alcohol was reduced. This access to drink made some soldiers take risks, as James Sims discovered after taking a drink of brandy offered by a sergeant. When they asked for someone to retrieve a Bren gun, Sims surprised himself by volunteering. As he later explained: 'It was almost suicidal as the whole area was sewn up by MG teams.' (24) Considering their location the phrase 'Dutch Courage' was never more applicable. Despite such actions, to the credit of the troops there were no recorded incidents of drunkenness.

The failure of Market Garden and the stagnation of the front for winter changed the way alcohol was treated. As the army became static there was an opportunity to relax. Inevitably this included parties. Canadian officers sent out invitations to the officers of units in their area requesting their company for a 'Get-to-know-your-neighbour Cocktail Party'. For such events they sent representatives to Antwerp to find alcoholic drinks more suitable for a party than issue rum.

The appalling winter weather resulted in alcohol-fuelled indiscretions even by men who were normally teetotal. Often non-drinkers were detailed to fetch rum rations safe in the knowledge they wouldn't drink it. However, the cold tempted some to sample the rum. One such individual did so whilst crossing a swollen river on a makeshift bridge:

It warmed him instantly. A second, third and fourth draught followed in rapid succession, and with one foot on the plank, he attempted a fifth large drink. Two unsteady steps on the narrow bridge, but the third missed and he fell headlong into the freezing river. The temperature was below zero, yet the sudden coldness produced an instant sobering effect, because after a struggle he threw off his greatcoat and struck out strongly for the opposite bank, where further difficulties ensued before he managed to get out of the water. (25)

He was never sent to fetch the rum ration again.

Though such episodes appeared comic, over-indulgence could be potentially lethal. In winter falling asleep without finding shelter could result in frostbite. When one gunner drank the rum ration for his entire crew and then fell into a drunken stupor, he was found barely alive and frozen to the floor. Even the Normandy cider was not without often unpleasant side effects as it caused stomach upsets in the men unused to its acidic qualities. Doctors also blamed it for an outbreak of gastroenteritis during the Normandy campaign. Yet the problems of drinking acidic cider were minor compared to some of the drinks available. Many illegal stills had sprung up to cope with wartime shortages. These were often controlled by profiteers who supplied the black market and many of their products were used to welcome the liberators. The unscrupulous distillers of these drinks showed little concern for the fate of their customers and concentrated on maximising profits. Analysis of 'brandy' – or as Canadian soldiers called it 'Ape Sweat' – confiscated during raids by MPs revealed it was often up to 95 per cent methyl alcohol and potentially lethal. In Amiens, December 1944 saw the deaths of six soldiers and the hospitalisation of many more. They had been drinking a crude homemade alcohol sold as brandy. Although the sale of spirits to soldiers was banned, the edict made little difference, and it was only after the poisonings that MPs reported a fall in the purchase of spirits.

The risks of consuming such products were many and varied. If the possibility of blindness and madness were not enough, there was also the risk of accidental injury whilst under the influence of overstrong alcohol. One soldier found himself inadvertently driving over an unfinished bridge and overturning his vehicle after having a fight with his mate whilst driving. The problem was not confined to the black marketeers and their back yard stills. There were also soldiers producing alcoholic drinks. One tankman recalled the behaviour of some of his comrades: 'One crew had a still. And they brewed up anything – they scraped the stuff off telegraph poles and used it. It was dangerous. They did a lot of silly things. One bloke got so drunk he walked out of his bedroom window, fell out and killed himself.' (26)

Although Montgomery was a well-known teetotaller he was tolerant of drinking. He knew soldiers would never forsake their beer and accepted drinking among his own staff, so long as there was no visible excesses. Fortunately for Montgomery those drinkers on the staff of TAC HQ carefully concealed their more exuberant behaviour. There is little doubt the Field Marshal would have frowned at the behaviour of some of his staff, amongst whom were men operating a still and secretly producing bathtub gin. In Germany it was later reported that a whole hospital was filled with soldiers who had gone mad after drinking a petrol-based concoction. They also began to unearth supplies of liquid that was obviously alcoholic but was unsuitable for human consumption and there were to be innumerable casualties. On closer inspection they discovered it was V2 rocket fuel. It was too strong for their bodies to tolerate and those who sampled the clear spirit often crumpled as if shot. The lucky ones lapsed into comas, the less fortunate went blind or died. After linking up with the Red Army some soldiers found themselves drinking all manner of potentially lethal concoctions, and one group of signallers were left temporarily blind after attending a Russian party. Others were offered drinks that were found to be strong enough to power blowtorches.

The latter stages of the campaign were marked by increasingly frequent alcoholic opportunities. The Germans had bought or looted much of Europe's alcohol, including the best French wines, champagne and brandy and the produce of Belgian and Dutch breweries and distilleries. There was also the prospect of the wines of the Moselle and Rhine vineyards and beers from local breweries. Once the troops reached Germany they began to encounter another unfamiliar brew – schnapps. This fierily famous fruit spirit replaced the calvados of Normandy and the gin of the Netherlands as favourite tipples. Again many troops were initially hesitant about this unfamiliar drink. Soldiers appeared from houses and farms sipping uncertainly from their mugs, asking comrades to confirm the identity of the clear fluid. The more experienced drinkers could put them right, leaving the soldiers to celebrate their latest advance and submerge the memories of their most recent losses. As had happened with calvados orders soon went round many units forbidding the consumption of schnapps in fear of its possible effects.

During the final weeks of the war soldiers began to relax. As resistance crumbled troops no longer had quite the same fears of immediate counter-attack – it was not that the risks had disappeared but they had diminished. This gradual respite from fighting was enjoyed by those with access to alcohol. Germany was in chaos – its towns destroyed, its population on the move, its armed forces destroyed. When towns fell to the advancing armies the men who had done the fighting were often able to let their hair down. The scenes of anarchy were emphasised by the appearance of officers and men toasting their successes with looted alcohol. Men stood on street corners, swigging warm champagne from tin mugs, using portraits of Hitler for target practice. Every shattered German beerhouse was entered by the conquering army, trying the taps to see if the barrels were still full, the lucky ones filling their mugs and waterbottles. They pulled chairs and tables from ruined bars and restaurants and sat drinking at improvised pavement cafés. Those detailed to dig graves or latrines began to unearth hidden stores of drink, which were soon dug up and shared out. When large supply dumps were discovered it was common practice to remove part of the haul to send as a gift to Divisional or Corps HQs. It was safer to pay a 'tithe' rather than have a senior office decide to requisition the whole dump. Since they knew the 'high ups' would soon be sending lorries to claim their share of the loot officers and men told to guard large dumps simply removed what they wanted before anyone turned up to count the stores. The usual course of action was for officers to confiscate what they could, securing some for their Mess, giving a share to the sergeants and spare bottles for barter.

The destruction and dislocation meant there was no certainty as to what drinks might be found and as the troops settled into the towns they had to make do with whatever was on offer. The limited quantities and unpredictable range of drinks resulted in some weird and wonderful concoctions. 'A' Squadron of the Sherwood Rangers Yeomanry were luckier than some when they positioned their HQ in a Bremen bar. A quick search of the cellar revealed a large sack of sugar which was mixed with apple juice and rum to make a punch.

Others in the city had no need to resort to devising cocktails. The Battalion HQ of 2 Lincolns was based in the Alter Korn gin distillery and the 1st Battalion Royal Norfolk Regiment occupied the Becks Brewery. In no time soldiers were sampling the drink and helping themselves to souvenirs from the Becks gift department. On hearing of the haul lorries began to arrive from other units. It was traditional that every unit within striking distance should try to get in on the act. Reacting to the threat the Norfolks put an armed guard on the brewery to defend their beer supply. Even the town major arrived to try to get his share only to be told that no one was allowed access to the brewery without a chit from the Norfolks' CO. However, it was too good to last and soon the infantry were on their way to the front again, leaving the brewery to the rear units, but not before loading every available vehicle with as much as they could carry.

For the men of the occupation forces there were interesting appointments to be had in the newly captured breweries and distilleries. There was no greater reward for the hard-working infantrymen than to find themselves in charge of such locations. Ken Hardy's reward was to be head of a distillery. He recalled:

> Alcohol didn't play a big part in my life at all – not until I got to Germany where I was put in charge of a distillery. It certainly didn't play much of a role in Normandy, I hardly ever had any. Then when we went to Le Havre I discovered Benedictine, and it was a revelation to me. It didn't last long, just whilst we were in Le Havre, but the taste stayed with me – always, right up to now. Then at Goslar I was in charge of the brewery and the distillery. It was a very important job. I used to go to bed sloshed – absolutely stoned out of my mind – then wake up, have a glass of water and start all over again. I used to take the brandy and put it in the beer to drink. That went on for weeks. But we ran it properly, security was tight and it was distributed properly. When I came back to this country my mother was appalled at my state and what it had done to me. I think we'd all gone out as innocent boys, we'd had no experience of life. She couldn't believe the change in me. (27)

In occupied towns follow-up units soon began establishing their own improvised bars. Units took over cellars – often the only undamaged locations – and settled in. Wood was found to construct bars, planks were nailed to walls to make shelves. Furniture was salvaged from the rubble of local homes to provide tables and chairs, then finally the all important stock of 'liberated' alcohol was brought in. In these newly formed bars supplies of free drink could be distributed fairly, with the social atmosphere helping to prevent over-indulgence and excessive drunkenness.

With the situation stablising, life became increasingly pleasant for units moving through German towns. At Rheine, the town major insisted a group of Pioneers could only be housed in a building on the proviso they did not loot its well-stocked wine cellar. Their company commander agreed. He took the keys to the house and its cellar and promised when they departed the bottles would all still be in place. Indeed they were. For each night of their stay the men were allowed to line up and collect one bottle of wine each, on the condition they handed back the empty bottle from the previous night. Thus when the Pioneers departed the house the cellar remained intact, albeit with empty rather than full bottles on the racks.

Of course, not everyone was so disciplined. Many of the warehouses and stores were raided by the troops with little care taken over the distribution of their contents. Even men sent to guard such liberated booze often found the temptations too great to resist. At Neumunster, MPs went to check up a wine store only to find the store unguarded and the commander of the guard drunk.

Such temptations were too much for many of the troops. With the end of the war rapidly approaching there was a marked rise in the amount of drinking among even the troops in forward areas. Although some officers started the morning with drinks of gin to accompany their breakfast, it did not mean it was yet safe for them to overdo it. There was a wide gulf between the revitalising morning 'nip' and day-long over-indulgence. Fortunately there were still few men who ever allowed themselves to get in such a state when in close contact with the enemy, but gradually the numbers appeared to be increasing and some soldiers began to take chances which would have been previously unthinkable. In the village of Wildeshausen, outside Bremen, tank crews of the 5th Royal Dragoon Guards held a party with captured alcohol in a schoolhouse. During the party Germans attacked the village and destroyed a number of vehicles before the British troops could respond.

With so much drink to be found, the troops sometimes had enough to spare and men going on leave were able to take some home to their families. In the final months of the war it was a common sight to see men heavily laden with 'liberated' bottles as they disembarked from leave ships. A Guards colonel reported his men were arriving home exhausted from the amount of champagne they were carrying. These were not just presents. With alcohol so strictly rationed in Britain the soldiers could tap into a lucrative black market, and were soon offering wine and spirits to eager landlords in local pubs. This trade in alcohol went two ways. With so much unfamiliar alcohol offered to the troops, British brands were at a premium. The Black Watch were able to arrange a supply of their favoured whisky by making a deal with the RAF. In return for the use of a 'liberated' generator the RAF agreed to send a plane back to Inverness to collect forty-eight cases of Scotch.

As the end approached many of the soldiers increased their drinking. With the men of the 6th Airborne Division reaching the Baltic all thought of the Germans continuing to resist was gone. Their armies were split. There was no continuous front line and their main pockets of organised units were far from the Nazi heartland – isolated in Norway, Denmark and Schleswig-Holstein. As the advancing troops reached their final objectives and were told to stay put awaiting further orders it was clear the end was near. They settled down, started to relax and awaited the party that would come once the final order was given to cease fire.

4

Sex Conquers Orders

'Do you really have to ask what soldiers get up to when they are sent to some large city for relief?' (1)

'It wasn't exactly prostitution was it? You picked a girl up, she wanted a bar of chocolate. Bang. Job done.' (2)

For centuries the man in uniform has been a potent symbol of male virility. The image of the dashingly handsome, red-coated cavalry officer has found its way into novels, plays, songs, films and television programmes. Soldiers have been surrounded by a sexual aura – powerful, dangerous, heroic, somewhat distant. Always at the call of King and Country – ready at any moment to abandon all he loved to answer the call of duty. Such men captivated women throughout the ages. During the First World War young women handed out white feathers to young men not in uniform. The message was clear, a man not brave enough to fight did not deserve their affections.

But what of the uniformed men of the Second World War? In the early summer of 1944 thousands were waiting to be shipped to France, most of them young men travelling abroad for the first time. They were heading for a Europe almost bereft of eligible young men. So many of the men of the occupied countries were away from home, either in POW camps or working in the factories of the Reich. Others were in hiding, like the thousands of Dutchmen wishing to avoid the onerous task of working for the Germans.

Into this environment came the British army and their allies, not the dashing red-coated soldiers of history but dirty and dishevelled men in crumpled ill-fitting khaki. Gone was the glamour of horses and swords, replaced by tanks, rifles and machine guns. However they still managed to conquer the hearts of Europe's women – attracted by their physical appearance or the gifts they bore. In a Europe so bereft of consumer goods men with cigarettes, coffee and petrol could conquer moral objections and buy their way into bed.

This sea change in sexual morals had begun long before the invasion. Uncertainty bred a new moral code. Life was increasingly cheap and people took their pleasure where they found it. Conscription split up families, women went into factories and their men into uniform. Men who for years had enjoyed the sexual comfort of a wife found barrack life difficult. Enforced separation did little to quell their libidos. All over the country illicit liaisons sprang up. Soldiers paired up with the women living near their camps. Waiting wives enjoyed the affections of men not in uniform, and latterly the glamorous GIs whose comparative wealth and smart uniforms ensured them a warm welcome. Without the steadying influence of absent fathers and working mothers, many teenage girls flirted with promiscuity, surrendering their virginity to young men they hardly knew, often oblivious to the dangers of disease and pregnancy.

Prostitution flourished, both as a way for soldiers to find relief and for hard-pressed women to earn extra money. It was not just on the street corners of Piccadilly or the darkened alleys around docks or railway stations that girls plied their trade. Brothels flourished in the heady atmosphere of wartime London. In some of the more exclusive establishments were found a better class of working girl. Madams recruited well-spoken secretaries and shop girls from some of the capital's most fashionable stores. They even attempted to bring in the wives of army officers whose husbands had been posted abroad. The names of the most respectable establishments were well known in the officers clubs of London. Those in the know would take hopeful comrades aside and direct them to places like the Cavendish Hotel in St James where the proprietress, Rosa Lewis, was always able to help. At Mrs Fetherstonhaugh's 'Private Hotel' in Knightsbridge one Coldstream Guards officer was shown to a room only to be met by his own sister.

Young soldiers from every perceivable background and all four corners of the land were thrown together. They soon learned the new moral codes of people whom they might never have met without the war. More innocent recruits were shocked by the sexual behaviour of their fellow soldiers as was recalled by Pioneer Corps Corporal Alexander Baron:

> I was still repeatedly taken aback by what I saw of sexual behaviour which was like that of dogs trotting about in the street. I remember one occasion when we picked up an Air Force girl while we were travelling in the back of a covered truck. She was fair and pretty. I took her to be the kind of girl toward whom one ought to be protective. Soon she was lying on the floor at the back of the truck with her legs up, giggling and gasping pleasurably. Among the men who went to her were some whom I had thought to be faithful husbands. She dropped from the tailboard outside an Air Force camp and walked off, as bright as ever, while the men waved and called cheerful goodbyes after her. I thought how do they know? Why are they so sure of each other? How can all these transactions take place so instantly and confidently without a word being spoken? I decided that I lacked some kind of psychic antennae which other people possessed. (3)

Most learned that if they made the effort of getting to know women there was often a chance to 'get lucky'. Artilleryman Doug Colls organised battery dances whilst in a camp in Berkshire. To find female dancing partners he telephoned a local ATS camp, where he was put in contact with a sergeant. Their conversation was most encouraging for Colls:

> 'Will you be coming to the dance?' I asked her. 'Of course.' 'Perhaps we could meet up?' I suggested. 'Why not.' 'How will I recognise you?' 'Well, my name is Holly.' 'Fine, but I can't go running amongst your girls asking who's Holly?' 'Well you know that I have three stripes, but I am 5 feet 5 and blond.' She told me. Things were falling into place! 'Fair blond, quite blond or very blond?' I asked. 'Well, I'm very blond, out of a bottle, I suppose like Jean Harlow. You know, blond on top and dark elsewhere.' AND SHE WAS! (4)

Older men regaled the young soldiers with lurid details of their sex lives, impressing their eager listeners with stories of delights they might expect when they left England. Pre-war regulars told bawdy tales of the brothels from Cairo to Calcutta where they had wiled away their years of service. Barracks were also home to unabashed masturbators, or in army parlance of the day men who went 'climbing up their rifle'. In some camps there was open homosexuality with the sight of men leaving each other's bunks at roll call a common occurrence, as an anti aircraft gunner recalled: 'Nobody commented on this or made any criticism.' (5)

However in the main the army was full of thousands of young men with little or no sexual experience, some eager to learn the ways of love, others too innocent or scared to experiment. Looking back, many of those innocents laugh about how sheltered their lives had been and if only they had known then what they learnt in later years. One of those innocents, Dr Ken Tout, looked back on the conversations between the men he served with, and remembered: 'Sex was much talked about but not as we now know it. With most young men of the day it tended to be much sublimated into romantic ideas about girlfriends rather than the frank, physical sex talk of today.' (6)

The constant spectre of death or disablement that haunted the fighting men led to a change in attitudes towards sex. If life was cheap then sex was cheaper still. No man knew how long he might last at the front nor when the next opportunity to sate his desires might arise. Consequently they took their chances whenever they came. Few had time to spend wooing potential conquests and instead concentrated their efforts on women who seemed obviously willing. Thousands made their way across northern Europe leaving behind them a procession of one-night stands and brief encounters.

The military authorities were well aware of the likely behaviour of the troops and the risk of disease. With great foresight, when one tank regiment was ordered to paint its vehicles with names beginning with the letter 'S' their doctor suggested he call his ambulance 'Syphilis'. The authorities had no intention of losing vast numbers of fighting men to the VD clinics and took steps to prevent infection. In the last days before D-Day the men were issued with contraceptives ready for their arrival on the Continent. Invariably some joker would shout 'I thought we were going to fight the enemy not fuck them!' They took the 'French Letters', some using them to waterproof wallets and watches, some inflating them and flying them from their rifles. Many more pocketed them in hope that they would live long enough to put them to use. Even at this late date, scattered amongst the troops were plenty of innocent young men who were unsure of what the 'rubbers' were supposed to be for. Nineteen-year-old artilleryman John Mercer recalled: 'We were all issued with condoms but I never used mine. We blew them up. I remember saying, in my innocence, "Where have they got all those balloons from?" And my mate said "They're not balloons they're French Letters". ' (7)

Despite the profligate sexuality of so many of the men of 21st Army Group there were thousands like Mercer who retained their innocence throughout the campaign. Many wondered what might be on offer from the women of the towns they liberated but never acted on their instincts, leaving that to other seemingly more worldly wise men. Signaller Stan Procter watched the activities of others in his unit: 'A young orderly, Private Franks from battalion HQ came out of the house in the morning and said he had been with a girl who could not get satisfaction from her boyfriend. She came out later dressed in a loose fitting pink dress. He went off with her again. I suppose this kind of thing must have been going on all the time but not for me.' (8) Looking back some were surprised at how innocent they were, as one commented of a leave spent in Paris: 'I wish I'd have known then what I know now!' (9)

Unlike these innocent soldiers many others soon found use for their condoms. It was not without reason that they had been issued. Plenty of men, of all ranks, made the most of any sexual opportunity. They were leaving behind the social constraints of home, abandoning the morality of Britain and preparing themselves for the personal freedoms war offered. They may have been subject to orders, facing death and incredible hardship, but in the wake of the fighting was to come a level of freedom few had experienced before or would know again. Anyone who chose to forget about the moral codes of civilian life was free to do so. Their personal behaviour wasn't influenced by the worries of wives, girlfriends or families. There were no gossiping neighbours reporting liaisons back to their parents. The sexually profligate and the abstemious served side by side yet in an exclusively male environment few would judge the behaviour of their fellow men.

Of course, not all of the men were just looking for sex, many were searching for true love. There was nothing like the day-to-day threat of death to instil a sense of urgent romanticism in soldiers. Serious relationships and marriages soon flourished. Even on D-Day some men struck up relationships with French women that were to blossom into serious relationships and culminate in long, happy marriages. A local girl who tended wounded soldiers on the invasion beaches soon found herself courted by and wed to an English soldier. When a Canadian officer reached the town of Le Touquet he was met by a young lady waving to him at a road junction on the edge of the town. The first of the liberators was soon to court the first of the liberated, culminating in their marriage in early 1945. Such was the enthusiasm amongst civilians for contact with British troops that many marriages were rapidly planned and executed. In the heady days following the liberation of Brussels relationships flowered and impromptu decisions were taken that this was the town to which they would like to return to live after the war. Many were to do just that, some waiting until demob, others just disappearing from their units and returning to the arms of their beloved.

In their sexual encounters with the women of the liberated countries, men of 21st Army Group soon realised there seemed to be significant differences between the women they had left at home and those they met on the Continent. Their enthusiasm, expertise and openness at first shocked, and then delighted the soldiers. Even some of the more sexually experienced were pleasantly surprised by the behaviour of the women they encountered. While for the sexually inexperienced soldiers, the women of Europe were a godsend. Some were shocked by the range of activities on offer in the bedrooms of their conquests. These were not the passionless encounters conducted hastily between the sheets of the marital bed, nor the furtive fumbling of teenagers in the darkened alleys of their hometowns. Instead the British and Canadian soldiers were taken into homes to fulfil the physical needs of women grown frustrated by the absence of their own men. These women, whose husbands had been the victims of war, were POWs or away working in the factories of the Reich, still had sexual longings. And then there were the younger women, who had reached their sexual maturity in war-ravaged lands and were seldom able to find lovers amongst their own men. All were eager to show gratitude to their liberators. Many young soldiers who were at their sexual peak, enjoyed the struggle to cope with the voracious appetites of the liberated population.

The liberal sexual displays of cities like Paris and Brussels opened their eyes to a whole world of previously unattainable opportunity. The soldiers who stepped out from hotels whilst on leave were immediately exposed to sex as a commodity. Prostitutes solicited openly on the streets and in every bar or café. Seedy looking men hustled them for entry into sex shows or attempted to sell them pornographic postcards. They learnt of sexual activities seldom mentioned back home. In their early encounters with the Continental women many of the soldiers were shocked by the willingness to perform, and the expectation of receiving, oral sex. The 'soixante neuf' or '69' became a thing of legend. And yet the irony was how few would be able to show off their newly-learnt tricks to their seemingly repressed girlfriends and wives when they returned home. How could they dare to claim 'my Belgian girlfriend liked it so why don't you?'

In the exhilarating days of the 'Swan' from the Seine to Brussels by General Horrocks' 30 Corps there were hundreds lucky enough to find brief satisfaction with the women whose homes lined the route of the advance. In some cases, even as the columns continued to roll forward, women were pulled onboard trucks and carriers to copulate with eager soldiers. As they entered each village, they were garlanded with flowers, showered with gifts and plastered with kisses. Once their vehicles stopped, the eager men soon got chatting to likely conquests. It was a tremendous boost to the morale of the soldiers just to see women, let alone meet with them. Even the flirting of the young women took the minds of the soldiers back to happier times and the romances of their youth. However, for many it went further than innocent flirtation. Young or middle-aged, attractive, plain or ugly - all seemed ready to claim a piece of their liberators. Inevitably, when the order came to move on the successful men would come tumbling out of civilian homes with women waving and blowing kisses as they departed. To the catcalls and jeering of their mates they ran to their vehicles frantically pulling on boots and buttoning trousers. With time, many of the soldiers realised their most eager sexual partners were the self-same women who had previously entertained the German occupation forces and were now hoping to redress the balance by granting favours to them. Not that the soldiers cared, all that mattered to them was the brief relief from the realities of war.

When the advance finally peaked with the liberation of Brussels, there were scenes that were forever to be imprinted on the memories of the soldiers. For days it seemed that officers had no idea what had happened to their men. They had simply disappeared into the homes of the local population. The whole city had erupted in joy with their arrival. In later years General Horrocks joked about how the memory of those days still had the power to make the veterans blush. When the tank crews of the 3rd RTR arrived in Antwerp they found billets in an upmarket brothel, with all fees being waived for the three days of their stay.

Every unit seemed to have one man who was constantly successful with the ladies. It was seldom the best looking man, instead someone who just seemed to be good at talking women into bed. They were constantly on the look-out for new opportunities and were often spotted sneaking away from their positions to take shelter in the arms of local civilians. A mechanic in the 1st Northants Yeomanry, known to his friends as 'Ram' because of his legendary success with the opposite sex, explained his tactics to his comrades: 'If you go into a dance hall and you see a lot of girls, go for the ugliest one. Why? Because they always come across, because they are desperate. And the safest 'cause no one else has had them.' (10) When the 90th Field Regiment RA's resident Lothario visited Brussels he was to have the greatest success of his career by meeting, courting and marrying a Belgian countess all in the course of a 48-hour leave. The 4th Battalion Somerset Light Infantry's own 'Romeo' attended a pre-wedding party in a French village and ended up spending the night with the bride-to-be.

However not all encounters were of the girls' choosing. In August 1944, during the breakout from Normandy, the men of D Company, Ox and Bucks Light Infantry stopped in a small French village. The schoolmaster wanted to thank the men for liberating the village. Having nothing of value to offer the British he brought forward his daughter whom he offered to Major Howard, the company commander. Howard refused. However some of his men were less concerned with the Frenchman's feelings and accepted his daughter for their pleasure. This was not an isolated case. A similar offer was made by a French farmer to a Canadian artillery troop. They were to pick a pair of gunners who were to sleep with his two daughters. The Canadians were happy to oblige and a lottery was organised by their NCOs to select the fortunate individuals. The only stipulation being that they be ready to move first thing the next morning. The two soldiers were pampered by their mates, given baths and fresh clothing, and made ready for their night of passion. Fearful of an error in the translation of the farmer's offer, the selected men made their way to the farm where they were wined, dined and eventually escorted up the stairs to the rooms of the girls. Similar stories came from Holland, where it was reported that one Dutch woman showed her gratitude to the liberators by having sex with every man in a platoon.

Not all soldiers waited to leave the front line before finding sexual partners. The prospect of imminent death was a spur to soldiers and every opportunity was taken to indulge, even in forward positions. At night some men sneaked away to abandoned German positions where they met up with young ladies for an evening's entertainment. Soldiers sat kissing and cuddling with local girls in the tangled undergrowth of Norman hedgerows whilst their mates sheltered in slit trenches just yards away. Even in the midst of battle men indulged themselves. One infantryman was spotted having sex with a woman in a barn. They laughed as they continued their lovemaking, oblivious to the sound of shellbursts, living for the moment. During the height of the fighting around Oosterbeek, during Operation Market Garden, a paratrooper was found having sex with a Dutch nursing auxiliary. The couple thought that the incoming mortar fire would distract other people and had not expected to be disturbed. The soldier was disciplined and the nurse dismissed from the hospital. Pioneers and Royal Engineers in Holland repairing roads took breaks from their work, stopped passing Dutch girls and for a bar of chocolate took the girls over a hedge for sex, whilst their mates continued working yards away. In one case that entertained his superiors and became something of a legend amongst his mates, one member of a tank crew contracted gonorrhoea after having sex with a woman in the heat of battle. Whilst under fire the trooper got out of his tank to go to the toilet. Instead he met up with a woman and had a 'quickie' beside the tank. His officers thought the circumstances sufficiently humorous for the soldier to be awarded a medal and sent a recommendation up to the Brigade HQ. They passed it on to the divisional commander who also thought the story funny enough to deserve a reward. It was only when the recommendation reached 21st Army Group HQ that the circumstances were questioned and the award quashed.

As autumn turned to winter and the once rapid advance of the conquering armies slowed to a halt, soldiers found an ideal opportunity to explore liaisons with the people of the liberated lands. With the front lines stagnating even the forward troops found themselves within easy distance of civilians eager to be wooed. Throughout the spiralling 'Line of Communications' thousands of soldiers settled into civilian billets, 'got their feet under the table' and settled down for winter. Suddenly relationships blossomed as the men went about their daily lives with the local women. During early morning raids on railway stations, intended to capture deserters, MPs increasingly discovered soldiers who were waiting for the first train to get back to their units. By day they went about their duty as normal but at night they returned to the homes of their girlfriends in much the same way they would have done in civilian life.

However, with the flourishing romances came a moral dilemma, just how serious were the soldiers about the relationships they formed? Of course, many pledged undying love and eventually returned to marry their girlfriends. Some even settled in the towns they had liberated. However many more simply passed out of their girlfriends' lives never to return.

One infantry NCO observed the behaviour of the soldiers who had fallen in love with local women. After showing obvious signs of being smitten and unable to cope with enforced separation they resorted to desperate measures: 'Let's be honest about it there were thousands who went to live with women they'd met. I knew at least two dozen people throughout the campaign who met a girl and then that was it. They just disappeared off the face of the earth. We didn't make any fuss about trying to find them. The Regimental Police had a go but they knew as well as we did what had happened.' (11)

Of course not all the soldiers were so faithful. Broken relationships caused heartache for their women and left some with a desire for revenge. Hussar John Reynolds recalled the opportunities that occurred whilst working in the kitchens of an officers' mess alongside French civilians. Out of loyalty to his wife Reynolds turned down the many offers he had from the women he worked with. However not all his comrades displayed the same self-control and a number of French girlfriends proved to be possessive, deliberately trying to break up the marriages of their soldier boyfriends: 'I was a good letter writer. I had to sit and write letters for chaps who had had letters from their wives because the women they'd been knocking off had wrote home to her. Yeah, they connived to get the address and wrote to them.' (12) Padres and NCOs repeatedly came across such problems, however they had little to offer but the suggestion to write home offering apologies.

The sexual marketplace was seemingly confused and certain questions had to be raised. What were the female participants? Girlfriends, mistresses or whores? And did it really matter? Certainly not for the soldiers and increasingly less for the women. Widows, housewives, students, mothers and schoolgirls all played a role in bringing comfort to the men.

Lines between physical relationships generated by affection and those embarked upon purely for profit were blurred. To many of the soldiers there was little difference. They could get sex wherever and whenever possible, whether it was free or they paid. Northants Yeoman Ken Squires didn't consider the women he met to be whores: 'It wasn't exactly prostitution was it? You picked a girl up, she wanted a bar of chocolate. Bang. Job done. And many of the guys married the girls that they first picked up like that.' Squires met one particular girl each night in the Dutch town of Zwolle, who didn't always expect payment: 'There was a certain girl I always met under the bridge by the river. And for some strange reason it was always sex. Sometimes I never had anything in my pocket but it was still sex.' (13)

For the women it could be an experience fraught with moral dilemmas. Initially most of the women gave themselves willingly. In the heady, post-liberation atmosphere there was seldom a question of deep emotional attachment, nor a desire to profit from relationships. Quite simply, they fancied their liberators or were caught up in the euphoria of the time. With time, if the soldiers stayed for long enough relationships developed, some with lasting emotional ties. But more often than not the soldiers simply moved on to fight their next battle and conquer more hearts elsewhere. As the first waves of troops moved on and the support troops arrived it became easy for the women to develop new relationships. There was a gradual realisation that the soldiers could offer much to their girlfriends. They were generous with their sexual partners, showering them with gifts, not necessarily intended as payment for services, but as tokens of genuine gratitude for the affection shown. Gifts could be simple, such as cap badges or mementos from Britain and Canada, but more often than not they were more practical. The women received cigarettes, food, chocolate, coffee and clothing. Some of the sex on offer was unbelievably cheap. One gunner reported how it was possible to get sex in Belgium in exchange for a bar of soap and still get change.

These gifts were a passport to a better standard of living. Commodities that could be traded and meant the difference between sinking into or rising above the mire of poverty engulfing the liberated territories. The realities arising from sex with soldiers led to an understanding of the benefits this could bring. Once a boyfriend's unit had moved on it wasn't easy for the women to return to a life of poverty. With hungry mouths to feed, sex became a simple question of economics – to eat or to go hungry. It was a temptation thousands were unable to resist.

With this came the blurring of the lines between prostitution and normal sociable behaviour. In societies where money had little true value and commodities were the currency of the day was sleeping with a man for gifts any different to walking the streets or working in a brothel? Without doubt the economic situation prevalent in Europe led to an explosion in prostitution. More and more women took up what was one of the few available employment opportunities. Parents accepted the behaviour of daughters and husbands turned a blind eye to men brought home by their wives. Young boys, sometimes less than ten years old, approached the soldiers offering their older sisters in return for cigarettes. Brothels flourished, just as they had back in Britain. Some were sumptuous establishments like 72 Rue Royale in Brussels, favoured by Guards officers, or the Vicomtesse de Brissac's home in Paris. Others establishments were less impressive, with farms, bars, cafés, restaurants and private homes all offering willing women to the soldiers.

There was somebody for every taste. Women from all four corners of the globe, plump farm girls, elegant models and actresses, the sophisticated daughters of Europe's wealthier families, dowdy housewives and lost and lonely refugees. Educated or illiterate, ugly or beautiful, expensive or so cheap it seemed hardly worth paying. All the flotsam and jetsam displaced by the tide of war were on hand to provide relief for the soldiers.

A wide gulf existed between the accepted ways of the British army and those of the Germans with regard to prostitution. During the years of occupation the Germans had allowed their men to visit brothels. Such visits were the norm rather than the exception. When Brussels was first liberated its prostitutes were found to have a low level of venereal disease that was attributed to the efficiency of the Wehrmacht's medical services, in that they made bi-weekly inspections of the working girls. Field Marshal Montgomery preferred this openness towards prostitution rather than the strict rulings of the British army. Monty had attempted to provide such supervised facilities for his men whilst serving overseas during the interwar years. He felt that since it was inevitable soldiers would seek out sex it was best they could do so in a controlled environment. Army doctors visited approved establishments and the women were inspected for disease. The system appeared to be a success, preventing disease and eliminating the need to take disciplinary action against men arrested in brothels. However, these ideas were too modern for the traditionalists of the military establishment. The moral codes of the time prevented open discussion of such behaviour and as a result the experiment was doomed to failure. Montgomery attempted to raise the question once again in 1940 whilst serving in France with the British Expeditionary Force, however it was clear the War Office would never allow the military to act as brothel keepers. By 1944, when he returned to France at the head of 21st Army Group, he realised that public opinion and the officers who inhabited the corridors of Whitehall would never tolerate British soldiers being openly allowed access to prostitution. The subject was dropped. For the next eleven months of campaigning the British and Canadian soldiers were denied access to clean, medically inspected females and told that officially, according to Standing Order Section XII paragraph 15, all brothels were out of bounds. However the desire for sex conquered orders and thousands of men took their chances.

Some didn't wait to get to rest areas before they visited brothels, instead they visited prostitutes who plied their trade close to the front lines. Fresh from the front lines the troops would stand in line waiting for their few minutes of pleasure with the girl of their choice. When they were finally ushered into the bedroom the first contact with the working girl would often dampen the soldier's ardour – before he would be allowed to have sex the prostitute would insist on removing his trousers and washing his genitalia. It was a shock to the soldiers but a wise move for the girls. While the intention was to prevent the spread of disease it was also recommended since many of the soldiers had been unwashed for so long and emitted unpleasant odours. Harry Free, serving with the 43rd Reconnaissance Regiment, paid a visit to one of these newly established brothels. He wrote: 'When we were in France, during combat, we pulled back one night and heard about two girls who were on the game. I went with a mate to this house where they were and joined a queue! Our troop captain, Jackson, found out and had us up before the troop as an example of how not to behave!' (14) With so many willing customers sex was a lucrative trade, so much so that many French women set up impromptu brothels in their homes. These were not the painted prostitutes so often seen in the towns and cities but amateurs – ordinary farmer's wives eager to make some money on the side. In these simple homes, with their flowered wallpaper and basic furniture, soldiers of all descriptions queued up for brief liaisons with the Norman farmgirls. A Northants Yeoman regaled his comrades with details of his visit to such an establishment: 'I heard this Frenchwoman was … inviting people in. The old mother was at the door in a filthy black dress collecting the subscriptions …. There were all these blokes … on the stairs – infantry, artillery, ordnance, even bloody pioneers …. I went up to see what was happening. There was just this farm wife on her own, with a bloke.' He added: 'The place stank like a midden in the middle of a sewage farm … I've seen better talent out in my old cow byre.' (15)

Despite the reputation of France as the world's capital of romance there was little evidence of this on display for the men of 21st Army Group as they made their way across the north of the country. This was not the France of legendary repute. This was not the Côte D'Azur, it was not even Paris. Instead of shimmering seas and bright, sunlit skies this was a land of mining towns, small farming villages and drab industrial towns. When it came to romance and particularly, sex, the French had a rival in their small, unglamorous neighbour – Belgium. With its ever increasing population of Allied military personnel, Belgium, especially its capital Brussels, became a sexual mecca. This was where the British and Canadian soldiers spent their leave and much of their spare time entertaining themselves with the local working girls. It was also the source of an ever increasing incidence of sexually transmitted diseases. By late 1944 syphilis, traditionally known as the 'French disease' had become the Belgian burden. Whilst official reports early in the campaign had described the disease as 'rampant' (16) in France, only when 21st Army Group had crossed into Belgium did they feel the full impact of the results of unprotected sex. Medical reports confirmed the situation, highlighting how the earlier low levels of VD: 'proved without doubt that the reason for the low incidence up to now was the lack of opportunity. Once the troops entered Belgium there was a marked rise in the number of cases.' (17)

This sudden rise in sexual activity and the accompanying rise in sexually transmitted disease had their roots in one simple factor – leave. With the once rapid advances slowing down and a number of large towns and cities under Allied control the authorities saw fit to institute leave for its battle-weary soldiers. Soon Brussels, Paris, Antwerp, Eindhoven and numerous smaller towns were full of men on 48-hour passes. They arrived onboard trucks they laughingly nicknamed 'Passion Wagons' and made their way to bars and cafés in search of sex.

Although all brothels were officially out of bounds it seemed to have little effect on the soldiers' behaviour. Men openly formed queues outside brothels waiting their turn to spend a few hasty minutes with the girls. This was no time to be coy about sex, there was no reason to hide the fact they were desperate to 'get their leg over'. Nearly everyone was in the same boat, most had gone for months without sex and libidos were raging. As one soldier recalled: 'we were only young and for some the anticipation was more than they could manage!' (18)

The more exotic establishments traded under names like 'Le Sphinx' whilst others were little more than cafés where enterprising owners allowed amateur prostitutes to ply their trade. Glamorous women approached soldiers offering themselves for the night at a price of a thousand francs, approaching the men in turn until they elicited a positive response. Outside the bars prostitutes walked the streets offering favours to the willing 'Tommies' whilst sex shows were touted by seedy characters skulking in darkened doorways. It was a great lure for the soldiers as one remembered:

> I visited Brussels twice, once during combat, once after. The first time I spent drinking and going to nightclubs where you picked up girls – the girls, they were prostitutes really, actually flaunted themselves in clubs and brothels. Brothels were legal and prostitutes weren't cheap. Soldiers visited brothels as a matter of course – we were only young! Some used protection others didn't. I did, as I had seen films of what it was like if you caught VD in the army – you got your pay deducted. I would say I was a jack-the-lad – always first in the queue. The second time I visited Brussels was after the war had finished. I was with my wife and we spent the time sightseeing – a much more sober affair. (19)

Every night, all over the city, red lights seemed to flicker on. If not in the established brothels then in the new ones that seemed to spring up wherever the soldiers gathered, some to indulge themselves with the prostitutes, others just to watch the comings and goings of the girls as they went about their business. There was little pressure on the men. Whether they bought beer or bodies they were spending their money. Alexander Baron frequented one such establishment on the Belgian coast. He wrote:

> We sat at small round tables in a room like a barn, its high walls were bare except for dirty, flaking yellow paint. The floorboards were bare and strewn with litter. A staircase open to the room ran up a side wall to a landing. A mass of men crowded on this staircase, making a lot of noise on the wooden treads. On the landing doors were banging open and shut all the time. Once in a while a girl came downstairs for a rest. The girls all looked like farm wenches with huge shoulders and fat, mottled red arms. Sometimes we offered one of them a drink. Wearing only, as far as we could see, a short dress and a pair of slippers, she would sit down heavily as if she had been doing a hard morning at the washtub. Not bothered by us with conversation she would sip her beer for a few minutes, then sigh, thank us, and go back upstairs. (20)

It seemed the whole of Belgian society openly accepted the behaviour of the soldiers and was complicit in their sexual antics. It became an accepted part of everyday life and few tried to hide the reality of the situation. A British gunner was shocked when he gave sweets to two small Belgian girls and they replied: 'We jig jig for English soldiers in the next war!' (21)

Some went to extraordinary lengths to find sex; whilst at a isolated transit camp in Belgium soldiers of the 43rd Reconnaissance Regiment found out the location of a brothel and decided to pay a visit. The problem was that, with no transport available, it involved a fourteen-mile walk. Eventually only one man decided to make the long night walk to the house where: 'all the delights of man were obtainable'. (22) The journey became an odyssey, a night of wrong turnings, stumbling into minefields, avoiding MPs, and hitching a lift in an ambulance. Eventually he arrived just in time to see the brothel raided by MPs and the girls and their Canadian partners carted off to the Provost guard post. The night ended with a disappointed soldier facing a long walk home, all without having achieved his aim.

Increasingly soldiers became involved in the operation of these brothels. They could help find clients from among the resident military population, provide security and procure the food and drink to sell to the clients. At Louvain in Belgium a British sergeant major ran a brothel next door to a barracks where he worked. The NCO's girlfriend worked for him and the inhabitants of the barracks were an obliging source of custom and income. Others accepted offers from individual prostitutes to desert, move in with them and act as their pimps. For the women it was ideal, who better to help them solicit for clients than men who spoke English and could approach the men on leave on an equal level. These deserters were the men who became the centre of the crimewave that engulfed north west Europe in 1944-45. When MPs raided the homes of prostitutes they often found deserters in hiding with vast hordes of stolen military supplies. With the failure of the military authorities to accept prostitution and allow it to operate in a controlled environment the criminal underworld had taken control and exploited the situation to the detriment of the army.

Not only prostitutes offered sexual entertainment to soldiers. There were also many sex shows in the towns used by troops on leave. In Louvain there was a renowned performer whose act was called 'Penny On A Drum', based on a UK radio show of the same name in which a band played when pennies were thrown onto a drum. In the Belgian version a generously proportioned lady would squat over the drum and pick up coins using her vagina to the delight of the onlooking Tommies. On one occasion a tin of corned beef was thrown onto her drum, without a pause she continued her act and the tin was picked up, to the astonishment of the audience. Other dubious pleasures included a fat woman with varicose veins who danced naked around the tables every time a man bought a drink. There were also 'clip joints' where girls worked the bars, chatting to the soldiers, keeping them talking and spending their money on the hope of a bed for the night. For every drink they purchased the girls received chits, cashing them in for wages at the end of the night. All the soldiers ended up with were empty pockets. As well as raiding brothels MPs attempted to prevent soldiers from attending sex shows. The clubs weren't just closed down when raided but military personnel were brought up on charges for having watched the shows. The activities of one officer were described in the antiquated legal language of a charge sheet: 'In a café entered a room together with other ranks for the purpose of viewing a lewd exhibition, and remained there in the presence of said other ranks whilst such an exhibition was given by two females.' (23)

In this sexually charged atmosphere it was little wonder that many of the soldiers approached physical encounters with a haste that would prove to be unhealthy. Despite the films the soldiers had been shown warning of the dangers of unprotected sex many failed to heed them. Those men who failed to use condoms were running a serious risk of contracting any number of infections. Syphilis, gonorrhoea, crabs, scabies – all could be picked up from the prostitutes, and all could render the men unfit for further service until the infections had been cleared up.

By September 1944 it was noted by the military authorities that rates of venereal disease were on the increase, and that they had already risen to 'unsatisfactory levels'. (24) Montgomery was alarmed by the increase, in October he wrote to all commanding officers on the need to control infection. He pointed out that the rate of new infections in the first week of the month would, over the course of a year, be equal to the strength of an entire division. He requested that men be directly addressed by their officers on the dangers of infection. The Field Marshal needed his soldiers at their posts, not languishing in hospitals being pumped full of penicillin. To counter the epidemic of sexually transmitted diseases a number of measures were taken. A booklet entitled 'What You Should Know about Venereal Disease' was issued to troops, MPs were ordered to approach soldiers seen in the 'doubtful company' (25) of undesirable prostitutes and to warn them of the possible consequences of their actions. There is little evidence to suggest such action had any effect on the men's behaviour and with little distinction between prostitutes and girlfriends some of the soldiers were very trusting of their partners. In the autumn of 1944, after the liberation of Brussels, the standard excuse given to medical officers was 'Oh, but it can't be VD Doctor – she's clean – she told me so!' (26)

To help prevent the spread of disease the soldiers were given regular check ups known as FFIs – Free From Infection. It was hoped that by finding men in the early stages of sexually transmitted diseases the spread of the infections could be curtailed. The soldiers were paraded in line with their trousers unbuttoned as the medical officer walked along the lines of men. Each man then dropped his trousers, his hands and fingers were inspected for signs of scabies or impetigo, then his genitalia was inspected for signs of sexual disease – doctors sometimes using sticks to lift the penis to check for sores underneath.

There were also attempts to prevent men contracting disease. The army introduced rules to regulate the sexual behaviour of soldiers as one sexually active soldier recalled: 'We were very well warned about sex. Nearly every unit had an Early Treatment room. And in there you went if you'd had unprotected sex and they used the tubes and what have you.' (27) Any man intending to have sex was supposed to sign for condoms prior to departing on leave and afterwards had to visit a 'Green Cross Station' where their penises were washed with antiseptic fluid and then wrapped in a bag for several hours. Of course few men bothered with such rigmarole, even with the classification of VD as a self-inflicted wound that carried a sentence of thirty days in a military prison. Doctors reported how the soldiers were happy to collect their condoms when heading out on the town but the numbers returning for post-coital washes were negligible. Those unfortunate enough to pick up an infection were given medical treatment for their condition, which was seldom carried out in a sympathetic fashion. For forty-eight hours they were pumped full of penicillin and then a fearsome catheter was inserted into the urethra to clear up infection.

The rate of infection, that had run at 0.42 cases per thousand men in the summer of 1944, rose sharply to 1.2 cases per thousand by April 1945. The steepest rise coincided with the start of three-day leaves to Brussels in October 1944. A study of new infections showed out of 226 cases 126 had originated in the Belgian capital. There was a dip in the level of new infections in December 1944 thought to have resulted from the announcement of the start of home leave. The logic was that men were prepared to wait until they got home before having sex and were afraid of picking up infections they could pass on to their wives.

However it didn't last long and in February 1945 it was reported infection had doubled in the space of a month. 2nd Army officials later admitted that condoms, preventative medicine, genital inspections, talks by officers and warning booklets proved to be insufficient to curtail the spread of sexual diseases. Except in the larger towns men were failing to use the 'Green Cross Stations' in sufficient numbers to prevent infection. What the army needed was more robust measures. Methods of treatment changed. Initially fresh cases of VD were treated whilst men remained with their unit with only relapsing or resistant cases and those suffering penile sores were referred to Venereal Disease Treatment Centres (VDTCs) at Corps level. Under the new system Field Medical Units were detailed to admit men with gonorrhoea and to treat them with penicillin whilst the recurrent cases and the men with sores were still sent to the VDTCs.

The use of penicillin had revolutionised treatment of syphilis. The new 'wonder drug' seemed a panacea, able to clear up all manner of infection. Previously, infected soldiers had made weekly visits for arsenic injections to attempt to control infection. Now the doctors at the VDTCs found the courses of treatment they administered were greatly reduced. After nine days of treatment soldiers were returned to their units and only needed to be readmitted for check-ups after two, four, six, nine, twelve and twenty-four months. These savings in man hours were vital to the hard pressed generals, freeing up the maximum number of men for front line service. Such was the success of the VDTCs that by the spring of 1945 medical authorities were stressing the need to open the centres at Divisional level rather than just one per Corps.

The medical authorities made attempts to trace the source of infections. Initially this was supposed to be the responsibility of Civil Affairs officers. However with the rapid spread of disease it was decided to bring in the Provost Corps to carry out the work. From December 1944 soldiers infected with venereal disease were given questionnaires to fill in detailing the women from whom they thought the infection had been contracted. MPs asked the soldiers for her name, address, her 'beat', bar, café or brothel. Of course few soldiers could supply a name for the girl and her 'location' could be as vague as 'near the railway station'. Therefore the questionnaire also requested they supply a description of her age, hair colour, height and any distinguishing marks. By locating the girls through these leads efforts could be made to put certain bars and cafés out of bounds to troops. To facilitate this, in early 1945 a new rule was introduced. If three infections were traced back to one source then that establishment was put out of bounds for a period of three months. However these prohibitions made little difference to trade. There was little hope that just by closing a bar they could halt the spread of disease. If the girls had no customers they would just move on and ply their trade elsewhere.

MPs also checked the ages of prostitutes, ensuring that no girls under twenty-one worked the clubs or streets. In Helmond in the Netherlands MPs enforced a curfew on all women under twenty-one, ensuring that they were home by sunset to prevent any liaisons with soldiers. They also cooperated with local police in keeping watch on the homes of women known to be infected with VD to prevent soldiers from visiting them. The army's medical authorities made efforts to work with Belgian doctors to help prevent the spread of disease. The girls traced as a result of the questionnaires were advised to receive medical treatment from their doctors. Initially some doctors were reluctant to cooperate, either refusing to pass on details or giving them certificates stating they were free from infection without first checking. Doctors had to be convinced to forego patient confidentiality so infected working girls could be given suitable treatment. In January 1945 the Belgian government intervened and published a decree on the subject. In the future there was to be a compulsory registration of all VD sufferers who were legally required to undergo a course of treatment. Additionally Provost sections liased with the city's medical authorities in an attempt to crack down on the spread of infection by arresting those women they suspected of passing on disease. January 1945 saw the apprehension of ninety-one working girls, sixty-nine of whom were infected with gonorrhoea, seven with syphilis and fifteen who were clear of any infection. It was a Herculean task. With so many girls working in such a wide range of establishments thorough checks were impossible.

However, venereal disease wasn't the only problem for those men involved in regular sexual activity. Because of the amount of sex on offer soldiers had to take care with their performance. A trooper of the 1st Northamptonshire Yeomanry visited his medical officer with an unusual complaint. One of his comrades recalled: 'I remember one poor bugger. He'd gone somewhere and he'd had something a bit different, and he'd gone to the E.T. room. But about three weeks later he produced a little bit of pus out of the end of his penis. So he thought "Christ, I'm in trouble". So he went up to the guy in the E.T. room and said about it, and the bloke sent him to the doctor. And apparently it was strain, not gonorrhoea. Because he had performed so well he had strained something.' (28)

Sexually transmitted lice were perhaps the most common complaint. Lice made their way easily between sexual partners. Although easily cured they were still a source of great discomfort. Northants Yeoman Ken Squires recalled: 'I came back through a transit camp after being on leave and after a day or two I was itching like buggery, especially around the scrotum. I thought "Christ Almighty". So straight over to see the medic. And he said "You've got a beautiful dose of crabs there". I said "What do you mean?" and he does something and says "There you are". And there was this little thing with its pincers out.' Although the treatment was relatively simple it had the effect of curtailing the soldier's activities for some weeks: 'He said "We'll shave it all off and I'll give you some blue unction and you'll be alright". I walked around with a purple penis for a long time. I didn't dare show any of the girls. They'd say "No good to me, I don't want your crabs". (29)

Scabies was also passed between sexual partners. A soldier, who picked up the infection in Normandy, explained the treatment: 'The treatment was to be coated with Benzyl Benzoate, applied by an orderly with a shaving brush. The stuff resembled paper hanger's paste. Quite painless except to a certain portion of one's anatomy when it stung like blazes.' (30)

Despite the bravado with which many soldiers approached sexual relationships and the willingness of so many of the women there was a downside to their behaviour. They left behind a legacy of fatherless children. Late 1945 saw the births of around seven thousand illegitimate children in the Netherlands, most of them believed to be as a result of liaisons between British or Canadian soldiers and local women. After the troops left, many of the women eager to avoid shame to their families were forced to give up their babies for adoption. Some of the fathers had stayed briefly, passed on to fight elsewhere and lost their lives on the battlefields. Others soon forgot their girlfriends as duty took them away to continue the fight and eventually returned home to be demobbed into the arms of their waiting wives. To this day many of these illegitimate children are still searching for the fathers they never knew. Some have their father's name and photograph, others details of his unit or mementoes from his civilian life, but for many there is no record and no hope of ever discovering their identity. Calling themselves 'The Children Of The Liberation' they attend veterans' parades across their homeland, searching for clues and hoping to meet men who might remember their fathers. A few are successful and after years of searching are able to locate lost fathers and previously unknown siblings. But for many more the hunt goes on with little hope of ever tracing their true origins.

For all the enthusiasm that greeted the men of 21st Army Group in the lands they had liberated from the Nazis the soldiers had little idea how they might be greeted once they crossed the borders of the Reich. They had expected the passionate reaction from those who had suffered at the hands of the Germans but what could they expect from the women who had so recently been amongst Hitler's most ardent supporters? How would the girls of the 'League of German Maidens', or the housewives who had proudly worn their medals proclaiming how they had bred Aryan children for the 'Fatherland', react to the arrival of an occupying army? How would they react to the sight of the men in battered brown battledress who had vanquished their fathers and husbands? In time the men of 21st Army Group were to be pleasantly surprised.

5

A Little Bit of Frat

'It is too soon for you to distinguish between good and bad Germans; you have a positive part to play in winning the peace by definite code of behaviour. In streets, houses, cafes, cinemas etc, you must keep clear of the Germans, man, woman and child, unless you meet them in the course of duty. You must not walk out with them, or shake hands, or visit their homes, or make them gifts, or take gifts from them. In short, you must not fraternise with Germans at all.' (1)

As the troops approached the German frontier they were faced with signs reminding them of their duty. The signs carried simple messages such as: 'You are now entering enemy territory. Don't fraternise.' (2) The message Monty had given to the men of 21st Army Group was unequivocal – there should be no friendly contact with the people of a defeated Germany. It was made clear to the advancing armies what type of behaviour was deemed unacceptable. As early as September 1944 it had been announced that marriage to German women was forbidden. Now the outlawed activities included 'ogling' women, shaking hands, allowing children into military vehicles or giving food or cigarettes to civilians. And although Monty didn't actually mention it, sex was totally forbidden. Instead, the Germans should be completely ignored unless it was operationally necessary to deal with them, and then contact should be perfunctory.

During the initial engagements on German soil the civilians kept their distance, little wishing to be caught up in the fighting. Even once all the territory to the west of the Rhine was clear there was little opportunity for the two factions to mix since vast swathes of land were cleared of civilians whilst preparations were made for the river crossing. In advance of the crossing clear instructions were given as to how the troops should behave once they had begun their drive into the heart of Germany. Not only was the ban on fraternisation reiterated but also the punishments for disregarding the order. The first offence could bring a seven to fourteen day stoppage of pay and for a second offence pay could be stopped for up to twenty-eight days. A third act of defiance would result in court martial. For officers the rules were even more severe – just one offence could result in a court martial and reduction to the ranks. However, in a country on the brink of disaster it would take more than a few well-placed signposts to control the behaviour of the incoming men.

For all the strict instructions, the troops seemed ready for the task ahead. Like any battle, they viewed the advance into Germany with trepidation and harboured their usual pre-battle fears. But somehow this was different. This was what they had been waiting for, a chance to bring the war home to the very people who had voted for Hitler back in the 1930s. If they relished the thought of finally bringing the battle into the Reich they also approached the border with caution. Now they would be fighting amidst the homes of their enemies rather than their allies. No one could be sure of how German civilians would react – certainly they didn't expect to see flags of celebration waved from the windows of the vanquished enemy or be greeted with food and flowers, as they had in the liberated countries. The soldiers were certain few would be pleased to see them and some would be dangerous, but there was one over-riding question in the minds of the troops – how would the local women react to the conquering army?

Upon crossing the border into Germany there was a widespread feeling of apprehension regarding possible resistance by the politically indoctrinated population among whom could be spies and die-hard Nazis. In the early days no one could be sure if an effective resistance movement would emerge. Everyone had heard of Hitler's planned Werewolf groups, who were supposed to attack Allied units and disrupt communications. However, despite all the Nazi propaganda, they failed to materialise on any significant level. There were isolated instances of sniping at lone soldiers and vehicles but no sign of coordinated, organised sabotage. But initially most soldiers seemed to expect the resistance movement to appear, with this fear contributing to some men offering extreme solutions to the question of civil affairs: 'civilians are expendable. It would be safer to shoot the lot' one Canadian officer suggested. (3) As they approached the German border a Scottish sergeant summed up the attitudes of many soldiers: 'Fraternisation? Blow their bluddy heids off.' (4)

This attitude of outward hostility permeated all levels of the army – as early as September 1944 Monty had written to friends that he would: 'look forward to turning the German families out of their best houses'. (5)

The question of how the local population should be treated was a vexing one. Every unit seemed to contain men with a mixture of emotions and this diversity of opinion caused numerous disagreements amongst the occupying units. Some men wanted to humiliate the enemy civilians, wreck their homes and loot their valuables, whilst others viewed them as the victims of dictatorship and war who should be treated with consideration. For every man who wished for nothing more than a chance to shoot Germans there was another who bore them no ill will. For every officer who wished to enforce rules on non-fraternisation there was another who was keen enough to befriend the local fräuleins. As one recalled: 'It was still possible to admire a nice looking girl, even though she was a German and we were busy killing them and being killed by them.' (6) And there were plenty who wanted to do more than just admire the local girls. As the troops made their way across Germany one thing was certain – if the army was to function, the authorities would have to turn a blind eye to the activities of those individuals who had no intention of complying with Monty's fraternisation order.

However most questions about more enjoyable contact with German civilians would have to wait until the fighting was over. Although few of the British and Canadian soldiers held any feelings of real malice towards the Germans many civilians were killed in accidents or by troops unprepared to take unnecessary risks. Whilst the men of 21st Army Group were never given to the large scale excesses perpetrated by the Red Army, neither did they behave like angels. The soldiers had a job to be done – to finish the war as quickly as possible so they could return home.

The men who had fought all the way across Europe were not taking any chances. Buildings thought to be concealing enemy soldiers were routinely attacked with all available weapons unleashing a hail of fire designed to subdue any opposition. With their greatest fear being the unknown and anything unknown being a danger, anything dangerous could expect to be shot. The reality was that it was almost impossible for soldiers to distinguish between an innocent civilian and a dedicated member of the 'Volksturm', many of whom had no more uniform than an armband.

The behaviour of the troops upset Germans especially when the victims were the very young or very old. When they complained to British soldiers about shooting old men or boys there was little reaction. There was no room for mercy, an old man armed with an anti-tank weapon was just as dangerous as a uniformed soldier. It was not that the soldiers didn't feel for the civilians they killed but that there was no time to dwell on death – when every day saw the death of a friend who could openly grieve for another dead enemy?

To prepare for the appearance of unwanted civilians some infantrymen were taught a simple phrase: 'Im hausen bleiben wir schiessen' which translated as 'Get into your house or you will be shot'. There was little doubt that they were serious. The soldiers of the 1/5th Queen's Regiment were instructed that: 'Civilians obstructing you will be shot if necessary in order to make them obey your orders' and that they were to: 'Show Civs that we come as conquerors and mean business.' (7)

There was little doubt that most infantry and tank formations adhered to such orders. As one Queen's NCO put it: 'If they are in the way, God help them.' (8) The well trained, battle hardened soldiers were often unable to stop firing in time to spare civilians – if they saw movement in a house there was no time for contemplation and any sign of life was greeted by a hail of fire. Such were their instantaneous reactions that waving white flags by anyone, soldier or civilian, was no guarantee of safety. Instead the soldiers blazed away with their weapons at any potential opposition. Consequently, many civilians remained hidden in their cellars whilst the houses were assaulted and cleared by the British soldiers. The men assaulting houses did their best to take care, most avoided throwing grenades into cellars if they thought them to be occupied by civilians. Some infantrymen, however, didn't trouble themselves to look, instead throwing grenades down cellar steps and continuing with their duties, ignoring the possibility they might have killed civilians and praying they had cleared out all the defenders. The situation with regard to civilians was complicated when the German changed tactics and made the infantry's job even more stressful. However, as one NCO recalled they soon adapted to the changing tactics: 'The Germans were bloody quick. They got wise to this and they hid down in the cellars with the civilians. So then we would put a tank through the corner of the house and watch the rest of the building come down on them. Then you could watch them coming up one by one, because the rubble would cover them.' (9) Sergeant Les Toogood was clear about the dangers posed from the occupants of cellars and had his own way to make sure both soldiers and civilians surrendered: 'Nine times out of ten you don't go into the cellar of a house. So our words were "Kommen sie hier. Flame Waffe!" Which the Germans knew meant either come out or we'll put a flame thrower down there.' On one occasion Toogood called down into a cellar only to be greeted by a nurse and a nun who insisted there was no one but wounded in the cellar. He decided to take their word for it and, leaving his rifle behind, went to inspect the cellar. However, he made it clear what the result of any deception on their part would mean: 'I said if anyone shoots me you're all going up in flames!' (10) Toogood was lucky, the Germans were true to their word and no one got hurt.

Many other civilians caught up in battle were less fortunate. When enemy troops used civilian air raid shelters as cover the attacking troops had little time to consider the consequences. They knew the horror that would be inflicted by using flame throwers on a tightly packed shelter. Deep in their hearts they could visualise the charred bodies of women and children, hear the screams, smell the charred flesh, but they had no intention of becoming victims. All that counted was staying alive, and there were few men in 21st Army Group who had any intention of risking death so close to the end of the war. Although there was little that could be said about such incidents, the burden of harming civilians weighed heavy on the minds of many soldiers, especially if they saw the results of their actions. As one infantry NCO recalled: 'In your own mind it caused a bit of bother. But then you come up and look around you and see the thousands of civilians killed by the bombers or the shells. You make excuses for yourself. You can always come up with some excuse – If you do something that may be wrong, you can always say if I hadn't done this to them they might have done something to me.' (11)   For all their concerns they had little time to grieve, as one soldier recalled in his memoirs: 'There was nothing I could say. They only thing was to get on with the job.' (12)

The ruthless behaviour of the advancing soldiers was a logical reaction to the realities of the battlefield. Pockets of resistance could be hidden anywhere, and snipers could remain hidden for hours, picking off their targets from well concealed positions. Thus the easiest solution was to burn down any building thought to be their lair. There was little opportunity to check whether civilians were also in residence. The early months of 1945 were not a time to be politely knocking on doors and asking questions. Instead tanks were brought up and used to demolish houses that stood in the way of the advance. Flame-throwing Crocodile tanks sneaked carefully into position and squirted their deadly jet of ignited fuel into row upon row of German homes. Or Royal Engineers in tanks were called up to launch their dustbin sized charges of high explosive that could flatten even the most sturdily constructed concrete buildings. Who owned the house, or whether it was occupied, was a question the soldiers didn't have the luxury of asking.

Only once the noise of battle had subsided would the local population tentatively make their way up their cellar steps and slowly make their way into the open. They were shocked to see the destruction wrought by the battle that had raged around their homes. Whole streets might be aflame and the roadways blocked with the rubble of collapsed buildings. Telephone lines and power cables were usually down, the contents of shops littered the streets, gas mains burned and water mains spurted. In just a few hours all they had known had been destroyed. In the aftermath of such destruction those Germans whose homes still stood had to face occupation by the conquering army. This was the moment of truth – the moment when the army would find out if the mass of khaki-clad men would heed Monty's orders.

In the immediate aftermath of battle most soldiers had little interest in the local population. Instead they were interested in relaxing and calming down after the stresses of combat. Civilians stood open mouthed as exhausted and filthy soldiers tramped past them, making their way straight upstairs to bed. Without removing any clothing, boots, or even equipment they crashed out *en masse* on the beds of their hosts, sleeping as if dead until raised from their slumbers to continue their duties. For those civilians who elected not to hide in the cellar there was a good chance they would be locked down there whilst the soldiers occupied their home.

In the early days of occupation the most basic forms of fraternisation were seen. Whilst searching houses soldiers would ask the occupants to provide meals from their well-stocked larders. There was seldom need to issue threats, since the presence of heavily armed men was enough to convince 'hausfraus' to don their aprons.

Varying attitudes were displayed regarding the suitable treatment of Germans and their property. There were countless arguments over how best to treat the civilians whose homes were occupied. Some officers made it clear to their men how they were to behave. With regard to billeting the CO of the 7th Battalion Cheshire Regiment instructed his men: 'Civilians may be ejected where it is considered necessary and they must accept the fact that we intend to live "one better" than they all the time.' (13) In February 1945 Major Douglas Goddard of 217 Battery R.A. recorded the varying emotions within his unit, when he wrote in his diary: 'A great storm arose today over the return to the house at the gun position of the German owners who tried to sort out some clothes from the shambles we swept from the house. Two schools. Heartless – kick them out, destroy their homes. Chivalrous – let them salvage their clothes, help them.' (14)

Major Goddard later explained his own position with regard to the treatment of the Germans:

My diary entry summarises the divergences of attitudes well. The British troops were probably less inclined to savagery and destructive reprisals than most armies, but there were many excesses. 21st Army Group rules against looting/raping were strict but the directive did not always penetrate to us in the front line. I never came across an incidence of rape by a British soldier. But it may well have happened elsewhere. Some took the view that Nazi tyranny, the holocaust, and indiscriminate bombing at home justified them in any destructive action and in looting and desecrating homes and evicting families. Some officers condoned this. Mine, and I believe the majority view, was that as a civilised people these sort of actions were against any normal moral code and particularly in my case Christian teaching. Furthermore it showed indiscipline and mob rule and brought the army into German contempt and disgust. Admittedly many Germans were still arrogant and provocative. There was a middle way which most of us condoned. When one came across an abandoned house or village it seemed reasonable to collect the odd item of value or collectors interest. (15)

In theory the rules for moving into a German home were simple but strict, the Germans were given a short period to take what were called 'personal belongings' and then told to leave. Where they went was not the concern of the incoming troops and what constituted 'personal belongings' was at the whim of the requisitioning officer. Often a cordon would be put round houses to prevent the Germans from taking any items the soldiers thought might be useful for their own comfort. Seldom were they allowed to take more than their clothes and basic bedding, and no more than could be carried by hand. Anything needed or wanted by the soldiers would have to be left behind – bedding, radios, coal, food and cooking utensils. Although the rules stated that civilian furniture should be locked in one room for protection, few actually adhered to it. Once the house was occupied it could be treated as the property of the army and thus its contents would not necessarily be intact when the homeowners finally returned. The civilians could do nothing but stand aside and watch as the soldiers carried away whatever they wanted. Stoves were torn out to be installed in HQs, mattresses taken to line slit trenches, armchairs taken to make comfortable latrines. Such actions were commonplace and the Germans had no one to whom they could complain, as civilians of a defeated nation they could not even claim for expenses for the billeting of soldiers in their homes.

In some cases the troops exhibited a degree of malice unexpected by some of their number. Women were left in tears when soldiers cornered them and forced them to hand over jewellery. Expecting sympathy they showed off their bruised hands, where soldiers had torn rings from their fingers, to anyone who would listen. Some more innocent soldiers were to have a rude awakening when witnessing the behaviour of their comrades. One newly arrived officer looked on in awe as the men of his platoon swarmed around civilians, taking their blankets and watches as they were evicted from their home.

A combination of the continued arrogance shown by civilians and misbehaviour by the occupying forces led to a number of confrontations between the two sides. Regular fights broke out by night in the German town of Bucholz, with rear echelon troops of the 7th Armoured Division confronting locals. News of the incidents reached senior officers in the division and efforts were made to clamp down on offenders. To prevent further clashes additional sections of MPs had to be drafted in to carry out extra patrols.

Whilst there was much discussion over how severely the Germans should be treated and what counted as fraternisation, there was little question over contact that helped to speed the progress of the war. Any contact with Germans that benefited the troops whilst in action was deemed acceptable. During the advance from the Rhine some units forced civilians to clear up the aftermath of battle. They were put to work dragging the corpses of horses and cattle, some of which had actually been slaughtered by farmers to prevent them falling into the hands of the occupying forces. It was essential to clear up the corpses to prevent the spread of disease. At first the soldiers took on the task, fixing ropes to vehicles and dragging the animals away. However, they decided the job should be forced upon civilians who should suffer for the misdeeds of their countrymen. It was entirely pragmatic, why should soldiers do the job when they would soon be moving on? It was logical for the inhabitants to clean up their own villages. In some cases gangs of jeering soldiers crowded round as the villagers used their bare hands to drag dead livestock into piles ready for burning. Whilst such scenes may have appeared distasteful to outsiders the soldiers were merely enjoying their brief period of relaxation prior to their next battle.

Some types of contact with Germans helped save the lives of both civilians and soldiers alike. It became common practice to use the German telephone network to contact the mayor of a town and request it be surrendered rather than face the full destructive force of any assault. Often the burgemeister would be ordered to telephone his opposite number in the next town to warn of what might happen. Instructions were blunt, leaving little doubt in their minds as to the result of continuing resistance. As one officer ordered: 'phone the mayor and tell him he had better surrender his town and so avoid houses being burnt down'. (16) In many cases it was successful, ensuring the advancing troops would be greeted by the welcome sight of white flags, hastily made from bed linen, hanging from every window. At Neumunster the burgemeister met the tank commander who arranged the surrender and presented him with the keys to the town, complete with ceremonial scroll. Some fraternisation even arose from physical necessity. When one NCO found himself with severe toothache he traced the local German dentist. He ensured careful treatment by pointing his pistol at the bewildered dentist throughout the operation.

In the chaos of the final days of war and the first days of peace the issue of relations with civilians was made increasingly complex by the state of virtual anarchy that existed within Germany. The advancing soldiers found farms where the inhabitants seemed to speak no German. They soon realised the non-German occupants were former slave labourers who had taken over farms and consigned their former masters to sleeping quarters in stables and pig pens. The troops had little sympathy, knowing as they did that in these well-stocked farms the animals were often those stolen from the countries who had suffered under the Nazi yoke. The immaculate appearance of the farmyards was also known to be a result of the fact that the farmers often had little to do except keep their farms tidy whilst the foreign labourers did all the hard work. However, as the war drew to a close British soldiers found themselves in the uncomfortable position of having to protect many of these farmers and many other civilians from the attentions of the many thousands of DPs – Displaced Persons – who roamed the countryside.

They came from all over Europe, former concentration camp inmates, slave labourers and foreign workers who had come to Germany for the high wages offered in her factories. Now, for many, revenge was foremost in their mind. In the chaos armed bands roamed Germany terrorising the population, shooting their former masters, taking any food and valuables they coveted, murdering those who resisted, raping any woman they wanted. It became the task of the British and Canadian soldiers to deal with the predominantly Russian and Polish gangs and play the role of protector to the German people. Of course, not all the troops were keen to play protector to civilians and in some areas those on guard duties were specifically told by their officers that their duties did not include protecting Germans from attack by DPs. A few even teamed up with the rampaging gangs after members asked British soldiers to join them in their nocturnal raids. The DPs made a point of stressing how they would treat the vanquished Germans, promising: 'Much shooting, many corpses.' (17)

The situation was further complicated since both the former slaves and their masters came to the British for protection in fear of what the other might do to them. In a paradoxical situation British soldiers found themselves both hunting down armed gangs of former slaves, guided by local Germans, and cooperating with the gangs in hunting down hiding SS men.

Although violent towards the Germans few of the DPs bore any malice towards the British soldiers and little resistance was shown to the troops carrying out these policing operations. However, it remained a dangerous and uncertain time for the soldiers and as late as July 1945 they were still coming under fire from gangs of Poles and a number of men were killed during these peacekeeping operations. After surviving the war they died in peacetime carrying out a task where they were often uncertain of whose side they should really be on.

Despite the official efforts to control the behaviour of the DPs there was a certain amount of sympathy for their actions, some coming from unlikely sources. Such was the sense of revulsion at the wartime behaviour of the Germans, and their enslavement of so many people from all across Europe, that even army padres were beginning to lose any desire to forgive. As one wrote: 'There is a good deal of rape going on, and those who suffer have probably deserved it.' (18) It was a seemingly uncharitable statement but it reflected the mood of the time. The discovery of the concentration camps and the forced labourers slaving in German industry had undermined feelings of sympathy for civilians caught up in the violence. Few had expected the Germans could ever behave in such a depraved manner and it had shattered many illusions about war. Even with the country in ruins, its whole infrastructure in chaos, its people homeless, it was not a time to be sentimental.

Into this chaos walked the officers and men of the Military Government, whose job it was to take control of Germany. In many cases they found the situation confused and quite often dangerous. At first their concerns were with any remaining pockets of German troops who might be lurking in houses and woods. There was no time to police the former slave labourers who roamed the land taking revenge against the people who had enslaved them.

In Hanover the situation had descended into anarchy – stores of food and wine were broken into and ransacked by DPs who killed the policemen who tried to stop their orgy of destruction. Rape and murder was the order of the day. It was the job of the British army's representatives to bring order from chaos. With limited resources, their priority was not to protect Germans but to prevent the ransacking of food stores in order that people could at least be fed. This small unit, made up of former British policemen, augmented by a squad of Dutch policemen and recruits from among the released Allied POWs who were flocking into the city, had to attempt to control the situation. Whilst the civilians continued to suffer the British slowly began to bring the former slaves to heel.

At first Germans complaining of having been attacked and their family members killed were told by the British: 'We only have time for living people here.' (19) They would take action only if they thought lives could be saved. The military authorities had enough problems in protecting British soldiers without worrying about the fate of Germans. The town major brought in Germans with records untainted by Nazism to help restore electricity and water supplies and slowly life began to return to normal. Committees of former slave labourers formed, with representatives of all nations, and it was made clear that it was their responsibility to control their people. To do their job they were given offices and cars. The policy paid off. Slowly but surely the reported levels of rape and murder began to fall. By taking the 'softly, softly' approach the situation had been calmed and normality began to return.

The British soldiers policing German towns had to cooperate with civilian leaders since the assistance of burgomeisters was essential in the restoration of order. The problem was that the British were forbidden to have anything but essential contact with the enemy civilians. So strict were the rules that they were even forbidden to shake hands. The embarrassment of having to refuse a man's hand was avoided by officers making sure their own hands were fully occupied whenever a German attempted such cordial gestures.

Once the initial chaos had subsided civil affairs staff began the process of organised occupation. Whilst curfews were imposed for civilians, cinemas and theatres were taken over for the exclusive use of the troops and civic buildings were taken over to house the incoming military authorities, other activities started that were to sow the seeds of the undermining of the non-fraternisation order. At the start they faced a wall of sullen hostility from many civilians. The Germans had little idea of what the occupiers might do to them. Men of the armoured units reported a particularly suspicious reaction from Germans since they wore black berets and overalls, a colour the Germans associated with the SS. As a result the Germans gave them a wide berth, fearing they might be a brutal British equivalent of the feared German force. Through the office of the burgomeister civilians were detailed to work for the occupying army. Cleaners, kitchen staff, waitresses, secretaries, laundry workers, all were needed to service the British. Although these civilian workers would eventually become essential to the smooth running of the machinery of occupation, it would be some time before most of the soldiers could really trust them and show them any real warmth.

The feeling that the Germans should pay for bringing devastation to Europe would not go away overnight. Although many British soldiers displayed a degree of sympathy for the innocent civilians whose homes were defiled in the pursuit of victory, there were plenty who had no compunction about perpetuating their misery. When efforts were made to salvage furniture from bombed houses it was a task unpopular with those who had themselves been bombed out in the air raids of 1940 and 1941. Though a minority, many such individuals refused to assist in salvage operations since they had no desire to help the Germans whilst their own homes lay in ruins.

With the prevailing mood of the occupying troops the local civilians still needed to remain cautious. It was a risk for German civilians to criticise either British troops or attempt to endear themselves to them. Soldiers had little time for those Germans who constantly emphasised their hatred of the Nazis. When one German farmer claimed he was happy to see the arrival of British troops since Hitler had ordained that all poultry was to be slaughtered the British troops responded with hostility, as one later wrote: 'We rewarded the creep by killing all the hens we could catch, and getting them ready for the pot.' (20)

Committed Nazis were lucky if it was only their livestock they lost. Some still gave Nazi salutes even to the soldiers who were occupying their villages and towns. Such behaviour infuriated the soldiers. The civilians who inhabited towns and villages in the vicinity of labour or concentration camps were often faced with irate troops who wished to extract some measure of revenge. At Celle Scottish troops of the 15th Division ordered four hundred townsfolk to carry the emaciated survivors of a labour camp through the streets of the town and into the local hospital. For all their annoyance at being forced to assist in the clear-up, they were fortunate to have received such lenient treatment. Other civilians were not so lucky. The foreign labourers, who had suffered so much at their hands were happy to cooperate with the occupation forces by pointing out devoted Nazis and led soldiers to hoards of buried arms. Civilians found to be hiding weapons were then taken away and executed – no trial, no defence, just a rifle and a bullet.

However, staying out of trouble was not simple. Even innocent civilians, with no intention of antagonising the occupying forces, could find themselves in difficulty. Prior to the crossing of the Rhine large areas were cleared of civilians to facilitate the build-up of military supplies. MPs were informed that civilians entering the prohibited zones should be shot at without challenge. However, the civilians in question did not necessarily know they were committing an offence since, as the MPs were told: 'For security reasons the boundaries of the prohibited areas will not be publicly disclosed.' (21)

Though acts of deliberate vengeance soon petered out, in the early stages of occupation many soldiers enjoyed reinforcing the sense of defeat and bringing a feeling of shame to a population who were powerless to react. In the aftermath of the fighting many soldiers made deliberate efforts to humiliate the population.

They sat in the streets and loudly played gramophone records of triumphal German military songs such as 'Marching Against England'. Embarrassed civilians crossed the roads to avoid having to see the conquering army revelling in their defeat. Others were left to walk in the gutter after being forced off the pavements by soldiers who deliberately strolled through the streets two or three abreast. Drivers of military transport forced civilian vehicles from the road, one man even admitted using his tank to knock trams off their tracks.

With little regard for the starvation rations endured by many Germans, especially in the larger towns and cities, in the months following the peace some soldiers were profligate with their own rations. Rather than saving leftovers and giving them to the miserable civilians they deliberately threw away surplus food and watched the desperate people scavenge from the bins. A few even reinforced their misery by waiting until civilians had found the food and ordering them to return it to the bin since it was a theft of military property. Others stood by and watched as the DPs heaped misery upon their former oppressors. Soldiers stood aside as civilians were beaten by the former slave labourers, or as the newly free gangs looted shops and robbed homes.

Despite widespread humiliation of the Germans, most soldiers were embarrassed by the sight of grown men following them through the streets anxiously waiting for their cigarette butts to fall to the ground. Fights even broke out among the desperate Germans in the rush to get the shreds of tobacco left unsmoked by the men in khaki. However, other soldiers deliberately upset the Germans by dropping cigarette ends down drains to the dismay of those expectantly trailing them.

In a demonstration of the servile position of the German civilians orders were given that civilians should doff their caps when passing some British HQs. Soldiers were sent to chase non-compliant Germans who were made to stand bareheaded facing the union flag. When Captain W.S. Brownlie of the 2nd Fife and Forfar Yeomanry found himself unable to get past a German lorry in his car he waited for the chance to chastise the German driver. Eventually he was able to get past, pulled up in front of the lorry and made the driver leave the cab. The unfortunate driver, uncertain of his fate, was then made to bend over as Brownlie gave him 'six of the best' across his bottom with a cane.

Not of all the humiliation heaped upon Germans was carried out by individuals. The military authorities organised activities designed to ensure the populace were fully aware of why they were being treated with contempt. Groups of civilians were bussed to concentration and labour camps to witness the crimes perpetrated in their name. They were made to file past the piles of rotting corpses and see the shuffling, skeletal figures of survivors. Others were forced to disinter the bodies of murdered political prisoners to give them a proper burial. Confronted by the reality of the regime few were left in a mood to show hostility to the occupying forces. People living in areas far from camps were forced into cinemas to watch films of the liberation of Bergen-Belsen. Anyone caught laughing or making light of the images that filled the screen was made to stay behind to watch the films again and again, until the message was absorbed. The occupying troops took pleasure in some of these activities. They were sent into the towns around Belsen to collect provisions for the survivors of the camp. In Celle, each household was ordered to hand over one blanket to ensure sufficient bedding for those who had survived the terror and every adult member of the town's population was ordered to provide one outfit of clothing, including shoes and underwear, to help clothe the desperate and dishevelled camp inmates.

Despite these displays of contempt there was little doubt that the 'frat ban' was doomed. In the aftermath of battle, as the chaos was finally stabilised, and the troops started to have contact with civilians, most British and Canadian soldiers treated the Germans fairly. Whilst few men had any qualms about the destruction they had brought while the fighting continued, few were able to sustain the feeling. Even those who had initially revelled in the sufferings of enemy civilians soon began to soften. One man later admitted: 'At the time this did not worry us as we knew that it was necessary to move the enemy, but later when we saw the terrific damage from bombing in Hamburg and the way people were having to live in the ruins, yes, I felt sorry for them. But there was always the thought at the back of your mind "well they did start it all".' (22) Even with these thoughts the men who saw the fate of the wretched civilians were soon moved to assist them. With so many in need of assistance there was little chance that many soldiers could stand by and let them suffer. Once the soldiers began to assist the Germans there was little chance the 'frat ban' would be a success. Sergeant Les Toogood passed through Hanover: 'The stench was terrific. There wasn't a town left. Those that came out of the holes were people after all. The lads soon fed them.' (23) This was soon to be the pattern – once a town was safely secured the troops were unable to stand aside and watch people suffer.

Alec Simons was one of those soldiers able to show sympathy for the dejected inhabitants of a defeated country. Simons, a Manchester-born Jew, serving with the Royal Army Ordnance Corps, recalled:

> We had the call to guard a coal train. This was considered a very good job because at the side of the wagons was part of a train similar to the Orient Express, where tea was going on all night. And we could sleep our four hours off duty on this train. The instructions we received; 'Don't let anyone steal this coal'. When I asked 'Say they try?' I was told 'Shoot over their heads'. About 1a.m. a woman in black, clearly seen as it was a full moon, crept with two children towards the train. Every two or three metres they stopped. I said 'Halt'. She said 'Don't shoot'. When she came forward I shouted to the other lads, they just pushed loads of coal down from the top of the wagons. Then dozens of people came out of the bushes to collect it. That day I was proud. (24)

The first few weeks of peace were a time of uncertainty for the soldiers of the occupying army. The imposition of a 'frat ban' seemed ludicrous to many of the soldiers as no one could be certain whether their officers or the MPs would attempt to enforce the ban. Fred Sylvester was serving with the 43rd Reconnaissance Regiment at Hermannsberg in Germany: 'On a walk through the woods I, with another soldier, came across a family who were sitting in the sun, and someone was playing an accordion. We two stopped to listen and at that moment a posse from the Regiment came to arrest the male in the German family. Among the posse was Major Milos Knorr – a Czech liaison officer, we thought that we would be reprimanded for fraternising but nothing was said.' (25) Like Sylvester, many soldiers were settling into a routine that ensured they would have some day-to-day contact with Germans. Indeed, it was often difficult for soldiers to know what behaviour counted as 'fraternisation'. Certain moral dilemmas arose – there were even questions raised by Catholic soldiers as to whether they would be in breach of the rules by attending mass. Furthermore, it was uncomfortable for men to deliver their laundry for local women to wash without any show of normal human emotions. Who could resist the smile of a child or a pretty girl? How could they ignore the sad faces and outstretched hands of the children who inevitably crowded around them in search of food? However, whilst the commonly pedalled explanation for the collapse of the 'frat ban' was that the soldiers were immediately drawn to handing out sweets to German children, there were certainly other emotions at play. Most knew it was not sympathy for children that caused breaches of the ban, rather it was contact with their mothers.

Upon arrival in Germany the soldiers had little idea of how they would be greeted by German women. The German women had been fed propaganda to attempt to convince them they would be raped and murdered by the invading armies. Even the 'high ups' at 21st Army Group HQ had expected the levels of rape to be higher than they turned out to be. But few of the soldiers had such violence on their minds. The reason was simple, why would they bother to rape women who could be bought for the price of a packet of cigarettes? They weren't averse to paying for sex, since they knew they could afford it and in the chaos of 1945 cigarettes, coffee and food would open many doors, and many more legs. All across northern Europe they had been fêted as liberators and been fortunate to meet women willing to express their gratitude physically. But this was no indication of what might happen in Germany, the question on every hopeful soldier's lips was would they be treated as eligible young men or as conquerors? They were to be pleased with the answer.

Even while the fighting continued the fraternisation ban had little effect on their sex lives and they were soon getting to grips with the German girls. The troops were pleasantly surprised to find the women just as amenable to their charms as the women of France, Belgium and Holland. With the local girls seeming so willing many young men snatched hasty moments of passion in the fields and farms of Germany, some even whilst the fighting raged around them. Like the women of the liberated countries they soon realised the economic worth of the liberators, reckoning on the men being a source of real coffee and cigarettes. Men were led into the bedrooms of women eager to show their willingness to please the occupying army. The housewives took down the photographs of their missing or dead husbands, hid any portraits of Hitler and did their bit for Anglo-German relations.

With the coming of peace the situation became even more entrenched. Once again the lines were being blurred between girlfriends and whores, as the devastation of Germany forced thousands of previously respectable German women into prostitution. It was not a question of morality but of survival. With the collapse of the transport and distribution network food was scarce. Inevitably the only way to guarantee a supply of food was to buy it on the black market at ludicrously inflated prices or earn it from the soldiers of the victorious armies. Women from all walks of life flocked to the barracks and billets of the British soldiers where they traded their bodies for coffee, cigarettes and food. Some of the more desperate individuals were seen at army camps wearing nothing more than shoes and coats, always ready to pleasure another man in order to save her family from starvation.

It was not only these desperate women who hung around the soldiers. As the soldiers started to be demobbed anxious German women made their way to camps and barracks to enquire after their boyfriends. They wanted to know why they hadn't received mail. It became the task of their former colleagues to explain to the women, as sympathetically as possible, that the men probably had wives and families at home and were unlikely to write to them. However, in contrast to this, there were also increasing amounts of men who pleaded not to be sent home, instead requesting that they be allowed to stay with their new-found loves rather than return home to their wives.

In the chaotic aftermath of war moral standards were slipping and soldiers made little effort to hide their exploits. Once the military situation had settled down, all across the British zone soldiers went off duty and straight to the homes of their girlfriends, returning just in time for the morning roll call. Men shared their beds with German girls even whilst the rooms were occupied by other soldiers and it was not unusual for men to offer the services of their 'girlfriends' to their mates. Some soldiers were not content with one 'girlfriend' and with free or subsidised access to rations could afford as many as they desired. A few even took up with mother and daughter combinations, figuring it would be cheaper and more convenient to keep all their partners under one roof.

Of course it wasn't just German women they encountered. Former slave labourers were also in abundance and many took up office jobs with the army. The newly recruited staff, who were often given battledress to wear fitted with the insignia of their home countries, all tended to display certain features. They were young, good looking and obliging. These female DPs were believed to be the source of the alarming rise in VD rates found in the spring and summer of 1945. As doctors reporting to 2nd Army HQ explained: 'Female displaced persons of eastern origin were quite willing partners and one may be justified in assuming that they have been the source of infection.' (26)

Some of the units within the advancing armies had a more readily available source of girlfriends than others. During the closing weeks of the war, at Oberlangen in Germany, an SAS patrol liberated a camp for Polish slave labourers. The 1,700 women had been taken prisoner during the failed Warsaw uprising and were lucky to be taken alive because, as partisans, they could have expected instant justice from the Germans. In a comradely gesture, Mike Calvert, the leader of the SAS group then arranged for men of the Polish Armoured Division to visit the women. In the aftermath of the camp's liberation the Polish Division seemed to disappear from the field of battle, their time taken up with celebrating with their countryfolk.

With the collapse of German resistance the conquering forces were able to relax. Throughout the British and Canadian armies men began to settle into the routines of occupation and enjoy the perks of victory – perks that would inevitably involve sex. Infantry subaltern Ken Hardy experienced the changing of emotions towards the local population. Initially he had felt strongly enough to stick to the rules and wanted the Germans to feel sorry for the suffering they caused:

> Of course Montgomery had issued an edict that we were to treat the Germans with contempt. There's no doubt about it, we used to do so. We would deliberately walk down the pavement three abreast and force them out into the road. We treated them with utter contempt. But non-frat didn't last long. People knew Montgomery for what he was. There was a certain amount of pleasure in the very early day s, but it didn't last, mostly because there were very few young German men around. And most of our men wanted desperately to get to know their womenfolk. They got on quite well with them! The blokes had a free run of the women – who were pining for them. It was a hell of a time…: 'Non-frat' was as dead as a Dodo from the time Montgomery closed his mouth. I didn't go out and chase my chaps away from the women. I didn't have time, I was doing it myself! (27)

As the attitudes of those men who had endured the worst of the fighting began to change it was no wonder the signposts that had greeted their arrival in Germany seemed increasingly obsolete. Signaller Stan Procter witnessed a blatant indication of the changes: 'Two or three weeks after the war had ended I was going somewhere and saw a notice by the road – 'No Fraternisation!' – and there were six condoms hanging from it!' (28)

Despite the softening attitudes towards the Germans some officers continued to prevent breaches of the rules by their men. As a consequence soldiers had to take care in their liaisons with local women. Harry Free of the 43rd Reconnaissance Regiment remembered: 'In our troop, our officer was really strict and enforced the 'non fraternisation' rule. But we found ways round it – what the eye doesn't see …..! So my experiences were not endorsed, or even known about by the officers. You'd have been for the high jump if they'd found out.' (29) The technique used to prevent detection was explained by fellow 'recce' veteran Roy Merrett: 'In public you did not obviously accompany German females, you strolled along with a mate either in front of or behind the two girls you were courting. When a secluded spot was found, you then exchanged your male friend for a female one.' (30)

With such encounters taking place across the British zone of occupation, the whole subject of avoiding contact with Germans started to become a joke. Soon the word fraternisation was bastardised to enter the vocabulary of soldiers. 'Frat' was used in many forms as they asked each other: 'Are you going fratting tonight?'

or spoke of their girlfriends as 'a bit of frat'. The editors of unit newsletters joked about the subject of non-fraternisation. 'Freelance', the journal of the 5th Kings Regiment, even published a list of 'Frat Patter', helpful phrases translated into German for the soldiers to use. Included on the list were: 'Will you marry me?' 'Will you come to the pictures with me?' and even 'Do you like Germany? I like it, but not the people.'

One of the readers of Freelance recalled his own involvement in the defiance of Monty's order. John Longfield, who as a nineteen-year-old had fought in Normandy with the Kings Own Yorkshire Light Infantry before being medically downgraded to serve in the 5th Kings Regiment, explained how the 'frat-ban' made little difference to daily life:

> We were not allowed to associate with the Germans. General Montgomery had sent us a notice saying you were not allowed to talk to anybody at all. I'm afraid to say that our blokes totally ignored his orders and associated with the local population. I was in Hamburg, I wasn't on duty, and I came across a cinema with a sign outside 'Out Of Bounds To Troops'. The film was Laurence Olivier in Henry V, so I thought 'Sod it!' and went in. I sat down and sometime later a rather embarrassed manager came and tapped me on the shoulder and said, in English, 'Out of bounds to British troops'. I said 'Don't worry, go away'. So he did and I just stayed there. I thought this was totally ridiculous, that you should be banned. It was typical of the British attitude. (31)

He also defied the authorities by breaking curfew to attend dances held by students at Berlin University. To avoid detection by the Army patrols that cruised the streets of the German capital the parties were timed to start just before curfew began and continued until breakfast time when the curfew was lifted.

Despite the flagrant violation of the fraternisation ban by so many soldiers there were some for whom it wasn't a laughing matter. Many officers were convinced their men were following Monty's instructions and remained determined to make sure they continued to do so. Lord Boardman, serving with the 1st Northants Yeomanry recalled: 'We continued to enforce the order and it was well observed.' (32) However, consider the words of one of the troopers who served in the Regiment: 'Every evening they got five or six big buses and send them all round the villages to pick the women up. And we'd have dances that used to go on all night. Half the chaps would go home with them and not come back till the morning. Everyone was having the time of their lives!' (33)

Some officers, NCOs and MPs rigorously enforced the rules, resulting in harsh punishments for the offenders. As little as a half hour conversation could earn a man eighteen months' imprisonment and men were put on charges for such innocent acts as slapping the backsides of German women. An officer of the Ayrshire Yeomanry was even posted to India for having allowed his men to mix with German girls. As a result efforts were made to deceive the authorities – badges with the emblems of Allied nations were purchased by soldiers so they could be worn by their girlfriends to give the impression they were any nationality other than German.

A LITTLE BIT OF FRAT

In the initial months of peace the soldiers of the newly designated BAOR –
British Army Of The Rhine – enjoyed their role as an occupying force. Although
few wanted to do anything other than get home as quickly as possible most had a
rough idea of how long they would remain in uniform and decided to make the
most of their remaining service. The economic situation was ideal for the occupiers since money seemed to have little value – as in the liberated territories most
trade was by barter. The products civilians wanted were the obvious – cigarettes,
coffee, petrol and soap. Other more luxurious items could be bought and sold but
these basic goods were the bedrock of any contact between soldiers and civilians.
Cigarettes became the most effective currency and the British soldiers, with their
continual supply of free tobacco, could live like kings and enjoy luxuries few had
known in pre-war years. Anything could be bought with tobacco, even people. For
cigarettes some German civilians betrayed their former leaders. Both Field
Marshal Von Manstein and Rudolph Hoess, the Auschwitz commandant, were
betrayed to the British by civilians in return for tobacco.

Some of the soldiers didn't like to think of the trade as a black market. One of
those who benefited, Ken Moore of the 5th Kings Regiment, thought the trade
should be likened to the magazine *Exchange & Mart* – the trade was a 'redistrib-
ution of material' where the soldiers got rid of their surplus and in return acquired
the luxury items that had long disappeared from British shops as a result of the
war. Clocks and watches, jewellery, crystal glasses, lingerie, silk stockings, furs –
all were exchanged and sent home to a country long starved of luxuries. Moore
was able to use the economic situation to produce his regimental newspaper. He
explained how it worked: 'I won't go into details but I'll say it cost 6d to produce,
it was sold for 3d and a profit was made! If Gordon Brown wants to know how
I'm open to offers! That was a very good commercial transaction. We wanted a
magazine printed, which we got. The Germans wanted cigarettes, that they got.
Net result everybody was happy.' (34)

For many of the fortunate soldiers it was a time of excess. They indulged themselves with food, alcohol and sex. Officers set up clubs in exclusive hotels like the
Atlantic in Hamburg where the porters ran the black market and could get almost
anything in exchange for cigarettes or coffee. They had access to people who wanted to sell cars, paintings, jewellery and could arrange prostitutes for the pleasure
of the officers. Many officers employed butlers, chauffeurs, riding instructors and
tailors and one went a step further and even kept his own private dentist. Again,
many of the staff taken on were chosen for being young, female and amenable.
One unit of field security police managed to acquire the strangest staff. They
employed a number of Chinese jugglers and acrobats who were formerly part of a
circus. By day they worked as domestic servants, then by night they entertained at
parties thrown by the officers.

It wasn't just the officers who benefited from the economic conditions and
enjoyed a high standard of living. After the discomfort of slit trenches many soldiers found themselves in barracks or billets. Life was made easier by the availability of a vast pool of cheap local labour that could be employed to fulfil menial

tasks. The soldiers could have their clothes washed and pressed or their boots shined, all for the price of a few cigarettes. They visited public baths where staff would run the water for them and clean the baths after them. It was a far cry from living off the land and washing in a biscuit tin of water. The services of maids, cooks and cleaners were within the price range of almost anyone and could be employed for nothing more than board and lodging.

Prices fluctuated as supply and demand dictated the market. If cloth was available tailors would make suits for the price of just ten cigarettes, whilst as many as 2,500 cigarettes would have to be handed over to acquire a Great Dane puppy. For those who chose, it was an ideal time to make money and enjoy the high life. They could visit funfairs and stay on the rides all night for the price of a cigarette. Men with the right jobs could exploit the situation to their benefit. Harry Free found himself in an enviable position: 'I was put in charge of the petrol station in Wuppertal – a very powerful position! – doling out petrol to army personnel. I had a Porsche car – and dated a very attractive and experienced German girl. A good time was had by all. Then I went on leave, and when I returned the petrol job had been given to someone else. I don't know about the girl! I was very sorry to lose that job!' (35)

In light of such open violations of the 'frat-ban' it became glaringly obvious that the situation couldn't be allowed to continue. Montgomery finally admitted it was impossible to continue to restrict the activities of the soldiers. To avoid serious breaches of discipline by the soldiers changes were gradually introduced. On 10 June Monty sent a message to the population of the British zone explaining why the restrictions had been in force. On the 14th of the month an order was issued that the soldiers be permitted to talk and play with the German children. Everyone knew the soldiers already spoke to and fed the children of Germany but now their conduct was officially sanctioned. According to Montgomery he was eager that the troops should be able to mix with the Germans and help to re-educate them. However, many observers thought he had simply realised he was losing the fight to control the behaviour of his troops and was just offering this explanation to cover up the truth. A month later a further change was introduced so that troops could now meet in public and talk with the Germans. They were still forbidden to enter private homes, marry Germans, or be billeted in their houses. In September the ban came to an end and the soldiers no longer had to worry about MPs breaking up the relationships which were flourishing all over occupied Germany. Northants Yeoman Joe Ekins was in Hamburg when the ban was lifted. It was not easily forgotten, as he recalled: 'The only thing I remember about Hamburg is the day the Frat Ban finished. You couldn't walk through the park without stepping on a courting couple. They were laying on the grass, all over the park.' (36)

By the time the 'frat ban' had been lifted the face of the British army in Germany had changed radically. With demobilisation well under way many of the former fighting men had already returned home. In their place came post-war conscripts and those who had missed the fighting. As they left, the 21st Army Group veterans finally relinquished the old attitudes of experienced soldiers. The last vestiges of antagonism, doubt and mistrust towards the civilians could at last be cast away. And with their departure for home they saw the tailing off of the voracious sexual urge that had sustained so many of them from the moment they first landed in France. This urge – that had followed them through the brothels of Brussels, the bedrooms of housewives across northern Europe, and into the homes of the Reich – would now have to be curtailed. Gone were the dangers and privations that spurred the desire for one last 'leg over' before facing death in battle. Gone too were the ever-welcoming arms extended to the fighting men, the sexual favours given as the prize for liberating Europe. Gone too was the opportunity to revel in the conquest of the Reich by buying its women for the price of a packet of cigarettes, a tin of coffee, or a hot meal.

The years of military and sexual experience had made men of so many British boys. They had learned things about life that might never have entered their consciousness had it not been for the war. Little wonder that for many the war marked the end of an age of innocence. Men who would never have considered visiting brothels found that such behaviour had become the norm. It was as if nothing could shock them any more. To many of the soldiers the women of Europe seemed a totally different breed from the women they had left at home. And no doubt many British women would not have believed the behaviour of their husbands, sons, fathers and brothers.

Of course, the women back in Britain had changed, in fact the whole world had changed – the pre-war standards had been swept aside, paving the way for the sexual revolution of the 1960s. The eyes of the wartime generation had been opened in a way few would ever forget. Jack Woods was one of the men who had been away from home, fighting his way across from Normandy to Germany. 1946 saw him transferred to Padua, in Italy, where, whilst working alongside the MPs he was to have one last shocking experience that was to show him how much his world had changed: 'This was an education, especially the nightly raid on the local brothels, which were out of bounds to all ranks, not bothering to knock, just bursting in on the girls at their work, I certainly saw some sights. The worst for me, I think, was to go to the NAAFI and see the British girls who had married Italian Prisoners of War, selling themselves outside for the money to get back home. It's a funny thing you know, somehow I didn't think of British girls that way, gave me something to think about.' (37)

6

Home Comforts

'Sleep! I must sleep! Count! What shall I count? The hours since I last slept! Since 8 a.m. yesterday. No, not yesterday. Some other day. Long ago. Far Away ' (1)

For any man joining the army during the Second World War there was an inevitable culture shock, since few experiences could have prepared them for barrack room life. For the majority of the new recruits it was the first time they had entered a world of strangers. The lack of freedom, discomfort and unappetising food, and no privacy was a shock for most new soldiers. They slept in draughty huts surrounded by their new comrades, often washed in cold water, dressed and undressed in large groups of men, and used toilets without doors.

Barracks were seldom heated by more than a single small stove, usually incapable of dispelling the cold and damp from either the huts or their inhabitants. In the depths of winter the concrete floors of Nissen huts were glazed with ice, plumbing froze in the ablutions blocks and toilets often failed to flush. Some COs instituted rules insisting that windows be kept open all night, regardless of the weather, to keep the air fresh and harden the men. In these conditions soldiers slept under blankets, without pillows or sheets, on straw-filled mattresses, crammed fifty to a hut where only twenty-seven or so had slept in the pre-war army. To emphasise the privations of military life, many camps were built in inhospitable locations such as windswept moors and cliff tops.

Life did get more interesting out on exercises living in tents or bivouacs and spending all day in the open air. Yet while the respite from stuffy barrack rooms could be enjoyable in the balmy days of summer, few relished life under canvas in the damp of autumn or the cold of winter.

The conditions endured by the soldiers were a deliberate attempt to toughen and prepare them for what they might expect in the battles to come. But if they thought barracks were uncomfortable they were in for a shock when they arrived on the Continent. Little wonder many soldiers attempted to provide themselves with a few basic home comforts to remind themselves of what they were missing.

The weeks after D-Day left many of the troops unbelievably tired. The hours of daylight were long, from 4.45 a.m. until 11.15 p.m., stand-to came before dawn and there were patrols and guard duties to be carried out at night, and that was before any threat from the enemy. Though the Germans were known for their dislike of fighting at night it didn't prevent them from sending out fighting patrols or stop their bomber crews from raiding the British and Canadian positions. The result of all this activity meant that any man who slept four hours a day was considered lucky. Fortunately most were young and fit, otherwise the effects of sleeplessness could have been much worse. Soon the ability to snatch sleep whenever possible became vital for the military machine to operate.

At times during the height of the fighting for Normandy it seemed that 21st Army Group was about to grind to a halt. From the riflemen in the forward slit trenches, catching a couple of hours sleep each night, to the senior offices spending all day following the course of battle and most of the night planning for the next day, to the surgeons working around the clock to save the lives of both friend and foe and the tank crews, alert all day before pulling out at dusk to refuel, rearm, carry out maintenance work and then hopefully rest, all were exhausted.

At 30 Corps HQ Lieutenant Colonel Bowring reported: 'The work of the staffs and units will suffer severely unless it is appreciated that human endurance cannot go on forever, and it is absolutely essential that one should work in such a way that some people are rested while other people are working.' (2) During the long days of June and July 1944 there were few khaki-clad men in Normandy who looked further ahead than their next sleep. When their day's work was complete they fell to the ground and slept. At times they slept so deeply that German patrols were able to penetrate the British lines without difficulty, even entering the houses occupied by the exhausted infantrymen. Throughout the campaign, whenever the fighting was at its height, there was nothing the soldiers desired more than sleep.

In the first days after the invasion it was the sailors and marines ferrying troops to and from the beaches who were to face the greatest levels of exhaustion. Arthur Jarvis was a coxswain on a landing craft working from D-Day to D+3 without a break:

> When you missed sleep you got used to it and could nearly sleep standing up or even marching. My worst was D-Day and the next two. I didn't stop to eat or sleep; toilet we done either over the side of the landing craft or, if the sea was too rough, in a bucket in the engine room. On the third day the troop ship we were about to unload blew up with over 2000 men onboard so instead of putting them on the beach we picked up the wounded and took them to the nearest ship with medical staff, leaving the dead floating around. When we finished after three days we jumped into our hammocks to sleep. It was then that it hit you, you jumped out and were violently sick, then you managed to sleep. (3)

Few had been fully prepared for the possibility of such fatigue. One man who had foreseen the likely problem was Major John Howard, whose troops had spearheaded the invasion with their successful capture of the canal bridge over the River Orne. During training he had tried to keep his men exhausted and had gone for long periods where he slept little more than two or three hours a day. It was his firm belief that he needed to be able to make quick, effective decisions however tired he might be. In the battles that followed D-Day his efforts were certainly of use since there were few chances for him or his men to rest fully.

The experience of Howard's men was shared by many assault troops. The commandos, who had first linked up with Major Howard's force and then moved directly to the eastern flanks to bolster the defensive positions set up by the paratroopers on the morning of 6 June, spent the first few days at almost constant alert, unable to rest for fear of counter-attacks – unfed, unwashed, unshaven and above all unrested. Their officers noticed how the lack of sleep affected them. All their actions were slow and laborious. They appeared oblivious to what went on around them, only stirring at the first sign of enemy activity and then relapsing when the threat had passed. In this state the men continued for days until they could take no more, eventually nature took over and men had no choice but to collapse into deep sleeps. Men reached their limit, their officers attempting to keep them alert, yet fighting a losing battle, not daring to sit down for fear of giving in. Men drifted off in the middle of conversations, or fell asleep while standing and collapsed to the ground. The commandos eventually spent eighty-two days and nights in action – from 6 June until 26 August. When they were finally withdrawn sleep was all they craved and for the first three days they slept an average of fifteen hours out of every twenty-four.

At the end of a day's advance it was common to see men unable to keep awake and they often crashed to the ground, too exhausted to dig trenches, instead they lay down, attempted to forget their thirst and hunger, then snatched a few hours of disturbed sleep. Others, at the very limit of their endurance, fell asleep whilst digging and tumbled head first into their half finished slit trenches, oblivious to the world around them. John Majendie realised his men were 'bloody knackered' and even watched as one fell asleep whilst having his hair cut. Some men soon found they could sleep whilst marching or simply standing still, leaning against their rifles – one soldier reported sleeping through an enemy barrage that blew the roof off the building he was resting in.

Ken Hardy recalled his exhaustion:

Lack of sleep was a hell of a problem – there were times when I didn't sleep for days. The day my friend Stan was killed – I can't tell you how depressed I was – I came back and found myself a concrete culvert. I eased myself in and went to sleep. It was the first decent sleep I'd had. The next morning I went with a farmer to fetch Stan's body. When we got back he said 'My wife's seen you and thinks you look dreadful. You're coming home, she's going to put you to bed and you're going to sleep for 24 hours.' And I did – I slept solid for a whole day. (4)

Overwhelmed with exhaustion some men slept with their eyes open and others fell into such deep sleeps their resting bodies became indistinguishable from corpses. Stretcher bearers found themselves waking sleeping men as they attempted to remove them for burial. Even soldiers out on night patrols fell victim to their exhaustion. Men told to lie still while enemy patrols passed by who closed their eyes momentarily found themselves drifting off and within seconds could be fast asleep. In such circumstances it became essential for NCOs to keep the men awake to prevent them from snoring and alerting the enemy.

It wasn't just the infantrymen who were suffering from the burden of their workload, tank crews too were feeling the strain. During the severe fighting in Normandy some tank crews were to remain almost constantly within their vehicles for eight days and nights. Whilst advances or actions continued they spent long periods of each day cooped up inside their vehicles, hardly able to stretch their limbs, fidgeting in the hard seats as the hours got longer. Even after they withdrew for the night their duties were not complete as they often needed to refuel, re a rm, cook and eat, all before they could allow themselves the leisure of sleep.

After entire days cooped up within tanks it was difficult to know who had the worst deal – the commander who had to stand upright or the others who were unable to stand. By the end of their ordeal tank crews discovered their feet and ankles to be swollen and footwear had to be discarded. Doctors began to diagnose a previously unseen disorder of 'Tank Commander's Feet'. Long periods of standing caused problems with circulation and serious swelling of the feet and ankles. In the worst cases sufferers had to be evacuated to hospital in England.

After Operation Totalize many tank crews involved were completely worn-out – one gunner told to traverse turned the turret twice round, having fallen asleep after being given the order. Tanks slipped into shell holes because drivers fell asleep. When they dismounted some fell asleep standing up leaning against the sides of their tanks; one passing lorry driver watched the staggering and stumbling of the dismounted crews and thought they were drunk. They couldn't sit down to eat because they would fall asleep. Northants Yeoman Ken Tout later wrote: 'Sleep! I must sleep! Count! What shall I count? The hours since I last slept! Since 8 a.m. yesterday. No, not yesterday. Some other day. Long ago. Far Away.' (5) He did his sums and totalled forty-one and a half waking hours. Men awoke screaming in the night, arguments broke out, only for the voices to fade out in mid-sentence as their owners drifted back to sleep.

Despite the fact that the infantry and tanks were in close contact with the enemy for much of their time it was not always they who suffered worst from sleep deprivation. The role of the most exhausted servicemen fell to the artillerymen – officers noticed their own gun crews sprawled as if dead beside their 25 pounders and as one man loaded and fired the rest slept, untroubled by the crashing of the guns. John Mercer explained the burden of work:

> As a wireless operator I was on duty four hours on, four hours off, for six months. You got very tired. In fact I fell asleep three times in action, I just couldn't keep awake. I was only nineteen and if I was tired I just couldn't keep awake. I was shouted at and called every name under the sun but no action was taken. I was taken prisoner briefly at Le Havre and when I got back I'd had forty-eight hours without sleep. I just conked out – couldn't be raised. We all have our limits. (6)

Battery commander Major Douglas Goddard explained:

> We artillerymen were probably worst off for sleep. The infantry were regularly – and very rightly – out of the front line in reserve and were able to have longish periods of rest and rehabilitation. We were constantly in action night and day supporting other formations or on harassing and defensive fire tasks. My recollection was that as

young and very fit men we soon adjusted to three to four hour sleeping limits and did not suffer too much exhaustion. The worst feature was attempting to sleep in wet trenches when for long periods there was pretty constant rain and no buildings were about. My personal diary constantly refers to sleeping problems. Many nights, when working out or firing extensive fire plans we had no sleep. It was on these occasions that we were under serious mental strain working out complex target data, very often under shell-fire, with the added strain of knowing that if our mathematics were wrong our infantry would suffer from what is now known as 'friendly fire'. I only recall one night where sleep overcame me which could have had serious consequences. At the start of Operation Market Garden on the night of 20 September we were moving terribly slowly up the axis towards Nijmegen and Arnhem and I was fairly well forward in the 43 Div column, leading our battery. The column was halted and, not having slept for well over 24 hours, both my driver and I fell asleep (I was actually standing up in the truck as was the requirement for a column leader). It was pitch black at about 3 a.m. when I suddenly woke to discover that the Divisional vanguard in front had moved on and I was holding up the main body of the Division. Fortunately I managed to catch up before the Division had to deploy. I made sure it never happened again. (7)

The fear of falling asleep tortured those men who needed to keep alert to protect their comrades. Such was the dilemma for artillery observers who desperately needed rest in order to function properly. Without a clear mind it would become impossible to guide the artillery fire so essential to protect the infantry. But to be alert and ready to react entailed keeping awake. It was a tortuous cycle in which by remaining alert they diminished their ability to function fully, all the time being aware of the possible tragedy resulting from their inability to call in accurate artillery support. The danger was demonstrated when one exhausted observer accidentally gave the coordinates of his own position as a target for the artillery.

Canadian gunner George Blackburn also felt the effects of sleep deprivation. Whilst on duty at his Normandy command position he dreamed he was calling fire orders and that the guns were firing. When he awoke to find the guns firing he was confused – he had received no requests for support, nor given orders to fire – until one of his men pointed out they hadn't realised he was talking in his sleep and had assumed he was actually giving them orders. During the winter of 1944 he collapsed in mid-sentence whilst at a meeting. His collapse led his colleagues to believe he had been hit by a sniper and searched his body for wounds but, noticing his restful breathing, they realised his true condition and left him to his slumbers. On a separate occasion he fell asleep leaning against a stove and managed to set his uniform on fire.

During the prolonged battles of the Normandy campaign the exhausted soldiers found each day blurring into the next. Day after day they fought, ate, slept, awoke – then started the process all over again. The names of towns and villages were easily forgotten, instead theirs was a world of fields and hedgerows. Some men lost all track of time, uncertain of the day, date, or even the month.

The breakout from the Normandy bridgehead saw little respite for some infantrymen who advanced constantly for as long as two weeks. Days were spent marching, digging in, marching again, sheltering from attacks from the air, attacking enemy positions and marching on. Advances were being made, losses were light but sleep was almost non-existent. After two weeks the officers and men who endured this finally dug in and stayed put as the advance bypassed them. Now they could rest. Some men fell asleep standing up or leaning against vehicles, others fell to the floor and slept for twelve hours or more. Too tired to find shelter men slept out in the open, simply lying down with their gas capes draped over them. One man recalled his best sleep during this period being a night on the stone steps of a church using his steel helmet as a pillow.

The extremes of exhaustion meant that even the ever present cigarette and cups of tea were no longer enough to keep the troops going. During night marches men fell asleep, but still kept moving – blindly trudging along, following the man in front. When columns stopped they kept walking, bumping into the man in front and being jerked back into consciousness. Such was the level of exhaustion that sentries were posted in pairs, if one man fell asleep the other had to wake him. When they were finally relieved the exhausted infantrymen collapsed to the bottom of their trenches – fast asleep before they even hit the floor. When their bodies finally reached the limit of endurance some men found they could take no more and fell into such a deep sleep nothing could wake them. One man recorded sleeping for fourteen hours, not even responding when a sergeant poured rum into his mouth.

It was not just constant activity that disturbed their slumbers – even at rest they were disturbed. The terrific concentration of artillery that was amassed to support all major offensives contributed to sleep deprivation. Soldiers occupying areas adjacent to artillery positions had little chance of sleeping through the noise of the softening up barrages. When the time came for the advance to begin many soldiers would already be utterly exhausted having only slept fitfully in the hours beforehand, a combination of noise and fearful anticipation. In Normandy, at Arnhem, or in the Reichswald – whenever battle raged the soldiers could expect little sleep.

Those officers and NCOs who were attempting to keep their men awake soon found themselves as exhausted as everyone else and when it came to the stage that the men whose job it was to give orders were too tired to think straight, the safety of whole units came into question. There were obvious dangers from officers and NCOs falling asleep during briefings and missing out on vital orders for forthcoming battles.

The effect of sleep deprivation was felt by Sergeant William Partridge, who attempted to snatch sleep as best he could:

> On Hill 112 my slit trench companion protected me from interruption by other soldiers during brief sleep periods but could not protect me from the noises of battle. Occasionally I was issued with tablets to make up for the lack of sleep. It was a problem, particularly when in a reserve role, when I would find the whole company asleep and only my own platoon sentries on duty. On Mont Pincon, after reaching our objective after day long fighting, I was awakened to be given important information but was fast asleep again before I realised its importance. (8)

The tablets he talked of were Benzedrine – or 'bennies' as they became known in the language of post-war drug culture. Although the recreational use of drugs has often been seen as a scourge of modern society, drug use has a chequered history. Many substances started their life as accepted parts of daily life only to later be outlawed. Certain sectors of nineteenth-century society were fuelled by the use of the opium derivative laudanum, and it became known as the drug that inspired the poets and artists of the day. The latter years of that century saw the widespread use of cocaine which was considered acceptable enough to be used in Coca-Cola before moral outrage saw it removed from the formula.

Another of the favoured drugs of the latter part of the twentieth century had an equally respectable start. The 1950s and 1960s saw the increasing use of amphetamines – or speed – that fuelled a generation of youths eager to keep awake for long nights. It was a drug that allowed teenagers to enjoy every minute of the weekend, only having to worry about the comedown on Monday morning. However, for all their thoughts of rebellion through drug use, the post-war youth wasn't the first generation to use the drug. Little did they know that many of their fathers had been familiar with amphetamine use and that the Second World War was fought by soldiers and airmen, thousands of whom had taken drugs to keep them awake.

First synthesised in 1887, amphetamine was a cure without a disease until the late 1920s when its use was studied with the thought of aiding treatment of a number of conditions including opium addiction, alcoholism, migraine, epilepsy and schizophrenia. In 1932 amphetamines were made available over the counter for the treatment of hayfever, asthma and colds, administered from a simple nasal inhaler. The new drug – marketed as Benzedrine – was soon found to have other uses. After doctors began to use Benzedrine for the treatment of narcolepsy, a condition in which sufferers fall into deep sleep, it became clear this was a drug worth investigating. Benzedrine was closely studied by the military and within years would be in widespread use by armies throughout the world. The British, Americans and Germans all favoured the use of amphetamines to help keep their men awake over long periods.

Although not issued to all the troops, it was believed the British military consumed as many as eighty million pills during the war. Their medical officers carried the pills ready to be handed out when the troops were reaching the end of their physical endurance. By giving them pills the soldiers soon found hidden reserves of strength, they found their eyelids were no longer heavy, their muscles no longer ached, hunger and thirst were suppressed and they were able to focus their minds on the battle. Yet there was an inevitable come-down as the effects of the drugs had to wear off eventually. After long periods without sleep or food and without the Benzedrine to support them the soldiers found themselves reduced to a zombie-like state. Their bodies ached more than ever, they yearned for nothing more than deep sleep, their thirst and hunger returned, their movements became slow and disjointed. Those who had chewed gum for hours on end found their jaws ached from the incessant movement.

Benzedrine became a particular favourite among the men of airborne units. Their often tenuous positions on the battlefield and uncertainty over relief by ground troops meant they had a vital need to keep awake. Men of the 1st Airborne Division discovered the extreme effects of Benzedrine during Operation Market Garden, when the drug became an essential part of their diet. Their ability to keep fighting for over a week with little food, water or sleep, could be attributed to its effects. Yet the combination of constant doses of Benzedrine, combined with extreme exhaustion and a serious shortage of food, began to get too much for the paratroopers and towards the end of the battle some were reporting that they were seeing double. Others were so tired they forgot to unbutton their flies before urinating. What little energy they retained was reserved for fighting, the niceties of everyday life were abandoned. They discovered that whilst the Benzedrine could keep them awake it did little to relieve the aches and pains of exhaustion. The chemicals played havoc with their bodies and whilst their bodies yearned for sleep, their eyes failed to close. Prolonged use of the drug had far reaching effects. To fill the waking hours they talked constantly, hardly pausing till their jaws ached. Others found themselves hallucinating, unable to distinguish between real and imaginary enemies. Their attention span was diminished as the drugs caused their minds to wander, the lack of co-ordination of their thoughts reflecting the disjointed movements of their exhausted bodies. Yet there was little choice but to keep taking the pills until supplies were finished – many of the soldiers realised that to abandon the chemicals would have sent them into deep sleeps, condemning them to inevitable defeat. Even in the last hours of the battle, as the men prepared to cross the Rhine, NCOs handed them out more pills to keep them awake and alert as they trudged towards the river.

Whilst those tired soldiers who were not given 'pep pills' had no difficulty falling asleep at night the same can not be said for their attempts to arise in the morning. Seldom were they able to sleep for long enough truly to refresh their bodies. Instead they were often woken after only three or four hours. On summer mornings they would be woken before the sun came up and in winter they awoke wrapped in groundsheets or blankets soaked with dew or stiff with frost. Not only were their bodies still tired but they ached from the discomfort of the night. Those whose exhaustion meant they could sleep in any position, found that come morning their limbs revolted against their ordeal. Added to these burdens they found foul tastes in their mouths – their breath smelling, their lips gummed together and their eyes encrusted with sleep – and all of this with no likelihood of relief.

To minimise discomfort most soldiers did their utmost to make their nights as easy as possible. The bare earth of slit trenches offered little comfort to their occupants. In hot weather the dry earth turned to dust that penetrated their lungs as they breathed during the night, and in wet weather the rain gathered in pools at the bottom of their slit trenches, soaking their already worn out bodies. With little to use as coverings at night, except the rubberised cotton of their groundsheets, many of the troops started to look around for anything that might make their existence more bearable.

The infantrymen started by cutting down crops and lining their slit trenches with soft sheaves of corn. They entered abandoned homes and took curtains, blankets or carpets to make improvised bedding. As they became more established the infantrymen attempted to construct the most solid dugouts possible. The standard slit trench was a six-feet-long hole, four or five feet deep and covered with a roof. This would be made from whatever was available such as doors, shutters, logs, and even wardrobes filled with earth. The lids of ration boxes were fixed across openings to act as covers for improvised escape hatches. Troops discussed how best to construct shelters, talking of roof support beams or how to construct steps. When the simple slit trench was found wanting men dug L-shaped holes so that if a mortar bomb landed in the entrance only their feet would be injured.

In time some men decorated their shelters, shelves were constructed upon which rested books, jars of flowers and photographs. They gave their shelters names and placed painted boards by the entrance with 'Mon Repos' or 'Home Sweet Home' on them. Londoners reproduced the London Underground logo with the name of their home station, and others gave their home address. Some added luxury refinements such as parachute silk linings, biscuit tin floors, shelves made from ration boxes, whatever could be scrounged was utilised.

The most luxurious of prepared positions were a triumph of art and ingenuity. One commando took a double bed, complete with mattress, from an abandoned house, dug a five-foot hole to put the bed in and then covered the hole with doors from abandoned houses. The earth excavated from the hole was then put over the doors resulting in a deep, dark, comfortable and safe dwelling. Some even contrived to ensure rain water would drain from their shelters. Alexander Baron constructed a shelter combining a tent with a cellar. He wrote to his family: 'Everyone else has been washed out at least once, but thanks to all the dodges and devices that I've installed I'm not bothered by so much as a drop of rain. I get in, close my little trapdoor above me, and climb into my bed (proper mattress) as snug, warm and dry as could be devised.' (9)

Winter saw the need to construct deep, warm positions that offered shelter from both the enemy and the elements. Felled trees, doors from houses or any available wood was used to construct submerged shelters that could be covered in earth. Men competed with each other to see whose shelter was the safest or most luxurious. Canadian artillery officers even constructed their own underground officers' mess. The walls of the ten by fifteen feet room were lined with bamboo matting and tapestries, the floor with an oriental rug. Lighting was provided courtesy of a 12-volt radio battery and heating from a coal-fired stove. Tables and chairs taken from local homes completed the picture and even empty shell cases were hammered together to make a chimney.

The problem for the infantrymen was that luxuries were not easily portable and when they moved they simply abandoned any comforts and started again at their next location. Marching for miles to a new location meant they could ill afford the extra weight of blankets, bedrolls and lamps. A few individuals carried comfort items including a private in the Black Watch who liberated a pink, lace edged silk cushion from a brothel and carried it until his death. One group of infantrymen who had occupied a silk factory, stole all they could, carried it on their unit transport and cut up the rolls to make silk sheets which were discarded as soon as they got dirty.

For the infantrymen such luxuries were rare, however the crews of tanks and other vehicles were more fortunate, and had no concerns about carrying extra weight. Tank crew could always retain a few luxury items to improve their lot at night. Bedrolls, inflatable beds, sleeping bags, mattresses, blankets, looted eider-downs – all were tied to their vehicles ready to be unpacked. Ken Squires went one step further than most of his comrades: 'My stepfather had got me a sleeping bag – sponge rubber with canvas on top – and my mother had put sheets in it. On the first occasion I used it I opened it and found a pair of pyjamas inside. That was great until the lads saw it. I kept using it until the sheets turned grey. I was at the front, wearing pyjamas, quite innocently but everyone was taking the mickey out of me. They called me Posh Squires.' (10)

Life could be quite intimate for tank crews. As well as carrying bedding, tank crews could also make themselves comfortable with the waterproof sheets used for covering the tanks. The sheets were spread on the ground to protect the crews from the cold and damp of the earth, then their bedding was laid on top and finally the engine covers were laid over the top of them. Beneath the covers all the crew members huddled together – officers included. Sometimes the crews dug deep pits which they then drove their tanks over to give them protection from incoming mortar or artillery fire.

When resting in buildings the tank crews could use their batteries to provide electric light, whilst those without access to power used whatever materials were available to make lamps. Oil lamps were improvised by the ever inventive soldiers. Firstly the bottom was cut off from glass bottles by winding string around and pulling vigorously at either end to heat the glass. This was then dunked into cold water thus making a clean crack in the glass. This was then stood up in a tin of paraffin and a wick placed inside. Others were constructed using cigarette tins, rifle cleaning cords and paraffin. The resulting lamps lit many an otherwise gloomy dugout.

For men at the front the notion of sleeping between clean sheets in a warm dry bed seemed an unattainable delight, yet when the chance arrived their bodies often revolted. Some men invited into civilian homes found themselves unable to sleep – the luxury of a soft bed was too much for them and they had to make their beds on the floor.

Sleep was not the only factor in their discomfort – they also had to endure being uncomfortably dirty. Hygiene was a constant problem for front line troops, especially since they were still expected to shave regularly. Military traditions dictated that the men remained clean shaven, soldiers being allowed to grow moustaches but banned from wearing beards. The strict discipline was instilled into most of the soldiers and there were few who failed to shave whenever the opportunity arose. Even on D-Day some soldiers made their way into barbers' shops and, still clad in wringing wet battledress, sat down to be shaved. But once the infantrymen were fully engaged with the enemy there were few opportunities to stay clean shaven and with little chance to safely boil water the only option was a dry shave. Consequently, the rules regarding shaving varied from unit to unit – some officers insisted their men remain clean shaven and others ignored their appearance so long as they were able to fight. In some of the stricter regiments men were put on charges for failing to shave despite remaining unshaven to prevent insect bites from becoming infected.

Knowing the paroxysms of fury it would have raised on parade back in 'blighty', they initially relished the idea of not shaving, yet the desire to be clean shaven went deeper than just discipline. Instead, they soon recognised the benefits shaving could bring. After days and weeks of living in slit trenches, the opportunity to purge their chins of stubble was a previously unrealised pleasure. Even if they dampened their skin with rainwater collected from a rut in the road, it was a joy for them to scrape away with razors – as if the stubble was a symbol of all the accumulated dirt and exhaustion. To have a clean face was one final link with civilisation, and to shave was a liberating experience, symbolically distancing them from the corruption of war – if only for a few minutes.

When it came to personal hygiene, shaving was the least of their worries. Their faces were easily accessible but what became really filthy was the rest of their bodies. There were few opportunities for washes that might have revitalised exhausted men. Instead they went for days or even weeks without being able to undress or properly clean themselves – and that was before even thinking about getting a change of clothes. Feet swelled up inside boots and the pressure of the laces cut into their feet and ankles. In the summer their socks became soaked in sweat – dried out, were soaked again, eventually becoming as stiff as cardboard. In the winter their boots were soaked with moisture, the feet inside them constantly wet and uncomfortable. If boots were taken off to dry out they became stiff and assaulted the feet with every step.

As the dirt seeped into their uniforms the men began to smell. Their crotches and scalps itched, some just with accumulated dirt others with lice. Inhabiting slit trenches surrounded by piles of excreta and pools of urine made for an unpleasant cocktail of aromas. Yet surprisingly few men were bothered by the smell since everyone smelt the same. For them there was a single overriding aroma that seemed to mask all others – the smell of death. A veteran explained:

> Sometimes you had to use bodies as cover, hide behind them to fire from. The smell of death got into your clothes, so it was there continuously and you didn't notice it. We didn't wash or shave – if I'd have taken my boots off my socks would have walked on their own, they were that bloody stiff. You were afraid to take your boots off next to anybody, the smell would knock the bugger out. But you didn't care if others smelled because you knew that you smelled. Sometimes you had to stand in water for an hour or two, by the time your feet came out they were putrid. (11)

In the first few weeks after the invasion there was no provision for washing and the army had more pressing matters than baths and showers. Instead the troops had to wash as best they could. Paratroopers were taught to take turns washing, with one man in three being allowed to strip off and wash whilst his colleagues remained alert. In Normandy one company of sixty men had to share five shaving kits between them, the rest having been lost in the initial drop. The same men were in action for fifteen days before they were able to change their underclothes, and it was another two days before they were able to get a bath by using a manger in an abandoned stable, carrying water to the bath under constant enemy fire.

Artilleryman John Mercer found an opportunity to have a bath: 'Six days after we first went into action six of us were sent down to a farmhouse to have a bath. They had this big copper for washing clothes and we all had a wash in it. We drew lots and I was last so I got all the dirty water. But at least I felt cleaner. We didn't have a proper bath till much later. In something like three months I was able to wash properly three times.' (12) Officers were just as likely to have to endure long periods without getting a bath; the letters home of one Guards officer revealed how it was not until October that he was able to have his first bath since leaving England in July.

Desperate times bred desperate measures and some men were reduced to rubbing their hands on dew-covered grass then rubbing their face in order to get a morning wash. Most found whatever water was available, stripped off and washed as best they could in the circumstances even if it was no more than pouring a bucket of water over themselves. There was little chance of getting clean but at least it was invigorating and provided a refreshing stimulus to cast away the feeling of grubbiness. During rainstorms men stripped off and stood beneath the broken guttering or drainpipes that made refreshing, if cold, improvised showers. Other innovations included digging pits, lining them with tarpaulins and then filling up with water heated up by the cooks, or improvising showers from perforated jerrycans.

Hygiene was of utmost importance, lice spread quickly between the men and, knowing the risk of disease, each man was issued with a 3 oz tin of anti-louse powder each month. More importantly the army brought in mobile bath units to keep the men clean. These were set up in fields or buildings, with water pumped from any available source and heated by oil burners. The filthy soldiers were ushered through a series of tents and whilst waiting some men noticed the bath staff avoiding them because of the revolting aroma of rotten flesh that clung to their uniforms. In the first tent they would strip off and leave their uniforms to be laundered, then they would dash through to the next where they would wash under the hot water. Often more than one man would have to share each showerhead but there was no time to worry about appearing naked in front of others – although officers admitted to a feeling of shyness at being seen unclothed by their men. As they waited to wash, the soldiers often wondered whether their skin colouring was dirt or a suntan, waiting until they had scrubbed their filthy bodies to find the answer. In the next tent they would dry themselves and move on to a final tent where a new set of underclothing and clean shirts were issued, seldom with any regard to the size needed. They then swapped garments until, hopefully, everyone had a complete set of suitable clothing.

During the winter the naked soldiers questioned the logic of standing in the freezing rain as they queued for a shower, as John Mercer recalled: 'We stripped right off apart from our boots then went in. I said to my pal "Is it better to be clean and cold or stay dirty and keep warm?" We said we'd better be clean and cold.' (13) Once dressed the soldiers revelled in the luxuriant comfort of soft, clean, freshly laundered underclothes, overjoyed to have cast off the grimy clothing that had been their lot for many weeks.

Not all visits to bath units were uneventful. Corporal Worthington of the 1st Royal Dragoons recalled his one and only visit to a bath unit during his time on active service in Europe: 'Whilst in the shower a German plane came and strafed the baths, we all ran out in the nuddy and jumped into the nearest ditch. Looking back that was all funny.' (14) Northants Yeoman Michael Hunt had an unusual experience upon visiting a Canadian bath unit in Holland:

> Before we went overseas we put our name and regimental number in our underwear. My first shower was the beginning of July. You got clean pants, shirt, socks, towel, all rolled up – so I gave mine in and got a new set. Then in March 1945 we were moving up to Calcar for the Rhine crossing and we had to stop in Nijmegen. So we decided to go to a Canadian bath unit, hoping we'd get some good kit. We handed our stuff in, then went to get our replacement kit and they gave us all the old stuff they could find. I was going to hand it back and I could see they'd been written on. So I said to the chap I was with 'Let's see which silly bugger these belonged to' and there on it was my name and number! (15)

After almost eight months his own kit out of the hundreds of thousands in circulation had come back.

With few chances even to take a shower the idea of a lying down bath was something most soldiers could only dream about. When such an opportunity arose it would be so rare it would warrant a letter home to announce the fact. Fortunately many of the towns they passed through had public baths and soldiers were sometimes able to stop for long enough to use the facilities. Some men were able to enjoy the relative luxury of communal pithead baths at the coalmines of Belgium where they could stretch out and immerse themselves. Yet for many of the men there were few opportunities for visits to the bath units, one veteran recalled only once visiting a bath unit in Normandy and then not seeing another until the end of the war. Instead he and his comrades had to use water heated over 'benghazi' cookers for washing. Having a bath in a biscuit tin was not unknown and in the most unfortunate cases men fought through the whole eleven months only ever washing with water from a mess tin. In their desperation, some entered German homes and made civilians prepare baths for them. Fearing a hostile reaction they made the Germans stay whilst they bathed, holding families at gunpoint until they had re-dressed.

Even if they could get their bodies clean the condition of their clothing remained a constant source of discomfort for the troops. In the early days after the landings in Normandy soldiers were responsible for their own cleanliness, since there were more important units to take their place on the battlefield than the mobile laundries. Consequently the troops went for long periods without changing their clothes. When one Canadian gunner finally undressed after fifty-three days, he found his socks could stand up by themselves. After long periods fully dressed they found their feet not only stank but had become soft and swollen – the skin white and puffy.

Whilst infantrymen had few opportunities to wash uniforms, for vehicle crews the situation was often different. During wet weather they could dry their boots on the engine of their vehicle, they could also carry more spare clothes and tins to boil water and wash clothes in. Some chose to improvise and took to washing their clothes in petrol – a primitive form of dry cleaning. Their shirts and underclothes were soaked in fuel poured from jerrycans and then left to dry. Only once the clothes were thoroughly dry could they be worn otherwise the petrol would cause itching and severe rashes.

Though the troops did their utmost to minimise discomfort by keeping clean there was one 'home comfort' that was rarely seen at the front – toilets. Right from the start of their training soldiers had learned that they would have to abandon any notion of privacy. The doorless latrines, in force to prevent impropriety taking place behind closed doors, meant the troops grew used to going to the toilet in the view of others. They learned this was part of daily life and although it would never be comfortable to drop their trousers surrounded by friends and colleagues, it was a foolhardy man who would take his chances out in the open whilst under fire.

Rules were strict in barracks but everything would change once they reached France. John Reynolds recalled a bizarre incident that undermined military discipline: 'One of my mates was caught urinating up against a lorry. Next day they posted orders forbidding us from urinating against vehicles. A few days later we went on an exercise on Dunstable Downs. Churchill came to inspect us. The first thing Mr Churchill does is, he gets out of the car and peed up against the wheel!' (16)

The start of the journey to France had seen the troops on troops ships and landing craft. On the ships the toilets frequently became blocked and on the small landing craft there were no toilets, leaving desperate men to squat over buckets. Once ashore the order of the day was 'Cat Sanitation' where individuals would dig a hole and cover their own faeces – wiping their backsides with the four sheets of toilet paper contained within their ration packs. For men at the front the prospect of using a prepared latrine was too dangerous, consequently there was little choice but to use their own slit trenches. The chosen method was to ask the man sharing the trench to scramble over to the neighbouring hole so as to afford a measure of privacy and then defecate onto a shovel, throwing the resulting mess away from the trench, and hoping it didn't land in someone else's. Alternatively they called for covering fire and scrambled to cover, hoping the enemy would not spot them. Abandoned German helmets were also used as makeshift chamber pots that could be squatted over and kept covered until an opportunity was found to empty them. For mortar crews trapped in their trenches by enemy fire the waterproof bags used to protect the bombs' tail fins came in handy as makeshift toilets.

Tank crews – cocooned within their vehicles – had no access to a toilet and were forced to use empty ammo tins or shell cases, only emptying them when it was safe to open the hatches. Care had to be taken when emptying the improvised chamber pots through escape hatches, many a driver was soaked when turret hatches were directly above the driver's compartment. Thoughtful officers ordered tanks to be parked up forming a square so that one by one the crew-members could drop through the escape hatches and squat in the enclosed area, safe from incoming gunfire. Other tankmen held on for as long as possible, clenching their muscles, controlling their bowels and by will-power alone resisted the urge to 'go'. For their persistence they were rewarded with constipation that caused the sufferers much discomfort.

For most troops improvisation would remain the standard mode of operation. In stable locations the most common latrine would be an upturned ration box with a hole cut in it, perched above an evil smelling hole. Latrines – dug by 'shithouse wallahs' – sometimes consisted of deep trenches with Y-shaped branches placed at either end with a tree branch between them forming a crude seat to perch upon. To improve latrines, chairs were taken from homes and the seat knocked out to allow the men to sit in comfort. Len Bennett remembered the lack of privacy at latrines:

> Toilet facilities were obviously primitive and makeshift at times, but organised wherever possible. There was no alternative. I think the majority of us recognised the need for hygiene, but that is not to say that an arrangement of a communal pole seating about six at a time was ever more than endured. I for one never felt at ease, but it was accepted. An unpalatable necessity would be my definition. (17)

Soldiers had many unwelcome encounters while going to the toilet. Some found Germans surrendering to them whilst they crouched with their trousers round their ankles. Others were shot in the backside by German snipers who took sympathy on them and chose to spare their lives. Others had unwelcome encounters with the contents of the latrines. One young tank officer found a recently dug area of earth which he confidently claimed was housing an anti-tank mine. He fitted explosive into the hole to detonate the offending device, the resulting blast showering the area in shit from a latrine neatly filled in by the previous inhabitants of the camp.

The difficulties in going to the toilet were made worse by 'Compo Tummy' brought on by a diet that lacked fresh food. The condition, also known as 'Beachhead Belly' or 'Compo Sickness' was most commonly called 'the shits'. The diet of rehydrated compo rations and lack of access to clean water left many soldiers affected by stomach upsets. Later in the campaign bottled fruit was to have a similar debilitating effect on the soldiers who-over indulged. It became a common sight to see soldiers heading at high speed towards hedges, one hand clutching a spade the other frantically undoing the trousers. Even once the food distribution system was functioning properly soldiers were still succumbing to sickness and diarrhoea. The summer sun left them with raging thirsts and, despite the pleas of medical officers, they drank from rivers and streams filled with the corpses of men and animals.

The soldiers were also plagued by the flies that fed on the rotting corpses of cattle that littered the fields of Normandy. Dysentery became rife with whole units laid up unable to fight with confidence. Officers reported their men too ill to rise from their slit trenches, sleeping as if dead, every so often staggering off to empty their bowels. Each movement sapped their already depleted stores of energy. The pills used to treat the condition soon ran out and seemed less than effective to sufferers.

Everywhere it was the same – infantry positions, artillery batteries, HQs – all were home to sick men. It took all the skills of the officers and NCOs to get their men to do anything. Shouting at them was a non-starter, only by encouraging them and coaxing them gently could men be made to rise from their sickening slumbers to fulfil their duties. For all the army could try to solve the problem, it was self-perpetuating. The flies that plagued the soldiers fed on the excrement that littered the battlefield, and the dysentery only produced more excrement. The only solution was to keep fighting and advance out into fresh countryside.

Once they broke out of the filth of Normandy new problems emerged. During the 'Swan', the rapid advance from the Seine to Brussels, columns were covering up to forty miles a day. Such was the speed of advance that lorried infantry were not able to make toilet stops and had to make do with going over the side of their trucks or standing on the back step with a comrade holding onto their webbing straps.

The troops yearned for the clean ceramics of civilian toilets. It was a simple reminder of home – the type of memory that sustained them in the dark days of war. When the opportunity arose they queued for the chance to sit in comfort – even when flushes were not working many of the soldiers continued to use toilets, filling them to the brim with excrement and paper. Filthy it may have been but it was a fitting reflection of their condition – normal men living a dirty existence and yearning for the comforts of home. Comforts that could only come once the enemy was defeated.

7

Recreation

'A.B.C. – Any soldier will tell you that Ale, Bacca and Cunt are the main topics of conversation among any group of soldiers.' (1)

'I wonder how many war histories record time spent on entertainment, the cinema, ENSA shows and playing Monopoly?' (2)

It is often said that the experience of war is made up of long periods of boredom interspersed with short bursts of intense excitement. This was certainly the case for a majority of the fighting men in 21st Army Group. Whenever there was no fighting to be done their lives continued as normally as possible, even in face of the most incredible obstacles.

Most of the men bound for Europe had spent their years in uniform without once seeing the enemy, instead filling their time with parades, exercises and training lectures. In their spare time they polished boots and brasses, attended lectures on regimental history, scrubbed floors and pressed their uniforms. Leisure was not top of the agenda – what counted was preparing for war. In wartime Britain leisure pursuits were somewhat limited. Many camps were miles away from large towns, the pubs had a limited amount of beer and British women seemed preoccupied with the attentions of American servicemen. Instead thousands of soldiers spent their leisure in the canteens of the Navy, Army & Air Force Institute, or as it was commonly known – the NAAFI. Its motto was 'Service to the Services' and it aimed to bring comfort to the soldiers. Here they could spend their meagre pay on subsidised goods such as tea and buns, then relax in easy chairs, read, smoke, chat, or play a game of darts. It was hardly exciting but it was a welcome change from the austerity of the barrack room.

For all the efforts to keep the men busy most officers knew that once their men had experienced battle they would have little time for the mundane details of barrack room life and what the soldiers would need was leisure. Only in rest and recreation could soldiers build the reserves of energy necessary to return to the fray. As a senior army chaplain wrote in 1944: 'A watchful eye needs to be kept on the over-zealous non-commissioned officer who takes a delight in finding odd jobs that need to be carried out in off-duty hours. This type is a menace to morale.' (3)

For some soldiers it was only in the final days before the invasion of France they were able to find time to relax. Pioneer Corporal Alexander Baron wrote to his family of how he was passing the days: 'We've been strolling by the sea and lounging lazily in deckchairs watching the holiday crowds (not inconsiderable) surge by and the children building their sandcastles as in happier days. During the day we have had bathing parades two or three times a week.' (4)

It was a deceptive calm – the balmy days of early summer 1944 would soon be washed away by a tide of violence that left the soldiers yearning for the return of a time when they could sit and relax. With only around ten per cent of soldiers serving in forward positions and the rest engaged in supply and support, that made for very little 'excitement' and plenty of leisure time. Whilst the army endeavoured to lay on a range of recreational facilities, the soldiers still had to find much of their own entertainment. Army Welfare Services may have played a vital role, and ENSA shows may have been acceptable, but they offered little in comparison to the nightclubs and bars of Brussels. The entertainers of the concert parties might have been able to make the troops laugh but nothing brought a smile to their faces like a night on the beer or in the arms of a willing female. For the men sent on leave a balance had to be found between relaxation and hedonism, and for every soldier wanting to keep out of trouble and have a quiet time there was another for whom nothing would stand in the way of the pursuit of pleasure.

Not everyone was convinced the army should be concerned with the leisure of its men. Winston Churchill, held an outdated opinion that caused conflict with some military leaders. He felt the war could be won by pouring men into battle and was scathing of the back-up required to keep the army in the field – to him winning a war was about blood and guts. Churchill had a scant understanding of the logistics required in a modern army and at times showed a disregard for the need for soldiers to relax. In his diaries Field Marshal Sir Alan Brooke, the Chief of the Imperial General Staff, noted how at the start of the campaign in Normandy: 'Winston began one of his long harangues stating that the army was bound to crowd into "dental chairs" and YMCA institutions instead of bayonets into the landing in France.' (5) As Alanbrooke also noted: 'It is appalling the false conception of modern war that he has got.' (6)

Churchill little understood the tremendous boost to morale given by a few hours' relaxation. The troops were positively buoyed by even the most simple pleasures.

To crowd into barns or farmyards and listen to George Formby was the perfect tonic. For many France was where his reputation was sealed, performing within the range of German guns. Despite the danger the helmeted Formby played for men who hours later would be facing the enemy. It was a gesture few would forget, despite the posturing of the prime minister. Formby was just one of the many top names brought in to entertain the troops. ENSA concert parties featured some of the most popular acts of the day – Flanagan and Allen, Kay Cavendish, Florence Desmond, Richard Hearn, Sylvia Sinclair, as well as numerous lesser-known performers including unicyclists, jugglers and dancing girls. By July 1944 there were six concert parties operating within the confines of the Normandy beachhead. In time the army also brought over highbrow acts like string quartets and even Sir John Barbirolli's Hallé Orchestra. The ENSA performers appeared everywhere a space was available – in fields, barns and factories as well as the more conventional venues of theatres and village halls. Where there were no stages they

Sex Conquers Orders
The advancing armies found many willing partners in the lands they liberated.
Here British troops entertain French girls in the ruins of Caen. *August 1944.*

A Little Bit of Frat
Many German civilians faced a hostile reception from the advancing
troops. Here British soldiers watch as civilians are forced to rebury
the bodies of 97 slave labourers murdered by the Nazis.

Home Comforts
The men did their utmost to make their lives comfortable. These men have
taken mattresses from houses to line their slit trenches. *December 1944.*

Home Comforts
Exhausted men found they could fall asleep anywhere. This officer of
the 5th Battalion Coldstream Guards is resting on his motorcycle.

Home Comforts
Where no washing facilities were available the men were forced to improvise.
Here Sgts Gill and Nunnerley of the 49th Division wash in floodwater.

Recreation
With cigarettes freely available there were few men who did not smoke. As one
remembered: 'Smoking was as much a part of living as eating and drinking'.

Recreation
Brussels became a popular destination for troops on leave. This British
soldier is enjoying the delights of a student bar 'The Wooden Leg'.

A Man in Uniform
Away from front line positions many men adopted unorthodox clothing. These
Canadian signallers have acquired civilian hats. *Normandy, August 1944.*

improvised, performing on tabletops or on the back of lorries.

James Byrom, a non-combatant airborne medic, attended an ENSA show in Normandy, which for many of the audience was the first sighting of glamorous female legs since they had left home. In his memoirs Byrom recalled: 'We were welded into one community voice, every soldier singing with a thousand lungs, laughing and stamping like a drunken giant, and whistling at the female performers with a full blooded lewdness that made the whole idea of sexual intercourse monstrously, delightfully obscene.' (7)

However, not all the acts suited their audiences. Lieutenant Douglas Goddard attended a show given by: 'six attractive, young and talented lady musicians – a soprano, mezzo soprano with accompanist, and a trio of piano, violin and cello. A delight for the musical connoisseur but, apart from the excitement of the lovely performers, it was not quite the entertainment for soldiers brought up on Max Miller and the Crazy Gang.' (8)

Many soldiers remained deeply cynical about the acts provided for them and could never accept the army was providing entertainments without an ulterior motive. In Ghent, troops reported that the standards of the ENSA shows were much higher than elsewhere and a rumour went round that this was designed to keep the soldiers off the streets to prevent the spread of VD.

The favourite mass entertainment of the pre-war period was also available – cinema. Unlike ENSA stars who were often reluctant to go to the front, the men of the Army Kinema Section had little choice since they were mostly projectionists who had been called up into the Royal Army Ordnance Corps. The travelling cinemas that followed the armies across Europe put on films anywhere they could. Like the concert parties, they set up in private houses, schools, town halls, theatres and farm buildings – anywhere that could conveniently be used to bring entertainment to the troops.

All the big movies of the day were shown – both Hollywood hits and home produced fare – and the khaki-clad projectionists observed how their audiences reacted to the various films on offer. They were surprised to find that sentimental stories were favoured by the soldiers. One unlikely success was the three-hour religious epic *The Song of Bernadette* which held the audience gripped despite its subject matter. One of the least popular films was a cinematic adaptation of *The Canterbury Tales* during which, as one projectionist noted, some men fell asleep, the sound of snoring had other men in fits of laughter, and people were continually walking out. Although those soldiers lucky enough to make visits to the cinema found all the most up to date films of the day on offer, not all of the available pictures were suitable for their audience. Transit camps thoughtlessly showed *The White Cliffs of Dover* a film about families saying goodbye to their men going off to fight in the Great War.

Reading matter was also sent out. The army purchased thousands of newspapers, magazines and old library books and surplus stock from magazine distributors. Mobile libraries were established to keep a regular flow of books to the fighting men who were able to purchase them at reduced rates. Efforts were also made to buy up as many wireless sets as possible for distribution to front line units, with the intention of making one available per seventy men.

A number of charitable organisations also played a role in bringing comfort to the troops. One such organisation whose activities were greatly respected, was the Salvation Army. Their 'Red Shield' mobile canteens appeared just behind the front lines and dispensed tea and sandwiches to the grateful soldiers. It was a simple touch of home. Whilst the religious message may have been lost on most the notion of helping out those in need was one they fully endorsed. Few ever forgot their generosity and courage, as Harry Free recalled: 'The Salvation Army was brilliant, the soldier's best friend. They came right up to the front (WI and WVS never did) – very courageous providing refreshments to soldiers on the front line. I had, and still have great respect for the Salvation Army.' (9) The American Red Cross vans also received a warm welcome. The fare they offered made a pleasant change from the British tea and sandwiches. Their popularity was guaranteed since attractive young women handed out the coffee and doughnuts, ensuring long queues at their vans.

Despite the provision of entertainments some officers were convinced what the men needed more than anything was time to themselves – a chance to collect their thoughts, read their mail, eat and drink without the fear of attack. In the early stages of the campaign although the situation was not stable enough to initiate leave it was still possible for units to be given short periods of rest. Visits to sea-side rest camps were a pleasant feature of life for those soldiers lucky enough to live to see them. The camps were established before the end of June, and were still within range of the enemy's heavy guns. They offered cafeterias, a post office, chalets with wicker chairs, cinemas, ENSA shows and a NAAFI. From August the camps also offered soldiers a quart bottle of beer each per four-day stay. The troops were able to enjoy a strangely calm holiday amidst the turmoil of war. When the weather was fine they spent long hours sunbathing on the beaches and where the sea had been cleared of mines they were able to go swimming. This desire to swim followed them across Europe and they indulged at any opportunity, whether it was the sea, lakes, rivers or ponds.

Two weeks after D-Day Arthur Jarvis was sent to a rest centre:

We were taken to a long pier like arrangement near the Mulberry Harbour and told to find our way to a place called The Normandy Fleet Club, near Bayeux, and to be back here by noon in a week's time. .... We reported to the RTO office and they got us a lift on a lorry taking supplies to the front. The driver dropped us off outside this big villa which had been used by the Germans. As we went in the gate a big notice said you can put your hands in your pockets and don't salute officers. In the huts in the grounds it said don't bother to make up your beds, breakfast is from 8am till 10am. When you went for a wash and a shave in the morning you'd look in the mirror and there was a big notice 'Don't bother to shave'. When you went into the villa there was writing paper etc and a notice saying 'Please write home'. (10)

Although such facilities were available, few were able to take advantage of them.

RECREATION

Many units pulled out of the line to rest had no time to be transported to seaside camps. Instead they stayed in fields and villages just miles from the front line and had to entertain themselves as best they could. Much of their time in such brief periods of respite was taken up with washing or changing their clothing, drawing new kit, maintaining vehicles or simply sleeping. There was little access to comforts. Churchill might have been mollified to find that although cinemas and libraries were supposedly available, some men reported never having seen either facility throughout the whole campaign. Infantry officer Ken Hardy, who was constantly at the front from June 1944 until early 1945, remembered: 'I never, ever had any experience of it at all. I never saw a mobile library, I never saw a cinema. I suppose the only recreation we had was a bath. I can't even remember reading a book in that whole time. I don't know how others found the time to do it.' (11)

In lieu of official rest centres many battalions established their own, paid for from regimental funds, to ensure those not fortunate enough to be sent on leave still had the opportunity to rest. They took over hotels, opening cafés and reading rooms, employing local musicians as entertainment and women to work as waitresses. Those soldiers that liked to go drinking or chasing girls could always find their own entertainment, so it was important to provide quieter facilities for the others. In these venues they could drink tea, sit and read in peace, or play chess.

Once disengaged from the enemy, some men still found their time fully occupied. Les Toogood was a sergeant in charge of a section of snipers, whose responsibilities meant he found little chance to relax:

> We got a fair amount of time out, but the point was that the first thing you had to do was to bury your dead. You had to make sure they were looked after and write a little note to their parents. Also to make bloody sure the lads were fully equipped and had time off. And to make sure the Bren gun carriers were in tip top shape. As for myself, all I ever did was sleep and eat. You don't have time for anything else. You see, the infantryman had time. But us, sometimes we went out three or four days before the attack, reccee-ing, coming back, making sure the lads who been out at night had a bit of a rest. And I'd take another section out to drop them off here and there. So snipers didn't have so much time, but in all fairness to the colonel, when we had time off nobody bothered us. (12)

It was only when the infantry and their iron-clad comrades withdrew from the front and pulled back into reserve that the soldiers had a chance to relax fully. In the hours immediately after being withdrawn few thought of anything else but sleep. If they marched back from the front many slept as they walked – supported by their more alert comrades. If they were travelling by lorry most were asleep before the engine roared into life. Arriving at their destination they wearily set to digging in, preparing the bare holes that might be their homes for days on end, and then would collapse into them, sometimes without even bothering to remove their equipment. When they awoke, the soldiers put their mind to doing the one thing they had yearned for whilst in the line – as little as possible. They sprawled around on the grass or in the mud – chatting, smoking, writing, eating – just taking it easy.

One veteran recalled: 'You'd do maybe a month or so in the line. Then you'd have two or three days in reserve. You went back but not very far, you were still under the guns. You'd have a wash and a shave, have a bath. Maybe change your clothing, stitch up the holes in your socks, unless you'd found a drawer full in a house or whatever. You were at peace. Not to think "where am I going to go?" Just to sit there was glorious.' (13)

Those men whose units were fortunate enough to rest in towns did not have to worry about devising ways to pass the time since all the entertainments of 'normal' life were available. However, many of the troops greeted these breaks with an unprecedented enthusiasm, and their behaviour was not always ideal. In November 1944 a number of Canadian units moved out of the line to spend five days in Ghent. The men were overjoyed to be able to relax in a real town, awash with both civilians and military personnel. Billets had been arranged within easy walking distance of the city centre and Mess halls established. There were no areas 'Out of Bounds' and public transport was free. All the soldiers had to worry about were shifts guarding their vehicles. In the words of one Canadian veteran: 'The city was our oyster.' (14) The arrival of the 13th Field Regiment signalled an inauspicious start to the stopover in the city. As their vehicles made their way through the streets one of the drivers faked an accident, choosing a particularly appealing street. The stalling of the column afforded the men an opportunity to sample the delights of the local bars. For the rest of the evening their officers and NCOs raced around the streets rounding up the offenders. By the time they were safely established in their billets the Canadians were already eight hours late.

During the remaining days their behaviour changed little. Drunks wandered the streets, day and night. Soldiers were seen throwing their mates into the canal. Aggressive drunks fought each other whilst others, having run out of money were forced to trade in their equipment to continue buying drinks. One soldier was spotted walking out of a bar in his socks after swapping his boots for beer. Gangs crowded onto trams, some hanging off the outside, all of them waving and shouting at passers by.

Eventually threats were made to force the troops to modify their behaviour. They were told if they didn't stop they would be ordered out of the city to spend their time in a sleepy village or waterlogged field. The threat worked and the soldiers altered their behaviour, little realising that some had upset the locals with antics worse than those displayed by the German occupation forces.

Only one thing was as vital for their relaxation as sleep – not food, not beer – just tobacco. Cigarettes and pipes were an ever-present fixture in their mouths and were a vital part of any post-battle comedown. As one remembered: 'Smoking was as much a part of living as eating and drinking.' (15) Even those men who had never smoked before they joined the army puffed their way through the campaign. It was an easy decision to start smoking since the army gave them a free ration. They received them and thought 'why not?' as one veteran explained: 'I wasn't a smoker until I went to the desert. I started and of course I kept on doing it. You had a round tin of 50 cigarettes and there was a little bit on the lid and all you had to do was to turn it and the cigarette came up. And every third day you'd get a tin of 50 free.' (16) They could also buy them at a reduced rate from the NAAFI. Furthermore, wealthy individuals and charities brought cigarettes by the thousands to send to their local regiments, whilst individuals received them from their families. Thus the soldiers often found they had a surplus. Alexander Baron, who spent the summer of 1944 in slit trenches in Normandy, recorded the details of his supply. The ration of a hundred and twenty-five cigarettes a week meant by 5 August he had one and a half pounds of spare tobacco and two weeks later he recorded having a thousand cigarettes in stock. All his comrades were in the same position and so he couldn't even give them away. Little wonder the soldiers were soon trading surpluses on the black market.

Even in the midst of battle the cigarette was a vital tool. As Len Bennett remembered: 'The cigarette was regarded as a form of medicine. The first thing they'd give a wounded chap was a cigarette. They just stuck it in his mouth whether he wanted it or not. It took the stress away.' (17) In the aftermath of battle cigarettes and pipes were the first thing the infantrymen pulled from their pockets. As one veteran NCO recalled: 'You could sit there afterwards and puff away. You'd think "Beautiful, beautiful", it was all over. Then you were ready for the next stage.' (18)

Many men going to war had prepared themselves for the periods when they would be able to unwind and relax. For the footsloggers this meant little more than a pack of playing cards but for those with transport other items could be packed. Dominoes, draughts and chessboards were taken and some even packed typewriters to record their accounts of the campaign, and thousands more carried illicit pocket diaries to record their thoughts.

Time would prove that few soldiers were able to record their experiences in depth. In place of real literary endeavours most soldiers contented themselves with writing home. The access to regular mail from home and the ability to write to loved ones became a vital factor in morale. As soon as the troops landed in France the army postal service prepared to deliver mail – the first deliveries were made on D+1, with a total of eight batches reaching Normandy by 14 June. Such was the efficiency of the postal service that it took just three days for mail to reach the front and sacks of letters left France twice a day for Blakehill Farm Airfield, near Swindon, where it was sorted for onward delivery. John Majendie, a company commander in the Somerset Light Infantry, recalled how highly mail was regarded: 'The order of importance of things coming up from the rear was the mail first, food and drink second, and ammunition third. The mail literally came up when you were in a slit trench and the Germans were the other side of the road.' (19)

A strong feeling of admiration developed for the men who drove through enemy fire to bring mail to the front. The regular supply became a lifeline as the troops awaited the next letter from friends and family. Mail gave the soldiers a sense of belonging – as if each delivery strengthened the link with home that the enemy strove so violently to break. The tenderly written words of wives, the pleas of mothers for their sons to take care, the kisses added by small children – all served to bring tears welling up into the eyes of men who knew they might never return.

Some soldiers became prolific, writing home at every opportunity. They would start a letter, stop, go into an attack and hopefully live to complete the letter. Others were less concerned and seldom bothered to write. One veteran recalled why it failed to interest him:

> I didn't have much time for it. My brother and sister were in the forces and my mother was at home. Now and again I would fill in one of the green forms – 'Hello, goodbye' – that was it. I didn't have much to say. You see, whatever you put on there was blue pencilled by the censors. You had some clever buggers writing 'I can't tell you where we are but the trees look very nice or the river is good.' That was out. So by the time they got it, you had about two words on the whole bloody letter. And they really did cross them out, there was no two ways about it. Even if only one word was left they would still send the letter. So I didn't send many. There were people who wrote regular, every night, every time we stopped. Rather than have a wash or a shave they would write, especially the married people. That was different. I wasn't one for that, I'm afraid. (20)

This question of censorship was the cause of much disquiet among the troops. Many failed to see the need to cut out details, since the Germans knew so much about them anyway. However, neither the men nor their officers had any say in the matter and they were forced to adhere to the rules governing content. Soldiers were forbidden from making any mention of specific incidents or locations for a period of two weeks. The intention was that if intercepted by the enemy their words could give away no information. Censorship was a task few officers relished since they had no desire to intrude upon the private world of their men. When censoring the mail officers came across many words in code. Some such as SWALK – Sealed With A Loving Kiss – were obvious, but others confused the officers, including NORWICH, a blatant refe rence for what awaited retu rning soldiers – (k)Nickers Off Ready When I Come Home. Another favourite was BURMA – Be Undressed Ready My Angel. BOLTOP – Better On Lips Than On Paper. GUTS – Get Up Them Stairs. On a less blatant note came ITALY – I Trust And Love You. One of the more bizarre codes used was SWOS – Sealed With Officer's Saliva, which of course was the reality since the envelope was sealed by whoever censored it.

Attempts to continue normal relationships whilst on active service meant that whole love affairs were conducted by post. The enforced separation prevented the usual development of romances and many foundered under this pressure with the despairing servicemen receiving 'Dear John' letters from home. Some felt the lack of understanding of what life was really like for them contributed to failure. In these trying circumstances Stan Procter attempted to continue his relationship with his girlfriend, and later wife, Audrey. It was not always obvious whether they would be able to patch up the differences caused by the unreal situation of enforced separation. After fifty years of marriage he looked back into his wartime diaries that recorded how he felt at the time: 'I received seven more letters including one from Audrey in which she said our troubles were my fault. I found it difficult to believe that she did not seem to appreciate that I was in danger of being killed day and night.' (21)

It was not just letters that arrived from home. The books and magazines that arrived in the post were a welcome tonic. Mostly the soldiers read for relaxation. Works of fiction, both serious and pulp, were devoured whenever possible. Whereas men reading cheap cowboy novellas seemed to fit perfectly into their surroundings there was something incongruous about the sight of officers reading *Tatler* in the midst of death and destruction.

The reading matter carried by infantrymen had to be light. Paperback books were about the limit that could comfortably be transported in their haversacks. Tank crews had an advantage since they could carry extra luggage on their vehicles. This meant that in times of rest their leisure options were greatly increased. It was simple for them to fill a pack with books, then strap it onto the tank's hull. One man even welded a small shelf inside his tank to provide a space for his paperbacks. Whereas most men reserved their periods of reading to time spent off duty a handful continued relaxing even when danger was near. Such displays of nonchalance may have helped them relax but they could also prove hazardous, as the crew of one tank discovered. When their tank came under fire from German positions they were unable to retaliate because their own gun was jammed. The tank commander had been reading when the attack started and as they fired their first shot the book became jammed in the recoil mechanism, preventing the gun from being reloaded. Fortunately both tank and crew escaped intact – more than could be said for the offending paperback.

In the close-knit world of the fighting men it didn't take long to learn each other's histories. Some men chatted incessantly as a way of attempting to take their minds off the terrifying situation they found themselves in. Men at the front found conversations limited, at the end of a day the soldiers wanted to find out the news of their pals, who had been killed or wounded. After that it was time to settle down to food, drink and tobacco. Ken Hardy found his talks with his men focused on one subject: 'It was "Why me? Why am I here? How did I find myself in this position?" We had this idea that it took seventeen people to keep one man at the front and we discussed it all the time. Everyone used to say "Why the hell am I the seventeenth?" There was an awful lot of whining about that, by the officers as well. It was pretty repetitive.' (22)

Although Hardy found his own conversations mirrored by those of his men it was not always the case. The strengths and weaknesses of particular officers was a common feature of the soldiers' conversations, in particular those officers who appeared to be blasé about the war and were thought to be willing to risk the lives of their men. A reconnaissance regiment veteran recalled: 'We often complained about our stupid CO who used to say things like "hunting Germans today, chappies". Had no respect at all for him, or any other senior officers who were seen as inept.' (23)

Most had adopted the traditional vocabulary of the British soldiers, words which originated in India or with the Eighth Army in North Africa – tea became 'char', a woman was a 'bint', 'doolally' meant mad, 'mufti' referred to non-regulation uniforms and 'shufti' meant to look. Now they introduced new words of their own. A 'charlie' was a coward, 'fratting' and 'a bit of frat' referred to relationships with German women, which were banned under Monty's notorious 'non-fraternisation' order. Another widely used word was 'Swanning', which had a number of meanings. Coming originally from the notion of rapid advances – sticking one's neck out – it came to have a variety of uses. To the soldiers it could refer to visiting friends, taking life easy, looting or skiving. 'Liberate' was much the same. Soldiers talked of 'liberating' a woman when they had sex with her. A town could be described as 'well and truly liberated', meaning it had been flattened and its shops thoroughly looted.

Certain subjects were at the forefront of conversation. Much time was spent discussing the course of the war, how much longer it might last and, in particular, when they would be demobbed. Above all other subjects stood the two main topics – women and alcohol. They talked of women they had had and women they hoped to have, of beer drunk in the past and to be drunk in the future. Older, more experienced soldiers regaled their younger comrades with lurid details of their sex lives. At times it was little different to discussions held in pubs back home. One man even noticed two fellow infantrymen, oblivious to the fighting going on around them, discussing the relative merits of rival football teams.

Artillery observer John Mercer recalled the chats he had with friends whilst resting away from forward positions:

> We all swore a lot, we were all foul mouthed. I haven't done it since I came out of the army. George, whose sister I married after the war, he educated me about music. He used to play classical music on the mouth organ. We talked about films and music, we were both keen on Laurel and Hardy, and Bing Crosby. We talked about home and our parents, books we'd read, what we'd done – I was a bank clerk, George was a lighterman. Like people talk about TV now, we talked about going to 'the pictures'. We were quite philosophical – we talked about religion, about God, about the stars, about the future, the past – what we wanted to do and didn't want to do. (24)

Once established on the continent, some politically minded soldiers organised impromptu debating groups. Pre-war Communist Party organiser Alexander Baron organised lively political and social debates in barns that became a mecca for men eager to escape their slit trenches and take their minds off the war. They sprawled on the straw-covered floors and hung from the lofts. It reminded Baron of the paintings he had seen of soldiers' Soviets during the Russian Revolution – here were vast numbers of armed men, the very men in whose hands rested the future of democracy, discussing the details of the life they would build in the post-war world. Baron opened his forums with controversial questions, designed to capture the attention of his audience and stir up debate. At one meeting he asked the assembled soldiers whether it was right to refer to women as 'a piece of cunt?' (25)

Such meetings became a launching pad for discussions that raged between the soldiers. They held views from across the political spectrum, reflecting the society from which the army had emerged. The war seemed to have polarised opinions, with advocates of socialism contrasting with those defenders of the status quo. Many with 'conservative' opinions held that they were fighting for individual free-dom – for the choice of the man against the machinations of the state as seen in the power of the Nazi Party. Others saw it as a fight for the maintenance of the leading role of Britain in world affairs. Those of a left wing persuasion stressed the need for the defeat of the Fascists in order to protect the working classes against the oppression of big business and its political allies.

Conversations invariably led to discussions of the latest rumours about the course of the war. There was always someone who claimed to know the exact time and place of the next attack, when they would be getting leave, or that the Germans were about to surrender. The men discussed the rumours avidly with the question of 'where are we going next?' followed by the inevitable 'why is it our turn again?' Usually the rumours were something heard from 'a friend with con-nections at HQ' or some other unattributable source. Good or bad, the news spread like wildfire, stories changing as they were retold until they were sometimes unrecognisable. Hopeful, or just plain ludicrous, rumours did the rounds until another more likely story came around to replace it.

As victory came closer men began to discuss what to do after the war – or as one described it in his memoirs: 'that vast and frightening era known as the post-war period'. (26) At this time the Beveridge Report was widely discussed and if there was one thing most agreed on it was the need to establish a welfare state. The men who were winning the war were eager to make the most of peace. Those offi-cers who talked politics with their men began to see a shift towards support for the Labour Party – Churchill for the war, Attlee for the peace. For most of the cam-paign such discussions were academic. The only peace that really concerned them was the peace that started once an action was finished and they found themselves in relative safety. Right from the start of the campaign card games were one of the most popular ways to pass time. Gambling was, is, and probably always will be a favourite way for soldiers to pass long hours of boredom. Although officially out-lawed, there was little that could be done to prevent gambling.

All manner of cards games were played – poker, fantan, bridge, whist, brag, pontoon. They even gambled on the turn of a single card. Or they played dice, pitch and toss, housey-housey – as bingo was then called, and gambled on the flip of a coin. Sweepstakes were also popular, with the players offered a choice of pos-sible locations on the French coast where the Second Front might begin. In the Hertfordshire Regiment it was reported that the winner held the ticket specifying 'near Bayeux'. Later in the campaign, as men grew hardened to the experience of war, some even organised callous sweepstakes as to when they thought a particu-lar officer might be killed.

The big domestic sports events also provided the men with a chance to gamble. Some men opened books on horse races such as the Derby that was held in June 1944. But with most major sports meeting cancelled for the duration they gambled on impromptu sporting events that took place behind the front line. Captured Wehrmacht horses were used for races and fox-hunting, in particular by the former cavalry regiments. Other sports were more unusual, reflecting a spirit of improvisation. Officers of the Coldstream Guards organised 'Point to Point' races between Bren carriers that careered over obstacles across French fields. Others used captured Wehrmacht motorcycles to play mechanised polo.

Football – the soldiers' favourite sport – needed little organisation. All that was needed was for someone to get a ball out and the men would be eager for a kick-about. There was no need to take equipment off, they could even play quick games carrying their rifles. It was quick, simple entertainment, just enough to take their minds off what lay ahead. At Waregam in Holland troops took part in a football match against a local team whilst their comrades attacked enemy positions. As one of the participants noted it was: 'incongruous but life was now lived for the minute'. (27)

The winter of 1944-45 was to provide an opportunity for sporting activity little known back at home. During the 'Battle of the Bulge' many British units were swiftly moved into positions alongside their American allies in case the enemy broke through. The move from the flat, sodden landscape of Holland and Belgium to the hills of the Ardennes was soon exploited, with troops borrowing skis from local civilians and taking advantage of the snow-covered slopes. Soon the soldiers were behaving like schoolchildren, those not able to ski resorted to borrowing toboggans and skidding down the hillsides. Whenever columns halted the soldiers dismounted and had snowball fights – including contests between officers and other ranks.

Some turned to artistic pursuits to fill their time. By concentrating their hands and minds on wood carving or sketching they could free themselves from everyday pressures. Little time was needed to reach into a pocket, pull out a pencil and sketchpad and draw. During the static fighting in Normandy soldiers searched the wreckage of gliders that had landed on D-Day. They removed perspex window panels and carved trinkets – including rings and pendants. Although officially banned for fear of giving away military information, others took up sketching, painting and photography. Many had packed cameras ready to record the good times shared with their mates and exposed photographic films were sent home for processing, accompanied by letters requesting contact sheets so pictures could be selected for enlarging. Stan Procter, whose work as a signaller at 214 Brigade HQ gave him sufficient time to indulge in hobbies, recorded his progress into Germany. He photographed everyday life – football matches, cooking, eating, swimming and resting. He got his materials from the wreckage of shops where he searched for chemicals to process his films. Gradually his wireless van became home to a grow-ing array of photographic equipment, including an enlarger. He recalled: 'As soon as we stopped for the night, I knew I had something to do. Where can I find some-where dark? Where can I find water?' (28) Whenever possible he went into the cel-lars of German homes and practised with the chemicals. Even over fifty years later he remains surprised at the results, since he was working totally in the dark with no 'safe light' to help him: 'I still can't believe it. Some of the negatives have crys-tallised but some are still perfect quality.' (29)

Not everyone could have such time-consuming hobbies, however nearly every-one had time to listen to the wireless. Music played an important role in the lives of many soldiers and provided a soundtrack to their experiences. On D-Day many ships and landing craft broadcast music as they approached the beaches. Signallers who listened to broadcasts recalled how they realised others were doing the same since they could hear machine guns in the distance firing bursts in time to the music of Glenn Miller. As well as Miller they listened to all the stars of the day – Tommy Dorsey, Jimmy Dorsey, Harry James, Alice Faye. Hits included – 'The Sunny Side Of The Street', 'Starlight Serenade', 'I'll Be Seeing You', 'Long Ago and Far Away', Bing Crosby's 'White Christmas' and the German favourite 'Lili Marlene'. Even the small '38' sets, designed to be used by one man in forward observation posts, were strong enough to pick up the BBC.

As well as being a photographic enthusiast, signaller Stan Procter was also a great music fan:

> When we were off duty I could tune into the BBC. And I used to put an extension speaker out for the infantry to listen to. We had the forces network and I remember that the signature tune was 'Opus One', Glenn Miller. The incredible thing to me was, when we were on 'The Island' between Nijmegen and Arnhem, and the battle was going on around us, I was off duty and somehow I had a set I could listen to, and I listened to Debussy's 'La Mer' while all this was going on. Nobody would think that anybody would be sitting listening to 'La Mer' in the middle of Operation Market Garden. It's the various moods of the sea, there's the storm and the calm. When I read my diary I think 'How extraordinary!' that this sort of thing was going on. It comes as a surprise to me! (30)

At times the music could be a bizarre accompaniment to their situation. Late on a Sunday afternoon, rolling forward to take part in the attack on Le Havre, tank crews tuned in to the BBC – ironically the tune that emerged from the speakers was 'This is a Lovely Way to Spend an Evening'.

Most units did not need a wireless to provide their music, as they had their own musicians willing to play, and there was always one man with a good voice who would sing to his comrades to help them relax. Wherever the troops stayed there always seemed to be a piano and a khaki-clad pianist ready to entertain his mates. However badly damaged an instrument someone would try it, often to the merri-ment of others. In wrecked churches enthusiastic soldiers repaired organs with tape or chewing gum and played to whoever would listen.

With the advance stalled for the winter the troops needed entertaining and many units formed bands that became a regular source of entertainment. Ken Squires joined a dance band in the winter of 1944:

> Obtaining the gear in the first place was fantastic! We said to Bill Fox 'Do you think you could find any instruments?' And up came the instruments, yeah – piano, a set of drums, Buddy Hare had his trumpet, he was the bugler, but he carried his trumpet anyway. Lockie had his clarinet and sax, Harry didn't have his drums until some arrived via Bill Fox. The first thing we did was rehearse in a school hall, and most of

our instruments were tuned English style but the bloody piano was continental pitch. This meant if he was playing on the white notes we were playing on the black notes. So we wrote it down and transposed it, and that's extremely difficult. So next time we made sure we got the right piano. So we had a dance band. We had a good pianist, a good bassist, a good drummer, a bloody good clarinet player, good trumpeter and an infamous chap pretending to be a good accordion player. We had a great time, we played every night of the week. It was fantastic. At Christmas '44 we were organised to give the kids a treat in Holland, but then on the 22nd of December – Bang – and we were off to the Ardennes. But after that, when we were in Germany we used to play for every squadron – A,B,C, and HQ. So we were busy every night of the week. (31)

The respites from war enjoyed when troops were held in reserve allowed some to indulge in the behaviour they would have enjoyed on any foreign holiday – they went sightseeing. The liberation of Paris saw numerous 'tourists' heading for the city. Among them were Lord Carrington and his friends who rushed to Paris to enjoy dinner at the Ritz. Luxuriating in the splendour of top hotels was out of reach for most soldiers, but it didn't prevent them from making the most of whatever opportunity arose. Many soldiers enjoyed sightseeing trips, even if it was only a quick trip around the local countryside on an abandoned bicycle. For others rest provided an opportunity to scrounge transport and visit friends stationed nearby. With foreign travel having been a dream to so many men in the pre-war years this was the ideal chance to visit many famous sights. Eager soldiers went to Bayeux in the hope of seeing the famous tapestry that recalled an earlier cross-channel invasion. In Belgium, officers took their men to visit the battlefields of Waterloo which was of particular interest to those whose regiments had been involved.

In the autumn of 1944, when it came to relaxing in a real city, there was only one name on the lips of British and Canadian servicemen – Brussels. The triumphal 'Swan' from the Seine to the Low Countries had culminated in the liberation of the city that was to become the epicentre of 21st Army Group's operations. In the days leading up to its liberation there had been a feeling that finally the British and Canadian armies would have a real prize, a city they could call their own. Few could have realised quite how right they were. The liberators were treated to an outpouring of emotion few had witnessed before or would ever know again. The drink, freely given kisses, food, and flowers that were showered upon the spearhead of 21st Army Group were to become a legend among the servicemen – the Yanks could keep Paris, now the Brits and the Canucks had somewhere they could be proud of. Brussels, possibly the least fashionable capital in all Europe, had suddenly become somewhere everyone wanted to visit.

As soon as the city was liberated everyone seemed to be trying to find an excuse to get there. The staff officers of 21st Army Group's Main HQ soon took up residence, as did the HQ of the British 2nd Army. Forces moved in to garrison the city, MPs entered to keep order, civil affairs staff arrived to smooth relations with the local people, and support staff found their units converging on what was to become the hub of military operations in the region. It was not only those on official business who were attracted to Brussels. Drivers deliberately made diversions into the heart of the city so they too could share in some of the largesse bestowed on the liberating forces. Officers of units stationed near the city freely gave out passes to their men so they could spend a day there. Everyone seemed to have a reason to make their way into the city and trawl the bars, restaurants and shops that were just crying out for them to spend their hard-earned wages. It was a wave of tourism the city had never seen before.

If the garrison staff and the unofficial visitors were not enough, soon there was another surge of tourists making their way into Brussels. They arrived in trucks they called 'Passion Wagons', with high hopes of their dreams being fulfilled. Their pockets were full with the accumulated cash of months of having nothing to spend their pay on, and alongside the cash were handfuls of condoms handed out by the staff of the 'Green Cross' stations. These were the men on 48-hour leave passes, who fully intended to enjoy every minute of their freedom.

Those fortunate enough to receive a 48-hour pass were given hotel rooms across the city. When leave started in October 1944 sixteen hotels were taken over by the army, rising to nineteen plus seven hostels by February 1945. Little wonder so much accommodation was needed – by December 27,000 men a week were receiving leave passes. Coming straight from the front lines it was like entering a strange, previously forbidden world. Some men found themselves in private rooms with their own toilets and washrooms. Sergeants could even expect en suite bathrooms.

The first thing most did upon arrival was to settle down into a deep hot bath. After months without washing properly they filled the tubs with as much water as possible and luxuriated in the steaming water. With soap and brushes they scrubbed at their bodies and washed their hair to rid themselves of the accumulated dirt. It was a desperate attempt to be rid of the aroma of death they had carried for so long. Some washed themselves, drained the bath of the filthy water, and immediately refilled it. It was as if they had stepped back into some long forgotten world of civility. In this alien world tea could be brought to their bedside, although some soldiers were disappointed that the chambermaids were somewhat older than the girls pictured beside the bells.

When they were finally scrubbed and shaved, had combed their hair and pulled on their best uniforms, it was time to go out on the town. There were no worries about getting ready since most hotels even had boot blacks they could visit before heading out. Then they were ready to take their first steps back into the civilian world. They checked their pockets to make sure they had their wallets, and were carrying their leave passes – they didn't want any interruptions from the 'Redcaps' – and opened the doors onto a world of unimaginable pleasures.

Their first stop was often the barber's to have their haircut, something many had not enjoyed since leaving England. The condition of some soldiers' hair was so poor that barbers washed it twice before daring to approach it with their scissors. Once suitably presentable they visited photographers' studios where they had formal portraits taken – portraits that still grace the mantelpieces of homes up and down the country to this day.

Then they were ready to seek enjoyment. Most knew exactly what they were looking for – as one veteran recalled: 'Do you really have to ask what soldiers get up to when they are sent to some large city for relief?' (32) The city was constantly brimming with troops, as one later wrote: 'most of them with girls, others drunk, others just wandering, lost and amazed in the back-line Babylon'. (33) For most people the trip to Brussels was their first real experience of a Continental city, and for some the visits were to end in drunken fights, whoring and confrontations with MPs. In the months of fighting the war had leapfrogged them from village to town, field to wood, seldom stopping in civilisation long enough to experience more than the very basics of life. But this was a real city, teeming with life and its temptations. It was a dream come true, they were treated like kings. Nothing had prepared them for this, the civilians seemed in awe of their liberators. Upon entering restaurants house bands played 'God Save the King', to the embarrassment of the soldiers and whenever they produced a cigarette, a waiter would appear with a light. However, there was so much more to the city than sitting in restaurants – as so many memoirs modestly state it was an experience: 'better left undescribed'. (34)

From October 1944 the brothels of Brussels were to see a surge in trade, with queues of men waiting to take their turn. Although they were officially out of bounds it made little difference and crowds of young men stood open mouthed, in expectation at what waited within. Cafés, bars, restaurants – everywhere the soldiers went there seemed to be someone selling sex. They couldn't walk down the street without being accosted by girls offering themselves at a price. Even if sex wasn't actually on offer there were other delights available. Shady characters hung around outside bars and lured them into dingy basement rooms where they could watch live sex shows or buy pornographic postcards. For forty-eight hours everyone was allowed to have their vices. Little wonder the army was to see a massive rise in venereal disease in the months that followed.

Along with sex, the other main preoccupation was drinking. In Brussels they found beers of every imaginable taste and flavour, and with civilians eager to please the soldiers many found they had little need to buy their own drinks, as one recalled: 'I got a two day leave in Brussels. But I don't remember much about it, other than I've got a photo of me and the bloke who went with me. We're sitting at a table and we've got about 20 pints of bloody beer in front of us. And there's only me and him sitting there! I'm sure we didn't drink it all.' (35) With beer flowing freely, hundreds of soldiers were arrested for drunkenness, spending their hard-earned leave in police cells. Others evaded the gaze of MPs as drunks were assisted by their mates, made to walk upright and kept quiet as they returned safely to hotels.

There was little the MPs could do to prevent drunkenness and the access to alcohol and women produced numerous disturbances in the city. During the day everything remained peaceful but the situation changed at night. In December 1944 MPs reported: 'The discipline of all troops on the whole is good although saluting is bad and it is very much regretted that drunks are seen in the town between midday and dusk, these mostly being Canadian.' (36) At the end of each day the MPs had plen-

132

ty of work to keep them occupied. They kept 'Black Marias' standing by at the main railway stations each night from 8 p.m. until 1 o'clock the next morning. 'Flying Squads' of six lance corporals and one sergeant and 'Riot Squads' of five lance corporals and one sergeant were on hand to deal with troublemakers. With the onset of the curfew and the closing of the bars they had to cope with any trouble involving service personnel. Drunks tumbled from bars, arguments started and fights broke out. They started from the slightest of provocations – the soldiers argued over girls, they picked fights with pushy pimps, or were enraged at the prices charged by bartenders.

At the end of each day it fell to MPs to enforce the 11 p.m. curfew and restaurants, canteens, cafés, bars, brothels and nightclubs were all subject to regular raids. With little warning MPs crashed through the doors and ordered the troops to stay seated. Others made their way to secure all possible exits and prevent escapes through lavatory windows. One by one the soldiers were approached and asked to hand over their papers, their faces were scrutinised and pertinent questions asked. Drunks, absentees and deserters were arrested, and over-exuberant revellers or those ignoring the curfew had their names taken.

Some nights the garrison guardrooms held as many as a hundred and fifty men, usually a mixture of absentees, deserters and drunks. Punishment for the troublemakers could be swift – men who had committed less serious offences had their leave passes revoked and were handed straight back to their units to face punishment by their COs. More serious offenders were transferred to Brussels-based units to be put on trial in the city – ensuring that most of the witnesses would be available to the court.

It was not just the lower ranks caught in these raids, their superiors were often involved. Not all of them behaved as 'officers and gentlemen' and representatives of a Guards regiment were forced to issue a formal apology to MPs for their behaviour whilst on leave. Openly flouting both curfews and restrictions on the carrying of weapons, drunken officers were spotted wandering the streets taking pot shots at chimneys.

In quelling disturbances it was not unknown for MPs to resort to drawing their weapons. RAF police even shot a man during a raid on a café in the rue de Zerexo. However, it was not only the MPs who were brandishing weapons in arguments. Although forbidden to bring their personal weapons on leave many carried pistols. After months of fighting some didn't feel at ease without a weapon to hand. Sergeant Les Toogood visited Brussels in early 1945:

The behaviour of the British soldier was abominable. They'd never been away from home, they'd never drunk. I'm not a saint, but I didn't drink and I didn't smoke. I had the privilege of getting ten days leave in Brussels, with the Americans. They gave me and five of my lads leave in Brussels. Also they gave us a house to go to, so we didn't have army restrictions. And the people there were wonderful. They were amazed by how rough we were. We were walking down the street past the Mannikin Pis. We were with the two Belgian ladies and their daughters. Coming down the road were five absolutely drunken soldiers, they were appalling, their language was absolutely foul.

My mate just drew his revolver and shot at the first one – he wouldn't hit him 'cause he knew what he was doing' and he said the next two shots will be in your knees, now shut up! And they sobered up just like that. Discipline was terrible, so I never bothered to go into towns much after that. (37)

With such incidents showing up the British and Canadians in a less than flattering light, the military authorities were desperate to keep standards of behaviour as high as possible. With the army occupying much of Belgium cordial relations with civilians had to be maintained. It was therefore considered essential for the men on leave to maintain high standards. There were dress codes to be enforced and MPs keen to ensure they were. Walking out dress for those on leave was battledress with a web belt, boots with anklets, or polished shoes. From later in 1944 the men were allowed to wear their battledress collars open to reveal a collar and tie, although few men actually had ties or shirts with collars. Many of those who had come straight from the front were less than concerned about polishing their boots or pressing their battledress than they were about getting out for a drink as soon as possible. Even the men who left their hotels correctly attired often let their standards slip after a few drinks. In just two days in November 1944 seventy men were charged by one company of MPs in the city, primarily for dress offences. In particular the MPs were instructed to pay attention to the non-wearing of belts which was prevalent amongst soldiers and, for some reason, was seen as an important offence – in one month in 1945 two hundred and forty-eight men were charged for failing to wear belts.

As the popularity of the city grew, brief stop-offs were made by many soldiers who claimed spurious reasons to pay a visit. Those with vehicles passing through the area took detours via the city centre to visit shops and restaurants until, like so many more enjoyable military pursuits, the Provost Marshal put a stop to it. He figured with so many people on official business in the city there was little room for interlopers.

To help contain the burgeoning population, from November 1944 residents of bases outside the city were banned from entering Brussels and MPs were ordered to crack down on all unofficial visitors. New traffic routes were devised and military convoys were deliberately diverted away from the city.

For those whose aims went further than sex and alcohol there were plenty of other pleasures to be sampled. Many took in the tourist sights – the Grand Place, the Tomb of the Unknown Warrior, and the Mannekin Pis. ENSA shows were put on in the rue de Malines, troops could listen to orchestras, choirs and jazz bands, or visit one of the sixty-six cinemas showing British and American films. Gamblers could watch horse racing at the Acropole racecourse or visit any of a number of greyhound tracks. For those with refined tastes both the opera house and ballet were open.

For the bargain hunters there were seemingly endless stocks of luxury items in the shops, goods not seen for years at home. Men went shopping for silk stockings, underwear and perfume to be sent home to wives and girlfriends. Ice cream parlours were open and doing a brisk trade and there were endless cafés selling egg and chips. Troops also had commodities they could trade when prices were prohibitively expensive. Some went to gundealers where they could get shotguns in exchange for looted Lugers. Those with less ambitious transactions in mind found they were able to exchange a single tin of corned beef for the equivalent of ten shillings, or could sell Lugers to American servicemen for the princely sum of £5.

Despite the delights on offer there were plenty of men who felt unable to enjoy their leave fully. It seemed like a reminder of a world that they had left behind and they found it hard to re-adapt to polite society. Without the company of their mates they felt lost and isolated. This emotion was to haunt many men in the post-war world – after life on the battlefields real life could never feel real again. They simply wandered the streets as if lost in the noise and confusion. Some who failed to settle down wished they had not accepted leave. They found the contrast between the teeming city streets and the front line too great, remaining tense and unable to unwind, all the time remembering what they would soon be returning to.

Officers had the run of the city's most exclusive establishments. Eager officers loaded their jeeps with wine and champagne, hoping to spend their leave in one big party. With the arrival of their jeeps full of looted booze there was soon a roaring black market trade that kept the hotels well-provisioned. Exchanges were made with waiters and hotel staff, the soldiers accepting the more readily available wines for the more scarce spirits. The Hotel Plaza was able to offer its officer guests captured stocks of German army gin and brandy for three francs, a fraction of the price on the black market. Among their favourite venues were the Eye Club – the private venue of the Guards Armoured Division, the Elysée Bar – famed for its martinis, Le Manoir, Gentrys, Maxims, the Atlantic Hotel, and the Gaiety. In January 1945 the Savoy was able to offer its guests lunches of oysters, caviar, woodcock and Lanson 1937 champagne. The Atlanta Hotel even kept a register of approved ladies whom officers could arrange to meet and dance with in the ballroom. The 11th Armoured Division established its own club where the bar was open all day and all night and white-gloved waiters served exquisite food to officers and their guests. During the winter of 1944-45, with little active campaigning, some officers made nightly four-hour round trips to enjoy the delights of the club. Driving from their billets they headed home at 4 a.m. to be back in time for roll call.

Although Brussels remained the epicentre of military recreation there were plenty of other towns and cities that played host to men on leave. The situation in Antwerp was different from that in the capital, since initially the town became home to crowds of relaxing soldiers whilst still on the front line. When the town had been captured at the climax of the 'Swan', the liberating forces had failed to press the advance and the line stabilised with outlying areas of the city in the hands of the enemy. Notwithstanding the obvious dangers, the city still became a centre for men on leave. Canadian gunners manned observation posts in the comfort of arm chairs whilst their mates, on five-hour leave passes, walked the streets of the town shopping, drinking and chasing women. Men could even leave forward positions to visit cafés and restaurants, cleaning themselves up in the washrooms prior to eating. The streets of the city saw a strange juxtaposition of soldiers and civilians as the dishevelled men mingled in the streets with the local population. Ken Hardy was one of those lucky enough to enjoy leave in the port: 'I went to Antwerp twice, it was really wonderful. It's difficult to describe how good it was. I came straight out of the front lines into the comfort of a four star hotel. It made you feel good to be alive. It was only ten miles back from the front. The first morning I woke up I heard a flying bomb going over.' (38)

When the war moved on the situation in Antwerp and similar towns settled down to the same patterns of behaviour as were seen in Brussels. The restaurants, bars and brothels of Eindhoven, Nijmegen, Louvain and many other cities were almost constantly full and the MPs spent their time dealing with troublemakers. Alexander Baron was in Ostend during the autumn and early winter of 1944 and with an author's eye for detail he recorded the scenes in the streets of the town:

> The bars and dance-halls were busy, although there was nailed to the door of nearly every one of them a printed notice: OUT OF BOUNDS TO TROOPS. During the day they were silent and empty of soldiers. One Military Policeman patrolling the pavement was enough to keep the men away. But at nights a tide of soldiers and girls surged in and out of them, flowing up and down the streets on pavements and roadways while music of many kinds mingled, little bands thumping, pianos playing, the voices of singers amplified, all in the darkness, for there were no lights or neon signs, all windows were covered by blackout curtains and the opening and shutting of doors threw only momentary shafts of lights across the pavements. From time to time the MPs swooped in their little covered trucks to carry out a 'Razzia', but they could do little against such a host, which melted away and, when they had gone, flooded in again. (39)

In the days following liberation Paris had been declared 'Out of Bounds' to British troops, and though accessible for some men on leave from October there were only two hotels available to British personnel. However, in January 1945 the French capital was opened to increasing numbers and seven hundred men arrived each day to enjoy forty-eight hours of rest. One officer, who was to find fame in later years, was lucky enough to spend his leave 'living it up' in Paris. He spent his time visiting the Folies Bergère and other places he admitted thinking more exciting than 'pilgrimages to the Rodin Museum'. (40) The officer in question whose leave was spent watching semi-naked dancers was none other than Robert Runcie, later to become archbishop of Canterbury.

By late 1944 it was not only the men on leave who had the chance to relax. With the onset of winter the whole pace of the war had changed. The weather seemed to work against any chance to continue the advance. The seasonal rains had flooded rivers and swamped whole areas of countryside. Tanks couldn't stray from roads for fear of bogging down and mine clearing tanks couldn't operate in the mud. The short hours of daylight limited operations and the men were left cold, wet and tired. It was little wonder the advance was slowed and the front line units given a chance to absorb reinforcements, re-equip and prepare themselves for the battles they knew would come in the New Year.

This change of pace meant that in the long, cold winter many men were able to rest for longer periods than during the hard fighting of the summer and autumn. Life was far from easy, but it was life. All the time the guns were silent was a bonus. Football matches were played between rival units or against local civilian teams. There were dances and even fancy dress balls to pass the time. The only thing spoiling the dances were the mothers and grandmothers who chaperoned young women. Civilians laughed at the comical scenes caused by the arrival of heavily armed soldiers who had to check their weapons in at the cloakroom before being allowed to make their way onto the dancefloor, and the shortage of women often resulted in men dancing with each other, shuffling across the floor in their heavy hobnailed boots.

In the last, relatively calm weeks of 1944 the soldiers were able to look forward to the event they had hoped would mark the end of the war – Christmas. The oft-repeated phrase 'over by Christmas' that had come from the lips of politicians, generals and civilians, was now a long-forgotten memory. The aim to be home for the festive celebrations was abandoned and instead they looked forward to the prospect of enjoying Christmas dinner and a few beers without any interruptions from the enemy. After all both sides were Christians. Despite this, care was taken to make sure too many units were not celebrating at the same time. In one Canadian division units were detailed to have their Christmas dinners by rota – spreading the meals a battalion a day over the last couple of weeks of the year.

Most units were able to spend Christmas Day in relative peace, and many enjoyed splendid meals courtesy of a mixture of rations, local produce and locally hunted game. Chickens were rounded up and fattened up on a diet of corn, bread and potatoes, ready for the festive celebrations. One cook even prepared wild boar, whose head arrived at the table complete with an orange in its mouth. Two-pint beer rations were given out to other ranks whilst officers and senior NCOs received spirits. Following army tradition, the men's dinners were served by their officers and NCOs, who then departed to enjoy their own meals. In some towns processions made their way through the streets as tanks pulled sleighs upon which santas were seated, dispensing largesse to the population courtesy of the generosity of individual soldiers and the 'blind eye' of cooks and quartermasters.

A typical Christmas Day for those lucky enough to be out of the front line consisted of an ENSA concert, or show performed by unit members, followed by Christmas cake and mince pies, with dinner served in the evening. The lucky ones feasted on delights that would not have seemed out of place on peacetime tables. The meal enjoyed by Norman Kirby, a sergeant at Monty's HQ, far surpassed anything the people back home could have dreamt of – turkey, goose, pork chops, Brussels sprouts, baked potatoes, Yorkshire pudding, red wine, Christmas pudding, mince pies, oranges, beer, whisky and cigars.

The CO of the 1st Battalion Royal Norfolk Regiment offered a prize of one hundred bottles of beer for the company who could provide the best Christmas dinner, although the meal itself was postponed until they withdrew from the front line. Soon enthusiastic officers were travelling to base depots attempting to find sufficient cutlery and plates with which to serve the meals. War couldn't stand in the way of military tradition which dictated that football matches be played between the sergeants and the officers. The participants clothed themselves in fancy dress borrowed from local women and Dutch workmen. Strange local hats appeared on the heads of the players, whilst their feet sported clogs.

Local knowledge was a prerequisite for having a successful Christmas party. The attachment of a Belgian liaison officer to the HQ of the Canadian 4th Brigade was a positive boon – in peacetime he had been an Antwerp wine dealer who was sent by the Canadians to fetch quality wines from the south of France. Many took the opportunity to get drunk, if sufficient alcohol was available, and joined in sing-songs around the piano. They relished the freedom to let their hair down, unconcerned about the activities of the enemy. At parties all manner of carefully hoarded stocks of drink were mixed together into vast bowls of punch, and cocktails prepared. Junior officers mixed with their men and got drunk together, much to the disgust of some senior officers, and many drunken soldiers were found the next morning having been sick in their billets. Those daring to look forward knew that the next big excuse for a party would be the surrender of the German army – but first they had to survive.

Not all parties were scenes of such delight and for some Christmas was a let down. Such was the clamour to get parties started that carefully hoarded stocks of alcohol ran out within minutes. Once the drink had run out there was little left to do and they made their lonely way back to billets. The feelings of these men was perhaps an omen for what was to come for some of the units in the 21st Army Group. As the Christmas football matches were played in the snow, the players looked up to the skies to see German aircraft on their way to hit Allied positions in the Ardennes. Although primarily remembered as an American engagement, the Battle of the Bulge involved thousands of British soldiers. General Horrocks' 30 Corps were quickly deployed to curtail any threat of a German breakthrough and there was no turkey or mince pies for those fighting in the Ardennes. Instead many Christmas dinners consisted of compo rations heated up in snowbound slit trenches or inside tanks.

Northants Yeoman Michael Hunt recalled the sudden shock of being told to leave from comfortable billets to move to the Ardennes: 'We were in this cinema and about half way through the film was stopped. Somebody came on the stage, "Would all Military Police report back to their units immediately." So all the MPs in the audience got up and left. The film started again and about ten minutes they stopped it again. Then it was "will all Ordnance Corps and Service Corps men report back to their units". This went on and on. It was only at the end, when we were called out, that we heard the Ardennes offensive had started.' (41)

As 30 Corps rolled south it was decided fresh infantry were needed. With few reserves available the men of the Parachute Regiment were rushed from UK bases to join the battle. All seasonal thoughts were soon forgotten. The glorious repast they had expected back home was replaced by cheese and jam sandwiches eaten on the back of open trucks as they drove across the frozen Belgian countryside.

In some units the order to move came as they were sitting down to Christmas dinner. In minutes they had gulped down their meals and taken their places on trucks still clutching their bottles of beer. A lucky few had their departure times delayed to allow meals to be finished before moving out. Some, such as the tank crews of the Coldstream Guards, were interrupted during their Christmas Eve celebrations and told to be ready to move at first light. Most of the drunken and disappointed officers and men rapidly made their way to bed with a few staying up all night to begin their journey still inebriated. The Gordon Highlanders received orders to move on Christmas Day, and despite a number of drunken drivers and a shortage of maps, they completed the move, despite some comical sights including a naked NCO riding in a Bren carrier and waving a red flag at civilians.

If the upheavals of war had disturbed Christmas, there was no disguising the joy that accompanied New Year. From 1 January 1945 British newspapers were finally able to report the first arrivals of men on leave. In late 1944 there had been some disquiet among troops who thought senior officers would be going home for Christmas. At Calais a train carrying a number of senior officers heading back to England was the subject of graffiti. As the officers approached the train they beheld the work of irate soldiers. Painted along the sides of the carriages were the words 'And We Shall Be Spending Our Xmas Here!' (42) The announcement that leave would start in the New Year helped to abate any rising resentment. Suddenly men had something good to look forward to. They travelled home on what they jokingly referred to as 'Monty's Magic Carpet'. For most it was a journey home that brought delight to their waiting families, but for many the respite from war was to bring little more than mental anguish. Seven days wasn't long enough to forget their troubles, and what troubled them was the knowledge they had to return to war.

In the first seven months of campaigning there had been little opportunity to spare men for such long periods. It was only in the winter lull the army thought it suitable for men to visit their families. Of course the soldiers who were granted leave remained cynical about it. Though grateful to have the chance to go home, most felt the sudden generosity of the authorities meant they were being rested because something was looming on the horizon. The battles that were to follow the January announcement would prove them right.

The criteria for leave was that a soldier must have served continuously in the operational theatre for six months and not have had any home leave during those six months. Those who fulfilled these conditions could look forward to a seven-day break, plus two days for travelling. Once it was determined how many men were eligible for leave, the lucky men were selected by lottery. The lists were then subdivided on a monthly basis so that the leave would be issued on a 'First out, first home' basis. The anxious soldiers, including those not eligible for the draw, crowded round to see the first names drawn from a hat, all hoping to hear their own names, the names of their mates, or of particularly deserving men.

Despite the ballots, leave remained a contentious issue, with many front line soldiers feeling they were cheated out of their entitlement. Since the rules were standardised across the army, it became evident men serving in rear areas were receiving more of the allocated places. It seemed unfair but the hard truth was that fewer of the infantrymen and tank crews survived the necessary qualification period without being wounded or killed. In their place men who drove lorries or worked in fuel dumps and offices, claimed the places on the ships heading home. Despite the antagonisms arising from this, January saw the tactless announcement that leave vacancies for fighting troops were being scaled down since the allocation for Line of Communication formations had been underestimated. It was another cruel blow for the men whose sufferings were bringing victory ever closer.

As the first batches of soldiers started to trickle back home to 'blighty', their minds were in turmoil. As one soldier lucky enough to get home leave admitted in his diary: 'For seven days we shall be extremely happy and then for the next seven weeks we shall be bemoaning it.' (43) They were so desperate to get home but as the time drew closer the uncertainty grew. They were all smiles as they left their units. Their mates walked with them to lorries waiting to whisk them away to what they mockingly called 'the real world'. Everyone gave them encouragement, advice on what to say to their families, tips for impressing the ladies. Friends gave them letters and parcels to post, or made them promise to look up their parents if they lived in the same area. Then it was time to depart.

The issue of leave caused a complex web of emotions. As they got closer to home their hearts began to pound, few remained unemotional at their first glimpse of the English coast. Yet many recorded a sense of anti-climax, a feeling they had become outsiders. The soldiers soon boarded the trains that were to take them home and as the carriages snaked through the London suburbs to the stations where they would change trains to reach their home towns, it seemed they were entering another world. Seeing London so soon after leaving the battlefield was an unreal experience and left them feeling ill at ease. The rows of suburban houses, neat gardens, cars, buses and people all going about their daily routines seemed strange and for many the homecoming they had dreamed of could not meet their expectations.

The married men were perhaps the most fortunate. They had someone with whom to share the emotion of their return. It was not cups of tea and fireside chats they had missed but the real physical intimacy that only marriage could bring. They and their mates could buy as many nights with Belgian housewives as they liked but this was different. Lucky men often discovered their wives had taken a holiday from work to be with them and most were greeted with outpourings of emotion. Many of the waiting women had packed off their children to the homes of relatives so there would be no one to disturb them. Their husbands hardly crossed the threshold before they were whisked upstairs for the sex they had long dreamed of. If the initial sexual thrill was enough for some married men there were plenty of others who were not able to throw themselves into home life with such gusto. Others found their wives and girlfriends were working in factories, unable to get time off to spend with them. Even their children had to go to school during the day and would only be home at night.

Single men returned to their family homes realising how much they had

changed. War had aged them, they had grown up physically, mentally and emotionally, and outgrown the bedrooms of their childhood. There was no hiding the
genuine delight at seeing parents and siblings, but they felt they needed something
else. It was hard to relate experiences to the visitors who flocked to see them, how
could they explain the details of what they wanted to forget? If they wanted to be
alone, how could they tell people without offending them? Once home they felt
lost, they missed the sense of belonging, and the feeling that you really could trust
your friends with your life. Often they sought the company of old friends, hoping
to recreate the jovial camaraderie of the slit trench or tank turret. Few found it,
instead they realised most of the people they knew were themselves away serving
in the forces.

Family members soon noticed the change that had come over the returning soldiers. Men returned to their homes with little fanfare, often saying a brief hello to
their families and then going straight to bed. Others arrived home late at night
and, not wishing to awaken the family by knocking, simply curled up on the
doorstep in their greatcoats and slept until morning.

Although most faced a welcoming reception, not everything was to their satisfaction. There was no lack of generosity – they were ushered to the front of queues
at cinemas as doormen found seats for them despite 'House Full' notices, and
wives and mothers were offered extra food by shopkeepers – but the generosity
masked a lack of understanding about the situation in Europe. The realities of the
front seemed a million miles away from the lives of civilians whose perception of
war was shaped by newspapers and newsreels. Civilians would talk about the war
and what 'they' were fighting for. To the fighting men the civilians' views could not
have been further from reality. Any thoughts of a moral crusade, a campaign of
good against evil had been submerged beneath the fight for survival.

There also existed a warped belief that the British and Canadian armies were
playing a minor role. Some thought the Americans were shouldering most of the
burden, others considered all the western Allies were playing bit parts in the drama
of war. When Alexander Baron met William Rust, the editor of the *Daily Worker*
newspaper, he asked for help from communist MPs to highlight the need for warm
clothing at the front. Rust's reply highlighted the gap between reality and public
perception – he told Baron not to worry about such details since the Red Army
was winning the war. Others were less than amused to see restaurants advertising
table reservations for the victory night. Many more miles of hard fighting lay
ahead, yet the civilians appeared to see the campaign as almost over, to the annoyance of those who would be fighting and dying to earn them the chance to use
these reservations.

However, these were idle concerns compared to the one big question mark that
loomed over their leave – 'when are you going back?' Tank commander Ian
Hammerton, who had been in the first wave on D-Day, was unable fully to enjoy
his leave, but knew how some soldiers coped: 'I expect the feeling of not being able
to enjoy UK privilege leave was general and understandable unless one went on a
seven day bender!' (44) Boozing their way through leave was a simple solution for

those who liked a drink, but others just concentrated on getting on with life. Ken Hardy went home in early 1945: 'The idea of going back was appalling, but I was terribly resilient. You accept it. Like anything else that approaches day by day, you forget about going back until almost the last minute. Then it looms up on you. I didn't think about my return at first. I had enough nous to know that you weren't going to enjoy anything like that. The thing was to go, enjoy it and worry about it for the last 24 hours.' (45)

Not everyone was able to adapt in the way Hardy managed. The emotional burden of leaving after so brief a stay was too much for some men. Their minds dwelled on return and affected their stay. Fears for the future invaded the calm of their leave and some refused to return, instead going AWOL. A handful refused even to take home leave in the knowledge that they would not be able to handle the return to normality whilst knowing they would soon be going back into action, and others were reluctant to make the journey knowing their wives had been unfaithful.

Stan Procter was one of those men whose home leave was not enjoyable. Although he was unable to express it, the whole experience was a disappointment, and nothing seemed to turn out how he hoped. His emotions at seeing his girl-friend had not been what he was expecting. It was difficult for Procter to explain what he was feeling, and perhaps harder still for outsiders to understand. At the end of his leave his family and girlfriend held a party to mark his departure: 'I felt so miserable I could not get into any kind of party spirit. My inside felt like lead as they saw me off at the railway station. Saying goodbye to Audrey was like leav-ing part of me behind.' (46)

When it came time to return many soldiers and their wives were unwilling to be parted, with MPs having forcefully to separate them at railway stations. Deep down, many of the women never expected their husbands to return, they had spent weeks and months awaiting the dreaded War Office telegram saying their man was dead. But he had returned, relief had come and all too soon he had to return to battle. Soldiers returning to their units often became depressed, trying to regain that hard edge which their friends had never lost.

For those men who missed out on leave other entertainments had to be found. In the relatively peaceful days of winter many units began to produce newsletters. These were many and varied, some being revived in the post-war period as the newsletters of veterans' associations. These journals were lighthearted and poked fun at officialdom, making jokes on such subjects as the policy of non fraternisa-tion referring to German girlfriends as 'a bit of frat'. (47) After the German sur-render they became increasingly professional – editors bought up supplies of newsprint and operated out of German printing works. The mechanics of produc-ing the newspapers were fraught with difficulties, electricity shortages meant printing had to be done at night, a job popular with the German printers since they were given food which helped to supplement their meagre rations. Despite the difficulties the 5th Kings Regiment's 'Free Lance' eventually reached forty-eight pages.

RECREATION

Despite the newletters, home leaves, 48-hour passes and leisure opportunities, the men of 21st Army Group knew one thing – war's end was approaching and they wanted to be alive to see it. Looking ahead they made the decision – real leisure could only return once the war was over. Then they could relax.

8

A Man in Uniform

'I saw how conceited men are, especially young men, how like little children they are in wanting to dress up, look showy and adorn themselves with tribal clothing and badges. They want to show off to the girls'. (1)

'On active service I was something of a rebel – whilst on recce duties I never wore a hard hat, I wore a black leather jacket, air gauntlets, gumboots, a yellow neckerchief and a beret. I was never challenged by senior officers, they seemed to be very lax.' (2)

Every year thousands of tourists descend on London to witness the pomp and pageantry of Britain's heritage. At the centre of this are the traditional military displays of the Changing of the Guard and Trooping of the Colour. These soldiers of the Guards regiments and the Household Cavalry, with their spotless uniforms and synchronised drill, are the very picture of British military tradition. These are the descendants of the men sent all over the globe to serve the Empire. It was a tradition where ability and efficiency was sometimes perceived as secondary to appearance. British military mythology is full of tales of men fighting colonial wars with their swelteringly hot woollen tunics buttoned to the neck – 'Mad Dogs and Englishmen' indeed.

For the traditionalists razor sharp creases, gleaming brass, shining boots and faultless drill were the bedrock upon which discipline was based. The scrubbing, polishing and creasing were supposed to give men pride in their regiment, its traditions and its former glories. New recruits during the Second World War were subjected to the same exacting standards, they were depersonalised and their identity was merged into that of the group. Little wonder many soldiers would use their uniform to express individuality as soon as the opportunity arose.

The basis of all uniforms of the period was the battledress, a two piece outfit of blouson jacket and loose fitting trousers made from rough khaki serge. Though of the same design as the British version, the Canadian battledress was cut from a superior cloth and came in a darker shade. Whatever the cloth, the battledress – either Canadian or British – remained an unpopular garment and most of its wearers thought they were the worst dressed army in Europe. Even to this day there is no mincing of words when describing their clothes: 'Our uniform? Nobody liked our uniform. It was bloody hopeless!' (3) They laughed that the jacket had the ability to make them look pregnant in front and hunchbacked in the rear. It was almost impossible to make battledress look smart – if the blouse fitted whilst standing up it would ride up as soon as the wearer bent down. The trousers were not much better. Tall thin men found they hung slackly, needing to be pulled in at the waist, the crotches hanging down towards their knees, whilst stout men found the trousers too tight across the seat. It was not just the design that irritated the soldiers. The rough, hairy material acted like sandpaper scratching at the tender skin of the crotch, leaving the flesh chafed.

What really mattered was not what they looked like but how they fared in battle. During the warm days of summer they might curse the rough serge but come the long cold nights of winter the battledress came into its own. The heavy cloth was considered far superior to the lightweight cloth of the American uniforms. The GIs may have looked smarter but in the life and death situations of a northern European winter the battledress was a clear winner. One Canadian veteran later noted how he retained his two pairs of battledress trousers to use as work clothes. The material was so strong it took him twenty years to wear out both pairs. The material needed to be strong – after all, as one signaller commented: 'the uniform was not for fashion shows'. (4)

For winter each man was issued with a thick double-breasted greatcoat. Unchanged since the First World War it was unsuitable for modern war. Instead brown leather jerkins were preferred in place of the greatcoat – having no sleeves they allowed a greater freedom of movement.

If the uniforms had changed little since the beginning of the war at least headgear had undergone many changes. The old style steel helmets, that had seemed outdated compared to German helmets even back in the Great War, were finally being phased out. In their place came a sleeker, tortoise shell-shaped model, that was used by most infantry units. This model offered greater protection to the head and neck and remained the basis for the British infantry helmet for years to come.

There were many other styles of headgear for use when the helmet was not needed. The ludicrous forage caps of the early war years had been replaced in all but a few regiments. The forage cap, commonly known as the 'cunt cap' due to its shape, had served little purpose apart from annoying drill instructors when it fell from the heads of new recruits. In its place most regiments had adopted the general service cap, a floppy brown hat not dissimilar in design to the tam o'shanters of the Scottish regiments. This cap – sloppy, misshapen and scruffy – was the perfect accompaniment to the battledress. Though smarter, the beret was only adopted by certain units. The men of the motorised infantry battalions wore brown berets, commandos had green, airborne forces maroon, and tank crews black. Men could also be identified by the angle at which hats were worn. The general rule was that berets, tams and caps should always angle to the right, except in Irish regiments who wore them to the left. Royal Armoured Corps men learned to wear their black beret to the rear of their heads whilst the Yeomanry wore them to the side. And paratroops tended to wear their red berets square upon the top of the head. It was all a matter of tradition, designed to bind the men into a cohesive unit.

As if the discomfort of battledress were not enough, boots seemed designed to heap more misery upon the troops. The peculiar nuances of the ammunition boot with its grained leather, hobnailed soles and 'horseshoe' heels was to be the bane of many a soldier's life as they shone them for parades and then dulled them for life in the field. The boots were impressive when stamping in unison on the parade ground but worn in the streets they took some getting used to. New recruits found themselves walking tentatively over cobblestones, especially when wet, and watched in awe as sparks shot out beneath their feet when taking new boots across gravel. At first painfully uncomfortable and unmanageable, the boots soon proved to be without equal – it was not without reason that the boot manufacturers of eastern Northamptonshire were famed worldwide for their military footwear. Almost unbearably hard to break in, the boots eventually moulded themselves to the feet of their owners offering them comfort and protection where lesser footwear would have been found wanting. Like the battledress they may not have looked stylish on the dance floor, but on the battlefield they knew no equal.

In the early years of the war as the infantrymen in the UK were complaining about the constant creasing and polishing, others were changing the look of their uniforms. As the war progressed a new realism crept into the way the soldiers dressed.

With the failure of the campaign in France in 1940 the public were in search of heroes. The first offering was 'The Few'. The young pilots of the Battle of Britain were to capture the imagination of the public. They flew in shirtsleeves, their feet clad in soft shoes, their necks wrapped in coloured scarves and hair worn fashionably long. They were followed into the hearts of the public by the 8th Army, the victors of El Alamein. These men were a breed apart, with an appearance that would have incurred the wrath of sergeant majors on the parade ground. Men wore a variety of headgear – tin helmets, solar topees, forage caps, bush hats, woollen cap comforters and even Arab headdress – whatever was comfortable. Pullovers, unseen and unacceptable back home, became *de rigueur*.

Clothes were worn to taste with men sporting a combination of tropical khaki drill and battledress, some men in long trousers others in shorts. Suede boots became popular. Many officers took to wearing comfortable civilian clothing, or as they called it 'mufti', purchased on visits to Cairo or Alexandria. One officer recorded going into captivity wearing a golf jacket, corduroy trousers, pink shirt, silk scarf and suede boots.

These were the men who fought and won the battles that turned the tide of war. Not the spotless Guardsmen whose image graced postcards and advertisements, but the unkempt men of some of the less fashionable regiments of the British army who continued the campaign through Sicily and Italy where their style underwent more permutations. In the blisteringly hot sun some took to wearing the wide brimmed straw hats favoured by the locals. The appearance of one soldier finally caused General Montgomery to act. After spotting a lorry driver minus his shirt, but wearing a top hat he issued his only order about uniforms – that top hats should not be worn in the 8th Army.

The public back home agreed with Monty, you needed victory before you could have a parade. By 1944 the soldiers waiting for the forthcoming landings in France, were aware of one thing – once battle began the barrack room standards would slip and comfort become the overriding issue.

The hard fighting of the Normandy campaign soon brought changes to the look of the men – gone were the parade ground creases, polished boots and shining badges – now the look of the survivors would have had their drill sergeants in paroxysms of fury. As Alexander Baron wrote to his family on the first anniversary of D-Day: 'If you wanted to dress like a comic opera pirate you could.' (5) In the heat of summer the soldiers had to adapt their clothing to make it more comfortable. The warm serge of the battledress was the first thing to go. It was too heavy and rubbed at their necks. At first they unbuttoned their blouses and rolled back the cuffs, then they removed them, strapped them into their webbing, and fought in their shirtsleeves. The ever busy artillerymen stood for hours under the scorching sun firing their guns. For comfort they stripped off their jackets and shirts, and in extreme cases even worked in bathing trunks.

The relaxation of the standards of discipline over uniforms allowed men to express themselves with small details of their attire. Whole units picked roses from the bushes that lined the roads of France to decorate their hats and the traditional English symbol shone out from the dull massed ranks clad in khaki. Men picked up umbrellas from the ruins of villages and marched en masse sheltering under the canopies. Among the regulated and restricted masses in uniform such displays were an expression of individuality. It said that they were bound, first and foremost, to their comrades as opposed to the army as a whole. By appearing casual they were attempting to feel casual, as Sergeant William Partridge explained: 'The psychological advantages of going into battle with your tunic collar turned up and one hand in your pocket, when possible, cannot be overemphasised.' (6) By January 1945 MPs inspecting standards of dress among troops found the practice of turning up collars was more than just widespread, it was 'universal'. (7)

These simple stylistic gestures were just the start of a movement among the soldiers towards making their own fashion statements. These were young men, with the same interests as all men of their age. Fashion was of interest in civilian life and remained of interest whilst in uniform. In the heat and glare of Normandy sunglasses became popular and throughout the campaign scarves were widely worn by the soldiers. For some it was decoration and for others just comfort. Scarves prevented the battledress collar from chafing against the neck. Even as adornments they were undoubtedly handy, being used as protection against the weather, as a facemask against smoke or dust, and for mopping up sweat. The scarves ranged between the extravagant and simplistically functional. For the most basic neckwear they tore strips from camouflage face veils and tied it around the neck like a choker. For more decoration they picked up tablecloths from the wreckage of houses and cafés, tore strips of coloured silk from the parachutes or simply took women's headscarves from abandoned homes. Various styles became popular – the airborne drop to the east of the Rhine left plenty of various coloured parachutes littering the fields. In the days that followed there would be a craze amongst soldiers for having the brightest silk scarf. The craze continued into the final days of the war with a German pilot reporting how he landed in a field only to be met by infantrymen who ignored him and instead cut up his parachute to tie around their necks.

The changes made by men in the front lines had to remain minor. Anything that made them stand out would also make them a target for snipers. Helmets might be abandoned when out of the line, but were essential protection at most times. However, there were few men who did take chances. During Operation Varsity Canadian paratroopers were seen going into action wearing bowler hats. One man even sported a multicoloured ice hockey sweater with a number five on the back. They may have looked relaxed but it was a look that was never going to catch on.

Whilst most riflemen could only make minor adjustments to their uniforms some of their colleagues were dressing up to a degree few could have expected before they arrived on the Continent. Vehicle crews noted how unlikely it was that anyone would be dressed alike – one man might wear battledress, another a tank suit, a third a leather jerkin, and so on. They had an unprecedented freedom, as one veteran recalled:

> We didn't wear the uniform as such. But being on the carriers, we had the engine between us, which was bloody boiling hot. So we didn't need a jacket and were mainly in shirtsleeves, rolled up. You mainly wore what you wanted to wear. Somebody would have a top hat, someone else a lovely coloured waistcoat. The chap with the top hat he wore it for a long time, he was on the carriers so nobody bothered him. Stupid things, all black humour. There were no problems with this, but it depended on the officers. Maybe if you fooled about in the front lines there would be problems, but if we were moving back or moving up to the lines, they didn't bother. We had a bloke on our carrier who wore slippers! The officers never saw it because he was in the carrier, but he always had his boots ready in case somebody came along. But he loved his slippers. It was just a way of expressing yourself. (8)

The top hat worn by the crewman in this carrier was not unique. It was a style that was one of the most popular throughout the campaign. While out of the line many men took to wearing non-regulation headgear – straw sunhats, fur hats, bowlers, trilbys – but it was the top hat that really caught their imagination. The upper class connotations of these hats amused the soldiers. What greater contrast could there be between the finery of a gentleman and the battered battledress of the Tommies and Canucks. In the moments before the start of Operation Market Garden General Horrocks noticed a complete carrier crew all sporting tall black hats. During the battles around Oosterbeek, outside Arnhem, one NCO kept his men entertained by walking around wearing an extremely tall top hat that he claimed made him impervious to shellfire. Somehow, once again, the 'high ups' in the army misjudged the mood of the men. Whilst the soldiers were fighting well – succeeding in their tasks, driving the enemy back, advancing slowly towards Germany – the Provost Corps were being told to check up on the headgear of the soldiers. With hundreds of men wearing comical civilian hats the MPs were being instructed to make sure berets and caps were being correctly worn on top of heads, rather than hanging off the side or the back.

Slippers and top hats were not the only unlikely items being worn by men at the front. John Mercer had an unusual solution to make the serge of his battledress less irritating to his skin: 'I was the most civilian of soldiers. Underneath my battledress I wore pyjama trousers. It was so the trousers didn't scratch my legs, because it was very hot in Normandy. I had eczema as a child and I was afraid of getting it again. So I wore the pyjamas. My friends used to kid me about it but I didn't care because those battledress trousers could rub you up in a horrible way.' (9)

Although most soldiers found pleasure in dressing down whenever they had an opportunity, they wanted to be as smart as possible when they came into contact with civilians. Men going on leave were irritated by their shapeless uniforms. Even after pressing out the creases they realised battledress would not compete with the GIs' uniforms. The Americans went on leave dressed in their best uniforms – smart trousers, skirted jackets, shoes and a collared shirt with tie. The British and Canadians feared the Yanks would 'pull all the good looking birds' leaving them with the dregs – all the cheapest, ugliest whores northern Europe had to offer. The Tommies and Canucks felt they looked like binmen compared to the distinguished-looking Americans. Indeed, even with their best uniforms, the officers of 21st Army Group could not compare to the average American riflemen.

In an attempt to redress the balance the soldiers defied regulations and contrived to get ties to wear whilst on leave. Such was the disquiet among the troops that the rules were changed to correspond with the unofficial changes. From late 1944 other ranks were permitted to leave open the top button of their battledress blouse and to wear collars and ties when off duty. For men going on leave it made a welcome change to appear smart and, hopefully, impress the women of Brussels. The only problem was that few had access to either collared shirts or ties. Once more the soldiers had to improvise and when MPs began to check on their ties and shirts they discovered many were wearing unauthorised patterns, including large numbers who had managed to acquire officer's pattern shirts and ties. Others had resorted to trading with their American allies, for whom ties were an integral part of the uniform. In some units the men would group together and share a collared shirt and tie. This would be given to each man in turn as he went on leave, ensuring a suitably refined image. When it came time for John Mercer to visit Brussels he and his mates were fortunate in the company they kept: 'We were allowed to wear collars, ties and shoes, but we hadn't got any shoes so we pinched some. One of my mates was a tailor's cutter. He sat down on his haunches and altered our shirts, making us collars and ties.' (10)

A number of men made further efforts to look their best and make subtle alterations to their uniforms. They took their trousers to local tailors and had them altered to fit. The soldiers wanted a better fit around the waist and seat and for the legs to be less baggy, similar to the GIs' trousers. However, some senior officers were not keen on these adjustments and ordered their officers to check for men making these changes. The commanding officer of the 1/5th Queens Regiment ordered checks to be carried out on its men. Between 15 and 17 January 1945 full kit inspections took place with prizes of 48-hour leave passes and free NAAFI issue for the best turned out men. Tailors' tickets, indicating unofficial alterations, were just one criteria of the inspections. Officers were also instructed to check uniforms for the correct number of buttons on shirts, that socks were correctly darned, there were no oil stains on battledress, boots were laced properly and that trousers hung in the correct manner. The timing of these checks seems strange since on the 17th the battalion took sixty-eight casualties – men who would not have been spared by having correctly laced boots and the correct number of shirt buttons.

In extreme cases some officers were downright antagonistic towards their men, shouting: 'Are you sunbathing?' (11) just because a man had his top button undone. Regiments with long, distinguished histories tended towards a greater emphasis on smartness. With such a wide range of standards, the Guards sought to uphold their tradition of being the best turned out soldiers in the British army. They held full 'spit and polish' parades whilst their comrades fought battles less than a mile away. Their officers noted with derision how scruffy most of the other British soldiers were, thinking them even worse turned out than the Americans.

Not all officers were concerned about the appearance of their men. There were plenty who thought what counted was their fighting ability. Many of these were the new, wartime officers, who were not tied up in military tradition. Ken Hardy, a twenty-one-year-old platoon commander in the Hallams, was none too impressed with the exacting standards expected within his unit: 'We were expected to dress up as far as we could on every single day. I know there were divisions out in Europe where you could dress down. But in my lot, the 49th Division, you couldn't.' With the emphasis on washing, shaving and keeping tidy, Hardy felt it possible the performance of the unit was affected: 'I sometimes feel it adversely affected their performance. Because time was taken up keeping clean that could have been better spent in other ways. It had rewards, but I don't think they were all that great. I think those units that came to a sensible compromise did better. But our discipline was pretty strict all the time.' (12)

Such beliefs were not uncommon. One anonymous veteran who 'dressed down', voiced his opinions of the time wasted on 'bullshit' rather more directly. As a member of a top Yeomanry tank regiment his attitude towards the uniform was more relaxed than might have been tolerated in some regiments: 'In our regiment you could get away with things like that. But the Guards couldn't, and consequently the Guards weren't any good. Well, they weren't as good as us.' (13)

The attitudes of such men showed how the disciplinary standards of the old elites were not carried through into some of the newer formations of the army. The tank regiments and armoured yeomanry regiments had a lax attitude towards clothing. The pioneers of tank warfare had been military revolutionaries, men who were looking forward to a new kind of war, not looking back at the battles of two hundred years before. This spirit was passed down to the wartime crews, some of whom seemed to have little more than a passing knowledge of the accepted dress codes. The officers of the Royal Tank Regiments considered themselves the elite of mobile armoured warfare, feeling they were more professional than the recently armoured Guards or the dashing figures of the newly armoured cavalry regiments. The cavalrymen thought likewise, they were an elite, they may have traded their horses for tanks and armoured cars but many were still determined to show their fighting abilities with the reckless abandon that had characterised cavalry warfare through history.

Hand in hand with the image of the brave warrior thrusting through the enemy line came a sartorial style that seemed a direct heir of the cavaliers of the English Civil War. Of all the men making stylistic amendments to their uniforms the tank officers were to display more abandon than most of their comrades. Unlike infantry officers, who needed to blend in with the other ranks to avoid observation by the enemy, tank commanders were already conspicuous since they usually sat on the rims of their turrets. There was no point in being disguised and so they dressed as they felt most comfortable. This was a spirit shown throughout the armoured units. In many regiments it became *de rigueur* to dress in the 'Eighth Army Style' of scarves, cords and desert boots. Not all were actually veterans of the North African campaign but they liked the idea of appearing to be confident, experienced soldiers.

Tank commander Ken Tout described the officers of his regiment, the 1st Northants Yeomanry: 'The officers look as though they are dressed for a fancy dress ball. One has a leather jerkin. Another is wearing denim overalls. One has a cricket sweater on. Others are in full battledress. One or two are in shirtsleeves. Trousers range from sloppy corduroys to sloppy serge.' (14) Other items of clothing seen in use by tank officers in Normandy included fur-lined leather jackets and even a Harlequins rugby shirt. Tout recalled seeing one of his officers being reprimanded for his appearance: 'Lt Tony Faulkner was wearing German jackboots, riding breeches and a coloured scarf in a remote outpost in Holland when the Brigadier unexpectedly appeared. Brig. Scott, a strict disciplinarian but respected leader, bawled him out – shouting "get some bloody proper uniform on and try to look like an officer!" '(15)

With the tank officers dressing up, their crews were taking dressing down to extreme levels. Supposedly they should have worn battledress, boots and overalls, with a tank helmet perched upon their heads. However there were few men who ever wore a complete uniform. They had been ordered to wear their helmets, yet they also had to wear headphones in order to communicate and the two could not be worn together. The inevitable result was that helmets were soon abandoned – one soldier reported losing his when his ship was sunk off the Normandy coast, yet eleven months later it had been neither replaced nor missed. Goggles were also a problem since many tankmen found the ones they were issued with were almost useless. They too were abandoned, replaced with sunglasses or substituted by captured German goggles. It was not only their eyes that were assaulted by dust. In the heat of the Normandy summer tank crews found that the ventilation system drew dust from the dry roads into their tanks. As a result crews needed facemasks so that they could breathe comfortably. With the usual spirit of improvisation they tore up strips of parachute silk that they tied around their faces to keep their mouths and nostrils clear.

If the discomfort of dust was not enough the tank crews had to endure high temperatures. With the summer sun beating down on their steel hulls and the huge engines constantly throbbing, tanks became unbearably hot. In the stifling environment of the tanks most abandoned battledress. Instead beneath their overalls they wore shorts or underwear. Many went bare chested, neckerchiefs became essential for wiping away sweat and webbing was discarded. The abandonment of belts and gaiters was an essential to survival. When their tanks were hit they had just seconds to get out. The crews were petrified belts and holsters would snag on the inside of the tank. The seconds it would take to get free could mean the difference between life and death.

Ken Tout recalled that only one man in his crew wore the full uniform, but even he wore civilian shoes, since the regulation hobnail boots were too dangerous to wear in a steel tank. They were too slippy, the hobnails making the men slide across the steel plates. Instead they chose footwear to give them purchase and civilian shoes, slippers and PT pumps were favoured. Even those who insisted on wearing their boots removed the hobnails and trusted leather soles over hobnails.

There was another good reason for not wearing boots. Sitting or standing almost motionless inside a cramped tank for hours upon hours in the heat of summer meant their feet were prone to swelling. Some tank men experienced excruciating pain as the leather and laces cut into their swollen flesh. To counteract this problem PT pumps were the preferred choice, sometimes they slashed them with razor blades to allow the feet to breathe.

The officers of the armoured regiments had little choice but to accept the appearance of their men. Since the officers were dressing up the men couldn't be stopped from dressing down. When a new squadron sergeant major arrived in a unit of the 1st Northants Yeomanry in September 1944 he was appalled by the state of the troopers. Their hair was long, their faces unshaven, brasses unpolished and battledress worn without creases. Much to the chagrin of the crews they were told to smarten themselves up, but luckily they had a friend in high places. The SSM was called in by the CO and told to abandon his infantry standards, what mattered was not the state of their clothing but the condition of their tanks. Members of the regiment recalled how he later faced retribution from officers for his attempts to enforce discipline. Ken Squires remembered:

> The SSM had a habit of having his cuffs turned up. Well, Captain Bill Fox and Lt 'Plonk' Faulkner both liked to do this. Hank Bevan was talking to Bill Fox and up comes the sergeant major. Bill Fox looks at him and says 'Sergeant Major, you are improperly dressed!' He looks at himself, there are no buttons undone, nothing wrong. Bill says 'Let me tell you this, Sergeant Major, there are two people in this squadron who are allowed to have their cuffs turned back. One is Lt Faulkner and the other one isn't you! So turn your bloody cuffs down.' And he never rolled his cuffs back again. (16)

Whilst the officers of tank regiments could dress up, the situation was very different in the infantry. Infantry officers, whether they approved or disapproved of the way their men were dressing, had their own concerns. Many officers adopted a deliberately relaxed image, as if offering a direct challenge to the precise military bearing of the German officer class. The immaculate, monocle-wearing Prussian officer with high collared jacket, shaven head and duelling scars had long been a comic figure in British eyes. This pompous, overbearing and unemotional character had become a figure of fun during the First World War, a satirised amalgamation of the Kaiser and his officer class. This stereotype was perpetuated by Hollywood throughout the 1920s and 1930s. And now British officers became a visual antidote to such military precision.

With service dress put aside for the duration of the war, officers wore battledress. They could choose either issue battledress or have an individual suit made by a tailor. If they wore the issue battledress blouse they could have the collar altered so that the jacket lining was not visible. Photographs of senior officers show a wide variety of styles – some wearing the most basic 'Economy Issue' blouses, without alterations, some wearing tailored jackets with various shapes and sizes of lapel. Men like Brigadier Roscoe Harvey favoured a modern image and wore a battledress blouse with a zipped front giving it the appearance of a civilian jacket. Others like Major General Thomas, commander of the 43rd Division, resembled a cross between a Great War general and the villain in a Victorian melodrama – wearing riding boots, breeches and a long leather coat.

Many of the new breed of officers did not have the financial backing to afford the luxury of tailor-made uniforms. Instead they wore exactly the same outfit as their men. For those in the front line this was to be a godsend. During their training they had been taught how German snipers would be able to pick them out by their apparel and therefore they should attempt to blend in with the rest of the men. John Majendie, commanding an infantry company, remembered: 'Dress regulations were relaxed. I think that when we went to France we were told Monty had said officers can dress as they like. Some people took that very literally, although you never saw officers dressed as civilians!' (17) Ken Hardy was one of those subalterns who enjoyed the anonymity of dressing to merge in with his platoon. He recalled:

> I knew about dressing down before I went out to Normandy. I never carried a pistol, I never carried a map and I never carried binoculars. If I did they were underneath my jacket. But I carried a rifle from the word go. I mean you want to live! We all realised you had to dress accordingly. The senior officers accepted this. They didn't do likewise, but they realised us platoon commanders weren't going to live very long if we didn't dress like privates. It stood me in hellish good stead. (18)

They also discarded compass cases and their ties and wore black boots rather than brown. No badges of rank were visible, officers removed the cloth pips from their epaulettes or hung their camouflage face veils over their shoulders, and NCOs removed the stripes from their sleeves.

In response to these visual changes some platoons transformed their whole manner of operating whilst on the battlefield. The men realised how strange the operations of some infantry platoons must have appeared to outsiders, since at times it would appear that no one was in charge. Everyone was equally scruffy and no one called each other by titles, instead to confuse the snipers, who might distinguish words and phrases called out in English, ranks were replaced with Christian names. The necessities of combat caused a gradual democratisation of units, and in some cases orders came not from the officers but from the man in the best position. Some officers even stopped using hand signals to guide their platoons. Instead they controlled the movements by blasts on a whistle, thinking that blowing a whistle was more discreet than obvious hand movements. It was as if there had been a sudden democratisation of the whole army. When the appearance of the officers shocked some civilians they deluded themselves that the officers and men dressed the same because as a truly democratic force there needed to be no distinction between ranks. Such was the homogeneity of the look that frequently German prisoners were heard to ask how an army managed to function when there seemed to be no officers.

Whilst most officers were dressing down to avoid recognition some were dressing to stand out. Though few and far between, they were the ones who made an indelible impression in the minds of the men who watched them go into action. Peter Young, commanding No 3 Commando, was seen wearing an Arab headdress during the fighting in Normandy. In the final anarchic weeks of the war the SAS were let off the leash in northern Germany to cause chaos and confusion behind the enemy lines. One officer led his jeep patrols wearing a top hat and corduroy trousers with the style and individuality that so characterised that unit's wartime activities. Others took to wearing two revolvers on their belts giving them the appearance of western gunslingers. Major Tatham-Warter, of the 2nd Battalion Parachute Regiment, actually went into action at Arnhem carrying an umbrella since he felt it would make him instantly recognisable to his men as no German would ever carry such an item. Such images of individuality were enhanced by the flamboyant actions of some officers – such as one who carried a fencing sword into action. He directed his troops by pointing out their objectives with the sword whilst standing in his jeep.

What made these men exceptional was that most were specialists, precious few infantry officers were prepared to take such risks. One who did was the commander of 18 Platoon, 4th Battalion Somerset Light Infantry, twenty-year-old Lieutenant Sydney Jary. Not only did he successfully lead an infantry platoon in battle but he managed it at all times dressed in his own variation on the dress code. His outfit should have acted like a beacon for snipers – brown cord slacks, a beret, a woollen pullover complete with badges of rank, a pistol, and latterly an umbrella. And yet somehow he avoided the attention of snipers, maybe they thought, like some American soldiers he met, that he must be a civilian? Or as the man himself commented: 'Put it down to luck.' (19)

Of the officers prepared to dress up for battle only a few were willing to make the supreme gesture of wearing the traditional dress of the Highland regiments. The traditional kilts of the Scottish and Canadian Scottish regiments had not been worn on active service since the early days of the Great War. It was considered too dangerous for bare legs to be exposed to the rigours of modern warfare. Despite orders some Scots officers were defiant and continued to wear their kilts in battle. Some thought it only correct to be 'properly' dressed for their moment of glory. A number of airborne officers wore their kilts in battle during Operation Market Garden much to the surprise of Dutch civilians who had never previously seen men in 'skirts'. However, one of the proud kilt wearers was to die when attempting to swim across the Rhine during the evacuation from Arnhem. The heavy woollen fabric became waterlogged and, too weak to continue, he drowned in the fast flowing river.

It was not only the soldiers' apparel that was undergoing changes – their hairstyles were also influenced by war. The extremes of the 'short back and sides' so favoured by sergeant majors was slowly to disappear from their heads. In its place came more relaxed styles. In preparation for D-Day some men adopted unusual hairstyles. Crew cuts became popular and some of the more adventurous, such as Canadian paratroopers, shaved the sides of their heads for the 'Mohican' look. One soldier even had his head shaved leaving the three dots and a dash of the 'V for Victory' morse code sign, and others shaved their hair into diamonds or square patterns. Haircuts were also used as a distinctive mark of identity. One tank commander noted how the crews of the recovery vehicles in his regiment went without headgear to show off their shaven heads.

Even on D-Day, as the fighting raged, those troops passing through villages and towns stopped for haircuts at barbershops. They sat silently, still soaked from wading ashore and still clutching their weapons, as they waited their turn in the barber's chair. In the months following D-Day hair became increasingly unkempt. With the escalation of the fighting there were few opportunities for the soldiers to get haircuts and their appearance deteriorated. As their hair grew it got increasingly greasy and dirty, matching their weatherbeaten skin and often unshaven chins. Unable to wash their bodies, the soldiers certainly had little interest in getting water to wash their hair. What attention it did get was from standing bareheaded in the rain, or dunking their heads in cattle troughs. What with sleeping in the open, not washing hair and wearing helmets for hours upon end their hair began to take on weird shapes. Vigorous combing would be needed to reintroduce partings, smooth out unruly curls and get the men looking suitable for the parade ground.

It would only be once the fighting had died down that the soldiers had a chance to visit barbers. Once leave had been initiated the soldiers were able to take advantage of their forty-eight hours of freedom to get a professional haircut. One of the first destinations of many soldiers were barbers, where they would have their hair lovingly treated. Once newly coiffured the soldiers would then go to photographic studios to have their portraits taken to be sent home to their families. The only problem was that Continental hairdressers seemed to have a different idea as to how men's hair should be treated from the barbers back at home. They left hair longer than regulation length and used oils and waxes to shape the hair in a way few soldiers had previously encountered. Men who found their hair treated in this way found themselves the subject of ridicule. Their mates laughed at them, calling them 'poofs' and comparing them to the pampered poodles carried by French women.

Despite the ridicule, hairstyles began to change, the shaven sides and backs disappeared and the tops got longer and wavier. Soon large waves of hair were appearing from the front of their general service caps as the off-duty soldiers pushed the hats back as far as possible to show off ever-growing quiffs. These changes would be fully realised in the post-war years when the former soldiers and the youth of Britain reacted to the regulation haircuts and wore their hair ever longer.

If the look of the soldiers had changed during the summer, it was nothing compared to the changes seen in winter. In the bitter winter of 1944-45 officers and men took to wearing any available items of clothing which would keep out the cold. Field Marshal Montgomery went so far as to wear as many as ten pullovers under his uniform. Despite this example, few went as far as the officer encountered by Dirk Bogarde at the HQ of a unit he was visiting. The officer, who was on the staff of a homosexual major general, was reclining on cushions, smoking a Balkan Sobranie cigarette, and wearing a mink-lined jerkin with lynx fur collar. He also admitted to wearing bathing trunks under his battledress trousers since they frustrated the advances of the major general when he tried to put his hands through his flies.

Few would be so luxuriously attired as this officer but with the onset of winter the soldiers needed more protection than that offered by their battledress, leather jerkins and greatcoats. The infantry were in a difficult position. It was essential for them to recognise each other during battle, their lives depended on it. They could not just dress up in any warm clothes they fancied for fear of being confused with enemy soldiers. There was also the question of comfort and mobility. Any extra clothing needed to be light enough to ensure they retained their agility and loose enough to allow them to operate their weapons efficiently. As the weather began to turn, long underwear and pullovers were dug out from packs, pulled on, and kept on for weeks at a time. Next came the greatcoats, designed to be worn over the webbing and equipment. The problem for the infantrymen was that these brown double-breasted coats were too cumbersome for use in action. To remedy this some soldiers cut the bottom off the coat, just keeping it as long as the skirt of a jacket. This innovation kept the upper body warm whilst allowing the legs to move unimpeded. The only problem with this was the wearer would also have to endure wearing the shortened coat at night. Without the extra material the coat just was not large enough to snuggle down in at night.

Fortunately with the lines static for much of the winter the infantry, like their colleagues in tanks and artillery, were able to acquire and wear all manner of clothing to help ward off the cold. Some traded with Americans and wore the GI combat over their battledress. Both Airborne smocks and the windproof smocks of mountain troops were increasingly requested by infantry units to help ward off the cold. The only men who were fortunate enough to be well catered for were the crews of tanks and other armoured vehicles. They were issued with a water-proofed, wool- lined oversuit, that was truly efficient at keeping the worst of winter at bay. The success and popularity of the oversuits was noticed by how often they were 'acquired' by men in other units.

Without sufficient supplies of winter clothing necessity once more became the mother of invention as the British and Canadian soldiers found extra clothing from sources closer to hand. They were forced to utilise whatever they could beg, borrow or steal. Men took to wearing multiple layers – possibly several pullovers, extra shirts and vests, two pairs of gloves or even more than one greatcoat. Shivering soldiers wrote to their mothers to send knitted scarves, gloves and bala-clavas. Some Canadian gunners cut the sleeves from greatcoats and sewed them onto leather jerkins to make warm jackets. The cold was such that this was not the time to worry about the niceties of relations with local civilians. Civilian homes were raided by soldiers to find spare clothing to be worn underneath their uni-forms. The soldiers rifled through drawers, stole jumpers, underwear, scarves and pairs of socks. They even took sheepskin rugs, wrapped them around their bodies and put their leather jerkins over the top to hold the skins in place. And if they didn't find rugs to use they could always make their own waistcoats from the pelts of the animals they killed for food. The most desperate individuals took to wear-ing all manner of rags – curtains, carpets and blankets were all worn by men eager to protect themselves from the elements. They also wore snowcapes made from bedsheets, since too few regulation outfits were available. In the absence of suit-able winter overboots Wellington boots became popular and in desperation sand-bags were filled with straw and these were tied around the boots to prevent the feet from freezing.

In time supplies were made available from official sources. The contents of the enemy supply dumps, liberated during the 'Swan', were now brought out of stor-age. With the German army equipped to fight on the Eastern Front they had numerous warm weather items. Fur hats and coats, sheepskins, and even parkas camouflaged with what appeared to be tiger stripes all began to appear on the backs of Allied servicemen. Vast stocks of the captured clothing were put to good use by individual units. Stocks also began to appear from the UK. All manner of winter clothing was issued to the troops – including duffel coats, fur-lined RAF boots, sea boot socks and even rabbit fur waistcoats. They may no longer have looked like soldiers but at least they were warm.

In Holland and Belgium some off-duty soldiers took to wearing the clogs favoured by the locals. They claimed the felt lining made the clogs warmer and more comfortable than boots. With all manner of winter clothing in use it was easy to tell who was a veteran and who was a new arrival. When reinforcements arrived in forward areas it was like a clash of two cultures. The veterans looked on in wonder at how the incoming men wore polished boots rather than Wellingtons.

Officers couldn't believe that map cases or holsters still existed.

Making jokes at the expense of the spick and span image of new arrivals was just one way the soldiers exploited their uniforms to provide light relief. From the very early days of the campaign the soldiers used dressing up in any clothes they found as a way of relieving the tensions of war. In the aftermath of battle soldiers went into houses and picked out the most ridiculous apparel with which to entertain their mates. Men were seen walking through the bomb-shattered streets dressed as if for a wedding, one man in a top hat and a fellow 'Tommy' on his arm, a wedding dress and veil over his uniform.

A veteran infantryman of the 7th Armoured Division remembered the behaviour of his comrades:

> If you were going down the road and there was a house that had been knocked about a bit, you'd go in and come out with a saucepan on your head. Everyone would have a damn good laugh. It was mainly just humour, all done just to have a laugh. And any silly thing goes …. They'd pick up a woman's handbag and wear knickers and a brassiere over their uniform. They'd come out of the house to where everybody was and just strut around. Or a chap on a woman's bike, that would be hilarious. That was a lovely spellbreaker, especially if you've had a rough time. It keeps you sane. Remember we were just kids. We didn't have minds. We didn't think as we did when we were in civvy street. We were children, with no minds. So anything like that was marvellous. (20)

Some of the most curiously attired soldiers seen in the British army during the European campaign were the men of the 1st Airborne Division who retreated over the Rhine after the failure of Operation Market Garden. Rather than wait for boats some braved the waters of the Rhine, and swam to safety. Arriving naked, on the south bank they dressed themselves as best they could and began the journey back to Nijmegen. They scrounged spare clothing off the troops assisting the evacuation, or pinched clothes from the Dutch homes. Some men were seen arriving in Nijmegen dressed in women's coats and dresses and one officer was spotted with yards of flannel wrapped around himself, held in place by a Sam Browne belt.

As the British and Canadian armies charged across northern Germany in the last days of the war little did they realise they were enjoying their last days of stylistic freedom and individual expression. They were making the best of the situation but it was too good to last. With the war nearing its end the senior officers began to look forward to the peace and plan for the role of their men in occupying the defeated Reich. Discipline would be the order of the day and they wanted their men to look like a conquering army, not a gang of tramps. In the first days of May 1945, as the 7th Armoured Division approached Hamburg, the men got the first taste of the new regime. Orders were given to them: 'No item of unauthorised clothing will be worn and it is the duty of all offrs & NCOs to enforce this order rigidly.' (21) The story was the same throughout 21st Army Group. The officers of the 9th RTR looked on aghast as their crews paraded in a curious mixture of uniforms, which had been altered to meet individual tastes, and looted civilian clothing. They were soon told to discard them. The story was the same throughout 21st Army Group, their freedom was too good to last. Harry Free of the 43rd Reconnaissance Regiment noticed the sudden change that accompanied victory: 'No one had to tell us when the war ended – it was "on parade", all brasses polished, marching here, there and everywhere – a very strict dress code enforced!' (22)

In the first weeks after the surrender of Germany the soldiers had to get used to all the old standards. Long neglected tins of blanco, brasso and boot polish were dug out from the bottom of packs and put to work. Buttons and brasses shone again. Belts and webbing changed colour. Sergeant majors could once again see their faces in the toe caps of the men's boots. Hats returned to regulation angles, no longer hanging off the backs of heads. Collars were turned down, scarves packed away and hands kept out of pockets. Vehicles had to be stripped of all the accoutrements that had been picked up along the way. Non-regulation boxes that had been welded onto tanks had to be removed, packs and haversacks had to stowed correctly, old pots and kettles were thrown away, mattresses, civilian bedrolls discarded, with the vehicle finally being repainted. What had been described back in Normandy as 'tinker's carts' were once again looking like military vehicles, ready for the victory parades.

Of course, these new standards could not be kept up forever. In the months following the parades and victory celebrations a malaise crept into many of those charged with occupying Germany. Those men who had seen their only military role as being to defeat the Nazis were anxious to be demobbed. Those who had already got their demob date, and knew they had but days to go, let their standards slip. One anti-aircraft artilleryman later wrote of the behaviour of himself and his mates: 'We slouched across our corner of a foreign field with hats on or off according to our fancy, collars undone, boots unpolished, hands in pockets, with many mouths drooping with our free allowance of fags. We could not have looked much like an all-conquering army.' (23) With one eye on 'civvy street' they began to make modifications to their uniforms with the intention of making them more fashionable. Tailors were employed to make uniforms more flattering. Battledress blouses were brought in on the body so as to fit better. Trousers had triangles of cloth inserted at the bottom of the legs to give the trousers a flared look, as one offender recalled: 'definitely against regulations but made the uniform a lot smarter'. (24) With the weight of war off their minds the people back home were finally able to get back to thinking about style and fashion, and the soldiers had no intention of being left behind. They may not yet have been able to call themselves civilians, but they did their best to look as stylish as the people back home.

9

Too Scared to be Frightened

'You can't be frightened all the time. You can only be frightened some of the time.' (1)

Amid all the uncertainties of war, one thing was certain. It was bloody dangerous. Yet for eleven long months – all across north-west Europe, every day without fail – someone, somewhere was taking appalling risks. They had no choice, someone had to do it. Despite their fears and apprehensions, despite the knowledge that death lurked around every corner, the men of 21st Army Group listened to their orders, awaited the command, and advanced into the unknown.

Many thousands of fighting men faced up to their fears and performed their duties in face of the very real threat of death. All their personal strengths and weaknesses were stripped bare for the world to see and with experience many were to admit that fear itself was their greatest foe, and their hardest battle was to control this. Thousands lost this battle, succumbed to the pressure and fell victim to the psychological traumas of war. Psychiatric problems, exhaustion and breakdown were not exclusive to weak characters, they could strike anywhere. From experienced men, to those going into action for the first time. From privates to brigadiers, heroes or cowards – all succumbed to the stresses and strains of battle. Their collapse had many names – shell shock, battle fatigue, exhaustion – or in the words of the soldiers, victims were 'bomb happy'. Whatever the name it amounted to one thing – soldiers unable to fight on.

It was a condition that had been seen throughout history, from Ancient Greece to the trenches of the Great War. Yet only in modern warfare, with its machine guns, massed artillery and airpower, were psychiatric problems witnessed on a wide scale. The relatively recent diagnosis meant that by 1944 doctors were still learning about both the cause and effect of 'battle fatigue'. It was not just the medical understanding of the condition that was changing. The interwar years saw the rise through the ranks of veterans of the Great War. This new breed of generals had been the junior officers of the previous conflict and understood the strain warfare inflicted on soldiers. It was the appreciation of these conditions that meant traumatised men would never again be put against a wall and executed.

The 'shell shock' of the earlier war was now a fully recognised medical condition – battle exhaustion – which would claim fifteen per cent of 21st Army Group's battle casualties. No longer was it a source of shame or a badge of dishonour – instead it was something people throughout the army were aware of.

161

Officers and NCOs could look out for the signs of imminent collapse and doctors could treat men before the condition became dangerous. No amount of practice could prepare them for the reality of war and as the men prepared themselves for the invasion of Europe there was one question at the back of their minds – 'How will I cope?' Even the veterans of the Mediterranean campaign faced the same questions over how they would perform in the battles ahead. Although they knew what to expect few relished the task. The question in their minds was how much longer could they continue before the well of courage ran dry?

As the first landing craft began their run in towards the beaches of Normandy their occupants watched and waited for the moment their questions would be answered. Arthur Jarvis was the coxswain on a landing craft carrying the first assault wave:

> As we approached the coast the battleships were firing over the top of us, and firing was coming from the shore, you can't explain the terrifying noise. Our flotilla went in first and only two of our craft out of fourteen got off the beach. I was frightened I was going to get killed and not know if I was on the winning side. Everybody was scared. I thought 'I am twenty-five, I shan't see twenty-six, and after five years of war I won't know who won'. But I was in charge so I couldn't show my fear, after all I was a man and they were nearly all boys of eighteen. My stoker had a breakdown, he went crazy, shouting and screaming. We had to tie him up, gag him and put him in the engine room till we had time to go to our base ship, hand him over and get a replacement. They told me he finished up in a mental home. (2)

If that could happen to the sailors it was little wonder the resolve of some soldiers would fail before they set foot ashore. Alexander Baron recalled a conversation with the commander of a landing ship: 'He told me that many of the Hampshires were young boys who clung to the ship's rails in terror when they saw men being killed in front of them. The sailors beat their hands free with clubs and forced them down the ramps on to the beach.' (3) Despite such obvious displays of terror it was to their credit that most men would retain their composure and go on to defeat the enemy.

Of all the experiences endured by the soldiers few were stranger than their first time in action. They had no idea what to expect, and for all their fears had precious little clue about what they were actually frightened of. Some men attached themselves to others, who they thought brave, in the hope that their strength would offer mutual protection. When the moment finally arrived some soldiers reacted in an entirely natural way – faced with the stark reality of war they cried, and at the first sight of corpses they vomited. These were not necessarily signs of weakness and a few minutes of quiet contemplation or a few words of encouragement were often enough to control emotions and allow a soldier to return to his duty.

An officer of the 5th Battalion Coldstream Guards attempted to explain the emotions he felt:

What do you feel about going into action for the first time? I think probably a dread of showing fear and not doing the best for your platoon. Then I suppose one is frightened of seeing the first corpse, the first hand to hand fighting, the first killing of an enemy. Funnily enough there was never a feeling that I myself would get killed or wounded and many of my friends said the same things, in other words 'It can't happen to me, surely'. (4)

The last hours and minutes of waiting were always an anxious time. Officers and NCOs worried that they would make mistakes, fail to capture their targets and suffer casualties. To observers there seemed to be a patient apathy about the soldiers as if they were storing up energy for what lay ahead. Waiting men found their bladders contracting and kept turning away from their mates to urinate as they awaited the order to advance. Officers made sure their men had a good supply of boiled sweets to suck to prevent their mouths from going dry, a common manifestation of fear. A commonly held feeling was that anticipation caused the stomach to knot, in the same way as experienced before a big sporting event – some likened the sensation to that felt as they walked out to bat during cricket matches.

The start of a major advance seemed to have an almost ritualised routine and soldiers became aware of a pattern of emotion. A veteran infantryman explained the apprehension he felt moving forward:

Coming along the road you'd come across the different size artillery guns. You'd see the heavy guns and think 'Uh oh! Twenty miles to go'. Then you'd see the 5.5s and know you were getting closer. Then it would the 25 pounders and you'd think 'Right, we're in it now'. And then the adrenalin would start as you came along the road. So then you knew you were going back in the line for another couple of months before you'd get a day off. Then before you go into the attack you go to the forming up point. That means if it's a big attack the whole division goes to an area and forms up exactly as the attack is going to happen. Now that's where the fear starts. I used to start shaking – my legs would shake, my arms would shake – no matter what I did I couldn't stop them. That was part of it. Also, I got a tightness in the chest. You then went from the forming up point to the start line. Once you got there you were still feeling the fear. Then all of a sudden the Verey pistol flare would go up, we would switch the carrier's engine on and the shaking would stop. The fear didn't stop though – just the physical signs of it. I think it was a good thing the fear did not stop. That fear kept me alive. Fear was alertness, they both go together. Once you were relaxed you were finished. Once the engines started up, I was still afraid but the arms and legs were functioning. But the fear is all inside you. (5)

Although fears manifested in many ways most soldiers experienced a number of common symptoms – crying, sweating, shivering, dry mouth, loss of control of the bladder or bowels, shaking, nervous laughter, inability to speak, and the most extreme of complete mental and physical collapse. Some men even found themselves yawning. Although it gave them an air of nonchalance it masked the reality of their fears. The soldiers grew to accept these symptoms as a part of their lives and Corporal Worthington of the 1st Royal Dragoons admitted: 'All the symptoms you have quoted I still suffer. In the early days every little stop we made I had to pass water. Fear – the only way that was dealt with was saying "get hold of yourself man". If you went sick to see the MO he would give you a laxative which wasn't needed, so that was a waste of time.' (6)

Of all the physical manifestations of fear the most worrying was the concern they might soil their trousers. Soldiers joked about how they were 'shitting themselves' with fear, but how many men actually lost control of their bowels or bladder? A study by Canadian researchers found that less than ten per cent of veterans admitted to having suffered this indignity and over forty per cent were acquainted with the churning stomach that might have made involuntary defecation seem imminent. That many asked may have preferred to give a less than honest answer is without doubt, as one veteran commented almost in passing: 'I know for a fact that dozens of us did something in our pants. Right, next subject!' (7)

Strangely, many found the opposite effect, as fear made the muscles clench tightly, preventing any attempt to empty the bowels. During the Normandy campaign, diets were so poor that many soldiers became constipated. John Majendie explained why this might have happened: 'Complete loss of appetite – you often didn't eat for a long time but you just weren't hungry. I don't know if it tightens the stomach or something. As far as I was concerned one's appetite just disappeared. You didn't even think about it.' (8)

Another of the more extreme physical reactions was vomiting, believed to have been experienced by around a quarter of the soldiers. Mostly it was caused by physical revulsion at the stench of dead animals or the swollen bodies of long-dead men, rotting and splitting open as gases built up inside them. At other times they vomited from fear. Unlike defecation, vomiting was easy to conceal. They could turn away for a few seconds, even just turn their head as the dry heaves of sickness engulfed them. Seldom would their mates even notice since they were worrying about their own fate, not that of the man next to them. Most commonly it was in the aftermath of battle that men vomited. With a position captured or an attack driven off many men suffered from shock. Though often minimal, it could still induce vomiting – revolted at what they had seen, upset by what they had done, incredulous that they had survived – it was difficult for them to control their bodies.

Given the certainty that death awaited many of the soldiers few ever openly cried in front of their comrades. They might shed a few tears in private over the death of a friend or cry themselves to sleep after seeing the effects of war, but few were prepared to do so openly. One veteran explained their reasoning: 'Emotion was never shown by anybody. It showed you were weak, so it didn't go down very well. You didn't want anybody to think you were soft.' (9)

There were other manifestations that were as much a part of their daily lives as eating, drinking and sleeping. There was nothing unusual about trembling limbs or minds that raced, unable to focus on anything except the horrors that lay ahead. They felt palpitations in the chests, with their hearts fluttering, seemingly missing beats, or beating so strongly they felt others must be able to hear. Many displayed the symptoms of mild shock – they shivered and felt chills where none existed as the blood drained from their skin. The hairs on their arms stood on end and their skin changed colour to a lifeless grey, the colour of the already dead.

The symptoms could manifest singly or simultaneously. Any combination could come and go at will, allowing the soldiers to recognise that there was nothing unusual in being frightened. This emotional and physical flux makes it difficult for veterans to explain fully exactly how they felt as infantry officer Ken Hardy explained: 'It's very complicated. I know it sounds like bravado but there were times when I had absolutely no fear whatsoever. And there were other times when I was pulverised with fear. I can't explain what the difference of circumstances was. Fear was awful, terrible. Loss of will. I don't know about the physical details but there was just an absolute loss of will.' (10) This emotional confusion was summed up by the soldier who noted: 'I was too scared to be frightened'. (11)

Just as the manifestations of fear varied from man to man, so did the methods used to keep emotion under control. For every man who succumbed to his fears there were plenty more who felt the same sense of hopelessness but never 'cracked up'. As a senior military chaplain wrote: 'The only difference between a brave man and a coward is that the fear of one is controlled whilst the fear of the other is uncontrolled.' (12) As they learnt the truth about war self-control became an increasingly important weapon and part of a deeply personal struggle. They battled against the desire to turn and run in the face of enemy resistance, and each man had to dig deep into his own resources of courage. It was a time for introspection – they were so obsessed with their own problems they could not consider other people's.

In order for them to understand fully how they were able to control their fear it was necessary to understand what they were actually frightened of. Strangely, few felt that death was their greatest fear. Instead they treated it with a nonchalance born of necessity, hoping if it came it would be quick and painless. Yet serious wounds played on their minds. Amputation terrified some men, others worried about being hideously burned – in particular the tank crews who went into battle inside potential furnaces. Few concerned themselves with losing their hearing but most were terrified of being blinded. An almost universal fear was of injuries to their genitals and some men went to sleep with their helmets protecting their 'meat and two veg' rather than their heads. They joked that a head wound would kill them, but if they lost their genitals they'd want to be dead.

Many were tormented by the fear they might fail in their duties. They understood how others relied on them and how if they failed others would suffer. Major Douglas Goddard recalled the pressure he faced in coordinating artillery fire:

My own recollection is that there were periods – particularly at the start of the Normandy campaign – when fear of not being able to cope under fire was dominant – when I suffered most of the symptoms you list, except possibly trembling and bladder. A churning stomach was the most distressing. One tended to become immunised and the symptoms lessened as time passed. The most intense stress for me as an officer was the fear that I would suffer mental paralysis when under fire and be unable to act decisively and rationally and as a result lose the confidence and respect of one's gunners. (13)

Although all these fears tormented soldiers, there was something stronger that played on their minds: their greatest fear was of the unknown. Tension was greatest before a battle, not during it. The real strain came whilst they thought about what would happen. There was no set pattern to battle, they could guess what might happen but everything else was unknown. As one infantry NCO explained: 'You didn't think of death but you thought about what you were going to come up against.' (14) It was less the fear of stepping on a mine than fear of whether there were any mines. They accepted machineguns would open fire at some point, but the fear was of how long they would wait and where would they be hidden? Were there tanks, if so where?

Everybody had their own ideas about their ability to withstand the fears encountered in the front line and what factors made some men into heroes and some into supposed cowards? To understand courage it was necessary to distinguish between two similar facets of the human psyche: bravery and fearlessness. Many have tried to understand how the differences affected soldiers, as one explained:

> An awful lot is talked about bravery, but I think there's a hell of a difference between being brave and being fearless. People are fearless because they don't feel any fear. People who are brave are probably shit scared at the time but manage to do great things. There were one or two people I met who appeared to be fearless. Whether they were very intelligent or very sick, I don't know. They had a very different outlook. Maybe they had no imagination? I don't know if you should envy the fearless chap. (15)

Few soldiers did envy their fearless comrades and most had to find a way to control what was going on within their minds. Self-control had to be learnt quickly. They needed to adapt to the situation and find a way to retain their sanity. Most found a simple solution. Activity was one of the most useful tools for soldiers in times of great stress. They needed to be kept busy – occupying their hands and minds to keep their thoughts away from the danger. Some opened fire at distant targets with little hope, or even intention, of causing injury to the enemy. The sounds of friendly artillery opening up and hitting enemy positions, a confident order from an officer, or the sight of an enemy to open fire on – all could provide relief from fear.

For tank crews their experience was somewhat different. They knew their armour might not withstand enemy fire and were conscious of how little time they had to escape if their tank was hit. Yet their fears were controlled by the isolation felt whilst cooped up in a large steel box. Their vision and hearing were limited. Communicating by intercom, they were unaware of much of the danger. Instead of explosions and the rumble of enemy tanks they heard orders fed to them via headphones. This sensory deprivation offered a barrier against the real world. The man facing the most stress was the co-driver. Commanders looked for targets, wireless operators concentrated on keeping their sets 'on net', gunners fired, and drivers attempted to manoeuvre thirty tons of steel. Yet the co-driver had little to do except, as tank commander Ian Hammerton recalled: 'pass ammunition back into the turret and bite their finger nails'. (16) Tank gunner Joe Ekins summed it up: 'I was alright because I've got the job of shooting. I'm focused on something. My fright has gone. But the rest of them, sitting in the tank, they were really brave, because they're just sitting there waiting for me to do something.' (17)

Like the tank crews, signallers also existed within their own world. With headphones on and ears straining to interpret the orders coming across the airwaves, they too became detached from reality – one called it an 'invisible cloak'. Unable to hear what was going on around them and occupied by their duties, there was little opportunity for the gravity of a situation to make itself apparent. The need to keep the wireless operating meant everything else was an irrelevance – neither deaths of friends nor the sufferings of others – all that mattered was their work.

The infantrymen, however, had no protective buffer. Yet they too found ways of mastering their fears – if only for a short period. The one job they constantly needed to do was 'dig in'. Wherever they stopped they had to find cover. Immediately they unstrapped their entrenching tools, pulled picks and shovels from behind their haversacks and began to dig. When enemy fire was coming in they thought not of the bullets but of the hole they were digging. All the time the hands were working the imagination was suppressed and mental strength preserved.

All manner of activities assisted the soldiers in the search for mental stability. Some were able to remain calm by attempting to behave as if nothing was happening. At Arnhem a paratrooper was seen playing the banjo whilst German artillery assaulted his position. Some men read books under shellfire, others made conversation, talking about subjects far removed from war. A war correspondent recalled chatting about gardening to an officer who broke off conversation to hunt snipers and another man toured slit trenches trying to enrol his comrades onto journalism courses. Using laughter to assuage tensions was also common, particularly when soldiers had suffered in battle. They figured it was better to laugh than to cry. It was usually ghoulish, black humour, laughing at death and making jokes about their misfortune. When friends died they quipped that it would leave more food for the rest of them, the comedy superseding both fear and remorse.

For all their efforts to suppress fear, nature played a role that was beyond the control of the individual. As they advanced into battle a wave of adrenalin surged through their bodies. Where minutes before their hearts had raced in anticipation, now they raced with the fuel of nature. They had craved activity to keep their fears at bay and there was no activity greater than battle itself. This adrenalin rush was explained by Fred Sylvester: 'When I was a child the thought of dying brought on a strange feeling in my abdomen. This was as though there was a hollow in my stomach, as if everything had shrunk to nothing. This was the same feeling I experienced when setting out on a patrol. Once the action started this feeling went away, or perhaps as my thoughts were elsewhere, I forgot about my fear.' (18)

However, once the fighting slowed and soldiers found themselves occupying static positions their minds began to wander. The impact of inactivity was first noticed in the weeks following D-Day. Initially 'bomb happy' soldiers were found behind the front lines, men not engaged with the enemy but living within range of enemy artillery. They had nothing to occupy their minds except the prospect of death. Yet as the advance slowed and the battle for Normandy turned into a war of attrition the situation changed drastically. From the beginning of July exhaustion cases in the rifle companies rose steeply, peaking towards the end of the month. Soldiers spent days on end in foxholes often only yards from the enemy. There was nothing to occupy their time except smoking, rereading old letters and making small talk with their comrades.

This creeping tension became evident wherever the soldiers served. From the deadly fields of Normandy to the dark, damp days of a winter in the Low Countries – the enforced state of inactivity shredded nerves. The time spent listening intently for the sounds of approaching danger from shells, tanks, aircraft, patrols and infantry attacks put an almost intolerable burden on the soldiers. Silence fully exercised the senses, straining every nerve: ears listened for any sound that might herald danger, eyes searched for the slightest movement, noses sniffed the air for the unique smell of the enemy, and hands felt the ground awaiting the seismic vibrations of tanks.

Newly arrived reinforcements were particularly vulnerable to fear spawned by ignorance. Arriving at the front they would be allocated to a platoon commander, who passed them on to his sergeant, who in turn passed them on to a corporal in charge of a section. The corporal might simply take them to a hole and leave them to their own devices. Never would they feel more alone – as the replacement for a dead man they were simply an outsider and could take days or weeks to be integrated fully into the section. It was not spite on behalf of the 'old hands', rather they were too preoccupied with their own problems to befriend a man who might be dead in a few hours. Little wonder some cowered in slit trenches, with hardly an idea of what they were supposed to do.

To break down in the first encounter with the enemy was not a sign that a man would never make the grade, rather that he needed firm guidance. NCOs sometimes found newly arrived men huddled together in shell craters crying. They could be treated with sympathy, shown care and understanding, and hopefully be returned to their place with their platoons. The role of strong and understanding leaders was vital. NCOs could prevent breakdowns by teaching men how to behave. They needed to know what was likely to happen – what signs meant danger, when they would get food, what their personal role would be, when they could safely sleep. Unfortunately it was not always possible to offer this support. When fully occupied organising their platoons and often deputising for wounded or dead officers, there was little time to help.

The failure of leadership was seen when entire sections refused to move forward into action. In early August 1944 eight men of the South Staffordshire Regiment were arrested for mutiny after they refused to follow their corporal into an attack. He was unable to move them forward and instead led them to the rear. When an officer arrived he asked each man in turn whether he would go forward. All bar one, Private Passmore, refused, instead asking what their punishment would be. At their trial the truth behind their mutiny was revealed. For most it was their first time in action and one man, Private Ryan, was a cook who had never received infantry training. The defending officer attempted to put forward a case for them to be treated with lenience, telling the court: 'They should not be blemished, and they should not go through their lives with this stigma on them for something that happened over which they had no real control at that time; their nerves were shattered, their morale had gone, and there was no one to assist and guide them on the right path.' (19) It was to no avail, all eight men received five-year sentences.

The knowledge that there were young men unable to comprehend the magnitude of the battles raging around them was a burden for some NCOs and they blamed themselves. William Partridge was one such sergeant, recalling: 'One young replacement soldier, faced with an incredibly frightening position, deserted. This, I consider, was as much my fault as his, as I should have explained to him more fully what we up against and how we all supported each other.' (20)

The best of the officers and NCOs, like Sergeant Partridge, had to be both a teacher and a friend, someone who could guide and listen. By understanding which men were best suited to which duties they hoped to ensure their soldiers wouldn't feel useless and demoralised, instead they would feel they were playing a vital role in defeating the enemy. Sometimes it was simple, if they thought the men were jittery they gave them basic tasks to carry out. Just by suggesting a man dig his slit trench deeper, or put a covering over the top, could be enough to steady them. They could also be sent out with a message for a neighbouring position or asked to fill Bren gun magazines. Alternatively they could be detailed to return to HQ on a spurious mission, the break from monotony and a few minutes of safety being enough to calm them. Rotas could be organised to ensure men who appeared on the verge of collapse were given regular periods of sleep and be allowed to recharge their emotional batteries. Commanders also made sure the men had all they needed to feel contented. Regular deliveries of mail, supplies of tobacco and hot food were all known to be of paramount importance in maintaining morale.

If none of these things worked there was another solution. NCOs and officers could spot those on the edge of a nervous breakdown and make them report sick. This way treatment could be given to prevent a man breaking down in battle, an occurrence which could spread panic. This had the benefit of allowing traumatised men to sleep for long periods and then hopefully return to the front refreshed.

Officers and NCOs were themselves buoyed by the knowledge of the good work they were doing and the influence they had on the survival of their men. One explained how responsibility helped him to keep his nerve:

Sometimes I used to think if I wasn't an NCO I'd have turned around and gone. I thought "What the hell am I doing here?' But because of your responsibility to the men you carried on and did your job. Then once you'd started you were totally embroiled in what you were doing, so you didn't think of running away. I was looking after the men, even though they didn't need it. I thought I was the one who needed looking after. (21)

There was another source of support – their mates. In times of stress peer pressure played a vital role in holding units together. Many of the soldiers felt camaraderie did more than anything to keep them going in the face of danger. Men who were so scared they wanted nothing more than to sit and cry kept going. They looked around them at their mates – their faces expressionless, their jaws moving slowly as they sucked sweets – and realised they could not let them down. They felt alone in their fear, little realising their mates felt the same. It was a cycle of deception that helped to sustain morale – hiding their true feelings so as not to be the odd man out.

The friendships made by the men at the front were like none other. Infantry sections and tank crews became like brothers, men tied by a shared history of sacrifice. They shared an intimacy few knew outside their own families. Some likened the bond between the soldiers to that in a sports team – a group of men who shared a talent and stuck together, win, lose or draw. What was essential was for everyone to play their role and support everyone else, without that the system would collapse and the team would fail. Even unpopular men, whose character made them stand out from their peers and who irritated others, could play their role in battle and earn the respect of their fellow soldiers.

With peer pressure sustaining the soldiers before going into action, and the adrenaline surge sustaining them in the heat of battle, the question was how would they cope with the aftermath of battle? Battles did not end in joyous flag waving – there was no cheering or celebrations of victory – instead most culminated in a period of deflated introspection. During action most men experienced lucky escapes, often near misses that killed others. These were not the clean, message-whispering deaths seen in the cinematic interpretation of war, but violent, bloody spectacles. Grown men screaming for their mothers, crying as life ebbed from their bodies. Men with hideous wounds or burnt, blinded, eviscerated, with jaws ripped off, bones shattered and blood spurting. The dead and wounded were friends and enemies alike, or civilians who could be old men, women, children and even babies. Such images burned into the consciousness of the men. Fortunately, in the immediate aftermath of battle there was much work to be done. Trenches needed to be dug, machine guns sited and bodies buried. As their heart beats slowed and their tense bodies relaxed, this flurry of activity helped to keep their minds away from the horrors they had witnessed.

Sometimes life was not so simple, the end of some encounters saw the soldiers in relative safety, perhaps holding a position whilst another unit pushed forward to pursue the enemy. With little work to occupy them the soldiers had to find their own way of coping. In this situation cigarettes were vital. As the smoke depleted the oxygen reaching their brains, the soldiers felt calmed. The light-headed, restful feeling allowed them to forget all they had endured and be ready for whatever else might come their way.

As the campaign progressed and some of the most experienced soldiers succumbed to fatigue it became clear the personal strengths and weaknesses of individuals was paramount in ensuring survival. As Eric 'Bill' Sykes explained: 'As a young man, I of course felt invincible and if anyone was going to die it certainly wasn't going to be me. I had, of course, anxious moments and was at times a little nervous but certainly never felt in need of the services of a psychiatrist. Remember – I was a street savvy youth and a survivor.' (22)

On the battlefield the soldiers were tested to the very limits of their endurance and would display their nature in a way few had previously revealed. They learned truths about themselves and not all was as expected. It was discovered that some of the best men in training were less than able once in action. Some NCOs who had been in their element during exercises and highly respected by both officers and men, failed to respond to orders. Others, who had previously appeared slow and lacking initiative, were able to adapt and understand what was needed of them and become resolute leaders.

Who better to understand the varying abilities of men than Sydney Jary? As a young subaltern he witnessed war at the apex of the advance, and all his preconceptions were quickly swept aside. In his memoirs he attempted to analyse what qualities were needed by his men:

> Had I been asked at any time before August 1944 to list the personal characteristics which go to make a good infantry soldier, my reply would indeed have been wide of the mark. Like most I would no doubt have suggested only masculine ones like aggression, physical stamina, a hunting instinct and a competitive nature. How wrong I would have been. I would now suggest the following. Firstly sufferance, without which one could not survive. Secondly, a quiet mind which enables a soldier to live in harmony with his fellows through all sorts of difficulties and sometimes under dreadful conditions. As in a closed monastic existence, there is simply no room for the assertive or acrimonious. Thirdly, but no less important, a sense of the ridiculous which helps a soldier surmount the unacceptable. Add to these a reasonable standard of physical fitness and a dedicated professional competence, and you have a soldier for all seasons. None of the NCOs or soldiers who made 18 Platoon what it was resembled the characters portrayed in most books and films about war. All were quiet, sensible and unassuming men and some, by any standards, were heroes. If I now had to select a team for a dangerous mission and my choice was restricted to stars of the sportsfield or poets, I would unhesitatingly recruit from the latter. (23)

The changes evident in the understanding of what made a good soldier were also reflected in their behaviour in the heat of battle. The men who did not allow their emotions to engulf them were often able to retain their sanity longer than those who succumbed to rage. The men who were gripped by swirling emotions, raging against the enemy, were usually less able to cope. Observers noted how the stoics among them were better suited to the realities of war than the men who actually became part of the savagery. Not everyone could maintain this detachment and there were plenty for whom the strain became too much. As they watched their friends die or be evacuated they felt their own end creeping ever closer.

The continual stream of highs and lows put a strain on the mental condition of many soldiers and pushed them to the edge. They found the danger-fuelled adrenaline surge pushed them to a point of insanity. With this 'high' feeling some found themselves laughing hysterically, their faces almost exploding in mad laughter. In the midst of battle and its immediate aftermath some soldiers were gripped by rage, showing it by shooting at POWs, wounded Germans, or even corpses. This 'high' was followed by a slump where the soldiers fell into a virtual collapse – and the greater the 'high' the further they had to fall. Once battle was over the sight of bodies or simple reminders of the beauty of life could cause them to break down in tears.

As stress played on the nerves of tank crews they became increasingly cautious. Fear of stepping out into the unknown kept some within their vehicles for longer than necessary. Whilst their crew mates got out to stretch their legs, nervous men sheltered inside, only emerging for the most urgent calls of nature. Only within the surrounds of their steel shell could they feel safe.

This tension, bred by isolation, was felt by many men. They did not want to be alone but wanted to be in company. Arthur Rowley of the 43rd Reconnaissance Regiment was detailed to return to HQ with a message but unfortunately the only available transport was a bicycle: 'I was very apprehensive at working alone for we usually operated as a team in a vehicle or in a foot patrol. Furthermore, the cycle had never been oiled and emitted the most terrible noises. Within a few yards I was wet with sweat, except my mouth which was bone dry. The ride back for me was more traumatic for my imagination was working overtime. Nevertheless I arrived back unscathed but quite a few pounds lighter.' (24)

Like Rowley, many in the reconnaissance regiments found their nerves pushed to the very limit. They had one of the most dangerous jobs imaginable and endured almost constant stress. Infantrymen could spend most of their days in foxholes trying to avoid the attentions of the enemy whereas 'recce' troops had to venture out to locate them. The price paid for any lapses of concentration was high. Harry Free, who also served with the 43rd Reconnaissance Regiment, remembered:

Being a leading recce driver meant that you were under constant strain from the moment you set off to the moment you returned. There was nothing in front of you but the enemy – somewhere – so you had to have your eyes all over the place. The strain was really horrendous – you didn't know when the enemy would appear – round the next bend, over the next hill. Roads were mined, German bazookas were hidden in hedges. Sometimes there was a German gun at the very end of a straight road just waiting for you. You were constantly looking for tell-tale signs so couldn't afford to be distracted by flippant conversations, jokiness or anything. I remember once a mate called Charlie, he was a sergeant with brilliant eyesight, put his head out of the turret of the car and a bazooka blew his head off. He hadn't spotted it. We often drove into enemy fire unexpectedly, and as the gunner engaged fire with them, we had to reverse back rapidly and I mean rapidly! I remember another sergeant bending down inside the vehicle and at the same time the gunner firing in response to enemy fire; the recoil of the gun hit him in the forehead and killed him outright. Shelling made you wary, apprehensive, wondering where they would land – though at least we had the protection from armoured cars whereas the infantry had no protection at all. I don't remember feeling fear, as such. In the job I was doing there wasn't time for fear, you were concentrating so hard all the time. (25)

Often it was not until leaving the front the soldiers realised how taut they had become. Once they were pulled back to rest the strain became noticeable. Historian Alexander McKee watched a group of young Scots infantry who had come back straight from the fighting in the Reichswald to a café. When the proprietor's baby began to cry one of the soldiers responded by threatening to bash its head in against the wall. The mother hurried her child away and McKee was convinced she had every reason to be afraid.

The growing tension was noticed at night when it was not unusual to hear the sound of soldiers crying in their sleep. Corporal Worthington had such an experience whilst serving in the 1st Royal Dragoons: 'You have a senior NCO that makes you dig a deep slit trench and then at night, when the enemy planes came over, he used to whimper like a dog with his knees tucked under his chin. He would tell me to listen for anyone calling for him further up the command and I would do this until I fell asleep, it stayed with me and affected me all my life.' (26)

With time increasing numbers of men found their nerves affected. Those approaching breaking point were obvious. Their speech grew slow and deliberate, their faces showed dazed expressions. Every movement became laboured, their bodies ached, they could not focus their minds. Some men found themselves laughing hysterically whilst crying at the same time and, looking back, felt they were teetering on the edge of madness, needing just one more incident to tip them into the abyss. Slowly but surely the psychological burden grew until the day it would finally come to a head. If they were not killed soon, surely they would go crazy. Alexander Baron described the tension: 'I felt ... that innumerable fine wires inside me were being tightened on violin pegs.' (27)

Most men attempted to conceal the tension building up inside them. Some wore dark glasses to hide the fear that showed in their eyes. Others kept their hands deep in their pockets for fear of revealing that they were trembling. Even those men who gave the impression of being lucky enough to cope were often carrying an emotional burden unseen by their comrades. In their endeavours to keep their minds closed, many soldiers were curt with their colleagues whose fears began to manifest. Men who broke down in tears often received little sympathy and instead were told to shut up. It was not that the seemingly heartless men felt no fear or sorrow but they were desperately trying not to succumb to the same emotions as the crying men – they were merely trying to stop despair from spreading.

Sergeant William Partridge tried to put into words the strain he was under during his nine weeks of fighting in Normandy. In a handful of highly evocative words he recalled the mounting pressure: 'There was an all embracing feeling of grief. You know the feeling as you are about to shed tears? That's how I felt day and night, week after week, without actually crying.' (28)

Although most exhaustion cases were found in the infantry or tank crews, others also suffered. Artillerymen endured the constant roar of their own guns that left their ears ringing. The crash of the guns drove some gunners to the brink of madness. They were no mere machine operators. Working in all weather conditions – their faces burned by the sun, their hands burned by the shells they fired –

sometimes hardly sleeping, on alert for incoming fire, or caught up in enemy counterattacks, many worked till they could take no more. A battery commander described the effect on one of his men: 'His mind wandered, his face was drawn and noises of any kind disturbed him, upsetting his balance and causing a buzzing sound in his ears.' Another man reached his limit when making an inventory of a dead friend's possessions. He lay sprawled in his bivvy: 'deprived alike of will and muscle power'. (29)

Surviving against the odds, even the most fatalistic of soldiers began to waver. The longer they lived the more the hope of survival began to re-emerge. It was a situation that played havoc with morale. Arch fatalist Ken Hardy, who defied the odds from Normandy until early 1945, explained:

> I didn't expect to come through and that went on for a hell of a long time. It was only when the feeling that you were playing russian roulette with your life every day, that I began to feel fear. The fear is of the unknown. You wake up in the morning and you don't think you are going to get through that day. And you wonder how it's going to happen to you. I remember being in one really ghastly fracas and you just hope it will be quick and clean and no messing about. (30)

As victory came closer and he realised he might survive Hardy could no longer accept the notion of death. Instead he began thinking there might be a future for him. The conflict between hope and fatalism pulled at his already worn nerves. Like thousands of others, Hardy knew he was approaching his breaking point, the only question was when would it come?

The 2nd Army's medical staff attempted to make an assessment of the reasons men broke down on the battlefield. In their report they stressed the effects of shelling and mortaring, inadequate leadership and training, ineffective integration of reinforcements, long overseas campaigning, previous neurosis and low intelligence. This was fair but missed one vital point – the effects of fear could be entirely random. The psychological make-up that allowed soldiers to withstand immense pressure was not shared by everyone. Many soldiers reported being surprised to see the most notable sportsmen of their unit – boxers, footballers, rugby players, PT instructors – being carried away from the battlefield trembling and crying. Men watched as these respected figures appeared helpless, almost like children. One of the unlikely victims was Private Walker of the Essex Regiment. He had served in the army for sixteen years, had an exemplary disciplinary record, had fought in Singapore, escaped via Burma and also undergone paratrooper training. When his own breakdown and involvement in mutinous behaviour came in November 1944 he told his court martial: 'I don't know, I just seem to have gone to pieces.' (31)

The reality of the situation was made apparent to those at 21st Army Group HQ who studied the figures for exhaustion cases. In the first thirteen weeks after D-Day there had been a reported 8,005 cases of exhaustion, with a majority of those coming from the infantry platoons. By the third week of July it was calculated that almost eleven per cent of evacuees were victims of exhaustion. For the whole of the Normandy campaign the rate of exhaustion cases among casualties was twenty per cent, by the end of the year it had dropped to fourteen per cent and in the first three months of 1945 the rate had again dropped to just 9.9 per cent. In all the figures came to an average of fifteen per cent of all battle casualties being as a result of exhaustion.

It was not necessary to study figures to realise the scale of the problem. That everybody cracked up in the end was soon made apparent to most of the soldiers serving in units alongside veterans of the fighting in the North Africa, Sicily or Italy. The 'green' troops who had joined such formations noticed there were plenty of men whose reserve of courage had been used up, who were increasingly 'shell happy' and showed a cautious attitude, nervous tension and a high rate of breakdown.

Few of those who suffered from 'battle exhaustion' could ever explain the stimulus that caused their breakdown. For those who experienced long-term tension it took as little as a single shellburst or near miss to tip the balance, as Ken Hardy explained:

> It was the most ghastly time of my life. It was humiliating, awful. I was already in a pretty bad way and I knew it wasn't going to take much to send me over the edge. Then I was sent to a Dutch village which had had no trouble at all. I drove into the church square, and no sooner had I arrived than they 'stonked' it with mortars. Before I arrived they hadn't had any trouble at all, then they got 'stonked', I thought 'This is a bit personal'. After that I don't remember a thing for five days. You may ask how I knew it was five days? Well, I had five days growth of beard when I came to. It was the most awful experience of my life. It was disgusting. My colonel, who had never been terribly sympathetic towards me most of the time – although he was towards the end – came up and said 'I think you've had enough. Thank you very much for all you've done.' I'd reached a point where I could never have gone back into action. I'd used up whatever reserve of courage I'd had. I think anybody who'd gone all the way through from the beaches had had enough by then. (32)

For some the source of their tension went back further than they realised. John Reynolds, whose breakdown came in September 1944, explained his experiences:

> When I got 'shell shock' was after we were badly hit. I looked and I could see a box barrage coming up towards us – I grabbed my revolver and rushed into the field towards where they were sending up some flares. In a lot of cases that would have been bravery, but fortunately I was pulled down by my mates, and brought back. I then reported sick, saw the M.O. and he said they'd have to send me back immediately as a psychiatric case. The psychiatrist put my collapse down to Dunkirk, traced it back to that period. (33)

For others their breakdown was triggered by incidents they witnessed – moments of pure terror that were too much to bear. An RAMC captain noted how it was often the death of close friends that had the most profound effect on soldiers, and despite the policy of labelling such cases 'exhaustion' they were nothing less than complete mental breakdowns.

The symptoms of 'battle exhaustion' could manifest in many ways. Some men were seen walking about in exposed positions singing at the top of their voices, others sat reading books oblivious to what was going on around them. Few of the men who succumbed can remember little more than waking up in hospital. One who pieced together the details of his breakdown from comrades was John Majendie, a company commander in the 4th Somerset Light Infantry. Having led his company in the successful consolidation and defence of Hill 112 in Normandy, Majendie suffered the strain of weeks leading a seriously depleted rifle company in some of the most savage fighting of the whole campaign:

> My memory of the events are spasmodic. We were in the 'bocage' country, which was terribly difficult. You can't see anything and it was getting a bit chaotic. We were taking casualties and we didn't know where the fire was coming from. I remember getting through a hedge and lying down to see what was going on. One of the men in my company came up and started to report something to me. There was a sudden crack and he went down, absolutely screaming his head off. It was horrible. For a few seconds you are just frozen. I helped him out of his equipment and got him get back through the hedge. I picked up his equipment because he had some spare Bren mags. Then I called an 'O' group – an orders meeting – further up the lane. I was giving out these orders, but I don't remember who was there.

A corporal who attended the briefing later recalled Majendie as incoherent, toying with his binoculars and compass yet doing nothing with them. The rest of the officers realised it was time to take positive action. Majendie took up the story:

> I vaguely remember my second in command suddenly saying to me 'Are you feeling all right?' I can't remember what I replied, but I wasn't all right. He later told me I was giving out orders but not making any sense. They thought I was going 'doolally'. My second in command asked if I'd like him to take over and carry on for a bit. So I said yes. And then we just carried on with the attack. I was physically ok, because I went on behind him with my rifle. We went through a couple more fields, just running across with fixed bayonets and so on. Then I got a message to go down to battalion headquarters to see the C.O., and he said 'Are you running the company or is John Scanlon?' I said 'John is at the moment'. So he told me he thought I could do with a rest. At that stage we suddenly came under a mortar stonk – I don't remember a lot about it – but years later one of the other chaps told me 'We all went to ground and you just stayed sitting there like a moron, oblivious to what was going on'. So I must have been very wafty. The second in command of the battalion gave me a lift back to the M.O. who gave me a knockout drop and I went back to where 'B' echelon was and slept for twenty-three hours. Quite honestly, when I woke up I'd had it. I think basically one was just knackered, we were very short of sleep. I'd had a shell burst almost in my face on Hill 112, and twice more I'd had shells burst within feet of me, and the M.O. thought I suffered from blast. Whether it is cumulative or one has a certain ration of tolerance, I don't know. I've often wondered if I'd have hung about a couple of days or so I'd have got back to normal again, but I obviously needed a bit of sleep. It's extraordinary, it's never happened before or since and you can't equate it with anything. (34)

Majendie's breakdown was a classic case of 'battle exhaustion' – the continued strain had sapped his mental strength, leaving him incapable of rational thought or coherent communication. Yet it was not one of the more extreme cases. Others went beyond the point of collapse and reached the point of temporary insanity. Men whose minds were completely gone did not always flee the battlefield, instead they ran straight into view of the enemy to be hit by volleys of fire. One doctor recorded how he had observed desperate men attempting to climb inside chimneys to escape shellfire, or trying to dig holes in the floors of jeeps with their hands. Others were found crawling or wandering aimlessly, unaware of their situation and in desperate need of treatment. Few cases were more unusual than an incident in the 1st Northants Yeomanry. In the midst of battle one tank commander ordered his gunner to cease fire. His shocked crew listened as he informed them they were to stop firing since he no longer believed in war and had declared a uni-lateral peace. Luckily a superior officer was at hand and arranged for his immedi-ate evacuation.

The most extreme cases could be picked up and carried whilst they still remained fixed in a seated position. In some cases they would have to held still so that their legs could be straightened allowing them to lie down. Such men lay sprawled on the dirt floors of the aid posts – unconscious, deep in sleep, unable to move. Others lay outside, even in the rain they failed to notice the sodden blankets that covered them and cared for nothing but sleep. These were the men who could fight no more.

In addition to the usual infractions of military discipline – desertion, cowardice, mutiny and absence – MPs were faced with a new, unexpected category – self inflicted wounds. These were common among men who were so desperate to escape the front they showed no fear of mutilating themselves. The two years' hard labour that awaited those convicted of the crime made little difference – if a man was desperate enough to shoot himself it was unlikely a prison sentence would deter him. It was first noticed in Normandy as men attempted to be evacuated by shooting themselves in the arms or legs. Many trigger fingers and toes were to be lost that summer as men attempted to book themselves a ticket back to 'blighty'. Men were even spotted holding their arms above their slit trenches in hope of being wounded by incoming fire.

In the three weeks ending 1 July there were fifty-two reported cases of deliber-ate wounding. A soldier of the 4th Wiltshires recalled that his company had lost fifteen men to them. Of course, few wounds were reported as self-inflicted, those who knew the truth covered up for their mates. Instead most incidents were report-ed as accidents or the result of enemy action.

As the practice spread it became difficult for the army to ignore what was hap-pening. Soon the military authorities began to notice a trend – there were just too many infantrymen arriving at hospitals with wounds to their hands or feet. To speed up identification of cases of self-inflicted wounds investigators were sent into the hospitals to interview suspects. The job was not made any easier by a ten-dency amongst medical staff to report all hand and foot wounds as possible SIWs.

Despite all the time spent on investigations they yielded few results. Of the hundreds of cases investigated there were few where witnesses could be found to corroborate medical evidence and ensure conviction.

Even in the closing weeks of the war soldiers continued to injure themselves deliberately. As the civilians at home prepared and planned for their victory celebrations some men were driven to desperate acts of self-mutilation to ensure they would still be alive when the final victory came. A few men took extreme measures, one soldier climbed on top of the train taking him to the front and deliberately hit a bridge so that he would be returned to hospital.

This question of punishments for offenders was fraught with difficulty. Failure to punish those men unprepared to fight could cause a wave of disobedience at the front. If the front line soldiers saw deserters treated with lenience they would figure 'why bother continuing to fight?' However, overly harsh punishment of exhausted men could cause resentment. Consequently one of the greatest challenges for the authorities was how to distinguish between those psychiatric cases who fled the field of battle in response to what they had endured and those men who wilfully avoided battle. In some cases officers and NCOs would fail to make this distinction – men transferred to The Black Watch were told in no uncertain terms that falling victim to the psychological pressures of war was not an option. The inference was that a man who went 'bomb happy' was not a victim but a coward.

This was an attitude shared by many senior commanders. Shortly before D-Day the men of 214 Brigade were addressed by Brigadier Essame who told them: 'Some of you will be blown to pieces – that does not matter. If anyone deserts he will be court-martialled and he will be shot.' (35) Although courts could no longer pass the death sentence for deserters, this did not stop some officers persisting with threats of execution and many soldiers discovered there were plenty willing to enforce discipline at gunpoint.

In the opening months of the campaign the army faced an unparalleled wave of desertion. The simple truth behind the figures was that the battle for Normandy was as tough as any of the war. Even Germans thought it worse than the Russian Front. The front line soldiers lived like moles, seldom straying from their holes, sleeping little, their energy sapped by the sun and their diet of tinned food and chlorinated water. Any advances were a slow process, fraught with confusion and marked by bloody slaughter. Hundreds of tanks littered the Norman countryside, their turrets blackened by fire, the corpses of their crews strewn around them. Whole waves of men were cut down by the concentrated fire of machine guns and mortars, the wounded being incinerated in the burning wheat fields through which they had advanced.

This experience was too much for many soldiers and sheer panic set in. As they crouched in whatever shelter they could find, seeing their friends die or listening to the screams of the wounded many soldiers just cracked up. Their bodies shook, their hands trembled, tears flooded out. Was this the blood, sweat, toil and tears Churchill had spoken of?

The moment when most made the decision to flee battle was the point when to do anything else seemed like certain death. Was it cowardice or terror? No one could truly say. All that was clear was that it was an act of desperation. When this was the action of a single man it was not too great a problem, but there was no guarantee desertion would be restricted to individuals. Some units faced the possibility of panic setting in.

In these circumstances only the rapid response of disciplined NCOs and officers could prevent panic. Despite the removal of the death penalty for desertion or cowardice the threats made by some commanders to shoot men fleeing the battlefield were carried out. They figured the only way to prevent panic from spreading was to shoot offenders. It was a situation that was replicated time and time again, as officers were forced to control those disobeying orders.

Such drastic action could only be used in extreme circumstances. It was on the slopes of Hill 112 that the officers of the 43rd Division were forced to take action to prevent the collapse of discipline. This was one of the fiercest battles in Normandy, since control of the heights gave an unrestricted view of the lands around. Initially the 5th Duke of Cornwall's Light Infantry were ordered to capture the summit, a task that cost them considerably. Many fled their positions to where the Somerset Light Infantry were holding the line. As they passed through the Somersets it became clear to one sergeant that his men were being affected by this panic so he took up a position on the edge of his slit trench and threatened to shoot anyone attempting to run away. With the threat of the panic spreading to the Somersets their CO, Lieutenant Colonel Lipscomb, took drastic action. He drew his pistol, rallied the Cornwalls, and told his own men he would shoot anyone running away. John Majendie watched the scene:

> In the chaos I remember seeing he had got his pistol out and was waving it about and I wondered at the time what was going on. Because these chaps came back at the double and it was a very dodgy moment, and I think if they had gone on I dare say a certain number of our chaps may have been tempted to go with them. Somebody I knew very well told me that he shot a chap. On the second or third night we were told to advance forward, only a matter of a few hundred yards. When D Company started to come back this chap said it was absolute chaos, and he said one chap was legging it 'so I shot him'. (36)

Even such drastic measures could not control men who were at the end of their tether. In the slaughterhouse of Normandy there was one battalion whose almost total collapse brought shame to its officers and whose failure remained hidden for many years. The 6th Battalion, Duke of Wellington's Regiment was unique in that it reached a point where it could no longer function. Suffering appalling losses of over three hundred and fifty men, their CO was replaced in an effort to steady the troops but morale plummeted. After only four days in his new command Lieutenant Colonel Turner realised the situation was hopeless and took the bold step of reporting the state of his battalion. All the original company commanders had been lost and nearly all the officers and NCOs at the battalion HQ. There was a rising rate of self-inflicted wounds and 'shell shock', and every enemy artillery attack saw large numbers of men fleeing their positions. With few of the officers and NCOs wearing rank badges and so many reinforcements, it became less a battalion and more a jumble of disparate individuals in which leadership and discipline were almost nonexistent. On two occasions in four days Turner drew his revolver to turn back panicking men. Recognising the desperate situation he asked for the battalion to be withdrawn, despite the knowledge that it would spell the end of his career. It was a brave move. Montgomery ordered the Duke of Wellingtons withdrawn and replaced by a fresh unit, the 1st Leicesters.

In periods of heavy fighting rear areas became scenes of chaos. Wounded men arrived back at regimental aid posts only to find large numbers of unhurt men had returned with them. Some men who thought they had reached the point of no return found the MPs disagreed with them – and they were declared fit to continue their duties. Few but the men who had really lost complete control of themselves would be treated with concern. MPs and regimental policemen awaited those fleeing, rounded them up at gunpoint, and attempted to restore order. Arrests were made, men were handcuffed and threatened with dire retribution. Even lightly wounded men were arrested if MPs thought they had left the field of battle unecessarily.

During major actions hospitals faced a constant influx of men who had lost the mental capacity to continue fighting. Seemingly callous measures were taken by doctors to segregate the real psychiatric casualties from those who might be faking it. The victims of breakdowns were simply left on the floor of aid posts to see their reaction. Any man pretending to be ill would eventually give himself away and genuine casualties would become apparent. In July 1944 the Canadians found they were admitting as many as one hundred men a day. Stocks of the sedative sodium amytal were almost exhausted as the soldiers were put to sleep. Drugged or sleeping naturally, they lay on the floor of hospital tents, oblivious to their surroundings. The weeks of fighting had taken such a toll on their bodies that little could now upset them. By putting men to sleep soon after the symptoms of battle fatigue were seen it was shown to be possible to prevent them from having to be evacuated. With rest many traumatised men recovered sufficiently to be able to return to their units.

Desertion was a difficult decision for any man. They all knew the consequences – letting down their mates who might die as a result, arrest, imprisonment – but soldiers at the end of their tether could do little else. To MPs this was cowardice or desertion, but to the men concerned it was desperation. They were not running away to avoid their duty but openly admitting they could carry on no longer. Some gave strange-sounding excuses – a Corporal Skingle of the 1st Dorsets refused to go into an attack on a machine gun position that was to be supported by tanks. His reasoning was simple – he did not like tanks. His fear cost him seven years' imprisonment. Likewise, men found crying in their slit trenches could be sent to report sick but equally could be ordered forward into battle, and they faced arrest if they refused.

Some men who found their nerve failing found a short-term solution to their problems. In the chaos of battle it was easy to get lost and then return once the fighting was over. If apprehended by MPs they could simply claim to be looking for their comrades. Others claimed to have been knocked out by blast or that they had been unable to locate their units since they had lost their glasses. There was little that could be done to prove otherwise. Only if a man regularly played the same game could action be taken and even then proof would be difficult to find.

Men who by chance found themselves separated from their units just decided not to return to the front. Instead they hung around the rear areas, got rid of their badges and mingled in with the crowds. They joined queues for feeding at kitchens and slept alongside legitimate occupants of camps. They soon spotted men in similar situations and teamed up to make their next move. Many had no intention of becoming long-term deserters, it was simply a matter of resting and clearing their minds of the terror they had experienced. These were the men who lived by the maxim: 'He who ups and runs away, lives to fight another day.' (37) They fully expected to be caught and usually were. Otherwise, once calmed they returned to their units to face punishment.

One of those who fled from the battlefield only to hand himself in after he had recovered his nerve was Private R.N. Jones of the 2nd Battalion Essex Regiment. A nervous eighteen-year-old with a history of panicking during air raids, Jones was a less than suitable infantryman. During his first action he lost his nerve and ran away. After he had recovered his self-control he gave himself up and was charged with desertion. In an attempt to convince the court to be lenient his father wrote to the boy's commanding officer:

> I appeal to you in your mercy to give my lad another chance. I am an old soldier, served in two wars. I do not know what the boy has done, he is very highly strung but he is a good boy, he does not drink or smoke and at the present moment his mother is in hospital on the danger list with pneumonia. The boy does not know. But please I ask you again, please give him a golden chance. Yours Faithfully, John Jones, a soldier in the 1st Div in the Mons Retreat and Boer War. (38)

His plea was read to the court but did little to help and Jones was sentenced to three years for desertion.

What punishments should be handed out was a contentious issue – there were still some who advocated execution or at the least that a deserter should be flogged. A few liked to make the point that up until 1879 the letter 'D' had been branded into the chest of deserters. Fortunately for the offenders such punishments were no longer available. Deserters also benefited from an understanding of the conditions on the battlefield and serious consideration was made of the reasons behind their decision. The outcome of a man's flight from battle was a lottery. If two men fled the field of battle at the same moment they might not expect the same treatment. If one had lost control of his mind he would be sedated by a doctor, admitted to hospital and evacuated as a psychiatric case. Yet if his colleague, who had shared all the same experiences and witnessed the same horrors, simply rested for a few hours and regained his composure before being picked up by MPs, he could expect to face imprisonment. In one case an NCO was jailed for two years after running away from his position. Under heavy enemy fire he jumped up, shouted 'Come on, I'm getting out of this' then disappeared. In his defence his colleagues claimed he was already suffering with his nerves, jumping into shell holes and taking cover at the sound of even the most distant shelling or mortaring – all classic signs of a man on the brink of nervous collapse. Yet he was treated not as a psychiatric case but as a coward.

To remedy these anomalies a number of measures were introduced. As early as July 1944 21st Army Group HQ requested that the courts have full knowledge of the defendant's military record: 'In the case of deserters, information as to whether the man "failed" on his first contact with the enemy or after some period of fighting, is invaluable.' (39) It was a tacit acceptance that a sympathetic ear should be given to those men who had been unable to withstand mounting pressure. Medical opinion was also sought, but a September 1944 report to 21st Army Group stressed that contradictions still existed:

> Some men went sick and were evacuated. Others in much the same state, ran away and were awarded penal servitude. The physical escape of the deserter and the psychological escape of the hysteric were expressions of the same mechanism but the former was severely punished and the latter treated with sympathy in hospital. As well as this legal anomaly there was also the fact that the number of deserters at the end of July was large, presumably due to the same conditions that precipitated neurotic breakdown. Many of these deserters belonged to seasoned units and considered that injustice had been done when they were awarded stiff punishment. (40)

In response to this steps were taken to improve the situation. It was decided to send medical officers on psychiatric courses to facilitate better understanding of the symptoms, causes and treatment of breakdowns. The experience of seeing the positive result of sleep left many doctors convinced that with sufficient rest far fewer cases of exhaustion would manifest and encouraged senior officers to make sure the soldiers had plenty of rest before any action. In response to this 21st Army Group HQ adapted their policies. No longer would men simply be put to sleep at aid posts and be left sprawled on the floor until they awoke, instead Divisional Exhaustion Centres were set up. In these all cases where men were not heavily traumatised were treated. They were held for four or five days, mostly under sedation. More extreme cases were sent to Corps Exhaustion Centres where the treatment lasted up to seven days. Behind these were two Army Exhaustion Centres that could handle any overflow and deal with men in need of more complex treatment. Being farther from the front, and out of the range of enemy guns, they were able to offer treatments such as hypnosis that it was hoped would aid rehabilitation. Those who completed their treatment yet were in need of further convalescence were then sent to the Second Army Rest Centre. Here they were assessed for a reduction in their medical category then reassigned to less strenuous duties. The policy worked and the figure for exhaustion cases returning to their units rose from thirty per cent to sixty-five per cent, with fifty per cent of them returned to full duties and fifteen per cent medically downgraded.

Arthur Rowley passed through the exhaustion centres with positive results. He recalled:

> We were occupying slit trenches on the approaches to the Siegfried Line. Shelling had been very heavy all that day and we had lost at least four lads in fwd listening posts. In the evening a slit trench next to mine took a direct hit and both lads therein were killed. I started firstly shivering, which eventually turned into uncontrollable shaking. I was evacuated through the RAP and spent about three weeks in hospital and then given the choice of being returned to unit or posted elsewhere. I opted to be RTU'd and remained with my unit until the end of hostilities with no further problems. (41)

Another response to the perceived injustice of jailing men whose only offence had been to succumb to stress was the decision to review the cases of the SUS – Soldiers Under Sentence. There was a general realisation that there were plenty of potentially fine soldiers languishing in the military prisons. Thus, three months into the sentence of a man convicted of desertion or cowardice a psychiatrist was sent to make an individual assessment of the case. They made some interesting discoveries about the supposed cowards and deserters. They found many considered prison to be like a 'rest cure' or 'rehabilitation' – a break from the torment of life at the front. It also emerged that in mutiny situations the real fault did not lie with the men involved but in a failure of leadership, allowing young men to be led astray by 'bad types'. The psychiatrists heard numerous reasons behind the actions of the deserters – some plausible and some downright bizarre: 'I went to sleep and when I woke up my company had gone ... Two fellows in my section were bomb happy and they got on my nerves to such an extent that I just hooked it ... It was just my instinct, sir ... When I heard the punishment for desertion was not shooting, I ran away ... I had trouble with my piles, sir, so I took the matter into my own hands ...' (42)

These studies resulted in a greater understanding of deserters, as the psychiatrists reported: 'The dividing line between real fear and neurotic anxiety is extremely fine. The outstanding impression gained by me is the great similarity between many of the cases reviewed and those that are referred through medical channels for psychiatric opinion ... The natural conclusion to be made from the paper is that a majority of deserters are not true cowards.' Seeing these results almost seventy per cent of the prisoners interviewed received suspension of their sentences and returned to full duties, twelve per cent were released from military prisons into the care of psychiatric hospitals and eight per cent were retained to serve out their sentence in full. The remainder were medically downgraded and released to work in the Lines of Communication. In the words of the doctors involved, the process weeded out the: 'neurotics, psychopaths, misfits and dullards'. (43) and made the good men available for service.

Few soldiers felt anything but pity for the so-called cowards and some felt a degree of envy that the 'cowards' had the courage to run away and face the consequences rather than stay to face the increasing likelihood of death, as one man recalled:

Let's be honest, there were thousands who turned the other way and deserted. We didn't make any fuss or try to find them. There were the Regimental Police, they had a go at finding them, but they knew as well as we did what had happened. But I'll be truthful to you, to this day I still don't know why I didn't turn round and run away. Many a time I felt like it. But you accept it. When you went home on leave and its time to go back, you think 'Bugger it I'm not going back'. But then you think if I don't go back somebody else has got to do my job and the squad will be one short, so somebody is going to get killed. That goes through your mind and so back you go. But of course not everybody can do that, and I don't blame them, not one little bit. Because I had exactly the same thoughts as them. (44)

Although the figures for men being treated for exhaustion were never to reach the levels of summer 1944, the following months continued to see a stream of men reporting sick. Assessment was made to discover what types of men were included and they pinpointed four distinct groups. Around fifty per cent were men who had been wounded in Normandy, evacuated to the UK, spent up to six weeks in hospital, a month in a convalescent depot, had a home leave, a month's training and then been sent back to their unit. Usually they went sick during the first hard battle after their return. It was clear evidence they had used up their stock of courage. The second group were the very young boys taking part in their first major action. Of the youngsters who became psychiatric cases most were boys who looked young for their age, had a poor temperament for combat and were of below average intelligence. Most admitted: 'They experienced grief reactions at the sight of their dead and mangled friends.' (45) The third group were the better quality reinforcements, youngsters who had arrived after the Normandy breakout and survived in action from October 1944 until the battles of early 1945. In that period they had used up the limits of their courage. The fourth group were the 'old campaigners', the men who had fought throughout the Mediterranean and had reached the end of their tether.

Helpful though such assessments seemed, there was one fatal flaw. These four categories could include nearly every man in the campaign. The most useful point 21st Army Group's doctors seemed to be making was something most of the soldiers at the front already knew – everybody cracks up in the end.

10

Burglary was not a Reserved Occupation

'… numerous complaints and reports of armed robberies, larceny from civilians and stealing WD transport by soldiers – both British and Canadian – deserters from their units.' (1)

With the whole of society mobilised for war it had to be accepted that conscription would bring people from all walks of life into the armed forces. This vast new army included thousands of men with little desire to be in uniform and many with backgrounds that marked them out as seemingly unsuitable for military service. This new breed of civilian soldiers mirrored the troubled society in which they had been raised. Following the Great War there had been a shift to the left in the political spectrum and the Labour Party had emerged as a real force in British politics. No longer did the voice of the establishment go unchallenged. This change, combined with economic crises and social strife, bred a generation of men less deferential to authority than their fathers.

It was not only those of a left-wing leaning who were a potential source of disaffection, there was also considerable disquiet in other sectors of society. The abdication crisis had torn asunder many preconceptions about 'King and Country'. Even in the eyes of traditionalists, the monarchy was tainted with an air of uncertainty. These doubts were augmented by the popular pacifist and disarmament movement of the inter-war years which, fuelled by the carnage of the Great War, had influenced people across society. The view that a modern war would cause irrevocable destruction was widely held.

Added to these factors, conscription brought in criminals, the work-shy, violent bullies and drunks. Once in uniform they served alongside religious men, teetotallers and thousands of boys just out of school – and everyone else in between. This potent mix of men made it likely disciplinary problems would arise.

21st Army Group contained a large contingent of Canadians, who were destined to be infamous. Rumours spread quickly about the men from across the Atlantic. Although they were all volunteers many were purported to be ex-jailbirds who had received suspended sentences on the grounds they agreed to military service. Other rumours suggested they were backwoodsmen whose life revolved around boozing and fighting. While they awaited the opportunity to prove themselves in battle, they posed problems for the authorities. They had a violent reputation, drank heavily and were regularly seen fighting outside public houses.

The situation was not helped by the attention paid to their activities by British newspapers. The troops resented the fact that every Canadian misdemeanour was reported, with emphasis placed on the man's nationality. In reality the Canadian soldiers, like their British comrades, came from all strata of society. However, their reputation was sealed and many civilians reacted to the uniform rather than to the man within. In London, while Canadian units waited for the drive south in preparation for D-Day, worried fathers kept their teenage daughters at home lest they stray into the clutches of the dangerous colonials.

In the run up to the invasion the office of the Judge Advocate General – JAG – whose job it was to oversee disciplinary matters, dealt with a bizarre array of crimes. Long hours of investigation were spent on offences that would seem farcical in light of what would happen in the following months. Soldiers were punished for giving lifts to civilians, allowing civilians into military bases, and making private phone calls. Charges were even brought against men who behaved improperly during the singing of the national anthem. In the last weeks before the invasion the JAG's office were called to investigate the case of an Italian POW who had: 'with indecent intent knelt behind a sow and placed the front of his body against the back of said sow'. (2)

When the time came to invade Europe past indiscretions were cast aside. The well-behaved soldiers lined up alongside all the malcontents and rogues the army had to offer. In the final days before the invasion fleet set sail, cell doors at barracks all over the UK were thrown open and all but the most serious offenders were given a chance to redeem themselves in battle. Absentees who handed themselves in were returned to their units and charges dropped. In the coming months all manner of men performed well on the battlefield, with many unlikely candidates performing great acts of heroism. However, it was off the battlefield where some men's lack of discipline would come into conflict with authority.

What surprised the military commanders was the level of indiscipline apparent throughout 21st Army Group. Although many of the offences were negligible, resulting from behaviour to be expected by men living in extreme conditions, others were of a more serious nature. Nobody was prepared for what occurred, and when MPs talked of a crimewave it was no exaggeration. Not without regret was it reported that: 'The Commander in Chief is satisfied there is serious and increasing indiscipline in 21 Army Group in matters of public and private property.' (3)

The discipline and behaviour of Britain's soldiers during the Second World War was influenced by one overriding factor – they were part of a new army, in which officers, NCOs and other ranks were overwhelmingly conscripts or 'hostilities only' volunteers. This was no longer the army of career soldiers who had policed the Empire since the time of Queen Victoria. Despite the discipline drummed into recruits by NCOs many retained their civilian values, shaped by the factories, offices and streets from which they came. At first many of the pre-war officers and NCOs had a difficulty accepting the attitudes prevalent among the conscripts. During basic training they did their best to impose the old standards and the traditional military regime was enforced upon conscripts. There were serious underlying social conditions that helped the military. As one veteran explained it: 'Britain was still a country where you had an upper class and people were used to obeying the upper classes. I think this was instilled in us. Any spark of rebellion was stamped out during the primary training. So I think we were more ready to accept discipline than the young men are today. The class structure had a lot to do with it, we were half way there already.' (4) Another explained how social structure worked within the military: 'It comes back to county regiments, because I first joined the local regiment. I knew who was the JP, the judge, the bank manager, and of course I paid the same deference to them in the forces as I did outside. Because I knew no difference.' However, he soon noticed changes once he was transferred: 'It was entirely different. It wasn't a county regiment. It was made up from part battalions because they had lost so many men. They weren't quite so "touch your forelock".' (5)

This remained the basis of many disciplinary problems. Officers and NCOs soon realised there was a difference between imposing discipline on new recruits and on veterans. The defeat of the British Expeditionary Force in 1940 saw the final flourish of the old peacetime army. John Reynolds escaped via Dunkirk only to be confronted by officers who thought the old standards could be maintained, he recalled:

> When we came back we got straight off the transport into the barracks. Next morning at six o'clock – reveille. I've got me shoes over me bloody shoulder, the shoes that they supplied me with I couldn't even get them on 'cause of blood all in me feet, where I'd walked. I stood there and the officer came along, he tapped me on the shoulder and asked 'Am I standing on your hair soldier?' So I just turned round and said 'I don't bloody well think so, I know it's long but I ain't had a chance to get the bugger cut!' 'I don't want no backchat from you' he said, 'Where's your shoes?' I said 'I can't put them on, I've seen the MO, I can't put them on, me feet are covered in blood. I marched 38 miles to get to that bloody boat!' He said 'We're going to give you some jobs to do so that you don't sit and get miserable and think too much about what has happened. You go and help to unload the coal wagons.' So I said 'I'm on light bloody duties'. He says 'Go and unload the bloody coke wagons!' Well, the coke's lighter than bloody coal! No, no sympathy at all.(6)

The backchat John Reynolds offered his officer was symptomatic of the change that was taking place within the army. Here was the new breed of soldier, happy to do his job as a fighting man, but wishing to be treated as an equal partner.

The new recruits were stunned by the calibre of some of the officers they found in the early days of the war. Many felt the senior officers were incompetent and that too many junior officers were veterans of the Great War who had been recalled to service. Some of the officers were men whose enthusiasm was genuinely frightening. Arthur Jarvis found himself under the command of the novelist Evelyn Waugh, with whom he and his colleagues were less than impressed. On overnight exercises Waugh incurred the wrath of his men by refusing to let them share two-man shelters, believing it unsuitable for men to sleep so close together. Some of them questioned Waugh over his enthusiasm for battle: 'He wanted to get into action. They asked him "Aren't you afraid of getting shot?" He replied "No, I won't worry about the Germans ". Jarvis explained: 'They said they weren't talking about the Germans. They were talking about his own men behind him! Because he was terrible.' (7)

Soon the officers of the 'old school' learnt there was more to military discipline than just giving orders. Although the other ranks would never be able to select their officers there was little doubt that soldiers would never respond to those who failed to earn their respect. Instead the new breed of officers had to be able to lead from the front and not resort to shouting and shoving from behind. It would take time, but somehow the army would eventually manage to get the balance right and officers who earned their men's trust, leading them with courage and treating them with respect, were repaid with a lifetime of friendship and thanks.

Whatever the strengths or weaknesses of their officers, this new breed of soldiers were more than just civilians in uniform and most devoted themselves to preparing for modern warfare. They wanted to get the war finished and get out of uniform as quickly as possible. From the ranks of this new army rose the leaders with the requisite skills to lead their men to victory. The new rising stars were the men who dedicated themselves to thorough training and the study of warfare. Many of their leaders were pleased to have a new breed of soldiers to work with: men who weren't influenced by the outdated dogma and rigid training of pre-war doctrines.

A new realism went into training, exercises dealt with simulations of what they might encounter on the battlefields of Europe, as they prepared to engage in the battles of the future rather than those of the past. The primary function of the soldier was no longer to slope arms by number and follow orders unquestioningly. Increasingly junior ranks were encouraged to think for themselves and attempt to understand how battles developed. In addition, as technology became more important, the soldier's individual talents were allowed to flourish.

If the officers and men were to think freely and develop in tandem with these new ideas there was little hope they would accept the old standards pertaining to discipline. If engineers and mechanics were to bring their personal levels of professionalism to the fight, there was little chance they would willingly accept the dictates of those without similar levels of skill. If a man could operate a wireless with proficiency and competently transmit and read Morse code why should he be reprimanded for failing to salute properly? In short, if a soldier was to face death in the name of democracy why could he not enjoy some of the freedoms he sought to protect?

Fortunately many of the NCOs and officers were realistic about the abilities of their men. The combination of efficient, thorough training and mutual respect between ranks ensured a majority of soldiers behaved as expected on the battlefield. As one former NCO explained: 'There was no lack of discipline. You didn't enforce discipline because it was there. Once you went forward to the line you did what you were told. Sometimes you looked around and thought "What the hell am I doing here?" But discipline was the not something you thought about, discipline was the normal thing.' (8)

The ability of the ordinary soldiers to remain disciplined in the midst of the most arduous of battles was a source of constant disbelief to many observers. Ken Hardy commanded an infantry platoon and was often surprised they followed his orders, despite the dangers: 'I am sometimes amazed at the way they did. In the early days it wasn't an issue, but later on in the middle of Normandy it became a big issue – that they would do what you said. Incredibly they did. In one after-noon, in ten minutes, I lost thirteen blokes out of my platoon. That's only because they were doing what I said. It's a hell of a price to pay for discipline.' (9)

Another successful leader, Sergeant William Partridge, was a good example of the new type of NCO. He blamed himself for the failings of his men. If replace-ments deserted or broke down in action he considered it his fault for not having taken sufficient care with them. He explained: 'From every soldier you expected the best that he could give, and you never expected too much from those who had lesser ability. In effect discipline was, within reason, tailored to meet the ability of the individual. Breaches, therefore, did not generally occur.' (10)

Despite the understanding shown by NCOs such as Partridge many troops remained deeply cynical about everything they saw or experienced. Arthur Jarvis, a coxswain on a landing craft, found himself embroiled in a confrontation with his officer on the morning of D-Day. Like many others Jarvis held the opinion that experience, and not rank, was what really counted. He recalled:

> I was put on a charge for direct disobedience of orders. On the first day I was com-ing back from the beach, I saw a landing craft, with 150 men on board, stuck on a wreck. So I got my deck hands to throw them some ropes. Just as we were about to try and pull him off, one of our craft with this young officer on board told me to leave it alone as we had more troops to put ashore. But I pulled him off, saving boat and crew, but got put under open arrest. A week later I was marched in front of this offi-cer who told me he didn't get 'made up' because he had a nice accent but because he knew more about landing craft than me. So I was to carry on till he could arrange a court martial. A few days later I had to take him to a meeting and he asked if he could have a go at the controls so I went to get out of the cockpit to let him get in but he said 'now you have to show me what to do' as he had only driven a small assault craft. So I said 'I thought you knew more than me? I had to learn to drive all types of craft to be a coxswain.' So in the end he dropped the charge. (11)

If disagreements between amateur soldiers and the amateur blunderings of some officers were not enough, there was also a gulf between 'civilian soldiers' of all ranks and older, more established regulars. The contrast between the peacetime and the wartime soldiers caused both confusion and conflict. Many of the peace-time NCOs expected soldiers to retain pride in their regiments and keep up cer-tain standards. Jack Oakley watched the behaviour of a senior NCO of the Kings Own Yorkshire Light Infantry: 'One of our chaps approached a CSM of the unit and asked "Can you tell me where the Koylis HQ is?" The Sgt.Major looked down his nose and said "Never 'eard of em". He then said "What you should say is the K.O.Y.L.I," emphasising each initial letter with a poke of his finger, "and not use the word Koyli"!' (12)

Most soldiers realised that the battlefield was not the place for dissent. The best hope was to follow orders and hope that by working as a team they would triumph. However there were inevitably many disagreements and arguments. When faced with orders to undertake dangerous jobs some married men openly refused, telling their officers to select a single man, or someone without children. Individuals pleaded with their superiors for the chance to remain in safety. Some NCOs even offered to give up their stripes in an attempt to be allowed to remain in safety rather than go to forward positions. These men weren't thinking of their careers, only their lives and the army needed them more than they needed the army.

Officers who made claims of forthcoming glory were treated with open derision or sullen indifference. Platoon commanders sometimes called for their men to follow them and got no response finding they were all alone as they charged enemy positions. Such bravery may have won medals but it also cost lives. Over-enthusiastic officers who were wounded were offered little sympathy and medics were often curt with those whose wounds resulted from their own foolhardiness.

With so many men and so many different attitudes, thrown together in a stressful environment it was little wonder soldiers sometimes disagreed violently with each other. Tempers became frayed, arguments broke out and sometimes blows were exchanged. In the heat of the moment these fistfights seemed important but could be forgotten in seconds as the men were once more submerged in battle. Specialists often became embroiled in disputes. Engineers detailed to clear mines often argued with infantry officers over how to get the job done and mortar crews refused orders regarding laying smoke, insisting they knew how best to do their job and should be allowed to get on with it.

The strain of battle also created disagreements between infantrymen and the tank crews supporting them. The infantry often felt the tanks refused to cooperate fully and support them in the requested manner. Tank commanders, on the other hand, had little choice but to refuse targets selected by infantry officers if they were complying with orders of their own superiors. When arguments started and infantry officers made threats of courts martial, the tank commanders openly ignored them, safe in the knowledge their own superiors would protect them. Frequently their orders were in direct contrast to the desires of the infantry. At night they had to leave the front line and retire to overnight 'lagers', leaving the infantry feeling vulnerable. It was not for a lack of courage but simply a matter of operational effectiveness. In the dark tanks were blind and at risk from attacks by German patrols.

Less traumatic, but no less heated were the rows between drivers caught up in traffic jams. During major advances vast tailbacks built up with various divisions all trying to use the same roads. While MPs sought to keep order, arguments and fights started as men insisted they should have precedence on the roads.

In this hot-house world it was rumoured that some soldiers used the ultimate deterrent against those issuing orders that were likely to result in a massacre – they shot their officers. Although few veterans have ever talked openly about such incidents there is little doubt some officers fell victim to attacks by their own men. A major in the Pioneer Corps was rumoured to have been shot by his own men during the Normandy campaign. His unpopularity had started in Sicily, where he paraded his men in the open, in sight of the enemy. Some thought him mad, others feared him and one man charged at the officer with fixed bayonet. By the time they reached Normandy his men could no longer tolerate him. Alexander Baron, serving in a neighbouring company, met a friend from the officer's company and asked: ' "Is he as crazy as ever?" "He's snuffed it, thank God," he answered. "A shell?" "Some bugger shot him," he said. This, in the English of the streets, referred without any doubt to a man in his own company. "He got us in the shit and then some bugger done him." ' Baron later discovered that according to official reports the officer and two other ranks were laying a smokescreen in front of an infantry advance when hit by enemy shelling: 'I know what wild rumours flew about among the other ranks. They saw him as a man looking for a medal. When they were given a dangerous job they assumed that it was his fault. "He got us in the shit." I could never know whether the wounded man's tale was the truth or wish-fulfilment.' (13)

Understandably, few are prepared openly to discuss such incidents, as one anonymous veteran recalled:

> There was a lot of shooting going on. A lot of officers got killed by their own people. Just because they wanted the medals like their fathers had got in the Great War. But they were getting them at your expense, because whatever you do it's the officer that gets the medal. They used to have accidents. Nobody's going to tell you that officially, but you can't get away from it. It happened. It was a fact of life. Why should you give up your life for some bugger who wants a medal? So we used to think why should we suffer? We didn't kill most of those ones, instead we maimed them. But there were one or two, that was it – an accident. (14)

With some men driven to such extreme acts it was little wonder they were in no mood to endure interference from outsiders when they spent time out of the line. Once away from the field of battle the army had to allow the men a measure of freedom. If they wanted their men to fight they would have to let them relax in the manner they chose. It was in everybody's interests that MPs kept clear of resting infantrymen. A hostile reaction faced officers or NCOs who attempted to make soldiers drill whilst serving in the field. Jack Oakely recalled the reaction of his comrades to their platoon commander, who was: 'The object of everyone's dislike although in hindsight I now realise that he was only doing his job and had to bear the awful responsibility of command. To us "Boys", for we were all no more than boys, the enforcement of discipline, route marches when not in line, rifle inspections, physical training, going for runs and a variety of other pursuits to which we all objected, was, by implication entirely the fault of the platoon commander throwing his weight about.' (15)

To be marched back from the front lines was unthinkable. Men who had spent weeks living in slit trenches had little desire to be treated like raw recruits on a parade ground. Such attempts were met with outright displays of fury. Soldiers refused to adhere to commands instead ignoring orders, refusing to salute or march in step. Faced with the mutterings of discontented men there was little choice but to back down and accept the matter.

It was not only the reluctant soldiers who proved a headache for their superiors. Those who had volunteered as paratroopers were eager to get into action and became frustrated by the tedium of barrack life. In the summer of 1944 the men of the 1st Airborne Division proved a constant source of problems for the military and civil authorities. As the war raged across France, they faced a period of enforced inactivity at bases in Lincolnshire. It seemed ironic, they had volunteered as paratroopers to escape the boredom of infantry life and now the infantry were getting all the glory. Numerous operations were cancelled as the ground forces advanced and in response they nicknamed themselves 'The Stillborn Division'. Their latent aggression boiled over into fights against American airmen and the theft of vehicles. On one occasion, paratroopers who had missed the last bus back to camp simply stole a bus. The inactivity also caused numerous absentees, who usually returned as soon as an operation was announced. On the second day of Operation Market Garden absentees reappeared at their camps, having seen the previous day's flights they knew it was time to return and take their place alongside their comrades. Subsequently officers were pleased with the performance of the miscreants. As Colonel John Waddy remarked: 'Some of those men with long bad conduct sheets did remarkably well and some showed leadership, even as privates, under fire.' (16)

This sense of duty was not the sole preserve of elite regiments, it was common in all front line units. A fierce sense of camaraderie gave the fighting men a feeling of independence and superiority over those who they saw as playing a less active role in the defeat of the enemy. As a result, there were many confrontations with authority figures and those outsiders they felt were doing little to win the war. Whereas back in blighty the common enemy had been the Yanks, in Europe it became the men serving in the rear areas.

When front line units came into contact with the rear echelons there was often conflict. The drivers, storekeepers and HQ staffs became figures of fun for those at the sharp end. The fighting men moaned that for every man in a slit trench there were ten or more others whose jobs ensured they never faced danger. This was the logistic reality of modern warfare, but it did little to mollify disgruntled soldiers. It was little wonder men of the two factions were to end up confronting each other in the bars and streets of the liberated territories as Ken Hardy recalled: 'I can remember quite a few punch ups when they met. And I suppose the meetings were pretty awful, the people at the back were patronising, that would ensure a big, big punch up. There could be quite a lot of bitterness.' (17)

Throughout the campaign the story was the same. After days of bitter fighting, clearing whole areas house by house and living in constant fear of death, the infantry would move on. In their place came the support staff – drivers, storekeepers, cooks, mechanics and clerks – all of whom enjoyed the freedoms of the liberator without paying the price. The long-suffering infantrymen, in their battered kit and soiled uniforms, laughed at their fellow countrymen – all parade ground creases, collars and ties – and called them 'the poofs' in reference to their pampered lifestyle.

In some cases infantrymen refused to allow other units into 'their town' for fear of them taking an unfair share of the spoils. They felt that liberating a town gave them the sole rights to the local hospitality. Tensions surfaced in the Dutch town of Breda where Polish troops, who resented the intrusion of other units, threw their rivals into the town moat and at Turnhout there was a riot when infantrymen were prevented from using the garrison cinema. In another incident Canadian troops told civil affairs staff they would have to fight their way in if they wanted to take possession of a building.

Bitterness over the supply of rations played a major role in the quarrels. Soldiers living on tinned food and 'dog biscuits' were shocked to see the vast quantities of stores in the rear areas. They concluded others were getting the pick of the rations and leaving them the dregs. Fred Sylvester of the 43rd Reconnaissance Regiment went to collect rations at Valkenswaard in Holland:

> It was discovered that the 14 man ration boxes were graded from A to G, with, in my opinion, decreasing quality. I realised that we had always had letters F and G. At Valkenswaard the 14 man packs were stacked in lettered piles and we were instructed to collect our own rations. Naturally we went to the nearest pile, not realising the significance of the lettering. A voice shouted that we could not have boxes from that end of the row but had to go to the other end. The boxes we had chosen were A and B. Having been told by the voice that we could not have them, we were determined to keep them. The boxes contained stewed prime steak instead of the meat and veg of the F and G boxes. An altogether better choice of rations. (18)

Little wonder some men deliberately antagonised the authorities. A senior infantry NCO recalled passing through a town his unit had captured: 'We were scruffy, we hadn't had a wash since God knows when and we never wore badges of rank. Everybody knew who everybody was, so you didn't need to.' As their column came to a halt the exhausted infantrymen dismounted and started to brew tea. They sprawled on the ground, smoking and blocking the pavements: 'We didn't mind how long we stayed there as long as we weren't going up to the line.' However, officious members of the Provost Corps took exception to the sight of the unkempt soldiers: 'Along came two very posh MPs, one was a corporal and one a lance corporal. Startling white belts, white holsters and gaiters. The corporal starts this spiel "Get up from there! You're supposed to be the British Army! What are you doing sitting down there? Get up!" and so on. He says "Who's your senior officer? I want a word with him. I'll put him on a fizzer." ' However, insults, oaths, and threats of charges brought little reaction from the infantrymen: 'On and on he was going and all of our boys were starting to grin now. They knew what was coming.' With the infantrymen displaying no badges of rank the 'Redcaps' had no idea they were addressing an NCO senior in rank to them. 'So I got up and said "Do you mind standing to attention!" Oh, that was it. I said "Who do you think you're talking to? I'll have you for insubordination." So he starts going on at me and I turned to my lance corporal and said "Get your book out. Put down insubordination to a senior rank."' His performance defeated the blustering MPs who could only argue their point until pay books were brought out exposing his superior rank. The NCO explained his attitude: 'We were only too pleased to do it. We enjoyed winding them up. Why should we suffer when there they are strutting down the road like that?' (19)

Although much of the wave of ill-discipline that swept through 21st Army Group was simply behaviour that would have been acceptable for the men as civilians, there was a hard core of individuals who could only be described as anti-social. Any army raised from all walks of civilian life will inevitably contain such individuals, but taking men raised in the harsh economic climate of the 1930s only added to the risks. The Scottish regiments numbered among their ranks some of the toughest men in the army – Glasgow gang members with a fearsome reputation, who carried razors with impunity and wore their scars with pride. Among the former gang members were men who would go on to earn honours on the battlefield, but many also caused nightmares for their superiors. Some continued their civilian ways, sewing razor blades into the seams of their caps, ready to strike at the first sign of trouble.

Authorities hopeful to build good relationships with the liberated populations found the behaviour of such troops a problem. There were elements who cared little for anyone but themselves, such as the Canadian soldiers who stole a bus at gunpoint outside the town of Limburg, sparking a hostile reception from the locals. Arguments among the liberating troops also spilled over into violence. At the start of July 1944 two Royal Marines were arrested in Normandy for the murder of a comrade. Despite the danger of spiralling indiscipline even murderers did not face the full force of military justice. When Guardsman Fairham shot and killed Driver Tilley after a argument outside a Normandy café he was sentenced to death. As in so many cases at the time the sentence was commuted to fifteen years' penal servitude. Fairham, who had a poor disciplinary record, was lucky to escape with his life. His service revolver fired the fatal shot, he admitted to firing it, and witnesses saw him do it. Maybe the leniency was related to the fact that all the parties involved, including the witnesses, were drunk, and that a fight had already taken place in which Fairham had sustained a black eye. In commuting the sentence the military authorities acknowledged these were exceptional times and men were reacting in exceptional ways.

More seriously, in the confusion of war those with a predilection for sexual crime found victims among the displaced and dispossessed. One of the earliest reported incidents took place in August 1944 when Mademoiselle Yvonne Niveau was raped and murdered by a British soldier. In time MPs were to deal with all the same sexual crimes encountered by policemen back home, including sexual assaults carried out on male civilians by men in uniform. In the closing months of the war and the start of peacetime there was to be a frightening rise in the reported murder rate – both of civilians and fellow soldiers – and of rape, indecent assault and offences against children. The rise of indecency with children had first come to the attention of the authorities in December 1944. With the army static for the winter, offenders befriended families in Holland and Belgium, often living among them in their homes. Here the abusers were able to exploit this atmosphere of trust and though the authorities attempted to investigate allegations, and some men were convicted, it was an issue that received little publicity.

The question of rape became a more public issue. Although not perpetrated on the scale experienced in the Russian zone it was a regular feature in investigations by British MPs. On a single day – 16 April 1945 – three women were reported to have been raped by British soldiers in the German town of Neustadt. While violence towards German POWs or civilians who obstructed the army could be ignored or made light of, violence against innocent civilians was another matter. Such behaviour was totally unacceptable. Many were to witness rape in those turbulent months. Sometimes soldiers with unblemished records, often drunk or suffering from the psychological effects of battle, behaved in a manner wholly unexpected by their colleagues. Rapes were committed or attempted against the most unlikely of targets – including elderly women. However, the impulsive actions of those suffering the effects of battle were of little concern compared to premeditated attacks. In one incident, in the German village of Oeyle, a lorry drew up containing two soldiers. The men gestured to two local girls to follow them to the woods. When the girls refused one was grabbed and dragged away by the soldiers. The girl began screaming and one of the soldiers pulled a gun to silence her. Whether intentionally or in error the gun went off hitting her in the throat and killing her.

Some officers failed to treat reports of rape with gravity. When a British medic had a rape reported to him he accompanied the MPs who went to apprehend the culprits. They were able to trace the men by the description of a bicycle stolen by the soldiers. After she picked them out of a line-up the two men were taken before their CO. His response was alarming. He insisted since the men were going on leave no action could be taken and that his word was final. As the medic left the office he noticed both the offenders were crying, although whether these were tears of relief or remorse only the rapists could know.

Not all the offences against civilians were carried out with such malicious intent. Some men reacted to circumstances in unlikely ways and seemed unable to deal with some of the realities of these trying times. Thirty-year-old Sapper Nye narrowly avoided execution when Field Marshal Montgomery commuted his sentence to life imprisonment. In December 1944 Nye shot and killed his Belgian girlfriend, nineteen-year-old Philomena Van Veeckhoven, in a fit of jealousy. Despite being married with two children, Nye had been seeing 'Philo' for two months. As yet he had neither met her family nor told her he was married, but as time passed he became increasingly jealous at her contact with other soldiers. On the night of her murder they had attended a Christmas dance where he spent much of the evening watching her dance drunkenly with other men. His jealousy was stirred when she took part in a 'kissing dance' where the participants formed a circle around one person who then stepped forward to put a scarf around the neck of another dancer whom they would then kiss. The recipient of the kiss then stepped forward, took hold of the scarf and took their place in the centre of the circle. And so it went on. It was light-hearted fun with everyone making the most of the occasion. Everyone except for one man. Nye did not like what he saw. Philo, his girl, was showing more enthusiasm than he thought appropriate and was embarrassing him. At the end of the evening, as they left the dance, his patience finally snapped. He took a friend's pistol and shot 'Philo' through the neck. His behaviour seemed ludicrous – a married man jealous of the antics of a girl eleven years his junior. Perhaps it was sexual jealousy. Perhaps it was a frustration born of love, knowing this was the girl he wanted but was unable to commit to. Whatever the reasons his actions almost cost him his life. At his trial he claimed it was an accident and was a shot fired in error from an unfamiliar weapon. The court, however, failed to recognise his claims. Instead, his public displays of jealousy, grabbing her and pulling her away from other dancers, convinced them of his criminal intent. In a strange twist of fate the court sat in the very room where the dance had taken place and Nye heard the death sentence read out only yards from where he had committed his crime.

The question of how they should respond to the few soldiers who committed serious criminal acts, such as rape and murder, was of little concern for the military authorities. It made good sense to arrest such troublemakers, bring them to trial and dispose of them to the military prisons. Such men were easily dispensable and best kept locked away. However the question of how to deal with the army's largest group of offenders, the deserters, was rather less simple.

During the opening weeks of the campaign the nature of the fighting was such that the figures for men deserting or going absent made uncomfortable reading for senior officers. Throughout the army there were rumours of a Deserters' Transit Camp, based close to the Normandy beaches, where two sergeants sold fake passes to men wanting to travel home. They allegedly expanded the operation to draw rations with fake requisition forms, collecting the food in stolen lorries. Eventually, so the story went, they had even devised their own brigade sign. Of course no one really knew the truth. No one ever admitted having been there. It was always a 'friend of a friend'. The story had probably grown from a mixture of rumour and experience, born of the confusion of having so many uniformed men loose in France, although there certainly were gangs of deserters living in abandoned positions in the fields of Normandy, surviving by stealing army rations. Members of these groups went on to form criminal gangs that plagued the liberated areas. By the time the campaign finished many fake units would exist, providing a headache for the authorities desperate to create a good impression with the local civilians.

The deserters were a serious drain on the army's resources. Thousands of soldiers deliberately disappeared in an attempt to avoid service in the front lines. They seldom took umbrage at being caught, knowing they would be kept in safety whilst awaiting trial. Once sentenced they would be sent to either a prison or a

Field Punishment Camp. It was a relatively easy life. Senior officers recognised the attitude of these men. Reports from 21st Army Group HQ explained the situation: 'There is no doubt in my mind that there are now in the back areas a large number of men without any sense of shame who have openly expressed their intention of not going forward and who can under reasonably comfortable conditions put through their service abroad without any risk to their necks either from the enemy or from superior authority.' (20) Staff at holding units began to notice a pattern of behaviour. In December 1944 the commander of 104 Reinforcement Group noted: 'The old trouble of committing crime with a view to avoiding or delaying a move forward seems to be starting on an organised basis again and I think the time has come when the question of disposal of crimes committed by Rfts (reinforcements) needs consideration.' The offences he noted were AWOL, theft and 'cases of insubordination generally "tried on" with the idea of being put in the guard room'. (21) The offenders tended to elect for trial by court martial thus further delaying their move by at least ten days and it was therefore suggested that offenders be given short periods of field punishment as opposed to detention.

Rather than play the system many men simply disappeared, merging in anonymously with the thousands in uniform. It was easy to avoid detection as long as they still appeared to be doing their duty. Riflemen Bourke and Wilds, of the 1st Battalion Rifle Brigade, disappeared from their unit between 20 July and 10 September 1944. After their experiences in Normandy they decided to desert and made off in a truck full of supplies. When apprehended all the ammunition they were carrying was found to be in place, although a hundred gallons of petrol had been used up. They had simply pretended to be on the road delivering supplies until an eagle-eyed MP noticed the truck was in the wrong area and questioned them. They accepted their arrest in good humour and when questioned admitted they had just spent their time 'swanning around'. (22) Although they had shown how easy it was for soldiers to go missing, Bourke and Wilds also showed how the authorities reacted to such crimes – both men received twelve-year sentences.

Many deserters made their homes in brothels, living with prostitutes and dealing on the black market. Some hid in transit camps, figuring they could remain anonymous among the ever shifting population. Others decided to attempt the journey home. It was relatively simple to hitch a lift to the coast and stow away on a ship or landing craft. Some came up with ingenious ways of outwitting the authorities to find a passage home. John Reynolds watched the ruses perpetrated by deserters in their attempts to get home. Some of their antics earned his admiration: 'A man stood on the side of the quay for the boat that was going over to England and he said "Aw, fuck 'em, I'm not going home. I don't care I'm not going home. She ain't been faithful to me." One of the MPs went up to him and said "Now come on soldier, come on we'll put you on the boat. You'll get straightened up over there, once she sees you." He'd got medals on his chest and everything. We felt ever so sorry for him.' The MPs forced the man onto the boat, seemingly against his wishes. Reynolds later witnessed the boat's return: 'He came back! He hadn't got permission, he'd got no pass, he'd got nothing.' (23)

Deserters who made the crossing without being detected then had to make it out of the docks and find their way to safety. Once in the home ports they mingled with men loading and unloading supplies until they spotted an opportunity to slip out of the gates unnoticed. Avoiding MPs they made their way into towns, stole clothing from washing lines, scrounged money, hitched lifts or jumped trains to make their way home. Hiding with friends or relatives, they bought black market ration books, changed their names and slipped back into civilian life. Some were to spend years on the run until an amnesty was finally passed. Others never returned to their former identity, living out their lives under adopted names.

Some men decided to keep out of the fighting even before the battle was fully under way. One paratrooper, misdropped on D-Day, took a job in a French bar, serving Allied troops but refusing all offers to be directed back to his unit. A soldier of the East Lancashire Regiment went one step further to avoid fighting. He sought sanctuary in a Trappist monastery, where he dressed in a monk's habit to avoid detection.

It wasn't always necessary to desert to avoid the fighting. Hospitals and aid posts were constantly full, and not always with the sick. Some found ingenious ways of defying the doctors. A favourite trick was the self-induced temperature. They put toothpaste under their tongues so when the temperature was taken the toothpaste would heat up the thermometer and register dangerously high. The trick was for the patient to keep his lips closed as the thermometer was withdrawn in order to wipe off all traces of toothpaste. Other tricks included chewing cordite from artillery shells that caused the heart to beat at high speeds and swallowing cotton wool balls, which appeared as ulcers on X-rays. One Canadian used an unorthodox method to get evacuated from the front, he faked bladder failure. Although doctors diagnosed his condition as faked the young signaller persisted. For weeks he walked around with a permanent wet patch on the front of his battledress trousers. Officers refused to let him into the command post and his mates wouldn't stand near him, all unable to stand the smell of the stale urine. Eventually the ruse worked, with a smile he was seen loading his kit into a lorry destined for hospital.

Those who elected to desert all faced one problem: how to live. The vast array of types on the run, such as men who deserted to avoid any fighting, those who intended to use the opportunity to make money, and those whose nerve had failed in battle, all had one thing in common, they needed to steal to survive. It was in this struggle for survival that criminal instincts were to triumph, and a shockwave of crime hit 21st Army Group. Criminal elements who had been called up for service found many opportunities to continue their work once in uniform. From the start of the war both the navy and RAF had refused to accept conscripts from borstals, even if they stated a preference for service at sea or in the air. Instead convicted criminals were directed for service in the army. Magistrates even joined in by recommending young offenders join up rather than serve a custodial sentence. Once in khaki they were to meet many others with similar backgrounds. John Majendie recalled some of the men he commanded: 'Undoubtedly there were some really "bad hats" in the army. You weren't in a reserved occupation as a burglar. We marched up to Hampshire where my mother lived. She had a loft where a lot of stuff was stored. The smartest chap I ever had serving in my troop pinched a whole lot of stuff from there. I never proved it but I discovered afterwards that he was a thief. A very smart soldier, always immaculate, and he was a professional thief.' (24)

In time MPs realised such men were at the forefront of criminal activity throughout the liberated areas, as one Provost diarist noted: 'it is not an exagge ration to say that a majority of long term deserters have civilian criminal records and are skilful and dange rous types'. (25) However, they were not alone in their activities. For many soldiers petty theft was not a matter of morality but of survival. In the midst of war rules regarding property were widely disregarded. Once in the field the excuse of 'lost to enemy action' became the norm. If something went missing they could simply indent for a replacement. Further more, when no spares were available from official sources most officers turned a blind eye to anyone who could magically procure replacements. The authorities were well aware of the wastage incurred as a result of such behaviour but were powerless to stop it.

Food dumps became a beacon for light-fingered soldiers and stocks of cigarettes and chocolate were their favourite target. They justified their actions by claiming cigarettes seldom reached the men at the front, instead being stolen for sale onto the burgeoning black market. The Provost Corps had a different opinion of such thefts. It became a vicious circle. Front line troops complained that rations were often missing chocolate or tobacco and so armed guards were put on the dumps with orders to shoot on sight. The victims were often those self-same infantrymen who wanted to get these rations before someone else stole them. To mollify their grieving relatives those men shot whilst stealing were listed as 'Killed In Action'.

Vehicles were also the targets for enterprising soldiers. If any transport was left behind it would quickly find a new home and be repainted with the badge of its new owners. Royal Marines who went ashore in Normandy found army motorcycles and laid claim to them by painting them blue with a white anchor on the petrol tank. Broken down vehicles were frequently stripped of everything that was of any use or value. Armoured car crews took machine guns from wrecked tanks or crashed aircraft and fitted them to their vehicles, or took tank periscopes and welded them onto their cars. The abandoned vehicles were soon bereft of all major mechanical parts – air filters, water and fuel pumps, carburettors, magnetos – anything that could be detached during a quick roadside stop. To counter this threat disabled tanks had their hatches welded shut until the mechanics arrived.

Vehicles were not the only things that found new owners. Luminous-faced wristwatches, issued to officers and senior NCOs, were coveted by the masses, and since they were written off by the quartermaster when the owner was killed his surviving comrades would 'acquire' the timepiece. However, not all the theft and pilfering was of abandoned equipment. Misuse of stores was reported on a wide scale. The main issue was one of comfort – soldiers stole to make their day-to-day life more pleasant. Waterproof car covers made comfortable bedding especially if used to line slit trenches. Car seat cushions adorned office chairs, stretchers and hospital pillows were used for healthy men to sleep on, kit was stored in ammo boxes and vehicle batteries used to light billets.

Even wounded men became victims of theft. The Royal Army Medical Corps, known by its initials RAMC, were nicknamed 'Rob All My Comrades' by the cynical troops. Although the vast majority of medics and bearers were honest there were enough rogues amongst them to cause concern and medics became known as 'robbers'. One officer reported losing a full month's pay and a pair of expensive civilian boots to unscrupulous hospital staff – the pay having been advanced to spend on leave. Others tied their boots to stretchers to deter opportunist thieves, and wounded officers often awoke to find their revolvers missing. This wave of theft was not confined to other ranks. A doctor in 141 RAC stole a marquee from an ordnance camp, erecting it to make himself a tent. Nor did thieves respect rank, with petty larceny taking place in the most unlikely locations. Major General Urquhart had his shaving gear stolen from his pack inside an HQ in Holland.

These, however, were petty offences – crimes carried out by soldiers who, for the most part, remained dedicated to their duty. What was of real concern was the shady activities of men who had little intention of doing anything other than make a profit for themselves. There were plenty of individuals who realised war was the ideal time for an enterprising man to make his fortune. Soldiers newly arrived on the Continent were shocked to see stalls where soldiers sold rations and NAAFI supplies. Looting, theft, armed robbery, stealing of army property and trading with civilians all offered opportunities for soldiers to supplement their meagre pay. For most this was merely a sideline as additional money meant extra food and drink in cafés, paying civilians to do laundry, haircuts and visits to prostitutes. For others the temptation was too great. Seeing the chance to get rich some, often those with a criminal past, deserted and descended into a life of crime, feeding off the turmoil that engulfed Europe. In time many of them teamed up into armed gangs – criminal syndicates that traded war department property with willing black marketeers. Their ranks were swelled by the increasing numbers of deserters and absentees who found the only way to avoid arrest was to join with others in a similar situation and embark on a life of crime.

Within days of D-Day evidence began to emerge about crime perpetrated by military personnel. Even members of elite regiments were accused of criminal activity with two Grenadier Guardsmen reportedly forcing entry to a café and threatening the proprietor with a pistol. As soon as provost units were established in France they began investigating robberies. After their arrival on 16 June, 70 Special Investigation Section – SIS – of the military police barely had time to unpack before they were thrown into the fray. The next day they were hunting down and arresting soldiers guilty of housebreaking. On the 23rd they began an investigation into the theft of 12,000 francs from a house in the town of Amblie, a Black Watch deserter being suspected of the crime.

In the first months of the campaign there was little opportunity for criminals to make their mark. The Normandy bridgehead was so crowded that it was hard to escape the gaze of the authorities. However with the breakout across France countless new opportunities arose. With the ever-lengthening supply routes and widely spread dumps of petrol and stores there were chances galore for those prepared to take the risk. Gradually MPs began to notice the large amounts of money in the possession of many of the deserters they apprehended. Despite claims that this was taken from German prisoners, a link was soon established between deserters and crime. In January 1945 a report by MPs outlined how deserters existed. Livelihood – 'Results of selling stolen WD stores to civilians. Sale of goods stolen from canteens. Scrounging from gullible British and American service personnel.' Sleeping – 'Mostly in private homes, farms, small cafés. Transit camps, trucks in railway yards and with units on various pretexts.' Feeding – 'At places where they sleep, on stolen rations, canteens and cafés.' Travelling – 'Stolen vehicles, hitch hiking, jumping trains.' (26)

It was not just criminals and deserters who played the black market. Troop trains stopping in towns soon took on the appearance of Middle Eastern bazaars, with soldiers hanging from the windows selling or swapping their blankets to eager civilians. In cafés and restaurants they were approached by shifty characters offering unbelievable prices for cigarettes. Willing soldiers hurried back to their billets to fill their pockets with as many fags as they could beg, borrow or steal. Often the soldiers were offered the currency of their choice. Those planning to save their money accepted sterling with which to purchase postal orders to be sent home. Those hoping to spend their leave indulging themselves opted for the local currency. Profits were vast with one Canadian estimating he could buy nine hundred cigarettes from Service Clubs for only $3.25. Yet he could sell a hundred cigarettes for $4.47 – a vast profit that he refused to accept in any currency other than sterling. If he needed local currency he could simply go into banks and exchange some of his profits.

The exchange rates were ever fluctuating and everything had a price. Chocolate could be sold for thirty times its price at home. In Belgium a kilo of meat costing less than fifty francs officially was worth up to two hundred on the black market. Similarly a kilo of butter could cost up to five hundred francs despite the shop price being only forty-three francs. Some of the transactions appeared innocuous but masked a web of dealing. When MPs arrested a soldier in Brussels for buying cigarettes from a man on leave it appeared an innocent deal between two individuals. But he was found to be buying from large numbers of men, carrying out single transactions for forty to a hundred cigarettes at a time. It was discovered that each week he bought thousands of cigarettes and sold them to civilians at a vast profit.

Some aspects of the trade, such as the sale of looted German goods, were of little concern to the authorities. However, other trades threatened to have more far-reaching effects, in particular the illegal currency market. Dealing currency between the various liberated countries was one of the growth crimes in the last months of 1944. From reichsmarks to francs, from guilders to gold coins, everything had a price, and the soldiers were keen to exploit it. Men on leave in Paris found they were able to enter the local branch of Lloyd's Bank and exchange any amount of foreign currency with no questions asked. They were simply given a form to sign and then were handed the requisite amount in francs.

The currency rackets became a simple source of income for servicemen. They sold goods on the black market, exchanged the proceeds into sterling, then bought postal orders to send home. Concerned MPs reported: 'the increase in this type of offence has reached alarming figures in amounts of cash recovered'. (27) The arrests of a number of miscreants highlighted their problems. Driver Chandler was caught carrying 27,847 Belgian francs, Driver Tanebourne was arrested with 16,775 Belgian francs and a Private Mercer was found with eleven pounds of fresh-meat, £9 in cash, £35 in postal orders and 3,000 Belgian francs. Eventually the exchange rates were altered to be less beneficial to the servicemen, and from January 1945 all postal order purchases had to be entered as a debit in pay books. No longer could the they purchase postal orders in excess of their own wages. The rules became an inconvenience, ensuring the soldiers drew their pay, as one explained: 'The soldier went for his pay. He didn't need it but he had to take it because he couldn't show where his money was coming from. They'd turn round and say to us "You haven't drawn any pay so what are you up to?" So he had to draw it each week.' (28)

However, the new regulations were soon sidestepped. Northants Yeoman Ken Squires remembered:

> Basically you lived on what you sold. 'You drew money to make sure you could get your postal orders off but to actually live it was a question of selling bars of soap, coffee and cigarettes. It was quite a huge black market. There was a big racket in Belgium because we were getting a fantastic rate of exchange. But then everything was stopped, everything was called in and we were re-exchanged. Whether we lost or not we didn't know, because if you wanted some money you just went down and sold a packet of fags and got what you wanted. (29)

Even if the soldiers were disadvantaged by the new rules they soon found ways to make up the difference. They soon introduced scams including selling coffee tins filled with sand or pouring a little petrol into a jerrycan of water. The petrol float-ed on top of the water and could be sold as unadulterated fuel. Royal Marines, based at Boulogne, had an even simpler scam, as Arthur Jarvis explained: 'We had a couple of sentries on the docks and they used to let the French chaps come down to see us. We'd have these tins of tobacco ready and they'd come along and buy it from the troops. Then as they walked away the marine would hold up two fingers to show how many tins he'd sold. Then the guard would stop them and confiscate the tobacco, bring it back and they'd go halves with the money.' (30)

Although the marines were able to perform their scams in relative safety others were not so lucky. A veteran of the Essex Regiment explained how such activities were a source of conflict with the locals:

> Ounce of tobacco, there's a point on there, to undo the lid. We used to take it out, put a bit of paper in, fill it with a couple of pebbles. Then we soldered the lid back

on and flogged it, so it looked alright, just like it ain't been opened. But that's illegal, things like that. British soldiers don't do that sort of thing, so they say. Done that in France and I hadn't got me gun with me. I had to run for it, a load of Froggies come after me. They opened the tin didn't they! See, in those days you carried your arms with you, but we'd left them in the barracks. That was your passport to happiness, your weapon. Showed it to 'em and they sort of cooled their minds, if they had any ulterior motives. You'd tell 'em to go away, politely. So this time we had to run for it. (31)

The military police were aware of the source of the problem: 'Black marketing is rampant owing to civilians possessing so much money. Military personnel have little money, but can procure foodstuffs, petrol etc, and as civilians in Holland and Belgium will buy any article without question, trafficking is rife.' (32) Vast amounts of supplies disappeared into the hands of civilians. In one month alone one section of ten MPs were able to recover four tons of rations from the homes of French civilians. There were reportedly scores of men who amassed sufficient funds to buy property to which they retired after demob. They purchased bars and cafés and settled down with their girlfriends, never returning to their former homes.

Whilst the majority of soldiers played the black market to finance their day-to-day lives, the criminal gangs responded to the burgeoning industry with an unmistakable glee. For these gangs the black market, theft and larceny were all part of the same game. Many soldiers would think nothing of blowing open a safe they found in an abandoned building – that was the spoils of war. However it was one thing to use explosives to 'crack' safes in the wreckage of banks and quite another for gangs to hold the staff at gunpoint and force them to hand over their money – as happened at Issum in Germany during a raid in which 95,000 reichsmarks were stolen.

As soon as Paris was liberated gangs began to run supplies directly to the city from supply dumps in Normandy. The 'modus operandi' was to break into stores, often with the connivance of the guards, and take anything that could be sold. In Belgium a group of fully armed deserters broke into stores and stole blankets which were taken to Brussels, sold for a hundred and fifty francs each, then converted into winter coats. The racket was exposed when a coat was spotted in a shop window in Lille. The supplier of the coat was traced to Paris where tailors in Montmartre were found to be converting blankets for civilian use, making handbags, hats, sports coats and even dressing gowns. Stolen greatcoats were also remodelled as civilian overcoats.

While the long-suffering infantrymen cursed those who stole their supplies, the trade continued unabated. The gangs found new enterprises to explore and exploit, and smuggling between the liberated countries became common. Using stolen lorries they attached themselves to military convoys and carried contraband over the Franco-Belgian border. Champagne and cognac passed from France to Belgium whilst cigarettes made the return journey at the behest of Belgian tobacco merchants. By the summer of 1945 the more professional of the gangs were even being investigated over alleged drug trafficking.

Investigations into criminal activities established that Brussels was the epicentre of the crime wave that included housebreaking, vehicle theft, theft from army stores, and even armed robbery. In December 1944 the garrison Provost Company reported that they were: 'having to deal with serious cases of larceny of WD property of all sorts and a certain amount can be put down to the activities of Absentees and Deserters who are at large in the town. Some .... who have already been in custody but have escaped are forming themselves into armed gangs and are living mostly in the small brothel cafés in the area east and west of the Gare Du Nord.' (33)

It was in these brothels that most stolen WD property was recovered during raids. Gang members were sometimes apprehended in spot checks on personnel but this was complicated when one gang started printing counterfeit passes which they validated with stolen stamps. As time went on the gangs became increasingly ruthless. Once apprehended many were unprepared to await court martial. On 11 November thirteen men escaped from the guard room of 120 Provost Company and in February 1945 five gang members escaped from detention at St Jean barracks with help from a guard. Despite the best efforts of the Provost companies the level of absentees at large in the city remained high. As soon as one man was captured another seemed to take his place. In November 1944 three hundred and twenty-two absentees were arrested, a single raid on the Café Blighty netting forty-three men. Early 1945 saw a fall in arrests that coincided with a drop in reported thefts, although the same period saw an increase in the number of armed robberies. The change in crime in the city reflected the military situation. As the war moved into Germany fewer troops were stationed in Brussels and fewer criminal opportunities arose. Thus the gangs followed the army into Germany with a notion to exploit the chaos.

Although on a lesser scale, the situation in Brussels was replicated in other towns. Antwerp faced major problems in the docks where war-damaged ships were stripped bare, and violent armed robberies were carried out by British, Canadian and US personnel. MPs struggled to cope with the burgeoning crimewave since a single officer with a staff of five sergeants had to patrol thirty-seven miles of docks. It was a hapless task. April 1945 saw £8,700 of WD property recovered after the arrest of forty soldiers and civilians caught pilfering from ships moored in the docks. Despite all their hard work, it was a drop in the ocean. In raids during the summer their haul included seven and a half tons of soap, 8,370 yards of hospital sheeting, 2,304 tins of salmon and three million cigarettes. By late 1945 the gangs were in complete control of the dock-based rackets and even MPs came under their influence with a number arrested for bribery and conspiracy.

Lesser ports, such as Ostend, also faced problems. In December 1944 investigations were made into a bogus unit of 'Field Security Police' all of whom were dressed as senior NCOs or officers. All the members carried forged ID papers and outwardly appeared to be a legitimate unit. In fact they were all private soldiers, deserters who spent their time stealing cars and committing burglaries. However, the officers in all gangs were not always imposters and MPs picked up a ten-man gang led by a lieutenant and a Canadian sergeant. It seemed the fabled 'Deserters Transit Camp' was not that far from the truth.

With a developing economic sense the criminals reacted to the demands of the market and they soon established there was one thing civilians wanted more than anything else – transport. Brussels was hit by an epidemic of vehicle crime. Stolen cars and lorries were repainted and passed off as civilian vehicles. It became unwise to leave jeeps unattended without immobilising them first, the usual method being the removal of the rotor arm. Even immobile vehicles were subject to thefts – everything of value, spare wheels, fuel, distributors, batteries and even windscreens were removed for sale on the black market. Even vehicles kept in guarded car parks were not immune as thieves cut the barbed wire then crashed vehicles through the barriers.

Although car crime was a major part of the criminals' repertoire they had another commodity that was even easier to dispose of – petrol. With the almost unquenchable thirst for petrol to keep the troops mobile, the army could not afford the emergence of a black market. With a jerrycan of petrol worth up to four hundred francs on the black market, and up to £50 offered for a single car tyre this crime was a temptation few were able to refuse. Wealthy civilians would pay anything to keep their cars going and there were soon more unauthorised than authorised cars on the road. It became the ultimate status symbol to be seen driving around when so many of their fellow countrymen seldom had enough to eat. In spot checks in Brussels at the start of October more than two hundred cars were caught illegally using WD petrol. Additional checks netted twenty-five cars using stolen wheels and tyres.

Whole sections of military police investigators became dedicated to tracking down those responsible. A single raid netted six hundred gallons hidden in civilian homes. In France, MPs arrested an armed gang of deserters responsible for thousands of gallons of petrol going missing in the Trouville and Deauville area. However, such raids were not simple affairs. To assist in raids MPs had to enlist the help of local policemen who were, they reported: 'not reliable, and whilst SIS are invariably bound to ask their assistance, I know very well it would be a folly to tell them overnight if we intended to raid a café or garage the next morning, because it is almost certain that nothing would be found when the raid took place'. (34) To avoid detection some gangs took to hiding contraband in unlikely places. In Ghent WD petrol was found stored inside the tombs and graves of a local cemetery.

The scale of organised crime eventually became too great to ignore and on 26 February 1945 'Operation Blanket' was launched. This was designed to round up as many deserters as possible. Starting at six in the morning and continuing for twenty-four hours, all available Provost resources were put into the apprehension of deserters and absentees and the search for stolen supplies. All non-essential movement was halted, leave passes were cancelled and units in rear areas were confined to their bases whilst searches were carried out. Cinemas, theatres and NAAFI canteens were closed for the duration of the search. In the course of the day four hundred and fifty arrests were made.

Of those apprehended as little as five per cent turned out to be long-term deserters, instead many had been absent for just a few days. Even searches of cafés and brothels failed to turn up any sign of the most wanted men. It was thought the operation could have netted more offenders had security not been compromised. Diaries of men on leave in Brussels reveal word had leaked out in time for deserters to make sure their papers were in order.

Amidst the chaos the men of the Corps of Military Police attempted to keep order. The 'Redcaps', as they were known from the colour of the covering worn on their service caps, shared a myriad duties. On the invasion beaches they shepherded men and vehicles to forming up points. They guarded POWs, fuel, food and ammunition dumps. They rounded up deserters, returned them to their units, gave evidence at courts martial, and policed the newly liberated lands. In leave towns they checked the dress of the soldiers, cleared bars, arrested drunks, broke up fights, and tried to keep soldiers out of the brothels. Most difficult of all was the job of the Special Investigation Sections whose task it was to investigate major crime. It was a task for which they received little reward and from the average soldier they faced little but derision. Most soldiers remembered them as men who curtailed their enjoyment of their spare time. The troops also resented the fact that MPs were automatically given NCO status and seen as 'lording it' over the infantrymen. These resentments often spilled over into trouble, with confrontations between MPs and men on leave. There were plenty of opportunities for MPs to utter the words of the formal caution: 'You are not obliged to answer any questions, or make any statements unless you wish to do so. But I must caution you that any replies you do make, or any statements you make, will be taken down in writing and may be used in evidence.' (35)

Northants Yeoman Ken Squires remembered the incidents: 'There was always trouble. Because you've got the super efficient lance corporal, MP bloke, and you've got a bloke who's been up the front line for a long time, he doesn't care whether his tie's knotted properly, or he doesn't care whether his beret's on properly or his shoes are dirty. And the lance corporal stops him, and if he's not bloody careful he'll get lamped. Especially if they're on their own or just two of them. There's a lot got hit. It was the officiousness of them.' (36)

Many officers understood their men's emotions and failed to take the MPs seriously, as John Longfield remembered:

I was coming back late at night and there was snow on the ground. I came across a road junction with Military Police standing there. I'd had a few to drink so I was feeling at peace with the world. So I strolled up to them to find out if they were lost. And they immediately said 'What's your name and number? You're on a charge, for having your hands in your pockets!' So I was up before the CO, and he said 'Did you have your hands in your pockets?' I said 'Yes'. He said 'Was it a cold night?' 'Yes.' 'Had you got gloves issued?' I said 'No'. He said 'Very sensible of you. Case dismissed.' And that was typical of MP's behaviour. They were not popular, not with me anyway. I thought why the hell didn't they join the infantry rather than the Military Police? (37)

Such was the unprecedented rise in criminal behaviour that MPs were hit with an unexpected workload. Every man arrested had to be thoroughly searched, have their personal property inventoried, and be prevented from speaking to other prisoners. It was all time-consuming work. As a result MPs called for the size of their units to be increased. Some believed their ten-man sections would need fifty men to deal with their workload. One section's monthly haul was seventy-one men arrested, mostly thieves and deserters but also including one man for murder, five for robbery with violence, two indecent assaults and six charged with sodomy. When the ten men of 73 SIS finally left Caen after nine months they calculated they had made a total of five hundred and fifty-six military arrests and recovered £50,000 worth of military property.

In August 71 SIS reported: 'It does occur to me that if the Establishment of a SIB Section was laid down by someone who knows the working of such a section, then I am sure we wouldn't be so reliant on what we can scrounge.' (38) Experienced detectives, some with long experience at Scotland Yard, were shocked to find they were forced to borrow fingerprinting equipment from local police stations. Each ten-man section had to share a single typewriter to write up reports and they became desperate for clerks to run their offices, and staff to provide their meals. Instead investigators were assigned to typing and cooking.

The crime wave meant it was not only MPs who found it difficult to cope. Offenders' units were hard pressed to carry out the necessary courts martial and to alleviate this a court martial centre was established. In theory this would allow the swift processing of offenders, allowing them to be tried and punished as soon as possible. Like so many seemingly good ideas it was less successful than hoped. They soon found the centre was overburdened, capacity had to be increased from two hundred to three hundred and fifty and an extra court had to be established.

This surge in prisoners was also felt at field punishment camps and military prisons, Which were reported 'choked up' (39) with absentees and deserters. To alleviate the overcrowding some men facing lesser charges were released 'without prejudice' to go forward as reinforcements. Inspectors found the resources of the punishment camps and prisons overstretched. Thus, on 12 December the court martial centre was notified that all the field punishment camps and prisons were full and unable to accept more prisoners. Again hasty decisions had to be made. Units were instructed to hold prisoners with short sentences of field punishment until they had checked if spaces were available. Latterly all men sentenced to up to 28 days field punishment were kept by their units where the punishment would be carried out.

For all the expedient changes in disciplinary practices there were still too many offenders to deal with. January 1945 saw two hundred and fifty trials, with two hundred and thirty-seven the following month – a majority of the defendants being deserters or absentees. Camps and prisons remained overcrowded, sanitation was overflowing and hygiene compromised. By March the court martial centre was averaging nine trials a day, and the camp designed for one hundred and fifty inmates held two hundred and fifty plus a further ninety men awaiting committal. It seemed no one had quite predicted the level of indiscipline.

The only thing helping keep down numbers was the amount of men escaping from detention. When one trainload of prisoners was moved from Normandy almost one-third of the one hundred and fifty men escaped. Similar problems were experienced at the holding units to which the offenders were sent upon completion of their sentence. At one unit desperate prisoners overpowered their guards, took their weapons then held them at gunpoint before escaping. Some even tunnelled out using knives and mess tins. Others, desperate not to be sent to the front, barricaded themselves in and had to be forcefully evicted. These were the men who had no intention of ever fighting. Even if the army could get them to the front, they were guaranteed to 'go on the trot' at the first opportunity.

By the spring of 1945 the authorities were reaching the end of their tether. Too many men were deserting or consciously offending to avoid risking their lives. Attempts were made to prevent this by announcing there would be no suspension of sentences at the close of hostilities. The message was clear – soldiers would stand a better chance of getting home quickly if they kept out of trouble. Fortunately for the authorities the nature of disciplinary problems began to change. The crumbling enemy resistance meant many soldiers perceived a lessening threat to their safety and had less reason to desert. However, other aspects of their behaviour began to worry their superiors. They were advancing into an anarchic wasteland. In the weeks immediately preceding the collapse of Germany chaos reigned. Thousands of displaced persons roamed Germany drinking, looting, raping, murdering and generally causing mayhem. Hundreds of thousands of people were on the move, all heading home.

It seemed that some elements of the British and Canadian armies were contributing to, rather than suppressing, the chaos. A number of observers felt that some soldiers were getting beyond control. In April 1945 it was reported that: 'the troops in Germany are not fully complying with the aims and spirit of the directions on behaviour in Germany. There is evidence that wanton acts of looting and pillage are taking place.' (40) At the close of hostilities General Dempsey issued a letter to the troops: 'Now that the fighting has ceased it must be realised by all ranks that wanton and unnecessary damage and stealing are NOT permissible and any case will be treated as a very serious offence.' (41) He was right to be worried. Looting and the destruction of property were an everyday occurrence. Livestock was openly stolen by soldiers to be cooked or transported to Holland and Belgium for sale to civilians. Germans were evicted from their homes only for the property to be ransacked, their valuables stolen, food consumed and furniture destroyed.

In light of the Dempsey letter, theft from civilians became an important issue. Once the hostilities were over, no longer could the victims of theft be casually brushed aside and the offences excused as the spoils of war. Instead looting became theft, an offence to which fewer officers could turn a blind eye. MPs soon established there were still plenty of soldiers who failed to distinguish between the two crimes and continued to behave as they had done whilst the war was still on. In June it was reported a group of servicemen had illegally confiscated eighty wirelesses from civilians in the town of Elmshorn. Later in the year seven officers were arrested for the theft of 3,941 bottles of spirits from a warehouse. During hostilities such acts had gone unnoticed, the only reaction from commanding officers would have been sending a truck to claim a share of the loot.

With the coming of peace the levels of theft from civilians began to fall. However, the decline in theft was accompanied by a sharp rise in the reports of violent physical and sexual assaults. Autumn and winter 1945 saw a continuation of this crime throughout the British zone, often involving servicemen using captured German weapons they knew were untraceable. A British sergeant was shot and wounded during investigations into the gangs of soldiers who roamed Berlin by night beating civilians and robbing them at gunpoint. July 1945 saw MPs on the trail of two British soldiers who had held up and robbed three Russian officers at gunpoint. In another incident a British soldier and a Russian soldier fought to the death with knives in the rubble of the city. It was a fitting precursor to the years of stand-off between the two sides that were to follow.

In Germany the workload for MPs was eased by the fact there was little sign of a black market for WD property developing. In the early days of occupation the soldiers had little need to trade – they simply took whatever they needed. However with the war over, and looting and theft once more regarded as crimes, the soldiers soon needed ways to earn extra money. In the months following the surrender, as the troops became more established, the black market started to thrive. Once the ban on fraternisation with enemy civilians was lifted, illegal trade became rife.

Berlin, like Brussels before it, became the focus of illegal trading, centred around stalls set up by civilians in the shadow of the Reichstag. The scale of trade was unacceptable and by October the illegal dealings had grown to such an extent tanks were used in a crack down on. A former member of the garrison recalled:

> The troops made millions of pounds in Berlin, they spent the bloody lot, but it was there for the taking. And that was only on small things, so what they made on the big things I really don't know. The fiddles going on in Berlin were tremendous. The market was full of deserters. You knew they were deserters, but they were in civvies. I can't tell you what they up to! Anything that could be moved they could sell! The scrap merchants were the biggest crooks. They could buy and sell anything. They were the ones with the money. They've still got it today because they made so much money it was unbelievable. (42)

With the war over and the men being demobbed offences changed, now the question of criminality would be one for the civilian authorities. Would the prediction of one MP be realised? 'Some of these crimes are committed on a fairly well organised basis and if this can be taken as a portent for the future, the Police in England and Canada are going to have a new type of crime on their hands when the troops evacuate.' (43)

Only time would tell.

11

The Khaki Locusts

'We had to win the war, if nothing else, to get Danish bacon on the table again.' (1)

Wherever they served, regardless of background or upbringing, most soldiers agreed on one thing – they hated army food. They didn't refer to the Catering Corps cooking for them, rather they had 'their wicked way' with them. (2) The criticisms were not without substance, as Alexander Baron later wrote:

> The thieving cook was a traditional figure in the British army. Many a cookhouse was run by a twentieth-century Bardolph who conducted a lucrative business on the side selling off the soldiers' food to civilians. Most of his staff might well be shirkers who had never boiled an egg but wanted a soft job and no parades. On the first night ..... an orderly brought a large bucket into the chalet. It was full of stew left over from the day. The recruits sniffed at it and told him to take his pig-swill away. The next morning in the dining-hall I filed past a succession of trestle tables and was given a bowl of porridge, then a kipper which was dropped on the porridge, then a spoonful of jam dropped on the kipper, then two slices of bread with sooty fingerprints on them, a lump of butter and a mug of tea. I got all this down me and continued on the same principle as long as I was in the army. (3)

Although most accepted these culinary delights, there were some who starved themselves rather than face the meals. Arthur Jarvis was among them:

> The first time I went to lunch, I walked into the dining room and the smell! I walked out, I couldn't do it. So I lived on sandwiches I bought from the NAAFI with my own money. When the Corporal asked us how we were getting on and what we thought of the food, I said 'I've never been in, I can't face it'. And he said 'How long you been here?' I told him a fortnight, and he said 'Give it another week, you'll be hungry enough to eat anything.' And I was. (4)

The cooks couldn't really be blamed for the poor taste of the food. Any organisation attempting to provide for so many people in such trying circumstances was unlikely to satisfy everybody. The rapid expansion of the military, both in mouths to feed, new cooks, new premises and the constraints of rationing meant emphasis had to be on filling bellies, not pleasing tastebuds. Time was to prove when men were exhausted, or in the cold and damp, little pleased them more than a mess tin of hot food – whatever it tasted like.

During the years of training the soldiers had little opportunity to supplement their diets. The whole population had been hit by rationing, production was geared to military needs and imports had been cut to save space on merchant ships for essential raw materials. Luxuries were scarce – cakes, jam, sugar, fruit, spirits, sweets and ice cream had all but disappeared from the shops, and most people longed for fresh eggs rather than the powdered alternatives. However, although many of these goods were unavailable in Britain there was surprisingly little hardship on the Continent. Despite orders that soldiers should not interfere with civilian food supplies, after years of waiting little could be done to prevent soldiers from making up for lost time – Europe had food and the British army was hungry.

Once the men of 21st Army Group arrived on the Continent they soon realised the routine of regular meals was over. With the fighting underway meals would have to be taken wherever and whenever possible, as Captain John Majendie of the 4th Somerset Light Infantry discovered: 'I can hardly remember a single meal, anywhere, of any sort. What did we eat? How did we eat it? I had a spoon with a regimental badge on it. I carried it in my field dressing pocket. That's all you needed, a spoon and a mess tin. You can't eat with a knife and fork.' (5)

When on the Continent the soldiers received sustenance from a variety of sources. The intention was for their daily meals to come from the field service ration. These were provided wherever and whenever kitchens could be established. Meals were prepared using a combination of fresh, frozen and dehydrated foodstuffs, and field bakeries were set up to provide fresh bread. However simple the meals might be, it was hoped that a hot meal could be brought to the forward positions every day to abate the hunger of the soldiers. The most common meals were meat stews, delivered in insulated containers. When the soldiers were operating in areas where kitchens had yet to be established they survived on 14-man composite ration packs. These packs, commonly referred to as 'compo' rations, were intended to provide for all the needs of fourteen men for one day. The packs contained tins of cooked meat and vegetables for the main meals, tinned bacon and sardines for breakfast or lunch, soup, cigarettes, chocolate bars, margarine, boiled sweets, powdered tea, sugar and milk, salt, dry biscuits, puddings, soap and toilet paper. The packs were designed, if evenly shared, to give each man a daily intake of 3,600 calories. A further innovation was that the compo packs were labelled A to G, with each letter designating the type of meat contained within for the main meals. The basic versions were stewed lamb, pork and vegetables, oxtail and haricot beans, beef and kidneys in gravy, steak and vegetables, or salmon.

It was intended to keep the use of such rations to a minimum, since the diet was not varied enough to keep the soldiers at the peak of fitness. They needed more variety and a greater range of fresh vegetables to provide roughage and prevent constipation. Although these rations were designed for minimal use there was one other ration available to the soldiers. This was the 24-hour ration packs, for use by troops engaged in assaults. The food came in individual cardboard boxes that fitted inside the mess tins carried in the soldiers' haversacks. Like the compo packs they provided sufficient calories for a single day. Contained within were ten 'hard tack' biscuits – commonly called 'dog biscuits' – a pack of dehydrated porridge, dehydrated tea and meat, chocolate, chewing gum, boiled sweets, four lumps of sugar, two cubes of meat extract for making hot drinks, salt and four sheets of toilet paper. It was intended that the soldiers should use breaks in the fighting to prepare their own meals, utilising individual 'Tommy' cookers to boil up the dehydrated foods.

On D-Day the British and Canadian infantry who stormed the 'Atlantic Wall' carried with them two of these 24-hour packs, in the hope that by D+2 the kitchens would be established and ready to start providing them with fresh food. Experience was soon to tell them that such hopes were forlorn and it would be weeks before anyone saw fresh food courtesy of the Catering Corps.

With the first units to land on D-Day remaining in the thick of the action for many weeks, the soldiers had to get used to living from 'compo' rations. The men of the Royal Norfolks went from 6 June until 12 July without the issue of bread. When they were finally pulled out of the line for a rest they received bread that had to be divided up sixteen men to one loaf. The cynical soldiers found it difficult to understand why it took so long to get bread when they were still operating so close to England, and the desperate desire for fresh bread led to some individuals paying up to £1 a loaf to French civilians.

During the long summer days water also became a problem, with some units issued with as little as a pint of water per day per man. Orders had been given that soldiers were not to drink from civilian water sources for fear of waterborne diseases. Even water that appeared clean and was used by civilians could carry microbes likely to cause stomach upsets in those unused to the germs. That a soldier was supposed to survive on such a small amount in the height of summer was unreasonable. There was little choice but to drink whatever was available. They could boil water, if it was safe to start fires, or use the purification tablets issued in their 24-hour ration packs. Until the army was able to establish suitable drinking water supplies many soldiers were forced to continue consuming whatever water they found, with the inevitable result of a serious outbreak of dysentery.

Instead of eating freshly prepared stews and soft white bread, the men became used to cooking their own meals from the 14-man daily ration packs. However, this distribution system left a lot to be desired. Nowhere in the army were there any groups of fourteen men. The most basic military unit, the infantry section, numbered ten men. As tank man Ken Tout wryly observed in his memoirs, these packs made little sense to five-man tank crews: 'The army only appears to cater only for seven men who eat six rashers of bacon between them every two days, or who … consume seven and three quarters hard biscuits each. So representatives of the four crews sit on the grass and barter for the odds and ends which are not divisible by four.' (6) When the rations were divided certain items would be put into a kitty, non-smokers donating cigarettes and smokers donating half their chocolate, so they had a supply of goods for trading with local farmers for fresh produce. It wasn't only tank crews who needed to be careful with their maths to ensure they consumed their meals fairly. Four-man carrier crews found themselves eating exactly the same meals for three and a half days, all the time hoping the next ration box wouldn't be marked with the same letter.

It wasn't only the strangely configured distribution of these rations that caused concern since the contents were also less than popular. The bacon provided in ration packs was imported from North America and was too fatty and heavily salted for men brought up on Danish bacon. Such was the way the bacon was delivered – rolled up covered in grease and canned – that even the Canadian soldiers were less than enamoured. Once cooked, the fat turned to liquid leaving the lean meat in unappetising red strings.

Nor was it only the soldiers who complained. 21st Army Group's medical representatives described the bacon as: 'very fatty and difficult to prepare in any appetising manner'. (7) The report went on to criticise many of the other rations. The meat and vegetable soups were 'too fatty … Salmon is grade 3 and of poor quality … Marmalade pudding is soggy and indigestible … Haricot Oxtail Stew has high percentage of bones and very greasy.' Furthermore the ration packs lettered 'E' and 'G' were particularly unpopular because the meat and veg stews contained too much vegetable. The haricot and oxtail stews were described by one tank man as: 'too foul to be true'. (8) If that wasn't bad enough, 'F' packs were found unsuitable for cold weather since they contained cold meats. The report also criticised the 24-hour ration packs with the compressed meat described as: 'tasteless, insipid and nauseating'. (9)

The ration chocolate, though vital for keeping up strength, lacked the taste and subtlety of civilian brands. It was thick, black, heavy and bitter – few soldiers could eat a whole bar in one go. To overcome the unpleasant taste some soldiers invented their own biscuits, melting the issue chocolate over the inedible hard tack 'dog biscuits' to concoct something more palatable.

The staple carbohydrate of the ration packs – hard tack biscuits – were designed to add bulk to the meals. The biscuits were hard, bone dry, tasteless and needed the addition of slices of meat or cheese to make them edible. However for men in forward positions, when the supply of fresh bread could be an unheard of luxury, the biscuits were their only source of the roughage needed to keep them 'regular'. The biscuits seemed to come forward in such numbers that there was often a surplus, until the enterprising soldiers found another use for them. Sniper Sergeant Les Toogood remembered: 'Tins of biscuits? We used to lay them on the floor of trenches, just to keep dry. We'd just leave them. If the farmer wanted them he could have them later. The hospitals had canopies from three ton trucks, but all the floors were tins of biscuits.' (10)

This surplus meant they could be experimented with. Biscuits were broken up or pounded into crumbs, then used for baking – being mixed with apples to make apple crumble. To carry out such experiments the troops needed ovens. The individual Tommy cookers may have been sufficiently powerful to cook for one man but they were of little value for larger groups. Instead portable gas cookers were available for use by the infantrymen. However, these had two major disadvantages – they were noisy and emitted highly visible flames and couldn't be used in positions where a flame was visible to the enemy.

Too Scared to be Frightened
There were many clear symptoms of fear shown by men on the battlefield.
This man, Sgt Getwood of the 15th Division, is visibly sweating.

A Man in Uniform
In the cold of winter many soldiers wore whatever would keep out the cold.
Here Field Marshal Montgomery, known for his own unconventional image,
admires a rabbit fur jacket worn by a Canadian infantryman.

The Khaki Locusts
Unimpressed by army cooks, the soldiers supplemented their rations
whenever possible. This tank crew of the Westminster Dragoons
have adopted a stray cow. *Normandy, Summer 1944.*

The Khaki Locusts
Once inside Germany the advancing troops found local homes well stocked
with food. These men of the King's Own Scottish Borderers are digging up
hidden stocks from beneath a German home.

The Khaki Locusts
Abandoned farms became a popular source of fresh meat. Here
Privates Speed and Callaghan of the 15th Division chase a pig.

Operation Plunder
Both civilian cars and captured enemy vehicles were used by the
advancing troops. These officers of the 50th Division have chalked
their divisional badge onto a looted Fiat. *June 1944.*

Operation Plunder
Souvenir hunting became a popular hobby. Lance Corporal Ware and Driver Rose
of the RASC collected these medals in the ruins of Berlin. *June 1945*.

A Masterpiece of Liberation
Most soldiers soon became immune to the scenes of destruction they
witnessed. These Scottish soldiers are posing for photographs in the
ruins of the German town of Goch.

In the accepted spirit of improvisation the preferred cooking apparatus became the 'benghazi'. Named after the North African town, the cooker had been the favoured domestic appliance of the men of the 8th Army and was the legacy of the desert veterans who'd joined 21st Army Group. It was usually a biscuit tin filled with sand or earth, soaked with petrol and set alight. They were quick, easy and ideal for boiling water or heating rations. Though energy inefficient and smoky, the cookers had the advantage that the wind seemed unable to blow them out and all but the heaviest rain failed to dowse the flames. Where the 'benghazi' came into its own was for preparing the soldier's favourite drink. If – as the saying goes – an army marches on its stomach then the collective stomach of 21st Army Group was awash with tea. Wherever the British army went, its movements were accompanied by the steady rattling of the tin mugs that hung from the packs of its men. At every stop these were detached ready for the inevitable brew. Before, after and even during battles soldiers stopped what they were doing, got a fire started and attempted to get a brew going. Before battle they used 'brewing up' as a pastime to occupy their minds and keep from thinking about what lay ahead. Brief moments of respite from battle were filled by the fizzing of the cookers and bubbling of water as soldiers tried to find something to keep their minds off the carnage around them. Then, with the fighting over, hot sweet tea helped to soothe the tattered nerves of the infantrymen as they tried to settle down.

Even before the first troops reached Normandy they were able to enjoy a soothing 'cuppa', since some of the aircraft taking paratroops to France had tea urns welded inside the fuselage. Reports of tea drinking has coloured some historians' judgement of the British performance on D-Day. It was noted how many British units achieved their first objectives then stopped to brew up, rather than pushing on inland. Although such reports were accurate – indeed the history of the South Lancashire Regiment proudly proclaimed they were the first unit to brew up on the beaches – they masked the reality of what was occurring. Many of the men seen brewing up on the beaches were simply passing their time whilst awaiting orders, choosing to brew tea rather than do nothing. This was a positive boost for morale, the younger men saw the veterans 'brewing up' and felt relaxed. Others accused of slowing up the advance by drinking tea in the shelter of the sea wall were men of the Royal Engineers whose job it was to clear beach obstacles. They had no choice but to wait for the tide to recede to let them continue their work. That anyone should begrudge them their tea was an insult. Landing in the first wave and clearing the beach for the infantry and tanks, they had earned their 'brew up' with blood.

The tea in ration packs actually bore little resemblance to their beloved drink, since it came in dehydrated cubes. The cubes contained tea, sugar and powdered milk, pre-mixed ready for brewing. The idea was that the cube or powder could be dropped into boiling water to make an instant cup of tea. It may have looked like tea and sometimes tasted like tea, but it was no substitute for the real thing. Despite this the troops made the best of their situation and consumed it by the pint. Every time a column of vehicles stopped the men inside dismounted, dragged out their 'benghazi' cookers and got a 'brew' going. Often the column would be moving before they had a chance to drink it but it was a habit they couldn't stop. Like the tea breaks in the offices and factories of Britain, the 'brew' became an institution – a reminder that despite their uniforms they were still civilians at heart.

With the troops desperate for hot meals cookers became an essential part of daily lives. Whilst in static positions the cooks improvised and made ovens from whatever came to hand – metal ammunition boxes, bricks and clay – all played a part in cooking meals for the troops. One ingenious, if dangerous, device was designed to operate like a blowtorch. Petrol was heated up inside a jerry can and as the fumes were emitted from a hole in the side of the can they were ignited with a match. This caused a long stream of blue flame that gave off immense heat. The jerry can was placed inside a brick construction topped with metal grills taken from a domestic cooker. It was noisy, volatile and evil smelling but cooked efficiently – a pan of water would come to the boil within two or three minutes.

Such weird and wonderful inventions were not always needed to heat food. Although the soup that arrived in ration packs was universally derided it did have one redeeming feature. They had a wick that ran through the centre of the can which could be lit by the soldiers to make a tin of boiling soup within minutes. To the great mass of soldiers, who were less interested in the innovations in weapons than in filling their bellies, the self-heating tin was considered one of the best inventions of the war.

Crews of some vehicles found themselves living off tinned rations whenever they were in forward positions. Tank crews carried boxes of rations and seldom had access to prepared meals. Instead the crews became virtually self-sufficient, preparing their own food from tins when they were pulled back from the line at night. Often they placed tins on the engines of their vehicles so the contents could heat up and as soon as the order came to halt a hot meal would be ready. The men of the Reconnaissance Corps experienced similar circumstances. From the Normandy breakout until VE Day they were almost constantly on call, patrolling ahead of the advance to record any enemy activity. It was a dangerous job that often entailed exposing their vehicles to enemy guns to draw fire and note positions of enemy guns. It was also a task they carried out on empty stomachs. In the mornings before their patrols began they would prepare their own breakfasts over 'benghazi' cookers, frying tinned bacon and sausages, or heating up tins of beans, all washed down with 'compo' tea. They soon found that everything they consumed carried the faint smell of the fuel used for heating the food. However once breakfast was finished there was little further opportunity to eat. Such was the tense nature of their work that they seldom had time for a break during the day, it was impossible for them to pull in at the roadside and cook a meal. Instead they had to remain alert and on the move, their eyes scanning the landscape around them. Total concentration had to be ensured since the slightest lapse could result in death or wounding. Breakfast had to sustain the crews for the whole day, with the first opportunity to eat coming as dusk fell, and they returned to the safety of their own lines.

The demoralising effect of existing on a diet of lukewarm tinned or dehydrated food led most commanding officers to make strenuous efforts to ensure cooks became operational as soon as possible. Conscientious COs ensured hot food was sent forward to their men at least once a day. These evening meals often consisted of heated tins brought forward by willing drivers. When positions were under machine gun fire they even used tanks to deliver food – arriving at positions, opening the hatches and throwing out the hot tins. Others arrived in carriers that barely stopped before the tins were thrown out to the infantrymen. When vehicles couldn't get through, courageous men carried the tins forward, risking their lives to feed their comrades.

The tins they delivered were prepared by heating them all together in a container of boiling water. It was quick and easy, however the tins became distorted by the pressure of the steaming liquid within and opening could be a hazardous task. It was vital to ensure they were facing away from the body to prevent being scalded by a jet of boiling liquid. The delivery of these meals was a lottery in which anything and everything could be mixed together. Even company commanders weren't exempt as Captain John Majendie recalled: 'I can only remember one meal, presumably we must have had more, they brought the tins up in the company carrier and chucked them out from one slit trench to another. Most of them the labels had come off, because they'd boiled them in a dixie, and so you kept a couple of tins and chucked the rest on. I had tinned sausage, the best sausage I've ever eaten, and tinned marmalade pudding. It was wonderful.' (11)

Once the field kitchens were properly established, and the supply of fresh food could be ensured, the cooks were able to get to work providing more substantial meals. Yet the vagaries of battle often meant that fresh food could not be delivered and the infantry had to go hungry. Once more the men at the front found themselves eating lukewarm stews that had been bravely carried up to their positions. Many mornings were to see the arrival of the previous evening's stew, now cold, ready to hand out as breakfast. On such occasions any meals were considered a luxury and when supplies were really short the soldiers found themselves eating cold baked beans straight from the tin or spread on slices of stale bread. It was little different from the early days of the campaign, except the food was fresh rather than dehydrated.

With limited supplies of fresh food it was little wonder the men of 21st Army Group endeavoured to liven up their meals. Even before they had reached Normandy troops were supplementing their rations in any way possible. One group of paratroopers waiting for their flight to Normandy, even roasted the carrier pigeons they were taking to use in the event of the failure of signals equipment. Whilst on board a landing ship heading for Normandy tank crews of the Northants Yeomanry were seen throwing 75mm shells overboard to make more space for ration boxes. As the convoys of ships and landing craft slowly approached the Normandy coast observers were also surprised to see fishing rods hanging over the sides of the craft. Others used buckets, wash bowls, mess tins and steel helmets to scoop up fish killed in explosions. This became a common way of supplementing rations, although later in the campaign it was to become more deliberate. Hungry soldiers threw hand grenades into the rivers and then waded out to collect the fish, scooping them up in helmets, buckets or even upturned umbrellas. Trout farms were subject to the same attentions, the destruction of their tanks leaving many fish to die as the water seeped away.

If the khaki-clad fisherman signalled an inauspicious start to the campaign, more blatant examples of men supplementing their rations were to occur once they were safely ashore. Both politicians and military authorities were mindful of potential problems between British soldiers and French civilians. Knowing that they needed to maintain good relations with the French it was decided that the army would be self-sufficient and not interrupt the supply of civilian food. They should not steal from, sell to, barter with, or buy from the French. The intention was to prevent hardships among the locals and the possibility of their reliance upon military supply. It was an order that proved impossible to enforce.

Such restrictions were of little concern to the troops. All that mattered was filling their bellies, and if their cooks couldn't help them they were more than happy to help themselves. As it became clear that rations would not be enough to keep them satisfied, most reached the same conclusion – to live off the land.

It was a choice soldiers had made throughout history. The hordes that had raged across Europe in the Dark Ages had pillaged all they needed for survival. That was the traditional right of the conquering soldier – Huns, Goths, Vandals, Tartars – all had done it. Now a new name was added to the list – 21st Army Group. Of course, the British and Canadian soldiers were not so extreme in their methods, but many of the farmers of north west Europe were to discover their stocks seriously depleted by the attentions of their liberators. With so many farms abandoned due to the battles raging around them, and with their owners evacuated from the front line, the soldiers discovered hundreds of cows in need of attention. Without regular milking their udders were swollen and many were in great distress. As if by instinct the cows approached the men sheltering in slit trenches. For the ever-opportunistic soldiers this was the ideal situation, free fresh milk available on demand. So, as the cows stood over their positions the soldiers reached up and milked their udders. Some units even established their own farms, adopting cows and keeping them in enclosures to enjoy the daily production of gallons of good quality fresh milk. They also set up enclosures for ducks and hens which were fed on army biscuits. The caged pets of French families also became a target for the troops and stewed rabbit was a common feature in their cooking pots.

Despite the rules about food, even the HQs of senior officers joined in. General Horrocks was surprised to find that 30 Corps HQ had its own mobile farm. Former farmers and farm labourers serving in his command were put in charge of stray animals and their produce was used to supply eggs, meat and milk to the HQ and wounded soldiers. When they were on the move bystanders were surprised to hear the sound of mooing coming from the covered trucks

With senior officers setting such a poor example it was little wonder the men of the Provost Corps were unable to enforce the rules. Farmers' fields, untouched by the Germans during the occupation, were soon stripped of crops. Barter became an instant hit with soldiers who wanted to liven up bland rations. And if legitimate trade didn't work there was always theft. Faced with a diet of tinned food and dry biscuits who could blame the soldiers for crawling into fields of strawberries and gorging themselves, or picking onions to liven up the bland taste of ration cheese. If they passed a greenhouse they went in and took the tomatoes. It was no big deal, no one made a fuss – like all good soldiers it was a case of get in, get the job done, and get out quickly. Some soldiers were reduced to sneaking onto farms, crawling through ditches and gullies to reach elusive potato crops that French farmers refused to sell. A few cautious individuals, mindful of the possible repercussions, went to great lengths to hide their work. They crawled into the fields, uprooted potato plants, dug up the potatoes and then replanted the stems in the ground.

The threats of MPs had little effect on the infantrymen and their attempts to prevent stealing food was not helped by the lack of cooperation from officers, many of whom joined in with the thefts. Ken Hardy, commanding a platoon of the Hallamshires, had little intention of subsisting entirely on tinned food: 'I can vividly remember in Normandy we were forbidden to take anything. But we suddenly discovered a liking for baked potatoes and butter. But the French farmers would only sell us the butter and wouldn't let us have any potatoes. So we used to go out at night and nick them. We didn't think of that as looting. It was foraging.' (12)

The scavengers were in for some surprises. Ken Squires, a wireless operator in a Sherman tank, attempted to use a crop of 'liberated' potatoes to liven up his rations: 'We picked up these bloody new potatoes, and we're home and dry or so we think. Until we "liberated" a pot to cook them in. The pot was absolutely bloody riddled with garlic, and the new potatoes just tasted of garlic. Of course we'd never had it before.' (13)

What the scavengers really wanted were not exotic Continental flavours, but the familiar taste of home – fresh foods they could remember from the pre-war days. Eggs in particular were beloved of the fighting men, as tank commander John Foley noted in his memoirs: 'Now you must know that in those days an egg was a rare thing of great beauty; a prize to be jealously guarded and cooked with care and attention.' (14) They were simple to prepare – frying, boiling, and making omelettes were all popular – they could be hardboiled and carried as a snack, or could even be consumed raw. Many farmers were eager to trade the produce of their hen houses and for the equivalent of sixpence Norman farmers would sell three eggs to the eager soldiers. Others resorted to swapping their spare kit, especially boots, in exchange for eggs.

If the farmers were not keen to part with their eggs it made little difference, there were plenty of abandoned farms that soldiers claimed as their own territory to prevent usurpers from stealing 'their' eggs. Wary soldiers set guards in farmyards for fear that others would come and pinch their supply. Such was the competition that some took extreme measures. It was rumoured that some men even waited with the hens and caught the fresh laid eggs before they landed on the straw. Their attitude towards eggs was opposite to that of the farmers and did little to endear them to the liberated population. Seaforth Highlander Alastair

Borthwick summed it up in his description of how soldiers were dismissive of what they considered: 'The narrow minded belief, obstinately held by civilians, that if a man owned a hen he also owned the eggs.' (15)

Later in the campaign the soldiers came across eggs in numbers that had previously been unthinkable. At Weert in Holland, the South Lancashire Regiment uncovered a battery farm and liberated two million eggs, originally destined for the Wehrmacht. Once the soldiers were fighting through the farms and villages of Germany they discovered, to their delight, that nearly every home appeared to have a hen coop. These were duly raided, the hens killed for the pot and the eggs taken for cooking. Such was the widespread availability that one man reported carrying fifty hardboiled eggs as a haversack ration.

With so many British and Canadian soldiers foraging and clearing farms of anything edible the local farmers had good reason to be annoyed. To add insult to injury the soldiers also destroyed many of the crops growing in the fields. Although the cutting of crops was forbidden many soldiers continued to do it. They used wheat to disguise dug-outs and to line trenches for warmth. The men who needed the crops had little intention of heeding the instructions, and were safe in the knowledge that few 'Redcaps' would venture into the front lines to enforce the orders. Furthermore, few officers were interested in the petty dictates of MPs, especially if they put the lives of fighting men in danger.

In summer it was possible for soldiers to supplement their meals without incurring the wrath of farmers. There were plenty of alternative sources of food that were freely available without upsetting the local population. Men went blackberrying, collected cherries, picked ripe fruits from the bushes that lined the gardens and roads of Normandy, then mixed them in with the tinned desserts of their ration packs. Some also gathered wild mushrooms to add bulk and taste to tinned stews. The most plentiful fruit in the region was apples. Wherever the soldiers travelled they seemed to encounter orchards where they picked apples that could be stewed or eaten fresh. Tank crews collected the apples that cascaded from branches of trees and fell through the open hatches of their tanks. They joked about how so many were squashed underfoot that if they waited long enough the floors of the tanks would be awash with cider.

Yet all the free fruit and vegetables could not quell the soldiers' desire for something more substantial. What they really wanted was fresh meat. With fatty tinned meats being the only fare on offer via official channels, and the ban on buying from farms or shops, there was only one option – theft. Former butchers soon became popular, able to prepare animals for their mates. Cows were plentiful in Normandy and in the summer of 1944 thousands were lying dead in the fields, bloated with gas and crawling with maggots. The surviving animals were roaming the fields, their owners having been evacuated, and many fell victim to former butchers who had swapped their striped aprons and straw hats for khaki serge and a tin helmet. It was fifteen days after the invasion that one airborne unit got their first taste of fresh meat. A small pig appeared near their trenches and was promptly killed with a pistol shot, shared out and cooked by the ravenous men. It was to set a trend that continued throughout the campaign, considerably diminishing the livestock population of farms.

Many officers happily involved themselves in schemes to feed their men on something more appetising than biscuits and corned beef. Murdoch McDougall, a commando officer hatched a plot to provide fresh meat. He arranged to take a section out to a farm in no-man's land supposedly to cover the return of a sniper. This gave the men an opportunity to kill a calf, some rabbits and a sheep. The dead animals were loaded onto a handcart and wheeled back through the Allied lines, but not before they had covered up the carcasses so that no one would find out what they had been up to.

When animals strayed into minefields and were killed their corpses were retrieved by the soldiers and the undamaged flesh cut to provide steaks for the soldiers. Soldiers were quick to find excuses for their 'crimes', many an officer was confronted by soldiers carrying dead animals and claiming they had been accidentally killed. Other excuses offered by men found leading livestock away for slaughter included informing the officers that the animals were being taken away from the front line to a place of safety. Those officers who attempted to stop men from stealing animals were sometimes ignored. When an officer stopped a Scottish soldier carrying a hen and told him he could be shot for stealing the soldier gave him a brutally honest reply: 'Well, Sir, we mae git shot any time so it makes nae difference.' (16)

The problem for many of the soldiers was not finding animals for food but what to do with it. Inexperienced butchers were unsure of the correct way to kill a chicken or skin a rabbit. Comical scenes were played out as soldiers around farmyards chasing chickens they had carelessly beheaded. There was also a down side to the consumption of fresh meat, prepared by unskilled butchers and cooked hastily over open fires. Many men found themselves struck down by gastric complaints after eating meat that had not been cooked thoroughly, or taken from animals unfit for consumption. As a result there were individuals who refused to eat the meat offered to them. Unless they had seen the animal killed they turned their noses up at steaks, fearing they might have been cut from the corpses of the long-dead cows that littered the countryside.

Nor were all the soldiers ready to kill farm animals. For some of the men there was a feeling of disgust at any killing, they experienced enough bloodshed not to want to be responsible for more. They knew they needed to kill men to stay alive, but animals were another matter, they offered no threat to the soldiers and so, they reckoned, should be left alone. When faced with captive animals on deserted farms, they preferred to free them and allow them to roam.

With the breakout from Normandy and the advance north came a new challenge. The main priority for those entrusted with supplying the advancing army was to keep them moving and fighting. Thus the supply trucks were full of ammunition and petrol – food was not the priority. Once again the men were living on tins and dehydrated rations. With lines stretched to their limit the shortfall in food had to be made up from raiding abandoned German supply dumps. In their hurry to avoid the rapid Allied advance many dumps, often capable of feeding thousands of men, were left to their fate. Whenever the advance halted the infantrymen and tank crews loaded up their vehicles with whatever was available. John Mercer was among them:

> When we were chasing the Germans across the Seine we came across one of their stores. There was an enormous amount of tinned ham, and cooking fat. Then we helped ourselves to potatoes from the fields and we had ham and chips, which we cooked ourselves. They were our own, personal rations. We crossed the Seine to the north of Vernon. We went bumping across a railway bridge, it had been blown up but it was just above the water. When we had got across the other side the bridge went down with a crash and we had no cooks' wagon for three days, so we lived off the ham, and the fat, and the spuds. That lasted us for a long time. Because we had our own transport we were able to carry the extra food, unlike the infantrymen – Join the Artillery and ride! (17)

Not all the liberated food was as familiar as ham and chips. Often what they found was not common British fare, but the foodstuffs beloved of the Wehrmacht. For a period such foods as cheese in 'toothpaste' tubes, dry breads, smoked sausages, strange tasting tea, caraway seed biscuits and ersatz coffee became the basic rations for many of the 30 Corps men. The unusual tastes of foods such as turnip jam were unsuited to their palates and left many of the soldiers regretting they had been so critical of the efforts of their own cooks.

The system of living off captured rations was repeated whenever a rapid advance was made. During Operation Market Garden the priority for supplies carried by road was once again fuel and ammunition. With one narrow road to supply an entire corps there was little room for cooks' wagons and abandoned food once more became the staple diet for many of the soldiers. The Guards Armoured Division were stationed in the area around Nijmegen. The salient created by the thrust through Holland meant they had German units on all sides and the situation remained fluid, with both sides unsure who was in control. The Guards drew their rations from three Wehrmacht supply dumps in the town of Oss. The dumps were thought to contain supplies for one million men for a year. The stores provided untold luxuries including tinned meats, bacon, Bols gin, sugar, cigars and apricot brandy. When the storekeeper, Mr Snoek, produced the ledger for British soldiers to sign it displayed the names of German soldiers, and it was discovered that the Germans were still using the facility – the two sides drawing their rations on alternate days.

The difficulties of supply were magnified for the airborne forces involved in Operation Market Garden and they had to rely on airdrops to replenish their supplies. The paratroopers had flown in carrying two 24-hour ration packs each but these were quickly finished, and there was little opportunity to establish field kitchens. Also, many resupply drops fell into enemy hands, further deepening the hunger of the beleaguered airborne soldiers. For one group of paratroopers their misery was compounded when a horse and cart, that had been requisitioned to carry their packs, bolted during an enemy attack. It was the first day of the operation and the unfortunate men were left with no food, and days of bitter fighting ahead of them.

Desperate times need desperate measures and the men on the ground had little choice but to fend for themselves. Soon the paratroopers were scavenging through abandoned homes to fill their groaning bellies. Fortunately many of the homes were well stocked and the troops were soon gorging on preserved tomatoes, french beans, jam and bottled cherries. Some even risked their lives to go out into gardens to dig up vegetables.

Within days the local homes were stripped of all edible goods, and all accessible shops were looted to sustain the soldiers. The airborne dressing station in the Schoonoord Hotel sustained its patients with stew made from two 'liberated' sheep and porridge made from a sack of oatmeal found by one of the medical staff. Towards the end of the battle, with food stocks exhausted, the soldiers were forced to eat anything. Some found themselves eating oleomargarine, the foul tasting greasy concoction that came in their ration packs, and was considered barely palatable even with bread and cheese to accompany it. In their desperation the ravenous paratroopers took it straight from the tin and consumed it by the spoonful.

The failure of Market Garden saw the stagnation of the advance towards the Reich. The slowing of the advance that occurred once the icy hand of winter clutched north west Europe meant food supplies could be stabilised. Kitchens became firmly established behind the front lines and ensured a good supply of hot food. With the port of Antwerp finally open supplies no longer had to be driven across hundreds of miles of open road before reaching the men at the front. The logistical nightmares that had characterised the early stages of the campaign were solved and the soldiers were able to settle down in the hope there would be no major advances until the worst of winter was over.

If the problem of the distance travelled by food supplies was solved by the stabilisation of the front, the stability brought with it new trials to tax the unfortunate men in the most exposed positions. Winter saw many units defending areas of low-lying flooded countryside that characterised the Low Countries. Often the British and Canadian troops occupied houses that were raised above the level of the land around them. The German policy of deliberately destroying dykes and flood defences changed the face of the battlefield. The homes and farms were slowly surrounded by water as the tides of floodwater rose, eventually becoming heavily defended island outposts of the Allied armies. Patrols were carried out in rowing boats and for men of both sides winter was miserably damp. If patrols had to be carried out by boat, then supplies had to be brought forward in the same manner. Once again many of the men at the front were cut off from the hot meals they needed to sustain themselves. However, a measure of salvation was on hand for them. Since much of the livestock was at risk the ever thoughtful soldiers rescued them and allowed them to live in the ground floors of houses. They didn't mind sharing their living quarters with sheep, cows and goats since the animals had been saved for the pot. In the Rhineland, amphibious vehicles swam through the floodwaters like latterday Noah's Arks – rescuing farm animals from the floods and bringing them back for consumption. For the first time since Normandy there was again a steady provision of eggs, milk and fresh meat with which to supplement their rations.

For some soldiers the main concern of late 1944 was would there be enough food to sustain them through the dark, damp days of winter? They feared neighbouring units might get the best of the edible loot, and became extremely protective of their own food sources. Some men even carried live animals into action with them, keeping the meat fresh ready for when an opportunity arose for cooking. On the Rhine crossing one British corporal was seen carrying a duck strapped to his webbing, its beak taped shut to prevent it quacking. In one village, where all the hens had seemingly disappeared overnight, it was discovered they had been herded into one room by the snipers who were fattening them ready for Christmas.

This was not an uncommon situation. The snipers were known for their foraging skills, indeed many of the best snipers were born countrymen. Ex-gamekeepers and former poachers worked side by side as they hunted for Germans. These were the ideal men for the job – they were used to killing, they knew how to stalk, how to use the land to their best advantage and how to creep up on their quarry unseen. In their offensive role of scouting ahead of the advance, they were able to ensure they got the pick of any available livestock, something that immediately made them popular with their officers. As Sniper Sergeant Les Toogood, who was raised on a Welsh farm, remembered:

> A couple of the officers used to come and eat with us because we had more food than anybody else. I was lucky, I had a ghillie in my section. Myself, I'd shot deer on Lord Lovat's and Lord Stirling's estates, with the meat being sent to the hospitals. We trained our snipers shooting deer, it was logical really. We taught them to skin the animals, treat the livers, cook the meat, and everything else. My particular section were highly suited to the country. On Dartmoor I was allowed by two farmers to shoot sheep. My lads had never shot at moving targets so I would take the farmer with me and he'd get the dog to chase the sheep. And I'd make sure my lads could shoot the sheep as they were being chased. (18)

It was not just the snipers who put such talents to use. In the quieter periods hunting became a favourite pastime throughout the British and Canadian armies, not for Germans but for game. The sport had started when the offensive had stalled to allow 30 Corps to advance towards Brussels. The units left behind found an ideal hobby. Whilst resting at the Seine, the men of the 43rd Division took to fishing in the river, whilst others used the opportunity to hunt wild boar. Ducks, geese, partridge, pheasant, deer were all targets for the hunters in uniform. It became a common sight to see both officers and men out hunting, looted shotguns hung across their arms as they searched for something to liven up their dull rations. Keen hunters even adopted stray dogs to use as gundogs.

As with most pastimes enjoyed by the soldiers someone in authority took offence and decided it was unseemly for the men to be hunting. From December

1944 poaching was designated an offence and game shooting was outlawed without the consent of landowners. Game was defined as deer, wild boar, pheasant, partridge, woodcock, snipe, pigeon, wildfowl, hare and rabbits. Once again the rules had little impact on the front line troops since the officers whose role it was to enforce such orders were also keen on the sport.

Once in Germany hunting weapons were easily acquired. Under the rules of occupation all weapons had to be handed in, this covered not only military weapons but also the hunting rifles and shotguns of the local farmers. Local men would be ordered to deposit all weapons at the Town Hall where the Allied servicemen had the pick of the weapons. Soon the familiar report of shotguns would be heard as the troops made their way into the countryside, picking off animals for the pot.

These shoots were not without risks, one brigadier stepped on a mine whilst partridge shooting, was badly injured and had to be evacuated to the UK. Others found themselves being chased by irate gamekeepers and as a result took their jeeps on hunts, ready to make a quick getaway. Shooting parties could also fulfil more than one purpose. Major General Whistler, GOC of 3rd Division, noted in his diary how he had bagged one partridge, a pheasant and several Germans whilst out hunting. Others did not only use leisure time for hunting. When the paratroops at Arnhem came under heavy attack on the second day's drop most soldiers were preoccupied with forming up with their units and returning fire. But for some others the first priority was attempting to shoot hares living on the landing grounds, and which they hoped would find their way into the cooking pots to supplement their meagre rations.

Those who chose a more sedate way of supplementing rations made trips into towns where luxury foodstuffs could be purchased. Officers of the Household Cavalry, waiting to cross the Rhine, sent men to Nijmegen to shop for whitebait and oysters to sustain them whilst they waited to restart the war. However in typical army fashion, as soon as such foods became popular orders came that all consumption of shellfish was to be outlawed for fear of possible outbreaks of typhoid fever.

Once they were across the Rhine there was little need to send men on shopping trips to find elusive foodstuffs. Upon crossing the Reich's last great barrier and driving into the heart of Germany, the troops were pleasantly surprised to find that German farms were well stocked with livestock, and their owners well fed. The towns and villages of the Reich seemed a world apart from the devastated landscape through which they had fought to reach the Rhine. German farmhouses did not seem complete without shelves of pickled vegetables, jams, preserved meats, smoked hams and bowls of dripping.

The wealth of livestock was shocking for the men who had fought across three countries in which the stocks of farms appeared depleted. For the front line soldiers this was an unacceptable state of affairs and many did their best to redress the balance after the hardships they had seen in the occupied countries.

The situation where many soldiers worried about the reaction of civilians was now long past. No longer were there any doubts about theft, the soldiers didn't worry if civilians saw them take the food and livestock – no one cared what they thought. In the words of Ken Hardy: 'When we got to Germany it was a "free for all", absolutely. It was fair game, with no problems at all. You had no qualms about pinching from the Germans.' (19)

The final months of the war were characterised by brief, albeit bloody, battles and rapid drives through the German countryside. In the breaks between these battles the soldiers acquainted themselves with the world of the German farmer. Whenever a column of soldiers stopped, eager men invaded the nearest farm and the clucking of disturbed poultry and the squeals of slaughtered pigs filled the air as the soldiers took their pick. Tank crews even welded wire cages to their tanks to house chickens. As Peter White, a junior officer in the 52nd Division, wrote in his diary: 'As each truck crunched to a halt the Jocks piled out to descend like a swarm of khaki locusts on the luckless farmers.' (20) With glorious abandon the soldiers used their looted cameras to record the scenes of triumph, as they paraded their edible trophies. Pigs hung from the barrels of tank guns as men gutted them ready for roasting. Geese and ducks had their necks wrung before being plucked and cooked. Men persuaded farmers' wives to boil water for tea and the clanking sounds of buckets and pails was heard from cowsheds as soldiers attended to the cows and fetched fresh milk to accompany the brew. It was the life they had dreamed of ever since landing in France.

The first meeting between one newly arrived subaltern and his platoon was the sight of them herding geese into the yard of their billet and calling for a butcher serving in the platoon. It was a rude awakening to the ways of an army at war but was increasingly to become a way of life whilst in Germany. The foods found in German homes provided surprisingly good meals for many of the soldiers. This lifestyle was a shock to new arrivals who expected to be living on a diet of hard tack biscuits. In one case, on his first day with his platoon, an officer was served chicken with boiled and chipped potatoes, beans, peas, bread and butter, tea, Xmas pudding and rice pudding, all washed down with whisky. It was a far cry from the rationing of home or the mess halls of the army.

In those final hectic weeks surreal scenes were played out all over Germany. Throughout Germany the infrastructure of transport and supply was in tatters, those goods trains not destroyed were unable to move for fear of attack and were left in sidings until looted by the advancing troops. Soldiers, civilians, ex-POWs and Displaced Persons all ransacked the wrecks of goods trains blown up by the unchallenged airforces. With no way of distributing foodstuffs factories and packing plants accumulated stocks which in turn fell prey to the hungry soldiers. British soldiers cleared civilians from their homes and sat in their place, dining in comfort at tables covered in pristine white tablecloths, eating their meals with silver cutlery, their meals accompanied by the best champagne and claret Europe had to offer. As they dined the displaced German civilians trudged wearily away from the homes now occupied by their conquerers, pushing their remaining possessions in handcarts and prams, eager to escape the turmoil of war.

THE KHAKI LOCUSTS

As the war drew to a close the men of the liberating armies were eating everything they could get their hands on. They knew the end was coming, they were doing their best to relax, and they wanted to live, once more, with full bellies. Perhaps subconsciously they were preparing themselves for the day they would return to 'civvy street' and once again be subjected to the indignity of rationing.

12

Operation Plunder

'It was a general rule that you couldn't loot from the French. And the Dutch had nothing left to loot. But when you got into Germany it was fair game, free for all.' (1)

History is littered with tales of marauding armies who travelled across continents destroying all in their path – laying waste to towns, villages and whole civilisations. The Mongols, the Huns, the Vandals and the Vikings, all were known for their excesses, rape, pillage and plunder was the order of the day. They lived off the land, taking all they needed before moving on.

The vast armies of the modern democracies were not supposed to function in this manner. History relates how the Nazis plundered Europe of its raw materials and art treasures. Retribution came in the form of the Red Army who smashed their way into Germany, taking all they needed to live from day to day and then later shipping back entire factories to rebuild their ravaged homeland. In this version of history the Germans destroyed, the Russians avenged and Britain and her allies liberated.

But history is seldom so simple. Looting was a part of war, all sides did it, and without doubt the British army enjoyed the perks afforded to the victors. In eleven months of fighting many of those liberated by the British and Canadian armies were to pay a high price, as were Germans whose land was occupied. Few took heed of the notices that proclaimed 'Looting Is A Serious Crime' or 'Looting Means Death!' For all the efforts of MPs to protect private property there was little they could do to prevent war-weary soldiers from taking whatever they desired.

It was only the authorities that ever talked of looting since the soldiers had their own language to describe and justify their actions. Goods stolen from homes and shops were described as 'liberated'. Searching for loot was known as 'swanning'. Privately, even senior officers turned a blind eye to the misdeeds of their men, referring to the crime as 'personal commandeering'. Despite all the warnings about arrest, imprisonment or even execution, there were few men not tempted to avail themselves of whatever was on offer.

Despite their fears and apprehensions, most soldiers attempted to live their lives in a manner little different from how they lived as civilians. Many treated war as an adventure, albeit one that could cost them their life. They felt the urge to collect souvenirs of their travels, mementoes of what for most was their first trip outside their homeland. Thousands of men wanted something to take home to their families, a record of their role in the defeat of the Nazis. Added to the desire to acquire anything that might help make life more tolerable, and the frequent opportunities to 'liberate' goods of real financial value, it made a potent mix that brought despair to many people and comfort to those who claimed the spoils of war.

The first souvenirs were very simple personal reminders of home. In their last moments on British soil men picked up stones to act as a physical talisman of what they wished to return home to. Others collected simple reminders of their journey, filling matchboxes with sand from the landing beaches – an innocent indication of what would soon be a worrying trend. At first much of the loot included things that were an operational necessity. So much equipment was lost during the landings that the men had to pick up whatever they needed to continue with the war. D-Day had seen commandos wade ashore carrying bicycles, upon which they were supposed to advance quickly inland. When these were lost to enemy fire or succumbed to flat tyres they had to find alternative transport. Green bereted stragglers were seen moving towards the front astride a variety of bicycles. Some rode heavy, black Wehrmacht bikes. Others were seen on ladies' bikes, complete with wicker baskets or on delivery bikes stolen from shops. In a comical moment a brigadier acquired a child's bicycle and pedalled forward to consult his battalion commanders. Others took the issue of improvised transport a step further, stealing horses and riding off to reach their objectives or catch up with their units. These latter day cavalrymen raised hoots of laughter as they outpaced the slow-moving convoys, their bareback riders clinging on for dear life as they urged their mounts forward.

In the first days after the invasion the men at the front had little opportunity to loot, and much of what they took were the basics necessary to keep them alive – spades, picks, shovels, saws, axes – all the tools needed for preparing slit trenches. Amidst the chaos some picked up items of little value. Fathers looked for presents for their children, knowing it might be the last gift they might ever send. John Majendie was one such man: 'When we were down at Etterville, we were dug in in an orchard, and there was a cottage. It was flattened. I picked up a wooden doll and I sent that home to my children. I don't know if that's quite classified as looting.' (2)

Whilst the infantrymen, sheltering in the hedgerows and shattered farms of the forward positions, found little worth looting it didn't take long for others to take advantage of the chaos. There were large contingents of sailors arriving in France and hunting for souvenirs. One soldier set up shop in an abandoned pillbox selling chunks of concrete which he claimed were authentic pieces of the Atlantic Wall. The venture was a success and he had a constant stream of patrons until closed down by an officer from his regiment. Even without his stall the sailors who came ashore were still able to find mementoes. They searched abandoned German bunkers, picking up discarded helmets, knives and binoculars, and even unscrewing the maker's nameplates from artillery pieces to take away. The visiting sailors were not only picking up the detritus of war as souvenirs. MPs carried out raids on the ships that were at anchor off the Normandy coast only to find that many sailors had been looting. A raid on a single ship unearthed an estimated £150 worth of civilian property.

As the bridgehead expanded so did the opportunity to loot. The numbers of troops arriving in Normandy made the task of the MPs difficult. They soon realised homes were being thoroughly looted throughout the liberated zone. The MPs immediately set about trying to tackle the problem. As early as June 1944 half of the men of a 49th Division Provost company were engaged in anti-looting patrols.

During August, after investigators set up office in Caen, they were visited by a constant stream of French civilians eager to report their homes violated by British or Canadian soldiers. They faced so many complaints they had little time left to carry out other investigations. On 7 August they recorded: 'In the majority of complaints received little can be done. Thousands of troops are moving through Caen and are undoubtedly responsible for a large percentage of the looting.' (3) They also concluded that officers were just as responsible as their men, not only by failing to enforce discipline but also by participating in the looting. Arrests included two captains and a lieutenant for theft and an artillery captain found in possession of a stolen car.

The concern over the active involvement of officers in the crime was recognised by the office of the Judge Advocate General. In July 1944 Lieutenant Colonel Backhouse reported that officers were implicated in many acts of looting, something that concerned him more than any other offence being committed by the troops. The following month he again reported on the subject: 'The only matter which concerns me is the number of cases upon which I have been asked to advise where officers have removed property from damaged houses.' (4)

The pattern of behaviour that emerged in Normandy was to set the tone for the rest of the campaign. To these soldiers it mattered little whether the civilians were friendly or not, loot was loot. The temptation of abandoned homes was too great for many of them to resist. There were many cases where towns were liberated only for vast amounts of civilian valuables to disappear in the vehicles and packs of the liberators. Even as civilians sheltered in their cellars unscrupulous British soldiers could be rummaging through drawers and stealing any valuables, as Jim Sims wrote of his own experiences at Arnhem: 'Looking round someone else's home is fascinating, especially when you can open drawers and cupboards as though you were a detective hunting for clues.' (5) In a world filled with violence and destruction many of the soldiers just wanted to find some small item of beauty, something they could carry to remind them of the world they had left behind. Some took ornate picture frames in which to house the photographs they carried of their families. These were set beside the sleeping men, as if on a bedside table at home.

Others wanted simple everyday items to send home. With industrial output geared towards war production there were shortages of most basic goods. Soldiers in Germany found factories full of watch springs, which were virtually impossible to find back home, and posted them back to be sold on the black market. The ravaged homes of Europe were also the ideal source of replacements for what had worn out, with soldiers searching houses for simple items such as sewing machine needles to send to their mothers.

Not all the loot was worthless trinkets. When the bodies of soldiers were searched for personal possessions to be sent home, they were sometimes likened to mobile jeweller's shops. For the infantrymen jewellery was the ideal loot – it had a high value, was easily sold and was easily transportable. Some of the more extravagant soldiers made public displays of their loot with numerous jewelled rings on their fingers and their pockets festooned with gold watch chains. To many of their comrades such displays were effeminate, vulgar and frightfully un-British but to the men in question it was a display of individuality and of their casual regard for the military regime. Others chose to hide the spoils of war, cramming their pockets with gold and jewels and hoping to live long enough to sell the loot.

The fear of boobytraps perhaps did more than anything else to control looting. The thought of dying was the greatest deterrent to all but the most dedicated of offenders. When the infantrymen captured positions directly from the enemy they felt relatively safe, knowing the enemy were unlikely to have prepared a trap. However, when they came across abandoned positions few wanted to be the first man in. There were too many stories about how doors, drawers, chairs and even toilet seats had been rigged to cause explosions. Hastily pulling open a drawer in search of jewellery could be sufficient to set off hidden mines. Truly determined looters developed ingenious tactics. One preferred method was to 'fish' for what they wanted. Lengths of telephone wire were fitted with hooks and used to snare selected items so the soldier could retire to a safe distance to pull it to safety. The fear that kept the average solider from taking such risks was ideal for the determined looters. The Germans were reputed to fit boobytraps to their dead. Upon finding dead bodies they told their comrades to stand back out of danger, then as the others took shelter they would approach the body and loot it without interference.

The looting caused friction between the liberated populations and the troops, and there was also friction between units. Many infantrymen felt they were deemed responsible for the looting and resented this. The infantrymen occupied towns before they were checked for boobytraps and knew the risks of entering unoccupied buildings. By the time a town was clear of the enemy the infantry might be moving on towards the next battle. They were convinced it was the follow-up troops whose behaviour was responsible for upsetting civilians. Few infantrymen claimed to be innocent, but they had important issues to think about. An extra weight in their pack might cause fatal delays, nor did they have the leisure time needed to ship truckloads of loot away from the front to be sold.

Despite the lack of interest shown by many officers in the indiscretions of the soldiers, there was one organisation that kept a close watch on the activities of the looters – the Claims and Hirings Directorate. Right from the start of the campaign, as MPs attempted to crack down on looting, the staff of the directorate, who were mostly former insurance assessors, handled claims for compensation from civilians. By the time the war was finally over the directorate were to have little to show for their efforts, except a huge compensation bill.

Before June 1944 was over the Bayeux-based Claims and Hirings' staff were well aware of the situation in the liberated areas of Normandy and reported back to the War Office: 'There has been considerable looting, some quite serious, which has made a bad impression.' (6) To study the cause of damage to each individual home was too time consuming as entire villages fell victim to crime and the assessors were instructed to lump them all into reports for each village. By September it was clear that a majority of the claims were for looting and theft and by October the total paid out was £69,030, out of which £60,731 was compensation for looting and theft – including 67,815 francs paid to a French general for the losses incurred when the British soldiers passed through his property, and a woman who received a payout of 137,220 francs after troops looted her home. And that was with over two hundred claims still outstanding. By January 1945 the Bayeux office was still striving to settle the outstanding claims for the misdeeds of the previous summer.

With the Claims and Hirings' staff tied up dealing with serious looting, there was no one to keep watch over the other potential source of loot – the enemy. There was no compunction about stealing from the Germans, since troops convinced themselves the Germans had stolen their possessions from civilians. Despite rules governing the treatment of prisoners many British and Canadian soldiers ignored orders and stole whatever they wanted. Many surrendering Germans went into captivity minus valuable personal effects, their captors feeling they had earned the right to rob from the men who had brought misery to so much of Europe.

High on the 'shopping list' of many British and Canadian soldiers were German weapons. Experience on the battlefield had taught them many of the enemy weapons were superior to their own. The Schmeisser machine pistol was highly prized, respected for its reliability and solid construction. Their bolt action rifles may have been powerful and accurate, but there was nothing like automatic fire to give them a sense of security.

Such was the proliferation of captured weapons that regular orders were issued for them to be handed in. Whenever there was a lull in the fighting it became routine for notices to be read out ordering all captured weapons to be surrendered. The crossings of the Seine and the Rhine both saw instructions that no enemy weapons should be carried. The army had no intention of being seen as scavengers and felt undermined by the idea that soldiers preferred enemy weapons to their own.

Enemy weapons were not the only things wanted by the soldiers. They also coveted goods the Germans seemed able to produce to a much higher standard than the British. These included binoculars which were particularly favoured by British soldiers since their magnification was greater than their British equivalent. Since the British only issued binoculars to officers and senior NCOs the role of looting was of military importance. Even the strictest officers considered them as an addition to their fighting ability.

These binoculars often featured the world famous Carl Zeiss lenses, the product of a factory whose output still remains among the best in the world. Carl Zeiss also made the lenses for the Leica cameras which featured high on the looters' shopping lists. At a time when many British soldiers surreptitiously carried Kodak cameras to take their 'holiday snaps' the Leicas were a godsend. They were small, lightweight and used 35mm roll film – anyone with an interest in photography knew these were the best in the world. So the soldiers took as many as they could, always knowing someone willing to buy one. They made their way back to the UK in their hundreds, some being kept as the family camera and others being sold to dealers. It is not without reason British auction houses still offer 1930s and 1940s Leicas at sales of photographic equipment.

The black-faced watches made by the Swiss firm Helios were another of the favourite spoils of war. In the British army luminous watches were issued only to officers and fortunate NCOs. At night sentries would borrow their sergeant's watch and pass it on to the next man on duty so an accurate track of time could be kept from the luminous dial, rather than light a match to see the face of a conventional timepiece. With the looting of German timepieces, the soldiers could convince themselves they were increasing their efficiency. An unexpected source of German watches came after the capture of the bridge over the River Waal at Nijmegen. The Germans launched a desperate offensive to destroy the bridge sending in frogmen armed with mines. They failed and the capture of frogmen or the retrieval of their bodies was a popular event since it meant a chance to pinch their waterproof watches.

It was not only the military issue timepieces which were coveted by the soldiers, they also wanted civilian models, in fact any working watches they could trade, sell or wear. Many were without watches and spare parts were hard to come by and broken watches had been left in drawers until industry realigned itself with civilian needs. With the capture of German soldiers, or by searching corpses, the British and Canadians were able to acquire watches. The stereotype of the soldier with watches from elbow to wrist was not confined to the Red Army. Indeed, medical officers reported having difficulty in taking a pulse from some wounded men since they had watches covering every available space on their forearms.

For many the best loot was money and to find piles of banknotes was their dream. French notes were found in such abundance they were used for lighting cigarettes and cigars by some soldiers. This profligacy stemmed not from a disregard for the value of money, as from confusion as to whether notes in use during occupation remained legal tender. Those who took the trouble to collect the notes found it was the right decision since they had no problems exchanging the money or depositing it in bank accounts.

When the soldiers found vast sums of money they were hit by a sense of shock. The obvious reaction was to scoop it all up, stuff it into pockets, haversacks, even their helmets. They acted instinctively, gathering the cash without first checking what currency it was. It was safer to take the money and sort it out later, away from prying eyes. It became a common practice for infantry sections or vehicle crews to work as syndicates, with standing agreements that any loot be shared out equally. Some kept the cash as a central reserve, using it to pay for food, beer or other luxuries. When armoured cars of the 11th Hussars destroyed a German convoy and found two full suitcases of French francs, the money was shared out between them and was sufficient to prevent them having to draw any pay for the rest of the war.

When collecting German money they often found the notes were worthless. Soldiers discovered bundles of notes left over from the period of high inflation in the 1920s. Some hung onto the notes in the hope that they might one day be transferable, as veteran Wilf Allen recalled of his 1923 issue 2,000,000 mark note: 'I'm still trying to change it!' (7)

There were some individuals who were unconcerned about the source of their loot. The less squeamish men were prepared to search the pockets of dead enemies in the hope of finding money, watches and jewellery. As troops became hardened the robbing of corpses became a common occurrence and they viewed bodies with a callous disregard. At first many soldiers were superstitious about robbing the bodies of the dead, fearful that they themselves might one day be the corpse being searched. Northants Yeoman Ken Squires recalled his own feelings: 'On one occasion I remember looking at a dead guy's wrist and thinking "Shall I have his watch?" But then I thought, "God no, I can't do it".' (8)

Those unused to such behaviour were shocked by the scenes they witnessed. One anonymous veteran recalled witnessing the handywork of the looters: 'There was the enemy, but he proved not to be too much of a problem. How long he had been there I do not know, he was lying on his back, his feet heavily bandaged, no doubt through endless marching, his jackboots placed neatly beside his body. I also noticed that his ring finger was missing …. Someone's son, someone's father, someone's brother, someone's liebe – what a ghastly business war is!' (9)

The aftermath of one such looting expedition was witnessed by Ken Squires when he went to see a corporal responsible for the burial of corpses. What he witnessed was a bizarre scene that could only ever arise in wartime: 'He's found all this bloodstained German money. He's washed it all and it's hanging out on a line to dry. I said "Why are you doing that?" and he says "There's a lot of money there mate, it's all good German Marks". And sure enough it was.' (10)

Some of those involved in robbing corpses were shocked by their own behaviour. John Mercer was initially one of the more innocent soldiers, but found himself hardened by his experiences. He noticed his behaviour changing when confronted with the aftermath of a successful infantry attack, and the fashion for wearing enemy belts: 'I did become callous. In particular I wanted a German belt and the infantry had just captured a place in Holland, and there was a German soldier lying on the ground, he was still warm, and I rolled him over and took his belt off. It was horrible. I shouldn't have done that.' (11)

It was not only the realisation of how war was personally affecting them that made the soldiers think about what they were doing. 'Grave robbing' was beyond the realms of accepted civilian behaviour, yet here were ordinary young men looking into the eyes of their deceased enemies whilst rifling through pockets, emptying wallets and even cutting off fingers. What really affected many of the looters was the discovery of personal effects that made them realise the dead were little different from themselves – young men, far from home, grieved for by wives, girl-friends and mothers. The photographs that were an ever present feature of the wallets of the dead made many think of their own families and what an unbecoming end it was.

Searching corpses may have appalled many soldiers but there was an understanding that the bodies of friends needed to be looked after. However, the death of a friend raised questions such as who would write to his family, who would bury the body, who would gather up his personal belongings? Not least of these questions was what should happen to his loot? The unwritten rules varied from unit to unit. In the Irish Guards it was accepted that the loot should be reclaimed from the body and sent back to the man's family. In other units it was the norm for a dead man's loot to be shared out among his mates.

From the start of the Normandy campaign it became clear there would be loot enough for everyone. However, few could have anticipated the windfall they would encounter when they defeated the German armies in the region. The humiliating blow experienced by the enemy when their forces were crushed in the Falaise pocket saw thousands of panicking soldiers attempting to flee the battlefield. In their clamour to escape the enemy left behind mountains of equipment. For the troops advancing through the detritus of defeat it was as if Christmas and their birthdays had all come at once.

As the dejected survivors watched the arrival of the Allied armies they had little thought for what they had abandoned in the streets and fields of Normandy, all that mattered was to have survived the maelstrom. For the advancing troops it was another matter and they set about looting the German columns with an unparalleled fervour. Troops took their pick from hundreds of abandoned and burnt out vehicles, thousands of prisoners and innumerable corpses. What the Germans were leaving behind was often their own loot – goods stolen from across Europe. It was clear to those scavenging amidst the wreckage of the defeated army that many Germans had deliberately attempted to escape with stocks of French civilian property. There were rich pickings among the wreckage, more trophies and souvenirs than could ever have been hoped for and most importantly there was time to go hunting for them. Men of 21st Army Group, from the lowliest riflemen to the most senior officers, grasped the opportunity.

At first they were like children let loose in a toyshop, snatching at anything of interest, much of which was soon abandoned. All their favourite loot was on offer: flags, money, jewels, weapons, plus expensive women's clothing, including furs, silks and lingerie. Many conquered their revulsion at the scenes and looted from the putrefying corpses of their vanquished foes. The wallets of the dead were stripped of money, rings were pulled from fingers and some soldiers were soon seen sporting as many as six watches per wrist.

As the men relaxed their 'expeditions' produced increasingly bizarre results, as if in competition to find the most unusual loot. A tank squadron of The Buffs started collecting German vehicles, including an Opel car, an amphibious Volkswagen, a half-track carrier, and a camouflaged bus. At first some of the officers tried to get rid of the vehicles, but were convinced the bus could be used as the squadron office. Gradually they were talked into keeping the cars and the half-track, all of which might come in handy. Eventually a line had to be drawn and it was reached when one man appeared driving a Panther tank.

Of all the loot acquired at Falaise these abandoned vehicles were among the most prized. The army had rules regarding abandoned enemy vehicles, that is that they should be handed over to the correct authorities to be repainted, serviced and issued to units most in need of them. Most officers disregarded this, simply taking vehicles and driving them until unserviceable. Everyone wanted to be mobile, infantrymen and their officers wanted cars in which they could go exploring, tank crews wanted motorcycles to ride when off duty and mobile units wanted extra vehicles to ease their loads.

Though vehicle theft had begun almost as soon as the troops arrived in France it was only after the victory at Falaise that the looting of vehicles became a widespread sport as previously there had been nowhere to drive to. Now with much of France open to them, German staff cars became the most prized 'booty', and a target for any self-respecting officer. As the playwright William Douglas Home wrote: 'Everyone has got a private car or so, and most of the British army consists of German vehicles left behind.' (12) Volkswagens, Mercedes, Hanomags – whatever the Germans had abandoned, were quickly repainted and were soon racing around the roads of France. They went sightseeing, visited friends, took trips to the seaside, went shopping, or simply motored through the countryside. The top quality German staff cars were so prized by the advancing troops that even broken down cars were towed behind their captors' vehicles until time came to fix them.

The next great opportunity for plunder was at Le Havre, where the possessions of the German garrison soon found new owners. The troops who captured the town behaved like tourists shopping for souvenirs. Alcohol stores were uncovered, leading to displays of public drunkenness. Soldiers 'liberated' suitcases full of money – the wage packets of the German garrison. The usual trophies of weapons, binoculars, cameras and clothing were scooped up and Nazi flags taken to be used as tablecloths. One soldier even made off with the silk sheets from the German garrison commander's bed.

Soon the liberators passed on, out of France and into the Low Countries. Much of Belgium was liberated with relative ease yet once the advancing armies reached the Netherlands the advance stalled. The Dutch greeted the liberators with a fervour that seemed to surpass the welcome offered elsewhere. Maybe it was that the people of the Netherlands were suffering to an extent not experienced by much of Belgium or France, maybe it was just they had waited longer. However, despite arriving to such a warm welcome there would be many problems resulting from looting during their stay. In the opinion of some observers the reputation of the British army would be eternally tarnished. It was to the credit of the Dutch civilians that despite everything suffered at the hands of the liberators they continued to show exceptional hospitality to the men of 21st Army Group.

During the winter of 1944 many Dutch civilians were shocked to find the behaviour of their liberators comparable to that of their occupiers. Although the Germans had stripped the land of its menfolk and livestock they had never stolen property on such a scale. Friendly soldiers warned civilians to keep doors locked and valuables hidden for fear of the behaviour of some soldiers. But it was to no avail – when the fighting had died down and they returned to their houses they found locks broken or doors kicked from their hinges. Some men admitted stealing money from homes out of curiosity – the house was empty, the money was there, so they took it. No malice was intended but that was of little consolation to the victims. In one of the more blatant outrages, homes in the town of Venray were stripped of furniture by soldiers who filled their lorries with loot. Men heading for leave stripped houses of linen that would command a high price back in Belgium. At one point a complete set of brass band instruments disappeared. MPs seemed powerless to stop what was happening – men were stopped, they apologised and then continued elsewhere.

In the eyes of some, the army was losing its reputation for fair play. Frustrated by their inability to act, the police in Venray drew up a list of complaints against the British, in particular that the soldiers used the cover of the civilian curfew to carry out their nefarious activities. They found numerous scenes of destruction – doors broken open, drawers opened, and floors ripped up to locate hidden valuables. In the village of Leunen Royal Engineers were thought to be behind the cracking of thirteen safes, and the theft of wood, furniture, stoves, sewing machines and even truckloads of coal. In their reports the crimes were listed under the heading of 'English damage'. (13)

The unfortunate inhabitants of Venray were not alone in making lists of wanton damage and looting by the liberators. Looting around Nijmegen caused serious problems for the staff of the Claims and Hirings Directorate. Such was the growing concern among local civilians over the behaviour of troops that there was a flurry of letters going to and from various headquarters trying to establish the truth of what had happened. In early December an official report was compiled highlighting the local concern, and at the end of the month a major from 12 Corps was sent to investigate the situation. His findings revealed that it was not only the soldiers who were to blame for the situation, and stressed how the looting presented a more serious problem than in other liberated countries: 'the Dutch civilians appear to be more adept at this form of sport, perhaps, than the most highly trained Canadian troops or troops under command of 30 Corps'. They had apparently set themselves up as: 'receivers of stolen goods and practically invite soldiers to loot by offering them substantial prices for any useful articles the soldiers can procure or deliver'. (14) In May 1945 the problem was resolved with the British and Americans agreeing to make a bulk payment of £220,000 for looting carried out by troops in the Nijmegen area.

The sufferings of the Dutch would pale into insignificance compared to the scale of looting perpetrated against the nation which had brought so much chaos to Europe – Germany. While many soldiers had looted throughout the liberated countries, bringing heartache to the local populations and a measure of embarrassment to those of their comrades who had hoped for impeccable behaviour, nothing would compare to the epidemic of crime unleashed within the Reich.

From the moment they reached the border until the cessation of hostilities, the advancing soldiers of 21st Army Group stole with impunity – it was not without a sense of humour the codename 'Operation Plunder' was chosen for the crossing of the Rhine. Officers and men alike helped themselves to whatever they wanted, even the men who had never been able to in the liberated zone had no compunction at looting German homes. As local homeowners looked on the soldiers marched in, searched for valuables and left, ignoring the tears and pleas of their victims.

The journalist Leonard Mosley observed the behaviour of the British advancing across Germany. In his book *Report from Germany* he attempted to explain the rationale of the troops involved in looting. It seemed they firmly believed that appearances were deceptive and that seemingly nice Germans were untrustworthy rogues. Using this logic they convinced themselves that anyone could be a secret Nazi, thus it made stealing from them acceptable. Soldiers decided that farmers couldn't possibly afford the fine things found in their homes and must have stolen them from the occupied countries, thus stealing such goods was not a criminal act.

What surprised Mosley was how looting was so rigorously carried out by troops of all ranks, many of whom, such as fifty-year-old officers, he thought should have been able to resist temptation. With the army firmly entrenched in Brussels, the city became a Mecca for men returning from Germany with loot to sell. Some men found a regular outlet for booty and attempted to corner the market in one product – be it sporting guns, adding machines, ball bearings or even slaughtered cows.

In face of extremes of misbehaviour, some officers remained proud of their reputation and considered their men were less prone to looting than other units. The 43rd Reconnaissance Regiment was one such unit, at least in the eyes of some of its officers. As they handed over the German town of Wesel to another formation it was noted that their replacements immediately began looting. Eric Gethyn Jones, their padre, was appalled by the behaviour of the incoming troops and later wrote: 'A few days later I and some others passed again through Wesel, and to our horror we found the place literally sacked, with stuff scattered all over the gardens and on the roads.' (15) Yet as one of his flock recalled, his own unit were less than innocent, but were careful to hide their misdeeds: 'I suspect the padre did not see the odd Nazi pig, wandering on the battlefield, disappearing into our rations.' (16) Nor did he spot his men going into gardens with iron spikes to probe the earth and search for buried valuables.

Soldiers soon became adept at finding the carefully hidden valuables left behind by the fleeing civilians. Homes were searched for newly built walls, put up to disguise secret chambers. Such hastily constructed walls were soon broken down by looters and the contents removed. In one such hidey-hole an officer of the Scots Guards found four brand new piano accordions.

As the advance continued, and such scenes became widespread, it became increasingly difficult to keep the troops under control. Even after representatives of the military government had sealed cupboards they returned to find the seals broken and the contents scattered. The thinking of the soldiers was obvious – if someone had taken the trouble to seal a cupboard it must contain something worth stealing. Soon every column of British soldiers marching through Germany would be characterised by the array of items hung from the packs and webbing of the men. Alongside the ever present picks, shovels and tin mugs hung oil lamps, umbrellas, stoves, blankets, baskets, musical instruments and slaughtered animals.

Towns and villages became scenes of chaos as soldiers brought the war home to the local population. A report from 21st Army Group HQ admitted: 'Troops in Germany are perpetrating wanton acts of looting and pillage.' (17) In the ruins of Cleve soldiers used knives to cut down tapestries from the walls of the medieval cathedral. As artillery officer Douglas Goddard recorded in his diary on 14 April 1945: 'Our chaps looting like mad.' (18) This seeming descent into anarchy led some to speculate on the future, thinking discipline was all but lost. Another officer of the Royal Artillery recalled in his memoirs: 'Was the army losing control, since here and there officers and men appeared to be indulging quite indiscriminately whatever wanton fancies entered their heads?' He watched furniture taken out of homes to fuel bonfires, while engineers hunted for buried treasure with mine detectors. Soldiers were seen pushing wheelbarrows and babies' prams loaded with loot. Accompanying these surreal scenes were soldiers riding horses through the streets, and armed men firing at stray domestic pets. To cap it all two soldiers were observed sitting in a van upon whose sides was written 'You loot, we buy, all the best prices'. (19)

Rather than attempt to stop their troops some officers preferred to issue edicts on what was acceptable loot, hoping this might restrain more criminally inclined individuals. Usually they concluded that acceptable loot consisted of anything that made life more comfortable, such as bedding or furniture, razors to keep themselves clean shaven, and luxury foodstuffs such as eggs which the German people could survive without. The Gordon Highlanders even included wine on their list of acceptable loot since it was thought most had been stolen from France.

Whilst most were content with just following such informal orders or stealing valuables from empty buildings, some made a concerted effort to steal whatever they could regardless of upsetting the locals. A gunner talked the owners of a German jewellery shop into giving him their stock by convincing them it would be destroyed in an imminent counter-attack. The ploy worked and the haul of watches was shared out in his troop, two per man. In the city of Cleve a group of Canadians emptied a safe of diamonds, estimated to be worth 20,000 dollars, although they were unable to benefit when they were destroyed by incoming artillery fire. In the chaos there were also vast amounts of reichsmarks to be found. Many men ignored them reckoning that the currency was worthless, expecting it to be withdrawn or totally devalued before they would be able to spend it. Others collected the money just in case. It was a wise move since it would be months before currency reform was introduced.

Those soldiers amassing a significant amount of loot were the talk of the army.

Many rumours went around about individuals who had vast stocks of money, gold and jewels. Often they were unscrupulous men, with little concern for where their newfound wealth had come from. Others were just opportunists who saw a chance to make a better life for themselves after demob. In time many of the newly wealthy soldiers would disappear, taking with them the secrets of their success – the man who dried bloodstained reichsmarks on a washing line disappeared after demob, heading back to Belgium to build a new life. The soldiers who witnessed the hoarding of wealth were seldom critical of the actions of others. Whether they themselves were involved was irrelevant, as one veteran wrote: 'It wasn't really seen as wrong, more a perk of the job. Some soldiers did sell things and made quite a lot of money – some even bought bars out there.' (20)

The soldiers who took part in the looting of German homes had their own reasons for their behaviour. Some were anxious to make money, others longed for the comforts of home. Whatever their reasons, many were surprised at how callous they had become. Signaller Stan Procter had taken goods from abandoned homes or shops but eventually resorted to pinching directly from the locals. Everyone else seemed to be looting but for him such behaviour was out of character:

> I'm very ashamed of it, but I pinched a wireless set. I've got a photograph of me sitting listening to it. That was dreadful – but it worked! I think the shame only came afterwards, at the time it didn't register. This poor old German lady said to me 'Please don't take it'. You get into a certain frame of mind, callousness must come into it because of what you had been going through. I don't know if anyone else is ashamed of what they did. When I think back, I think of that poor old lady. She's in a battered house, her son was up in the loft hiding – we had to turn him over to MPs. What a dreadful thing for me to do, but at the time it was just part of life. I suppose war changes people, you do things you would never do in normal circumstances. (21)

Even amidst the rubble and burning buildings, not everything was chaos. As Germany came under the control of the occupation forces the soldiers had officially sanctioned opportunities to acquire goods. It had been decided that civilians should hand over all weapons to the occupation forces. The soldiers confronted local burgomeisters who were told to collect all weapons, cameras and binoculars and have them ready for the patrol to collect. Weapons included hunting rifles and shotguns, often antique weapons not used for many years, and even swords. There were no inventories taken, no records kept and no intention of ever allowing the Germans to get their possessions back. Instead it was a free-for-all, as one British soldier recalled: 'These were taken back to the squadron where they were available to any of us, but I still remember all the guns being smashed across the corner of the armoured cars to bend the barrels and then thrown into a pond. These items were supposed to be taken for our security but I thought what an utter waste.' (22)

Such was the scale of looting that the staff of the Claims and Hirings Directorate made an appeal to Field Marshal Montgomery. As early as February 1945 a message was sent to 21st Army Group's commander requesting he send out an order to help curb the crime levels. They requested he direct the message at those in positions of authority who might be able to alleviate the situation: 'The seriousness of the subject should be brought to the notice of officers who ... were turning a blind eye to undisciplined acts of their men, particularly in forward areas.' (23)

Despite appeals, most officers were realistic about the crimes carried out by their men. Rather than attempt to prevent looting they simply ordered all loot to be hidden within vehicles so that outsiders should remain unaware of what was being carried. Since the desire to loot was not the sole preserve of other ranks it would have been hypocritical to enforce the rules too stridently. One officer who attempted to stop his men from looting, instead making them continue fighting, decided it was a fruitless task. He realised he could hardly question his men's behaviour whilst wearing two pairs of German binoculars.

A number of officers organised looting for the benefit of their men. Officers of the 1st Northants Yeomanry made very definite efforts to ensure the comfort of their tank crews. Ken Squires remembered:

> When we were in Goch preparing to do the Rhine crossing, we had a few days when nothing much was happening. I was 'earwigging' to some officers. One said 'We've got very little funds in the squadron PRI'. And the other said 'Well, we worry too much about that'. All of a sudden a 3 ton lorry appeared. We were near to the Bechstein piano factory. I've heard that three of these bloody Bechsteins were loaded onto the back of this lorry, run down to Antwerp and sold. Then two trucks come back with loads of beer. That was the sort of thing that was going on. (24)

As the advancing troops overran Germany, cars once more became the most desirable loot for officers. At Munster Robert Runcie, later to be the Archbishop of Canterbury, found a Delage staff car still flying the pennant of its former owner. He took the vehicle and used it until it was claimed by a brigadier. The behaviour of the future archbishop was reflected in the antics of many of his fellow officers, who could afford to be reckless with the vehicles. Ken Hardy soon acquired a car for himself: 'You had no qualms about pinching from the Germans. I had a car – a convertible. I can't remember the make. I busted it in the end. I broke it in two. But it was alright, if you lost one you could just get another.' (25)

This cavalier attitude towards cars meant many British units took on a motley appearance, with a multitude of unauthorised vehicles in their columns. Eventually the situation became ridiculous. There were so many looted cars that one commander found his division taking up twice as much road space as before. The need to move quickly was vital but there were frequent blockages and traffic jams. When specialist equipment was needed at the front it was found increasingly difficult to move quickly, instead being caught up in columns of stolen cars, vans and trucks. To remedy this efforts were made to stop the theft of vehicles. After the crossing of the Rhine MPs were ordered to check all vehicles for permits, and any without a permit were forced off the road where the engines were destroyed. Of course not everyone obeyed the orders. One Pioneer officer managed to get round the orders about cars by having his looted car crated and shipped home as part of his unit's equipment. Others found even more simple methods to defy the ban. Clerks simply typed out notices to be stuck onto car windows. The note stated the owner of the car had freely donated it for use by the British army. The 'certificate' just had to be handed to a German who could be persuaded to sign and the vehicle could be claimed to be legitimate.

Some had good reason to ignore the orders. Units of the 6th Airborne Division were detailed to move quickly across Germany to the Baltic. Since they had insufficient transport of their own they were forced to improvise and soon became unexpectedly mobile. The paratroopers simply stole anything that could move, with no time for questions about requisitioning or repainting. War correspondents watched the progress of the column and reported them riding in all manner of civilian transport – bakers' and butchers' vans, post office trucks, fire engines, horse drawn wagons, even a steam roller.

The progress of this motley collection of vehicles marked the end of the advance across Germany. With their arrival on the Baltic coast the majority of German troops were effectively cut off from the rest of their country and had little choice but to surrender. The final days of war and the first few days of peace were the last chance for the men of 21st Army Group to acquire loot before the authorities reintroduced peacetime discipline.

With the coming of peace there was a flurry of looting by troops who realised it might be their last chance for enrichment. Even Monty's HQ staff were suspected and upon departure from their billets in Ostenwalde orders were issued that all kit was to be inspected for loot. The officers were found to have furnished themselves with books, typewriters, silk nightdresses, linen and towels.

Whilst his own staff were enjoying the fruits of the victory, Montgomery was forced to act to prevent an orgy of looting from the now defeated Germans. While the fighting had still continued he and his fellow commanders turned a blind eye to looting. A realist, Montgomery knew his soldiers were involved, but as he wrote in his memoirs: 'In the heat of battle certain actions are often overlooked'. (26) However, in peacetime the behaviour had to be confronted and controlled. The authorities soon realised that they had to build a strong relationship with the Germans and such a relationship could only be based on trust. On 5 May the men of the 1st Battalion Cheshire Regiment heard orders from their commander: 'From now on all looting will be rigorously suppressed. Any cases coming to light through civilian reports or censoring of parcels will be severely dealt with.' (27) On 6 May Monty issued the order that all looters would face court martial.

For the men of 21st Army Group the final victory over the Nazis had been a curiously muted victory. Throughout history the surrender of an army has traditionally been the moment at which the victorious warriors claim the spoils of war. In ancient history the victors took the womenfolk from the defeated city. Later armies claimed the crowns from the heads of defeated kings and the battle flags of their vanquished foe. Modern conflicts had seen the ceremonial handing over of officers' swords and revolvers. The climax of the campaign was not a triumphant entrance into the capital of the enemy with a ceremonial handover of flags and swords. Instead it was a simple ceremony in an anonymous tent on a heath.

With few formal opportunities for generals to collect trophies they received their souvenirs in much more muted affairs. In Berlin, Field Marshal Alanbrooke was to acquire a souvenir in circumstances that so poignantly reflected how much war had changed the world. Rather than leave the city with a beautifully engraved sword or the sidearm of a defeated German general he took with him a single German medal, silently handed to him by a Russian soldier during a visit to a Gestapo HQ.

There were thousands of individuals collecting reminders of the victory – some were elegantly symbolic of all they had suffered, others simple mementoes reflecting how the defeat of the enemy had been the victory of the 'ordinary men'. John Reynolds was working in Calais when the Germans surrendered. Now was the moment when the British would finally be able to re-enter Dunkirk. It was a poignant moment for Reynolds who five years previously had suffered so much agony on the march back to the coast. He recalled:

> One of the officers said 'Reynolds, weren't you at Dunkirk?' I said 'Yes, Sir'. He said I could go with him to get a souvenir. So I got dressed up and went with him. When we got there all the German soldiers were standing in line and they'd got their arms laid out in front of them. I was standing with this officer and he said 'Now get yourself a souvenir'. So I thought I'd take a sword. In fact I took two! They had the German emblem, the eagle, one decorated in silver the other made from Solingen steel. I used to have them up on the wall in my house, with 'Dunkirk' and the date painted on them. (28)

The victory mementoes acquired by John Mercer were less spectacular but no less symbolic. Unlike many of his comrades he was not interested in valuables, rather in simple reminders of his role in the defeat of the enemy:

> I know this sounds like I'm 'shooting a line', but me and my friends were the first British troops to go into Hitler's Chancellery. We drove up to the Chancellery and thought let's go in and have a look. The Russian guard presented arms, he obviously didn't know who we were, we were only greasy gunners after all. So we went in, climbed through all the glass, into the Hall of Mirrors, into Hitler's study. We looked out and saw where there had been the fire where his body was supposed to have been burned. We went all through the Chancellery, looking at things. On the way out we came to the door leading down to the bunker, but we all said no since we'd come across booby traps before. I came back with an armband, a set of SS photographs and a typewriter brush! I thought I could do my dubbin or blanco with it. (29)

Mercer was not the only one snooping around Berlin looking for souvenirs – one British officer was arrested, caught smuggling two carpets into Belgium that he admitted had come from the Chancellery.

When the time came for the soldiers to head home most were carrying some form of looted goods – up to March 1945, 286,384 claims had been settled by the British authorities, most of which compensated for looting. Even with the war finished the costs were still being calculated. May 1945 saw the Claims and Hirings Directorate still investigating more than 2,000 cases of hard core looting from west of the River Seine and by the end of June 2,797 claims were still awaiting the attention of assessors.

Those soldiers who had never been caught or had their gear searched by MPs, thought they would be able to get home without losing any of the spoils of war. However, they had reckoned without the intervention of the one organisation that might be able to thwart them – His Majesty's Customs and Excise.

Customs officers had few illusions about how much loot would arrive with the soldiers. The experience of dealing with men returning from the Mediterranean had left them with little doubt about what would be contained within the haversacks and kitbags of the returning men. From pineapples to motorcycles, all manner of goods had been illegally imported.

Unlike Lieutenant Colonel Brewis of the 6th Airborne Division, who was caught transporting a motorcycle in regimental baggage – or the soldier seen carrying a small piano – most soldiers were restricted by what they could fit into their luggage. That is not to say they were not loaded down with souvenirs. Their kitbags, haversacks and pockets all concealed items they thought might interest customs staff. There were individuals who were carrying thousands of reichsmarks, whose personal wealth far exceeded the four hundred marks they were officially allowed to change back into sterling and one soldier was arrested attempting to exchange 40,000 marks.

Returning troops soon realised it was best to make sure all loot was carefully concealed from the prying eyes of customs staff. Word went round that when the ship was approaching the port they should look out for tables being set up on the dockside. This was the sign they would be subjected to a thorough questioning. Some soldiers used carefully planned ruses to prevent closer inspection of their kit. When one man declared a camera without a lens, the customs officials laughed at him, explaining that minus the lens it had no value since it would be impossible to purchase a replacement. With that he was waved away, later he showed his mates that the rest of his luggage was packed with fully operational cameras. Another ingenious man concealed yards upon yards of silk inside his army issue water bottle in order to evade customs duty. Growing wise to such tricks, customs officers were on the lookout for men who seemed unnaturally fat under their clothing – they were taken aside and their coats opened, revealing lengths of cloth wound around their bodies.

The problem of getting large items past customs officials in the UK vexed many soldiers. A captain in the Intelligence Corps was rumoured to have found the perfect solution. Whilst most of them simply broke down their loot to make it fit inside their kitbags, he went one step further. Having stolen an antique carpet from a German castle, the officer paid someone to construct an oversize kitbag capable of holding his loot without attracting any attention.

Many soldiers found the customs men actually showed little interest in them, asking only a few simple questions before waving them through. Stan Procter, who'd been forced to leave his stolen radio behind, found his souvenirs failed to raise interest: 'They stopped me and asked what I'd got. I started reeling off this list of stuff that I thought they might be difficult about – dress material, drink, cameras. And they said "Go on, off you go". They weren't a bit interested really. More interested in gold bars, probably.' (30)

The reason for this disinterest was that customs men had more pressing concerns. Whilst unlicensed imports might have implications for the exchequer there were other imports with longer-term consequences. Of particular concern were the large numbers of weapons arriving in the country. As early as March 1944 Customs and Excise reported that they didn't want to be responsible for searching the baggage of returning soldiers, instead insisting that it be the responsibility of the Home Office to stop the illegal importation of goods into the UK at source. They wanted a crackdown that would prevent loot being taken onboard troopships, yet were also keen to avoid any conflict with returning personnel, as was noted in departmental reports: 'We have ample evidence of the irritation caused to service personnel by the detention and seizure of arms and ammunition in their unaccompanied luggage', and that they faced: 'opprobrium for what service personnel are apt to regard as high handed action'. (31)

The arguments over who was responsible for preventing such imports continued throughout 1944 and into 1945. Whilst civil servants discussed barrel lengths, air rifles and whether it made a difference if weapons were carried in luggage or on the person, the country was being flooded with illegal weapons. Soldiers were caught with rifles wrapped inside greatcoats, and the forces mail depot at Bournemouth regularly found guns hidden in packages. In fact, specific orders had been issued forbidding the posting of guns and ammunition after a lorry load of mail was lost when concealed explosives exploded during transit. However, with 120,000 packets to sort each week it was clear they could not intercept everything.

In the long run it would be the weapons that slipped the net that would be of greatest concern. A Home Office report of 1946 estimated that 76,000 weapons had entered the country illegally as souvenirs whilst as few as two hundred had actually been seized after August 1944. The majority of the weapons thought to have arrived illegally were handguns, but there were also thousands of rifles and machineguns, and over two million rounds of live ammunition.

Steps were taken to clamp down on the import of weapons. From August 1945 random searches of fifteen per cent of all leave-bound soldiers was made prior to embarkation. MPs were sent aboard troopships heading across the channel and made announcements about the penalties for smuggling. They also took definite action, and one journalist reported how MPs and customs officers were seen breaking the points off SS daggers to render them harmless. The announcements highlighting the penalties for bringing back loot struck fear into the hearts of homebound soldiers. The threat of being returned to their unit and missing leave was enough to send them rushing to the rails of the ships and divesting themselves of their trophies. Kitbags were emptied of all manner of loot – daggers, helmets, swords, bayonets and guns. Infantry officer Ken Hardy was one of those who heard the warnings:

Customs were the only thing that worried us. I was an avid collector of German machine pistols, they were lovely things. I had a complete collection of them, and I was determined to get them back to England. When I got on the boat there were dire warnings about jail terms for anyone bringing weapons back. And I can remember standing at the back of the boat chucking all these guns into the water. Newhaven harbour must still be full of stuff! (32)

Not everyone heeded the warnings. John Raycroft, a homeward bound Canadian, devised a plan he hoped would outwit the customs officials. He covered his pistol in grease, wrapped it in waterproof fabric and bound it with adhesive tape. His plan was to excuse himself from the inspection queue, conceal the weapon in a toilet cistern, then return for his loot once he had been given the all clear. In the end his precautions were unnecessary since they were sent immediately to board a train, never once seeing a customs official.

Weapons were not the only concern for the excisemen who waited on the docksides to supervise the arrival of returning troops. The collapse of the German regime meant there were plenty of valuables hidden in kitbags and pockets.

When it came to the question of loot of artistic value customs officials initially used a simple logic – they thought since import was forbidden none would enter the country. What they failed to realise was that many soldiers ignored the regulations. It was a case of 'fiddling whilst Rome burns'. As customs officials discussed precisely what constituted loot of 'artistic value' the men of 21st Army Group were furiously looting, and paintings, tapestries, antique furniture, gold and silver tableware, and even exhibits from museums, were being hidden in kitbags. The problem for officials was that most returning men made an effort to hide their loot. If they had large antiques then they could be shipped back in unit transport, in which case there would little chance of spotting them. The other loot of real value would be gold and jewels, which could easily be hidden about the person. Short of detailed searches of every man and every vehicle there was little hope of finding looted jewels. One soldier reportedly made his fortune smuggling home the watches confiscated by the Nazis from the inmates of Belsen concentration camp.

The customs officials were also powerless to act in the face of organised action. The ultimate act of evasion came when the SAS arrived at Tilbury in the spring of 1945. Knowing the enemy had never been able to stop them, they figured there was no reason to be thwarted by civil servants. They simply revved up their engines and sped past the waiting officials, their loot safe from inspection. Their next attempt to outwit the customs officials was to no avail. On the return trip from Norway they attempted to smuggle fur coats hidden inside the spare petrol tanks of their jeeps. The problem was that it was decided to ship the men back separately from their vehicles, which were returned anonymously to depots in the UK, the loot lost forever.

Though Customs and Excise were unable to act against groups of determined men, they were able to hound individuals even after their return home. Some of those hoping to profit found valuables were difficult to dispose of. In the summer of 1945 Corporal David Robb of the Argyll and Sutherland Highlanders was arrested when he attempted to sell a selection of jewellery. Thinking them stolen, the jeweller had alerted the police. The items included a gold cigarette case, diamond brooches, gold earrings set with rubies, bracelets, platinum brooches, amethyst cuff links and a gold compact, estimated at a value of £1,020. After investigations it was revealed that Robb had spent five years in a POW camp and upon release had gone on a looting spree in the company of some Russians. The police believed his story and accepted no crime had been committed and let the matter drop. However, customs officers were less understanding. They pointed out that since no duty had been paid upon importation, the jewels should be held awaiting payment. Despite the circumstances of their import, the fact the military authorities thought the items should be returned to Corporal Robb, and that he was in hospital recovering from TB, there was little sympathy from the customs officers who wrote: 'It is fairly obvious that goods wrongly dispossessed do in fact reach this country by returning members of the forces and that it is practically impossible to prevent such happenings. At the same time I do not feel at all happy that we should give it our blessing and approval.' (33) So in December 1945 the jewellery was officially confiscated.

For all their successes loot flooded back into the UK, where much of it still resides to this day. Most of the weapons have long gone, handed in to the police during gun amnesties held since 1945. However, much else still remains – from Leica cameras on sale at auction houses, to paintings that still hang on the walls of veterans' homes. From the stolen rings that grace the fingers of the veterans' wives, to the men who keep their wartime portraits housed in photo frames that had once sat on the dressing tables of German homes. From the men who earned enough to buy property for themselves, to those whose corpses were stripped of loot to be sent home to their grieving families. To the victor the spoils.

13

A Masterpiece of Liberation

'By and large, I was indifferent to the destruction of property. I saw it as something necessary and so long as it made sure there were no German soldiers left
to kill me, then it was justified. There was so much destruction of property that
you got used to it and didn't really notice it after a time. I personally never saw
or heard of soldiers actually enjoying destroying things – but if, for example, to
eliminate a sniper, it meant knocking down a Church or a farmhouse, so be it.' (1)

In May 1945, as six long years of war finally came to an end, Europe lay wasted.
From Normandy to the Caucasus, from the toe of Italy to the tip of Norway, and
from the harbour in Malta to the Glasgow docks, thousands of towns, villages and
cities were in ruins. Bridges rested on riverbeds, railway lines lay twisted, and thousands of wrecked vehicles were slowly rusting in fields as farmers raised their crops
around them. Great cities such as Berlin, Dresden, Stalingrad, Leningrad and
Warsaw were in ruins, their buildings destroyed and populations dispersed.

Countless other towns and cities had suffered immense destruction from the
ground and the air. Five summers on from the Blitz some British cities were still
struggling to rise from the ashes. Vast areas of London, Bristol, Portsmouth,
Coventry, Liverpool and other industrial centres were reduced to wasteland.
Rubbish-strewn bomb sites, once teeming with life, were now playgrounds where
young children acted out the battles fought by their fathers and stray cats chased
mice and rats where once they had been pets.

The level of destruction was unprecedented, far surpassing what had been seen
in the First World War. Although some areas had been totally devastated during
the earlier conflict the extent of the damage had been limited, covering a small
area of the Continent. The aerial bombing of Guernica during the Spanish Civil
War, which had caused such widespread terror and outrage, now seemed minimal
compared to the deliberate firestorms that had raged through the cities of the
Reich.

Such was the confidence in the destructive power of high explosive that the commanders of the bomber fleets thought they alone could bring victory. Sheer ton-
nage of bombs, they argued, could bring a country to its knees eliminating the
need for heavy ground losses. However it was soon made clear to the footsloggers
the policy had failed. If German industry was all but destroyed where were all the
guns, bombs and bullets coming from? Even during the heaviest Allied bombing
the Germans were able to raise their military output, producing aircraft and tanks
the Allied servicemen could only dream of.

In the end it still fell to someone to clear and hold the ground essential for victory. That someone was usually the infantry and their armour-clad friends in the tank regiments. Nobody was taking any chances. The rule of advance was – if in doubt hit it with everything you've got – air attacks, artillery, mortars, machine guns, flamethrowers, rockets, tank fire, small arms fire, and whenever possible even the heavy guns of offshore battleships. And then hope. Hope that no one had survived or that the infantry could reach their objectives before the defenders recovered. More often than not someone would survive even the heaviest onslaught, and it took only a handful of survivors to bring an offensive grinding to a halt.

So the advance continued, leaving a trail of destruction that followed the Allied advance from Normandy to the Baltic. There were many notable victims. The Norman city of Caen was destroyed by Allied bombers to clear a safe passage for the British and Canadian infantry. It was callous but honest, leaflets were even dropped informing civilians of the oncoming devastation. The Dutch city of Arnhem had its centre burned to the ground and its suburbs emptied of civilians, their homes thoroughly looted. The island of Walcheren on the Scheldt estuary was flooded by Allied bombing of the dykes designed to swamp the German defences and open the sea route to Antwerp. Even the medieval city of Cleve in Germany, once the home of King Henry VIII's fourth wife Anne, was 'taken out' by the RAF to make way for the advance of the Canadian 2nd Army through the Reichswald forest up to the banks of the Rhine.

The price of liberation was high, both for Allied and enemy civilians. For the soldiers the very use of the word 'liberation' became a joke. It was a word that was used in different ways to convey different meanings – as a verb 'to liberate' meant to loot, whereas used as an adjective 'liberated' implied total destruction of an urban area.

All over Europe the picture was the same, thousands of civilians were returning to homes defiled by soldiers of all nations, their furniture wrecked, possessions missing, floors stained with mud, shit and blood. Everywhere the whole landscape was scarred with bomb craters and trenches, walls were pockmarked by bullets, hardly a pane of glass seemed to survive. Tanks marked their progress through Europe by leaving a trail of demolished walls, flattened telegraph poles and churned-up roads. Even soldiers seemed out of place among the ruins. They took tables and chairs from wrecked buildings, laid them with table cloths and cutlery from the houses and sat down to consume their rations, as if celebrating the destruction they had brought to the town. It was a strange juxtaposition, the men who caused the destruction relaxing amongst the rubble as if everything around them was normal.

Even as the twentieth century drew to a close some of these scars remained. Some obvious, like in Berlin where vast new developments fill the wastelands formerly occupied by the Berlin Wall and its accompanying 'Death Strip', themselves both legacies of the Second World War. Others less obvious, such as charred fragments of walls, tucked away in the corner of an open car park, once somebody's home and probably someone's grave. Or less fashionable areas of a city where a single road leads nowhere, with one lonely lamp post the only reminder of what once stood .

But what of these men who laid waste to Europe, so many of whom now rest in the cemeteries marking the route of the advance? How did they feel about the destruction they caused, buildings they levelled, furniture they smashed and people they left homeless?

The army was aware most soldiers were reluctant to overcome the morality of civilian life. They knew men would not want to cause unnecessary destruction but it was something the soldiers had to be prepared for. Whilst the soldiers sat and debated the rights and wrongs of the destruction of the Benedictine Abbey at Monte Cassino their leaders were attempting to get them accustomed to the life-saving realities of destruction. Whilst preparing for the opening of the 'second front' tank crews were initiated into this new life. Early in their training they had been told to keep to the roads and avoid damage. Then instructions changed and drivers were deliberately told to proceed across fields of crops. At first drivers hesitated, concerned about the reaction of the farmers. The morality of wilful damage was questioned – yet this was the very reason they were ordered to do it. Once in action there would be no room for hesitation.

Such problems arose as soon as the troops landed in France. Some tank crews faced with obstacles like high walls carefully skirted around them trying to locate an opening. In time they learnt to just charge straight through leaving rubble in their wake. Eventually they would think little of parking a tank inside a house, as it gave perfect camouflage and the satisfaction of flattening German property.

Despite all the training, preparations and motivation there was little that could be done to ensure when it came to the crunch soldiers would not remain sentimental about the wave of destruction they were about to unleash. For the invasion to succeed it would be essential for the soldiers to forget 'An Englishman's home is his castle', forget about the sanctity of homes and possessions and instead remember that homes were just bricks, mortar and potential shelters for the enemy. In those last days before the invasion signs of a new attitude became evident amongst the troops preparing themselves for the assault. Men began to cast off the vestiges of civilised society in displays of wanton destruction. Through destruction they prepared to begin a new phase in their lives.

At last we got the expected order, (wrote Pioneer corporal and aspirant novelist, Alexander Baron), Field Service Marching order. Confined to billets. All kit to be jettisoned except the gear we wore and some small requisites. This last order was unprecedented. Kit was usually collected into stores or kept to be sent on to us. Our billets were in a row of little houses. In the evening the men in my billet went out into the back garden and lit a bonfire. .... We brought abandoned kit out of the house by the armful, trousers, tunics, underclothes, and good boots; we threw everything into the fire. Someone threw petrol on and the flames roared high. We were all squatting on the lawn like Boy Scouts in camp, drinking beer from bottles that passed from one man to the next. We did not drink a lot but the act of flinging away kit was itself intoxicating and so were the flames. A soldier threw three or four nine-millimetre bullets into the fire. One by one they popped and squealed past us, each time provoking a whoop and shouts of laughter. I was standing at the back with a manila folder in my hands. Well, I thought, goodbye to all that, and threw my (unfinished) novel into the fire. (2)

With that last, supreme gesture Baron and his friends were ready to go to war.

Despite such destructive gestures the soldiers took time to adapt to conditions on the battlefield. However they were, in the most part, afforded a gradual introduction to the realities of war and what they might expect by the time they took their place in the forward positions. They usually arrived in the front line through a landscape of destruction. They marched through ruins, along roads pitted with bomb craters, lined with the burned-out wrecks of military vehicles and the detritus of abandoned military hardware. They looked on silently as the streams of ambulances brought wounded men out of the line and refugees trudged away carrying their meagre possessions. And slowly, as they approached the forward positions, they saw the corpses of the fallen that brought a personal, human touch to the sights they had witnessed. There was no more certain reminder of the need to do anything in order to survive than seeing corpses dressed just like them, men who had carried rifles like theirs, and now lay sacrificed to the same cause they espoused. So they learned to destroy the homes of their allies and demolish buildings that held up an advance, all in the name of survival.

The very real and emotional dilemma over the destruction of property was illustrated by the fate of Cleve during the battle to clear the Reichswald Forest and secure the west bank of the Rhine. General Horrocks was asked the unenviable question: 'Do you want the town of Cleve taken out?' (3) Horrocks understood the full horror this implied. The whole town and many of its population would be destroyed by aerial bombardment. This was a medieval town, steeped in history, filled with architectural treasures. It was not an easy decision, and was one that was to haunt him for the rest of his life, but Horrocks knew by levelling the town it would delay the arrival of German reinforcements and thus protect the advance of his own troops. Knowing the lives of his men were his primary concern, Horrocks answered 'Yes' and condemned the historic city. With heavy heart Horrocks watched the flight of the bombers as they made their way to flatten the historic city. The raid was a success – that night Cleve died so that British soldiers might live.

Yet from the destruction grew hope – hope that the trail of destruction led to the lair of the beast, that only from the ashes of war could a new, peaceful Europe rise. In this hope were sown the seeds of a new morality, born of realism, that survival and victory over the enemy were worth it whatever the price.

Nowhere was this new morality more evident than in the attitude toward churches, the very fabric of the religions to which a vast majority of the men professed. No longer could churches be seen as places of worship but instead as the shelters for enemy snipers, machinegunners and artillery observers. Any reticence about sacrilege was misplaced. It was soon clear that knocking down towers and steeples was essential to the progress of war. Canadian officers, with a high level of French-Canadian Catholics amongst their troops, were worried that the destruction of churches would cause upset so they were often careful to ensure obliging Catholic soldiers were given the task to prevent dissent. There was no shortage of volunteers, all of whom understood that churches were primarily enemy observation posts rather than places of worship.

If churches were fair game there was little hope for civilian homes. Even in friendly villages men casually threw furniture from the windows of homes they occupied. They needed space and this was the quickest way to get it. Few would have behaved in such a way at home but morals were changing. This wasn't vandalism or wanton destruction it was just making space to sleep. This learning process for soldiers in a battle was brief, bloody and often fatal. Failure to adapt could mean death. Waiting outside a door meant staying out in the open longer than was really necessary and was an open invitation to enemy snipers. Failure to smash windows when occupying a house meant the danger of being cut to ribbons by flying glass if a mortar bomb landed nearby. Even mirrors and picture frames were smashed with rifle butts to render them glass free. Leaving curtains hanging in windows increased the risk of fires. So the soldiers had a brief education, doors were kicked open, windows smashed with rifle butts, curtains torn down and used for sleeping on and furniture destroyed to make barricades and offer safe firing positions. Libraries were cleared of books that were then packed into wardrobes of wooden cabinets to fill up the windows not needed for shooting from, in the hope they could stop bullets or shrapnel. It was unavoidable, if clothes were found in a wardrobe they would be strewn on the floor, if crockery was found in a cupboard it would be thrown to the floor. There was precious little time to worry about the niceties of occupying a building, however friendly the owner might be, or how many people were being made homeless by their actions.

By and large it was the sight of very personal items littering the battlefield that had the greatest effect on the soldiers as they brought back memories of family and heightened the desire to be at home in safety and comfort. As they sprawled in the rubble they found themselves surrounded by family photographs lying in shattered frames, the ragged remains of civilian clothing, and in particular the possessions of children. Never was it more heartbreaking for the soldiers than to see the toys, cots, prams and dolls that littered the wreckage of the buildings they had destroyed. Hallamshires subaltern Ken Hardy recalled his emotions at occupying civilian homes:

> You did do it, especially in Holland where you couldn't dig in because it was waterlogged. So you had to fortify houses and that meant a lot of destruction of things you knew people were coming back to. That was pretty awful. Really tough, the idea that people were going to come back to something you had deliberately destroyed in order to survive. You comfort yourself with the fact that you're doing it for them, but it don't go very far. You did it because you had to but it was always with a pang of guilt that somebody's going to come back to this. (4)

As artillery observer John Mercer recalled: 'One of our observation points was a chateau in Normandy. I remember walking through the ruins of it in the lull and picking up pictures, bits of photographs and thinking "Oh dear, you've done this". It had to be done ... I did become callous.' (5)

Like Mercer, it was essential for the attacking troops to harden their hearts and accept the results of their actions. There was no time to dwell on the realities. Tankman Ken Squires wasn't worried about the buildings, merely the Germans concealed in them, in particular the artillery observers. He explained: 'Destruction? Didn't matter. A church spire? What about the guy who's up the top there? Bang, no problem. Water towers were great fun. Oh yeah. All the water that came out of them. Houses, farmhouses, drive through them, it didn't matter. Hope to God there's nobody in them. If you've got to go, you've got to go through them. No frigging about.'

His fellow Northants Yeoman Michael Hunt recalled that: 'The only time Mr Brown, my commander, had a qualm was when we fired at the hospital in Caen. He was right, he had no alternative. A field piece was sheltered in the corner behind the wall, and he was firing at us, the only thing to do to get rid of him was fire at the hospital. And the easier way to get the gunner on him was to take down the hospital wall.' Squires knew they had to become callous and remain strong willed: 'As far as I'm concerned with that sort of thing, I was loading for the gunner, and for me I'd look out of my periscope and think "Oh, that's good he's done that. Thank God for that. Me, saved." Thinking about it I was probably hard hearted about it.' (6)

One of the standard techniques employed in street fighting was 'mouseholing'. After the infantry fought their way into one house Piats would be employed to blow an opening through the wall into the adjoining house and so on through a terrace. The infantry would fight their way into one room then proceed through a building room by room. Grenades were thrown into rooms, doorways and stairways raked with automatic fire. The soldiers worked their way up to the top of the house and then 'mouseholed' through the walls of the top room before working their way down, floor by floor to clear the next house. Once a house was entered there was little chance for the defenders to surrender as the British soldiers methodically cleared the house room by room. In this way the soldiers could make their way safely along a row of buildings without having to reveal themselves in the open. It was a dangerous job with the risk of either side firing through the thin walls, floors or ceilings. As much firepower as possible had to be used to suppress the enemy. Even to kick a door down risked showing oneself to the defenders. Instead doors would be blown off and rooms cleared without giving the enemy a target. Such were the dangers inherent in house clearing that whenever possible the soldiers preferred to call in armoured assistance. Tanks were used to knock the corners off buildings exposing the positions to fire from the attackers or leaving the defenders buried in the rubble.

The technique brought untold misery to civilians but it saved the lives of countless soldiers. Similar methods were also used to prepare defensive positions. Pickaxes were used to hack through interior walls allowing soldiers freedom of movement between buildings.

The destruction of homes came to be just another part of life for the soldiers engaged in total war. It was difficult to be sentimental when personal comfort was involved. In the front lines officers and men would often kill all the livestock abandoned by householders to prevent them interfering with the soldiers' work. Despite orders to the contrary soldiers took sheaves of corn to make a comfortable lining for their slit trenches or to use as camouflage. In addition machinery was wheeled out of farmyards to act as impromptu armoured covering for their positions. When Royal Engineers were ordered to clear fields of mines, they didn't work carefully through the crops. Instead they used flame-throwers to burn down the crops allowing them a clear view of where they were working.

There was no time to be careful. Even when houses were to be left unoccupied, and instead the gardens fortified, then the furniture was smashed up and used to make walls for slit trenches and doors torn from their hinges to use as roofs. If there were no doors left in the homes with which to construct shelters men simply smashed up chicken coops or rabbit hutches, taking what they needed to ensure their comfort and safety. However, when positions were more permanent soldiers would often create something out of the destruction – farmhouse tables were removed, their legs sawed off, and a tarpaulin tacked onto the top to make beds for soldiers.

The desire for heat also led to destruction. Living in half-ruined buildings in the middle of winter it was understandable men wanted a working stove. They would search through rubble to find what they needed, take it back, fit it and attempt to generate heat. If they didn't work they were abandoned and another one located and fitted. The rearrangements only added to the chaos. If they found a good stove when the time came to move on it would be loaded onto transport and refitted wherever it might be needed. Some willing infantrymen even found small Dutch stoves they could carry on their backs ensuring that wherever they stopped for the night they could always keep warm.

The fighting around Arnhem during the doomed Operation Market Garden saw some of the most extreme displays of destruction. Where this fighting differed from that seen at other times during the campaign was that the British began the devastation even before the battle had fully commenced. In his memoirs of the battle published in 1958, Major General Roy Urquhart, the commander of the British Airborne troops, recalled the behaviour of the men serving under his command and their attitude towards Dutch property during the battle. He knew from previous experience that British soldiers had a respect for property and the houses of those they were fighting to protect.

For many of the soldiers faced with homes which had to be occupied there was an initial shock – how could they enter someone's home and defile it, albeit necessarily? This was a typical first impression for men who were experiencing combat for the first time. These were the homes of their allies, people they had come to liberate. The soft furnishings, family photographs, carefully ordered shelves, neatly tended gardens, were all reminders of home. How would they like foreign soldiers rampaging through their homes? Some soldiers had even agreed to requests from civilians not to occupy buildings and took up positions in the streets where they were without suitable cover. Others knocked at doors and asked permission to search houses. Urquhart considered this time wasting but was fortunately able to report: 'They soon lost this politeness.' (7) Indeed they did. Soon paratroopers were fortifying semi-detached houses by demolishing the dividing walls and burning down buildings to provide illumination at night.

These were problems particularly found in airborne units. Unlike ground troops who had a long journey, often of many weeks, before reaching the front, airborne men arrived straight from the comfort of their barracks. Only hours before they had been waking up to a cooked breakfast and preparing for their flight to battle. Unlike the infantry who seldom entered a town until after it had been assailed by artillery barrages or aerial bombing, the paratroopers brought the battle to towns previously untouched by war. They proceeded towards battle through streets where well-tended gardens flanked tidy houses, where vehicles in the streets were undamaged and where civilians lined the roads to cheer. Hence their arrival on the battlefield and the chaos it was to bring was a sudden shock, both for themselves and the civilians whose homes they had come to liberate. With this harsh introduction it took time for the paratroops to reacquaint themselves with the realities of war.

Despite the initial reluctance witnessed by Major General Urquhart his men were soon barricading themselves into Dutch homes in an attempt to ensure their safety. There seemed a resigned acceptance of what had to be done. A 1st Airborne sergeant major set up his position in a house still occupied by its owners, mounting his machinegun on the top of a mahogany table, the muzzle protruding through the smashed glass of a bay window. Turning to the terrified Dutchman lying on the floor he uttered the simple words of apology: 'Sorry, dad.' (8) There was a heavy feeling in the hearts of many men as they used antique furniture to build barricades knowing it would soon be destroyed. Curtains and bedding were used to provide comfort for the men lying in fire positions on the hard floor of houses, and were torn into strips to wrap around boots so that they wouldn't make a noise when moving around at night. To make firing positions for snipers roof tiles were knocked out, allowing them to fire from a concealed and well-protected position. Once more the house and all its contents became nothing more than a shelter, somewhere to hide from the very real threat of death.

There was little choice but to destroy the homes and possessions of their Dutch allies. Every precaution had to be taken in an attempt to win the battle. It was not only the soldiers who became resigned to the fate of local property. The civilians accepted the fate of their homes with pride, their freedom was worth more than bricks and mortar. Few complained of the behaviour of the soldiers in wrecking their homes. As some buildings collapsed into piles of rubble others were engulfed in flames. In order to prevent the Germans from sneaking troops across the bridge under cover of darkness, and give the British troops light by which to shoot, a small building was chosen and set fire to, illuminating the whole area.

At times it was necessary to burn buildings for health reasons rather than personal safety. With the battles in Normandy raging through the farms of the region there was little time to bury the livestock that became casualties of the fighting. As a result stables full of dead horses and cattle were put to the torch to prevent the spread of disease and try to curb the all-pervading smell of rotten flesh that hung over the battlefields.

Whilst most soldiers were unmoved by the sight of wholesale destruction inflicted on towns in the support of their operations many disapproved of the damage done by indiscriminate aerial bombing. Before most major attacks the RAF and USAAF were used to bomb German positions. The idea was that the defences would be shattered, anti-tank guns crews wiped out, tanks blasted from their hiding places, infantry buried in their trenches. At worst it was claimed the defenders would be too numb from the effects of the blast to offer any serious resistance. The tactic of using sheer weight of high explosive to blast the enemy from their positions was understood and it was acknowledged that lives were saved, however it was not always successful nor totally appreciated. In the aftermath of such an aerial onslaught some men complained the extent of the damage hampered their movements. Tank crews found the only roads capable of holding their weight pitted with impassable craters. The armoured cars of the reconnaissance regiments, detailed to pass through the enemy defences to probe in advance of the main body of troops, were sometimes unable to move. In bomb-cratered towns they were left helpless and unable to exploit the opportunities bombing was supposed to have created. It was impossible to move quickly through the rubble-strewn streets. They were left vulnerable to attack by surviving German infantry without even the possibility of a quick escape.

Despite the lack of desire to damage property and the very real emotional turmoil caused by seeing the results of their work, some soldiers admitted to getting a genuine feeling of delight in wielding the power that caused so much destruction. The enthusiasm for the power they wielded led to a profligacy in which the resulting destruction far outweighed necessity. Lone enemy soldiers were fired on by rapid-firing anti-aircraft cannons, or subject to the attentions of high explosive or even armour piercing shells. If such assaults could be made against men it was little wonder so many buildings fell victims to the firepower of the liberating forces.

Few tank crews admitted to enjoying the results of destroying property although some tried to explain the bloodlust involved, recalling how in the fear, noise and excitement the experience was almost orgiastic.

These were difficult emotions for soldiers to understand fully . They realised the sad results of their work, and knew they really shouldn't enjoy flattening civilian homes, yet seemed to get a certain guilty thrill out of it. The awesome destructive power of hundreds of heavy bombers left the men standing in wonder. The ground heaved, the air was filled with noise like thunder. Anything that wasn't tied down seemed to rattle. They knew the effect such raids could have on a town since many had experienced bombing during the Blitz. In the face of such firepower who could not but marvel at the spectacle as it unfolded before their eyes? Dr Ken Tout tried to explain how he felt as a tank gunner, blasting a path for the infantry from

Normandy to the Netherlands. He was always rather sorry to knock down part of a house or farm and saddened to have to shoot wounded cows or horses as a humanitarian act.

> However, there was a kind of mass enthusiasm, rather than hysteria when the entire squadron of 19 tanks lined up and started firing 4x17 pounders, 15x75mm canons, and 38 Browning machine guns at, say, the line of cottages ringing a village and held by an enemy rearguard. It was like the enthusiasm of a crowd at a football match, or perhaps a larger Guy Fawkes party. The property became a simple target. It was only later, if we were able to walk around the destroyed village, that regret set in. (9)

Fellow Northants Yeoman Joe Ekins remembered a very specific example of the delirious appetite for destruction: 'I quite enjoyed blowing a house down. It's an exhilaration to drive a tank through a house and see it fall down either side of you. I think we all enjoyed destruction.' Ekins and the tanks of his squadron found themselves supporting a group of infantry in the half-light of dusk. He explained: 'Tanks didn't fight at night 'cause somebody could creep up and drop a bloody hand grenade down your top.' As they approached the village they received orders over the radio to withdraw for the night. When they attempted to explain the situation to the infantrymen the situation soon became heated. The infantry NCO told the tank commander: 'Its bloody stupid, I've got to take this row of houses which are full of Germans. We're being fired on and we've got to take them. We haven't been ordered to go back. Come on, come and do this for us.' There was growing dissent among the crew of Ekins' tank as they insisted their commander comply with the order to withdraw: 'I said "You stupid bugger, come on let's go!" I was shouting at him "Come on, bloody hell, we've been ordered to bloody go back, you stupid bugger. We'll be killed if we go up there."' However the commander overrode their objections:

> He said that we were going to go on, so we did. All we did was we just revved up, in a line and went straight through the row of houses. One through one house, one through another, and flattened 'em. I thoroughly enjoyed it. As soon as we got through we turned round and high tailed out of there as soon as possible, I mean, the infantry can look after themselves then. Complete destruction, we did absolutely destroy, we just went up to this row of houses and knocked 'em down. And the infantry finished them off. Yeah, I enjoyed knocking them houses down. (10)

However there was a degree of damage that could have been avoided. With this scale of destruction it was unsurprising some individuals showed scant regard for private or public property. Although few in number, a significant minority of soldiers cared little for the niceties of liberation. The necessary destruction of homes and property degenerated into wanton vandalism, often in the search for hidden loot. MPs reported on the behaviour of some troops. They told of the desecration of roadside Calvaries where troops left the ground strewn with litter, carved their names, scrawled graffiti and hung signal wires from the figure of Christ. A French scientist also submitted a written report to the military authorities on the behaviour of his liberators. He had returned to his laboratory to find his office ransacked, doors broken down, drawers opened, tablets upset and valuable scientific instruments broken or stolen: 'I am sorry to report that I must use the same terms that I used when I submitted an account of the occupation by the German army. Now, as then, the troops have behaved, not like men of culture in a sanctuary of science but like barbarians in a hostile country.' (11)

Graffiti has traditionally followed victorious armies. Soldiers carved their names into wood or stone as a defiant declaration of their survival against the odds. For the soldier, who faced death with such regularity, and for whom it could come so suddenly, it was natural to leave his mark whilst he could. They carved initials, love hearts and unit signs onto trees or any wooden surface. They scribbled across the walls of the homes they occupied, leaving their names or pencil drawings of glamorous women, in the manner of a condemned man decorating his cell.

The army seemed to be struck by a wave of disrespect from tired fighting men towards property. Nothing seemed to have any value, except their lives. The weather also contributed to the casual destruction of property. Troops billeted in the railway station in the Belgian town of Limburg blew off the back of a safe door and used it to crawl from room to room rather than face the cold outside.

Alexander Baron observed the behaviour of one group of infantrymen: 'We spent the night in an empty seaside villa with a party of front line soldiers going on home leave. They tore up the staircase plank by plank and banister by banister to keep a fire going all night. The house was a shell next day when another truck came for us and took us to Ostend.' (12) Within the 49th Division MPs noted how 'wilful damage' was done to the fixtures and fittings of the railway carriages in which the soldiers departed on leave, as if the departing soldiers retained little respect for the comforts of the civilian world.

Although relatively few of the soldiers condoned wanton acts of vandalism, it was difficult for them to condemn it. There was little desire to be judgemental about the behaviour of their comrades. Each man knew how his own behaviour had changed and how the emotional burden of war had caused a shift in attitudes. They could easily understand how men who saw that life had so little value could have no regard for the property of others. What price could be put on a broken window or graffiti carved into the pews of a church when so many corpses littered the streets?

In late 1944 those soldiers who had seen the homes of the people they had come to liberate flattened beneath the ever advancing steamroller of military firepower, finally reached the German border. For one unit their very first sight of the enemy's homeland was the wreckage of a frontier customs post. Appropriately the gate to the Reich now lay torn from its hinges, abandoned alongside the other detritus of war. The roads were potholed and houses little more than piles of bricks, waiting to be shovelled into bomb craters by the untiring army bulldozers. It was fitting that the very edge of the Nazis' homeland should be the scene of such devastation, for now was the time for all the pain and heartache that the Germans had exported to be brought home in one last wave of destruction. In the hearts of so many soldiers there was but one feeling, now was the chance to pay them back for the Blitz.

Trooper John Reynolds had experienced the Blitz in East London whilst on honeymoon. He explained: 'I came and I saw a lot of damage. I'd seen Liverpool Street station where a bomb had gone straight the way down and killed 200 people. So how could I feel any bitterness about them. I've seen a thousand bombers go over, no I've got no sympathy, cause I'd seen so much myself. They didn't sympathise when they seen four or five hundred bombers over here.' (13)

As the men of 21st Army Group moved into Germany there was a noticeable shift in attitudes towards the destruction of property. Although there were relatively few examples of vandalism for the sake of it there were many examples of buildings being destroyed rather than taking any chances. During the Normandy campaign, and the progress through the Low Countries, it had been a common feature of any advance for tank crews to rake hedgerows with machinegun fire, hoping to dislodge any hidden enemy or discourage them from approaching the Allied flanks. When entering villages thought to be occupied by the enemy the tanks crawled through the streets firing high explosive shells into each home as they passed – swinging their turret from side to side and unleashing their fury into the menacing darkness that lurked behind windows.

Slowly but surely this appetite for destruction increased and this methodology was magnified once they crossed the German border. During the advance into the Reich men were less and less prepared to take unnecessary risks. Anything that might conceal a German was raked with fire. No one wanted to be first around a corner for fear of what might be waiting so it was easier to make sure any house that might offer the enemy shelter was destroyed. No longer was it just machine gun fire that was used to deter the hidden enemy. Houses, farms or factories, which could harbour the enemy, were reduced to rubble or set ablaze. If enemy troops were found hiding in wooded areas the 'Crocodiles' were called up and the whole area engulfed in flame. When troops came under sniper fire every house that could shelter a sniper was blasted by tank fire, and whenever possible the preferred method of suppressing snipers was to bring up a flame-throwing tank and burn down all the surrounding buildings. There was no time to discriminate. Whole areas of towns and villages fell prey to the all-engulfing fury of the flames. As petrified German defenders fled their positions they were cut down by hails of rifle fire. The crews of the flame-throwing tanks were getting highly professional at their work, with their officers noting how the crews had a barely concealed lust for burning down buildings. Among others, the Irish Guards gained a reputation for lighting up the places in which they stayed overnight by burning down houses and haystacks.

All sentimentality regarding homes and the fate of their owners dissolved, once the border had been crossed the general attitude seemed to become 'couldn't care less'. If something stood in the way of the advance it was levelled. The troops had long become used to the sight of the wreckage left in the wake of war. Many expressed genuine surprise to enter a village where buildings stood intact.

Destruction was so widespread it was just a part of their lives. From top to bottom the army displayed a ruthlessness seldom seen in the earlier stages of the campaign. This attitude was recorded by a 49th Division Provost company: 'Damage done through actual military operations to German property may very well have a salutary effect upon the population by bringing home to them something of the horrors which have been perpetrated by their armies.' (14) The observed ruthlessness even extended to the possessions of the army itself. Major General 'Tiny' Barber of the 15th Scottish Division ordered that any vehicle blocking the axis of his division's advance be bulldozed into a ditch. Ironically his own jeep was the first victim of the edict. When Brigadier Michael Carver found his way blocked by lorries of another unit at a crossroads, he ordered a tank to drive straight through a nearby house thus clearing an alternative route. The drivers of the offending lorries were then told if they did not move their vehicles the tank would crush them. Carver soon found his advance able to continue. Here was one of many officers who was open about his feelings towards the Germans and later admitted to having no charitable feelings, thinking that the Germans had brought it upon themselves.

For soldiers whose very survival depended on the efficiency of their operations there was little room for sentimentality. Anything blocking a road during an advance was a danger and ruthless methods were used to facilitate the speedy clearing of a safe path. John Groves, an officer with the 43rd Reconnaissance Regiment, recalled the prevailing conditions: 'During my own advance in Germany we were held up in a village by a crater between a house and high bank. A tank came up with a petard mortar and destroyed the house. A bulldozer followed and pushed the rubble into the crater. We went through. Whether anyone was in the house I do not know. We wanted to push on and finish the war.' (15) The bulldozers plied their ugly trade all across the collapsing Reich. If there were no rubble available to fill craters they simply put a long chain around a house and drove off, pulling the house down behind them. Where the craters were too large to be filled easily engineers were summoned forward and a new route was flattened through the surrounding buildings. If bridges were destroyed, houses were demolished and the riverbed filled with rubble to create a ford. The issue of destroying property was of little concern – the issue of military efficiency and self-preservation was.

Prior to the move into Germany there had been little deliberate destruction by soldiers. Now acts tantamount to vandalism began to spread throughout the army. Antique furniture from the medieval Rhineland towns made its way onto the bonfires the men used to keep warm at night. Pianos were pushed from the windows of upper floors just to watch them smash on the ground below, other men slid pianos downstairs just to hear the sounds they made during the descent. At the sixteenth century Schloss Moyland, once the home of Frederick the Great, Canadian soldiers paraded around in the top hats found in cupboards and threw furniture and paintings into the courtyard to make fires for cooking. In Cleve Tom Gore described a 'scene of utter destruction'. He and his mates reacted to their new environment: 'There was a roofless shoe factory that had hundreds of new shoes scattered around. The only thing not broken was a big, glass-fronted clock. My mate said "Why isn't that broken?" and picking up a new shoe, threw it at it, smashing the glass. It seemed to fit in better with the surroundings now.' (16)

All over the country soldiers ate their rations from fine china plates then threw them from the windows, deliberately letting them fall and smash in the streets. Seeing this a soldier commented to a watching war correspondent: 'The washing up. You just chuck it out of the window. Nothing has any value any more ....'. (17) In the chaos many soldiers seemed unmoved by the scenes of devastation; they knew that life and death were the only things that had any real value, not the few 'odds and ends' that were disgorged by the wrecked homes. As buildings burned soldiers used the heat to good effect, putting eggs into buckets of water and leaving the buckets to boil in the burning houses, safely retrieving the eggs to eat when hardboiled.

At a trout farm near Luneberg the farmer complained that British troops had come to his farm and destroyed his fish. He was waiting for them with nets so they could take what they wanted but they had other ideas. They rushed past the farmer, ignoring his pleas, and started throwing hand grenades into the pools. The explosions killed many trout but yielded few edible fish. When their officers arrived their behaviour was little different. They drew their revolvers and shot the fish remaining in the water.

Germans who failed to show remorse for the actions of their countrymen or offered active resistance to the advancing armies also faced severe retribution. Civilians were sent into towns as messengers for the advancing armies promising that unless towns were surrendered they would face the full fury of a planned assault. The official diarist of the 11th Hussars recorded how the policy worked at one northern German town. He stated: 'A civ was soon afterwards contacted and directed to the Burgomeister of Harsefeld with a message that if all German soldiers were not out of the town by 1400 hours something very nasty would happen to the town.' (18) When, on 9 April 1945, the 23rd Hussars found themselves facing 12th SS Training Battalion in the village of Steimbke, they took decisive action. There was no holding back and all possible firepower was called for to: 'convert this large village into what has been acknowledged as a masterpiece of liberation'. (19) What the Hussars' diarist had couched in hyperbole the diarist of their accompanying infantry recorded in more stark terms: 'most of the village left in ruins'. (20)

Once in occupation the soldiers took suitable revenge against some members of the population, in particular any unrepentant Nazis they encountered. Tanks were deliberately parked in the once neat gardens of German homes. If a house contained photographs of Nazi atrocities it was burned to the ground. If householders gave Nazi salutes their homes were torched. If weapons were found concealed in the home, once more, fires were started.

Such was the dilemma over the extremes of their behaviour that many soldiers made efforts to explain their emotions. Letters to families, from writers who thought they might be shocked by the descriptions of the scenes of destruction and chaos, carried notes to express their own emotions about the situation. As one letter writer added: 'I sense a touch of pity in your heart as you read this description. I must confess to feeling no such sentiment this time.' (21) The chaos imposed on the occupied countries by the Germans had been enough to harden the hearts of even the most sentimental of soldiers.

Despite the levels of destruction inflicted on the population of Germany by the invading armies there were relatively few cases of wanton and overzealous destruction. Certainly, individual homes had been destroyed out of a pure thirst for revenge but seldom had rage caused larger areas to be put to the torch. However the behaviour of the Canadian Argyll and Sutherland Highlanders in April 1945 was to buck the trend. When they were fired on by civilians in the village of Soegel they reacted with a show of force. They sent in their engineers who removed the population at gunpoint and proceeded to burn the whole village to the ground. Four days later, when their CO Lieutenant Colonel Wigle was shot and killed by a sniper, thought to have been either a civilian or a German soldier dressed in civilian clothes, they repeated the performance and another town fell victim to fire. After so many months of hard fighting, all the way from Normandy, they were in no mood to tolerate civilian misbehaviour. Once again the soldiers fixed bayonets and marched the locals out of their homes. The Germans pleaded to be allowed to remove even a few of their possessions but to no avail. With the civilians clear of the area, every single house was razed to the ground.

It was natural that in the final days of the campaign the troops should behave with such a wanton lust for destruction. Now everywhere seemed to be rubble. From the villages that offered any resistance, to the towns that could act as channels for enemy reinforcements and the cities that seemed to have been long since wiped from the map. From industrial centres to sleepy farming villages. Modern apartments and medieval homes, none were spared. Dortmund, Essen, Cleve, Bremen, Hannover, Hamburg – the list seemed endless.

Then, as April turned to May, the German will to fight on finally crumbled and only as the enemy resistance collapsed did the destructive urge finally wane. In the stirring of the spring sunshine the victors finally began to bypass villages; to drive through whole towns without needing to stop to burn down homes. Towns went past in a blur of white flags that fluttered meekly from so many windows. No longer were the flame-throwers needed, nor the airstrikes, the artillery barrages, the mortar fire, the high explosive or the suppressing fire of the machineguns. Only in peace came restraint.

14

Rage, Revenge & Retribution

'I don't think anyone took many SS prisoners. Not if they could get away without being caught doing it.' (1)

There are many rules of war. These rules, standardised and codified by the Geneva Convention, set out the correct behaviour of soldiers within the parameters of what is considered acceptable in a civilised society. But to the soldiers whose job it is to fight the battles one unwritten rule stands out above all others – ensure your own survival.

Laws concerning battlefield behaviour, and recriminations stemming from contraventions of these laws, are often irrelevant to men who actually fight the battles.

The treatment of POWs is at the very heart of the rules of war. The Geneva Convention states that prisoners should be taken from the battlefield to a place of safety, they should not be robbed of valuables and personal effects, nor should they face threats, coercion, or torture to reveal military secrets. If put to work whilst in captivity then their labour should have no connection with military production. POWs should be fed the same rations as the soldiers of their captor's army and given sufficient clothing and shelter. During the Second World War these conditions were often not met and life as a prisoner could be harsh, although at least it was life. For the surrendering soldier, of all sides, the primary concern was not how life would be in a POW camp but could they reach a camp in safety?

Such was the ferocity of many battles that all sides were guilty of what could be termed war crimes. Contraventions of the Geneva Convention were not the sole preserve of the Nazis. It is widely known that Russians and Germans fought each other with a bitter hatred and with a knowledge that to be captured was tantamount to death. Both sides regularly executed prisoners and those who survived were employed as slave labour. The Nazis and the Communists, from opposing ends of the political spectrum, were fuelled by a mutual loathing. Both were anti-democratic and illiberal, with their armies under a measure of political control, a control thought to influence their soldiers' behaviour.

But what of the Germans who surrendered in north-west Europe – many of whom claimed the fighting in the west was more intense than that in the east? How did they fare in the hands of soldiers from democracies? How did the soldiers entrusted with restoring order to Europe react to conditions on the battlefield and the day-to-day struggle for life?

There was a history of massacres even before the start of the campaign to liberate Europe. In the dark days of 1940 around one hundred men of the 2nd Battalion Royal Warwickshire Regiment were massacred by SS troops at Wormhoudt in Belgium. The prisoners were herded into a barn and butchered with only a few living to tell the tale. A similar number of soldiers from the Royal Norfolk Regiment met the same fate at Le Paradis on the same day. Although the campaign in North Africa has generally been seen as 'clean' there were occasional extremes of behaviour. The Germans even claimed that a hundred and eighty doctors, medics and wounded were killed in cold blood when the New Zealanders overran a Wehrmacht Field Hospital.

Such incidents, and others occurring in Italy and during the raid on Dieppe, were an indication of what was to come once the liberation of Europe began in earnest.

If there is one story about the treatment of German prisoners that continues to shock forty years after its first publication it is the experiences of Edward Ashworth, whose story was first published in Cornelius Ryan's groundbreaking D-Day history *The Longest Day*. Hoping to get a German helmet as a souvenir Ashworth, a sailor unloading supplies on Juno Beach, made his way to where he had seen a Canadian soldier leading a group of six German prisoners. Upon reaching the group he found the Germans lying in the sand and upon closer inspection found that each had had his throat cut by their guard. Such behaviour was exceptional, in its unrestrained brutality it went beyond the limits of what even the most hardened soldiers considered justifiable. This was not a killing in the heat of the moment but a calculated execution, the type so often associated with the SS. However the incident was a fitting prelude to the increasingly bitter fighting in Normandy where both sides stood accused of mistreating their prisoners. In the words of the historian and war veteran Charles Whiting it was: 'the first recorded war crime of the campaign. But it wouldn't be the last.' (2)

Many of the German soldiers taken into captivity in the first days of fighting after D-Day fully expected to be executed by their captors. The experience of those who had fought against the Red Army had exposed them to a harsh reality – mercy was a quality little found on the Eastern battlefields. Further to this the Nazi propaganda machine had portrayed the British and Canadians as monsters. In an attempt to encourage their soldiers to fight to the bitter end they were indoctrinated with the belief they were facing ruthless killers who would show them no quarter. However, most Germans soon learnt that their captors meant them no harm, as one infantryman remembered:

A lot of the soldiers in Normandy had been fighting in Russia. They had a different perspective to those I'd fought against in Italy. They thought we were going to kill them immediately, there was no two ways about it. They had so much in their mind from fighting the Russians that they were sure they were going to be killed. They were glad to come to us to be killed, they knew they would be shot – end. But with the Russians they would be tortured and all the rest. Then when they did come over to us we just sent them back and on the whole they were treated very well. (3)

Royal Marine Arthur Jarvis ferried Germans back from the beaches to ships waiting to take them to England. Before making their way into captivity they had to help unload supplies:

> I had to get the Lewis Gun off the mounting to get them off the landing craft to start unloading because they thought they were going to be shot. But when they were at work and we started giving them cigarettes they just couldn't understand it. Then afterwards, when they realised we weren't going to shoot them, they used to show us photographs of their families. They seemed just the same as us. (4)

Throughout the campaign Germans were put to work in contravention of the Geneva Convention. Rather than send them immediately to a safe position, they were sometimes kept at the front to carry out a variety of tasks. Such breaches of the rules were often necessary when, with insufficient men to carry out many important tasks, prisoners were the only available alternative. Thus POWs often found themselves digging slit trenches or carrying away injured men. During 'Operation Plunder' heavily laden commandos employed prisoners to carry their heavy weapons and packs, and onlookers were perplexed to see their grey uniforms intermingled with the brown of the commandos.

Any activity that helped protect those fighting could be justified, if not according to the rules of war according to the realities of it. It was not unusual to see captured Germans acting as stretcher-bearers, carrying their wounded conquerors from the battlefield and on the D-Day beaches captured Germans were made to dig graves for Allied soldiers while the fighting still continued.

In extreme cases prisoners were forced to perform tasks that not only contravened the Geneva Convention but must also have appalled them. In early 1945, whilst fighting outside Bremen, soldiers of the 3rd Infantry Division captured some German 88mm guns. At bayonet point the captured gunners were forced to turn their weapons around and open fire on German positions. Such acts were illegal but acceptable to the British soldiers.

There were occasions when the use of prisoners overstepped the boundary between necessity and cruelty. Some prisoners were put to work clearing minefields. To ensure the job was done properly the POWs were then marched across the minefield to check it was clear.

Although the vast majority of surrendering Germans were treated with care and consideration by their captors, the realities of war were to destroy many reputations. The British 'Tommy' has gone down in popular history as a man who treated his enemies fairly. Solid and dependable in battle, kind and caring in the aftermath, treating the enemy with consideration. Such an image was born of stories of how German soldiers were captured only to be faced with the line 'Fancy a cup of tea Fritz?'.

The stereotype was only part of the picture rather than the whole scene. For many veterans, acts of violence against their enemies make for uncomfortable memories. These were not the stories their families wanted to hear. Soldiers who returned from the battlefields wanted to fit back into society, not to remain outsiders. They knew no one would understand the violence they had experienced nor the behaviour it spawned. To civilians the war had been black and white, good versus evil, us against them. They wanted to remember their soldiers as kind-hearted heroes, not cold-hearted killers.

Yet their public faces masked the ferocious reality of how war had shaped their behaviour. It was not the behaviour of benign individuals who caused the Germans to make official complaints through diplomatic channels regarding the treatment meted out to their prisoners. In the last eleven months of war, it would be Germans in the front lines, particularly the SS, who paid the price for the vainglorious ambitions of their political mentors and faced brutal treatment at the hands of the conquering armies.

As the first waves made their way ashore on D-Day a feeling of rage took hold of some among them. Groups of prisoners were mown down by passing infantrymen incensed by the slaughter on the beaches. They were enraged that the Germans were safely out of the war whilst the invading men still faced death at every turn. On Gold Beach the 1st Battalion of the Hampshire Regiment faced stiff resistance. With his comrades pinned down by fire from a pillbox, CSM Bowers of the Hampshires positioned himself ready to attack it with grenades. As he prepared his first grenade, a white flag of surrender was pushed through the firing slit. Having crawled through minefields, eliminating German positions along the way, he was in no mood for leniency. Ignoring the flag of surrender, Bowers forced his grenade into the pillbox. The resulting explosion brought the survivors of the attack tumbling from the door, their hands raised above their heads.

Within hours of the landings men of the Middlesex Regiment saw one of their platoon commanders killed by a grenade thrown by a surrendering German who was in turn killed by their sergeant. All this before they had even left the beach area. Such incidents were to have a profound effect on the attitudes of the soldiers and set the standard for the battles ahead.

At the start of the campaign most troops were unsure of 'the form' on treatment of prisoners. Men who had not previously come into close contact with the enemy stuck closely to the rules as to how prisoners should be dealt with. Looking back many veterans laugh at how they treated their first prisoners – allowing them to keep their money and watches. In time few German prisoners left the field of battle without first being searched by their captors for loot and many were thoroughly humiliated.

With insufficient manpower available to guard surrendering Germans no chances could be taken with groups of prisoners marched to the rear. Belt, braces and boot laces were often cut in two, their tunics slashed open and fly buttons sliced off. A man holding up his trousers with one hand was unlikely to use a weapon with his free hand. Truculent prisoners even found themselves gagged by their captors until they could be handed over to MPs. Throughout the campaign prisoners were dealt with roughly. Rifle butts, bayonets and even whips were used to keep them moving. They were pushed, punched, kicked, made to run, and even made to goose step.

Their treatment depended on both the situation on the battlefield and the attitudes of their captors. Different men had different rules concerning what behaviour was suitable. Depending on the situation they might lose just their money or in some cases all their personal effects including badges, medals, watches and wedding rings. There were others who just wanted pistols and knives, such as sniper Sergeant Les Toogood who recalled the methods used by one of his colleagues:

> He hated the Germans. He would halt them in the field and tell them in no uncertain terms if they had any guns, knives or anything – we didn't want their watches or anything personal – but if they had guns, knives or anything they'd better drop them now because he's going to pick six blokes out and shoot them. He'd go you, you, you, you, over there, go behind a barn and then he'd go 'brrrrrrrr'. He wouldn't shoot them – well he has shot them and sometimes he would shoot them – but it's amazing the amount of stuff that would be dropped. Then the blokes with him would gather all the rifles and sell them for three or four quid. We were mercenary, it was part of the spoils. This was a fund so that if any bloke got a 'blighty' wound, he had 25 quid. We were quite organised. (5)

Few of the soldiers were quite so methodical. Many prisoners were just stripped of all valuables. Eager men pounced on them, tearing watches from wrists, pulling rings from fingers, emptying wallets of currency and taking gold jewellery, fountain pens, badges and medals. MPs were sent to the POW cage at Banville to arrest a corporal who had stolen 51,000 French francs from POWs. As a result of such behaviour some Germans even offered their watches to the men who captured them explaining they would be robbed anyway and preferred their valuables to stay with front line soldiers.

Despite the efforts made by MPs to punish men who stole from prisoners there were plenty of officers who happily joined in the search for valuables. One officer who showed enthusiasm for stealing from prisoners was Ken Hardy, a twenty-one-year-old subaltern in the Hallamshires. Although many other soldiers were searching for souvenirs he had one priority:

> For me money was most important. I used to line them up and take all their wallets, take all the money out. I'd give them their pictures and love letters back. I found my blokes were quite squeamish about it, they wouldn't do what I did. I think they had some kind of superstition about it, they weren't as keen to do it as me. I liked their money. At Le Havre I found a full suitcase of money belonging to the German Commander. I didn't get all of it, it had to be shared out! When I came back to this country I had about £1500 in the bank all of which I had taken off the Germans. I had an uncle at Lloyds Bank and I used to put it into an envelope and send it back to him, he banked it for me. I lived the life of Reilly for three months. (6)

Not everyone approved of such behaviour. John Mercer, a Royal Artillery observer, who had himself been briefly captured by the Germans, was against such thefts: 'I argued with the infantry because they said to the Germans "Give us your watches, give us your rings" and I said "Hang on a minute, they were taken prisoner honourably". But they said "No, when they get back to the prison place they'll be stripped anyway." I was very idealistic, very straightforward, and I had great admiration for the German soldiers.' (7)

As the Germans learnt about the economic reality of being captured, the British and Canadians were themselves learning other truths about war. This brief and bloody education was to shape their behaviour in the coming months. Unwashed and exhausted, living off tinned rations, burned by the sun and soaked by the rain, they faced the best-trained, most professional and experienced army in the world. In the face of such extreme conditions it is not surprising that the veneer of civilisation began to slip and they indulged in behaviour that would have shocked their families back at home. In such circumstances it was little wonder that POWs were seen being led into captivity as an officer shouted to the escort: 'Take him back, and don't shoot him.' (8)

It may have been easy for outsiders to condemn battlefield killings, but reality was not so simple. History records the Germans as the offenders, safe in the knowledge that 'the British don't do that sort of thing'. However to the man in a foxhole, knowing that death stalked his every move, there was always one good reason to break the rules – survival. The soldier's perception of war became more important than codes, laws and conventions and those men who survived learned realities unappreciated by the people at home. Sergeant Les Toogood, MM experienced life at the very apex of the advance, from D-Day to VE Day. Toogood, who had joined the army to escape the poverty of life on a small Welsh farm, spent his war scouting and sniping in no man's land. He saw at first hand the dangers of taking prisoners: 'You can't in action, you can't, you can't ….. Everybody's got the wrong conception of fighting, you see it in the films, but you're there to kill the bastards, they're there to kill you.' (9)

They had to learn the enemy did not always play fair. In the months preceding the invasion the officer commanding the British 49th Division, General Barker, addressed his men on the tricks likely to be faced. He warned of the dangers of Germans pretending to surrender and then opening fire on the soldiers who exposed themselves to collect prisoners. They were told to make prisoners come to them rather than move out into the open. Barker was right. Throughout the campaign there would be numerous examples of the Germans pretending to surrender and then throwing themselves to the ground as concealed machineguns opened fire on the soldiers accepting their surrender. Other Germans were known to feign death, laying prone on the ground until a tank passed by, then opening fire with their deadly anti-tank weapon, the panzerfaust. Such experiences taught them to be wary of any attempted surrenders. What General Barker had not told his men was there were two ways of dealing with surrenders. Firstly soldiers could follow his instructions and stay under cover, not showing themselves until prisoners were safely away from any supporting fire. The second option was more extreme – death.

In the weeks after D-Day, as the Allies fought to maintain a foothold on the Continent and expand the bridgehead, the men at the front became accustomed to the German methods and responded accordingly. The soldiers who survived trickery learnt their lesson and attuned themselves to a type of warfare where they could neither expect mercy nor be able to show it. One witness to the ruses explained: 'When we were taking a prisoner we would do it in the right way. If they showed the white flag we would call them over but we would stay in cover in case they did some tricks.' However, he explained how some men fell victim to ruses: 'That was all due to greed on the part of our soldiers. They wanted watches, Lugers, anything at all. As soon as the prisoners stand up and come over they wanted to be the first to loot him. And loot they did. That's why the Germans played these tricks, they knew our men would come. No matter how much you told them not to do this the greed was there.' If the Germans reacted with trickery, then the rules changed: 'So then of course you wouldn't take them prisoner. You wouldn't bother. No way. They'd collaborated in a massacre so they'd get massacred.' (10)

As the battle for Normandy raged and more soldiers realised the threat posed by German tricks the reaction to attempted surrenders became more extreme. At the peak of the fighting it seemed that the rules were all but forgotten by many front line infantrymen. In the words of one Canadian soldier: 'When the Jerries come in with hands up, shouting "Kamerad", we just bowl them over with bursts of Sten fire.' (11)

By the end of the Normandy campaign the 'green' soldiers had become hardened to the realities of war and set about passing this knowledge on to the reinforcements absorbed into their units. Men joining the 4th Dorsets, who had suffered so much in the Normandy fighting, were told by their sergeant: 'not to take any prisoners but to shoot them!' (12) In the aftermath of the death and destruction on the battlefield the mask of compassion often associated with the 'Tommies' was beginning to slip.

The dangers of trickery were also apparent to medical staff, since wounded Germans were known to attack those attending them. In time such acts of mercy were to become something many soldiers carefully avoided. Some officers ordered their men – including medics and stretcher bearers – to leave them to die rather than offer assistance for fears, born of bitter experience, that the wounded man might be concealing a weapon.

The 3rd Royal Tank Regiment learnt, to their cost, the danger of failing to search prisoners. After the capture of St Anthonis, on the border between Belgium and Holland, a group of SS prisoners were marched through the town. As they passed the tanks of 3rd RTR one prisoner threw a hand grenade at a group of British officers, killing the regiment's commander Lieutenant Colonel Silvertopp. The tank crews took swift revenge and every one of the SS prisoners was shot. However, the deaths of those prisoners was no consolation for the loss of a popular commander. In reviewing the retribution exacted for the death of Silvertopp one of his men admitted that under the Geneva Convention their behaviour was a war crime, yet the morality of such acts of revenge was irrelevant to the officers and men involved. The killing was not premeditated but a reaction to the situation that had been imposed on them. There would be no reports, no enquiries and no punishment. The most significant legacy was a heightened awareness of the threat posed by POWs.

As with all claims regarding battlefield atrocities it is necessary to view incidents from more than one angle. It is important to remember whilst British and Canadian histories and memoirs record the tricks played by the enemy, much less is said about similar actions by their own soldiers. Although often referred to as a gentlemanly battle, as a result of the acts of kindness shown to wounded British prisoners in the aftermath of battle, the bitter fighting during Operation Market Garden was the scene of many breaches of the rules regarding the treatment of prisoners. After the war Sepp Krafft, whose deployment of German units around Arnhem did much to thwart the success of the operation, claimed that paratroopers of the 1st Airborne Division had deceived his men by calling out 'Don't shoot!' in German and then opening fire as the enemy approached. Whether these claims were accurate or not there was little doubt not all men of the 1st Airborne Division were playing fair. One group saw their NCO shot by Germans as he attempted to escort a surrendering German into their position. This betrayal hardened the attitudes of the survivors. From that moment on they followed their own unwritten rule – no prisoners. If the Nazis could be play dirty to defend their political aims then so could the Allied soldiers to win the right to finish the war and go home.

The realities of the battlefield meant the Red Cross flags employed by medical personnel of both sides were frequently ignored and abused. Neither side felt able fully to trust the other when under the protection of the Red Cross and soldiers of both sides were prepared to open fire on those under its protection. British and Canadians often felt certain the Germans used the Red Cross flag as cover for intelligence gathering. Thus they reciprocated and local ceasefires to pick up wounded were used by both sides to reconnoitre enemy positions.

It was not only the army that developed a rather cavalier attitude towards the protection of the Red Cross. The RAF also became embroiled in controversy after it was claimed they had deliberately attacked German ambulances. William Douglas Home serving in 141 RAC wrote to his local newspaper, which published his letter. In a subsequent letter to his parents he explained he had seen: 'no less than 25 white German ambulances – and they were ambulances – which had been blown up by Typhoons'. (13)

The potential danger posed by prisoners was not the only concern for the British and Canadian soldiers. Even when prisoners had no hostile intentions they were an unwanted encumbrance. Detailing men to escort prisoners to the rear diminished a unit's fighting strength, and during battle it became easier to shoot anyone surrendering rather than expose others to danger. Tank crews of the Northants Yeomanry saw how infantrymen dealt with the problem. Michael Hunt was among them: 'A couple of Jocks came up with five or six German prisoners and asked Mr Brown to take them. Mr Brown said "I can't take them. I've got nowhere to put them in a bloody tank. Take them back to command". They said "ok" and they wandered off. Within a minute or so I heard "brrrrrrrr". I'm bloody certain it was these two infantry blokes, they thought "sod you buggers" and shot them.' (14)

They understood the infantrymen's behaviour as Hunt's fellow Yeoman Ken Squires explained: 'Well in the heat of the moment ... really and truly, I wouldn't have worried about it if it was me. Because I would have thought "I wonder how many other poor buggers you've done that to from our side?" When you come to think of all the things we've actually seen that they've committed against humanity. Shoot a few of the buggers, it didn't matter if you think about it? ... no bugger 'em, shoot 'em, get them out of the way.' The tank crews did not feel the infantrymen were motivated by malice: 'You've got to think of the others ... This is the comradeship, the infantry wanted to get back. They were leaving their mates in the lurch. ... you don't need the problem. Get them out of the way.' (15)

The problem of attending to prisoners worked both ways. The issue of how tank crews could deal with prisoners was fraught with confusion since they could only be rid of prisoners if supporting infantry were amenable. With a preponderance of the deadly anti-tank weapons available to the enemy, tank crews knew how vulnerable they were to attack from pockets of German infantry roaming around the battlefield. In light of the dangers many tank crews felt they could ill afford to take chances and when unaccompanied by infantry they had little choice but to wipe out surrendering troops.

Such actions appear callous but to a man responsible for a crew of five it was an act of expediency designed to save lives. RAMC medic W.A. Blackman heard of such behaviour by British tank crews from a wounded German. The German explained how the tank crews were ignoring white flags and opening fire. The story caught Blackman's attention and he soon repeated it to friends. When it became known he was circulating the story he was approached by a sergeant major and told: 'You are ordered not to repeat such stories told to you by German wounded otherwise you will find yourself in very serious trouble. Do you understand?' (16) The implication was clear, although the military authorities would take little action against breaches of its own rules it had no intention of allowing rumours to spread.

These difficulties were illustrated by an incident during the assault on the Belgian town of Bourg-Leopold. A tank crew of the 13/18th Hussars captured a group of twelve German paratroopers. The tank commander had little choice but to keep the prisoners with him or execute them. They were disarmed and made to sit at the front of their captors' tank as it continued the battle for control of the town. The prisoners became an insurance policy against attack by the enemy. Such behaviour was an obvious breach of the Geneva Convention, and much criticism was levelled at SS troops who used injured paratroopers in the same manner at Arnhem. But for tank crews wanting to survive a battle it was an obvious action, carried out not through malice but from a genuine desire to survive.

Such incidents showed how the fate of surrendering enemy soldiers was dictated by the circumstances of the battlefield. For most of those involved battles were a time of utter confusion. A soldier might be certain the enemy were to his front, possibly to either side, and hopefully not to his rear. Some men reacted to the sight of enemy uniforms regardless of the situation or behaviour of the enemy. Soldiers new to battle often fired at prisoners not out of vindictiveness but from excitement at their first close-up encounters. Other more experienced soldiers reacted instinctively. One officer recalled how he was travelling in a Bren carrier when a lone German ran towards him. It may have been an attempt to surrender or a desperate plea for medical assistance, but he was never to find out, the quick thinking soldier behind him reacted immediately, killing the German.

There was little opportunity to take prisoners when clearing the enemy from houses. If the Germans failed to surrender before the initial assault they had little chance to do so later. The assaulting troops had no time to waste concerning themselves with the fate of the enemy. Instead they operated like clockwork – grenade through the window, rake the room with fire, move on to the next room. Stopping to help the wounded or encumbering themselves with prisoners only made them targets. Their task was to get the job done as swiftly as possible, moving from room to room, killing all in their path. In such circumstances sentimentality meant death, something they were all striving to avoid.

Learning these truths was the first step that could tie their behaviour into a cycle of rage and revenge. Fully aware of the tricks the enemy could play they learned that death could come at any time and how even the slightest error could give the enemy the chance to kill them. Above all they learned that to survive they would need to be every bit as strong as their enemies. To survive they would have to kill. The ability to kill without mercy was often brought to the fore by a feeling of rage that gripped some men on the battlefield. Many soldiers recalling the last apprehensive moments before commencing an attack reveal themselves lonely and confused. These were moments of introspection. With their senses struggling to cope with the sights and sounds of battle other emotions tend to be submerged beneath the instinct to survive. A platoon commander in the 5th Battalion Coldstream Guards summed up these feelings when he wrote: 'The emotions in a battle go from fear on the start line, anger when one is fired on and I regret to say complete blood-lust when you eventually reach the objective – grey uniforms were not men but just targets.' (17)

The German tactic of making the Allies fight for every inch of territory resulted in scenes of both ferocious defence and merciless assault. The Germans pursued lost causes, continuing firing when surrounded – knowing that delaying the advance for even a few minutes would help their cause. The casualties they inflicted enraged the attackers, especially when they finally threw up their hands and surrendered. Often these were futile gestures. When white flags appeared many of the British and Canadian soldiers were reluctant to accept surrender. In their fury they exacted retribution for the senseless slaughter, shooting anyone surrendering.

It became vital for officers and NCOs to control this rage, and prevent men succumbing to their emotions. Some took a strong moral stand, refusing to allow violence towards prisoners. Ken Hardy noticed how he experienced difficulties in controlling his men in the aftermath of battle:

I was always amazed that one infantry soldier would view the lot of another infantry soldier with compassion. So there was never quite that hatred between the infantrymen of our army and the infantrymen of the German army. However that wasn't always the case, it was really dependent on how the Germans behaved. I can vividly remember occasions where the Germans used to fight up to the last minute and then put their hands up. And, on more than one occasion, I had great difficulty in stopping my fellows just letting them have it. Oh yes, you could stop them .... with difficulty I think, on the basis of 'You fire and I will fire at you. I've told you not to do it and that's that!' Discipline is everything in the infantry, you lose discipline and that's it. (18)

Despite the moral standpoint of such officers, a threat of mob violence hung over the battlefield. Individual rage could spill over and spiral out of control. There was the ever present danger that rage could descend into savagery. Of an assault on Carpiquet airfield outside Caen the official historian of the Canadian Regiment de la Chaudière wrote: 'No prisoners are taken this day on either side.' (19) When Canadian positions came under attack at night the troops became brutal. They were seen with knives, slitting the throats of wounded Germans, and Canadian officers were forced to draw their pistols to regain control.

Not all officers were themselves merciful towards prisoners. One Somerset Light Infantryman, recalled how at Château Fontaine in Normandy they managed to capture a sniper who had been harassing them. He was called for by his company commander and ordered to remove the prisoner to the rear. This order was then followed with instructions to execute the prisoner as soon as he was out of sight. The soldier, feeling no personal hatred for the sniper, simply marched him away to be handed over to regimental police.

Despite efforts to control rage there were times when there was little hope of preventing excesses. Whilst holding precarious positions on Hill 112, one of the most hotly contested locations in Normandy, men of the 4th Battalion Somerset Light Infantry came under attack by German tanks. One of the tanks was stopped and its crew attempted to surrender but as they approached, the Somersets opened fire. The officer commanding the company recalled that he was told: 'just about every survivor in the company had a bang at them and they were all shot. The probability was, and I'm 99 per cent certain, they were coming out to surrender, either that or run away but they weren't going to take any action.' (20)

One witness to the incident failed to understand their actions until shown the bodies of men killed during a previous attack, when tanks had used their heavy guns on men cowering in trenches. What he had discovered was that what initially appeared to be an example of rage was more than that. The action of the soldiers was inspired by a thirst for revenge against the enemies who they felt had murdered their comrades. This desire for vengeance was to become important in the self-perpetuating cycle of revenge that characterised the campaign in Europe.

Captain John Majendie, the officer commanding 'A' company of the Somersets, was to experience this. Whilst remaining non-judgmental of his men he noticed how individuals approached the enemy with a differing outlook. Majendie felt little hatred towards the Germans, but this was in contrast to some of his men. As prisoners came in he found few to be defiant, rather they were unshaven, dirty, smelly and very frightened. He noted:

> One's attitude towards them? I certainly didn't feel any antipathy towards them. I was rather intrigued. A German soldier takes his steel helmet off he looks exactly like a British soldier. As we were trying to consolidate on Hill 112, a Boche suddenly came in from the side of my company, looking extremely frightened. And my company sergeant major upped his rifle and took a bang at him. He missed, but I said 'Don't do that again'. I didn't ask him whether he meant to miss him or not, but I don't think he did. Well, he'd been a long time with the company and he'd seen a hell of a lot of his friends killed or wounded. And later on, I remember when three prisoners came in – one was wounded in the face – asking for water, and the sergeant major said 'Don't give the bugger any water!' I said get a mess tin and give him some. I think he had a very genuine hatred whilst I found them rather intriguing. (21)

Differences in opinion were sometimes seen in the heat of battle. One NCO who believed that prisoners involved in trickery should be shot explained how not all his men agreed and spoke out against executions. His feared dissent could have serious repercussions for discipline:

> You had the holier than thou types. According to them you shouldn't kill in the first place. They could cause bother you see, they talk to one man, tell him these little things. He'd start niggling, he'd tell the next man and so on. Before long they'd all be not wanting to fight. So you had to stop it there and then. So what we used to do then was make them a stretcher bearer. That wasn't the end of the problem, he could still yap, but he couldn't cause much bother with the front troops. (22)

As men became progressively stressed by the psychological impact of war their tolerance for the enemy diminished especially when they witnessed the death of friends. During a hunt for German snipers, a group of men from the 59th Division forced some SS men to surrender, but as they herded their captives along the road another Nazi stepped out of a trench and opened fire. In the chaos one of the British patrol was hit in the head and killed. His best friend took revenge against the SS prisoners, charging them with his bayonet and killing a number of them.

Others' experiences were quite different. Sydney Jary, who commanded 18 Platoon of the 4th Battalion Somerset Light Infantry considered that he and his men were not brutalised. Despite prolonged service at the front his men were never responsible for violence against any of the Germans who surrendered. Jary became convinced that war did not brutalise and that, conversely, he and his men became more sensitive as the campaign progressed. He was certain the nature of a man influenced how he responded to the enemy rather than the experiences: 'I would not suggest that the naturally brutal might not find in war an outlet for their brutality. However, that war does not brutalise the type of decent and fair-minded young Englishmen whom I had the very great honour to command, I have no doubt.' (23)

That certain individuals were more inclined towards the abuse of prisoners was without doubt. Ken Squires of the 1st Northants Yeomanry recognised certain qualities evident in men known for their mistreatment of POWs: 'Hardnuts in the army would think no more of shooting a bloody prisoner as not. The characters that you knew within the regiment, you knew who they were. I'll tell you what it was like. He was like a bloody poacher. Take Northampton and all us guys living there, the guy who was the hard one was the poacher.' (24)

For all the debate over whether or not the fighting men became brutalised one thing was certain – 1944-5 was a very dangerous time for certain German service-men attempting to surrender. Without doubt the men of the Wehrmacht stood a greater chance of reaching POW camps than any SS troops. The troops soon learned to take no chances with SS prisoners and acted accordingly. Recce trooper Arthur Rowley recalled: 'From experience we knew that the SS Troops were more difficult to deal with than the normal Wehrmacht. Furthermore, the display of arrogance shown by captured SS did not go down well with us. Generally we showed the Wehrmacht more consideration and understanding than the SS. After all they were like us, they didn't want to be there either.' (25)

The Waffen SS were an enemy unlike any other. Arguably without equal as a fighting force they were also without equal for their reputation for brutality. Their very name became a byword for all that was wrong with the Nazi regime. It was they who became woven into tales of revenge that haunted the battlefields, and it was no surprise they were often seen surrendering with their insignia freshly torn from their uniforms to avoid recognition. Of course, the German military had many other formidable units in their ranks, such as paratroopers and Panzer Grenadiers, but few names struck such terror as that of the SS. As signaller Len Bennett explained: 'I think it was the SS the animosity was towards. You may have an animosity in hot blood towards anyone, but in cold blood it was towards the SS.' (26) In the words of one man: 'I don't think anyone took many SS prisoners. Not if they could get away without being caught doing it.' (27)

There were also many civilians who longed for revenge against them and it was often the men of 21st Army Group who took revenge on their behalf. One veter-an NCO recalled: 'There were a lot of areas where they had killed the people in the towns or the villages, and we'd get to hear about it. There weren't too many prisoners taken in a place like that.' (28)

It was primarily against the SS that some units were dragged into a bloody cycle of revenge and retribution. The incident which caused the greatest controversy and was widely seen as changing the attitudes of so many soldiers, took place on 8 June 1944 when SS men executed a group of Canadian prisoners at Ardenne Abbey. It was later claimed that the next day their commander, Kurt Meyer was taken to see the bodies of Germans who had been lined up and executed by Canadians – whose crimes were avenged at the Abbey. In court Meyer stated his men had found their comrades with their hands bound behind their backs. It was also claimed that on 7 June they had found a notebook on a Canadian officer stressing that no prisoners were to be taken. Despite his protestations about the behaviour of Canadian troops Meyer, who was not present at the time of the executions, was tried and sentenced to death for the actions of his men. The sentence was later commuted to life imprisonment after representations by Canadian veterans who, like Meyer, well knew the cyclical nature of such incidents.

It has also been claimed by French historian George Bernage that the massacre was in revenge for the murder of seven Germans by a British unit on 8 June. They had allegedly captured nine Germans before being forced to retreat. Unable to carry more than the two most senior Germans in their vehicle, the decision was made to execute the rest of the prisoners. Whatever the truth of the allegations – of who executed whose men first and whose atrocities were the worst – the men of the invading armies found themselves with a 'cause célèbre'. In the aftermath of the slaughter at the abbey it was to be the Canadians about whom most atrocity stories were to circulate. At the height of the fighting they appeared to be caught up in a tit-for-tat cycle of revenge. It was not just the Germans who thought the Canadians responsible for war crimes. A soldier in the Royal Engineers serving alongside Canadian infantry recorded how they dealt with a sniper responsible for the death of their officer. Just three days after D-Day, in the town of Banville, they found the sniper hiding in a church steeple. The unfortunate German was taken to a farmyard, made to kneel and then beheaded with a woodman's axe. Such cold-blooded acts were few and far between but helped to enhance the reputation that the Canadian infantry were not to be messed with.

It was not just the Canadians who were caught up in such feuds. Many units had individual scores to settle, incidents that led to revenge throughout the campaign. These incidents could be real or rumours that had grown from something half heard and half remembered. Among the infantrymen of the 7th Armoured Division there was considerable antipathy towards the Waffen SS. Few of the infantrymen of the division expected mercy if captured and engagements against the SS routinely became a matter of 'no quarter asked no quarter given'. (29) Even to this day few veterans like to openly discuss the acts of revenge they were involved in, as one man recalled: 'Strictly off the record, if you wore the "Rat" on your shoulder and you came up against Germans with the SS flash on their collar, no prisoners were taken. That was from the desert days. We never took prisoners, they never took prisoners. It wasn't expected. But that rivalry was not to be spoken about.' (30) The desert veterans felt the Germans singled them out as the men who had turned the tide of the war and such feelings helped perpetuate the cycle of revenge and retribution. There was reportedly a running feud with the SS Langemarck Division, whose men were responsible for an incident the repercussions of which were felt for many months. When men of the 1/6th Queens Regiment counterattacked the enemy at Livarot they found SS men mercilessly executing wounded 'Rats' with pick axes. The word soon went round: 'Never take prisoners in the "Langemarck" Division!' (31)

Likewise the men of the 49th Division found they had become infamous when German radio broadcast a speech outlining their notoriety. Identified by their divisional 'Polar Bear' badge they were nicknamed 'The Polar Bear Butchers' and were claimed responsible for the murder of surrendering Germans. As a result the

German troops were instructed never to take prisoners from the division. Whether the claims were true or not was immaterial, what counted was that the men of the 49th Division expected no mercy.

The broadcast influenced the minds of many 'Polar Bears'. No longer could they afford to take chances – no man wished to fall victim to German soldiers hungry for revenge. Private John Longfield was sucked into this cycle of violence. During one attack he found himself alone except for the corpse of a Bren gunner. The incident that followed was to haunt Longfield for the rest of his life. As a German soldier approached him he attempted to open fire but his Sten gun jammed. Realising he could expect no mercy he threw the useless weapon at the smiling German, grabbed his dead neighbour's Bren and emptied the magazine into his enemy at close range. In more innocent encounters Longfield might have expected to go quietly into captivity but in light of the broadcast he could expect no mercy. As he explained: 'The only effect that had was to make people more bloody minded.' (32)

The Germans grew to expect acts of bloody revenge from the British and Canadian infantry. Yet there were others with a deeper hatred of the Germans. 21st Army Group also included the men of the 1st Polish Armoured Division. They acquired a fearsome reputation and were believed by many never to take German prisoners. These were men who had escaped when the Germans invaded their homeland in 1939, and who had endured great hardship before they finally arrived in Britain. For them it had already been a long war, waiting almost five years before they had a chance to avenge their earlier defeat. These were men with a score to settle. For the German soldiers there was an appreciable fear of falling into their hands. In Normandy Polish tanks drove straight over retreating Germans, allowing no chance of escape or surrender. Reports on the battle for Arnhem recorded Polish paratroopers shooting prisoners and opening fire on Germans enjoying the safety of the Red Cross. In later years stories emerged suggesting some Poles may have taken revenge against the Germans in a more systematic fashion. An American captain reported how he was sent to accept the handover of 1,500 German prisoners from Polish forces in the aftermath of the closing of the Falaise gap. When the Poles arrived they had only two hundred prisoners with them. The American officer refused to accept the two hundred men stating his orders had been for 1,500, and asked about the missing 1,300. The Pole reportedly explained how they had shot them. When the American asked why they didn't execute the remaining Germans the Pole apologised: 'Captain, we can't shoot them. We are out of ammunition.' (33)

While many soldiers were involved with what might be termed as collective acts of revenge others were involved in personal acts of retribution. The ranks of the British army were peppered with volunteers from throughout Europe who had escaped into long exile, and who were fighting to liberate their homelands. Their hatred was more personalised than that of their British comrades. Sergeant Les Toogood served alongside a foreign volunteer: 'He didn't like the SS or Panzer Grenadiers, and if there was an officer or equivalent to an RSM in the group we were lucky to get them back alive. And when you hear his story about what they did to his sisters and his mother. I mean, if they'd done it to my parents I wouldn't have had any qualms.' (34)

Not all killings were done in the heat of battle. The proud Nazi bearing of some prisoners was to be more than some soldiers could bear and it took just one comment from a prisoner to invoke the fury of the Allied soldiers. In March 1945, when Major General Friedrich Deutsch attempted to surrender, he faced men of No.6 Commando who were in no mood for dealing with arrogant Nazi officers. He approached a commando lance corporal who called out 'Hands up!', foolishly the general replied 'I am General Deutsch and I will only surrender to an officer of equal rank'. The unimpressed commando replied 'Well, this will equalize you' (35) and cut down the general in a hail of fire from his Tommy-gun. The NCO's only punishment for this murder was to dig a grave and bury the corpse. In similar situations many Germans professed to their captors how they would happily die for their Führer. It was a foolish speech – there were many British and Canadian troops happy to oblige.

For German snipers there was little opportunity to surrender. They adopted the tactic of allowing forward units of the Allied armies to pass by and then creating chaos behind the front. Their methods upset the sense of morality of many soldiers who thought sniping was a dirty, underhand tactic. So when German snipers were finally flushed from their positions they could expect little mercy. In the words of a soldier who had lost friends to snipers: 'no worry about the Red Cross Convention'. (36)

These cold-blooded shootings of Germans who had already surrendered raise more emotion than acts carried out in the heat of battle. To so many of the British public the very idea that 'our boys' could or would have behaved in such a manner was unthinkable. Though such killings took place on a smaller scale than the acts of rage they occured throughout the campaign. Men who were disgusted with what they had experienced and blamed the Nazis, men who could not be bothered to trouble themselves with prisoners, or men who simply saw no moral dilemma in executing a surrendered enemy – took the law into their own hands.

In the days following D-Day the situation was so fluid that the killing of POWs could be little more than an act of expediency. During a German counter-attack in Normandy one commando found himself in an uncomfortable situation. With a German attack closing in on their HQ he was ordered by his CO to execute three prisoners, insisting he could spare no one to guard them. When the commando hesitated the colonel pulled out his revolver and told him he would either shoot the Germans or himself be shot for refusing an order. Faced with so stark a choice the prisoners were swiftly executed.

That infantrymen at times behaved in such a callous manner is unsurprising, however, that medical staff could display similar attitudes dismayed many infantrymen. Enemy wounded were supposed to be afforded the same treatment as Allied wounded but this could be at the discretion of doctors. It was known for doctors to refuse to allow German patients to remain in the wards with Allied wounded. Even when medics brought in wounded Germans their efforts could be in vain. In one incident a medic watched as a seriously injured young German soldier was left tied to a stretcher and ignored as two doctors discussed the iniquity of the Germans. They continued their conversation, pausing only to tell the medics to keep the dying soldier quiet. When they finally examined him it was too late, and he was despatched to the mortuary. Such nonchalant behaviour upset the medics and stretcher-bearers who risked life and limb to rescue wounded men regardless of their nationality.

In such a climate it was inadvisable for German wounded to show any signs of hostility towards their would-be saviours. A wounded officer of the 2nd Fife and Forfar Yeomanry recalled an ambulance journey accompanied by a liberated Canadian POW, a starving Polish concentration camp inmate and a truculent German officer whose foot had been blown off. During the journey the German offered cigarettes to the soldiers but refused to share with the Pole. When told to give the Pole a cigarette the German spat in the starving man's face. Despite his wounds the German was shown no sympathy, his behaviour had outraged both the ambulance crew and the wounded men. Unceremoniously he was taken from the ambulance, dumped into a ditch and left to die.

Surrendering Germans who made their way safely into captivity could still face danger. Despite rules governing the treatment of prisoners many Allied soldiers used threats and violence to force prisoners to divulge information. The formula of 'name, rank and number' was of little concern to those who believed the ends justified the means, and that the welfare of Allied soldiers was of more importance than that of their prisoners. Enemy soldiers were expected to offer the sort of information British soldiers had been warned against revealing. Some prisoners found themselves beaten by both the soldiers who captured them and the MPs to whom they were handed over, with intelligence officers threatening them with further beatings in the hope of extracting information. Mental and physical cruelty were useful tools. On one occasion a British sergeant with four uncommunicative SS prisoners left the room to return with four grave marking crosses. The message was clear, they were destined to rest beneath these, and so they began to talk.

Threatening behaviour was not the sole preserve of lower ranks and on occasions senior officers were involved. When a German sniper was brought to the HQ of 214 Brigade Stan Procter watched the scene:

> An officer held a pistol to his temple as the Brigadier tried to interrogate him. He said nothing. I watched horrified in case the officer pulled the trigger. I can still see the expression on the prisoner's face as he expected to have his brains blown out. Eventually the Brigadier grabbed his arm and hurled him away. He was only trying to frighten this chap, but I could see this chap standing there with this gun at his head, I thought 'Oh my God, what is he going to do?' My sympathy was with the poor chap. (37)

Trooper John Reynolds of the 15/19th Hussars witnessed a deliberate display of cruelty towards a wounded German:

He'd had his arms shot off, he was put into an ambulance after he'd been treated. One of my mates got wounded, and he was sat in the same ambulance. The German officer said 'Cigarette, cigarette'. So my mate got half a cigarette, gave it to him, put it in his lips. But he left it there. He sat and watched him burn his lips. He said 'You fucker, I've just been into a field where there were about forty Americans shot down, by your machine guns up the top of the hill and if you think I'm enjoying sitting watching you with a fucking fag you've had it.' (38)

By April 1945, with the Rhine crossed and Germany all but defeated the men of 21st Army Group were growing increasingly careful. With the end in sight no one wanted to fall victim to the last desperate Nazi attempt to ward off defeat. This was not a time to take chances and had not the messages from the political leaders been unequivocal? The enemy should be totally destroyed -Winston Churchill himself had spoken of the Nazis as an 'evil gang' that would be 'wiped out'. (39)

In the face of increasingly embittered troops, many Germans would be fortunate to survive the act of surrender. Although, as evidenced by the thousands upon thousands of prisoners taken, the killing of prisoners was not carried out on a large scale it was without doubt widespread. Fortunately for everybody concerned, most German soldiers were more than eager to give up, and had no intention of fighting to the bitter end. In the final weeks of war many thousands surrendered without firing a shot – in April 1945 more than 1,500,000 Germans surrendered to the Allied armies, including a hundred and fifty generals and admirals.

With so many happily trudging into captivity the dogged resistance by some German units revived a sense of ruthlessness in the Allied armies and they increasingly resented the efforts of the Germans who contrived to hold up the advance. Every roadblock, mine, machinegun or sniper seemed to prolong the agony. In small towns and villages continued resistance sometimes meant every house had to be cleared individually. By now well practised in the art of clearing houses, the British and Canadians acted with ruthless efficiency. Very few who attempted to hold out against the hail of PIAT bombs, grenades and automatic fire would survive to reach POW camps. This was the period of which the war correspondent Alan Moorehead reported: 'At times the skirmishing grew so bitter prisoners were being shot.' (40)

New soldiers, both young and old, were coming into the infantry. These eighteen-year-old boys and men in their forties were nicknamed the 'six week killers' after their short courses of basic infantry training. In the final weeks of the war they were introduced to the harsh life of the battlefield and were not taking any chances. Some officers noticed a difference between the veterans and the newcomers, as one later wrote: 'New troops had a more civilian and brutal outlook.' (41) They were less inclined to see their prisoners as fellow victims of war, as did the veteran infantrymen. Some expected to see the execution of the defenders who had killed their mates and expressed surprise if prisoners were simply robbed then marched into captivity.

With the end of the war within sight many soldiers were in no mood to show tenderness towards prisoners. Those who survived battle often began their journey to the POW cages with punches or kicks from their captors. It became common to make POWs run or march 'at the double'. This was despite orders that the 'Doubling' of POWs was banned as it was considered bullying and: 'not worthy of British soldiers'. (42) However, few heeded such instructions and POWs attempting to slow down were often met by volleys of shots fired at their feet. As they ran into captivity, their greatcoats flapping around their ankles, their captors offered little sympathy, laughing at them and shouting 'Schnell, Schnell'. In one incident a Canadian despatch rider was seen knocking down a prisoner with his motorbike. Each time he attempted to run the DR revved up his machine and sent the despondent POW sprawling into the mud.

Those who failed to keep up with the speed of the march could sometimes meet a violent end. Two British soldiers were even seen herding POWs along a road using a whip. One of the men was cycling and the other running beside them – regularly changing places so as to preserve their energy. When asked what they did with any prisoners who could not keep up they admitted that the man on the bike shot the stragglers. Understandably, few of the prisoners decided to risk such a fate.

Despite the willingness of so many Germans to make their way peacefully into captivity many others had no such intention. The route of the British army took it across northern Germany, the traditional training ground of the Wehrmacht. Across their path were camps home to those being trained to fight for the survival of their 'Fatherland'. These camps were staffed by experienced soldiers, often virulent Nazis and veterans of fighting throughout Europe. The ad hoc units fielded in the final weeks of the war were not the defeated, demoralised men seen elsewhere. Hitler Youth, the staff and pupils of the training schools, Marines and Luftwaffe pilots – all were prepared for one final attempt to stem the Allied advance. Increasingly some very young German soldiers fell into the hands of the British soldiers. It was difficult for many of the British soldiers to feel hatred towards them, and some of the older men had sons waiting at home who were older than these proud Nazi warriors. Once they had dropped their weapons and had been stripped of their helmets, they were revealed as what they really were – very young, tired and scared children. Some, often as young as twelve, were treated like naughty, if somewhat dangerous boys and sent into captivity after a good spanking. However, not all were to face mercy. In the battles around Teutoberger Wald men of the 1st Herefords came into contact with boy soldiers from a Wehrmacht training camp. As one of the British soldiers later admitted, those who did not raise their arms quickly enough were shot without compunction.

As if killing schoolboys was not enough, nothing could prepare the advancing troops for the horror they would next encounter. It would soon be revealed that these were not the only children falling victim to war. With the collapse of the Nazi regime the course of the war took a horrifying new turn as the advancing armies uncovered some uncomfortable truths about their enemies. The discovery of the concentration camps seemed to change the world forever. No longer could war be viewed as an art – a noble pursuit of gentlemen and dedicated professionals. Now all the glamour was stripped away exposing the full horror of man's inhumanity to man. This was war against the innocent – women, children, old people, the handicapped. Here was the proof of what they had been fighting for. This was not a fight of one country against another – it was a war between the Nazis and civilisation.

The tragedies that were revealed when the British army entered the concentration camp of Bergen-Belsen were to have a profound effect and once and for all dispelled the notion that the Nazis could be a noble enemy. Many who saw the results of Hitler's policies found it hard ever to speak of their experiences. To later generations the scenes have an uncomfortable familiarity as images of piles of corpses and of the plight of the starving have been burned into the consciousness. Genocide as witnessed in Rwanda or Bosnia, starvation as seen in Ethiopia, have filled the television screens for many years – yet acts against innocent civilians are always compared to the Nazis' crimes. Those British soldiers entering Bergen-Belsen on 13 April 1945 had no such preparation. They knew they were fighting an evil aggressor and rumours of such camps had been in circulation for years. But finally here was the evidence, stacked like firewood or crawling around in front of them. When the advance units of the 11th Armoured Division reached the camp they found around 40,000 prisoners, many on the edge of existence. Typhus, typhoid, dysentery and tuberculosis were rife. Naked bodies lay scattered everywhere, some slumped where they had fallen and died, others in piles sixty to eighty yards long. Some, too weak to move, lay cramped on bunks in damp, unlit sheds where the dying shared their beds with the dead. Everywhere was evidence of cannibalism, with fleshless corpses having been cut open and the hearts, livers and kidneys removed by the desperate inmates.

Many of the soldiers felt bewildered, how could they ever again view the enemy as human beings? The journalist Alan Moorehead noticed a change in the men he encountered after the liberation of Belsen. He reported British soldiers with: 'hard rigid expressions on their faces, just ordinary English soldiers but changed by the expression of genuine and permanent anger'. (43) Was this the time to follow General Eisenhower's order to 'Destroy the enemy whenever and wherever you can'?

Guards in concentration and slave labour camps could expect little mercy from the liberating troops. Many prisoners took instant revenge against their guards and the liberators seldom intervened. At the Oberlangen camp in northern Germany the prisoners sorted the guards into 'good' and 'bad' and the 'bad' were openly executed. At Bergen-Belsen the British initially encountered 800 Wehrmacht soldiers and 1,300 Hungarians, however these were not their primary quarry. What they wanted were the SS men and women who had inflicted the reign of terror on the inmates. At first the guards remained at liberty helping to control the camp whilst a truce, that allowed the British free access to the area, was still in effect. Although the SS men initially retained their weapons they were warned that for every internee shot by them one of their own would be executed. They remained at liberty until the truce ended and military records state that twenty-eight male guards and twenty-five female were taken into captivity on 17 April. The senior staff, including the commandant and the camp doctor were soon rounded up and held in cells, where many were subject to beatings. One was seen lying in a pool of his own blood pleading with his captors to finish him off. Another, resigned to his fate, committed suicide.

The story of the Belsen guards illustrated the new consciousness of 21st Army Group. Upon entry into the camp many of the guards were rumoured to have been executed. It was considered just treatment in light of their crimes. As one veteran recently wrote to a national newspaper: 'When we liberated the concentration camps, those savages who called themselves "guards" – the SS – were given fair treatment. In the main it was a bullet where it hurt most – in the stomach.' (44)

The scenes were such that many of the liberating troops were reluctant ever to discuss what they had witnessed, as if the crimes of the Germans were so monumental they had degraded the liberators and forced them into acts of violence they would rather never have committed. Some reported seeing Germans rounded up and executed by military policemen, their bodies dropping into the pits already occupied by their innocent victims. Others were beaten by British troops who were described by witnesses as: 'mad with rage'. (45) Such was the feeling of fury that orders were issued that civilians wearing white armbands within the 'forbidden area' were helping with the relief effort and were not to be shot on sight.

The surviving guards, male and female, were put to work burying the dead, always running at the double as they carried corpses. They lived on starvation rations of mildewed bread and scraps of bully beef, similar to those they had previously given the inmates. They were not given plates or mess tins, instead their food was thrown onto the ground where the once proud SS men were forced to scramble among corpses if they wished to eat. No facilities were offered for them to wash and they had no access to toilets, instead they were forced to drop their trousers and squat in full humiliating view of their tormentors. Men and women alike were afforded the same treatment. When they collapsed from exhaustion they were beaten with rifle butts, kicked or prodded with bayonets. No mercy was shown by bulldozer drivers some of whom deliberately pushed the SS men into the pits of bodies, burying them alive under mounds of dead flesh. Those attempting escape or disobeying orders were shot without question. When one guard was wounded whilst attempting escape he was thrown into the pit and buried alive among his victims. Official reports by 21st Army Group Headquarters that none of the guards had survived, all having succumbed to typhus, seemed to mask the truth – in the spring of 1945 there was little pity in the hearts of the Allied soldiers.

Within days the news spread throughout the army. Men who visited Belsen returned to their units full of tales of horror. A German-speaking wireless operator in the 1st Royal Dragoons was sent there on a viewing party as his officer considered him to be friendly to the Germans, thinking it would change his opinion. One of his comrades later wrote: 'he came back considerably shaken at what he had seen, when his views were passed around I think this did affect the attitude of most of us. Shortly after we had a number of SS POWs to look after for one night and I know that there would be none of those allowed to escape.' (46) The atrocities of the concentration camps certainly had their effect. Patrick Delaforce who served with the 13 RHA, part of the division that liberated Belsen wrote: 'Yes, SS were often shot as a matter of principle, certainly after Bergen-Belsen. .... Very little mercy was shown by my battlegroup. .... I am not saying 'retribution' was on a large scale but it occurred all right!' (47)

Many soldiers felt the scenes they witnessed changed them forever. When the rumours had emerged many had been sceptical and the truth was to shock them:

> We had a couple of days out of the line and the officers said 'You will go and see this' so a certain amount of us were sent to look at it. That was mainly a PR exercise. So we'd come back and say it did happen. To quash all the rumours that were going around that nobody would do this. I think they were afraid that people would go soft. So we were sent to go then come back and give the details. Then everybody was right-minded again to have another go at the enemy. That's my side of it. Why did they bother to send a few of us? They could have just said it did happen. During the fighting everybody must have thought why am I doing this? Why am I bloody standing here getting killed? For what? You looked at a dead enemy and said 'what has he ever done wrong in his life?' Then, of course, when you saw the horrors of the concentration camps you thought there is a purpose to it all. My mates admitted this, it really gave them a reason to carry on and do the job without grumbling. So it really helped. (48)

As soldiers men were brought into Belsen as witnesses to the Nazi crimes others were engaged in an urgent struggle to save the surviving inmates. The medical staff of the liberating units were thrown in at the deep end, attempting to care for the dying inmates, trying to prevent the spread of disease and endeavouring to supervise the rehabilitation of the survivors. There was little time to worry about the fate of the guards. As prisoners of war they were, in theory, entitled to full protection by the British. However there was little chance of the British medics lifting a finger to help them. Instead many were willing to see them executed. Captain Barer of the RAMC had no sympathy with the SS as a result of his experiences after the liberation of Sandbostel, a satellite labour camp of Bergen-Belsen. His experiences left him believing complete extermination of the SS was the only solution. He wrote: 'I am quite aware that many non Nazis were forced to join the SS in recent times, but I feel it would be better to let the innocent suffer rather than let one guilty man escape ..... After a war which has cost us so many fine and useful lives it would be wrong to be unduly squeamish about worthless lives. ..... They must be exterminated.' (49) *

---

* The extreme attitudes conveyed by Captain Barer did not reflect his true feelings towards the German people, as his widow Dr Gwen Barer explained:

    In late April my late husband Captain Robert Barer MC, an MO in the Guards Armoured Division was detailed to enter and report on the Typhus-infested POW/concentration camp, Sandbostel. 'No words could possibly convey the horror of the place,' he wrote on 3 May 'the SS are just not human, they must be exterminated – better to kill a few thousand innocent ones than allow a single man of them to escape.' As they made their way out he asked his companion, 'Did you feel any pity?' 'No' he replied. 'It was true, the things we had seen were so terrible that all feelings of sympathy and pity had been driven out. All I felt was horror, disgust and I am ashamed to admit it – hate'.......

Captain Barer was not the only one promising a violent end for SS men. Events were conspiring to harden the hearts of the advancing armies, yet some of the incidents that inspired revenge were not all they might have seemed. Rumours spread quickly through 21st Army Group, some based on facts and some entirely fiction. One had a great effect on the men who heard it. A story emerged of how a Private Parry of the 1/5th Welch Regiment had seen a group of his comrades executed by SS men at Rethem on the River Aller. The story spread like wildfire and had a profound effect upon the troops. The infamy of the incident was ensured when the scene was sketched by Brian de Grineau of the *Illustrated London News* and published on 21 April 1945. Who would now take the chance to surrender or would accept the surrender of German soldiers? For many soldiers revenge was uppermost in their minds. When the town was finally captured, some German prisoners were repeatedly beaten by their captors with other British soldiers having to resort to armed threats to restore order. Yet it was soon revealed the story of the massacre was false and the supposed victims were safe and well in a German hospital. Despite this discovery the damage had been done and the rumours had reinforced the stereotypical image of how the Germans behaved.

In the days that followed it seemed that mercy was a quality little evident among some formations. As the 7th Armoured Division advanced in the direction of Hamburg they became embroiled in bitter fighting around the village of Vahrendorf. The 2nd Battalion Devon Regiment had taken the village on 20 April only to be counter-attacked on the 26th. The Devons and the 1/5 Queens Regiment were attacked in the village by an improvised battle group consisting of an SS training unit, Marines, Hitler Youth and Wehrmacht. For several hours the battle raged through the streets of the village. 'A' Company of the Devons were surrounded and for two hours they fought hand to hand with the enemy, men of both sides were intermingled with each other in a fight to the death. Eventually, with the streets littered with the fallen of both sides, the enemy were routed. The Devons had lost seven men killed, seven wounded and twenty-two missing. The Germans too had suffered heavy losses and were to suffer even more. As the final Germans surrendered it appears the British soldiers allowed their emotions to take over. According to reports by civilians a large group of SS men were rounded up and herded into a shellhole. Then, with the civilians confined to their houses, the prisoners were executed by men under the command of a British corporal. One local woman recalled seeing at least twenty bodies in the shell crater. Within days the British had moved on and the villagers exhumed forty-two corpses from a mass

One possible explanation of why the SS had done those things – the only emotions the guards could feel were loathing, disgust and hate. Robert did not retain his extreme views and was even accused of being pro-German. Within weeks he visited (illegally) pre-war friends of mine. He wrote, 'The people obviously have not the slightest idea of what the Nazis and SS have done...... every nation has the responsibility of what goes on in prisons... the Germans have shirked their responsibility.... We have seen the greatest degradation of the human race of all time. The camp commandant said he was ashamed of being German but I'm ashamed of being human.' Asked to see a sick old man in the cellar of a destroyed town, he helped get him to hospital. As he left a girl said, ' You see they are good, not as we have been told' – particularly poignant as Robert was Jewish. A friend recalls how. as a delegate at the first post-war conference that Germans attended, Robert befriended them while most delegates shunned them. He never got over his experience at Sandbostel. In 1971 we were dining with American friends in Munich. One asked him a relevant question. Robert simply burst into tears.

grave. To this day stories circulate about the fate of seventeen anonymous Hitler Youth rumoured to have been executed with bullets through the back of their necks who now rest in the local cemetery. The locals had no idea why the British troops behaved that way on that particular day, but if the reports were true it was without doubt a war crime comparable to the murder of Canadian troops in Normandy, or the massacre of US soldiers at Malmédy during the Battle of the Bulge.

To German eyes this was a massacre, a slaughter of innocents on the battlefield. However to the infantrymen of the 7th Armoured Division it was all in a day's work. These were men grown accustomed to war, for whom killing was nothing, a daily occurrence few enjoyed but all knew was their job. And it was a job they were good at. Many of them had fought in North Africa, Sicily, Italy and then from Normandy to the Elbe. And on the final lap they were still facing the best units of the German army. Since Normandy they had encountered the tricks and deceits of the Germans, seen their friends killed without mercy and replied in kind. Many fought by the maxim 'no quarter asked no quarter given'. Ever since the crossing of the Rhine they had been prepared for desperate attempts to contain their advance. Troops of the 1/5th Queens had been told by their CO to expect trouble from both soldiers and civilians, and were ordered to respond with severity: 'Civilians obstructing you will be shot if necessary in order to make them obey your orders. ... Civs using arms against you will be SHOT. ... Show civs that we come as conquerors and mean business.' (50) The Devons had also been spoken to by their CO who: 'stressed the need of increased severity towards the German people'. (51)

In the face of fanatical German resistance and the unequivocal orders of their officers it was little wonder the final week of April was to build into a crescendo of violence. On the 22nd of the month, just days before the battle for Vahrendorf, the Queens had suffered seven casualties as a result of German trickery. The Germans, thought to be from the 12th SS Battalion, had approached men of the Queens Regiment waving white handkerchiefs. The battalion diarist recorded: 'The Germans adopted the old ruse of the white flag and as our patrol prepared to make them PW they were shot down by a concealed enemy covering party.' (52) With the end of the war in sight such occurrences were a tragedy. To the Desert Rats it seemed vindictive that the Germans were fighting a lost cause and unnecessarily causing casualties. Coming in the wake of the discovery of the horrors of Belsen the British infantrymen were in no mood to be lenient with the SS and they vowed not to be the final martyrs to Hitler's fading dreams.

Whatever really happened in Vahrendorf that day those British soldiers involved would never answer for their actions – there would no investigations and no war crimes trials. Those Germans whose bodies were found in the shell crater in Vahrendorf were paying the price for their loyalty to the Führer, for crimes committed that day and for crimes committed all across Europe. With their 'Deaths Head' collar badges they could but pray for mercy from the conquering infantrymen. Whether it was a cold-blooded execution, a calculated act of revenge or an act of rage in the heat of battle, made little difference. The fanatics of the SS had vowed to fight to the death and the British and Canadian troops were happy to oblige.

In those final days there were battles such as this taking place all across northern Germany. Seldom did they last more than a few hours, sometimes as little as a few minutes. Few of the formations involved in these battles escaped without casualties – sometimes heavy, sometimes not, but always sad. With the fate of Germany all but sealed so many observers switched their gaze to the future shape of Europe rather than the realities of life at the front. The continuing slaughter was glossed over and recorded as an untroubled 'swan' from the Rhine to the Baltic. The cameras and pens of the media remained focused on the thousands of surrendering Germans trudging slowly into captivity, rather than on the corpses of those who failed to survive the final battles. The rooting out and grinding down of the last defiant Nazis did not fit into the new mood of optimism for a better and brighter Europe.

Eventually as resistance crumbled and the Germans began to accept defeat, fewer troops showed defiance and little stood in the way of the advance. As April turned to May only a handful of Germans seemed to retain the will to fight. There was less and less fighting but it was still too early for the Germans to relax their guard. In the chaos during the last days of war and first days of peace the German soldiers were often uncertain of their position. Any show of resistance was punished with extreme violence and most just poured towards the victorious Allies, eager to make their way into the relative safety of POW cages.

Even senior German officers suffered at the hands of the victors. The ceremonial handover of weapons to their captors seemed an irrelevance in a war where thousands of civilians were dying as a result of the barbaric treatment afforded them by the Nazis. Such was the feeling of fury that some British officers used the opportunity to humiliate their prisoners. Brigadier Mills Roberts, of the Commandos, had been appalled by the sights he had witnessed at Belsen and expressed his anger during the surrender of Field Marshal Milch. When offered the Field Marshal's baton as a token of surrender he broke it over his captive's head.

Despite this the transition to peace came relatively smoothly. The hard hearts of the British and Canadian infantrymen soon softened. They passed whole columns of forlorn Wehrmacht soldiers, their vehicles stopped for lack of fuel, their faces bewildered as the might of the victorious military machine was displayed to them. They sat by the roadside as thousands upon thousands of fully armed tanks and vehicles sped past them into the heart of Germany. Only days before the men of 21st Army Group had been clamouring to kill them, to get the job done, to book their ticket home. Now they ignored the bewildered Germans. As the threat had passed so had the urge to kill.

Eventually the surrendering troops were rounded up. They were concentrated into large areas under the command of their officers who awaited orders from the victors. In the aftermath of war the British remained responsible for over a million

German prisoners. Included among them were many former SS men who thousands of people all across Europe held responsible for crimes and who expected retribution. Whilst the men of the Wehrmacht were slowly released to undertake vital reconstruction work the SS were kept prisoner. Their life was not easy, surviving on rations of six ounces of pressed meat and six ounces of biscuits per day. Considering the alternative was death on the battlefield or slavery in Siberia most of the inmates were content with their lot. For those selected for interrogation there would be little peace. When asked about their treatment the words of one man who worked in an SS camp revealed much about the mood of the British army: 'No comment.' (53)

Whilst a few soldiers still harboured ill will towards the German prisoners attitudes amongst the majority began to soften. With the end of hostilities most had little desire to punish their former enemies – they were looking forward to 'demob' and this was reflected in their behaviour. Joe Ekins was sent to guard SS prisoners in the Ruhr:

> Soon after we got there, they decided they couldn't do without a lot of the officers so they put their demob numbers back six months or so. So the officers said 'Jesus, bugger it', you know. They didn't give two monkeys about anything. We appointed guards from among the SS and said 'Right you'll look after each other, you're the guards on the other prisoners'. Every morning there used to be a dozen of these SS men come in, take your suit and get it pressed. And every evening about five or six buses went around the villages to pick up the women. They'd all come for dances that used to go on all bloody night. Half the soldiers would go home with them and walk back in the morning. Anyway this went on for some time. ....They had a check up and found about 50 of these SS prisoners were missing, but they didn't do anything to the Regiment they just bundled the SS up and sent them off to France. (54)

With the war over there was another tool to be used against unrepentant Nazis – humiliation. It was clear that violent retribution could create martyrs and there was a far greater need to re-educate the Nazis. One German naval captain told his captors he was still proud to be a Nazi in spite of learning the truth about the regime. In an effort to shame him into admitting the enormity of their crimes he was escorted to Sandbostel. Here he witnessed the horrors of disease and starvation among the inmates and met with former camp guards who revealed the truth of their deeds. The shocked sailor returned to his ship and called his crew together. His humiliation now complete, he forced himself to admit the truth and committed an act that would previously have been unthinkable. To his assembled crew he announced: 'I am ashamed to be a German officer.' (55)

With the uttering of such admissions the cycle of rage, revenge and retribution was broken. Now the men of 21st Army Group could finally abandon violence, try to forget their experiences and attempt to rebuild their lives free from the memory of the acts that war had forced them to perpetrate.

15

Life Behind the Wire

'It may appear to outsiders a little childish for men to cheer at the sight of something as mundane as food. Accept that there is very little of interest that happens in a prisoner of war camp; boredom rules so grant them this small expression of pleasure.' (1)

On 6 June 1944, all across Germany and eastern Europe, thousands of prisoners of war listened to the news they had long awaited. The invasion had begun and the Allied armies had started the campaign that would lead to their liberation. It was a time for celebration but above all it was a moment that gave them hope. Yet for all their positive emotions as they could foresee a future free from imprisonment there were others who were about to start their journey into captivity and looked to the future with trepidation.

From the first moments the men of 21st Army Group landed on French soil some of the men were captured by the enemy. For these men the final year of war would be one of hardship and conflicting emotions. It would be a time of fear and hunger, disease and death, pain and suffering, until eventually the moment of liberation arrived.

It was a time for mixed emotions. Many entered POW camps relieved they had survived and were convinced that victory was inevitable. They thought they would survive. They hoped and prayed they would survive, but few could have imagined what awaited them. Between the summer of 1944 and spring of 1945 they would have to survive the depredations of the weather, starvation, forced marches, Allied air raids, disease, attacks by their guards, assaults by civilians, and even conflict with their Russian allies.

Even in the first hours of the invasion some men were destined for captivity. The parachute drops of D-Day left many of the airborne soldiers isolated. Eric 'Bill' Sykes of the 7th Parachute Battalion was among them. Although headed for the River Orne he was dropped further to the east. He remembered how the crew of their plane had told them they 'knew the exact field', as Sykes recalled: 'They may have known the exact field but they sure as hell didn't know the right river.' Eventually he teamed up with seven similarly stranded men and they attempted to make their way back to Allied lines:

Finally on the thirteenth day, unlucky for some, the group of seven that I was with, eventually got ourselves into a predicament where we were pinned down in a ditch by machine gun fire and suffered the ignominy of capture. To our questionable credit, I must say that we were some of the first of the all conquering liberation army to enter the city of Paris, albeit under armed guard with a German tour director. The German guards were very proud to show us their real estate acquisitions – the Eiffel Tower, the Arc De Triomphe, etc. (2)

The emotional response to capture was often extreme, coming as it did in the aftermath of violent battles. John Mercer was briefly taken prisoner during the assault on Le Havre, being held overnight then being released upon the surrender of the German garrison. Although only a POW for hours the experience had a distinct effect on him:

> I suffered a mild form of hysteria. I was introduced to some press people and they all gathered around me and talked to me, but I could not tell them where I lived. I just couldn't articulate. I wanted to but I just couldn't. I couldn't tell them how old I was. I could get my name out that's all. They went away and came back about half an hour later and I still couldn't. I was traumatised. But it passed. I slept it off. I thought that was very strange. (3)

Most soldiers were alone when taken prisoner. Torn away from the familiar surroundings of their unit they were thrust into an alien world. This sense of isolation upon capture had a great effect on the morale of prisoners. For many life in the army had only been made bearable by comradeship and to be stripped of this security was an intolerable burden. Private George Marsden of the 7th Battalion Duke of Wellington's Regiment was one of those who suffered. Marsden was captured in an attack on a farm and anti-tank ditch in Holland in late 1944. The position had changed hands a number of times in the course of the fighting when it was finally retaken by a German counter-attack. Many of his comrades were killed and Marsden was himself shot in the arm and shoulder. He regained consciousness to find he was being carried away on a door by two Germans. From then until liberation he was to endure a life of almost unrelenting loneliness. The uncertainty of the first few hours of captivity shattered any illusions about POW life:

> I didn't feel fear and certainly not relief, I had lost a lot of blood and was in and out of consciousness. I appeared to be the last of our group, the others killed or taken prisoner. I was carried into the coal cellar of a house, when I got used to the dim light which came through the cellar grate above me, I saw two German soldiers lying in the far corner, they were wounded, had their heads bandaged, when they realized who I was, they crawled towards me and started shouting and punching my head, I shouted out, the men were dragged away, then they attacked me again. I was then taken away, carried down a street to a house where a lady tried to wash blood away from me before the street lower down was attacked by a RAF plane firing rockets. (4)

Having been wounded then beaten by enemy soldiers, Marsden was refused admission to a hospital and was instead left in the street. Eventually he was admitted to a makeshift hospital where his wounds were treated. For days his only contact was with German wounded and their medical staff, and this remained the case until he finally entered Stalag XIB.

Upon capture they faced many hazards, not least of which was the long and arduous journey back to Germany. In the heat of summer men crammed into railway wagons designed for horses soon became dehydrated – one man reported that it was not until 10 p.m. that he received his first drink of the day. Similarly many went for weeks without washing, as their trains were shunted around Germany in search of accommodation. Other factors also heightened their discomfort. With their almost total domination of the air, the RAF and USAAF attacked many trains carrying prisoners back to Germany. One carrying prisoners from Arnhem to Germany was attacked twice in four days.

The single biggest influx of prisoners during the campaign came in the aftermath of Operation Market Garden. In just over a week of fighting, over 6,000 men of the 6th Airborne Division were taken prisoner and travelled en masse into captivity. The individual reactions to capture were varied. They were not always stoical, some men broke into tears and a few were physically sick. Despite the danger of showing defiance in the face of their captors some of the new prisoners still showed their spirit giving 'V' signs to German photographers who recorded their journey into captivity. Others laughed and some groups broke into song despite the obvious displeasure of their guards. Jim Sims, captured at Arnhem, explained his personal emotions: 'I have often been asked what my feelings were on being captured and my answer seems to upset those asking the question. I felt RELIEF that I was still alive, although badly wounded, and with luck would see my parents again.' (5)

Despite the fears of the prisoners most were treated well by their captors. John Waddy was one of those who received assistance from an unlikely source:

> After the battle I was taken to St Joseph's Hospital, Appledorn and carried into a ward full of SS walking wounded. I was covered in bandages, plaster and brick dust. A SS Corporal came to me and gave me an apple but as I was wounded in the jaw I couldn't eat, so he sat down and cut and peeled the apple and fed it to me, piece by piece. I had come in an ambulance with a very badly wounded parachute soldier. I asked him later to find out how he was, and he went off, coming back later he said respectfully 'Der Junge ist Todt'. (6)

Others faced more severe treatment. One paratrooper who argued with an SS man who stole his wallet was executed on the spot. This seemingly unnecessary brutality shocked the other prisoners who complied with further orders without question. The prisoners were initially held in warehouses outside Arnhem awaiting transfer to camps in Germany. Conditions were appalling, the toilets were blocked and the prisoners were forced to use the corners of the room, leaving it swimming in urine and excrement. This was made worse by the fact their boots had been taken away to prevent escape.

In these camps, few seemed prepared to attempt to escape. Those planning to make a break from the camp found the response lacklustre, with their comrades admitting they were physically and mentally exhausted from their ordeal and looked forward to captivity. There were a number of escape attempts on the train transporting prisoners to Germany. The Germans reacted to escapes with threats to execute every third man if the hidden escapers did not give themselves up. After that many prisoners felt escape was not worth the risk, and they prevented any further action being taken by the more enthusiastic men.

Conditions on these trains were terrible, with little food or water provided for the prisoners. There were occasional issues of bread but the only water was often that given to the men when the trains stopped in stations, but with no receptacles in which to collect the water they were forced to drink their fill and wait until the next stop. The situation was even worse for the wounded men, many of whom were transported with a complete lack of medical attention. This had a predictable result of large numbers dying during the journey. With the Germans insisting the numbers would have to tally upon arrival at the POW camp the prisoners were forced to complete the journey side by side with corpses. Upon arrival at their destination some wounded men, even ones with leg wounds, were classed as fit to walk the mile from the station to the camp. During the transfer some immobile prisoners were not even allocated stretchers and had to be dragged along the ground on sacking by their comrades. Those who had been forced to hand over their boots to prevent escapes, arrived to find all the boots thrown in a pile from which they had to try to find a pair their own size.

Unlike many of the infantrymen who entered the Stalags, the unwounded men captured at Arnhem passed through the gates of their camps with pride. Wearing their coveted red berets and marching in step, they entered the camps with a discipline and sense of unity that enabled many to survive their time as POWs without a significant drop in morale. The successful integration of the arrivals at Stalag XIB was ensured by the behaviour of one of their number – RSM Lord. Regimental Sergeant Major J.C. Lord, nicknamed 'Jimmy Jesus' by his fellow prisoners became a legend amongst POWs. He was a pre-war warrant officer, one of the 'old school' for whom discipline and cleanliness were the order of the day. Determined not to let his men sink into apathy he attempted to make order out of chaos. He was appalled by the appearance of the British soldiers, considering shirts made from wood fibre unsuitable garb for British soldiers. He harangued the camp authorities and arranged new clothing for them. In return he expected men not to slouch around the camp with their hands in their pockets but to behave like soldiers. Lord also attempted to get the various nationalities in the camp to pull together and show a united front to their guards. However despite his efforts this was not to be, as one of the paratroopers revealed: 'There was a great deal of bad feeling between the various inmates of Stalag XIb. The Americans shared our camp but would have nothing to do with us. … The French disliked everyone, especially the British who had run away at Dunkirk and betrayed the gallant French. The atmosphere in the POW camp was dog-eat-dog and one soon adapted. The British were the best looters.' (7)

Despite his undoubted success, Lord's efforts did not alleviate the suffering of many prisoners. For men such as George Marsden this sense of comradeship was never attained during Stalag life. In the daily battle for survival there were few opportunities to make friends: 'I never saw anyone I knew in our compound and never saw all the foreign POWs in their compounds. It was just small talk about how people were taken prisoner. I didn't get to know anyone in particular, most people were sullen and quiet. They talked as they walked never ending round and round the perimeter. I just lay around, didn't feel up to walking around and move-ment pained my shoulder.' (8) Lucky men often had just one good friend, their 'mucker' with whom they shared everything and could protect each other's prop-erty from theft. Less fortunate men, like Marsden, had no one.

Upon arrival at their new homes the incoming prisoners were often shocked by the conditions of the long-term inmates. Even before the cruel winter of 1944 many had lost vast amounts of weight and were suffering from numerous ail-ments. They were, however, often better clothed than the incoming men and suffi-cient clothing kept out the winter chills was vital. With little fat left covering many of their bodies greatcoats and woollen jumpers were highly prized and closely guarded. Even in the heat of summer POWs often wore all their heavy clothes, or at least kept their greatcoats with them all day – knowing if these invaluable win-ter clothes were out of sight they would be stolen. The unfortunate men taken prisoner in the latter stages of the war had no opportunity to build up stocks of clothing and many were dressed in rags by the time of their liberation. George Marsden was unable to change his clothing between capture and liberation: 'I still had my cellular pants on, stiff with dried blood, my trousers fastened down the front with safety pins. I'd ripped them diving over wire before being captured, plus my left sleeve was missing from my jacket.' (9)

The new prisoners had much to learn about life behind the wire and were often wholly unprepared. One of the first shocks was the all-pervading stench in the camps. The stench came from unwashed bodies, blocked toilets, cesspits and fes-tering open wounds. It was a difficult life to settle into. They took time to adapt to a life of fear, boredom, hunger, exhaustion and cold. New prisoners suffered terrible or disappointing dreams, reliving their last hours of battle or believing they were at home and waking to a terrible sinking feeling.

Even the process of collecting rations was a hurdle for the new prisoners. Arriving at camps without plates, cutlery or even mugs, they had to improvise. Utensils were always in short supply – one POW, without a mug or bowl to hold his first meal, was forced to drink soup from his shoe. Throughout his captivity George Marsden never used a mug, a plate or cutlery: 'Our daily food was man-gels, usually used as cattle feed, brought to us in a bin of hot water, you had to stand in line for a scoop full of this to be placed in a tin that was begged from someone who'd collect them on a rubbish heap whilst out on a working party, no eating implements except fingers.' (10)

Although the Germans were supposed to give prisoners the same rations as their own soldiers they seldom did so. An average day's ration might be a tenth of a loaf and some soup in the morning, repeated for lunch and tea. At first many prison-ers found the black bread, so favoured in Germany, unpalatable and threw it away. The paratroopers captured at Arnhem had only recently left England and their memories of soft white bread were still strong in their minds, but to survive they had to overcome their prejudice, and were soon swapping their valuables for the hated black bread.

Such was the paucity of the rations that immense care was taken over preparation and distribution, as Bill Sykes remembered:

> The rationing of the small amount of available food was a lengthy and precise process, which took the wisdom of a saint and the accuracy of a surgeon to ensure fair distribution. You wouldn't believe the delays that hungry men will endure to ensure that they get their fair share. For instance, the oil drum filled with soup had to be continuously stirred so that the body of the soup didn't sink to the bottom of the barrel when each 'Oliver Twist' presented his tin bowl for a ladle of sustenance. Potatoes were counted and sized on numerous occasions during the chain of distribution. The cutting of a loaf of bread, five men to a loaf, was an object lesson in concentration worthy of a master chess player. The pieces were measured for accuracy and handled by each party for weight assessment, before cutting the cards for priority of choice. Remember, the loaves of black bread had rounded ends, so an allowance had to be made for this small discrepancy. The one meal of the day took untold hours of deliberation and patience, but then, when it may be your last supper why not savour the fruits of your labour!!! (11)

Doug Colls, an inmate of Stalag XIIA at Neubrandenburg, spent all day looking forward to 3 p.m., the magic hour at which the bread ration was issued. One afternoon Lance Sergeant Colls found he faced a dilemma:

> It was my job to divide the loaf, as accurately as possible into ten equal parts and the performance of this task was the cause of aggressive looks on the one hand and apprehension and embarrassment on the other. All these emotions arose from the state of the loaf; one end of it was mouldy to the depth of at least two inches. Why were we issued with a mouldy loaf when the roster showed my name as the 'bread cutter'? The job was difficult enough with a normal loaf to ensure that ten equal slices came from the loaf when considering that the bread cutter got the tenth slice when the other nine had made their choice.

Various suggestions were made to solve the problem. One that few were prepared to accept was to cut off the mould and divide up the rest. Rations were small enough already and no one wanted to have less than normal. Eventually it was decided he should return the loaf to the bakery, although this involved sneaking into a separate compound. The plan worked until Colls was spotted by a German NCO: 'I dived for the opening under the wire; halfway under I felt something holding me back. The back of my battledress had caught on the barbed wire!' As his friends pulled him through the wire the German caught up with Colls and beat him with a wooden stake. Such was the desire for bread the prisoner had risked his life, barely escaped the wrath of the guard and eventually lost the precious loaf. Despite the despair of Colls and his fellow prisoners they had no idea of how lucky they had been. When Colls was taken before the commandant to explain his behaviour the commandant directed his fury at the German NCO and an interpreter explained: 'In the future if any prisoner is seen going through the fence the sergeant major has been instructed not to hit them with a wooden stake but to shoot them!' (12)

Most prisoners found their daily rations insufficient to maintain a good level of health and as the months progressed the spectre of starvation became apparent. One prisoner recorded his daily ration. Breakfast – acorn coffee. Dinner – half a pint of watery soup and three small potatoes. Tea – tea made from rose leaves, a slice of black bread, a portion of margarine, and a spoonful of ersatz jam complete with wooden pips. Such meals became the norm, and for some even the sight of ersatz jam became a luxury. In this environment Red Cross parcels were essential for survival, bringing vitamin pills, tinned food, chocolate and cigarettes.

With the increasingly chaotic situation in Germany this tobacco became vital for survival. Cigarettes had become the main currency within camps and prisoners were able to bribe guards to acquire all manner of goods. Whole packs, when available, were left on top of kit bags so that during searches the eager guards would agree not to search for the contraband hidden below. Twenty cigarettes were worth a whole loaf of bread and could mean the difference between survival and starvation. Most importantly the cigarettes could be used to purchase food and medicines – commodities that could mean the difference between life and death.

One problem with the food within the parcels was that most needed cooking. Since there was seldom enough fuel, beds were pared down and the wood used in the stoves. Soon men were forced to share bunks and even to sleep on the cold, hard floors of the huts as their beds were burned to cook meals. At Stalag XIA there were not even enough beds to accommodate all the prisoners even before the beds were broken up. In many cases they didn't have their own allotted spaces instead at night there was a mad scramble as prisoners attempted to get a place in the top level of the three tier beds. The desire to sleep on the top level became apparent during the night. It was not just the theory that heat rises or that the bugs fell from the upper levels onto the men sleeping below. They knew that by vacating their hard won bed space even momentarily someone else would occupy it, as a result they dared not leave even to go to the toilet. Thus the fortunate men occupying the top bunks were the only ones safe from being urinated on during the night.

The toilets provided in camps were seldom anything more than an open pit with a basic structure above, used by large numbers of prisoners at the same time. There was little or no privacy. In the worst cases the facilities were no more than a row of poles where men would squat over the open pit. There was no division between them and no cover around them, just the foul smelling pit below. Some unfortunate men slipped from the poles and fell into the pits where they were left to drown in the foetid pools of excrement since there was no way their fellow prisoners could have rescued them. George Marsden recalled the facilities available: 'Disgusting, there was one toilet in a concrete building, a hole in the ground which had running water under it, until someone must have been upset because the water was cut off. This was for the use of hundreds of men, most having dysentery, imagine when the stone building was filled and the trail of excrement ran across, sometimes in to the hut.' Washing facilities were little better, with few men having access to hot showers: 'there was just a cold water tap at the back of the hut somewhere, no towel so no wash. It was a good job that I was brought up in the recession when people struggled daily to feed their large families'. (13) Some toilet facilities were even more basic, even if the prisoners eventually came to make light of the situation: 'All in all it was a difficult time, but it had its lighter moments, have you ever sat on a tall oil drum, acting as a lavatory, facing a large audience during the performance of your daily bodily functions? You can imagine the initial embarrassment. But when you've got to go, you've got to go, especially after standing in line for some length of time.' (14)

Lice flourished in these conditions and became a nightmare for the prisoners. The precautions associated with preventing infestation – regular showers, hair washing, properly laundered clothes – were unknown in many camps. They were well aware of the risk of typhus and the effects the disease would have on their malnourished bodies and as a result a daily delousing had to be carried out. In the long boring winter days, when the weather confined them to their huts, the hunt for lice became a way to pass the time. POWs sat in their bunks for hour upon hour, searching their clothes and yet even then few men were ever completely rid of them. They paid particular attention to the seams of clothing where the bugs thrived. The insects were pinched between thumb and fingernails or thrown into the flame of a candle. The prisoners paired up to search each other's hair, yet despite their efforts it was a hopeless task – as soon as they were deloused the vermin appeared from elsewhere. In an effort to dissuade the lice some men took extreme action and shaved off all their body hair.

In spite of the appalling conditions for many prisoners the overwhelming feeling was one of unrelenting boredom. Most had little to occupy their time, and activities that in civilian life might have occupied a few hours each week now had to fill every waking hour. Many tried to sustain their morale by teaming up with likeminded souls so that they could stimulate each other with conversation. However, others were never able to form friendships within the camps, at best forming a series of unfulfilling relationships that went no further than sharing food parcels and cooking for each other. This sense of loneliness was encapsulated in the title of Robert Kee's book on POW life – *A Crowd is not Company*.

This isolation meant some men were unable to cope and became suicidal. There was a combination of factors that influenced the mental deterioration of inmates. Some endured the ever-present fear of being considered cowards by friends and family at home and most felt life was passing them by. They missed seeing children grow up, missed anniversaries, births and funerals. Regular soldiers struggled to come to terms with the fact that whilst they were languishing in POW camps their contemporaries were being promoted and capitalising on the opportunities opened by war.

In the camps the delivery of mail and the chance to write regular letters back home became vital to sustain morale. The letters had to be short since they were filled in on specially printed postcards supplied by the Germans, but despite the limitations it provided a link with the outside world. The size of the forms ensured the men wrote as small as possible, trying to fill every space. Though they received news from home and kept up to date with the lives of their families they themselves had little to say. The monotonous routine of daily attempts to keep warm and abate the pangs of hunger did not make for interesting reading for the families who read them. With little to discuss their letters became repetitive featuring continual pleas of undying love and longing for the day they might be reunited.

Despite surviving on ever-diminishing rations, some soldiers were forced to labour in German industry. Few found this an easy life. Hours were long – sometimes shifts lasted as much as eighteen hours – but any who refused to work were told in no uncertain terms they would be shot for such displays of disobedience. The prisoners were employed throughout German industry, some toiled in factories, others went to farms, mines, quarries, forests and building sites. It was little more than slave labour, few were given protective clothing – in winter men without gloves found their hands sticking to metal they touched. Some of the worst labour involved men who were harnessed like animals and forced, like biblical slaves, to turn a large wheel. Sometimes they worked seven days a week and if they refused their guards simply fixed bayonets. When it became a choice between working or dying few had any illusions about what was the best course of action. 'Bill' Sykes was among them:

> We worked on an open-cast coalmine from six o'clock in the morning until late afternoon, doing menial hard labour such as filling 20 ton railway hoppers with sand, carrying lengths of iron rail, and wooden rail ties. It takes a lot of shovelling for a bunch of undernourished men to shift 20 tons of sand. Although I must admit the long handled shovels made admirable leaning posts. The winter months were particularly rough, as food was not in plentiful supply and the bitter cold took its toll. (15)

Over the years some prisoners had settled into their jobs and seemed to accept their place. In particular those engaged in agricultural work enjoyed their jobs, they kept healthy, ate well and the guards left them alone. This acceptance of their role led to disagreements between various factions of prisoners. Some men worked hard whilst others did just enough to convince the Germans they were pulling their weight. Some actively sabotaged the factories whilst others were rumoured to have earned medals for the scale of their endeavours. For most the primary issue that caused disagreement was the speed at which the work was undertaken. Groups of men worked quickly to finish their allotted tasks in the knowledge that once complete they would be allowed to return to their barracks and relax. Opposing factions considered such haste as treachery, preferring to take as long as possible to finish jobs, spinning it out and slowing down production.

Not all the men sent on work parties had the luxury of debating work rates. The shortage of food and lack of a balanced diet resulted in wounds recovering very slowly. Open wounds and sores persisted for months as the weakening prisoners found less and less energy to raise themselves from their beds. For men still not fully recovered from wounds heavy work was almost impossible. Instead the prisoners who were too weak to fulfil the allotted tasks relied on the good will of sympathetic guards to allow them to avoid any strenuous exercise.

Whether fit or healthy there was one major advantage gained from being sent to work in factories – women. As the war had progressed more and more German men had been required to leave their jobs in industry and been conscripted into the Wehrmacht. Their place in industry was taken over by women and foreign labourers. By 1944 the British men were to face unforeseen opportunities to enjoy relations with these women. In a period when few men were prepared to face the daunting prospect of escape tunnels were still carefully constructed. However these were 'Tunnels of Love', dug to connect the prisoners' compounds with those inhabited by the female labourers. By night the POWs made their way along the dark tunnels to emerge in the foreign labourers' enclosures and spend the night alongside their girlfriends, at dawn retracing their steps to take their place at roll call.

It was an environment where love, and sex, flourished. It was not only the foreign labourers who formed relationships with the POWs. With so many men in uniform the young German women longed for the company of men their own age. Many of the British prisoners were more than willing to help relieve their sexual frustrations. J.H Witte was offered the chance to meet a German girl in the cab of the crane she operated. Knowing sex was on offer he readily agreed. After a long period of enforced celibacy, and perhaps daunted by the surroundings and the fear of capture, he found himself unable to respond to her advances. Ironically, for the rest of the day, cursing the missed opportunity, he kept getting erections.

In some camps foreign labourers arranged girls to prostitute themselves to the prisoners. In one incident a group of prisoners all had sex with a nineteen-year-old Belgian girl. The POWs drew lots then each took their turn, handing over a packet of cigarettes each for her favours. She seemed nervous, visibly trembling and not enjoying her task. For the men the sex was intense, passionless and very quick. They couldn't help but realise her plight, but they too were desperate. They longed for physical intimacy and she for the purchasing power of cigarettes. Though the prisoners realised it was degrading, they still took their place in line, relieving the sexual tension of imprisonment. With death and starvation as common companions, there was little room for the niceties of pre-war morality. With life so cheap who could afford to worry about the welfare of one unlucky woman?

Those not on working parties were denied this pleasure. Instead they had to make do with the traditional substitutes – masturbation or homosexuality. The strains of incarceration caused some prisoners to behave in ways they would never have thought possible, as one inmate recalled: 'Liaisons sprang up between all kinds of people, tall and short, fat and thin, and the good, the bad and the ugly. Relationships took many forms from parcel sharing, holding hands, heavy petting and actual indulging.' (16) Some formed inseparable couples, embroidering matching monograms on their jumpers, as if to seal their relationship in lieu of marriage.

Others relieved the tension with masturbation and pornographic photographs commanded high trade prices. Those married men who had experienced full sex lives prior to incarceration were among the most active masturbators. Some prisoners used it as a way to pass time and kill the boredom, escaping the boundaries of the camp with their sexual fantasies. They became known as 'mutton floggers', 'bishop bashers' and 'wire pullers', their penis known as the 'one eyed milkman'.

The prisoners may have viewed human life as worth little more than the price of a packet of cigarettes but they had no illusions about how precious they considered their own existence – and in 1944 staying alive meant not escaping. In the wake of the executions of the fifty prisoners who escaped from Stalag Luft 1 in spring 1944 it had been decided by the British authorities to wind down the escape organisations. With victory coming ever nearer it was deemed illogical for men to risk their lives, especially when so few escapes were successful. Despite this some men still decided to break out, if only for a change of scenery. 'Bill' Sykes was working as a labourer in a quarry when he decided to get away:

> Escape from our particular work groups was relatively easy, you could just walk away when the armed civilian guards were otherwise occupied. A couple of times during my incarceration, I took off for a few days using the 'Sykes' confidence approach. I was very much a loner when it came to 'escaping', no cloak and dagger stuff, just walk freely amongst the German people as if I had every right to do so. The obvious difficulty was, you can fool some of the people some of the time, etc. It was pretty obvious that I was a POW from my uniform with a large red circular patch on my back, but it's surprising how much you can get away with by using the 'I have a right to be here approach'. Travelling by local trains was, in my case, not very difficult. Get into conversation with someone, preferably an older couple who spoke a little English, and hope that the ticket collector didn't call your bluff when you explained to him that the guard that you were travelling with was in the toilet. I was eventually caught and apprehended by local police for obtaining food without having any local currency. It's called stealing. Or in my book, appropriation by reason of necessity. I was heading north for Berlin, why, who knows, just a whim that perhaps I could get lost in the big city. My contrarian period. The first escape, cost me seven days in a strafelager on a punishment diet of bread and water and a transfer to another camp. The second pathetic attempt, was more like a weekend affair, modesty forbids me to elaborate upon the precise circumstances. This cost me another week in the 'cooler'. After that, I resigned myself to waiting for the Allies to come to me, instead of vice-versa. I'm afraid that these two disappearing acts of a few days duration cannot be classified amongst the great escapes of World War Two. (17)

The notion of disappearing into a big city may have seemed like a novel way of escaping POW camp but the reality was less than ideal. Even those prisoners sent out under guard on work details in German towns and cities faced many dangers – from disgruntled guards, civilians and not least Allied air attacks.

As the war progressed, and the Allied air armadas brought increasing levels of devastation to German towns, more and more prisoners were detailed to help clear bombsites. This work offered the opportunity to loot bombed out shops and find the food necessary to sustain them. Items stolen by the POWs included food, jewellery, clothing and even pornographic photos. Knowing the reputation of the

British prisoners for stealing, the guards ensured that on return to the camps POWs were searched and most of the contraband was taken by the guards.

In the final chaotic months of the war countless POWs were caught up in the air raids. James Sims, a paratrooper captured at Arnhem, was sent to clear bomb damage in the town of Uelzen. It may have given the prisoners hope to see the damage inflicted by the bomber fleets, until they realised the bombers didn't only hit a target once – they often returned day after day to hit the same target. Nothing could have prepared him for the experience of being on the receiving end of bombing raids. The first thing they noticed was a lone Flying Fortress dropping marker flares near where they were working. Without warning the sky filled with bombers and everyone ran. In fear there was no distinction between friend and foe: 'We fled from the station area and it was a race between POWs, Guards, women, kids and SS as to who got to the dubious shelter of some woods.' (18)

Sims found himself sheltering in curious company – between a German mother attempting to comfort a crying child, and an SS officer. The destruction caused by the raids had little effect on the POWs, and to some extent raised morale, until they saw corpses of children killed by the bombing: 'It all seemed such a waste'. (19) However, their problems began after the raid when a crowd assembled, mainly women, carrying carving knives, bricks and sticks, and attempted to attack the prisoners in retribution for the destruction of their town. Only the intervention of the guards was to save them.

Living conditions within camps deteriorated sharply in the final months of the war. Food supplies became increasingly erratic as infrastructure collapsed under the pressure of constant bombing raids. Slowly prisoners began to starve, their malnourished bodies falling prey to all manner of diseases. Those final months of captivity were in many ways to be the most uncertain of the whole war. Prisoners despaired at knowing the date of liberation could not be far off, yet realising that if it were delayed many of them might fall victim to sickness and starvation. By the beginning of 1945, in one camp alone, there were reported to be seven funerals a day of men who had succumbed to malnutrition. Some prisoners became too weak to bear the burden of the inevitable roll calls that characterised life in the camps. Sick men, forced to stand for hours in the cold and damp collapsed and died as their guards carried out innumerable unnecessary counts, and funerals became an almost welcome relief in the monotonous routine of Stalag life.

With hardship the whole social structure within the camps was turned upside down. In the early days of captivity men had focused their minds on a number of subjects. Everyone had initially spoken of escape but that had now been erased from their minds. After that they had all talked of sex, but now even that seemed a distant dream.

Once hunger had struck they talked of nothing but food, their favourite foods, meals eaten in the past and meals they would eat when they were free. However with the threat of starvation hanging over them many found themselves unable to discuss what they couldn't have. Jim Sims watched as the changes struck his fellow prisoners: 'Freud reckoned everything we did was motivated by Sex. Not true –

when women and food were not available – there is still FEAR!' (20)

In the atmosphere of uncertainty tensions ran high. Friendships were put under great strain and many broke up after years together. Friends even fought each other as they scavenged through the dustbins searching for the peelings that might sustain them for a few more hours, curbing the ever present pangs of hunger until the next issue of watery soup. If scraps couldn't be found men resorted to sucking the leather of their boots in the hope that it might give some sustenance.

The trials of the long, cold winter placed an intolerable strain on their health. Not only had food stocks diminished but medical supplies were at a critical level. Medics were reduced to injecting men with alcohol to knock them out for minor operations. Such was the level of debilitation that even the trade value of pornography began to fall within the camps. As prisoners found themselves unable to get erections there was little need for visual stimulation to aid masturbation.

The worsening conditions may have demoralised the prisoners, wrecked them physically and threatened their entire existence, but they did not crush their spirit. Many had been too weak to dedicate themselves fully to camp life but there was still a genuine effort to keep morale as high as possible. By the end of 1944 those prisoners in Germany were celebrating. They were aware of the Allied situation and knew this was the beginning of their last year in captivity. Xmas and New Year was the party season, food had been saved where possible and those lucky enough to have spare potatoes and raisins had distilled evil tasting, foul smelling 'hooch' to raise the party atmosphere. Men labouring in an oil refinery even stole petrol which they unwisely consumed to celebrate the supposed 'holiday season'.

The year may have ended on a high note for some prisoners but the most they had to look forward to were more months of misery. Even as prisoners in Germany were settling down to enjoy their meagre Christmas rations or starting another day's work in a factory, thousands of their comrades were already setting out on the first steps towards home, on forced marches out of Poland. With thousands marching along the frozen roads of the east, and thousands more facing starvation, 1945 was not going to be the year of triumphal victory. Instead it would be a year of doubt and uncertainty. Their hopes for the future hadn't vanished, rather they had been subsumed beneath a wave of deprivation. After surviving the trials of battle, capture and imprisonment, the POWs had one last ordeal to survive – liberation.

16

The Gates Open

'One really cruel guard had deserted but was discovered hiding in the next village. He was dragged back to face a 'kangaroo' court and sentenced to be hung. He was hoisted aloft and this didn't bother us one bit.' (1)

As the first snows of winter began to fall and the advancing Red Army rolled ever westward, the fate of POWs held in the Reich's eastern provinces became more uncertain. Thousands were incarcerated in camps across Poland, Czechoslovakia and eastern Germany. With the Russians steadily approaching the German border it seemed the prisoners could be caught up in the Germans' defence of their homeland – few POWs had any illusions about their fate if they were trapped between these two bitter enemies.

While POWs held in western Germany settled down for what they knew would be their last winter in captivity, those in the east hastily prepared for what would be their most trying period in captivity. Few prisoners bothered with dreams of escape or liberation, instead they focused on day-to-day realities – food, heat and lice.

As the Red Army advanced, the POW camps flooded with continuously conflicting rumours. One minute they heard they were to be left to be liberated by the Red Army, the next they were to be evacuated west. No one could be certain of their fate until the guards finally issued definite instructions. Eventually it became clear most prisoners would have to face the deprivations of winter and march to safety, across hundreds of miles of frozen roads. The prisoners had come to expect little comfort but they realised sticking together was the most likely way to ensure survival. If that meant evacuation of the camps under continued German control, so be it. At this late stage escape was only an option for the extremely brave, desperate or foolhardy.

There was a shiver of excitement whenever word went round it was time to leave. In some camps departures were postponed on countless occasions and prisoners assembled only to be kept waiting and then returned to their huts. Eventually men grew weary of the cancelled departures and gave up trying to prepare. It was a time of unprecedented anxiety and anticipation. It seemed the normally efficient German organisation had been reduced to chaos.

And then, often with only hours to spare, the order was finally given. After months or years of captivity, dreaming of what lay behind the wire, they began what was to become the long journey home. At one time prisoners' efforts had focused on the construction of the tools and provisions for escape attempts. Now their labours were directed at the necessities for survival. They knew the weather would spare no one and clothing and footwear were repaired in an attempt to provide protection from the elements. Their last hours in the camps were spent sitting on their bunks or at benches, sewing and darning in preparation for the march ahead. Fearing the cold one soldier began the journey wearing two vests, two pairs of long johns, two shirts, a cardigan, battledress, greatcoat, balaclava and gloves. He wore his socks in rotation hanging one pair under his greatcoat and putting on a dry pair each morning to help prevent frostbite.

Normally peaceful huts became scenes of feverish activity. They hastily constructed rucksacks, sometimes sewing up the bottom of shirts then tying the sleeves together to make straps, hoping to carry as much as possible on the journey. Some constructed carts and sledges to transport their kit. Red Cross boxes, slats from their beds and any spare wood was hammered and screwed together to fashion improvised transport. Old tins were battered into shape to act as smooth covers for sledge runners. Others used tins to make small stoves that could be used to cook food, boil water and warm their bodies.

All the organisation of years was ignored and cast aside. Carefully constructed furniture was destroyed to provide wood for carts. Books, lovingly hoarded, read and reread, were dumped to save space in rucksacks. Even valuable stocks of cigarettes were abandoned in the haste to pack, and surplus foods were cooked and consumed to help build up strength for the trials ahead.

After these frantic hours of preparation, the prisoners heard a single whistle, or a barked order, and it was time to step out into the unknown. In some camps departing POWs were issued with Red Cross parcels from stores that had been hoarded by the guards. They looked in amazement at the stocks of provisions they had longed for as hunger had gnawed at their bellies. Now, in a final agonising twist they were forced to abandon boxes of food they were physically unable to carry. Some men ripped them open taking only essentials like tinned meat or chocolate. Others hoarded cigarettes, relying on their trade value to buy food in the days ahead.

Finally the gates opened and they passed beyond the wire. Now they could finally see what lay beyond the hills and woods that had obscured their vision for so long. They saw the farms and fields where the camp latrines had been emptied and saw civilians who had carried on with their lives just miles from where thousands of prisoners were incarcerated in stupefying boredom. The wonder at seeing what lay beyond the barbed wire initially lifted their spirits. In the first days of the marches some men found an almost holiday atmosphere. For the lucky ones it was relatively easy going, hopes were high and while the weather was still good the miles were covered without difficulty. One group spent their first night in a concert hall that resounded to the noise of happy prisoners. Singing, laughing and playing music they celebrated the start of their journey westwards towards home. However, they were soon to have a rude awakening.

The prospect of marching for mile upon mile, day after day did not appeal to some POWs. As the columns trudged onwards some decided to take advantage of the chaos. Some men who had been working on farms simply returned to the homes of people they had worked alongside, returned to their work, settled down and awaited the Russian arrival. Those who had formed relationships with local women moved in with them, some with little intention of rejoining the army or returning home. Others slipped out of the columns and hid, hoping to take shelter with local people or hide until the Russians caught up with them.

Such were the conditions on the marches that with hindsight some prisoners felt they should have taken their chances and escaped to the countryside. Within days the strain became unbearable. After years of captivity their feet were unaccustomed to the rigours of walking. Within days they had abandoned most of their possessions, keeping only essential items and leaving a trail of debris behind them. Books, spare clothing, musical instruments, plates and coffee pots, were left in the snow. The only thing remaining in rucksacks was food.

The old routines of camp life were thrown into disarray, no longer did they know what time they would eat or where they would rest for the night. There was a new routine – endless hours of marching across an inhospitable landscape – their faces burned by the wind, feet blistered and muscles wearied by constant walking. In this exhausting chaos, men who had for years shared every day together were now split up. The familiarity of the same faces day in day out was soon lost. Friendly faces were lost and soon forgotten. Few could think any further into the future than the next meal and thoughts of liberation were beyond contemplation.

Many shuffled along in the wooden clogs that had long since replaced their army boots. Those boots worn by prisoners were often decrepit, their soles patched, stitching coming undone and laces replaced with knotted string. Those without socks wrapped their feet in towels or rags in an attempt to keep frostbite at bay. Despite the hardship some men continued to keep diaries: 'Agony is almost unbearable now. We marched until 2 a.m., they told us that it was 20 below freezing, and made us wait for two hours on the road. We froze to the marrow, not used to this at all. When almost asleep on our feet, were taken into a large barn. Shivered all through the rest of the night …… no interest in anything at all.' (2)

If the food they had survived on within the camps was so poor it had driven them to desperation, rations on the march brought them to the edge of starvation. If the prisoners were lucky, after twelve hours of marching they would be fed on horse meat or weak soup, although some days they were given little more than bread and honey. Occasionally they went for days without even the issue of bread. With the guards providing little in the way of hot food they survived on what they carried or what they could steal.

Their one hope was with the Reich collapsing there would be chances to trade with the desperate population. Enterprising prisoners took advantage of the chaotic conditions by breaking off from the columns to break into homes and farms. Sneaking into farmyards they milked cows, and stole piglets which were hidden in rucksacks until they could be slaughtered. In a rare show of community spirit, one column pooled its money to buy a horse for a hundred and fifty marks which was cooked and shared between both prisoners and guards. The desperate marchers ate anything they could get their hands on, even mouldy bread and rotten vegetables filled bellies. When they saw potatoes being fed to pigs they kicked the animals away and scrambled in the muck to rescue the food. After the thaw even dandelions were picked and cooked by desperately hungry prisoners and strange concoctions such as cakes made from a combination of grain husks and molasses were baked.

The conditions soon took their toll on the prisoners' physical and mental welfare. Men, who had started out full of hope, soon began to lose spirit and argued amongst themselves. The rigours of the march pushed relationships which had survived the rigours of camp life to breaking point. Trivial arguments broke out. Good friends fell out over the ownership of sledges and whose packs should be transported. Partnerships were broken and new ones formed in a desperate quest for survival. If the cold and hunger were not enough, there was soon another burden – disease. As each day went by conditions deteriorated and starved and exhausted men began to fall sick, many with dysentery. As they marched men found themselves passing blood when they went to the toilet. One group of sixty-eight prisoners who marched from East Prussia lost thirty men from dysentery during their ordeal.

Nights of sleeping in barns and stables and pigsties compounded their agony. On arrival in barns there was a rush as men attempted to find space in the upper levels knowing that those underneath would endure soakings with urine as the men above, too tired to move, used the floor as their toilet. If they were lucky they slept on straw, shoulder to shoulder with fellow prisoners, sharing their makeshift beds with mice and rats. Prisoners awoke to find themselves bitten all over by insects living in the straw. During the night desperate men crawled over their comrades to get outside to defecate. The unlucky ones, often suffering from dysentery, who couldn't get out quick enough were left with watery faeces running down their legs. In the cold of night they had to strip off and attempt to clean themselves with snow covered rags. For such men their humiliation was all but complete. No longer would they worry about where they were, instead they dropped their trousers whenever necessary and went to the toilet. There was no modesty and no shame. Survival was all that counted. These night-time scenes were recorded by one diarist: 'My faith in humanity is now completely gone – and I shall never forget that barn with the darkness, overcrowded, boys crawling out to the lavatory, snarls and curses from men trodden on in the process – shouts about potatoes, groans and cries of the sick, my God! It was hell!' (3)

Following a night's sleep in freezing buildings the prisoners dragged themselves wearily from their improvised beds to prepare for the arduous task of another day marching through the snow to an unknown destination. Men who had failed to sleep in their boots or wrap them up in protective cloths, found the leather frozen and impossible to put on. They soon learned to take care for fear of being forced to march barefoot. Some perceptive men carried sacks of straw in which to keep their boots at night to prevent freezing. Most did their utmost to keep clean, washing and shaving where possible, breaking the ice on horse troughs to get water. In a desperate attempt to keep the lice at bay some POWs cut off all body hair and rubbed themselves with cow fat.

Their humiliation deepened as threadbare uniforms wore out leaving many prisoners clad in rags. The hasty repairs made by the prisoners soon fell apart, patches fell from clothes, stitches came apart and men were left in tatters. One soldier took off his trousers for the first time in three weeks to find his underpants had disintegrated. Some removed clothing only to find their bodies covered in sores and abscesses.

As the days passed the columns lengthened as prisoners struggled to keep up with the main body of marchers. Feet softened by years of imprisonment became blistered. In the mornings many POWs struggled to get their boots back on and were pained at every step. Soon the rear of the columns was made up of men slowly shuffling along, their blistered feet bound in rags, just waiting for the agony of frostbite to strike them.

It wasn't long before the sick began to be left behind. Those who fell out of the columns were often shot where they lay, as their friends trudged onwards, concentrating on their own survival and unconcerned about the fate of others. However, many healthy men were happy to team up again with their mates as soon as the sick men were issued Red Cross parcels from the Germans' ever diminishing supply. Fortunately, the Red Cross were attempting to keep track of the columns of prisoners. They pursued them around the countryside trying to continue with the fair distribution of parcels, an act that saved many lives.

When food was available there was a mad scramble to be head of the queue as the old-fashioned British notion of orderly queuing was abandoned. The strong took the best food and men fought to get second helpings even though others had none. Diarists recorded the scenes: 'Without any bias or prejudice, our boys, myself included, are a rotten crowd. Each one wishes to be head of the queue, and the result is a rush and a push, brawling, cursing, crowd jammed round the cook house. Animals and starving at that.' (4) It was little wonder that discipline began to lapse and in the worsening conditions some men stole from their comrades. However, the punishment for being caught could be dire. One offender was sentenced to run a gauntlet of two hundred men who summoned up enough energy to administer a brutal beating.

Such was the deterioration of comradeship that prisoners began to denounce their fellow countrymen to the enemy. When men in one column stole tinned meat from the Germans the guards announced all issues of Red Cross parcels would stop unless the culprits admitted responsibility. When only a few of the guilty men stepped forward their fellow prisoners began to issue threats, pointing out the culprits to the guards and forcing them to accept their punishment. It was a far cry from the days in the camps where men had openly protected their fellow prisoners from recriminations and defiance was a game that livened up the long days. Now defiance was a matter of life and death, the well-being of a fellow prisoner was not worth the risk of starving to death on a snow-covered road. Now they were being pushed to the very limit of their endurance: 'The British people are pleasant people in or under pleasant circumstances, but otherwise.....' (5)

For some prisoners the psychological strain also bore heavy. Near starvation rations, the freezing cold, exhaustion and constant bickering took a toll on their mental wellbeing. Their minds began to crack, some hallucinated, others withdrew into themselves shunning contact with their former friends. For a time it seemed they were men with no future and only the most optimistic could find anything positive in their situation.

By the time the long columns of prisoners had reached the relative safety of Germany many had little energy left. The weather, starvation, disease and guards had all contributed to the thinning-out of the ranks of men awaiting liberation.

Some kept a record of how far they had walked. One POW reported that between 10 February and 1 April 1945 he marched 593 kms. Others recorded marching on average 23 kms per day. At the end of their odyssey, the men eventually trudged into established camps. The northernmost columns were directed to Stalag XIB at Fallingbostel on the plains of northern Germany and the southern columns headed for Moosburg near Munich. Entering camps that would be their homes for the last weeks of the war, many of the POWs had reached their physical and mental limits. Fortunately time was on their side. The arrival of spring saw a rise in temperature, the thawing of remaining snows and an easing of rains. And the armies of the liberators were coming ever closer. With the brightening of the sky the forlorn POWs saw a brightening future.

The problem now was to survive life in the camps. Both Moosburg and Fallingbostel suffered from dramatic increases in inmates in the final months of war. Huts were overcrowded, with men forced to sleep two or three to a bunk whilst others slept on the floor. These were the lucky ones – others were forced to sleep in tents or makeshift shelters where their beds lay deep in mud. The increasing prison populations meant the Germans were unable to feed them and the hoped for salvation from hunger became a distant dream. Once more, starvation became a reality. Even those with food were often unable to enjoy it since they suffered from dysentery and emptied their bowels almost as soon as they had eaten. With the men even more crowded than before maintaining hygienic conditions was almost impossible. Toilets became blocked and raw sewage spilled out into the compounds. Hot water became a precious commodity as the camp infrastructure collapsed and showers were unknown for many, instead they were reduced to washing under cold taps.

The final, hectic days of captivity were amongst the most dangerous. Just as they had been uncertain of their fate at the moment of capture they were no more certain what might occur at the moment of release. Yet, whilst the guards stayed at the gates of the camps the prisoners had little choice but to await their fate. Men opened books on the likely date of liberation, harmless diversions from the worrying reality of what their captors might do in the final days. No one could be sure of the Germans' intentions, for the Germans themselves had no clear policy and little remaining framework to administer the camps. Even if guards seemed friendly there was always the ever present fear of retribution by SS units determined to

Rage, Revenge and Retribution
After the horrors witnessed during the liberation of Belsen concentration camp,
troops became increasingly intolerant towards SS prisoners. In a picture suppressed
by the censor at the time SS men are allowed to 'rest' in a grave at the camp.
Rumours soon spread that many 'rested' there permanently.

Rage, Revenge and Retribution
Here SS prisoners are made to run 'at the double' by their captors.

Rage, Revenge and Retribution
Many enemy prisoners were put to work clearing minefields. This line of men is
being marched across a minefield to make sure they haven't missed any.

The Gates Open
Once liberated many POWs set about destroying their camps. These men, captured
at Arnhem, are breaking up their barracks to provide fuel for cooking.

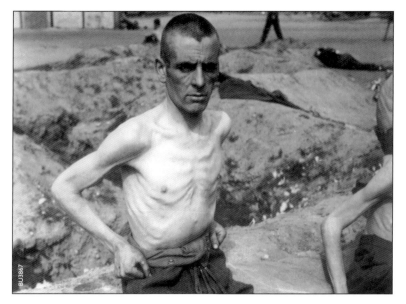

Life Behind the Wire
The reality of life in POW camps was far removed from the fictional image
popularised in the post-war years. By the end of the war many were starving. This
man, Private Morris from Wales, was liberated from Stalag XIb in April 1945.

Victory, The Moment of Reckoning
One of the traditional signs of victory. Cameron Highlanders
display a Nazi flag captured in Rheine, Germany. April 1945.

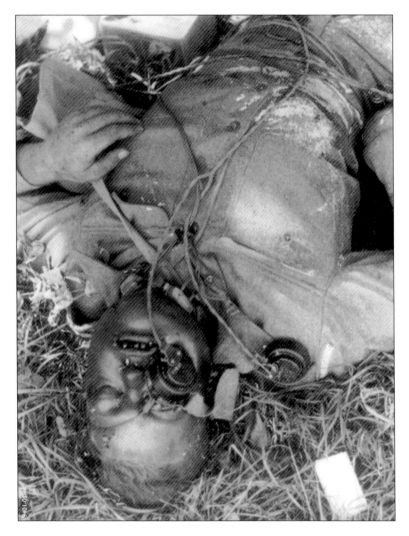

The Sadness Endures

This was the terrible reality of war that many veterans struggled for a lifetime to forget. Since any pictures of Allied corpses were suppressed by the censor this photograph, taken by an officer of the 5th Coldstream Guards, is one of the few to show a dead British soldier. In his photo album the officer, Michael Bendix, wrote beside it the words of Rupert Brooke's poem 'The Soldier': 'There's some corner of a foreign field that is forever England.'

make a stand. Fears about reprisals had hung over the camps on many occasions throughout the war. The Germans had threatened action in reply to the bombing raids that paralysed the Reich. The sense of dread that hung over the camps in such circumstances was known as 'The Clutching Hand', (6) and in the last months of the war its icy fingers once more gripped prisoners' hearts.

In the final weeks many prisoners decided the moment had come to break away from their guards and the threat of organised retribution. Some inmates from Stalag XIB, who had been on a working party clearing bomb damage, found themselves being marched towards British lines by their guards, but despite the constant Allied advance their future was far from sure. There were SS formations in their area and it was later discovered that eleven British prisoners had their throats cut by SS men. Most of the prisoners decided to stick together and their senior NCO suggested their guards hand over their rifles to the prisoners and head toward the Allied lines. The guards readily complied but soon took them back when an SS detachment was sighted. Once they had gone the prisoners took back the weapons and made their way to the nearest British unit.

Paratrooper 'Bill' Sykes, suffering from dysentery and weighing just a hundred pounds, was one such prisoner who decided to go it alone:

> On or around March of 1945 when the Russians were approaching the river Elbe from the east, and the Allied forces were approaching the river Mulde from the west, I decided enough was enough and took it upon myself to make one more 'dedicated' try to escape from captivity. The other ones had just been half-hearted one-man protests against the German guards. When I say escape, I use the term loosely, I just walked away. During a march south between the two rivers, the prisoners were incarcerated in a wooded area surrounded by German guards at 50 metre intervals with orders to shoot anyone approaching the perimeter. I, having reached a point of no return, approached one of the guards who asked me where I thought I was going, I answered that I was going back to England and nothing but nobody was going to stop me. He appeared to find some humour in this statement, or perhaps it was just my poor German interpretation of my intentions, so to my amazement he turned his back and allowed me to pass through the cordon. This led to a chain of events of many days of pure misery, constantly soaked to the skin by cold torrential rain, no food, a bad case of dysentery. What a miserable specimen of the human race I must have appeared. But salvation was at hand, a German family took me under their roof for a few days and gave me a share of the little food that they had and so I survived. I will be forever grateful. (7)

There remained many dangers for the prisoners – would the Germans hold them hostage, execute them, or simply leave them to be caught up in battles. However, the biggest danger was to be from the air. With the Luftwaffe all but eliminated Allied fighters had a virtual free reign in the skies above Germany. They roamed at will shooting up any possible target. Lines of marching men were assumed to be columns of German infantry and were obvious targets for the airmen. POWs marching from Eichstatt camp were spotted by American planes which had been seen attacking a train on the other side of the valley. Most of the prisoners thought they would be recognised as POWs since the end of the column was still within their camp. A few realised the pilots' intentions and dived into ditches as machine gun fire raked the column. Thirteen men were killed and a further fifty injured, only days before they would eventually be liberated. In another incident RAF Typhoons attacked a column of prisoners until a brave group of men used their greatcoats and laid them out on the ground to spell out RAF. The pilots broke off their attack but the damage had been done and up to seventy were reported dead.

The prospect of dangerously anarchic conditions within Germany, and the realisation that not all prisoners would be healthy enough to make their way back to Allied lines unassisted, made Allied powers prepare for the time the prisoners would be freed. One of their primary concerns was the welfare of those whose health had failed in the final months of the war, especially during the long marches westwards. Sick and wounded men languished in vast hospital camps staffed by doctors and medical orderlies from the myriad nationalities incarcerated in the German camps. Their provisions were few and improvisation was the order of the day. At times the workload looked like overwhelming the staff. All manner of sickness and disease was rife as the privations of incarceration took their toll. The medical staff did their best for patients who inhabited wards whose floors were awash in faeces, the air thick with flies. If the patients of such hospitals were to survive they would need help, and fast. Recognising the potential problems the Allies had a vast organisation ready to administer the health and welfare needs of the released prisoners. The 'PWX' were detailed the task of rounding up prisoners from their camps, bringing in medical assistance, feeding and clothing them, and arranging for their transport back to Britain.

Their task was not easy since they had to ensure the safety of the prisoners and yet make sure they were not kept locked up for any longer than was absolutely necessary. The only logical way to deal quickly and efficiently with them was to ensure they remained within their camps, something few could be expected to agree with. The War Office issued instructions about their treatment and how they were likely to behave:

> These men after years behind barbed wire, under strictest enemy discipline, will have violent hostility towards any attitude, organisation or individual reminiscent of what has been described as 'the regimentation of Stalag life'. It would obviously be desirable to transfer them immediately to other accommodation but this unfortunately will not be possible. Although, in handling large numbers, it is extremely difficult to introduce a personal touch, it is at least possible, in most cases, to ensure that there is a complete absence of any unnecessary rigidity and regimentation to which these men are extremely sensitive. (8)

It was therefore decreed that prisoners should stay within their camps to await liberation and then fully cooperate by staying put and not wandering off into the countryside. In the hope of enforcing this 'stay put' order it was announced those who left their camps would be treated as Displaced Persons and lose their right to rapid evacuation.

Despite the edicts issued from London little could be done actively to influence the behaviour of some POWs. Slowly, as the camp guards realised the Allied armies would soon be with them, they began to disappear. Few wished to be around to face the wrath of their captives when the moment of liberation came. Overnight, camps were abandoned, with prisoners awakening to the prospect of freedom. At first bemused, unsure of what lay beyond the wire, the prisoners took their first tentative steps of freedom. In some camps the trickle became a flood as the full realisation hit them.

It was at this moment that many prisoners decided to ignore instructions about staying put and instead try to find their own way to the Allied lines or enjoy their freedom. In some camps discipline all but disappeared. At Wesertimke, forty Guardsmen who took on the task of arming themselves and protecting the camp after the departure of the guards found their job almost impossible. There was little chance of keeping order and soon the inmates were roaming all over the area in search of their most longed for commodities – food, drink and women. They soon gave up and left the liberated POWs to their own devices.

Similar scenes were played out across Germany, although in some cases the prisoners reacted violently. Some guards made threats against prisoners, incurring their wrath. In some camps crowds of enraged prisoners rushed their guards, beating them, stealing their weapons and stripping the most unpopular Germans, before ransacking camp offices. Prisoners broke open storerooms, gorged themselves on food and alcohol, then looted the guards' possessions.

The men who had been working in German factories watched as the final vestiges of order were abandoned throughout the Reich's industries. They saw scenes of anarchy unfolding and decided to act on their own initiative. Some departed to their girlfriends' homes and soon 'got their feet under the table'. Others decided to head west in the hope of making their way to the Allied lines and finding their way home as soon as possible. Many ex-POWs had no intention of bothering with London's 'stay put' orders. They weren't interested in being processed, numbered and asked to wait for transport, instead they found their own way home. All over Germany men started appropriating cars and flocking westwards.

The grimy, bearded, scruffily attired men appeared incongruous behind the wheels of elegant German vehicles. With petrol shortages across Germany prisoners raided stores for strong alcoholic spirits. Some they drank and some they poured into vehicle petrol tanks. Many happily drove the captured vehicles until they met Allied units who relieved them of the cars stating that they were needed for the fighting men. Once again the prisoners were left to walk. One group were told by their liberators they could spare no transport since everything was moving forward. Instead their best bet was to make their own way to Brussels. The best available vehicle was the local fire engine which became home to the former prisoners who made their way west ringing its bell and cheering the advancing troops. Others were fortunate enough to be allowed to keep their vehicles and made their way to Paris or Brussels where they made the most of their freedom before cadging flights home.

Although many prisoners found transport many more were once again marching. Right across the Allied front thousands of men, alone or in small groups, headed towards liberation. The group of former prisoners who had taken possession of their guards' rifles finally linked up with the British forces and made their way to the nearest town, Vinstedt, where for a number of days they indulged themselves in an orgy of eating and looting. They were desperate – one, Jim Sims had gone from 11st 7lbs to just 7st in just six months. He later recorded his emotions: 'Being liberated was one of my life's greatest experiences.' (9) Despite their actions relations with the German civilians were not too strained. The Germans knew there was little they could do but acquiesce, the only law that existed was that the British army chose to enforce and they had more pressing concerns than the behaviour of POWs. The ex-POWs occupied the burgomeister's house and thoroughly looted it. The burgomeister himself talked with the ex-POWs as they took what they wanted from his home. Prisoners showed him family photographs and even discussed literature with him as they looted his book collection. Some prisoners were soon to be seen sporting watches from wrist to elbow, although others refused to join in since the Germans had never stolen their personal possessions.

Paratrooper 'Bill' Sykes was one of the lone men roaming the highways and byways of Germany:

> Eventually after many days and nights of aimless wandering, I was picked up by forward echelon troops of the American forces and dispatched to a hospital near Nuremburg, suffering from a bad case of dysentery and malnutrition. During my time at this location I met an American sergeant who indicated that he had a jeep and was going to travel to a concentration camp at Buchenwald, and seeing no one else had volunteered to travel with him, would I be interested. I said certainly, why not. I had travelled this far and survived, so why shouldn't I see for myself the crimes of man's inhumanity to man. Anyway, I figured that in my current physical condition I would be right at home amongst the skin and bone fraternity. Once again how wrong could I be. The scene that I witnessed was one of infinite horror where piles of dead bodies, in various stages of decomposition, were scattered about the camp. The living could not be distinguished from the dead. A place of horror, disbelief and anger against the perpetrators. To those unbelievers out there, I can attest to the fact that Hitler's 'Final solution' the 'Holocaust', or whatever one wishes to call the terrible acts of inhumanity, did occur and was as violent and horrific as portrayed in later documents. (10)

The men who had stayed put in camps now awaited the arrival of the liberating armies. The first POW camps liberated by the British were Stalag 357 and Stalag XIB at Fallingbostel to the south of Hamburg. The camps contained almost 20,000 allied POWs, including some 7,000 British servicemen, of whom around ten per cent had been captured at Arnhem. When the advance units reached Fallingbostel they were met by wildly cheering crowds. For some it was all they could do to stand upright and cheer, but they felt they had to make the effort. Soon the released men were lining the roads as their liberators drove quickly on to continue the war. It was a sudden clash of cultures. One prisoner, who for almost two years had drunk from old tins, was confronted by an English tank command-

er who offered him tea from a china cup and saucer. The sense of shock was reinforced by the weight loss so many of the prisoners had suffered. To the liberators,
often young men of eighteen or nineteen years, these seemed to be old men.

Tears of sadness and joy were spilled as the inmates finally realised they were
free. The first reaction of many of the prisoners was to ransack the camp offices
and guards' quarters. Food and clothing stores were raided, men searched the
commandant's offices for their files, alcohol was located and the joyous crowds
began their parties. The discovery of Red Cross parcels in the German quarters
only helped to heighten the sense of rage felt by so many prisoners towards their
captors. Soon many drunken prisoners had discarded their ragged clothing and
dressed themselves in the uniforms of their departing guards. The sight of some
liberated POWs was a shock to the advancing armies. Men reported they had been
uncertain why they were being waved to by men dressed in German uniforms.

However, in the midst of the festivities, not all the inmates were celebrating.
Even among those who were not considered sufficiently sick to be admitted to hospital there were plenty who lacked the strength to leave their beds to watch the liberators arrive. For them the situation was unreal, they knew the significance of liberation but were too debilitated to express emotion. The experience left them
dazed, knowing how they should feel but unable to express it.

These were turbulent times as a wave of anarchy engulfed the German countryside. All over Germany the scenes were the same as a vast army of ragged POWs
were unleashed into the towns and villages of the crumbling Reich. Their first
desire was to find food and to eat as much as possible. They acquired weapons and
were prepared to use them when doing business with German civilians. Pigs were
taken from farms, slaughtered, roasted and devoured by the ravenous men. Many
soon found themselves violently sick as their shrunken stomachs were unable to
cope with sudden intake of rich food. Farmers were sent to live in their now empty
pigsties as the liberated POWs took over their homes. Flour carefully hoarded by
the farmers was baked into loaves to satisfy their huge appetites.

For many, freedom meant souvenir hunting. Released prisoners joined in the
sprees of looting enjoyed by so many DPs and liberating troops. The German civilians had little choice but to surrender their valuables. They acquired anything they
desired, beer steins for their fathers, tablecloths for wives and mothers. From the
most elegant jewels to the cheapest pens, all had a place in the haversacks and
rucksacks of the men from behind the wire.

This was not a safe environment for some former camp guards. The officers in
charge of the welfare of ex-POWs admitted they expected significant numbers of
prisoners on working parties not to return to their camps immediately since it
seemed likely they: 'have decided to take disciplinary measures against certain
Germans'. (11) Their intuition proved right. Many prisoners did indeed have
scores to settle, as CSM Baggs of the Black Watch later recorded of his encounter
with three SS prisoners: 'You can imagine what they received.' (12) Many of those
who had treated the prisoners badly were to pay the price. When one group of
POWs was liberated by American troops at Moosberg in Germany they pointed

out a particularly brutal guard who just days before had shot and killed a prisoner. The guard, a ruddy faced farmboy, was taken away and executed by the Americans. Some prisoners discovered their guards hanging from trees in the woods. They were uncertain of who had carried out the executions – liberating soldiers, former slave labourers or disgruntled ex-POWs?

Some British POWs were certainly involved in lynchings. At Vinstedt British POWs singled out a guard for retribution. Jim Sims remembered: 'One really cruel guard had deserted but was discovered hiding in the next village. He was dragged back to face a "kangaroo" court and sentenced to be hung. He was hoisted aloft and this didn't bother us one bit. The Rifle Regiment who had relieved us rescued him, which caused an uproar.' (13)

Many acts of retribution were carried out but no one was on hand to record the numbers of guards killed. Whoever perpetrated the deeds was an irrelevance, what was certain that in the spring of 1945 being a POW camp guard was not the safest occupation. Some prisoners refused when offered weapons to shoot their German guards, they were too dazed by liberation to consider revenge. Others sat at the roadsides of Germany calling on Allied soldiers to shoot at the columns of German prisoners trooping into captivity.

Some prisoners was housed in comfort at the expense of their former captors. One group of former prisoners was housed in individual rooms in an SS barracks and given SS men as servants. One ex-POW used the floor as his toilet and ordered his SS servant to clear up the excrement with his hands. When the German refused guards were called and he was held at gunpoint whilst he completed his humiliating task. Pitiful scenes were repeated all over Germany as wretched former prisoners, some almost too weak to stand, summoned up their last vestiges of energy to throw stones at guards or beat them with sticks. It was a long awaited moment and even in their debilitated state little could be done to stand in the way of the desire to exact some measure of retribution. Some were even assisted by their Russian liberators, who gave them weapons with which to execute unpopular guards.

With ample opportunities to indulge themselves at the expense of their former guards many healthier ex-POWs were in no hurry to return home. Plenty hoped to be liberated by the Americans and so get their hands on the seemingly exotic foodstuffs they knew were contained in GI ration packs. One man even joined up with his American liberators and became the gunner on a half-track, operating the machinegun as they continued their advance. Prisoners liberated by the Russians were also offered the opportunity to continue the fight against the Nazis. The liberating troops could see no reason why the British prisoners would not want to join up with them and continue to fight the common enemy. No records were kept of how many accepted the offer although no doubt many young men lost their lives in their eagerness to strike back at their former captors.

However, most men had more basic matters to attend to. After long periods behind the wire of the Stalags hundreds, if not thousands, were desperate to reassert their sexuality. Many left captivity and set up home with local families, where they sought all things they had been denied in captivity – comfort, shelter, good food and sex. Artilleryman J.H. Witte met a German war widow yet despite attempts to woo her with American rations and alcohol, his initial advances were rebuffed. Witte had spent too long as a prisoner to give up easily. However, enforced abstinence affected his performance:

> This time she allowed me to play with her breasts. Greatly heartened by this, and somewhat hardened, I put my hand up her skirt and let it stray to the flesh above her stocking top, but when I slid my eager fingers up her suspenders and towards her knickers she stopped me. By this time I had a great erection which she couldn't fail to notice. I mentioned this to her, whereupon she undid my trousers taking my penis out. I ejaculated right away much to her amusement. (14)

Eventually the widow relented but only after Witte promised to marry her. He had little intention of keeping his promise as physical needs overrode any pre-captivity morality.

Morality did have an effect on other ex-prisoners. Some were disgusted by the way their comrades had behaved, particularly on the forced marches westwards. Normally staid Englishmen had been reduced to an almost animalistic state – fighting each other for food, abandoning sick friends and stealing from fellow prisoners. Some former prisoners felt so uncomfortable with this behaviour they had little desire to re-enter the society that had spawned them. They wanted a breathing space, a chance to reassess their experiences. It was only once they became acclimatised to the new feeling of freedom that a longing for home resurfaced and they made their way to the evacuation centres.

As the great mass of POWs surged westwards there were many whose safety seemed less assured. It was an uncertain period for those liberated by the Russians. For a while some enjoyed their freedom, driving around in stolen cars, but these were soon stolen by the Russians who were short of motorised transport. The prisoners were hustled back within the wire of their camps, ostensibly to prevent them getting mixed up in battles. Their liberators were not the disciplined troops they had expected. Their first sight of Russians was often of soldiers on horseback, riding carthorses or small ponies, their boots trailing along the ground. Soldiers rode on the back of farm carts or on women's bicycles. Some travelled in broken-down cars pulled by horses or oxen. And scattered among the front line soldiers were women, something previously unseen and unexpected by the western troops. Although orders that prisoners stay within camps were intended to make evacuation easier, prisoners soon realised they seemed to be prisoners of the Russians – being held as bargaining tools to force the Allies to hand back ex-Soviet nationals caught fighting for the Germans. The Allied officials sent to organise prisoner exchanges were unaware of Russian intentions and believed the Red Army's excuse that delays were due to administrative difficulties within the Russian zone. Officials were denied access to camps and prevented from travelling into areas where British POWs had reportedly gathered. At Luckenwalde British soldiers had their hopes raised when American trucks arrived to move them west to freedom and a flight home. However, to their surprise the Russians opened fire over the trucks and forbade movement of any prisoners.

It took months for thousands of those men liberated in the east to get home. Some, distrusting their liberators, escaped and made their own way back. The rest were eventually repatriated by rail to Odessa and then shipped back home. Despite the fears over Russian stalling and the barriers that seemed to be in place to prevent proper investigation of the numbers of men held in the Soviet zone some POWs simply accepted their fate. They had learnt enough of the chaos of war not to worry unduly about the circumstances of their journey home. All that mattered was they were heading home, albeit on a strange route. Many accepted their fate and endured the long journey, as Arnhem veteran Clifford Taylor wrote: 'Trust me to be one of the last to be free, after the war has ended!' (15)

Many years later dark rumours began to circulate about the fate of some of those men whose camps had been overrun by the Red Army. Sources in Russia seemed to suggest that large numbers of men who should have been repatriated had actually disappeared. Aroused by this information researchers began to examine the available documents in the hope of determining the truth. Alarming figures appeared. Ministry of Defence records showed the names of 168,476 British and Commonwealth prisoners repatriated in the spring of 1945. This contrasted with the 199, 592 POWs that the Germans claimed to have held. Where had the 30,000 missing men gone? One author suggested they had been pressed into service for Stalin, that they were swallowed up into the vast system of Siberian labour camps. Whilst not suggesting that the Soviets took no British POWs into captivity, there may be a simpler explanation.

Witnesses described how many hundreds of sick men fell out from the columns of POWs as they trudged westwards through the snow. Many were left to die or were shot by their guards. No one stopped to record their names or keep a tally of their numbers. Others, hoping to take their chances with the Russians, walked away from the columns of prisoners and disappeared into the countryside. A group of forty men was reported to have died when the ice broke as they crossed the frozen Vistula. Many more were rumoured to have been left behind by the Germans – too sick to move. Their fate is unknown. Whether they froze to death, were shot by retreating Germans or civilians, or ever actually linked up with the Red Army no one knows. Few Soviet soldiers had any knowledge of languages and it is possible POWs were executed in the same way as so many Germans who attempted to give themselves up.

Without doubt some of their more adventurous prisoners joined the Russians. Men held in those camps liberated by the Red Army recorded how they were offered their freedom to take up arms against the mutual enemy. Again, no one was there to record the numbers of those who accepted the offer or how many of the volunteers survived their adventures.

There were also the soldiers working on farms across eastern Europe. Some of these had little intention of rushing home. They had learnt the local language, romanced local women, and settled down. In no hurry to be separated from their new families some simply stayed on their farms. Others were caught up in the battles raging across Poland, losing their lives in the process with no one to bury them or mark their graves.

The final weeks of the war were some of the most chaotic ever seen in Europe, and with armies converging on the Reich, central power began to collapse. Vast bomber fleets battered German cities, their indiscriminate attacks killing both civilians and POWs sent to clear bomb sites. Allied fighter bombers ranged the skies with impunity, striking at whatever targets they could find. And then, with the final collapse of Nazi rule, thousands of POWs were set free into this anarchy. Some who found themselves in the Russian zone, refused to obey orders from the occupying forces and attempted to make their own way back towards British or American lines. Red Army guards opened fire on anyone attempting to cross the rivers that marked the borders of their zone and westward-bound former prisoners were among their victims.

There were also plenty who felt they had wasted their youth and decided to make up for lost time rather than return home to finish their service. Many cadged flights back to the UK, simply got onto trains home and restarted civilian life. Others, with an eye on making a profit from the chaos within Germany, slipped into civilian clothing and began to work the Black Market. Who can say how many lost their lives in the chaos or how many simply disappeared into society?

For those not caught up in the chaos, the transport for ex-POWs back to the UK started as quickly as possible. Flights from airfields in Lübeck and Luneberg areas brought 13,700 men directly back to England. Others were transferred to Brussels then despatched to airfields back home. With so many former prisoners to be processed ready for repatriation there were some delays in Brussels. The shuttle flights were inadequate to deal with the large numbers and eventually 70,000 men were to pass through the area. Once in the army camps they faced the unwanted return of army 'bullshit'. After so long with restricted freedom they were once more behind wire, although this time they were given passes to stay out in the city until 10 p.m. Many had no intention of complying with such restrictions and were determined to enjoy the city fully and Brussels' bars and brothels did a brisk trade from men making up for lost time. This was finally a chance to let off steam and release their pent-up sexual longings. They drank, smoked, whored and ate their fill. Nightfall found many too inebriated to stand, let alone return to camp. Fortunately MPs were sympathetic, and the drunks were delivered safely back to their beds.

Though the authorities were eager to process them quickly it was essential thorough checks were carried out on POWs' identities. Close inspection revealed interesting details such as privates who upon capture had elevated their rank to officers so they would have an easier life in captivity. They had fooled the Germans but were unable to fool those supervising repatriation.

Close inspection also revealed how most ex-prisoners were infested with lice. The threat of disease meant the journey home had to be delayed until they had been thoroughly deloused. Some men were treated as many as three times before leaving Europe – each time being told they should not have a bath for a period of twenty-four hours after the treatment. Constant dusting with powder, spraying and squirting with liquid wasn't a pleasant experience but the POWs had known worse in the camps and at least this time was the last time. Or so they thought. Back in England they would undergo the ordeal for one last time before they were considered safe to return into society.

Many of the prisoners had vast amounts of luggage they hoped to be able to bring home, although the maximum allowed on flights was forty kg. For some it was items they had constructed in captivity and wished to take home as keepsakes. Others carried pets they had acquired after liberation. Mostly the luggage was loot, German goods brought home either as presents or for sale.

Once all the paper work had been carried out they were ready to return home. Carrying their luggage they waited expectantly on airfields for the craft due to fly them home. At Rheims former POWs had to wait a day longer than expected for a flight back to England. They had expected to fly home on 8 May but the VE Day celebrations had interrupted the schedule – word went round that flight crews had got 'blotto' during the victory celebrations and been unable to fly. Bombers and transport planes were employed as a shuttle service picking up men and disgorging them on the home airfields. As the men were carefully counted on board some had to leave friends behind. After years of shared company, through boredom and deprivation, some POWs found themselves alone, as their mates were left waiting on the tarmac for the next flight. Many made their final wartime journey in quiet contemplation, uncertain of what lay ahead and unsure of how they would rebuild their lives. Others just sat silently nursing hangovers, the legacy of their final days of freedom.

The prisoners arriving back in England were a shocking sight. Some of those captured in the latter months had retained much of their own uniforms, but most long-term captives were unrecognisable. The war correspondent MacDonald Hastings travelled with a flight of ex-POWs from Belgium and recorded their appearance for the weekly magazine *Picture Post*: 'Scarcely any of the men had proper clothes; some of them even arrived without trousers, just a blanket thrown round them.' (16) They were malnourished, some had dysentery and many carried lice. Beards were widespread, as was long hair and those dressed in uniform were not necessarily dressed in a British one. Upon liberation many had ransacked the guards' quarters to replace their own worn out rags and were wearing German uniforms including greatcoats, jackets and jackboots – some even wore German officers' peaked caps, complete with badges. Also in evidence were German belts, camouflage parkas and fur-covered Wehrmacht packs. Their luggage provided another surprise for the onlookers – consisting of little more than souvenirs, including ceremonial swords, daggers, helmets, razor blades, cameras, scent and fountain pens.

The returning men were confronted by an unfamiliar sight – the smiling faces of British servicewomen. The women who handed them tea and sandwiches were totally unexpected. Many had been captured long before women had been conscripted. It was a much appreciated shock – the first of many in the days and weeks ahead.

Arriving in the UK men faced their final delousing. They were told to strip off, then their clothing was incinerated, although some made efforts to retain items of threadbare clothing to illustrate the hardships they had faced. They were put into baths where all their body hair was shaved off and they were painted with white lime. When they were considered clean the men were finally issued with new uniforms, with care taken to sew on the correct medal ribbons and badges so the men could make their way home with pride.

Armed with their leave passes and travel warrants the ex-POWs said goodbye to their mates, shouldered their kit bags and made the long-awaited journey home. Few found the journeys a comfortable experience as they experienced a sudden sense of isolation. For the long-term POWs, the conversations and concerns of commuters and chattering housewives reinforced the feeling of being outcasts whom time had forgotten. They took time to adapt. The smallest details of home life seemed out of place – the ticking of clocks, tablecloths, open fires rather than stoves, even the taste of vegetables. Where there had once been no choice now they had choice – whether to stay in or go out, what to eat, which radio station to listen to. They overheard conversations on subjects they knew nothing of. Accepted details of everyday life such as the Mulberry harbours were a complete mystery to them. All were small, seemingly insignificant details of normal life, but were complicated dilemmas to men who had endured captivity.

Rationing was also to cause stress and confusion to those who had sustained themselves with thoughts of the meals they would eat on release. They were disappointed to find many of their favourite foods unavailable. Simple conversations between housewives on the subject seemed alien to ex-POWs. How could they understand problems about meat shortages, or the lack of bananas in the shops, when only days before they had been fighting over crusts of bread? On returning to his local railway station one prisoner attempted to purchase a longed for bar of chocolate from a vending machine only to find the machine had been empty and unused for many years. Such delights would have to wait.

The appearance of British women also shocked prisoners, they expected the clean fresh-faced appearance of Continental women only to find most British women wearing full make-up. To them British women appeared to be wearing masks. These problems were perhaps greatest for the single men, since at least the married men had someone to return to. Despite the yearning for female company some men found they could no longer approach women. Years of captivity had eroded their confidence and they felt uncomfortable in mixed company. Some attended dances but found themselves unable to ask women to take the floor. It would take time for them to learn to live fully, and soon many families realised the brave face shown in the letters from the POW camps had been little more than a mask concealing a reality few could have imagined.

Many ex-prisoners wished to be left in peace. After so long in enforced captivity, crammed into huts alongside other men, they yearned for solitude. Instead many became curiosities, constantly receiving visitors who wished to view them.

Few wanted the attention, preferring to rebuild their lives quietly without the constant questioning of well-intentioned friends and relatives. Above all they wanted to fit back into society with as little fuss as possible.

They also knew they would have to modify the habits acquired during captivity if they were not to upset their families. They had to remember to use cutlery and not to lick plates clean. The army had made some attempts to prepare them for such problems, although the advice given was not always appropriate. At one lecture men were told to modify their table manners, being told: 'When you go home, don't say pass the fucking butter! Say pass the fucking butter – please!' (17)

However, not all prisoners were fortunate enough to be worrying just about the niceties of table manners. The lean months of winter had left many too sick to face the trials of reintegrating into society. Their weakened bodies fell victim to all manner of sickness and disease. Many were admitted to military hospitals and treatment prevented rapid reunion with their families. Some men implored their families not to visit them. They had gone off to war in the prime of their lives, as strong fit young soldiers but had returned as shadows of their former selves. The poor diet had weakened their teeth, left their skin drawn tight over fleshless skulls and their hair had lost its lustre, fallen out or turned grey. These were young men inhabiting the bodies of the middle aged. In this condition some preferred to save their reunions for the day they could walk confidently into the family home.

Time in hospital gave men time to think. Now they were finally free they had to reconcile the plans they had made in the long months and years of captivity with the reality they found back home. It was not be an easy process. For some there was ill feeling towards the Germans, particularly those men who had endured the rigours of forced labour. As Jim Sims wrote to his parents: 'Am putting in for a nice steady job starting the ovens when Uncle Joe sets up some in Berlin!' (18)

Once the ex-POWs had enjoyed a brief leave, then returned and completed their military service, they were finally released back into civilian life. There were no fanfares, no parades, and precious little recognition of their suffering. With the tales emerging about the conditions endured by prisoners in the Far East or the horrors of the concentration camps, the ex-POWs felt they had been lucky. Few wanted to tell tales of their own suffering – surely, they reckoned, they should just be glad to have been prisoners of the Germans rather than the Japanese? In the years that followed few admitted the realities of their experience.

As they merged quietly into society all they took with them were a set of new clothes, a certificate of service to show potential employers, and their memories. It seems strange to read the release certificate of anti-tank gunner Doug Colls, who had fought for five days at Arnhem, been captured and held on starvation rations for seven months. His testimonial read: 'Employed as battery clerk and does the job very well. Good at taking charge of the men and organising an office. Trustworthy, hardworking, cheerful and willing, a good typist and all round clerk.' (19)

Perhaps it is fitting to conclude with the words of the long-suffering George Marsden, who flew back from Germany in a Dakota which landed at Aylesbury.

The plane was so crowded many were forced to stand during the flight. They had long dreamed of the day they would return home and now the moment had arrived. Such was the feeling of anticipation that as they took their first steps on home turf a sense of let down was almost inevitable. Following delousing and two days of medical treatment he was sent home on leave. After the traumas of capture and the deprivations of POW life Marsden had a typically subdued homecoming: 'Made my way home on the train alone, caught a bus to Sheffield, and sat on the doorstep waiting for my mum to get back from shopping. So that was that, no flag waving, no fuss, the end of an exciting time of my life, some happy, some not very good at all.' (20)

17

Victory - The Moment of Reckoning

'What the hell do we do now?' (1)

8 May 1945 – a day that has become ingrained in the memory of people throughout the world – a day of celebrations and rejoicing. In Britain the crowds flocked onto the streets, blocking roads and filling squares to rejoice at victory. The images of London are unforgettable – Churchill and the Royal Family on the balcony of Buckingham Palace, cars swamped by flag waving revellers, men and women dancing in the streets. Yet apart from the uniformed men and women amidst the crowds of civilians, in this version of the defeat of Germany the front line soldier is nowhere to be seen. The recorded images are mainly of civilians, people remote from day to day contact with the war. For most of the soldiers – exhausted by years of war, tired of seeing their friends die, sick of devastation they witnessed around them – the experience of victory was very different.

As the Nazi war machine finally ground to a halt, the world breathed a sigh of relief. For almost six years war had raged across Europe causing innumerable casualties, and now it was over. Those at the centre of the fighting had seen the end approaching for months, as the Germans slowly but surely retreated, seldom panicking and seldom without a fight. The reality of the dying days of the Third Reich was much more violent than many historians have recorded and to the end many German soldiers put up bitter resistance. Whilst thousands of their comrades marched eagerly into captivity many fought on – never giving up the struggle or betraying their Führer. On the northern German plains the advancing British continued to meet stiff resistance from improvised battle groups made up of ardent Nazis – SS, Hitler Youth, Officer Training School candidates, Marines, paratroops and the instructors from Wehrmacht battle schools.

It was not only the Germans who were desperately trying to find reinforcements. By spring 1945 21st Army Group was a very different organisation from the one that had stepped ashore in Normandy the previous summer. Casualties had proved a serious drain on the resources of both British and Canadian units and many of the troops fighting their way into Germany were men who had never expected to fight. Among them were the 'six week killers', teenage recruits and men in their thirties, conscripted and given a hasty course in infantry fighting. Others were soldiers from cushy jobs as holding units were cleared of cooks, clerks and drivers. Scottish regiments brought forward their pipers and even battalion tailors found themselves in the front line. Whole regiments were broken up to provide reinforcements to other units. Ack-ack gunners and coastal artillerymen had retrained as infantrymen, with the fit men joining rifle companies and the rest serving as anti-tank gunners or mortar crews. RASC and RAOC men, pioneers and engineers – all found themselves picking up rifles they had hardly touched since basic training. Even the military prisons were combed out to find suitable reinforcements.

Manpower was also found from other sources with hundreds of Royal Marines transferred to the army. RAF clerks, storemen, groundcrew and even trainee aircrew were also transferred. By the end of 1944 fifty per cent of the 2nd Battalion Scots Guards were believed to be former RAF men. One bemused company commander even found himself with two RAF pilots among his men, both still wearing their 'wings' on their battledress blouses. Likewise, many Scots regiments had infantry platoons consisting almost entirely of Englishmen.

Yet despite the desperate search for suitable reinforcements some platoons fought from Normandy to the Elbe without ever being at full strength. One company of Gordon Highlanders even reported having just two officers when they should have had twelve and by the start of the Reichswald battle Canadian units reported that up to seventy per cent of their men had never previously heard a shot fired in anger. In some units the standard of the replacements was so poor that company commanders simply left some of them out of battle, not daring to risk them in action.

For the men at the front seeing the new recruits was often a shock. They joked how they could spot the 'six week killers' – they wore greatcoats that had never been slept in. Age differences could also be a problem, as one young NCO remembered: 'At nineteen-years-old my age was a hindrance. Giving orders to a thirty-five or forty-year-old man was difficult, you felt a bit strange. But it worked out, they were very good.' (2) It was little different with the younger arrivals. Battle-hardened nineteen-year-old John Longfield watched the young reinforcements absorbed into his unit after their losses in Normandy: 'I remember getting reinforcements and you felt quite old compared to them. I remember them saying to me "I couldn't kill anybody". And I used to say "For Christ's sake you must change that attitude or you're dead!" And most did change their attitude.' (3)

Not all reinforcements felt comfortable in their new units, as one young subaltern recalled: 'It was very disappointing. We weren't welcomed, we were just replacements for friends. The men were wonderful, they accepted us. But the top officers didn't make us welcome. But I can understand it. They had been together as friends for so long, and here we were – strangers stepping into dead men's shoes. Not a nice phrase but very apt.' (4)

It was also an uncomfortable time for the men whose units were broken up, as John Mercer recalled:

> We were devastated when the regiment was broken up. We didn't expect it. We really thought we were the best regiment in the British Army. We spent Christmas Day in a holding camp and the tradition in the army is that the officers and senior NCOs

come round and give you rum and tea in bed, but I turned over and went to sleep. That was the only time in my whole life that I felt homesick. I thought what am I doing here, for goodness sake – what's going to happen now? (5)

Yet somehow, despite all the difficulties the army had managed to absorb these reinforcements and push forward into Germany. To their credit most of the new breed of infantry had adapted to their task and stood on the threshold of a great victory – as long as they could survive. The closer it got to the end of hostilities the more cautious the advancing troops became. After six years of war, nobody wished to die with the end in sight. As the spearhead of the army surged through Germany others were left behind, enjoying every moment of their salvation. After the Rhine crossing some units found themselves conveniently far from the front. Northants Yeoman Joe Ekins was among them: 'We came back from Essen and had to wait to get our tanks back. Everybody could see the end in sight. Anything you did to keep out of the fighting was a bonus – if you ain't got to fight today it might all be over by tomorrow! One day closer. So everybody was as pleased as Punch. Other silly sods were going on into Germany but we'd come back.' (6)

Those not blessed with the fortune to be left out of these final battles began to develop a new way of fighting, resorting to increasingly ruthless actions to ensure their survival. There were plenty of men who thought the best course of action would be to use heavy bombers on every centre of resistance and simply pound the defenders into the ground. Relentless bombardment and a slow war of attrition would certainly have prolonged the war but they cared less for when the war would end, rather whether they would be alive to see it. Hoping to help ensure survival, they began to call down increasingly heavy fire on relatively small targets. As the advance penetrated into Germany Patrick Delaforce, a young FOO – Forward Observation Officer – noticed: 'more reliance on artillery stonks – barrages for infantry attacks – and calls for "limejuice" – Typhoon air support – on relatively small targets – pillboxes, hamlets etc.' (7) It was a most sensible option. It may have been harsh on the German soldiers – who were given fewer opportunities to surrender – but the cautious soldiers had little choice.

Right up to the end of the war boobytraps still exploded and mines destroyed vehicles. Even with the enemy all but dissolving into the night, few men felt comfortable enough to drop their guard. Rather than drive straight through roadblocks or attempt to remove them, the fear of boobytraps made soldiers order German civilians to remove them. None of the advancing soldiers wished to chance being blown up just to save a few minutes. Instead they would happily wait for the Germans to do the job before continuing.

The soldiers became increasingly profligate. Hedges, woods and homes – any possible cover – became targets for tank crews and infantrymen. They knew ammunition was expendable, but their lives were not. Carrying bandoliers of spare ammunition, troops advanced, firing from the hip, regardless of whether there was a target. All that mattered was that the enemy keep their heads down or be scared into surrendering. If a potentially hostile face was seen at a window flame-throwing tanks would be called forward to douse the building in flame.

Only once the target was ablaze would the advance continue.

This new nihilistic attitude made life uncomfortable for German civilians. If the enemy opened fire from an air raid shelter that might be housing civilians it made little difference to the soldiers – all available firepower would be used to suppress the enemy fire. If that meant assaulting a shelter with flame-throwers, so be it. It may have been distasteful for the men involved but civilian lives were expendable.

When they saw the results of such behaviour it weighed heavily on the hearts of the soldiers. Civilian corpses – women and children dying in the streets – none of it was what they wanted to see. They didn't want the civilians to get hurt unnecessarily, but what was necessity? Nothing was more important than to survive.

With victory in sight few men were keen to win medals. They were not caught up in the whirl of over-excitement seemingly engulfing some observers. They resented the media involvement and the idea that they should be racing towards the heart of the Reich. The soldiers cursed as enthusiastic BBC journalists broadcast details of the advance, telling the enemy the route to be taken and allowing vital bridges to be blown. The job was difficult enough without ill-informed amateurs getting excited by the prospect of victory – especially when it was not the journalists whose blood was being spilled.

Commanding officers began to notice the reluctance amongst the soldiers to take chances. It seemed the longer a unit had been active the slower it became in the final weeks. It was noticed that the battle-hardened 5th RTR lost fifty per cent fewer tanks in the final weeks of the war than their junior colleagues in 7th RTR. Yet no one could blame them. Even the fatalists could foresee survival, and in some units those who had long defied the odds were offered a lifeline by their officers and withdrawn to spend the final days in safety. This was a policy that could not be used throughout the army. There were plenty of long-serving men who knew there would be no respite until victory was sealed. For the men of Reconnaissance regiments the knowledge that the end was imminent was of little comfort. Every day they still had to carry out patrols, probing the enemy lines to locate any likely opposition. Even in the first few days of May 1945 the threat of death was a constant companion. In the final days the 43rd Reconnaissance Regiment lost a popular troop commander and a three-man armoured car crew. A sergeant from the Regimental HQ was among the dead, having asked for the opportunity to take part in a patrol before the war was over, paying the ultimate price for his eagerness to experience action.

These events took their toll on some soldiers. Included among them was a brave officer who refused to take a patrol out for fear of not surviving the last few days of war. For these soldiers there was precious little chance to be increasingly cautious, their work had to continue however dangerous. Harry Free was among those who dared not think of the end: 'Somebody must have known the war was coming to an end but the rank and file didn't until the ceasefire was announced to us the night before. On the day it was due to finish we were ordered to do a patrol but our officer, Jackson, wasn't taking any chances. He put us in a lay-by and we sat and waited. I don't remember changing the way we operated at any stage, apart from that. We just carried on as usual.' (8)

Whilst most of the troops were desperately attempting to keep out of trouble there were a few whose behaviour changed in an opposite way. A number of men were gripped by an urgent desire to play an offensive role, as had the 'recce' sergeant who had lost his life on his first patrol. An extreme example of this eagerness was exhibited by an officer who hitchhiked from hospital in the last days of the war and attached himself to a forward unit. Once there he borrowed a Bren gun. His intention was to charge an enemy trench in a last desperate attempt to win a military cross, without which he thought he would be considered a coward by his friends back in London.

In the final days there was a clamour for men to get back to their units. Some felt a need for glory but most just wanted to be back with their mates and to experience the end of the conflict in the company of the few people who could really understand them. These were the men who absented themselves from hospital and holding camps and hitched lifts in any available vehicle to be reunited with their mates. Others, who found themselves back in the British Isles felt they were missing out on what would be one of the most memorable moments in European history. Recuperating at a base in Northern Ireland Alexander Baron wrote home, telling his family how he wished he could be 'on the other side' making history: 'tasting the fruits of all that we and everyone else have gone through in these last five years. I do so want to get across before it's all over.' (9)

With the end in sight many grasped onto an abstract concept of what the final victory would be like. They made grandiose plans and schemes, laughing about what they would say to their officers and how they would get drunk like they had never been drunk before – but in truth few could make concrete plans for the future. The men who suffered the most at the hands of the enemy had their own personal celebrations at the end of each day of war. Every day of battle they lived through was their reward, and for a few short hours they could rest easy, safe in the knowledge they had earned the right to see another dawn. Little wonder they felt uneasy when they heard of the celebrations being planned by civilians back home. As early as winter 1944 Alexander Baron wrote home:

West End restaurants planning their victory night guzzles for those with fat enough wallets etc seems a pretty poor joke to me. Do these people think there's a picnic going on out here? Don't they know how bitter and gruelling and inch by inch the struggle has become along the entire Western Front? Does the tragic but wonderful story of the first Airborne Division mean nothing to them? Perhaps if some of the wishful thinkers could be sent out here to have a basinful they'd pipe down a little and do a bit more themselves to bring victory nearer instead of indulging in all this shoddy junketing. (10)

This sense of interference by the outsiders was heightened in the dying days of the war. The newspapers and radio broadcasts seen and heard by the soldiers were full of rumours. They speculated on the fate of Hitler and his henchmen and reported the supposed negotiations that the journalists thought might end the war. All of which was entertainment for civilians but of little comfort to the soldiers who still had targets to capture. As civilians prepared for victory, soldiers once more stepped out into the unknown.

Casualties continued and by the start of April 1945 nearly 21,000 of the 35,000 hospital beds in 21st Army Group were occupied, and the final month of war saw almost 12,000 more battle casualties. Between 28 April and 12 May there were 2,364 battle casualties – and that was in a period when all hostilities had ceased from 5 May. For the newspapermen and reporters these were the 'dying days' of the war and those were truly appropriate words – plenty of men were still dying to bring a victory everyone else seemed to take for granted.

Right up to the end 21st Army Group continued to meet stiff resistance. True, there was no longer a continuous front line, instead merely pockets of resistance – some large, some small, all needing to be neutralised or isolated. This was no time to be taking chances, it took just one fanatic armed with a panzerfaust to destroy a tank, or a lone sniper to bring a man's life to an end. All manner of hazards were encountered, from booby traps to terrifyingly destructive naval mines buried beneath roads. Plenty of men lost their lives when the end was tantalisingly close.

A week before the eventual collapse there was a precursor to the surrender. After weeks of speculation about his fate, German radio announced the death of Adolf Hitler. With the figurehead vanquished there seemed little point for the Germans to fight on – or so most Allied soldiers thought – but it was not to be. There was little time for celebration and many more actions had still to be fought. These weren't the glorious set piece battles so beloved of generals but minor encounters to secure single farmhouses, insignificant bridges and hamlets. The soldiers had to clear buildings defended by schoolboys. The men who had cheered, wept or simply listened in silence to the announcement of the Führer's death had little desire to risk their own lives now the architect of the destruction around them lay dead in the ruins of Berlin.

With the remaining territories of the 'Thousand Year Reich' rapidly diminishing the new German government was beginning to lose control. Already many of the towns and cities in northern Germany had fallen to the Allied advance. The great industrial cities of the Ruhr – Dortmund, Essen, Düsseldorf had been forced into surrender. From there the advance had continued, capturing Magdeburg, Hanover and Bremen. Against such an onslaught Admiral Karl Doenitz, Hitler's successor, knew he could do little but delay the final capitulation. He had no desire to sacrifice the lives of his men unnecessarily, but knew for every day his men continued to resist in the west, more of his forces could escape the advancing Russians to surrender to the British or Americans. After a few days of rapid retreat in the east it became clear there was little point in resisting any longer and from his headquarters in Flensburg, Doenitz issued orders that would see the conflict draw to a close.

The great northern port of Hamburg was one of the first to surrender. With much of the city already in ruins – courtesy of the British firebomb raids in 1943 – there seemed little point sacrificing the city and its population for a cause that was already lost. With large formations of the British army ready to attack the city Major General Wolz received the order to arrange the surrender. On 3 May elements of the 7th Armoured Division drove unopposed into the heart of the city, where the adjutant of the 1/5th Queens Regiment – a battalion whose war had taken them from North Africa, via Italy and Sicily, through France, Belgium and Holland, then into the heart of the Reich – raised the regimental flag over Hamburg's town hall. Though their job was not yet complete it was clear there would little more for them to do before the enemy finally capitulated. A feeling of relief began to spread through the ranks. Some men found themselves with no more duties to carry out and began to find other things to keep them occupied. John Mercer was a signaller working with a counter-mortar group. With no incoming fire from enemy guns they were given less taxing jobs to fill their time:

> So we used to guard prisoners and that sort of thing. We also captured Hamburg airport – just six of us. We spent three days there going through every hanger trying to find weapons. We found a few, but there was no resistance. Luftwaffe pilots were flying in from Denmark and Norway, just landing and surrendering. There were all types of Displaced Persons – French, Belgian and so on. Those who were lucky were walking home. We were also meeting Russian prisoners of war and we were more afraid of them than we were of the Germans, because they were hungry, they were after the German women, they'd got knives, they were quite desperate. They were strange days. (11)

With Hamburg occupied, Doenitz and his increasingly isolated government knew the moment had come to negotiate surrender and a delegation was despatched to Luneburg to open discussions. Arriving at Field Marshal Montgomery's TAC HQ they held the destiny of many thousands in their hands, yet were met with an almost casual disdain. Although knowing victory was inevitable, Monty remained aware the slightest delay could cost lives among his men. Attempts by the German delegation to procrastinate, to earn their forces in the east extra time to flee from the Russians, were given short shrift. The Germans hoped to surrender all their forces to Montgomery, but he was having none of it. To Montgomery this was a political irrelevance, a non-military matter that was none of his concern – his opinion was clear, if German forces were fighting against the Russians then they should surrender to them, not the British. For all the efforts of the delegation their situation was hopeless. They were despatched back to Flensburg to see Doenitz with a simple instruction – he was to surrender his forces immediately or face the immediate fury of the assembled Allied forces.

The message was clear and the surrender delegation duly returned to TAC HQ with his answer. At 6.20 p.m. on 4 May the act of surrender was signed, to come into effect from 8 a.m. the next morning. With their signatures the German delegation sent into captivity all forces based in north-west Germany, Schleswig-Holstein, Holland, Denmark, the Frisian Islands, Heligoland and the garrison at Dunkirk – a total of almost one and a half million men. Effectively it was over. Whilst there was to be a three-day delay before the Germans admitted total defeat and capitulated on all fronts, for 21st Army Group the job was done.

News didn't take long to spread. Just ten minutes after the document was signed General Dempsey at 2nd Army issued the order that all the four corps under his command were to stand fast on the line between Domitz, Ludwigslust, Schwerin, Wismar, Neustadt, Bad Segeberg, Wedel, Stade, Bremervorde and Bremen – his personal order went out: 'No advance beyond this line to take place without orders from me.' (12)

For most the surrender came not a moment too soon. Despite the knowledge that surrender was imminent many of the troops were still fully engaged against the enemy when the news reached them. For Sergeant Les Toogood and his snipers the ceasefire notice was perfectly timed:

> I had been told to take a patrol out against some Panzer Grenadiers, and if you're scared anyway then you're bloody scared to go up against them. It was flat ground, pasture land, the hedges were small – there was no cover. There were two woods and the ground sloped up, so we knew we hadn't got a hope in hell really. We'd been out for three nights recceeing it, and we'd had a bash at them previous to that. Then the 'old man' came up and said we had to have a go at them again. I was talking to 'A' company's commander to tell him what I was going to do, then the Intelligence Officer came up with the 'Don R' and said 'Hold Everything!' Oh, Christ – that was better than my bloody wedding! (13)

The arrival of the message was the signal for the inevitable celebrations to begin – although their war would officially continue until 8 a.m. the following morning there was little that could be done to prevent the parties from beginning. All over northern Germany it was time for a double rum issue, as commanding officers decided their men could start relaxing.

The senior officers of Highland regiments were quick to react. Transport carrying the men's kit was rushed forward. Ceremonial uniforms of kilts and sporrans were unpacked, pressed and made fit for the parade ground, as the troops were prepared for the inevitable ceremonial duties that would accompany surrender. Pipers put away the stretchers they had previously carried into battle, dusted off their instruments, and soon appeared suitably dressed to accompany the festivities.

Many less formal musical displays were soon to be heard amidst the ranks of the celebrating soldiers. In Hamburg troopers of the 8th Hussars 'liberated' some brass instruments and serenaded their colleagues with 'oompa music' whilst dressed in bits and pieces of Nazi uniforms. Radios were tuned into Allied radio stations so the troops could listen to the news broadcasts that told of their victory. Once the troops had heard the news, radios were left playing the more familiar dance music that would accompany the celebrations. Those lucky enough to be billeted in suitable buildings put on impromptu shows. No longer did they need to worry about the blackout, instead stages were lit with whatever candles and hurricane lamps the men could find. Singers sang, musicians played, comedians told jokes – anyone who could entertain in some way joined in. In some places soldiers formed bands with instruments improvised from tin cans, anything to make a noise. One section of MPs dressed up in Nazi uniforms and joined with civilians to stage mock arrests, trials and punishments of what they called 'the Hitler Gang'.

John Mercer remembered the beginning of the celebrations:

> It was quite something. We'd gone to a place called Itzerhoe – where they made cement at a big works there – I said to some of my mates 'The Kiel canal is just five miles away, let's go and have a look'. So we drove there. They said 'Shall we go on into Denmark?' but I said 'No, let's get back'. When we got back most of the troop were as drunk as owls, including the officers. They'd been firing their guns up into the air, like Arabs – bang, bang, bang, bang! They'd brought all the telephone wires down! Well, we hadn't been drinking and we thought what shall we do? 'Let's set fire to this haystack.' So we set it alight, I threw my cap into the flames and we danced around the haystack. Then we went to bed. (14)

If anything was to characterise that night of celebration it was displays of noise, light and fire. Les Toogood, freed from the responsibility of having to take out his patrol watched as the celebrations began:

> As soon as we were told to 'stand down' – that there was to be no more fighting – literally everybody behaved like it was Guy Fawkes night. The searchlight boys lit up the sky, everybody was firing into the night – bofors guns – it was just like a fireworks display. It was great – I could sit down and relax. I said to the lads 'You can clean your rifles in the morning'. It was absolutely wonderful. (15)

All manner of weapons were discharged, flare pistols lit up the sky, as did seemingly endless streams of tracer. At Oldenburg in northern Germany British tank crews reported Canadian infantrymen throwing hand grenades into the street and firing machineguns, provoking comments from some that it was their most dangerous moment since D-Day. Smoke generators belched out vast black clouds – in contrast to the dumps of captured ammunition that were ignited in jubilation.

The searchlights, so often previously used to guide troops advancing at night now lit the sky, as described by one of the celebrating men: 'No longer did their stabbing beams resemble probes, controlled, systematic and purposeful, in reconnoitring an arc of sky. Instead, their beams whipped crazily across the darkness, intersecting and recrossing each others tracks in giant sweeps, high and low, as if chasing phantoms or translating the confusion of dreams into gesticulations.' (16) At Monty's HQ on Lüneburg Heath one man climbed a pine tree and poured the contents of a jerrycan over the branches of the tree. When he safely reached the ground a match was thrown and tree ignited. The men then joined hands and circled the blazing tree, dancing and singing.

In other areas jubilant soldiers cut enormous 'Vs' into the earth and filled it with flame-throwing fluid which was ignited to illuminate their celebrations. Others caught sheep and shaved the 'V' into their coats, and RAF groundcrews – drunk on liberated schnapps – celebrated by burning down their mess tents. In many units such scenes of drunken revelry became the order of the day – where there was no obvious threat from the enemy both officers and other ranks joined in by consuming whatever alcohol they could find. Many had been accumulating stocks of liberated alcohol ready for the inevitable party and with the announcement of the ceasefire it was time to break into their supplies.

The men of the 6th Airborne Division, who had raced from the Rhine to the Baltic coast in an attempt to prevent the Soviet advance reaching Denmark, had settled in the town of Wismar. One group of men occupied the home of a local Gestapo official in readiness for a party. All available alcohol was emptied into a bath to mix a gigantic cocktail. When the time came to celebrate they really let their hair down. Drunken men unwittingly stuck their heads through glass window panes in their rush to vomit into the street – the chandelier was torn from the ceiling and liberated POWs lay sprawled across the floor, on tables or slumped in chairs. The following morning those men nursing hangovers nailed down the piano lid to prevent the more rumbustious among them continuing the party. However, the nails were pulled out and the music restarted. Then paint was poured over the piano – all to no avail as it was simply wiped off. Eventually wire cutters solved the problem. When the partygoers were informed their CO planned to inspect their billet the enterprising soldiers dug a large hole in the garden, filled it with furniture and the carpets, leaving a spotless shell for the officers to inspect.

When tank crews of the 'Buffs' held their party – delayed until 6 May – one officer was sent out into the surrounding countryside to locate whatever alcohol had not been looted by other units in the area. All stores not already emptied by the Canadians were found to be under guard. Unperturbed, the lieutenant returned from Bremen with two barrels of beer and a canister of unidentified liquid later found to be the propellant for a V2 rocket. Despite the unusual mix of drinks all present thought it a great party.

In the aftermath of the endless drinking some individuals wanted to take their entertainments one step further. Whilst many soldiers happily shared their drink with defeated enemy soldiers and civilians, some wanted to take revenge. There were suggestions by some partygoers to: 'Burn all the German property we can find,' (17) although few such attacks were actually carried out. Here and there men threw bricks at German homes or attempted to burn them down but most were restrained by their friends. Amid the celebrations the relieved soldiers shook hands with their mates, as if congratulating each other upon survival. That a sense of excitement existed is undeniable, but how deep it went was unclear. They were celebrating en masse – like members of a victorious team – but as they rejoiced in their continued existence, one question arose – what price victory?

Slowly, amidst the jubilation, some minds wandered away from victory and moved onto the reality of what they were celebrating. There was a joyous outpouring of emotion that they had survived a war in which so many had lost their lives. But these victorious emotions went so much deeper than personal survival. Slowly it dawned on them – whilst the news brought joy and long-saved champagne was cracked open, they realised all the bubbles of all the champagne in the world couldn't revive the friends they had lost.

For all the madcap celebrations there were many soldiers whose memories of the German surrender eschew such scenes. The feeling of ecstasy was not experienced by all servicemen and the massed crowds of London were certainly not replicated by many fighting men – indeed some have absolutely no recollection of any parties nor even any memories of the particular events of those days. Stan Procter was operating the radio at 214 Brigade HQ when the message came over the air that the surrender had been signed. His relief was tempered by his need to fulfil his duty and pass on the message to his commander, Brigadier Essame who was talking with the commander of the 43rd Division, General Thomas:

> There were no celebrations. In fact, the first thing that happened once the war was over was the Brigadier came round to inspect where we were living and make sure everything was 'shipshape'. No, there was nothing. I think one or two people did go out and get very drunk, but I didn't see them. And some people fired off their guns into the air, but that was all. It was very downbeat. You know how back at home everyone was out in London celebrating, but there was nothing for us over there in Germany, nothing that I saw. We were in Germany, so they weren't celebrating. For us the celebrations didn't come until fifty years later. (18)

There were thousands of men for whom emotion had been blasted away by war leaving just one simple feeling – relief. Douglas Goddard, a Royal Artillery battery commander spoke for many when he said: 'By this time we were a pretty emotionless lot and took most things in our stride, including peace. Where do we go from here?' (19) They all felt joy for their personal survival, grim satisfaction that they had performed their duties and pride in their achievements – but nothing could fill the void left by the loss of so many friends.

Despite the celebrations, for many who had suffered – seeing their friends die, being forced to kill men for whom they felt no personal animosity, experiencing life at its most extreme – there was a dark side to their emotions. Tank commander Ian Hammerton wrote: 'VE Day +1 was a holiday! We were still euphoric! But having had my 2nd sergeant and his gunner killed the day before the end our feelings were muted – we held their funeral. I can only imagine the state of mind of the two crew members who had escaped alive from that tank and found themselves back in Brussels for the celebrations there.' (20)

Plenty of soldiers felt ill at ease with the joyous mood. They felt they should join in the revelry and should rejoice at the victory they had fought so hard for, but found little enthusiasm. Instead when victory was announced many of them felt little more than relief. They had expected the final victory to be an exhilarating experience, but few found it so. There was little pleasure in victory and plenty of the men who had experienced the horrors of the front line were simply too exhausted to celebrate. Instead they just went to sleep and with a great weight lifted from their shoulders got the first full night's sleep for many months. A few chose the moment to reflect – to avoid any raucous parties and spend the moment alone in quiet contemplation. Others had a quiet drink with friends or even with lone enemy soldiers. Life was never going to be the same again. This feeling of anti-climax was particularly felt by the infantrymen – many who had served from Normandy to the Elbe experienced a curious sense of deflation. Everything definite about their lives had been swept away, in its place was left the void of uncertainty. One of those veterans whose war had started back in North Africa recalled how vague his memories were of what should have been a momentous occasion:

> There was no emotion. Emotion was never shown by anybody, because if you showed you were weak it didn't go down very well. So there was no emotion – it was over and that was it. There was some drinking and shouting, but not amongst us. It was among the others, not the ones at the front. It's fair to say those who suffered the most reacted the least. Because we'd lost so much, there's no doubt we were not the same people as before. There's no way you can be the same person after something like that. So we had a different outlook on life compared to the troops in the rear areas. I don't think there could be celebrations because of friends you had lost. We had a drink or two, but I don't really recall much about it. We didn't have the facilities, people at the back had the NAAFI and all that, but all we had was a camp. That's all I can remember, just carrying on work as before. We were soon doing garrison work in Berlin – that was a full time job. We had to do guard duties and so on, Berlin was a shambles. Lots of people must have had a good time – I would have if I'd been in a position to, but I honestly can't remember much about it. (21)

Some of the troops found there was little reason to celebrate since for them the future was so uncertain. Many of the exiles who fought within 21st Army Group saw victory not as a joyous time but as one of uncertainty and apprehension – for them the defeat of the Nazis had been the aim that had sustained them for so long, but with the Germans defeated that part of their quest was over – now they turned their minds to the prospect of finding out what had happened to their families. Most of the Poles, Czechs, and even German and Austrian Jews, had no idea as to the fate of their loved ones nor any clue as to what would be their own fate now that the war had finished. For many of these men there seemed to be an uncertain future, their fight for freedom apparently wasted as the Communists tightened their grip on eastern Europe, not knowing whether they could ever safely settle into a Communist controlled land. The Jewish soldiers seldom had any clue as to the fate of their friends and relations, and could only suppose them dead. They soon realised that to return home to Germany was impossible – how could they live among the people who had condemned their families to the gas chambers?

For some their enthusiasm for celebrations brought little more than pain and despair. At the moment of victory lives were to be lost as a result of the dangerous mix of explosives and alcohol. A number of men died after putting a German bomb onto a bonfire, making the party go with a bang with unexpectedly tragic results. Another group planned to go one better by collecting a V2 rocket that they hoped to explode to liven up their celebrations. Whilst transporting the rocket it exploded prematurely, killing the soldiers and levelling a German village.

Some units found there was another good reason not to be involved in celebrations – they simply had too much work to do. Soldiers' duties did not finish just because the war was over, instead they were fully engaged in preserving the fragile peace. There were plenty of German units that needed to be disarmed, Displaced Persons who needed to be controlled, former POWs who needed to be processed and returned home – and all that was before they could even begin to think about the fate of German civilians. Furthermore, there was the delicate question of preventing any further advance into Germany by the Red Army. Paratroopers of the 6th Airborne Division had raced across Germany to forestall a Russian advance into Denmark. In the Netherlands British and Canadian units worked long and hard to restore order to the country and ensure the smooth distribution of food to prevent starvation among the local population. SAS and airborne units were rushed to Norway to deal with German units who were stranded there at war's end, and other units rushed through to Denmark to supervise the surrender of German forces and prevent clashes between the defeated army and local resistance forces.

Wilf Allen of the 1st Royal Dragoons was in Denmark when news of the surrender came over the radio:

It was a strange feeling of emptiness and relief, relief to have got through but at the same time you remembered those of your pals that weren't with you, especially one of our cooks who had been killed the day before when his lorry hit a tree, ... I suppose our celebrations were seeing the joy of the Danish people at being liberated. No, I don't think I personally celebrated, there was that feeling of emptiness and 'so what happens to us now?' (22)

Also heading towards Denmark was Ken Moore of the 5th Kings Regiment:

Let down. That might sound strange. Because you had been living a life, for the years previous looking forward, not knowing when, but knowing eventually the day of peace would come. And when it came, in a sense we weren't prepared for it and frankly I think we didn't know what to do. To realise that you – suddenly – were reasonably safe and there's no more fighting, you didn't know how to handle it. We felt so lost. Because you had this target in front of you, we were going to fight until the war was over. Nobody ever dreamt about days or months or years, it's going to come sometime. When it came I think you didn't feel prepared for it. If you'd have been able to, say three months ahead, you could have wound yourself down. (23)

Ken Hardy was leading a unit of 'T-Force' whose job was to secure German industrial and military facilities. Having suffered so much in the previous eleven months, Hardy had mixed emotions at the news:

My memory of it is enormous relief – that I could wake up next morning with no more fear. I had been sent forward to reconnoitre a way into Lübeck. And the next day I led the company – plus a company of paratroopers and a company of Marines – into Lübeck, ready to go to Kiel. When we got into Lübeck we heard on our looted radio that the war was over and there would be no further troop movements. But the Major in charge of the Paras wasn't going to put up with that. He said 'My orders are that we go to Kiel tomorrow morning, and unless I hear personally from the commander, I'm still going – and you're coming with us.' So we went. That was VE Day for us. And it was absolutely hilarious, we rolled into Kiel and the German population – who thought the war was over – stood aghast as this mob marched in. But there was this enormous relief that we weren't going to do anymore fighting. We were still having to work but no one was going to get killed. There was a wonderful sense of freedom. We had a party – we had lots of parties! It was all a bit childish, we put up masses and masses of flares – it was a lovely time. But there was an sense of anticlimax and sadness – it was all over and life was never going to be as exciting again. (24)

There were plenty of others whose work meant there was no chance to celebrate, instead normal duties had to be performed without a break. Although the nature of crimes under investigation had changed, the work of the MPs went on unabated. There was little time to celebrate the end of hostilities since there was no shortage of crimes to investigate. Such was the continuing workload that few provost war diarists bothered to mention victory in their monthly diaries and whilst the soldiers began to dream of demobilisation and the return home the MPs realised there was still much work to be done – indeed, with the troops idle the MPs would have their work cut out keeping them out of trouble. The situation was much the same for the civil affairs staff, they were now fully in charge of a defeated nation – there would be no opportunity to relax, instead they would be fully occupied attempting to restore order amidst the ruins of the defeated Reich.

Plenty of units found the situation was less than stable. Men of the 43rd Reconnaissance Regiment heard Churchill's victory speech whilst travelling across Germany to set up roadblocks, but there was no time to stop and celebrate and their work continued. Recce trooper Harry Free recalled:

It was 'spit and polish' for us. On VE Day we were in civvy billets patrolling near Celle, maintaining a curfew. If we saw anyone out after curfew we took them back to base. VE day was a routine day for us. It was different for others as they were waiting to go home, but as a regular I had to complete my seven years service, which would be in 1947. We heard the celebrations in London on the radio – I remember feeling envious because all we were doing was patrolling. (25)

He and his 'recce' comrades had little opportunity to relax, and exhibited little emotion other than quiet relief. To some it seemed that in the chaos the surrendering Germans seemed to have more freedom than the victorious troops. On the night of the ceasefire John Groves, a 43rd 'recce' officer, was shocked when he went to visit his troop: 'To my amazement a platoon of German soldiers cycled past, doing a smart "eyes left" when they saw me.' (26)

Michael Hunt of the Northants Yeomanry was another of those who missed out on the celebrations: 'I was on a 24 hour guard duty in Zwolle. Bill Fox came out and said the surrender had been signed. The rest of the lads were out celebrating but we were still on guard. There was no doubt about it, a different feeling came over you – you weren't going to die there and then, nobody was going to drop a shell on you. Funnily enough I was on a 24 hour guard again when the Japanese surrendered.' (27)

For those who missed the initial celebrations there would be plenty of opportunities to make up for it in the weeks that followed.

The scale of drinking and the style of the parties held in the period following the collapse of Germany is illustrated by a story from 'Spearhead', the newsletter of the 43rd Reconnaissance Regiment, detailing an event in the sergeants' mess: 'Like all good parties it went with a swing, helped along by the band and everyone grew merrier and merrier. The barman was doing a brisk trade but we all kept pace with him. Someone decided he was Tarzan and proceeded to swing from some electric lights, others showed their zeal in more spectacular ways, while others just sat and sat!' When it was decided that the party should end, the author of the article was delegated to dispose of the remaining whisky:

> We carried the twelve bottles outside to the sink and started our unpleasant task. We withdrew the corks from the first two bottles and poured the contents down the sink with the exception of one glass each, which we drank. We extracted the corks from the next two and did likewise, with the exception of one glass each, which we drank. And so they continued until: When we had everything emptied, we steadied the house with one hand and counted the corks, bottles, glasses and sinks with the other, which were 29. To make sure we counted them again and had 79 and as the house came by, we counted them a third time. Finally, we had all the houses, bottles, glasses, corks and sinks counted, except one house and one bottle, which we drank, after pouring the last house down the cork. (28)

In some units the parties seemed to continue endlessly and alcohol became a prevalent feature of their lives. After officers of 112 Field Battery sent two lorries to the Moselle region to collect wine, their consumption went up substantially. One of the officers had to be medically treated after he began to drink four bottles each morning in lieu of breakfast. The officers and men of 272 Battery Middlesex Regiment continued their celebrations until 13 May. All-day drinking of whisky and lemon juice was the order of the day. The gunners raided their officers' drink supply, drunken officers gave away ties to their men who would now be allowed the privilege of wearing collared shirts and in a gesture of light hearted defiance beer was poured over officers. The process simply went on and on – as some men passed out others continued the party. In Hamburg Brigadier Michael Carver had to order the victory celebrations to stop since his officers were throwing wild parties night after night, getting drunk on 'liberated' alcohol and starting fights. He allowed one final party at his own HQ, which turned into a riotous affair. The next morning Carver was approached by a rather concerned doctor who had treated an injured officer in the wake of a fight that had taken place the previous evening. The man had lost part of his ear when an urn was thrown from a balcony. The concerned doctor feared that in his drunken state he had sewn the unfortunate officer's ear back on upside down.

In some cases the barriers of rank began to break down, with officers and other ranks mixing freely – discipline, they decided, should be left for the hours on duty. In one particularly raucous party, sergeants of the 2nd Fife and Forfar Yeomanry threw out all the furniture from the house their mess was based in and used it to build a bonfire in the garden. They then gatecrashed the officers mess and poured drink over them. The officers found the incident amusing until they discovered the drink had been stolen from their cellar.

The units who had missed out on the victory celebrations whilst en route to disarm the German troops garrisoned in Denmark found numerous opportunities for belated celebrations. Upon arrival in Denmark the liberation forces found themselves besieged by the ecstatic population. Families, farmers, shopkeepers – all seemed eager to adopt a serviceman, usually plying him with the local brew, Carlsberg. Wealthy locals put servicemen in their best horse-drawn carriages and paraded them around the streets to cheers from the population. Each night lorries were sent out from bases to deliver soldiers to parties in celebration of liberation. The lorries stopped at town halls, civic centres and inns and the waiting population picked out the men they wanted to join their festivities, from which they returned bleary eyed and exhausted the following morning. Both officers and men took advantage of this generosity – one officer was found inspecting the guard on a morning after he had over-indulged. It was obvious to the men he had been drinking, since during the inspection of one man's rifle he even failed to notice that the bolt was missing.

Unlike some of the other liberated peoples, the Danish hospitality didn't revolve around what they thought the soldiers could give to them. Theirs was a land of plenty – the rationing and food shortages that had tormented so much of Europe had been avoided. The soldiers found themselves offered all manner of food – pure white butter, thick rashers of bacon – all the produce denied to the export markets during occupation.

Some soldiers were taken to official functions where they were seated around vast tables in city and town halls and fed to the point of bursting. After years of rationing and basic military cuisine their shrunken stomachs were assaulted by the rich food. However, it was not only the food that they were unused to:

> First night we got there, I'll never forget, they wanted a Guard. We went into the Town Hall, they grabbed me out of the lorry, put me in a car with two or three women. Of course when you're 18 every woman is about 90, everyone looks old. I was sitting between these two women – they was old dears, well I suppose they were about 30 – old dears to me. They gave us this Schnapps, first time I've ever had Schnapps. I said 'What's that?' they said it was made out of potatoes. I said I'd had better water out of the tap at home. It don't taste too bad, just swigged it down. When I went outside I hadn't got a clue, woke up next morning in bed. All me equipments out of the lorry, rifle the lot. Who done it? I dunno. I haven't got a clue. Somebody enjoyed them bloody self, but not me. I hadn't got a clue.

If the victim of the potato schnapps thought that was the end of his alcoholic torment he was wrong. He and his colleagues were also challenged to a football match against the locals: 'We had to play them at football, they took us down, eleven of us. In the Danish paper it was headline news – British Troops lose 22-0 or something like that. Two or three hours before they had us on the booze, got us well going. I could see about 14 balls. I was more than half cut!' (29)

Of course, such partying could not continue indefinitely. Whether joyous or morose – rejoicing or remembering – a new reality crept up on the men of the triumphant armies. The evening parties and morning hangovers could not last forever – nor could the hollow sense of relief sustain them in the months ahead. The world was changing and survival was a fact – how much longer could it be celebrated? All the grief in the world could not bring back their lost comrades. Now that victory had given them a future, the troops could ask themselves just one question – 'What the hell do we do now?' (30)

With the war over the soldiers could take a long hard look at themselves. Like many, veteran infantrymen John Longfield was uncomfortable with how much he had changed:

> Two days after the war was over one of my chaps was shot accidentally. So we had to give him a decent funeral. I was on a party to take him, so we put him in a truck. He was on a wooden bench in the middle, wrapped in a blanket and we sat on either side. It was quite a long journey and one of the guys said 'How about a game of cards – a game of pontoon?' I said 'What the hell do we use as a table?' 'Well, he's there, use him as the bloody table!' So we start playing pontoon on this bloke's body. And blood started leaking through the blanket. And I thought 'Christ, what has this war done to me?' I was quite horrified, I didn't want to be like that. (31)

18

The Sadness Endures

'Oh, those days damn those days!' (1)

'I came across one incident, which horrified me, of a British soldier who had chopped off a dead German's finger to take the ring. I can only assume that he had seen so much killing that he had a callous disregard for human life and dignity. I often wondered how he later fared in civilian life.' (2)

After six years of conflict the war was over and the first soldiers began returning home. In those years they had faced the realities of war. Mostly it had been a fight between two groups of frightened, unwilling men. In the harsh glare of the shell burst they had grown up, grown cynical, seen hopes fulfilled and dreams shattered. The final, supposedly glorious, victory left them mentally and physically exhausted and it was with trepidation many faced the return to 'civvy street'. After danger, discomfort and horror they returned to rebuild their lives, though few would ever really be able to return to normality. Few were unscarred by the conflict and could admit, like one veteran, who described war as: 'just an episode in my life, kill or be killed, now all in the past'. (3) Most lived the rest of their lives unable to believe they had actually survived.

In the wake of such destruction it was hard for many to settle down to pre-war standards. For some it was initially hard to contain destructive urges that had been essential to their survival. It seemed their whole moral code had been erased and replaced by a new sensibility where nothing had a value. Even with victory secure many could not forgive the enemy's sins. The troops held power and civilians had little recourse against soldiers who exploited it. Some men took their revenge in petty acts of vandalism, as one tank driver recalled: 'I took some delight in knocking German trams off their lines – a touch of the tiller bar did the trick.' (4) Such behaviour was common – late night entertainment for some included shooting out street-lights and fuel shortages were solved by smashing wooden furniture into firewood. This sense of nihilism took time to erase.

Most men in the occupation forces had a clear idea of when they would be demobbed, since their release group number was marked inside their pay books. Men with long overseas service went first, others whose skills were essential for reconstruction also departed early as did teachers and policemen. Others waited anxiously as the days passed until their turn came to be demobbed and demob calendars appeared on the walls of billets as they counted the days.

However, not everyone was in a hurry to get out. Many enjoyed the opportunities offered in Germany – a land devoid of healthy young men offering unrivalled sexual opportunities to soldiers with access to coffee, soap, cigarettes and petrol. Home leave was also a chance for the import of valuable commodities as presents or for profit. With rationing still in force who could blame them for wanting to milk the land of their enemies? Ken Squires took advantage of the black market: 'My stepfather was a great fan of the open razor. He said to me "See if you can find any from a place called Solingen". They made the most fantastic cut throat razors in the world. I managed to find a pouch of seven razors – one for each day of the week, for the price of a couple of packets of fags.' (5) This was the start of a brisk trade and Squires accumulated as many sets as possible, selling them to British barbers at fifty shillings a set.

Spare time was filled with leisure activities. Endless football matches and card games were played. Mechanics spent hours tinkering with motorbikes, using them for racing or motorcycle polo. There were also educational classes including book-keeping, shorthand and photography. With time on their hands men also used military equipment for profit. One officer used a long-range wireless to contact friends back in England and began to play the stock market, the profits smoothing his transition into civilian life.

Troops also lived comfortable lives in liberated countries. In Denmark the local population played host with an enthusiasm that made many eager to stay. There was food, beer, cigarettes and girls in abundant supply. All the things they had talked and dreamed of, whilst sheltering in ditches and ruins, had now come to fruition. As one lucky veteran recalled: 'it was like a Club 18-30 holiday'. (6) As another admitted: 'We played football most of the time and had a lovely time. It was a hell of a life. We were never going to get that again.' (7)

One lorry driver found his own journey back from Copenhagen delayed by the antics of men who were in little hurry to leave. With a smile he recalled:

'The lorry stopped. The fitter came along and asked if I was alright, I said yes but I still couldn't get away, as someone had put sugar in the battery. There's me, the bloke by my side and four chaps on top of the load, in the back of the lorry. The Danes said "we will get you a new battery". Well a week later they got a new battery so away we went again. Went off, came to a stop. Someone had put water in me petrol. Week later we got some petrol. We had to go to Hamburg to pick up the Regiment. I got back to camp about three weeks too late. I got run into the nick straight away.' There was a simple explanation for why the delays occurred: 'Superb, I thought so. Hadn't got a clue what I was doing, it was all free. If we had to pay for it I would have been sober, but on 7 bob a week .....' (8)

There were plenty of men who couldn't understand why they should continue to follow orders, or keep their uniforms and billets tidy. Many felt the army had no place imposing its rules and regulations on them in peacetime. In one base gangs of men waiting to be demobbed demanded cigarettes from storekeepers, threatening to steal them if the issue was not forthcoming. Orders of 'lights out' were refused, and officers and NCOs were told by the miscreants to leave them in peace. The behaviour of some officers in attempting to enforce standards on men who had 'done their bit' and wanted to go home, upset many. As one wrote: 'These officers forget sometimes that they have grown men to deal with and not school children.' (9)

With all the changes going on the authorities were sometimes uncertain who had been demobbed and who hadn't. Some men simply disappeared. Others failed to sign in upon return at night and many failed to return at all, spending the nights with their girlfriends, sometimes only returning to draw pay and rations. Many officers simply told their men when they would be needed and, as long as they turned up for vital duties, allowed them freedom for the rest of the day. Despite such infractions they soon settled down. Few had any intention of remaining in the army any longer than necessary but the majority accepted the situation and settled into the cushy life of occupation. With cigarettes as the major currency the soldiers took advantage of their NAAFI supplies. They could afford maids and servants to clean their rooms, do the laundry and clean their boots. Poverty-stricken Germans cooked their meals and did the washing up, glad to save the scraps to feed their families. Many basic duties were taken over by Displaced Persons or civilians, giving the soldiers even more free time. It was a life few had known before and few would ever experience again.

Despite the perks, most longed for their 'demob'. Slowly, but surely, friends began to separate. Some units were disbanded altogether and the men transferred to holding units or posted into unfamiliar regiments. Even those who stayed with their own regiments often found themselves surrounded by strangers as newly conscripted men replaced their mates. There was a strange feeling of emptiness in barracks and billets as friends packed their bags, swapped addresses and said goodbye. Friendships that had survived the rigours of combat were terminated courtesy of a number in their paybooks. Men who had lived together for years – sharing food and cigarettes, getting drunk, chasing whores, watching their mates die – shook hands for one last time and never saw each other again.

Demobilisation grew into an entire industry in which vast stores and depots were the last port of call for returning troops. These camps could be strangely anonymous, as individual soldiers seldom knew more than a few men around them. In seemingly endless lines they waited for the final issue of pay, travel warrants, discharge papers and civilian clothing. They handed in uniforms and gave back belts and brasses that would never again need polishing. In exchange came a complete set of civilian clothing chosen from a selection of basic items. In the following years the ubiquitous suits, raincoats and hats marked these men out as veterans.

Leaving barracks for the last time was often an emotionally charged moment. Feelings were mixed – a combination of relief and trepidation, happiness and sadness. Even simple things like demob clothes sent thoughts racing. Some had been little more than schoolboys when conscripted, others had been working in low paid jobs or unemployed – few could ever have dreamed of getting so many new clothes in one day. Some younger men had joined up in clothes bought by their mothers and now left the army dressed as men. Looking at themselves they were shocked at what they saw. Arthur Jarvis remembered the reaction of his colleagues: 'We felt like a load of blooming gangsters – with the suit and the hat and everything.' (10) As they walked through the gates, newly clothed and shod, few felt any jubilation. They were happy to be out of uniform and most looked forward to their new lives. They had long dreamed of being able to do what they wanted, when they wanted, not to be at the beck and call of officers. As one recalled, they joked about how they never again wanted to get involved with anything official: 'We said we would never join anything again "Not even join a piece of string together".' (11) One chapter in their lives was finished – a new one was about to begin.

Having taken the first steps away from the army, they began to settle back into life. They returned home to a changed world – one in which the men who had fought the battles had voted overwhelmingly to get rid of Churchill and the Conservatives. To outsider observers this seemed strange – ousting a successful leader at the very moment of victory. But Britain had fought for democracy and their vote was their democratic right. John Mercer explained: 'We thought Churchill was a great wartime leader. But I didn't vote for him afterwards. I voted Labour. It was an odd time, a shock. We thought it was a new world. Well it was, the first Labour government changed the face of Britain.' (12) Mercer and his fellow soldiers, like many others, had decided 'Churchill for the war, Attlee for the peace'. In doing so they voted for the Beveridge Plan with its public health insurance, pensions, employment protection. They had gone to war from a society ravaged by poverty and had vowed never to return to it. With their votes they had paved the way for a society where the weak would be protected, the sick treated and the old cared for. The welfare state was the reward for their sufferings.

The return to civilian life wasn't always easy as society had undergone many changes. War had torn families asunder. Husbands and wives were strangers and children had little perception of their fathers – many asked their mothers who this person was and when would they leave again. In intervening years grandparents had died, brothers and sisters grown up, new babies been born, and homes completely obliterated by bombing. Those at home had adapted, but returning soldiers had to accept it overnight.

There was no great outpouring of emotion when they returned nor were there grand parades with hometown regiments parading the streets flanked by hordes of flag waving civilians. Instead their arrival was usually a quiet affair. Most arrived home alone, and a few in groups, having 'palled up' with other ex-servicemen they spotted on homebound trains. They stepped down from trains, to be met by wives and families. Greetings were simple – hugs, kisses, a few tears – then a walk or bus ride home. It could be bewildering. They suddenly realised life was about to begin again. It was not always a pleasant experience. Some men felt helpless without the company of their mates, as one man recounted: 'It was lucky they'd taken my pistol off me, or I'd have shot myself sooner than walk out under that arch at Waterloo.' (13)

Their first and most important challenge was to find suitable employment. Many were able to walk straight back into their old jobs, taking up their pre-war careers and hoping to make up for lost time. However, not all relished the idea of returning to their old jobs. Service had opened up new horizons for many who now wanted a better life than their pre-war jobs could ever offer. One former policeman serving in the Military government explained his uneasy feelings about returning to civilian life to journalist Leonard Mosley. After a day attempting to control gangs of rampaging ex-slave labourers he wondered: 'Can you imagine us back in Cambridge after the war, trying to look grave with someone for having no rear light?' (14) It was an emotion that rang true for so many. For some the shock of becoming an anonymous university student, alongside people just out of school, was uncomfortable and confusing. After months enjoying power in an occupying army could they feel at home surrounded by students with little experience of the outside world?

Those whose experiences had given them a desire for an education, to learn a trade, or improve their social position, could use what they had learned. Not all former soldiers drifted into anonymity, among them were men who would rise to high positions, such as Lord Carrington, Lord Whitelaw and Robert Runcie. Lord Boardman, who as Captain Tom Boardman served with the 1st Northants Yeomanry, embarked upon a political career. He had always hoped to be an MP and felt he could put his experience to good use: 'It gave me a much wider experience than I could have achieved without it ..... I learnt from – and admired – a wide selection of men who served with me.' (15)

Others with more modest aspirations found their experiences could help even in simple ways. Unassuming men, who had never considered career advancement found experience had changed them. Those who had 'put up' stripes discovered they retained the potential to lead and could now supervise staff. As one veteran recalled: 'Being promoted gave me the feeling that I could better myself, and I did. Lorry driver to depot manager.' (16) Such small steps may have seemed unspectacular, but for men whose confidence had been enhanced by military service they were significant.

The interruption caused by service had also given many soldiers a chance to think about their lives. Men with little formal education discovered themselves learning from better educated comrades and grew in confidence. This allowed them to develop lives that would otherwise have been beyond them. Mixing with people from all walks of life opened new horizons and allowed them to make important decisions about the future. John Mercer was one who never returned to his old pre-war job: 'I didn't go back to the bank. One of my friends, Maurice, had been a schoolteacher and I thought I wanted to do something else. I was a red-hot socialist in those days, so I thought I didn't want to deal with other people's money. So I decided I wanted to be a schoolteacher. My mother didn't like it, she thought being in a bank I was respectable and would be a bank manager one day. But I didn't want that.' (17)

The desire to control their destiny that made such men switch occupation, made others more determined to make the most of life when they returned to their pre-war jobs. Ken Hardy, like John Mercer, had started his working life as a bank clerk but, unlike Mercer, decided to stick with it and build a career. Having led a platoon into battle, Hardy was unafraid of the challenges of banking. Realising his potential as a leader he acquired the confidence to confront senior staff:

> I once stood up at the staff college in Westminster and said to the powers that be, 'Where the hell would you be if it wasn't for the management skills we learnt in the army? Not learnt at your expense, but you benefit from it!' Management skills were learned in the officers' mess, and you came out and applied them in life. Once you've enjoyed life in an officers' mess you don't really want to go backwards. You want to make the most of it. To live that kind of life, you don't really want to go back to being a junior in a bank. (18)

For Hardy the efforts paid off and in time he became a bank manager.

After demob Leonard Bennett again took up uniformed employment, this time as a policeman. The former signaller found himself in a career where his wartime experiences could be of assistance. Despite little desire to remember army life he could never escape the memory of war: 'I joined the Norfolk Constabulary, where there was considerable emphasis on smartness, discipline and deportment. I had to wear my medal ribbons every day and once a year on Armistice Day I had to ride around with my medals on. The more gruesome aspects of police work did not affect me as they might have done had I not been through my army service.' On one occasion he was sent to clear a body hit by a train. 'There were several of us picking up bits off the railway line. We were making jokes, which people would have said were awful, "I've got a bit of a leg here, can I fit it on to the bits you've got". ' (19) His military experiences also meant he was able to be dispassionate when required but retain an understanding for those who were more unfortunate than wilful.

Others were less able to adapt. After seeing so much suffering and destruction they felt unready to settle down. Cosy domesticity was an alien concept and they longed for the freedom they had found in uniform. They missed the camaraderie, cheap women, booze and the whole uncertainty of life. Suburbia seemed to shackle them as they yearned for the life that at the time they had been so desperate to escape. Some who longed for the old friendships of the war years found themselves heading back into uniform, rejoining the army in the hope of once more experiencing a sense of belonging.

Whilst for some 1945 was year zero – a start of a completely new life – for others it was the point where they restarted their old life, turning the clock back to catch up on years of missed opportunities. Arthur Jarvis had been away for six years when he was demobbed: 'I found it hard to settle down again, I had only been married about a month when I was called up so I had to get to know my wife all over again.' (20) Jarvis had been in church hearing his wedding banns being read out by the vicar on 3 September 1939 when the service was interrupted to hear Chamberlain's radio broadcast announcing the declaration of war. Within weeks he was married but was soon in uniform. In his years away he had only seen his wife four times. It was little wonder peace was seen as the beginning of a new life.

The veterans returned to a society with little understanding of what had happened in those last few months of war. To many outsiders it seemed the war had petered out. There had been no crushing of a last symbolic bastion and no triumphant storming of Berlin. Instead it had concluded in the anonymity of a tent on a heath. It seemed the role of the Americans and the Soviets had surpassed British efforts. It seemed 21st Army Group had been relegated to a sideshow, protecting the flanks of the great American advance into the heart of the Reich. This was just the beginning of public ignorance that blurred the reality of the British and Canadian role. Although most veterans were staunchly proud of their efforts, few boasted of their exploits and many failed to discuss them at all. This tendency to downplay the 21st Army Group's contribution was to a great extent the failing of the veterans themselves. Many veterans downplay the significance of their own role, never making claims of heroism but always seeming to know someone whose valour went unnoticed. Stories abound of the arbitrary nature with which medals were given, being allocated to units to be awarded to deserving men. Many brave men were justly awarded honours in recognition of their heroism, but many more acts went unheralded. Ludicrous situations arose where men were offered the choice between a medal and a week's home leave – few could refuse a trip home.

Even men who were recommended for an award could not be certain of receiving it. After one successful assault a commando officer was recommended for a DSO. However on its progression through various departments the order was successively downgraded until the courageous officer was awarded a Certificate of Merit. On the day he received his certificate the same award was given to a member of the Army Postal Group for his efforts in sending mail from England to the men serving abroad. This situation was replicated throughout the army. Veterans of the Northants Yeomanry still fail to understand why Joe Ekins received no recognition for having destroyed three Tiger tanks. To his comrades this was an outrage, whilst Ekins received nothing, others received the medals for performing relatively minor acts – including one man who was decorated for throwing a smouldering haversack out of his tank after the rest of the crew had baled out.

The scandalous treatment of some deserving men resulted in some veterans feeling unhappy with their own medals. Many never bothered to collect campaign medals whilst others left them untouched for years. Leonard Bennett had little interest in the awards: 'As for medals, I used to have to wear them once a year, but otherwise the kids played with them. I feel different about them now. I've made it clear I eventually want my son to have them, because I know he'll look after them. I think you value the medals now, but you didn't then. I suppose there was this anti-armed services thing, you had an anti feeling about it when you came out. But as time goes on, you begin to put things into perspective.' (21)

Despite the desire to put the past behind them and rebuild their lives, many carried a deep psychological burden. Experiences had been burned into their minds, scarring them for years. It was difficult for many to escape the knowledge that survival had been little more than stroke of fortune. Arthur Jarvis explained his own brush with fate:

I was taking an officer to a meeting and as I drew alongside he jumped off just as a shell exploded on the deck. It killed him and where my head stuck over the top of the cockpit the blast blew my helmet off and gave me slight concussion. When I got demobbed I went into the canteen and bumped into a marine I knew. He said 'We all thought you were dead!' because a lorry had brought a load of equipment into camp and he saw my helmet, we all had our numbers stamped on the chin strap, and when he asked the driver about it he said 'All this lot came off the dead on Sword Beach'. So my helmet must have got blown all that way, so you can guess what would have happened if I had had my chin strap under my chin instead of on the back of my head. (22)

This reliance on fortune is echoed in the words of Eric 'Bill' Sykes: 'Anyone who goes to war and survives is "Lucky". Anyone who goes to war and survives with their life and a whole body and mind is "Extremely Lucky". ... I was fortunate that my involvement was of relatively short duration and I came out of the experience with a whole mind and body and with a justifiable sense of participating in an action that was vitally necessary to the future of Europe and its people.' (23)

Others are not so fortunate. Many veterans returned home physically scarred by the wounds they had suffered, some serious and some no more than superficial. Most physical scars faded over the years, merging with the lines of old age. Those facing the greatest difficulties were the seriously wounded – many of whom struggled for years to recover. There were around 10,500 amputees during the course of the war, of whom some 2,500 survived to see out the century. For others the damage was less spectacular but became just as problematic. Gunners and tankmen have often lived for years with a constant ringing in their ears courtesy of the noise of their guns. There was no reason to complain and no one to complain to. They suffered in silence, enduring the pain and not sharing the problem until it became too obvious to ignore. When the damage became sufficiently serious it was too late to argue for a disability pension from the army, as too many years had passed to prove the source of damage.

Other scars were not physical. Some veterans failed to come to terms with their experiences. Few displayed any sign of their inner trauma, instead suffering in silence with their memories. For others the mental strain was too much and they failed to fit back into society. Mark Benney, a writer and a pre-war prison inmate, wrote a study of conditions in British prisons after the war. His book, published in 1948, stressed some of the causes for a wave of lawlessness observed in the aftermath of war. He noted how first-time offenders were often men with no previous convictions whose first offence had been desertion from the army. Without papers or ration books they had to play the black market and join gangs of organised criminals. Such men fell into a spiral of crime, once they had offended there was little way out except for giving themselves up to the army and taking their punishment. Some of these deserters had gone from being law abiding citizens to men capable of committing: 'senseless, brutal robberies' .(24) They posed a challenge to society and Benney pointed out: 'Young men by the hundreds of thousands have been given a really scientific training in violence, but have had no opportunity to learn a trade.' (25)

The rise in criminality was indicative of the failing of some veterans to readapt to society. Among those unable to forget what they had seen or experienced were unfortunate men who became outsiders – unable to settle back into civilian life some turned to alcohol, eventually becoming unable to hold down steady jobs.

Mercifully few lives were ruined by trauma. Those suffering serious psychological damage could turn to The Ex-Services Mental Welfare Society for help, but less traumatised men eschewed professional help and suffered alone. In the years immediately after the war, in streets throughout the country, the calm of night was shattered by the screams of men reliving their experiences. By day these individuals tried to live a normal life but once asleep the scenes of horror imprinted on their memories came flooding back. Recurring nightmares plagued their slumbers, and wives were bruised as husbands hit out violently in their sleep. The dreams that still disturb the sleep of some veterans remain so vivid they are no longer dreams in the traditional sense but fully detailed, sleeping memories. These recollections can be replayed night after night – real memories of events that seem as fresh as if they had happened only days before. John Majendie, a victim of 'battle exhaustion', explained his experiences: 'Initially the nightmares were quite vivid, but they diminished. But even now I still dream about it. The geography of things isn't right but I dream about advances and attacks through Normandy. But the mental picture of the ground isn't the same these days.' (26)

For others it was years before their wartime ghosts returned to haunt them. Infantry veteran John Longfield recalled how his subconscious memories eventually came back: 'You never shake it off. After I was demobbed I tended to forget it. I went to university. I was occupied with that. You think about it more when you retire. You wake up in the middle of the night and be absolutely horrified about the narrow escapes you had, and think Christ, it's a miracle!' (27)

Some of those afflicted by dreams find their minds need a stimulus, a switch that once it is tripped sends their mind racing and restarts the cycles of haunting dreams. One veteran recalled how his dreams resurfaced on a return trip to Normandy:

> We happened to go down a road that had been particularly horrible. There must have been a whole battalion on the move. They were crafty, they let us go down the whole length of the road, then they opened up and got the whole convoy. It was an absolute massacre. I went down that road again and it brought it all back for a couple of nights. People say us veterans have a different way of thinking. I don't think you could take the mind through something like that without some effect. I don't mean there's necessarily any harm done, but there's always something on your mind. (28)

Sleep is not the only time thoughts return from the depths of their memories. The association of certain smells, weather, or landscape, can stir memories. There are those who refuse to drink rum because of its connection to the vomit-splattered landing craft that took them to France. For some simply driving along a country road can bring back vivid memories. Former tank commanders once more feel alone and vulnerable, as if danger still lurks around every corner. Unconsciously they peer at hedges, search for hidden enemy soldiers in the shadows and scan the fields for enemy tanks, their guts churning in the expectation of an attack. Then suddenly the appearance of another vehicle or a modern building breaks the spell and returns them to reality.

Whether racked by dreams or able to sleep untroubled, the face many veterans presented to the world was often a mask hiding uncomfortable memories. Many found these tensions could not stay hidden forever as recce veteran Harry Free recalled: 'I was told after the war that I had a very blasé attitude, appearing not to have a care in the world. It wasn't a front – it was just my nature. Some years after the war I suffered severe bouts of depression and I often wonder if that was a belated response to the tensions of my experiences during the war.'(29) Others find their minds filled with anxieties that cause them to spend days in contemplation, worrying about incidents from their wartime careers. This question of what might have been is one that constantly haunts many veterans. Most would willingly give back their medals in return for the lives of lost comrades. The 'if only' question hangs over them – if only they had given different orders, if only they had given better covering fire, if only they had reacted more quickly.

Among those who returned from war there were some whose experiences scarred their lives and influenced their behaviour. Some returned home a shadow of their former selves, unable to express their feelings or share their memories. To outsiders they could appear rude or hostile. Only by breaking through this barrier could the reason be discovered. In time some could share details of their lives that highlighted their suffering. One Dunkirk and D-Day veteran, who spent years refusing to talk, eventually admitted how he still carried the burden of having lost one group of mates in 1940. Four years later he returned to France with new friends. Soon they too were dead and for a second time he was faced with the unbearable burden of loss. He would never make friends easily again.

For these veterans every day became a battle with their memories – carrying a burden of grief that put a strain on their relationships at home. Veronica Taylor, whose husband Clifford was captured at Arnhem remembered their life together:

Clifford would not talk about German interrogation. He refused point blank during our farming life to be questioned by anyone 'official'. Tax inspectors, rating officials, ministry of agriculture inspectors, milk board officers etc, etc, all got very short shift with Cliff! Difficult for me left to pick up the pieces! Cliff would say 'The Germans were the last to interrogate me!' No one could order him to do anything! A milk board man said to him 'You have to have a bulk tank instead of churns' and Cliff replied, 'I don't have to do anything – I'll sell the cows first'. He disliked policemen, although he knew several ex-Airborne who entered the police. I was thankful we could farm and be self-employed – as he could never have worked for anyone and taken orders! One terrible event which gave him nightmares occurred after his release from the work camp in Czechoslovakia. His train passed near a concentration camp, and there was a pile of bodies in striped pyjamas. The horror was the rats, which gave Cliff – a farmer's boy – his life-long complete horror of rats. We had the most rat free farm in Devon! If he saw one he spent hours washing his hands, and he only handled hay or straw bales with a pitchfork. Whatever his experiences – he talked about it so little – they affected his life. He suffered badly from depression. His first wife left him. It affected our marriage, his relationship with his two daughters whom he loved dearly, his friendships and ability to get on socially with people. He would cut himself off for days – fortunately, we had the farm and space – he would get in the most violent tempers about nothing, or so it seemed to us. It was impossible to reason with him sometimes. I was always impressed that Cliff did not try and glorify war – he wasn't ashamed to say 'I was frightened in the glider – I didn't want to kill – I was afraid in the POW camp' etc and yet stoically faced all these things. In the 1st Edition of the National Ex POW magazine they published a poem of mine for Cliff. I think I wrote it because I felt guilty after his death because so many things were not his fault and I didn't always understand. Does that make sense? (30)

To most veterans her memories make perfect sense. The emotional burdens carried by former POWs are perhaps the most poignant. Many could never shake off the feeling they had contributed little to the eventual victory. They had been defeated in battle – in itself regarded by some as a humiliation – endured hardship and boredom, and relied on the sacrifices of others to liberate them. POWs faced a lack of understanding about their experiences from people whose knowledge of POW life came from films or the escape literature of the 1950s. Their experiences were also submerged beneath the horrific experiences of men held by the Japanese. Whilst the plight of the Far East prisoners has been highlighted, the realities of imprisonment in Europe have received scant attention.

Some children of former POWs report being denied normal childhood treats by their fathers. They did not want to visit zoos and see animals held in small cages, nor allow caged pets to be kept in their homes. Nor could they tolerate watching food be rejected by ungrateful children. To men who had scavenged in dustbins for potato peel such behaviour was an insult. For many the trauma diminished over the years but for some the battle with their memories remained a lifelong struggle. George Marsden was among them: 'My life was affected, in that I became subdued. I think every night about certain things and have been unable to go away on holidays or be away from home. I have been back to Normandy, but was agitating to return home again, we have never been abroad on holiday, but I have a good wife who has looked after me.' (31)

The psychological scars of war are many and varied. Feelings of guilt for the fate of others hung over many like a cloud. Few veterans feel remorse for having killed – since they killed to survive – but are torn by guilt for the loss of friends. Veterans find fault with their own performance in battle, faults they perceive as having cost the lives of friends. Few could be blamed for any failings – nor would surviving comrades apportion blame – but the emotional impact of supposed blame remains. Officers and NCOs carry the burden of lives lost under their command, as Sergeant William Partridge explained he has long felt guilt: 'that I was still alive when so many of my comrades were dead, consequently I should expect nothing from life but accept anything, however disagreeable, that came my way'. (32)

Some veterans have spent their lives feeling guilty, punishing themselves for making decisions they made in good faith. Ken Hardy was the only survivor of a group of friends, all subalterns, who were among the first reinforcements in Normandy:

> Three of us decided to stick together. It was a great mistake. We had a choice of which regiment we would like to go to. So we read up the histories and came across the Hallamshires, who sounded romantic beyond belief. So all three of us went and we kept together as long as we could. I was the only one to come through, the others died within weeks. It was a great mistake for friends to stick together, because you have to watch your friends die. When we went out there we had neighbouring platoons. On one occasion I was leading my platoon supporting my friend's. I witnessed his death, which was an absolutely appalling experience. He was shot by a 20mm anti-aircraft cannon. His death was something I never really got over, I realised none of us were immortal. I still think 'There but for the grace of God'. It was a terrible mistake, we should not have stuck together. He watched me go through hell and I watched him go through hell and die. It has a profound effect on me because if he had chosen the other platoon, it would be him alive now. (33)

Grief and guilt became partners in the psyche of many veterans. Even those who played no roles in the death of others could be affected, feeling guilty for the lack of grief felt at the time of their friends' deaths. When Stan Procter used his wartime diaries as the basis for his written memoirs he found he wrote from a perspective that did not fully explain his actual feelings, rather how he felt in later years. He reread his diaries and used the original entries in an attempt to understand the differences between what he had felt then and his retrospective emotions:

> I have been pondering the question of attitudes and was wondering to myself why I seemed not to have been affected by grief when my friends were killed, at the time they were killed. So I looked in my diary to see what I had written. In my book for 30 June I wrote about Dick Sheppard being killed. I said in the book 'we were shattered.....' The entry in my diary for that day was 'Arrived back before midnight. Got tents up and all set for the night when we had to pack again and move at 2am. As soon as we arrived we were mortared. Hastie was killed and Dale injured. Moved back and we were mortared twice again. Sheppard killed and Hazlehurst injured. ...'. 'Shepherd killed' is simply recording what I had been told by a mutual friend and that is about all the emotion I felt at that time, but being thankful it was not me. ... I think my book tells of what I should have thought about the loss of those two friends but I think it must have been concern for one's own skin that was uppermost at the time. Seeing their graves 50 years later brought the tears. (34)

Experience continues to influence how veterans view the world. For some their distaste for violence is such they vent their fury on those who practise field sports – the slaughter of helpless animals seeming too close to their own memories. An Essex Regiment veteran explained how he felt when a work colleague began shooting pigeons:

> I said 'What are you doing that for?' He said 'They're a pest'. I said 'Tell you what, I'm a lot older now but I used to be a crackshot'. I said 'Give me the gun and see how

you feel if I fire at you. I could miss – I didn't years ago – but I could miss now!' He didn't shoot any more pigeons. They think they've got no feelings when they shoot 'em. Put them on the other end of a gun and see what happens then. Like those who do fox hunting, give them a couple of minutes head start and see how they feel. (35)

This distaste for violence was reflected in the post-war lives of so many soldiers. Few had been excessively brutalised by war, instead most were ready to enjoy the quietest possible life. Most learned to appreciate home life, realising most day-to-day problems were minute compared to the horrors of war. A comfortable bed, chairs to sit in and home cooking are appreciated by men who realise how lucky they were to survive.

Those who endured life at the front could be forgiven for thinking the conflict portrayed in books and films since 1945 was very different from the war they knew. For all the efforts of the soldiers the mainstream media has all but ignored much of the campaign – distilling the contribution of the British and Canadians to little more than D-Day and Market Garden. Few films, novels or TV dramas have focused on the campaign, instead concentrating on dramatic tales of spies, code-breakers and POW escapes. The failure to promote the scale of 21st Army Group's role in the victory comes from the lack of serious literature on the subject and without obvious cultural reference points to look to, the general public became unable to perceive the reality of war. Whilst factual memoirs have been many, there have been few novels relating to the British role. Those few novels of the period are mainly forgotten and there exist no works that have won the critical acclaim of the novels and poetry of the First World War.

Only one author wrote of the conflict in north-west Europe with an accuracy and honesty that won the attention of readers and the admiration of his peers. Alexander Baron served as a Pioneer in Sicily, Italy, France and Belgium, landing with a Beach Group on D-Day. Baron came to the public's attention with the 1947 publication of his novel *From the City, From the Plough* – a depiction of fighting in Normandy as experienced by a fictional Wessex battalion. His heroes were not members of an elite unit but average men in an average battalion. Baron based the novel on his own observations of life within the Normandy bridgehead and on tales he heard whilst undergoing infantry training that winter. Much of what he wrote of D-Day was taken directly from his own recollections but in rereading his work he realised what he had written had actually replaced his own memories, as if the cathartic experience of writing about war had erased much he wished to forget. The novel was an instant success, eventually selling over a million copies worldwide.

Acclaimed by reviewers and fellow novelists it became one of the few war novels to earn the praise of veterans who recognised its realistic portrayal of life and death. Men of the 5th Wiltshires wrote to the author stating they recognised Baron's 5th Wessex as their own unit, readily identifying with fictional characters that mirrored men they had served with.

Baron followed this success with a collection of short stories published under the title *The Human Kind*. The stories were brief glimpses of the lives of servicemen with Baron plundering from personal experiences and observations of his comrades' lives. It was a subdued and somewhat melancholic portrait, perfectly capturing the mood of the time. Of all the books Baron penned during his career *The Human Kind* was the only one adapted for the cinema. Here came the twist. By the time it was adapted for the screen the title was changed to *The Victors*. To Baron's eternal regret his affectionate portrayal of the men he had served alongside was brushed aside, his characters did not wear khaki battledress but olive drab – the uniform of American GIs. In an effort to appeal to the US market the film makers cast aside the very essence of the historical basis for the film and made all the characters Americans.

This failure of film makers fully to appreciate and reflect the role of British and Canadian troops in the final defeat of the Nazis was influenced by one important factor – the dominance of Hollywood. The American film industry had its own heroes to bring to celluloid and had little need or reason to import Allied heroes. Consequently most major war films have been dominated by the American role. Hollywood's dominance did not excuse the failure of British film makers to cover the European campaign. There were numerous films about the RAF and Royal Navy, or about the war in North Africa and Burma, but almost none about the ground war from D-Day to VE Day. Instead the public watched POW dramas, such has *The Wooden Horse* or *The Colditz Story*, depicting a war unknown to the average soldier. Despite the popularity of the escape stories, few former POWs could take them seriously. Many found these films unwatchable. The 'holiday camp' environment where inmates do good-natured battle with their guards and live to plot escapes, bears little or no resemblance to reality, failing to record the misery, boredom and deprivation.

A similar reaction is given to American-made films. Few found Hollywood's output matched their memories and recognised little on the celluloid battlefields. The soldiers' aggressiveness depicted in many films, failed to ring true. Dr Ken Tout explained: '*The Dirty Dozen* features criminals being recruited from prisons because only they would be tough enough to carry out the most desperate missions. In fact, front line heroes were usually the quiet guys. Braggarts and petty criminals knew how to escape and were not around when the crunch came.' (36) However some veterans reserve a sneaking affection for *Kelly's Heroes* – the story of American troops stealing gold from a bank. Although seeming ridiculous it mirrored the looting and theft carried out by many. As Ken Squires noted: 'A lot of it is very true. It was hilarious, but we were doing exactly the same sort of things. I remember going down a train tunnel in the tank, thinking "what the bloody hell's going to happen when we get to the other end?" So you put a few HE shells down in front of you as you were going along.' (37)

If the public were unready to accept the roguish reality of war few could have been prepared for the literature that emerged in the 1970s when a series of books became popular that showed war in all its gory details. The only problem was that the heroes were no longer from the Allied armies.

A string of hyper-realistic war novels emerged from the pens of writers such as

Sven Hassell and Leo Kessler. Both wrote of the war from the German perspective, often on the Russian front. Hassell's books originally appeared in the late 1950s, when he wrote of his experiences as a Dane in the German army. His first efforts were well received, as they focused on the horrors of war. However, later books became ridiculous. The cast of characters – some of whom had died in the original book – were seen fighting throughout Europe, always escaping by the skin of their teeth. The action went from Paris to Stalingrad, from Warsaw to Bulgaria, with each tale seemingly more ridiculous than the last.

Normandy veteran Dr Ken Tout was one of those dismayed by the lack of accurate literature about war. Ironically he could remember the words of a captured German: 'knowing the British ability for self criticism, it is quite likely that your future generations will cast you as the villains,…. And turn even to our SS for their heroes!' (38) Now the German had been proved right, Tout set out to redress the balance. Yet when he approached publishers with the manuscript of a novel he was shocked by their response. In the light of the success of books showing the war from a German perspective, Tout felt there must be a place for similarly realistic books about British tank crews. His completed novel was rejected by numerous editors who thought such things never happened to British soldiers and if published, readers would find them unbelievable. In face of such ignorance Tout tore up his manuscript and concentrated on writing his memoirs.

Only in the 1990s did veterans finally find dramas to which they could relate. Films like *Saving Private Ryan* and *Band of Brothers* were lauded for achieving a realistic recreation of combat. Veteran signaller Len Bennett recalled how these films: 'very effectively bring out the atmosphere of war – the squalor, the realistic way men fold when hit, the fear and loneliness, the tension of quietness with unknown danger there somewhere, and the horrific nature of wounds caused by high explosive and projectiles. Few others I have seen really match those.' (39)

It was not only the media that helped mask the reality of the British efforts. The image of the campaign suffered much at the hands of its participants. Many veterans remained reticent to talk of their role, unwilling to see themselves as heroes, and unprepared to accept they did more than 'their job'. The traditional British reserve can be seen to contrast with the excess and hyperbole with which some, in particular those in Hollywood, viewed their role in defeating Hitler. That is not to say either faction was right or wrong, simply that the more vividly presented view of history had an obvious attraction for outsiders. For all their desire to downplay their role in the war most veterans felt nostalgic about their experiences. The camaraderie of the war years left them realising what was lacking in civilian life. As civilians they lost the sense of belonging – that their platoon or crew was a new family. It was an allegiance born of blood and these ties were hard to break.

Only those who had shared their experiences could appreciate this depth of feeling, and many returning soldiers felt unable to talk about war with outsiders. This need to belong drew many veterans towards Old Comrades Associations and the British Legion. In such groups they could relive the feeling of group identity that had sustained them through the traumas of war. This bond caused many veterans to try to locate former comrades who had never bothered to attend reunions. Some they had little hope of finding, including those who deserted to live with Continental girlfriends. Most could be located easily with little more than a name and the telephone directory for their hometown. Efforts to find others proved fruitless, with some deliberately avoiding contact. There were many reasons why they didn't want to be contacted by former colleagues. Some had happily moved on and had no desire to look back to the war years. Others were frightened of reawakening long-suppressed memories and restarting the terrifying nightmares. Joe Ekins was among those who long avoided reunions. Distinct among his comrades, he had been responsible for a remarkable feat – the destruction of three Tiger tanks in a single action, including one containing the legendary SS tank ace Michael Wittmann. Post-war historians made much of the incident yet Ekins was loath to take credit for it. He explained his reasons:

> After the war I came back and I'd done six years. I was still young. I thought every-thing was going to be good. Wars were finished forever, we could pack up making guns. After a few years I was approached about what I'd done. But I'd seen what had happened and I considered that I'd wasted six years of my life. 'Cause the first thing that happened was that Krupp got their bloody factories back. Just years after the war. The bloke who'd been making all the bombs they'd been dropping on us, you know – the very reason we'd gone out there. Wars don't do any good, they got rid of Hitler, but Stalin was still there. I still think wars aren't a sensible way of doing things. So quite frankly I was really sick of it. I gave me kid the medals to play with. I thought nothing had happened that was any good. Then suddenly up came the sto-ries about the death of Wittmann. One of our blokes decided our regiment was going to get the honour – if it is an honour. But I was still in the same frame of mind – the local paper rang me up and said they wanted a photo of me. What they wanted to do was stick him on one side and me on the other, like a duel. The CO and Sergeant Major phoned me, they all wanted me to tell the story. I wouldn't do it. Ever since then, I've been approached maybe twenty times by people wanting me to talk about it. People started to write books about it but they were writing things that weren't right at all. Then Ken Tout came along and he said he was going to write the story and do it properly. I decided if that was the case I'd do it.

Although Ekins decided to tell his story he still felt no real hatred for the man he killed, nor did he want anyone to feel it was a personal battle between two men. All he wanted was for the truth to be told:

> After the war I didn't hate the Germans, as long as they aren't trying to kill you. I've felt more about it having watched films of their crimes than I did at the time. I think I'd have felt more if I'd known what were going on. 'Cause the Germans must've known what was going on. They say they didn't but they must've. You see a lot of people on TV who were very close to Hitler. I hate these people. They must've known what was going on. I hate them far more than I did the Germans back then in the war. I didn't realise the chap I'd killed was as bad as that, when the papers came on to me I said 'I'm not proud of what I've done.' (40)

To this day veterans regularly attend reunions across the country. These events can be times of humour and emotion. The entry of each man is a chance for his former comrades to assess how time has treated him. Meeting again for the first time in many years can be an intense shock. Some recognise their old mates immediately, spotting those whom time has left unaltered. Men who have kept their hair or never gained weight are instantly greeted with nicknames they haven't heard for years. Others find themselves forgotten, unrecognised faces from a time when a friendly face meant everything to them. Even now a gulf remains between those who served in the front lines and those who served in the rear. The front line veterans continue to light-heartedly rib them about their cushy lives, as one veteran explained:

> The poofs! We still call them that. We've got a bloke and all he can talk about is when he was billeted in Holland and Belgium. We were never billeted, we didn't know what he was talking about. But he was part of the back up – the B echelon. We make fun of him but we don't blame him. He was there, he did his job. Why was he living in a house? The shops were open! Where the bloody hell had he been? He must be winding us up. He talks about the war but – the poor bugger – I don't think he ever saw a shell let alone fire one. He was certainly in a different war to us! (41)

Reunions are often marked by another type of humour. Once among their own veterans laugh about death in the way they did years before:

> We still do the black humour. At every meeting someone will come up with some black stuff about somebody dying. That's the way with a British person anyway. This is how we survive. It's the same whenever we're together. Outsiders might talk about money or politics, but we would immediately come up with some stupid remark. I can't explain it, but it's still there, but it's only among our type of people – people who were in the war. If someone fell down and broke his bloody neck, you'd laugh at him. It's a way of getting over it. Maybe that's what the mind is doing, it's doing us a favour by going to these extremes. Because some of it is extreme. But there's no thought behind it, it's just a way of living. (42)

The depth of camaraderie is such that few attending reunions have ever witnessed rancour between former comrades. Michael Hunt recalled:

> Sixty years on those of us who are left are all good mates. I don't think I've ever heard a cross word amongst the comrades, and there are a lot of hard drinkers among them, but there is never any animosity. It's always a laugh. There have only been a couple of incidents, about ten years after the war a chap who had deliberately stopped his tank and pretended to have run out of petrol – an act that cost the life of one of the chaps – turned up for a reunion banquet. And one of the ex-corporals went berserk, he ordered the chap out of the drill hall. And he got him out. (43)

Occasionally veterans have used such events to exact revenge for unforgotten incidents. One recalled attending a post-war reunion at which he was greeted by his wartime nemesis – an officer who had put him on a charge for supposedly having sworn at a senior NCO. He remained bitter about his treatment:

> This sergeant came and told me I was on a charge for having swo rn at him. He said I'd
> told him to F-off. I did a week in 'clink' for that. Years later we went to a reunion in
> London and the major was at the door. He stood at the door, welcoming all the troops
> and shaking hands with them. The major went to shake my hand and I told him exact-
> ly the same as I was supposed to have said before. I told him to F-off! It was ve ry rude
> of me, but I was hurt they'd put me on a charge for something I never did. (44)

For some outsiders these organisations appear militaristic, celebrating war in an age when war has become unfashionable, but for the veterans nothing could be further from the truth. Some might loudly proclaim their martial deeds, but they are a minority. Instead most concentrate on recounting comical incidents, or chat of the good times they shared and friends they lost. After a few beers some might become maudlin, others increasingly expressive – admitting to acts of violence that would shock their families. They reminisce tenderly of wartime girlfriends, or laugh about the whores they bought for the price of a tin of coffee.

Revisiting the battlefields of their youth has also become important. For some the opportunity came in the immediate post-war world. Whether hoping to lay to rest their ghosts or merely wishing to show their wives the scene of their exploits, some men made the trip back to Europe. Armed with their cameras they recorded the places that meant so much to them. In the immediate post-war years there was much to remind them of their travels – the rusting hulks of abandoned tanks, buildings bearing the scars of battle, and abandoned slit trenches all marked the route of the advance.

Time may have healed these physical scars but it can not erase the memories of those who fought there. Most left a part of themselves on those battlefields. For many the loss had been physical – suffering wounds that dogged their civilian lives. Most had lost close friends and few could not claim to have lost their inno-cence in the fury of war. Good or bad, the battlefields of Europe were where their characters had been shaped. This was what drove them back.

At first return trips were haphazard but as time passed they became more organ-ised. Once retired the veterans found time on their hands. Freed from the respon-sibility of full time employment they could reflect on their lives and remember their youthful experiences and regimental groups, the British Legion, and organi-sations such as the Normandy Veterans Association all started to offer trips to their members.

For the organisers 6 June 1994 was a turning point. John Majendie, who acted as a guide on battlefield tours remembered:

> Ever since the fiftieth anniversary far more people are going back to France. Some
> people won't miss an opportunity to go back and yet for years they didn't bother
> about it. Hardly a day goes by without thinking about Normandy, about what hap-
> pened to oneself and so on. I used to be quite surprised by people who didn't want to
> go back. I can understand people, when they finally did go back and being so shat-
> tered by the memories, they said never again. But for people who disregard it and say

'Ok I was a soldier, I'm not a soldier anymore' and forget about it – to me that would have been very difficult. (45)

Ken Hardy was one of those who made his first trip back for the fiftieth anniversary. The return visit brought back memories of the friend he had watched die:

> For years and years I never thought about the war at all. I forgot it had ever happened, I never thought about it at all. And then along came the fiftieth anniversary and it all came streaming back to me. I don't think I had ever forgotten Stan Hume, but suddenly his death became tremendously intense. I go up to see his grave as often as I can. It's deeply moving. Partly because I was leading a very busy life I didn't have a lot of time to think about these things. I think that I do regret that I went on with my life ambitiously and competitively, because at that point I didn't think an awful lot about Stan. I don't think I was being ambitious to try to forget, I just forgot. It was only when work came to an end that I thought about him. (46)

Visits to the graves of their fallen comrades are the centrepiece of their trips. These are private moments, a time for solitude, to put away the cameras and stop the jokes. Usually in silence, often in tears, they walk along the lines of graves until they find the names they are searching for. Then for a few moments their minds go back. They don't see a stone with its engraved badge, name and number. They see the man. They remember the good times and the bad, the laughter and the fear – and above all they ask 'Why?'

Returning to specific locations can be an eerie experience. Just to see the same buildings and hedgerows that once struck fear into their hearts can conjure ghosts of the past they thought had long been suppressed. Artillery veteran John Mercer made a number of return journeys to the battlefields:

> I've been back to Normandy twice. I actually found my old gun positions where we had dug out the gun emplacements in an orchard. Then in 1993 I went on a tour of Operation Goodwood. I must admit I felt very peculiar there. I had the shivers. When you went outside our hotel you could see the big ironworks at Colombelles. The towers had dominated the area completely, and they were still there! The Germans had observed us from there. That was how we lost our men in their counter battery fire. It was uncanny. I didn't like that. (47)

While return trips are a personal pilgrimage, the act of visiting memorials fails to keep alive the public appreciation of their achievements. For many veterans the greatest fear is their endeavours will soon be forgotten. Some try to prevent this by teaching children about their experiences. In a world in which for many people war is something that can be escaped from by simply pressing a pause button on a games console, some old soldiers try to make a positive contribution to the public's understanding of its realities. One group have used their time to share their knowledge of war with a new generation of schoolchildren. The men of the Norfolk branch of the Normandy Veterans Association have tried to educate children via their School Visiting Team. The group was started by Royal Corps of Signals veteran Redmond Broderick, a man described by his local newspaper at the time of his death as a 'pioneering preacher of peace'. Since the late 1980s they have made regular visits to schools to keep alive the memory of the suffering endured in wartime. The title of the project illustrates their message: 'There is no glory in war'. Eric Davies explained their methods:

> We go into assembly and sit in front and join in either singing or prayers. The head will introduce us and then hand over to our spokesman who explains why we are at the school, and give a short resume of the job done by each one of us in the war. We then break up into groups, swapping over so the children get a chance to talk to each of us and get to examine the bits and pieces of memorabilia we take along. Our aim is to make children aware of the futility of war and that with few exceptions it is not as portrayed on the cinema or on TV. (48)

The veterans discuss their war experiences with the children. Proudly, they show gas masks, helmets, mess tins, photographs of weapons and medals. Often the children's perception of the conflict is challenged. Sometimes they ask 'Did you meet Hitler?', 'How many people did you kill?', or 'Did you know my granddad, he was in the war?' But above all they listen and they learn. They learn of fear, death and the unifying bonds of comradeship. The tales they hear are of hungry, tired, fed up, miserable men, who day by day motivated themselves to keep going in face of overwhelming odds against the hope of survival. They learn of how soldiers on both sides were just ordinary men, doing an extraordinary and unenviable task.

Former paratrooper Eric 'Bill' Sykes is another veteran who attempts to educate about the reality of war by answering questions from schoolchildren. In doing so he is attempting to repeat the education given him by his own father in the 1930s: 'I had seen some war films including one that my father had taken me to see as a very young boy... *All Quiet On The Western Front*, which shows in detail the horrors of war in the trenches. I think my Father's objective was the same as mine is today, to show the youth of your generation that war is not full of heroics like John Wayne dashing up a hill to plant a flag. War is bloodshed and killing.' (49)

These veterans have much to offer the world. They know the realities of war and have been able to use it for good. Thousands of other veterans, who learnt more about their fellow human beings by watching their behaviour than could ever be learnt from books, have been able to remain positive about the experience. Looking back they are proud, both of themselves and their entire generation. It may be a pride that appears unfashionable to outsiders — but it has sustained them through years of hardship and trauma.

From this sense of pride springs the right to complain, the right to feel bitter about how society has treated them. The problems of war pensions, disability rights, standards of hospital care – all things the veterans feel they fought for – aggrieves them. Many of the generation who won victory now feel cheated. Some feel society – the state, the government – has taken the credit for the victory without fully repaying or protecting those who suffered. Harry Free, who served through the campaign, is among them:

I feel quite cynical about what's happened since the war. I believe that it is totally wrong that they should be dependent on charities like the Poppy Day appeal. Leaving wreaths in memory of those who have died is sentimental and does nothing for the men who survived. They're not valued as they should be. The countries that lost the war provide more for their ex-servicemen than our government has done. I believe soldiers gave their lives so that people could have their freedom today. I think parades – at the Cenotaph etc – are hypocritical. I've never had any time for them. People who fought in the war can sit at home and remember their fallen mates quietly and in private without the hullabaloo and all the superficiality organised by 'nobs' who've never fired a gun in their lives. I think that soldiers are used as tools – bureaucrats who have no experience of war make decisions and gamble with other people's lives. After they've gambled, those remaining are forgotten and some have to depend on charity to survive. I think that young people today looking back at what's happened to ex-servicemen wouldn't come out and fight for their country. (50)

With their memories of war few veterans could not claim to have lived an interesting life. As they grow old and look back at those times their minds are awash with emotions, some good some bad – camaraderie and loss, laughter and tears, violence and love, terror and relief, achievement and bereavement. Of all these it is the sadness that endures. From the lowliest rifleman to the mightiest general, all know what it feels like to live with the memory of the loss of their closest friends.

Perhaps it is suitable to end on the words of Lance Sergeant A.G. Herbert who in the post-war years endured long courses of electric shock therapy in an attempt to return to 'what passes as normal'. He was one of those who suffered and would never forget, and later wrote: 'I have seldom attended a Remembrance Day parade. Every day is remembrance day for me. I shall never forget my lost friends.' (51)

Notes

CHAPTER 1 The Landscape of Battle

1   Anonymous – Interview.
2   Wilf Allen – Letter to author.
3   Anonymous – Interview.
4   John Majendie – Interview.
5   Arthur Rowley – Letter to author.
6   Arthur Jarvis – Interview.
7   Anonymous – Interview.
8   Anonymous – Interview.
9   Public Record Office - WO171/177.
10 Ken Hardy – Interview.
11 Anonymous – Interview.
12 Public Record Office - WO205/422.
13 Public Record Office - WO 171/5275.
14 Public Record Office - WO 205/422.
15 *18 Platoon* – Sydney Jary (Sydney Jary Ltd 1987)
16 *The Lonely Leader Monty 1944-5* – Alistair Horne (Macmillan 1994)
17 Wilf Allen – Letter to author.
18 *Mailed Fist* – John Foley (Panther 1957)
19 Public Record Office - WO 205/422.

CHAPTER 2 The Ordinary Men

1   Alexander Baron – Letter to family, May 1944.
2   *From the City, From the Plough* – Alexander Baron, (Jonathan Cape 1948)
3   John Mercer – Interview.
4   Len Bennett – Interview.
5   *The Guns of Victory* – George Blackburn (Constable & Robinson 2000)
6   *Articles of War- The Spectator Book of World War II* (Grafton Books 1989)
7   Anonymous – Interview.
8   Anonymous – Interview.
9   Len Bennett – Interview.
10 Arthur Jarvis – Interview.
11 *Letters Home* – Brian Johnston (Weidenfeld and Nicholson 1998)
12 Joe Ekins – Interview.
13 Stan Procter – Interview.
14 Alexander Baron – Unpublished memoirs.
15 Colonel John Waddy – Letter to author.
16 John Majendie – Interview.
17 *Accidental Journey* – Mark Lynton (Overlook Press 1995)
18 *Accidental Journey* – Mark Lynton (Overlook Press 1995)
19 Sydney Jary – Letter to author.
20 John Majendie – Interview.
21 Ken Hardy – Interview.
22 Ken Hardy – Interview.
23 Len Bennett – Interview.
24 Quoted in *Monty's Marauders* – Patrick Delaforce (Sutton 1993)

25 Quoted in *The D-Day Landings* – Philip Warner (William Kimber 1980)
26 Dr Ken Tout – Letter to author.
27 Dr Ken Tout – Letter to author.
28 Alexander Baron – Letter to family, June 1944.
29 *The Whitelaw Memoirs* – Willie Whitelaw (Aurum Press 1989)
30 *A Full Life* – Lieutenant General Sir Brian Horrocks (Collins 1960)
31 *Tank* – Ken Tout (Sphere Books 1986)
32 Reproduced from *Reflect On Things Past* by Lord Carrington (Copyright Lord Carrington 1988) by permission of PFD on behalf of Lord Carrington.
33 Public Record Office - WO171/139.
34 Michael Hunt & Ken Squires – Interview.
35 Stan Procter – Interview.
36 *Tank* – Ken Tout (Sphere Books 1986)
37 Andrew Charles – Imperial War Museum - 99/46/1.
38 William Partridge – Letter to author.
39 Anonymous – Interview.
40 Ken Hardy – Interview.
41 *Arnhem Spearhead* – James Sims (Imperial War Museum 1978)
42 James Sims – Letter to author.
43 Les Toogood – Interview.
44 Anonymous – Interview.
45 *Argument of Kings* – Vernon Scannel (Robson Books 1987)
46 Michael Hunt – Interview.
47 Public Record Office - WO285/18.
48 Anonymous – Interview.
49 William Partridge – Letter to author.
50 John Majendie – Interview.
51 Ken Hardy – Interview.
52 Anonymous – Interview.
53 Joe Ekins – Interview.
54 Arthur Jarvis – Letter to author.
55 Anonymous – Interview.
56 John Majendie – Interview.
57 William Partridge – Letter to author.
58 John Mercer – Interview.
59 Eric 'Bill' Sykes – Letter to author.
60 Dr Ken Tout – Letter to author.
61 R.G. Mead – Letter to author.
62 Anonymous – Interview.
63 Sydney Jary – Letter to author.
64 Harry Free – Letter to author.
65 *The 8.15 to War* Peter Roach (Leo Cooper 1982)
66 Anonymous – Conversation.
67 Anonymous – Interview.

CHAPTER 3 Dutch Courage and the Calvados Campaign
1 Joe Ekins – Interview.
2 Public Record Office - WO171/281.
3 Joe Ekins – Interview.
4 Joe Ekins – Interview.
5 *The Commandos - D Day And After* – Donald Gilchrist (Robert Hale 1982)

6   *Summon Up The Blood* – J. A. Womack & Celia Wolfe (Leo Cooper 1997)
7   Ken Squires – Interview.
8   Jack Oakley – Diary.
9   *Tanks Advance* – Ken Tout (Robert Hale 1987)
10 *Reflect On Things Past* – Lord Carrington (Collins 1988)
11 Ken Squires – Interview.
12 Ken Hardy – Interview.
13 Ken Hardy – Interview.
14 Michael Hunt – Interview.
15 Ken Squires – Interview.
16 G. Worthington – Letter to author.
17 Ken Squires – Interview.
18 Fred 'Vic' Sylvester – Letter to author.
19 Wilf Allen – Letter to author.
20 *Flame Thrower* – Andrew Wilson (William Kimber 1956)
21 Public Record Office - WO71/1103.
22 *A Quiet Little Boy Goes To War* – Stan Procter (Privately printed 1997)
23 *A Territorial Army Chaplain in Peace and War* – Eric Gethyn Jones (Gooday 1988)
24 James Sims – Letter to author.
25 *2500 Dangerous Days* – Patrick P.J. Bracken (Merlin Books 1998)
26 Joe Ekins – Interview.
27 Ken Hardy – Interview.

CHAPTER 4 Sex Conquers Orders
1   Roy Merrett – Letter to author.
2   Ken Squires – Interview.
3   Alexander Baron – Unpublished memoirs.
4   *The Past is always Present* – Doug Colls – Unpublished memoirs.
5   R.H. Lloyd Jones – Imperial War Museum - 89/1/1
6   Dr Ken Tout – Letter to author.
7   John Mercer – Interview.
8   *A Quiet Little Boy Goes To War* – Stan Procter (Privately printed 1997)
9   Michael Hunt – Interview.
10 Ken Squires – Interview.
11 Anonymous – Interview.
12 John Reynolds – Interview.
13 Ken Squires – Interview.
14 Harry Free – Letter to author.
15 *Tanks Advance* – Ken Tout (Robert Hale 1987)
16 Public Record Office - WO171/281.
17 Public Record Office - WO222/275.
18 Harry Free – Letter to author.
19 Harry Free – Letter to author.
20 Alexander Baron – Unpublished memoirs.
21 Major A.J. Forrest – Imperial War Museum - 91/13/1.
22 'Spearhead' – The newsletter of the 43rd Reconaissance Regiment Old Comrades Association.
23 Public Record Office - WO171/4456.
24 Public Record Office - WO171/167.
25 Public Record Office - WO171/3379.
26 Captain R. Barer – Imperial War Museum - 93/11/1.

27 Ken Squires – Interview.
28 Ken Squires – Interview.
29 Ken Squires – Interview.
30 Jack Oakley – Diary.

CHAPTER 5 A Little Bit of Frat
1 Letter from Field Marshal Montgomery given to troops before the crossing of the Rhine, March 1945.
2 *Report From Germany* – Leonard O. Mosley (Victor Gollancz 1945)
3 *A Territorial Army Chaplain in Peace and War* – Eric Gethyn Jones (Gooday 1988)
4 Lieutenant Colonel W.S. Brownlie – Imperial War Museum - 92/37/1.
5 *Monty - The Field Marshal* – Nigel Hamilton (Hamish Hamilton 1986)
6 *A Quiet Little Boy Goes To War* – Stan Procter (Privately printed 1997)
7 Public Record Office - WO171/5275.
8 Anonymous – Interview.
9 Anonymous – Interview.
10 Les Toogood – Interview.
11 Anonymous – Interview.
12 Lieutenant Colonel W.S. Brownlie – Imperial War Museum - 92/37/1.
13 Public Record Office - WO171/5170.
14 Major Douglas Goddard – Diary.
15 Major Douglas Goddard – Letter to author.
16 *Leakey's Luck - A Tank Commander With Nine Lives* – Rea Leakey & George Forty (Sutton 1999)
17 *1100 Miles With Monty* – Norman Kirby (Sutton 1989)
18 The Reverend C. Cullingford – Imperial War Museum – 90/6/1.
19 *Report From Germany* – Leonard O. Mosley (Victor Gollancz 1945)
20 Lieutenant Colonel W.S. Brownlie – Imperial War Museum - 92/37/1.
21 Public Record Office - WO171/4143.
22 Wilf Allen – Letter to author.
23 Les Toogood – Interview.
24 Alec Simons – Letter to author.
25 Fred Sylvester – Letter to author.
26 Public Record Office - WO 205/275.
27 Ken Hardy – Interview.
28 Stan Procter – Interview.
29 Harry Free – Letter to author.
30 Roy Merrett – Letter to author.
31 John Longfield – Interview.
32 Lord Boardman – Letter to author.
33 Joe Ekins – Interview.
34 Ken Moore – Interview.
35 Harry Free – Letter to author.
36 Joe Ekins – Interview.
37 *A Trooper's Tale* – Jack Woods – Unpublished memoirs.

CHAPTER 6 Home Comforts
1 *Tank* – Ken Tout (Sphere Books 1986)
2 Public Record Office - WO205/422.
3 Arthur Jarvis – Letter to author.
4 Ken Hardy – Interview.

5   *Tank* – Ken Tout (Sphere Books 1986)

6   John Mercer – Interview.

7   Major Douglas Goddard – Letter to author.

8   William Partridge – Letter to author.

9   Alexander Baron – Letter to family, summer 1944.

10 Ken Squires – Interview.

11 Anonymous – Interview.

12 John Mercer – Interview.

13 John Mercer – Interview.

14 G. Worthington – Letter to author.

15 Michael Hunt – Interview.

16 John Reynolds – Interview.

17 Leonard Bennett – Letter to author.

CHAPTER 7 Recreation

1   Fred Sylvester – Letter to author.

2   *A Quiet Little Boy Goes To War* – Stan Procter (Privately printed 1997)

3   *Psychology and the Soldier* – Norman Copeland (Allen & Unwin 1944)

4   Alexander Baron – Letter to family, May 1944.

5   *Triumph in the West -The Alanbrooke War Diaries* – Arthur Bryant (Collins 1959)

6   *War Diaries – Field Marshal Lord Alanbrooke* (Weidenfeld & Nicolson 2001)

7   *The Unfinished Man* – James Byrom (Chatto and Windus 1957)

8   *12th Wessex Field Regiment RA, TA 1938-1946* – Douglas Goddard (Privately printed 1997)

9   Harry Free – Letter to author.

10 Arthur Jarvis – Letter to author & Interview.

11 Ken Hardy – Interview.

12 Les Toogood – Interview.

13 Anonymous – Interview.

14 *A Signal War* – John Raycroft (Babblefish Press 2002)

15 Len Bennett – Letter to author.

16 Anonymous – Interview.

17 Len Bennett – Interview.

18 Anonymous – Interview.

19 John Majendie – Interview.

20 Anonymous – Interview.

21 *A Quiet Little Boy goes to War* – Stan Procter (Privately printed 1997)

22 Ken Hardy – Interview.

23 Harry Free – Letter to author.

24 John Mercer – Interview.

25 Alexander Baron – Unpublished memoirs.

26 *The Enemy Within* – John Watney (Hodder & Stoughton 1946)

27 *What Did You Do In The War Grandpa?* – Bob Price (Watermill Press 1989)

28 Stan Procter – Interview.

29 Stan Procter – Interview.

30 Stan Procter – Interview.

31 Ken Squires – Interview.

32 Roy Merrett – Letter to author.

33 *Flame Thrower* – Andrew Wilson (William Kimber 1956)

34 *Armoured Guardsmen* – Robert Boscawen (Leo Cooper 2001)

35 Joe Ekins – Interview.

36   Public Record Office - WO171/833.
37   Les Toogood – Interview.
38   Ken Hardy – Interview.
39   Alexander Baron – Unpublished memoirs.
40   *Robert Runcie, The Reluctant Archbishop* – Humphrey Carpenter (Hodder & Stoughton 1986)
41   Michael Hunt – Interview.
42   John Reynolds – Interview.
43   *Summon Up The Blood* – J. A. Womack & Celia Wolfe (Leo Cooper 1997)
44   Ian Hammerton – Letter to author.
45   Ken Hardy – Interview.
46   *A Quiet Little Boy Goes To War* – Stan Procter (Privately printed 1997)
47   John Groves – Letter to author.

CHAPTER 8 A Man in Uniform
1   Alexander Baron – Unpublished memoirs.
2   Harry Free – Letter to author.
3   Anonymous – Interview.
4   Len Bennett – Interview.
5   Alexander Baron – Unpublished memoirs.
6   William Partridge – Letter to author.
7   Public Record Office - WO171/4475.
8   Anonymous – Interview.
9   John Mercer – Interview.
10   John Mercer – Interview.
11   John Reynolds – Interview.
12   Ken Hardy – Interview.
13   Joe Ekins – Interview.
14   *Tank* – Ken Tout (Sphere Books 1986)
15   Dr Ken Tout – Letter to author.
16   Ken Squires – Interview.
17   John Majendie – Interview.
18   Ken Hardy – Interview.
19   Sydney Jary – Letter to author.
20   Anonymous – Interview.
21   Public Record Office - WO171/5171.
22   Harry Free – Letter to author.
23   *Gunner Green's War* – L.J. Green (The Pentland Press 1999)
24   Wilf Allen – Letter to author.

CHAPTER 9 Too Scared to be Frightened
1   Public Record Office - WO171/7805.
2   Arthur Jarvis – Letter to author.
3   Alexander Baron – Unpublished memoirs.
4   Captain M. Bendix – Imperial War Museum - 98/3/1.
5   Anonymous – Interview.
6   G. Worthington – Letter to author.
7   Ken Squires – Interview.
8   John Majendie – Interview.
9   Anonymous – Interview.
10   Ken Hardy – Interview.

11   A.G. Herbert – Imperial War Museum - 98/16/1.
12   *Psychology and the Soldier* – Norman Copeland (Allen & Unwin 1944)
13   Major Douglas Goddard – Letter to author.
14   Anonymous – Interview.
15   John Majendie – Interview.
16   Ian Hammerton – Letter to author.
17   Joe Ekins – Interview.
18   Fred Sylvester – Letter to author.
19   Public Record Office – WO71/902.
20   William Partridge – Letter to author.
21   Anonymous – Interview.
22   Eric Sykes – Letter to author.
23   *18 Platoon* – Sydney Jary (Sydney Jary Ltd 1987)
24   Arthur Rowley – Letter to author.
25   Harry Free – Letter to author.
26   G. Worthington – Letter to author.
27   Alexander Baron – Unpublished memoirs.
28   William Partridge – Letter to author.
29   Major A.J. Forrest – Imperial War Museum - 91/13/1.
30   Ken Hardy – Interview.
31   Public Record Office - WO71/948.
32   Ken Hardy – Interview.
33   John Reynolds – Interview.
34   John Majendie – Interview.
35   *A Quiet Little Boy Goes To War* – Stan Procter (Privately printed 1997)
36   John Majendie – Interview.
37   *Fear is the Foe* – Stan Whitehouse & George Bennett (Robert Hale 1995)
38   Public Record Office - WO71/911.
39   Public Record Office - WO171/139.
40   Public Record Office - WO222/275.
41   Arthur Rowley – Letter to author.
42   Public Record Office - WO285/25.
43   Public Record Office - WO222/275.
44   Anonymous – Interview.
45   Public Record Office - WO222/275.

CHAPTER 10 Burglary was not a Reserved Occupation
1   Public Record Office - WO171/7805.
2   Public Record Office - WO84/70.
3   Public Record Office - WO171/7821.
4   Leonard Bennett – Interview with author.
5   Anonymous – Interview with author.
6   John Reynolds – Interview with author.
7   Arthur Jarvis – Interview with author.
8   Anonymous – Interview with author.
9   Ken Hardy – Interview with author.
10   William Partridge – Letter to author.
11   Arthur Jarvis – Interview with author.
12   Jack Oakley – Diary.
13   Alexander Baron – Unpublished memoirs.
14   Anonymous – Interview with author.

15   Jack Oakley – Diary.
16   Colonel John Waddy – Letter to author.
17   Ken Hardy – Interview with author.
18   Fred 'Vic' Sylvester – Letter to author.
19   Anonymous – Interview with author.
20   Public Record Office - WO171/3708.
21   Public Record Office - WO171/3708.
22   Public Record Office - WO71/919.
23   John Reynolds – Interview with author.
24   John Majendie – Interview with author.
25   Public Record Office - WO171/4475.
26   Public Record Office - WO171/4475.
27   Public Record Office - WO171/3414.
28   Anonymous – Interview with author.
29   Ken Squires – Interview with author.
30   Arthur Jarvis – Interview with author.
31   Story told to author at T Force/5th Kings Regiment reunion.
32   Public Record Office - WO171/3409.
33   Public Record Office - WO171/833.
34   Public Record Office - WO171/3410.
35   Public Record Office - WO71/1103.
36   Ken Squires – Interview with author.
37   John Longfield – Interview with author.
38   Public Record Office - WO171/3410.
39   Public Record Office - WO171/141.
40   Public Record Office - WO71/4240.
41   Public Record Office - WO171/7821.
42   Anonymous – Interview with author.
43   Public Record Office – WO171/7805

CHAPTER 11 The Khaki Locusts
1   Norman Farmer, 5th Kings Regiment, interviewed in Danish newspaper *Aarhus Stiftstindende* 20/5/45.
2   Arthur Rowley – Letter to author.
3   Alexander Baron – Unpublished memoirs.
4   Arthur Jarvis – Letter to author.
5   John Majendie – Interview.
6   *Tank* – Ken Tout (Sphere Books 1986)
7   Public Record Office - WO222/275.
8   Ken Squires – Interview.
9   Public Record Office - WO222/275.
10   Les Toogood – Interview.
12   Ken Hardy – Interview.
13   Ken Squires – Interview.
14   *Mailed Fist* – John Foley (Panther 1957)
15   *Sans Peur 5th Seaforth in WW2* – Alastair Borthwick (1946)
16   *So Few Got Through* – Martin Lindsay (Collins 1946)
17   John Mercer – Interview.
18   Les Toogood – Interview.
19   Ken Hardy – Interview.
20   *With the Jocks* – Peter White (Alan Sutton 2001)

CHAPTER 12 Operation Plunder

1   Ken Hardy – Interview.
2   John Majendie – Interview.
3   Public Record Office - WO171/3411.
4   Public Record Office - WO171/735.
5   *Arnhem Spearhead* – James Sims (Imperial War Museum 1978)
6   Public Record Office - WO171/177.
7   Wilf Allen – Letter to author.
8   Ken Squires – Interview.
9   'Normandy Star' – Norwich Normandy Veterans Association newsletter.
10 Ken Squires – Interview.
11 John Mercer – Interview.
12 *Sins of Commission* – William Douglas Home (Michael Russell 1985)
13 *The Forgotten Battle* – A. Korthals Altes (Spellmount 1995)
14 Public Record Office – WO171/177.
15 *A Territorial Army Chaplain in Peace and War* – Eric Gethyn Jones (Gooday 1988)
16 John Groves – Letter to author.
17 Public Record Office – WO171/7821.
18 Major Douglas Goddard – Diary.
19 Major A.J. Forrest – Imperial War Museum - 91/13/1.
20 Harry Free – Letter to author.
21 Stan Procter – Interview.
22 Wilf Allen – Letter to author.
23 Public Record Office - WO171/3916.
24 Ken Squires – Interview.
25 Ken Hardy – Interview.
26 *The Memoirs of Field Marshal Montgomery* (Collins 1958)
27 Public Record Office - WO171/5169.
28 John Reynolds – Interview.
29 John Mercer – Interview.
30 Stan Procter – Interview.
31 Public Record Office - CUST106/857.
32 Ken Hardy – Interview.
33 Public Record Office - CUST 106/847.

CHAPTER 13 A Masterpiece of Liberation

1   Leonard Bennett – Letter to author.
2   Alexander Baron – Unpublished memoirs.
3   *A Full Life* – Lieutentant General Sir Brian Horrocks (Collins 1960)
4   Ken Hardy – Interview.
5   John Mercer – Interview.
6   Michael Hunt and Ken Squires – Interview.
7   *Arnhem* – Major General R.E. Urquhart (Cassell 1958)
8   *Five Days In Hell* – Jack Smyth (William Kimber 1956)
9   Dr Ken Tout – Letter to author.
10 Joe Ekins – Interview.
11 Public Record Office - WO171/742.
12 Alexander Baron – Unpublished memoirs.
13 John Reynolds – Interview.
14 Public Record Office - WO171/4240.

15   John Groves – Letter to author.
16   Tom Gore – Imperial War Museum 99/85/1.
17   *Men Under Fire* – R.W. Thompson (Macdonald & Co)
18   Public Record Office - WO171/4690.
19   Public Record Office - WO171/4693.
20   Public Record Office - WO171/5257.
21   C.J. Charters – Imperial War Museum.

CHAPTER 14 Rage, Revenge and Retribution
1   Anonymous – Interview.
2   *44: In Combat From Normandy To The Ardennes* – Charles Whiting (Spellmount 2000)
3   Anonymous – Interview.
4   Arthur Jarvis – Interview.
5   Les Toogood – Interview.
6   Ken Hardy – Interview.
7   John Mercer – Interview.
8   *My Life* – Bert Hardy (Gordon Fraser 1985)
9   Les Toogood – Interview.
10   Anonymous – Interview.
11   Quoted in *Caen, Anvil of Victory* – Alexander Mckee (Souvenir Press 1964)
12   Quoted in *The Fighting Wessex Wyverns* – Patrick Delaforce (Alan Sutton 1994)
13   *Sins of Commission* – William Douglas Home (Michael Russell 1985)
14   Michael Hunt – Interview.
15   Ken Squires – Interview.
16   W.A. Blackman – Imperial War Museum 99/85/1.
17   Captain M. Bendix – Imperial War Museum 98/3/1.
18   Ken Hardy – Interview.
19   *Caen Anvil of Victory* – Alexander Mckee (Souvenir Press 1964)
20   John Majendie – Interview.
21   John Majendie – Interview.
22   Anonymous – Interview.
23   *18 Platoon* – Sydney Jary (Sydney Jary Ltd 1987)
24   Ken Squires – Interview.
25   Arthur Rowley – Letter to author.
26   Leonard Bennett – Interview.
27   Anonymous – Interview.
28   Anonymous – Interview.
29   Anonymous – Interview.
30   Anonymous – Interview.
31   *The Only Way Out* – R. M. Wingfield (Hutchinson 1955)
32   John Longfield – Interview.
33   *War From The Ground Up* – John Colby (Nortex Press 1991)
34   Les Toogood – Interview.
35   Quoted in *The Conquest of The Reich* – Robin Neillands (Weidenfeld and Nicholson 1995)
36   Quoted in *Churchill's Desert Rats* – Patrick Delaforce (Alan Sutton 1994)
37   *A Quiet Little Boy Goes To War* – Stan Procter (Privately printed 1997) & Interview.
38   John Reynolds – Interview.
39   *Daily Telegraph Story of The War* - David Marley (Hodder & Stoughton 1946)
40   *Eclipse* – Alan Moorehead (Hamish Hamilton 1945)

41   *Esprit De Corps* – W.A. Elliott (Michael Russell 1996)
42   Public Record Office – WO171/510.
43   *Eclipse* – Alan Moorehead (Hamish Hamilton 1945)
44   *Daily Mail* Letters Page 22/01/02
45   *Report From Germany* – Leonard O. Mosley (Victor Gollancz 1945)
46   Wilf Allen – Letter to author.
47   Patrick Delaforce – Letter to author.
48   Anonymous – Interview.
49   Captain R. Barer – Imperial War Museum 93/11/1.
50   Public Record Office – WO171/5275.
51   Public Record Office – WO171/5171.
52   Public Record Office – WO171/5275.
53   Interview at T Force/5th Kings Regiment Reunion.
54   Joe Ekins – Interview.
55   *Living History* – Chaim Herzog (Weidenfeld & Nicholson 1997)

CHAPTER 15 Life Behind the Wire

1   *The Past is Always Present* – Doug Colls - unpublished memoirs.
2   Eric 'Bill' Sykes – Letter to author.
3   John Mercer – Interview.
4   George Marsden – Letter to author.
5   James Sims – Letter to author.
6   Colonel John Waddy – Letter to author.
7   James Sims – Letter to author.
8   George Marsden – Letter to author.
9   George Marsden – Letter to author.
10   George Marsden – Letter to author.
11   Eric 'Bill' Sykes – Letter to author.
12   *The Past is Always Present* – Doug Colls - Unpublished memoirs.
13   George Marsden – Letter to author.
14   Eric 'Bill' Sykes – Letter to author.
15   Eric 'Bill' Sykes – Letter to author.
16   J.H. Witte – Imperial War Museum - 87/12/1.
17   Eric 'Bill' Sykes – Letter to author.
18   James Sims – Letter to author.
19   James Sims – Letter to author.
20   James Sims – Letter to author.

CHAPTER 16 The Gates Open

1   Jim Sims – Letter to author.
2   W.Bampton – Imperial War Museum - 94/49/1.
3   W.Bampton – Imperial War Museum - 94/49/1.
4   W.Bampton – Imperial War Museum - 94/49/1.
5   W.Bampton – Imperial War Museum - 94/49/1.
6   *The Guarded Years* – Douglas Baber (William Heinemann 1955)
7   Eric 'Bill' Sykes – Letter to author.
8   Public Record Office - WO205/193.
9   Jim Sims – Letter to author.
10   Eric 'Bill' Sykes – Letter to author.
11   Public Record Office - WO171/3872.
12   C.Baggs – Imperial War Museum.

13   Jim Sims – Letter to author.
14   J.H. Witte – Imperial War Museum 87/12/1.
15   Veronica Taylor – Letter to author.
16   *Picture Post* - 12/5/45.
17   *Travels with a Leros Veteran* – Pauline Bevan (PB Books 2000)
18   J. Sims – Imperial War Museum 83/52/1.
19   Doug Colls – Army release papers.
20   George Marsden – Letter to author.

CHAPTER 17 Victory – the Moment of Reckoning
1   Fred Sylvester – Letter to author.
2   Anonymous – Interview.
3   John Longfield – Interview.
4   Ken Hardy – Interview.
5   John Mercer – Interview.
6   Joe Ekins – Interview.
7   Patrick Delaforce – Letter to author.
8   Harry Free – Letter to author.
9   Alexander Baron – Letter to family, 13th April 1945.
10   Alexander Baron – Letter to family, late 1944.
11   John Mercer – Interview.
12   Public Record Office - WO285/12.
13   Les Toogood – Interview.
14   John Mercer – Interview.
15   Les Toogood – Interview.
16   Major A.J. Forrest – Imperial War Museum 91/13/1.
17   Major A.J. Forrest – Imperial War Museum 91/13/1.
18   Stan Procter – Interview.
19   Major Douglas Goddard – Letter to author.
20   Ian Hammerton – Letter to author.
21   Anonymous – Interview.
22   Wilf Allen – Letter to author.
23   Ken Moore – Interview.
24   Ken Hardy – Interview.
25   Harry Free – Letter to author.
26   John Groves – Letter to author.
27   Michael Hunt – Interview.
28   'Spearhead' – 43rd Reconnaissance Regiment Old Comrades Association newsletter.
29   Anonymous – Interview.
30   Fred Sylvester – Letter to author.
31   John Longfield – Interview.

CHAPTER 18 The Sadness Endures
1   Alexander Baron – Letter written home on first anniversary of D-Day.
2   Major Douglas Goddard – Letter to author.
3   Cyril Spencer – Letter to author.
4   Harry Free – Letter to author.
5   Ken Squires – Interview.
6   R.G. Mead – Letter to author.
7   Ken Hardy – Interview.
8   Interview at T Force/5th Kings Regiment Reunion.

9   J.Y. White – Imperial War Museum – 87/12/1.
10   Arthur Jarvis – Interview.
11   Arthur Jarvis – Interview.
12   John Mercer – Interview.
13   Alexander Baron – Unpublished memoirs.
14   Quoted in *Report From Germany* by Leonard Mosley.
15   Lord Boardman – Letter to author.
16   Arthur Heyworth – Letter to author.
17   John Mercer – Interview.
18   Ken Hardy – Interview.
19   Leonard Bennett – Interview and letter to author.
20   Arthur Jarvis – Letter to author.
21   Leonard Bennett – Interview.
22   Arthur Jarvis – Letter to author.
23   Eric 'Bill' Sykes – Letter to author.
24   *Gaol Delivery* – Mark Benney (Longmans, Green & Co 1948)
25   *Gaol Delivery* – Mark Benney (Longmans, Green & Co 1948)
26   John Majendie – Interview.
27   John Longfield – Interview.
28   Anonymous – Interview.
29   Harry Free – Letter to author.
30   Veronica Taylor – Letter to author.
31   George Marsden – Letter to author.
32   William Partridge – Letter to author.
33   Ken Hardy – Interview.
34   Stan Procter – Letter to author.
35   Anonymous story told at T-Force Reunion.
36   Dr Ken Tout – Letter to author.
37   Ken Squires – Interview.
38   *Tanks Advance* – Ken Tout (Robert Hale 1987)
39   Leonard Bennett – Letter to author.
40   Joe Ekins – Interview.
41   Leonard Bennett & Arthur Jarvis – Interview.
42   Anonymous – Interview.
43   Michael Hunt – Interview.
44   John Reynolds – Interview.
45   John Majendie – Interview.
46   Ken Hardy – Interview.
47   John Mercer – Interview.
48   Eric Davies – Letter to author.
49   Eric 'Bill' Sykes – Letter to author.
50   Harry Free – Letter to author.
51   A.G. Herbert – Imperial War Museum – 98/16/1.

Unpublished Sources

Imperial War Museum

From the Department of Documents the author accessed the following private papers:
T.Austin (92/31/1)
C.Baggs
W.Bampton (94/49/1)
Captain R. Barer (93/11/1)
Captain M. Bendix (98/3/1)
W.A. Blackman (99/85/1)
Lieutenant Colonel W.S. Brownlie (92/37/1)
E. Chapman (conshelf)
Andrew Charles (99/46/1)
C.J. Charters (conshelf)
The Reverend C. Cullingford (90/6/1)
Major A.J. Forrest (91/13/1)
R. Gladman (92/1/1)
Lieutenant Colonel M.W. Gonin (85/38/1)
T.A. Gore (99/85/1)
A.G. Herbert (98/16/1)
Derrick Jones (83/52/1)
R.H. Lloyd Jones (89/1/1)
J.H. Parker Jones (01/10/1)
G.C. Miller (83/18/1)
J. Sims (83/52/1)
J.Y. White (90/6/1)
J.H. Witte (87/12/1)

Public Record Office

WO 365/39 Department of the Adjutant General
WO 365/62 Department of the Adjutant General: Statistical reports
WO 205/5(G) 21AG Military HQ Papers
WO 123/208 21AG General Routine Orders 1944
WO 123/209 21AG General Routine Orders 1945
WO 171/138 21AG HQ 'A' Branch June 1944
WO 171/139 21AG HQ 'A' Branch July 1944
WO 171/140 21AG HQ 'A' Branch August 1944
WO 171/141 21AG HQ 'A' Branch September 1944
WO 171/142 21AG HQ 'A' Branch October 1944
WO 171/143 21AG HQ 'A' Branch November 1944
WO 171/144 21AG HQ 'A' Branch December 1944
WO 171/228 2nd Army 'A' Branch 1944
WO 171/3870 21AG HQ 'A' Branch January 1945
WO 171/3871 21AG HQ 'A' Branch February 1945
WO 171/3872 21AG HQ 'A' Branch March 1945
WO 171/3873 21AG HQ 'A' Branch April 1945
WO 205/88 Resistance Groups (Relations With)
WO 205/89 Relations With Resistance
WO 205/90 Resistance Groups and Relations With Army
WO 205/91 Resistance Groups and Relations With British
WO 205/160 Equipment Reports, Early Stages Of Overlord
WO 205/422 Combat Reports May 1944 to April 1945
WO 205/998 Combat Lessons/After Action Reports
WO 205/152 Availability of Forces
WO 205/360 Reinforcements Demands and Procedure
WO 205/760 Operation Redcoat

WO 205/764 Additional Infantry Brigades
WO 222/275 21AG Medical Reports 1944
WO 285/12 Dempsey Papers – The German Collapse
WO 285/18 2nd Army Health Reports
WO 285/25 2nd Army Medical Services Outline History
WO 285/18 Dempsey Medical Papers Dec 1944 to June 1945
WO 222/275 21st Army Group Medical Reports
WO 205/139 Maintenance & Evacuation Of Allied POWs From Germany Part 1
WO 205/1026 PWX Reports
WO 171/5275 War Diaries 1/5th Queens Regiment 1945
WO 171/5171 War Diaries 2nd Battalion Devonshire Regiment 1945
WO 171/1295 War Diaries 2nd Battalion Essex Regiment 1944
WO 171/4693 War Diaries 23rd Hussars 1945
WO 171/5257 War Diaries 8th Battalion Rifle Regiment 1945
WO 171/4690 War Diaries 11th Hussars 1945
WO 171/4708 War Diaries 3rd Royal Tank Regiment 1945
WO 171/4773 War Diaries 63rd Anti Tank Regiment R.A. 1945
WO 171/5169 War Diaries 1st Battalion Cheshire Regiment 1945
WO 171/5170 War Diaries 7th Battalion Cheshire Regiment 1945
LAB 6/20 Call Up of Borstal Boys
WO 171/833 Brussels Provost Company 1944
WO 171/4601 Brussels Provost Company 1945
WO 171/3482 91 Town Major (Brussels) 1944
WO 171/7617 91 Town Major (Brussels) 1945
WO 171/3401 610 (VP) Company 1944
WO 171/3379 120 Provost Company 1944
WO 171/3386 241 Provost Company 1944
WO 171/7819 102 Provost Company 1945
WO 171/7820 108 Provost Company 1945
WO 171/7821 109 Provost Company 1945
WO 171/7822 110 Provost Company 1945
WO 171/3726 ATS Provost
WO 213/55 Adjutant Generals Records
WO 93/55 Court Martial Summaries 1944/45
WO 71/900 Court Martial Pte Payne
WO 71/902 Court Martial Ptes Passmore, Flavell, Evans, Hulme, Dingly, Griffiths, Ryan & James
WO 71/904 Court Martial Corporal Skingle
WO 71/907 Court Martial Pte Chamberlain
WO 71/908 Court Martial Gunner Dunleavy
WO 71/909 Court Martial Pte Mullen
WO 71/910 Court Martial Pte Cameron
WO 71/911 Court Martial Pte Jones
WO 71/914 Court Martial Private R. Jones
WO 71/917 Court Martial William Douglas Home
WO 71/918 Court Martial L/Cpl Orange
WO 71/919 Court Martial Rfn Bourke & Wilds
WO 71/924 Court Martial L/Sgt Potter
WO 71/943 Court Martial Ptes Twite, Lockley, Johnson, Brinley, Elliott
WO 71/948 Court Martial Ptes Dance, Lewis-Jones, Gallacher, Bell, Walker
WO 71/1026 Court Martial Guardsman A. Fairham
WO 71/1103 Court Martial Sapper Nye
WO 71/1110 Court Martial Pte Alf Wraight
WO 84/70 JAG Charge Books
WO 171/167 21AG Provost Marshall Sept to Dec 1944
WO 171/735 JAG Branch HQ Line of Communications 1944
WO 171/4456 JAG Branch HQ Line of Communications 1945
WO 171/182 DJAG Office 21AG 1944
WO 171/281 Assistant Provost Marshall, 1st Corps HQ 1944
WO 171/727 Provost Branch HQ Line of Communications 1944
WO 171/4475 Provost Branch HQ Line of Communications 1945
WO 171/742 Provost Branch 4th Sub Area Line of Communications 1944
WO 171/3936 Provost Marshall Branch 21AG HQ 1945

WO 171/423 War Diaries 3rd Division Provost Company 1944
WO 171/4143 War Diaries 3rd Division Provost Company 1945
WO 171/4182 War Diaries 7th Armoured Division Provost Company 1945
WO 171/510 War Diaries 49th Division Provost Company 1944
WO 171/4240 War Diaries 49th Division Provost Company 1945
WO 171/539 War Diaries 51st Highland Division Provost Company 1944
WO 171/177 21AG Claims & Hirings Directorate 1944
WO 171/3916 21AG Claims & Hirings Directorate 1945
WO 171/190 21AG Court Martial Centre 1944
WO 171/3922 21AG Court Martial Centre 1945
WO 171/3691 HQ 105 Reinforcement Group 1944
WO 171/3708 47 Reinforcement Holding Unit 1944
WO 171/8210 36 Reinforcement Holding Unit 1945
WO 171/8216 42 Reinforcement Holding Unit 1945
WO 171/3347 No4 Inspectorate Military Prisons
WO 171/3349 No5 Field Punishment Camp 1944
WO 171/3350 No6 Field Punishment Camp 1944
WO 171/3351 No7 Field Punishment Camp 1944
WO 171/3352 No8 Field Punishment Camp 1944
WO 171/3353 No 23 Field Punishment Camp 1944
WO 171/7863 No4 Field Punishment Camp 1945
WO 171/3409 70SIS CMP 1944
WO 171/7804 70SIS CMP 1945
WO 171/3410 71SIS CMP 1944
WO 171/7805 71SIS CMP 1945
WO 171/3411 72SIS CMP 1944
WO 171/7806 72SIS CMP 1945
WO 171/3412 73SIS CMP 1944
WO 171/7807 73SIS CMP 1945
WO 171/3413 74SIS CMP 1944
WO 171/7808 74SIS CMP 1945
WO 171/3414 81SIS CMP 1944
WO 171/7809 81SIS CMP 1945
WO 171/3415 82SIS CMP 1944
WO 171/7810 82SIS CMP 1945
WO 171/3416 83SIS CMP 1944
WO 171/7811 83SIS CMP 1945
WO 171/7812 85SIS CMP 1945
WO 171/7813 86SIS CMP 1945
WO 171/7814 87SIS CMP 1945
WO 171/7816 89SIS CMP 1945
WO 205/193   Civil Affairs Reports 1944/45
WO 171/739 Civil Affairs HQ 4th Line of Communication Sub Area 1944
CUST 106/857 Reports on Arms in Baggage
CUST 106/847 POW Loot
CUST 106/846 Customs and Excise War Division work reports
CUST 106/829 Reports on Illegal Exports
CUST 106/697 Loot of Artistic Value
CUST 106/700 Disposal of Smuggled Arms

Bibliography

Books

A Bridge At Arnhem, Charles Whiting (Futura Publications - London 1974)
Accidental Journey, Mark Lynton (Overlook Press, New York 1995)
Achtung! Minen!, Ian Hammerton (The Book Guild - London 1991)
A Crowd Is Not Company, Robert Kee (Eyre and Spottiswoode - London 1947)
A Drop Too Many, John Frost (Cassell & Co - London 1980)
A Fine Night For Tanks, Ken Tout (Sutton - Stroud 1998)
Aftermath Of War, Everyone Must Go Home, Sir Carol Mather (Brassey's - London 1992)
A Full Life, Lt General Sir Brian Horrocks (Collins - London 1960)
A Journey From Blandford, B.A. Jones (Woodfield 1994)
A Mind Of My Own, Elizabeth Maxwell (Sidgwick and Jackson - London 1994)
A Quiet Little Boy Goes To War, Stan Procter (Privately printed 1997)
Argument of Kings, Vernon Scannel (Robson Books - London 1987)
Armoured Guardsmen, Robert Boscawen (Leo Cooper - Barnsley 2001)
Arnhem, Major General R.E. Urquhart (Cassell & Co - London 1958)
Arnhem Doctor, Stuart Mawson (Orbis - London 1981)
Arnhem Lift, Louis Hagen (Hammond & Hammond, London)
Arnhem 1944, The Airborne Battle, Martin Middlebrook (Viking - London 1994)
Arnhem Spearhead, James Sims (Imperial War Museum 1978)
Articles of War - The Spectator Book of World War II (Grafton Books - London 1989)
A Signal War, John Raycroft (Babblefish Press, Prescott, Toronto 2002)
A Soldier's Story, Ronald Grimsey (Capella Publications - Stowmarket 1987)
A Teenager's War, Ron Tucker (Spellmount, Staplehurst 1994)
A Territorial Army Chaplain in Peace and War, Eric Gethyn Jones (Gooday, East Wittering 1988)
At the Fifth Attempt, John Elwyn (Leo Cooper - London 1987)
A Well Known Excellence, Dennis Falvey (Brassey's - London 2002)
The Battle for Normandy, Eversley Belfield & H. Essame (Batsford - London 1965)
The Battle Of The Bulge, Britain's Untold Story, Charles Whiting (Sutton - Stroud 1999)
The Black Bull, Patrick Delaforce (Tom Donovan Publishing - Brighton 1997)
The Bloody Battle For Tilly, Ken Tout (Sutton - Stroud 2000)
Bloody Bremen, Charles Whiting (Leo Cooper - London 1998)
The Bolo Boys, Mac MacIntosh (Victoria Press - Maidstone 1989)
Breaking the Panzers, Kevin Baverstock (Sutton - Stroud 2002)
By Tank Into Normandy, Stuart Hills (Cassell & Co - London 2002)
Caen, Anvil Of Victory, Alexander Mckee (Souvenir Press - London 1964)
The Cauldron, Zeno (Macmillan - London 1966)
Churchill's Desert Rats, Patrick Delaforce (Alan Sutton - Stroud 1994)
Churchill's Secret Weapons, Patrick Delaforce (Robert Hale - London 1998)
Cleared For Take Off, Dirk Bogarde (Viking - London 1995)
Commando Despatch Rider, Raymond Mitchell (Leo Cooper - Barnsley 2001)
The Commandos, D-Day And After, Donald Gilchrist (Robert Hale - London 1982)
The Conquest of the Reich, Robin Neillands (Weidenfeld and Nicholson - London 1995)
Corps Commander, Sir Brian Horrocks (Sidgwick and Jackson - London 1977)

Daily Telegraph Story Of The War, David Marley (Hodder & Stoughton - London 1946)
Dangerous Liaison, Derek Cooper (Michael Russell - Salisbury 1997)
Dawn Of D-Day, David Howarth (Collins - London 1959)
D-Day 1944, Robin Neillands & Roderick De Normann (Weidenfeld & Nicolson - London 1993)
The D-Day Landings, Philip Warner (William Kimber - London 1980)
D-Day June 6, 1944, Stephen E. Ambrose (Touchstone, New York 1995)
D-Day, Those Who Were There, Juliet Gardiner (Collins and Brown - London 1994)
Dear Bill, W.F. Deedes (Macmillan - London 1997)
The Desert Rats, Robin Neillands (Weidenfeld & Nicholson - London 1991)
The Devil's Birthday, Geoffrey Powell (Buchan & Enright - London 1984)
The Devil's Own Luck, Denis Edwards (Leo Cooper - Barnsley 1999)
Eclipse, Alan Moorehead (Hamish Hamilton - London 1945)
1100 Miles With Monty, Norman Kirby (Sutton - Stroud 1989)
The 8.15 To War, Peter Roach (Leo Cooper - London 1982)
18 Platoon, Sydney Jary (Sydney Jary Ltd - Carshalton 1987)
The Enemy Within, John Watney (Hodder & Stoughton - London 1946)
Esprit De Corps, W.A. Elliott (Michael Russell - Salisbury 1996)
European Victory, John D'Arcy-Dawson (MacDonald & Co - London 1948)
Fear Is The Foe, Stan Whitehouse & George Bennett (Robert Hale - London 1995)
The Fighting Wessex Wyverns, Patrick Delaforce (Alan Sutton - Stroud 1994)
Five Days In Hell, Jack Smyth (William Kimber - London 1956)
Flame Thrower, Andrew Wilson (William Kimber - London 1956)
Flashback - A Soldier's Story, General Sir Charles Richardson (William Kimber - London 1985)
The Forgotten Battle, A. Korthals Altes (De Bataafsche Leeuw & Uitgeverij de Arbeiderspers, Amsterdam 1984)
Forrard, The Story of the East Riding Yeomanry, Paul Mace (Leo Cooper - Barnsley 2001)
44: In Combat from Normandy to the Ardennes, Charles Whiting (Spellmount - Staplehurst 2000)
From Arctic Snow To Dust Of Normandy, Patrick Dalzel-Job (Nead An Eoin - Dublin 1991)
Gaol Delivery, Mark Benney, (Longmans, Green & Co - London 1948)
The Grey Goose of Arnhem, Leo Heaps (Weidenfeld and Nicholson - London 1976)
The Guarded Years, Douglas Baber (William Heinemann - London 1955)
Gunner Green's War, L.J. Green (The Pentland Press - Durham 1999)
The Guns Of Normandy, George Blackburn (McClelland & Stewart, Toronto 1995)
The Guns Of Victory, George Blackburn (McClelland & Stewart, Toronto 1996)
I Bought a Star, Thomas Fairbank (George Harrap - London 1951)
The Iron Cage, Nigel Cawthorne (Fourth Estate - London 1983)
I Was A Stranger, General Sir John Hackett (Chatto and Windus - London 1977)
The Killing Ground, James Lucas & James Barker (Batsford - London 1978)
Kingsley Amis, A Biography, Eric Jacobs (Hodder and Stoughton - London 1995)
Last Days Of The Reich, James Lucas (Arms And Armour Press - London 1986)
Leakey's Luck - A Tank Commander With Nine Lives, Rea Leakey & George Forty

(Sutton - Stroud 1999)

Letters Home, Brian Johnston (Weidenfeld and Nicholson - London 1998)

Living History, Chaim Herzog (Weidenfeld & Nicholson - London 1997)

The Lonely Leader Monty 1944/5, Alistair Horne (Macmillan - London 1994)

The Longest Day, Cornelius Ryan (Victor Gollancz - London 1960)

Mad Mike - A Life Of Brigadier Michael Calvert, David Rooney (Leo Cooper - Barnsley 1997)

Mailed Fist, John Foley (Panther - London 1957)

The Man The Nazis Couldn't Catch, John Laffin (Sutton - Stroud 1984)

Marching To The Sound Of Gunfire, Patrick Delaforce (Sutton - Stroud 1996)

Marilyn, Hitler and Me, Milton Shulman (Andre Deutsch - London 1998)

The Memoirs Of Field Marshal Montgomery, (Collins - London 1958)

Men at Arnhem, Tom Angus (Leo Cooper - London 1976)

Men Under Fire, R.W. Thompson (Macdonald & Co, London ?)

Monty, The Field Marshal, Nigel Hamilton (Hamish Hamilton - London 1986)

Monty's Highlanders, 51st Highland Division in WW2, Patrick Delaforce (Tom Donovan - Brighton 1997)

Monty's Ironsides, Patrick Delaforce (Sutton - Stroud 1999)

Monty's Marauders, Patrick Delaforce (Sutton - Stroud 1993)

Monty, The Man Behind The Legend, Nigel Hamilton (Lennard Publishing - London 1987)

Monty, The Making Of A General, Nigel Hamilton (Hamish Hamilton - London 1981)

Monty, Master of the Battlefield, Nigel Hamilton (Hamish Hamilton - London 1983)

The Moon's A Balloon, David Niven (Hamish Hamilton - London 1971)

My Life, Bert Hardy (Gordon Fraser - London 1985)

Nothing Less Than Victory, Russell Miller (Michael Joseph - London 1993)

Number Rank And Name, Bill Jardine (Fine Publishing - Beccles 1990)

112th Wessex Field Regiment RA, TA 1938-1946, Douglas Goddard (Privately Printed 1997)

One More River, Peter Allen (Dent - London 1980)

The Only Way Out, R. M. Wingfield (Hutchinson - London 1955)

Operation Victory, Major General Sir Francis De Guingand (Hodder & Stoughton - London 1947)

Out Of Step, Michael Carver (Century Hutchinson - London 1989)

Overlord, Max Hastings (Michael Joseph - London 1984)

The Password Is Courage, John Castle (Souvenir Press - London 1954)

Paths Of Death And Glory, Charles Whiting (Severn House - London 1997)

Pegasus Bridge, Stephen Ambrose (Touchstone, New York 1985)

The Polar Bears, Patrick Delaforce (Sutton - Stroud 1995)

Psychology And The Soldier, Norman Copeland (Allen & Unwin - London 1944)

The Race for the Rhine Bridges, Alexander McKee (Souvenir Press - London 1971)

RAMC, Anthony Cotterell (Hutchinson & Co, London)

Reflect On Things Past, Lord Carrington (Collins - London 1988)

Report From Germany, Leonard O. Mosley (Victor Gollancz - London 1945)

Rhineland, The Battle to End the War, W &S Whittaker (Leo Cooper - London 1989)

Robert Runcie, The Reluctant Archbishop, Humphrey Carpenter (Hodder & Stoughton - London 1986)

Sans Peur, Alastair Borthwick (Eneas Mackay, Stirling 1946)

The SAS At War, Anthony Kemp (Penguin - London 1991)

Silent Invader, Alexander Morrison (Airlife - Shrewsbury 1999)

Sins Of Commission, William Douglas Home (Michael Russell - Salisbury 1985)

Six Armies In Normandy, John Keegan (Jonathan Cape - London 1982)

So Few Got Through, Martin Lindsay (Collins - London 1946)
Striking Back, Peter Masters (Presidio Press, Novato, California 1997)
Summon Up The Blood, J. A. Womack & Celia Wolfe (Leo Cooper - London 1997)
Surgeon At Arms, Lipmann Kessel (William Heinemann - London 1958)
Sutherland's War, Douglas Sutherland (Leo Cooper - London 1984)
Swiftly They Struck, Murdoch C. McDougall (Grafton Books - London 1988)
Taming The Panzers, Patrick Delaforce (Sutton - Stroud 2000)
Tank, Ken Tout (Robert Hale, London 1985)
Tanks, Advance!, Ken Tout (Robert Hale - London 1987)
Thank God And The Infantry, John Lincoln (Sutton - Stroud 1994)
The Tiger and The Rose, Vernon Scannell (Robson Books - London 1983)
Travels with a Leros Veteran, Pauline Bevan (PB Books - Reading 2000)
Triumph in the West -The Alanbrooke War Diaries, Arthur Bryant (Collins, London 1959)
True Canadian War Stories From Legion Magazine, (Prospero Books - Toronto 1989)
True Stories of the Commandos, Robin Hunter (Virgin Publishing - London 2000)
Two Sides of the Beach, Edmund Blandford (Airlife - Shrewsbury 1999)
2500 Dangerous Days, Patrick P.J. Bracken (Merlin Books - Braunton 1998)
The Unfinished Man, James Byrom (Chatto and Windus - London 1957)
Victory In Normandy, Major General David Belchem (Chatto & Windus - London 1981)
War Diaries, Field Marshal Lord Alanbrooke (Weidenfeld & Nicolson - London 2001)
War From The Ground Up, John Colby (Nortex Press, Austin, Texas 1991)
Wars and Shadows, General Sir David Fraser (Ian Allen/Penguin - London 2002)
What Did You Do In The War Grandpa?, Bob Price (Watermill Press 1989)
When The Grass Stops Growing, Carol Mather (Leo Cooper - London 1997)
The Whitelaw Memoirs, Willie Whitelaw (Aurum Press - London 1989)
Wings Of The Wind, Peter Stainforth (Falcon Press - London 1952)
With the Jocks, Peter White (Sutton - Stroud 2001)
Years Not Wasted 1940-1945, Keith Panter Brick (The Book Guild - Lewes 1999)
You, You, & You, Pete Grafton (Pluto Press - London 1981)

Magazines

Picture Post 12/5/45

Others

Daily Telegraph Obituary Sir Martin Beckett 6/8/01
Daily Telegraph Obituary Major General Matt Abraham 6/6/01
Daily Telegraph Obituary Lieutenant Colonel Alec Chalmers
Daily Telegraph Obituary Major David Jamieson VC 8/5/01
Daily Telegraph Obituary Colonel Sir John Lawson 14/12/01
Daily Telegraph Obituary Sir Derek Bibby
Daily Telegraph Obituary The Earl of Kimberley 29/05/02
Daily Telegraph Obituary Donald Stones 25/10/02
Daily Telegraph Obituary James Baron
Daily Telegraph Review 'The Others' 02/11/01
Daily Mail Letters Page 22/01/02
Independent Interview with Alexander Baron
Other Words, December 1988
The Oldie, February 2001

Index